PIANO • VOCAL • GUITAR

The New Illustrated Treasury of

SONGS

The following songs are the property of:

BOURNE CO.
Music Publishers
5 West 37th Street
New York, NY 10018

Baby Mine
Give A Little Whistle
Heigh-Ho
Hi-Diddle-Dee-Dee (An Actor's Life For Me)
I'm Wishing
I've Got No Strings
Some Day My Prince Will Come
When I See An Elephant Fly
When You Wish Upon A Star
Whistle While You Work
Who's Afraid Of The Big Bad Wolf?

ISBN 978-0-7935-9365-1

Disney and Disney/Pixar characters and artwork © Disney Enterprises, Inc.

For all works contained herein:
Unauthorized copying, arranging, adapting, recording
or public performance is an infringement of copyright.
Infringers are liable under the law.

Walt Disney Music Company
Wonderland Music Company, Inc.

DISTRIBUTED BY

7777 W. BLUEMOUND RD. P.O. BOX 13819 MILWAUKEE, WI 53213

In Australia Contact:
Hal Leonard Australia Pty. Ltd.
22 Taunton Drive P.O. Box 5130
Cheltenham East, 3192 Victoria, Australia
Email: ausadmin@halleonard.com

Visit Hal Leonard Online at
www.halleonard.com

Printed in Hong Kong

Sgt. Garcia - Phil Ross as Monastario - Jan Arvan as Torres
Music Composed and Conducted by William Lava.
Zorro song by Norman Foster
and George Bruns.
RECORDED BY WALT DISNEY MUSIC CO
1228
MOUSE CLUB
BUENA
Vista
RECORDS
Wonderland Music
BMI
Title Song From Walt Disney's Motion Picture
"THAT DARN CAT"

CONTENTS

MICKEY MOUSE
MINNIE MOUSE

INTRODUCTION

Walt Disney didn't read or write music. In fact, he never even played an instrument, unless you count an unsuccessful stab at the violin during grade school in Kansas City.

And yet, his influence upon music was, and continues to be, so profound that the great American composer Jerome Kern was moved to say, "Disney has made use of music as language. In the synchronization of humorous episodes with humorous music, he has unquestionably given us the outstanding contribution of our time."

"There's a terrific power to music. You can run any of these pictures and they'd be dragging and boring, but the minute you put music behind them, they have life and vitality they don't get any other way."

—Walt Disney

That's lofty praise, especially coming as it did from a musical legend like Kern. But what makes his words all the more amazing is the fact that he said them in 1936, *before* the release of *Snow White and the Seven Dwarfs*, arguably one of Walt Disney's greatest moments not only in animation, but music as well.

Still, the question remains: if Walt didn't write any songs or compose any scores, how could he have had such a deep and lasting impact on music?

The answer, simply enough, is the same way in which he had such a profound effect upon animation without so much as drawing even one mouse or dwarf.

Walt was the mover and shaker, the man of vision who gathered around him some of the most talented writers, artists, composers, and musicians, who bought into his dreams and schemes and made them happen, all under his watchful eye.

Walt and Roy Disney with the special "Oscar" awarded to Walt in 1932 for the creation of Mickey Mouse.

Disney's imprimatur is stamped onto every song...

He once described his role this way:

> My role? Well, you know I was stumped one day when a little boy asked, "Do you draw Mickey Mouse?" I had to admit I do not draw anymore. "Then you think up the jokes and ideas?" "No," I said, "I don't do that." Finally, he looked at me and said, "Mr. Disney, just what do you do?" "Well," I said, "sometimes I think of myself as a little bee. I go from one area of the Studio to another and gather pollen and sort of stimulate everybody. I guess that's the job I do."

Of course, that doesn't explain Walt Disney's uncanny feel for what worked and what didn't, be it in music, films, or theme parks. Perhaps Eric Sevareid summed it up best in his tribute to Walt on the *CBS Evening News* the day Disney died: "He was an original; not just an American original, but an original, period. He was a happy accident; one of the happiest this century has experienced... People are saying we'll never see his like again."

Maybe it was his Midwestern upbringing and mid-American, mainstream appreciation for music and movies, or maybe he was just "a happy accident," but Walt Disney aimed to create entertainment that he himself would enjoy. Could he help it if hundreds of millions of people around the world happened to agree with him?

So although he didn't write "When You Wish Upon a Star," "Zip-A-Dee-Doo-Dah," or any of the other hundreds of tunes that make up the Disney canon, his imprimatur is stamped onto every song and score. When you hear "Whistle While You Work," you may not know that the words were written by Larry Morey and the music by Frank Churchill, but you certainly know it's a Disney song.

It didn't matter what a composer's background was, whether he was a honky-tonk pianist from Los Angeles, a jingle writer from New York's Tin Pan Alley, or a pop star from England, when he wrote for Walt Disney, he wrote in a style that was, consciously or not, immediately recognizable not as his own, but as Walt Disney's.

"No matter what I or anyone else in the music department wrote, people always recognized it as being the 'Disney sound,'" says Buddy Baker, a longtime Disney staff composer. "But if I was asked to define the Disney sound or how we got it, I would have to answer that I didn't know. It's not something I thought about while I was writing the music.

"I think a clue to the Disney sound, though, comes from the man himself," he adds. "Walt Disney had a wonderful concept of what the music should be, which is a great clue for the composer. For instance, if he wanted a big, symphonic score, he'd tell you that and he'd even tell you what he'd want it to sound like."

Disney songs represent a style and sprightliness that makes them eminently hummable and totally unforgettable. They were very much a reflection of their patron, who concentrated on melody and didn't like anything that was too loud or high-pitched.

Music lightens a story session in the mid 1930s as Walt Disney visits (from left) Webb Smith, Ted Sears, and Pinto Colvig.

Even the "Disney" songs and scores being written today, decades after Walt Disney's death, reflect the spirit and influence of this man who had a special ability to recognize what kind of music best fit a scene or situation and, more importantly (and more to the point), what was good.

It was Walt's direction and influence that led his composers and musicians to pioneer musical concepts and technologies that influenced both the film and music industries for decades—and continue to do so to this day.

But the music did not start out as Disney's own. In the first several Mickey Mouse cartoons, produced in 1928 and 1929, the music was either borrowed or adapted. An example was Mickey's very first cartoon, *Steamboat Willie*, released in November, 1928, and featuring the songs "Steamboat Bill" and "Turkey in the Straw."

(Top) Walt Disney's classic portrait with Mickey Mouse, taken at the Disney Studios on Hyperion Avenue in the 1930s. (Right) In 1938, Disney purchased undeveloped property in Burbank, which soon became the permanent home to the new Walt Disney Studios.

Still, even if the music wasn't written by members of Walt's staff, it was arranged in such a way that it sounded as if it just might have been. For instance, "Steamboat Bill," written in 1910, was whistled by the mouse himself during the opening moments of the cartoon.

THE EARLY YEARS

The sound that played the key role in Disney cartoons was music.

"Turkey in the Straw," which dates as far back as 1834 and is arguably a sing-song classic in the tradition of "Camptown Races" and "My Darling Clementine," was not arranged for normal instruments, such as guitars, flutes, or pianos, but was instead configured to accommodate the variety of "instruments" Mickey plays during the cartoon, including a washboard, pots and pans, a cat, a duck, several suckling pigs, and a cow's teeth. ("Turkey in the Straw," by the way, was selected for *Steamboat Willie* because it was one of the only tunes a young assistant animator named Wilfred Jackson, the sole musician at the small Disney Studios, could play on the harmonica.)

It could be said that the Disney musical legacy actually did begin with Walt himself. In 1929, he teamed with his then-musical director Carl Stalling to write a song that would become an anthem of sorts for his already famous star, Mickey Mouse.

That song, "Minnie's Yoo Hoo," was first heard in the 1929 short "Mickey's Follies." It is the only song for which Walt Disney ever took a writing credit.

Mickey Mouse and the musical improvisation that made him famous in his debut film, Steamboat Willie.

But that doesn't mean Walt didn't play an active role in the creation of the music heard in all succeeding Disney Studio cartoon shorts and animated features. He simply entrusted it to more accomplished composers and arrangers, the first of which was Stalling, an old friend from Kansas City.

In "Silly Symphonies" the music would rule

It was Stalling who persuaded Walt to begin the Silly Symphony cartoon series, which grew out of disagreements the two had over the use of music in the Mickey Mouse shorts. Walt wanted Stalling to fit the music to the action, while Stalling felt the action should fit the music.

The Silly Symphonies were a compromise. In the Mickey cartoons, the music would continue to play second fiddle to the characters and the action, but in the Silly Symphonies the music would rule.

Stalling stayed with the Studio less than two years, jumping from Silly Symphonies at Disney to Looney Tunes and Merrie Melodies at Warner Brothers, where he created his own musical legacy, composing scores for the likes of Bugs Bunny, Daffy Duck, and Porky Pig.

Despite Stalling's departure, the Silly Symphonies continued. In fact, they became so popular that Walt Disney began beefing up his music staff in the early '30s to handle the increased need for music for them.

The surprise hit song from Three Little Pigs *spawned a range of merchandise, including (left to right) sheet music, a board game, and records. These rare 1933 items are treasured by collectors today.*

One of the composers he hired was Frank Churchill, a young musician who had studied at UCLA and gained experience playing honky-tonk piano in Mexico and performing on a Los Angeles radio station (as well as serving as a session player in recording sessions for Disney cartoons). This heretofore unsung musician would play an important role in Disney music over the next decade. And he started off with a bang, writing Disney's first big hit, a song that came out of the most famous of the Silly Symphonies, *Three Little Pigs*.

Released in 1933 during the depths of the Depression, *Three Little Pigs* and its famous song, "Who's Afraid of the Big Bad Wolf?" provided hope and humor to a country that was badly in need of both.

As with many Disney films, *Three Little Pigs* comes from a children's story. But to Churchill, it also represented real life. While growing up on his family's ranch in San Luis Obispo, California, he was given three little piglets to raise by his mother. All went well until a real "Big Bad Wolf" killed one of them.

As legend has it, when Churchill was asked to write a song for the cartoon, he recalled his horrifying childhood experience and penned "Who's Afraid of the Big Bad Wolf?" in about five minutes, patterning the song loosely on "Happy Birthday." When it was released as a single and in sheet music, it featured additional lyrics by Ann Ronell.

"Who's Afraid of the Big Bad Wolf?" provided hope and humor to a country that was badly in need of both.

With "Who's Afraid of the Big Bad Wolf?" Walt Disney and his staff had created their first sing-a-long classic. It certainly wasn't going to be their last.

In 1929, the Disney Studio's creative team included (standing from left) Johnny Cannon, Walt Disney, Bert Gillett, Ub Iwerks, Wilfred Jackson, Les Clark; (seated from left) Carl Stalling, Jack King, and Ben Sharpsteen.

A COMING OF AGE

The next step for Walt Disney and his staff was the creation of the first full-length animated feature. But Walt wasn't content to "just" create and produce a feature-length cartoon. He envisioned something more.

From its beginnings, *Snow White and the Seven Dwarfs* was planned around music. However, early attempts at songs did not satisfy Walt. He complained that they were too much in the vein of so many Hollywood musicals that introduced songs without regard to the story. "We should set a new pattern, a new way to use music," he told his staff. "Weave it into the story so somebody doesn't just burst into song."

That last line, as simply stated as it is, has been the guiding principle in Disney animated features from *Snow White* and *Pinocchio* all the way through the more recent efforts, including *Beauty and the Beast*, *Aladdin*, and *The Lion King*.

What Walt wanted with *Snow White and the Seven Dwarfs* was something closer to Broadway musical than Hollywood motion picture.

Frank Churchill and Larry Morey were assigned the task of writing the songs for *Snow White*. By the time all was said and sung, the pair had written 25 songs, only eight of which ended up in the film. But what an eight they were, each one a classic in its own right.

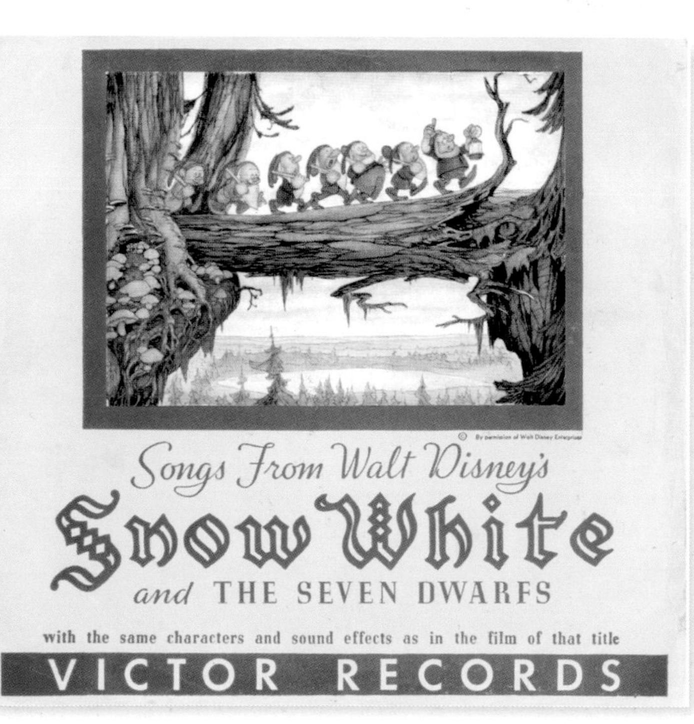

The first original motion picture soundtrack record album was Snow White and the Seven Dwarfs, *released by Victor Records in 1937.*

"We should set a new pattern, a new way to use music"

Walt Disney didn't write any songs for *Snow White*, but he played an active role in defining the content of each song and how it would fit into the film, as these notes from a story conference on "Whistle While You Work" demonstrate:

> Change words of a song so they fit in more with Snow White's handing the animals brushes, etc. Snow White: "If you just hum a merry tune"...and they start humming. Then Snow White would start to tell them to "whistle while you work." She would start giving the animals things to do. By that time, she has sung, of course... Birds would come marching in. Try to arrange to stay with the birds for a section of whistling. Orchestra would play with a whistling effect...get it in the woodwinds...like playing something instrumentally to sound like whistling...
>
> Get a way to finish the song that isn't just an end. Work in a shot trucking [moving] out of the house. Truck back and show animals shaking rugs out of the windows...little characters outside beating things out in the yard...
>
> Truck out and the melody of "Whistle While You Work" gets quieter and quieter. Leave them all working. The last thing you see as you truck away is little birds hanging out clothes. Fade out on that and music would fade out. At the end, all you would hear is the flute—before fading into the "Dig Dig" song [which precedes the song "Heigh-Ho"] and the hammering rhythm.

Snow White and the Seven Dwarfs ushered in not only the Golden Age of Disney Animation in the late 1930s and early 1940s, but the Golden Age of Disney Music as well. While Disney's animators were creating some of the most beautiful screen images ever seen, the studio's composers were producing some of the most memorable songs ever heard, including "When You Wish Upon a Star" from *Pinocchio* (1940), "Baby Mine" from *Dumbo* (1941), and "Little April Shower" from *Bambi* (1942).

World War II brought an abrupt end to the Golden Age. At the Disney Studios, the emphasis changed from creating animated features to producing cartoon shorts and instructional films to aid the war effort. Even after the war was over, Walt Disney didn't immediately return to animated features. Instead, he concentrated on "package" pictures (movies that featured a series of animated shorts rolled into one motion picture) and films featuring both live action and animation.

But Disney's staff of composers continued to play a significant role in these efforts, writing such memorable tunes as the Latin-influenced "Saludos Amigos" and "You Belong to My Heart" from the two South American travelog-style films *Saludos Amigos* (1943) and *The Three Caballeros* (1945), "The Lord Is Good to Me" from *Melody Time* (1948), and one of the most popular Disney songs ever written, "Zip-A-Dee-Doo-Dah," the irresistibly upbeat tune from *Song of the South* (1946).

Composer Frank Churchill (left) and sequence director/lyricist Larry Morey in the mid 1930s creating songs for Snow White and the Seven Dwarfs.

SONGS FROM TIN PAN ALLEY

The creation of the Walt Disney Music Company and Disneyland Records enabled the Disney Studios to release its own music, rather than rely on other companies. Shown here, a 1959 Disneyland record album and 1950 sheet music for Cinderella.

In 1950, Walt Disney returned to animated features with the release of *Cinderella*, but instead of relying on his music staff for the film's song score, he turned to writers from New York's Tin Pan Alley, something he would continue to do for his animated features throughout the 1950s.

Originally 28th Street in Manhattan, Tin Pan Alley was home to many of the largest song publishers in the United States. Each publisher employed an army of songwriters who worked out of small offices furnished with nothing more than pianos and music stands. During the summer, the writers would open their windows in a futile effort to get some relief from the stifling New York heat (the buildings weren't air conditioned). The noise of the pianos echoing through the street gave one the impression of people banging on tin pans, hence the name "Tin Pan Alley."

Walt didn't consciously set out to use Tin Pan Alley writers for *Cinderella*. While in New York on business prior to the start of production, he kept hearing on the radio a catchy novelty song, "Chi-Baba Chi-Baba," written by the team of Mack David, Jerry Livingston, and Al Hoffman. He was so taken with the song that he ended up hiring the trio to write the songs for *Cinderella*. Perhaps it's no surprise, then, that one of the songs, "Bibbidi Bobbidi Boo," is in the same vein as "Chi-Baba."

Walt again turned to Tin Pan Alley for *Alice in Wonderland* (1951), primarily because he felt the film would need an abundance of novelty songs, something the Tin Pan Alley gang was quite adept at producing. In all, 14 songs were written for *Alice*, including "I'm Late," one of nine tunes written for the film by Bob Hilliard and Sammy Fain, and "The Unbirthday Song" contributed by the *Cinderella* trio of David, Hoffman, and Livingston.

The renaissance in Disney animation continued through the 1950s and early 1960s with the release of such animated features as *Peter Pan* (1953), *Lady and the Tramp* (1955), *Sleeping Beauty* (1959), and *101 Dalmatians* (1961). The bulk of the songs continued to be written by Tin Pan Alley tunesmiths, such as Sammy Cahn, Sammy Fain, and Jack Lawrence. The notable exception was *Lady and the Tramp*, which featured songs by Peggy Lee and Sonny Burke.

The increasing reliance on outside writers for songs for the animated features presented no danger to the jobs of Disney's crack staff of composers and arrangers. At least they didn't seem worried by it, perhaps because they were so busy.

"[The 1950s were] a hectic time at the Studio," recalls Buddy Baker, who joined the Disney music staff following a career in big bands and radio. "We had the weekly series [*Disneyland*, which later became *The Wonderful World of Disney*, among other titles] to write music for, plus the daily show [*The Mickey Mouse Club*]. This was in addition to the feature films the Studio was producing. And Walt demanded quality, whether it was music for a multi-million dollar animated feature or a television show."

Walt's staff of composers was so busy writing the music they often turned to anyone who was ready, willing, and able to write the lyrics, be they animators, scriptwriters, story editors, or, in the case of "Old Yeller," Studio nurses (the lyrics for that song are credited to Gil George, who was in fact Disney Studio nurse Hazel George).

Disney staffers at the time included music director Oliver Wallace ("Old Yeller" and "Pretty Irish Girl"), Jimmie Dodd ("The Mickey Mouse March"), and George Bruns ("Zorro" and "The Ballad of Davy Crockett").

Bruns's experience writing "The Ballad of Davy Crockett" for the *Davy Crockett* series of TV shows was typical of the way songs were written for Walt Disney in the harried '50s, though the results were far from typical.

"Walt needed what I call a little 'throwaway' tune that would bridge the time gaps in the story of Davy Crockett," recalled Bruns. "He needed a song that would carry the story from one sequence to another. I threw together the melody line and chorus, 'Davy, Davy Crockett, King of the Wild Frontier,' in about 30 minutes."

Tom Blackburn, the scriptwriter for the *Davy Crockett* series, had never before written a song, but that didn't stop him from adding the lyrics, 120 lines of them (the completed version has 20 stanzas of six lines each).

Even before the television series went on the air, "The Ballad of Davy Crockett" took the country by storm. Bruns and Blackburn's little "throwaway" tune became a national sensation, much as coonskin caps would when the show premiered.

"It certainly took everybody at the Studio by surprise," said Bruns. "The irony of it was that most people thought it was an authentic folk song that we had uncovered and updated. Usually when you have a hit song, there are always lawsuits claiming prior authorship. In the case of 'Davy Crockett,' not a single suit was filed."

"The Ballad of Davy Crockett" became the fastest-selling record of 1955.

Composer George Bruns created a diverse range of music for Disney, from the award-winning score for Sleeping Beauty *to the hit song "The Ballad of Davy Crockett."*

THE SHERMANS MARCH THROUGH DISNEY

If the 1950s were characterized by Walt Disney's reliance on Tin Pan Alley songwriters, the trend in the 1960s could be summed up in two words: Sherman Brothers.

Hired by Walt Disney in 1961 as staff songwriters, Richard M. and Robert B. Sherman proved versatile and prolific during their almost decade-long association with Disney, writing more than 200 songs, many of which have become timeless classics.

The pair penned songs for animated features (*The Sword and the Stone* [1963], *The Jungle Book* [1967], *The Aristocats* [1970]) and featurettes (*Winnie the Pooh and the Honey Tree* [1966]), live-action musicals (*Summer Magic* [1963], *The Happiest Millionaire* [1967]), live-action non-musicals (*The Parent Trap* [1961], *In Search of the Castaways* [1962], *The Monkey's Uncle* [1965], *That Darn Cat* [1965]), musicals combining live-action and animation (*Bedknobs and Broomsticks* [1971]), theme parks (*The Enchanted Tiki Room* [1963]), and even the New York World's Fair (*Carousel of Progress*, *It's a Small World* [1964]).

Perhaps the greatest achievement of the Sherman Brothers' Disney career came in 1964 with the release of *Mary Poppins*, for which they wrote 14 songs and earned two Academy Awards, one for Best Song ("Chim-Chim-Cheree") and the other for Best Song Score.

"Writing songs for *Mary Poppins* was a songwriter's dream. Each song we did had a purpose, a reason for being," says Robert Sherman, echoing the long-held philosophy of Walt Disney about music in motion pictures.

Typical of their experiences composing tunes for *Mary Poppins* was the inspiration behind one of the most popular and memorable tunes in the film, "Supercalifragilisticexpialidocious."

"When we were little boys in summer camp in the Catskill Mountains in the mid 1930s," explains Richard Sherman, "we heard this word. Not the exact word, but a word very similar to 'supercal.' It was a word that was longer than 'antidisestablishmentarianism,' and it gave us kids a word that no adult had. It was our own special word, and we wanted the Banks children to have that same feeling."

"Supercalifragilisticexpialidocious"

Songwriters Richard Sherman (left) and Robert Sherman (right) review the music for Mary Poppins *with the film's co-producer and writer, Bill Walsh (center).*

Mary Poppins also proved to be the crowning achievement of Walt Disney's long and storied career. Combining live-action, animation, and the Sherman Brothers song score, it was the culmination of everything he'd been working toward in his more than 40 years in the film business.

When Walt Disney passed away on December 15, 1966, there was concern that his studio would not be able to survive without him. But Walt had confidence it would. "I think by this time my staff...[is] convinced that Walt is right, that quality will win out," he once said. "And so I think they're going to stay with that policy because it's proved that it's a good business policy... I think they're convinced and I think they'll hang on, as you say, after Disney."

Throughout the 1970s and 1980s the Disney Studios continued producing animated and live-action features, but all of them, with the exceptions of *Robin Hood* (1973) and *Pete's Dragon* (1977), were non-musicals. That didn't mean there weren't any songs in Disney movies. Such animated features as *The Rescuers* (1977) did feature songs, but these songs were usually performed during the opening or closing credits and were not essential to the story.

A MUSICAL RENAISSANCE

All that changed in 1988 with the release of *Oliver & Company*, Disney's first full-scale animated musical in more than a decade.

The film featured five tunes written by a Who's Who of pop songwriters, including Barry Manilow, Dan Hartman, and Dean Pitchford. But the key was that all of the songs adhered to an old Disney maxim: music should play an integral and prominent part in the story without overshadowing or disrupting it.

"Music should come out of the dialogue," said the film's director, George Scribner, reemphasizing a point Walt Disney had made many times years before. "The best music advances the story or defines a character. The challenge was to figure out areas in our film where music could better express a concept or idea."

Perhaps no one knew this better than a New York-based lyricist named Howard Ashman, who co-wrote "Once Upon a Time in New York City" for *Oliver & Company.*

With his longtime writing partner Alan Menken, Ashman redefined and revitalized the animated musical, bringing to it a style, wit, and sophistication that hadn't been seen or heard since the early 1940s.

"Animation is the last great place to do Broadway musicals," said Ashman, explaining the inspiration for *The Little Mermaid* (1989), *Beauty and the Beast* (1991), and *Aladdin* (1992). "It's a place you can use a whole other set of skills and a way of working which is more the way plays and musicals are made. With most films, the story seems to come first and the songs are an afterthought.

"Coming from a musical theater background," he continued, "Alan and I are used to writing songs for characters in situations. For *The Little Mermaid* we wanted songs that would really move the story forward and keep things driving ahead."

The seven songs Ashman and Menken wrote for the film did that and more. The result was the beginning of a New Golden Age of Animation that continues to this day.

Ashman and Menken followed the success of *The Little Mermaid* (for which they won an Academy Award for "Under the Sea") with *Beauty and the Beast.*

"Animation is the last great place to do Broadway musicals."

A review of the film in *Newsweek* magazine says it all: "The most delicious musical score of 1991 is Alan Menken and Howard Ashman's *Beauty and the Beast*. If the growing armada of titanically troubled Broadway musicals had half its charm and affectionate cleverness, the ships wouldn't be foundering."

The duo wrote six songs for the film, including an unprecedented three songs that were nominated for Academy Awards: "Be Our Guest," "Belle," and the eventual Oscar-winner "Beauty and the Beast."

The songwriting team of Howard Ashman (left) and Alan Menken received Academy Awards for their work on The Little Mermaid *and* Beauty and the Beast.

Before his death in March of 1991, Ashman had written lyrics for three songs in the next big Disney animated feature, *Aladdin*, including "Friend Like Me." Once again, the composer was Alan Menken. For the rest of the score, Menken collaborated with lyricist Tim Rice, a theatre veteran who, earlier in his career, wrote *Evita* and *Jesus Christ Superstar* with Andrew Lloyd Webber. Menken, Rice, and the film were honored with an Academy Award for Best Song for "A Whole New World."

Disney's live-action musical tradition continued with the 1992 release of *Newsies*, a full-scale production about the organization of newsboys in New York early in the 20th century. The score, by Alan Menken and Jack Feldman, includes the boys' inspirational anthem, "Seize the Day."

As the 1990s continued, Disney definitely reaffirmed its place as the world's best producer of beautiful and successful animated films. The next animated musical, released in 1994, was the universally beloved *The Lion King*, the allegorical story of the love between a lion cub and his father. Tim Rice was signed first to write the lyrics. "The studio asked me if I had any suggestions as to who could write the music. They said, 'Choose anybody in the world and choose the best.' I said, 'Well, Elton John would be fantastic.'" The producers were at first hesitant to approach the legendary rock star, but as it turned out, he was anxious to come on board. "I actually jumped at the chance," John confessed, "because I knew that Disney was a class act and I liked the story line and the people immediately."

Has there ever been a musical number on film, live or animated, that surpasses the emotional beauty of the opening number, "Circle of Life"? Rice, who first wrote the words for the song, was amazed at the speed with which Elton John composed. "I gave him the lyrics at the beginning of the session at about two in the afternoon. By half-past three, he'd finished writing and recording a stunning demo." Disney added another Academy Award to its collection when "Can You Feel the Love Tonight?" was cited as Best Song.

Pocahontas was the first Disney animated feature inspired by factual history. It brought another major theatre talent into the Disney Studios in Stephen Schwartz, who wrote the lyrics for the score, with music once again by Alan Menken. Schwartz knew success at a young age on Broadway as the composer and lyricist of *Godspell* and *Pippin*. The combined talents of Menken and Schwartz produced yet another Academy Award for Best Song for "Colors of the Wind," a chart-topping hit for singer Vanessa Williams.

Toy Story, the first full-length feature film animated entirely on computers, takes place among the magical lives of a six-year-old's collection of toys. A special film like this needed a unique kind of song, and Disney found that in singer-songwriter Randy Newman. "You've Got a Friend in Me" is the chummy song that expresses the easy goodwill of the enchanting story of Woody, Buzz, and Andy.

Alan Menken's sixth score for Disney was another collaboration with Stephen Schwartz—the adaptation of the classic 19th century Victor Hugo novel *The Hunchback of Notre Dame*. This was an incredibly ambitious undertaking in every regard. Just the task of adapting a screenplay from the sprawling novel is difficult enough, but creating a satisfying animated musical from this complicated story was a monumental task. The resulting critically acclaimed film is evidence of just how splendidly all those involved succeeded. The score contains an extensive, expressive collection of songs borrowing influences from gypsy music, French music, and traditional liturgical music. The richly emotional songs include "God Help the Outcasts," which, beyond the film score was recorded by Bette Midler, and "Someday," which became a hit for the vocal group All-4-One.

For *Hercules*, Disney turned to a new source for a story: ancient Greek mythology. But this was no dull classroom textbook topic as realized by Disney Studios. The film is a marvelously entertaining tale of the triumph of a true hero, enlivened by new songs, once again by Alan Menken, with lyrics by David Zippel, a Tony® Award winner for his work on the Broadway musical *City of Angels*. Rock singer Michael Bolton had a hit single with the expansive, soaring "Go the Distance," certainly an anthem befitting the mighty son of Zeus.

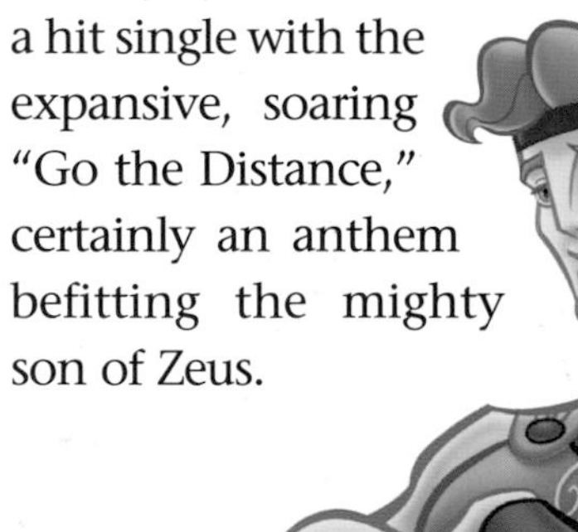

In the early 1990s Disney developed an animation studio in Orlando, Walt Disney Feature Animation Florida. *Mulan* is the first feature film largely created there using amazing state-of-the-art computer-assisted animation. This 2,000-year-old tale is of a courageous young Chinese woman who enters the army disguised as a man so that her ailing father can be spared military service. Technology allowed panoramic camera effects never before possible in animation, with especially amazing crowd scenes and the attack of the Huns. The songs, by Matthew Wilder and David Zippel, include "Reflection" and "Honor to Us All."

One of the most exciting developments at Disney has been the expansion of the company's business to include Broadway musicals. *Beauty and the Beast* was adapted for the stage in vivid fashion, with additional songs by Alan Menken and Tim Rice. The show opened on Broadway on April 18, 1994, and at this writing has just celebrated its tenth anniversary and become the sixth longest-running show in Broadway history. A touring company of the musical has been a smash success on the road.

Disney's claim to a piece of Broadway became even more tangible with the acquisition and renovation of the New Amsterdam Theatre. Built in 1903 and restored to its original splendor, it is now a cornerstone in the major redevelopment of 42nd Street in New York. The New Amsterdam is home to *The Lion King*, one of the most innovative musicals ever to open on The Great White Way. The stage adaptation from the animated film opened on Broadway on November 13, 1997, and contains additional songs by Elton John and Tim Rice, as well as songs by Hans Zimmer, Lebo M, Mark Mancina, Julie Taymor, and Jay Rifkin. The stunning production was also directed and co-designed by cutting-edge talent Julie Taymor. The musical won the 1998 Tony® Award for Best Musical, and is the biggest hit New York has seen in many years, with sold-out houses booked many months in advance.

On the heels of its Broadway success with *The Lion King,* Disney triumphed once again with another Elton John/Tim Rice collaboration, 1999's *Aida*. Inspired by the Verdi opera of the same name, *Aida* is the story of Egyptian prince and war-hero Radames, who, although betrothed to Princess Amneris, enters into a forbidden romance with the war-captured Aida, herself also, but secretly, of royal bloodlines. The play captured four Tony® Awards in 2000, including Best Original Musical Score, and a Grammy® that same year for Best Musical Show Album. A single of one of the show's most beloved songs, "Written in the Stars," as recorded by Elton John and LeAnn Rimes, reached No. 2 on *Billboard's* Adult Contemporary Charts and No. 4 in Canada.

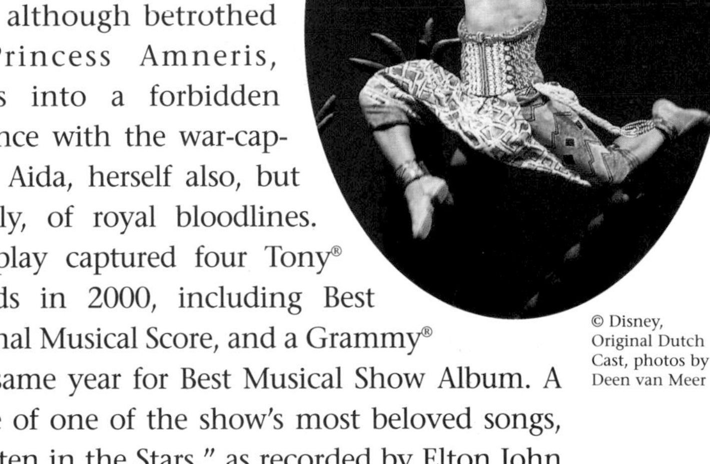

© Disney, Original Dutch Cast, photos by Deen van Meer

© Disney, Original Dutch Cast, photos by Deen van Meer

That same year, Disney released two hugely successful animated features: *Tarzan*™, an adaptation of the Edgar Rice Burroughs classic, and *Toy Story 2*, a follow-up to the 1994 landmark computer-animated blockbuster. Scored by pop-rocker and longtime Genesis member Phil Collins, the *Tarzan*™ soundtrack included the world beat infused "Two Worlds," and the No. 1 Adult Contemporary hit "You'll Be in My Heart," which beat out Randy Newman's *Toy Story 2* nominated song "When She Loved Me" to win the 1999 Grammy® for Best Original Song from a Motion Picture.

Disney closed the final year of the twentieth century in its customary grand style with a Walt Disney World-Epcot Center event featuring original songs performed by the incomparable London Symphony Orchestra. Having successfully encapsulated the zeitgeist of the dawning millennium, conductor Gavin Greenway's uplifting yet dynamic compositions of goodwill and camaraderie were recorded and released on 1999's *Millennium Celebration Album*.

A NEW GENERATION

With the new century came new Disney escapades—including 2000's original animated feature, *The Emperor's New Groove*, the story of Kuzco, a young, self-absorbed Incan emperor. He vexes a scorned sorceress who, botching a plan to poison him, turns him into a talking llama instead. Scored by John Debney, the film also features songs by composer David Hartley and lyricist/performer Sting, who earned a 2000 Grammy® nomination for Best Original Song for their collaboration on "My Funny Friend and Me." Other notable artists who lent their voices to this madcap Disney offering were Tom Jones, Eartha Kitt, and Shawn Colvin.

Like the two *Toy Story* films and *A Bug's Life* before it, *Monsters, Inc.*—the fourth creation by computer-animation giant Pixar—featured the latest in computer animation technology. The film is about two monsters who, as employees of a scream-inducing factory called Monsters, Inc., frighten children and "collect" their screams which then provide power to the monster's city. Although losing the Oscar for Best Animated Feature that year, *Monsters Inc.* did garner a Grammy® for Best Original Song for composer/lyricist Randy Newman's "If I Didn't Have You."

A lonely, orphaned Hawaiian girl adopts a ukulele-playing, genetically engineered pet in 2002's endearing tale of misfit friendship, *Lilo and Stitch*. Unbeknownst to Lilo, her new friend Stitch, who possesses a high intelligence and superhuman strength, escaped to Earth after being created by an extraterrestrial mad scientist as a weapon. The *Lilo and Stitch* soundtrack, which features Elvis Presley's "Blue Hawaii," and the popular "Hawaiian Roller Coaster Ride," hit No. 1 on *Billboard*'s Soundtrack chart, and went as high as No. 11 on the *Billboard* 200.

Walt Disney, July 1944

Swashbuckling made an enormous comeback with Disney's live-action *Pirates of the Caribbean* films. Born as a Disneyland ride in 1967, the Pirates phenomenon hit the big screen in 2003 with *The Curse of the Black Pearl.* Disney's first PG-13 film, it featured sweeping, original music by Klaus Badelt. Two more *Pirates* films followed: *Dead Man's Chest* in 2006 and *At World's End* in 2007.

The Incredibles features animation as only Pixar can do it. The 2004 feature film finds a pair of retired superheroes raising a family in quiet, suburban anonymity, but yearning for adventure. When evil rears its ugly head, the family, foibles and all, is spurred to heroic action to save the day. Michael Giacchino's jazzy, splashy "The Incredits," won a Grammy for Best Instrumental Arrangement.

Romeo and Juliet go to high school with the wildly popular Disney Channel Original Movie, *High School Musical.* Inspired by Shakespeare's timeless romance, the film finds a pair of high school students from rival cliques auditioning for roles in the school musical. The tidal wave of *High School Musical* popularity began with the film's release in January 2006. David Lawrence's soundtrack was the best-selling album that year. A concert tour in 2006 was followed by a stage version, television sequel, and ice version in 2007. A feature film sequel was released in 2008.

Whether she's called Miley Cyrus or Hannah Montana, the songstress daughter of country singer Billy Ray Cyrus is a teen sensation and role model. Her wholesome image and upbeat vocals have been showcased in a television series that debuted in 2006, a "Best of Both Worlds" tour and 3-D concert film, and a film planned for theatrical release.

Traditional Disney animation returned to the big screen in 2007 with *Enchanted.* Mixing artful traditional animation, computer-generated fantasy, the realism of live action and the music and lyrics of Alan Menken and Stephen Schwartz, the film finds a fairy-tale princess dropped into the middle of New York City's Times Square. Her handsome prince follows to rescue her, as does a good deal of magic and charm.

Perhaps it was Walt Disney himself who summed up best the reasons for the important role and the incredible success music has enjoyed in Disney animated features, live-action motion pictures, and theme parks:

"Music has always had a prominent part in all our products from the early cartoon days. So much so, in fact, that I cannot think of the pictorial story without thinking about the complementary music that will fulfill it... I have had no formal musical training. But by long experience and by strong personal leaning, I've selected musical themes, original or adapted, that were guided to wide audience acceptance.

"But credit for the memorable songs and scores must, of course, go to the brilliant composers and musicians who have been associated with me through the years."

G A7 D G D/F# A7/E D G D/F# A7/E
la. Long a - go, there were three pigs, lit - tle hand-some pig - gy wigs. For the
Came the day when fate did frown and the wolf blew in - to town. With a
D G D/F# D#dim7 A7 D A7 D G
big bad, ver - y big, ver - y bad wolf they didn't give three figs. Num - ber one was ver - y
gruff, "puff, puff" he puffed just e-nough and the hay house fell right down. One and Two were scared to
D/F# A7/E D G D/F# A7/E D G D/F# D#dim7
gay and he built his house with hay. With a hey - hey toot, he blew on his flute and he
death of the big bad wolf - ie's breath. "By the hair of your chin-ny-chin, I'll blow you in," and the
A7 D D7 G C#7 F#m B7 Em A7
played a - round all day. Num - ber two was fond of jigs and so he built his
twig house an-swered yes. No one left but num - ber Three to save the pig - let

D G D/F# G C#7 F#m B7 E7 A7
house with twigs. Heigh did-dle did-dle, he played on his fid-dle and danced with la - dy pigs. Num - ber
fam - i - ly. When they knocked, he fast un - locked and said, "Come in with me!" Now they
D G D/F# A7/E D G D/F# A7/E D
three said, "Nix on tricks, I will build my house with bricks." He had no chance to
all were safe in - side and the bricks hurt wolf - ie's pride. So, he slid down the chim-'ney and,
G D/F# D#dim7 A7 D D7 no chord
sing and dance 'cause work and play don't mix! Ha ha ha! The two lit-tle, do lit-tle
oh, by Jim-'ney, in the fi - re he was fried. Ha ha ha! The three lit-tle, free lit-tle
1 2 D D.C. al Coda
pigs just winked and laughed, ha ha!
pigs re - joiced and laughed, ha ha!
CODA
G
la.

I'm Wishing

From Walt Disney's *Snow White And The Seven Dwarfs*

Words by LARRY MOREY
Music by FRANK CHURCHILL

Slowly

Bb/G Bb/F Bb/D Bbm/Db C7

mf

Gm Gm7 Gm6

It's so sad and lone - ly, wish - ing well,

Gm C7 F F6 Fmaj7 F6

long - ing for some - one you nev - er see.

Copyright © 1937 by Bourne Co.
Copyright Renewed
International Copyright Secured All Rights Reserved

Gm
Gm7
Gm6
Make him love me on - ly, wish - ing well,
him
Dm7/G
G7
Gm7/C
C7
won't you grant this fa - vor to me?
I'm
F6
C9
wish - ing for the one I love to
F6
find me to - day.
I'm

F6
hop - ing,
and I'm dream - ing
C9
of the nice things,
F6
he'll
she'll
say.
Cm7
F7
Tell me, wish - ing well,
B♭
will my wish come true?
Dm7
G7
With your mag - ic spell,

C7
won't you tell my loved one what to do? I'm
F6
wish - ing for the one I
C9
love to find me to -
1
F6 B♭/C F A♭dim Gm7 C7
day. I'm
2
F
day.

Some Day My Prince Will Come

From Walt Disney's
Snow White And The Seven Dwarfs

Words by LARRY MOREY
Music by FRANK CHURCHILL

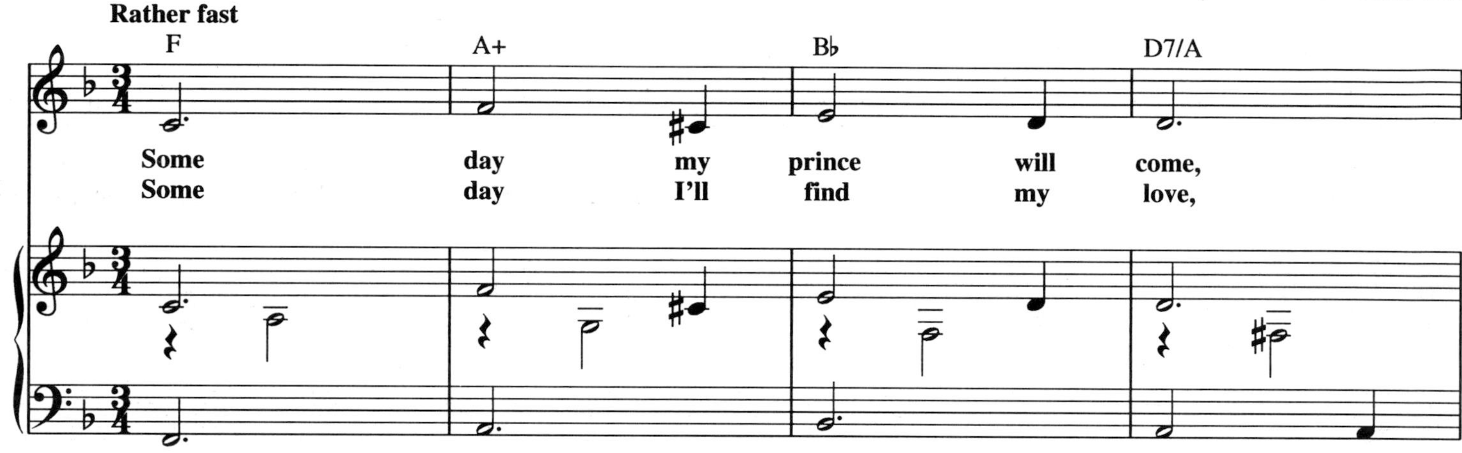

Rather fast
F
A+
B♭
D7/A
Some day my prince will come,
Some day I'll find my love,

Gm
B♭
B♭+
C7/E
F/A
some day I'll find my love, and how thrill - ing that
some one to call my own, and I'll know her the

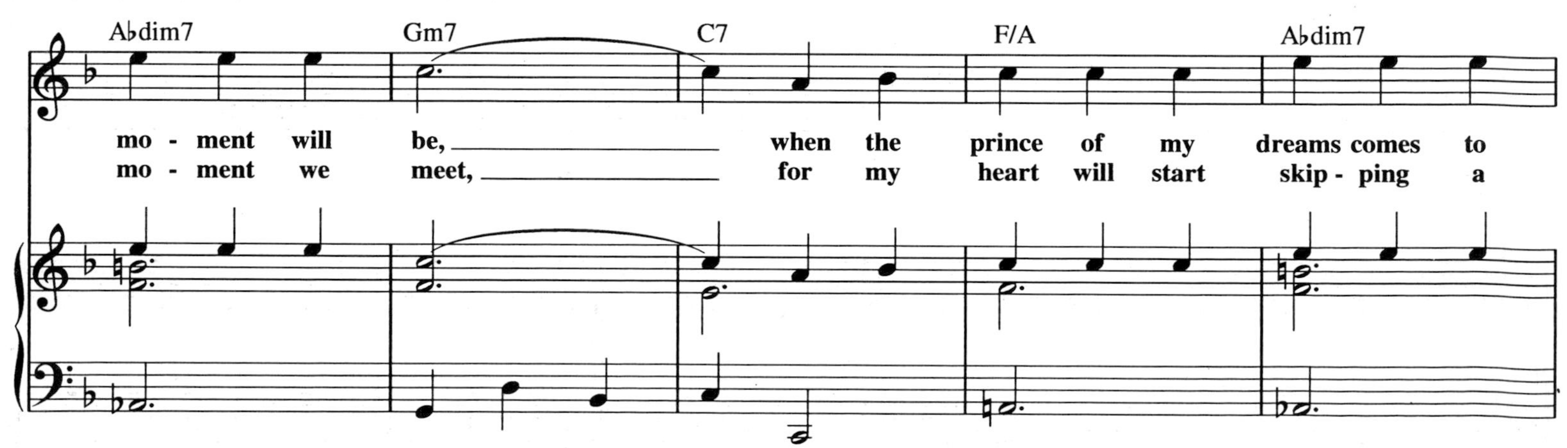

A♭dim7
Gm7
C7
F/A
A♭dim7
mo - ment will be, when the prince of my dreams comes to
mo - ment we meet, for my heart will start skip - ping a

Copyright © 1937 by Bourne Co.
Copyright Renewed
International Copyright Secured All Rights Reserved

Gm7
C7
F
A+
B♭
me.
beat.
He'll
Some
whis - per
day we'll
"I love
say and
D7/A
Gm
B♭
B♭+
C7
you"
do
and
things
steal
we've
a
been
kiss
long
or
- ing
two though he's
to though she's
F
A7
A+
B♭+
Bdim7
F
F♯dim7
far a - way I'll find my love some day some day when my
Gm7
C7
1
F
A♭7
Gm7
C7
2
F
dreams come true.
true.
8va

Whistle While You Work

From Walt Disney's
Snow White And The Seven Dwarfs

Words by LARRY MOREY
Music by FRANK CHURCHILL

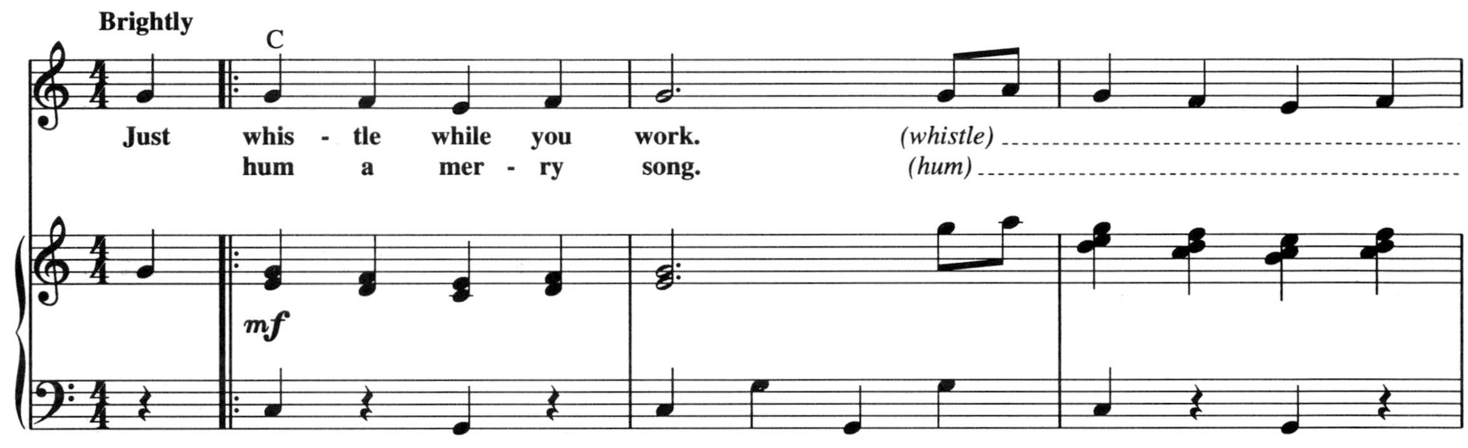
Brightly
C
Just whis - tle while you work. (whistle)
hum a mer - ry song. (hum)
mf

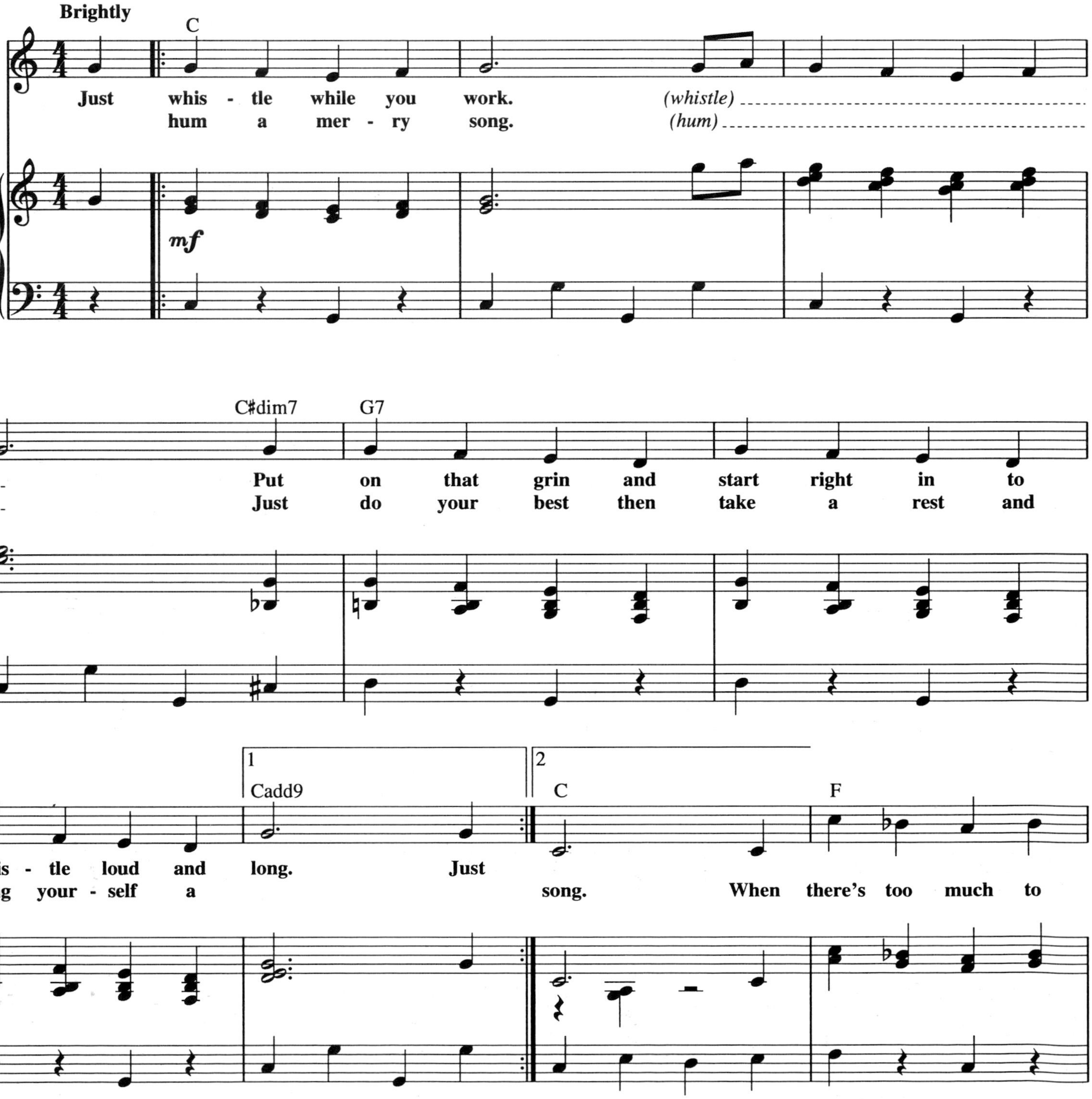

C#dim7 G7
Put on that grin and start right in to
Just do your best then take a rest and

1 Cadd9 2 C F
whis - tle loud and long. Just
sing your - self a song. When there's too much to

Copyright © 1937 by Bourne Co.
Copyright Renewed
International Copyright Secured All Rights Reserved

Fm
do, don't let it both - er you. For - get your trou - bles,
C6 C#dim7 Dm7 G7 C
try to be just like a cheer - ful chick - a - dee. And whis - tle while you
C#dim7 G7
work. (whistle) Come on, get smart, tune
C C6
up and start to whis - tle while you work.

Heigh-Ho

The Dwarfs' Marching Song

From Walt Disney's

Snow White And The Seven Dwarfs

Words by LARRY MOREY
Music by FRANK CHURCHILL

March tempo

G Em Am7 D7 G Em Am7 D7/F# G Am/C B7

mf

We dig dig dig dig dig dig dig in our mine the whole day thru. To dig dig dig dig dig dig dig is what we like to do. And while we dig we
dig dig dig dig dig dig dig and we try to do our bit. We dig dig dig dig dig dig dig un - til it's time to quit. And then we war - ble

Copyright © 1937 by Bourne Co.
Copyright Renewed
International Copyright Secured All Rights Reserved

Em Am/C B7 Em
al - ways sing, for when you dig there ain't a bet - ter thing than a
down the scale as we all go march - ing down the trail right a -
Eb+ D7 Am7 Fm6
tune, than a tune, you can whis - tle or can
long, right a - long, to the rhy - thm of the
D7/F# D7 G B7 C
croon.
song.
"Heigh - ho, heigh - ho." To
ho, heigh - ho." It's
A7 D7 C G/B
make your trou - bles go, just keep on sing - ing
home from work we go. (Whistle)

C B7/D# Em Cm6/E♭ G/D D7
all day long, "Heigh - ho, heigh - ho, heigh - ho." "Heigh -
"Heigh - ho, heigh - ho, heigh - ho." "Heigh -
G B7 C A7
ho, heigh - ho." For if you're feel - ing
ho, heigh - ho," all sev - en in a
D7 C G/B C B7/D# Em Cm6/E♭
low, you pos - i - tive - ly can't go wrong with a
row. (Whistle) with a
G/D D7 1 G D7 2 G
"Heigh, heigh - ho, heigh - ho." "Heigh -
"Heigh, heigh - ho."

Hi-Diddle-Dee-dee
(An Actor's Life For Me)
From Walt Disney's *Pinocchio*

Words by NED WASHINGTON
Music by LEIGH HARLINE

Brightly
N.C.
Cm7♭5 F7
Cm7
F7
f
sfz

B♭
Fdim7
F7
The grass is al - ways green - er in the oth - er fel - low's yard. No
mf

D
Cdim7
A7
mat - ter what your life may be you think your life is hard. If

Copyright © 1940 by Bourne Co.
Copyright Renewed
International Copyright Secured All Rights Reserved

E♭m7
Gm7
we could pick and choose and na - ture was - n't a fac - tor,

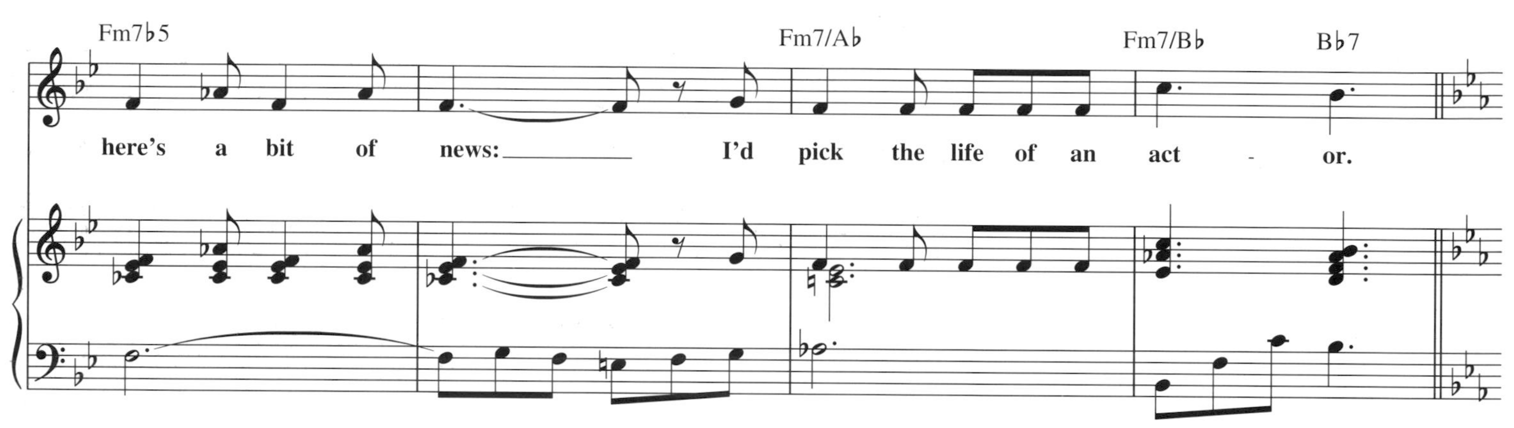
Fm7♭5
Fm7/A♭
Fm7/B♭
B♭7
here's a bit of news: I'd pick the life of an act - or.

E♭
B♭7
E♭
Hi - did - dle - dee - dee, an act - or's life for me, a
mf - f

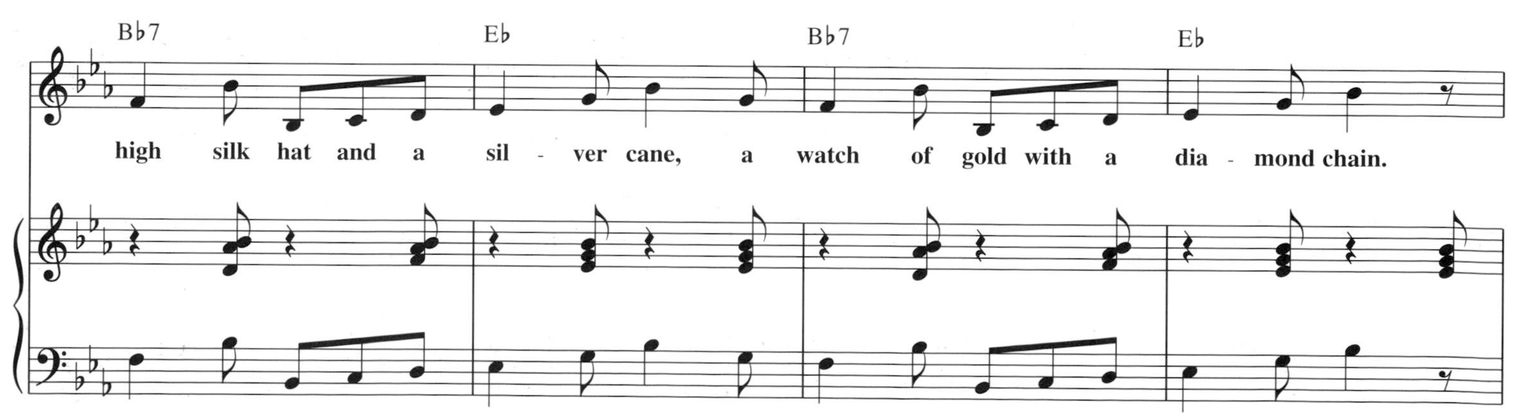
B♭7
E♭
B♭7
E♭
high silk hat and a sil - ver cane, a watch of gold with a dia - mond chain.

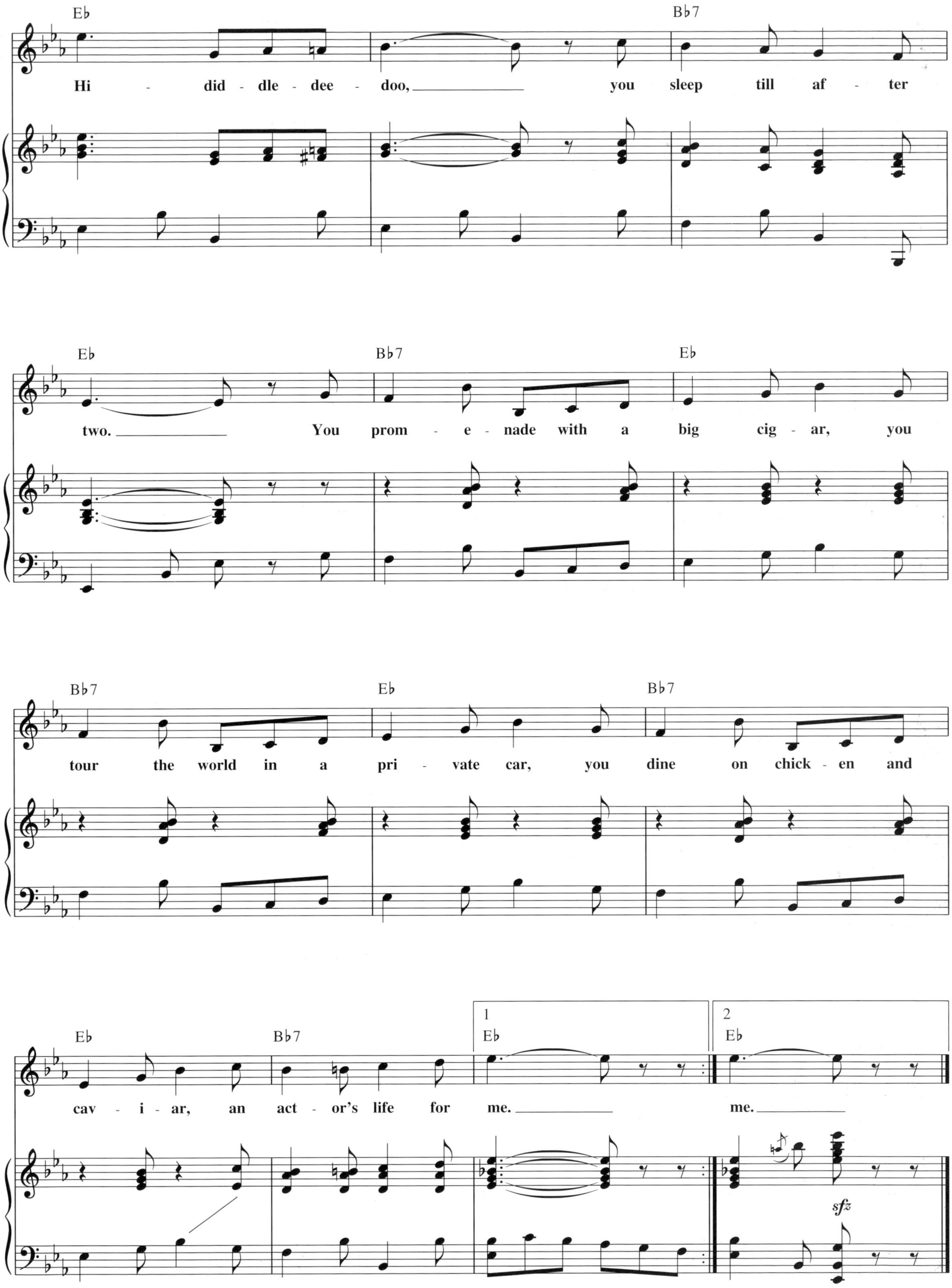

Eb Bb7

Hi - did - dle - dee - doo, you sleep till af - ter

Eb Bb7 Eb

two. You prom - e - nade with a big cig - ar, you

Bb7 Eb Bb7

tour the world in a pri - vate car, you dine on chick - en and

Eb
Bb7
1
Eb
2
Eb
cav - i - ar, an act - or's life for me.
me.
sfz

Give A Little Whistle

From Walt Disney's *Pinocchio*

Words by NED WASHINGTON
Music by LEIGH HARLINE

Moderately fast

Eb F#dim7 | Bb7/F Bb7 | Eb

When you get in trou - ble and you don't know right from

mf

Edim7 | Bb7/F F#dim7 | Bb7/F Bb7

wrong, give a lit - tle whis - tle! *(Whistle)* ___ Give a lit - tle

Ebmaj9 Eb6 Fdim/Ab | Eb/G Bb7 | Eb F#dim7

whis - tle! *(Whistle)* ___ When you meet temp -

Copyright © 1940 by Bourne Co.
Copyright Renewed
International Copyright Secured All Rights Reserved

B♭7/F B♭7 E♭ Edim7 B♭7/F F♯dim7
ta - tion and the urge is ve - ry strong, give a lit - tle whis - tle! (Whistle)
B♭7/F B♭7 E♭maj9 E♭6 Fdim/A♭ E♭/G D7♭9 Gm
Give a lit - tle whis - tle! (Whistle) Not just a
Adim7 Gm D7/F♯ Cm6/E♭ D7
lit - tle squeak, puck - er up and blow. And if your
Gm F♯dim7 B♭7/F A7/B♭ B♭9 E♭ F♯dim7
whis - tle's weak, yell "Jim - i - ny Crick - et." Take the straight and

B♭7/F
B♭7
E♭
E♭
Edim7
nar - row path and if you start to slide, give a lit - tle
B♭7/F
F♯dim7
F♯dim7
C7/G
G♯dim7
whis - tle. (Whistle)
Give a lit - tle whis - tle (Whistle)
C7/G
Fm7
B♭7
B♭9
B♭7♭9
and al - ways let your con - science be your
1
2
E♭6
Cm7
Fm7
F♯m/B♭
B♭9
E♭6
Fm9
B♭9
E♭6
guide.
guide.

When You Wish Upon A Star

From Walt Disney's *Pinocchio*

Words by NED WASHINGTON
Music by LEIGH HARLINE

With expression

C A7 Dm Dm7 G7
When you wish up - on a star, makes no dif - f'rence

Cdim7 C C6 C/E E♭dim7 Dm
who you are. An - y - thing your heart de - sires will

Dm7/G G7 C6 G7 C A7
come to you. If your heart is

Copyright © 1940 by Bourne Co.
Copyright Renewed
International Copyright Secured All Rights Reserved

Dm Dm7 G7 Cdim7 C
in your dream, no re - quest is too ex - treme.
C/E E♭dim7 Dm Dm7 Dm7/G G7
When you wish up - on a star as dream - ers
C Dm7♭5/G G13 Cmaj7 C6 G9 Gdim7 G7
do. Fate is kind, she brings to
Cdim7 C Am7 D7
those who love, the sweet ful - fill - ment of their se - cret

Fm6
G7
G7#5(♭9)
G7
C
A7
long - ing. Like a bolt out
(♮)
Dm
Dm7
G7
Cdim7
C
C6
of the blue, fate steps in and sees you thru.
1
C/E
E♭dim7
Dm7
Dm7/G
G7
When you wish up - on a star your dream comes
C
G13
2
Dm7/G
G7
C
true. dream comes true.

I've Got No Strings

From Walt Disney's *Pinocchio*

Words by NED WASHINGTON
Music by LEIGH HARLINE

Moderately

Moderately
G D7 G D7 G D7 G Fdim D7 D+
mf

G D7 G D7 G
Why does the gay lit - tle dick - y bird sing? What put the "zing" in a
mf

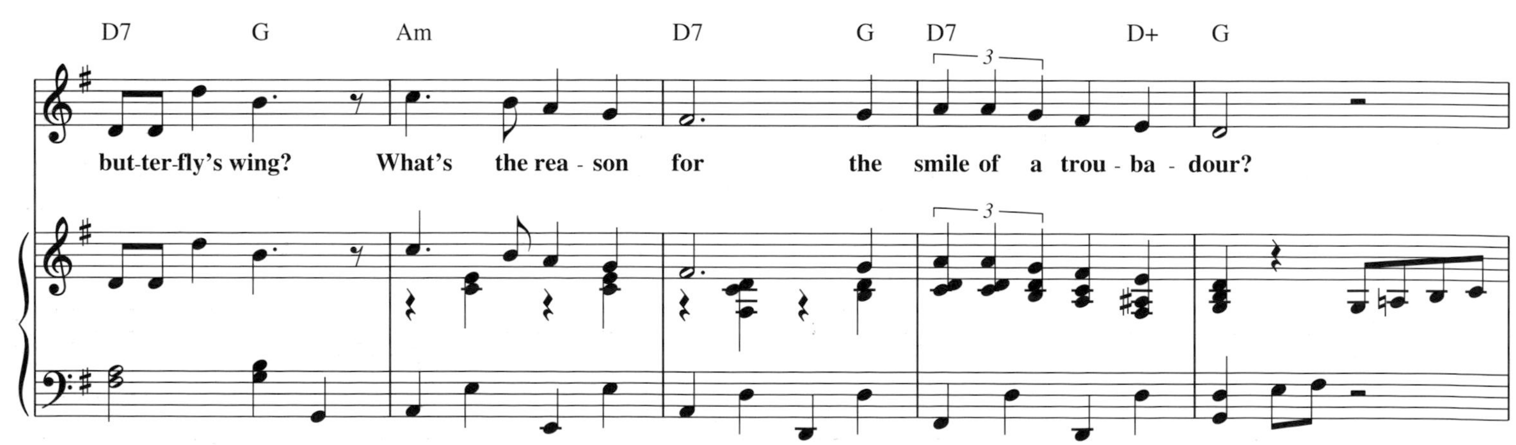
D7 G Am D7 G D7 D+ G
but-ter-fly's wing? What's the rea - son for the smile of a trou - ba - dour?
3

Copyright © 1940 by Bourne Co.
Copyright Renewed
International Copyright Secured All Rights Reserved

D7 G D7 G D7 G
Why does a breeze have a bar - rel of fun? Ev - en the bee who's a son - of - a - gun, it's
A7 D G A7 D7
all be - cause they're free, and string - less the same as me.
D7#5 G G6 D7sus D7 D7sus D7 G
I've got no strings to hold me down, to make me fret or make me frown.
mff
G6 D7sus D7 D7sus D7 G6
I had strings but now I'm free, there are no strings on me.

B7
Em B7 Em
B7
Em
Hi - o the mer - ri - o I'm as hap - py as can be.
A7
D A7 D
A7
D Bm D7/A
I want the world to know nothing ev - er wor - ries me. I've
G G6 D7sus D7 D7sus D7 G
got no strings so I have fun, I'm not tied up to an - y - one.
G6 D7sus D7 D7sus D7
1
G6 D7♯5
2
G D7 G
How I love my lib - er - ty, there are no strings on me. I've me.

Baby Mine

From Walt Disney's *Dumbo*

Words by NED WASHINGTON
Music by FRANK CHURCHILL

Moderately slow

Eb Bb/D Cm Cm/Bb Ab6 Abm6 Abm6/Bb Bb7

Ba - by mine ___ don't you cry. ___

mf

Eb Bb/D Cm Cm/Bb Ab6 Abm6 Abm6/Bb Bb7

Ba - by mine ___ dry your eye. ___

Ab Ab/G Fm7 Ab6 Abdim

Rest your head close to my heart, nev - er to part, ba - by of

Copyright © 1941 by Walt Disney Productions
Copyright Renewed
World Rights Controlled by Bourne Co.
International Copyright Secured All Rights Reserved

Eb/G
Fm7
Eb
Bb9sus
Eb
Bb/D
Cm
Cm/Bb
Ab6
Abm6
mine.
Lit - tle
one
when you
play
Abm6/Bb
Bb7
Eb
Bb/D
Cm
Cm/Bb
Ab6
Abm6
Abm6/Bb
Bb7
don't
you
mind
what they
say.
Ab
Ab/G
Fm7
Ab6
Abdim
Let
those
eyes
spar - kle
and
shine,
nev - er
a
tear,
ba - by
of
Eb/G
Fm7
Eb
G7#5
Somewhat faster
Cm
mine.
If
they
knew
sweet lit - tle

Dm7 Dm7/G G7 Cm
you, they'd end up lov - ing you
Dm7 Dm7/G G7 Cm Cm/E♭ Gm
too. All those same peo - ple who scold
Gm/B♭ Cm Am7♭5 D7 Gm D/F♯
you, what they'd give just for the right to
Fm7 B♭7 E♭ B♭/D Cm Cm/B♭ A♭6 A♭m6
hold you. From your head to your toes,

A♭m6/B♭ B♭7 E♭ B♭/D Cm Cm/B♭ A♭6 A♭m6 A♭m6/B♭ B♭7
you're not much, good-ness knows,
A♭ A♭/G Fm7 A♭6 A♭dim
but you're so pre-cious to me, cute as can be, ba-by of
E♭/G Fm7 E♭ B♭7 A♭dim B♭7♭9 E♭
mine. be, ba-by of mine.
A♭6 E♭ A♭6 E♭

When I See An Elephant Fly

From Walt Disney's *Dumbo*

Words by NED WASHINGTON
Music by OLIVER WALLACE

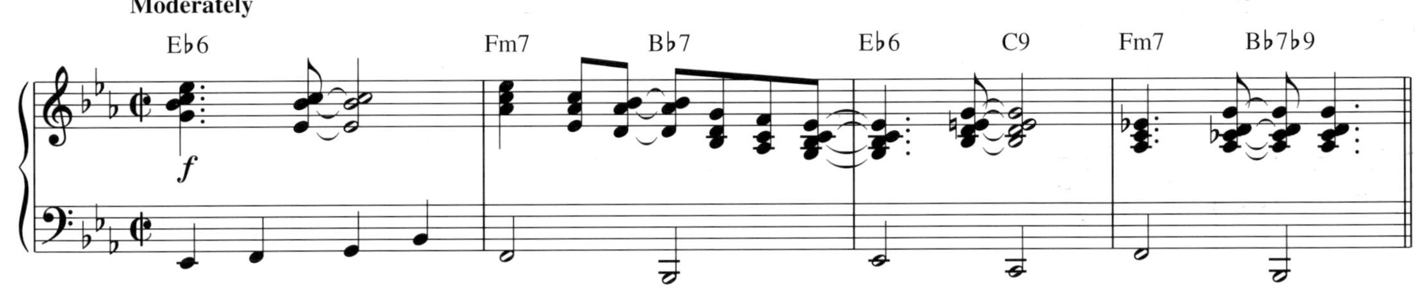

Moderately
Eb6 Fm7 Bb7 Eb6 C9 Fm7 Bb7b9
f

Eb Eb/G Fm7 Fm7/Bb Bb7 Eb Eb/G Fm Bb9 Eb Bb7
Ho! Ho! When I think a-bout it, Ho! Ho! I have to laugh
mf

Eb Eb/G Fm Fm7/Bb Bb7 Cm7 F7 Bb7
Ho! Ho! Just to think a-bout it bends me right in half.

Copyright © 1941 by Walt Disney Productions
Copyright Renewed
World Rights Controlled by Bourne Co.
International Copyright Secured All Rights Reserved

Fm7 Bb7 Eb D7 Eb
I saw a pea - nut stand, heard a rub - ber band, I saw a
gar - den walk, a ba - nan - a stalk, I saw a
mf - f
Bb7 Bb/Ab Eb/G Ebm/Gb Bb7/F Bb7 Eb Eb7#5
need - le that winked its eye. But I think I will have seen
pig with an aw - ful sty. But I think I will have seen
3
Ab B9 Eb/Bb F7 Fm7/Bb Bb7
ev - 'ry - thing when I see an el - e-phant fly. I saw a
ev - 'ry - thing when I see an el - e-phant fly. I saw the
Fm7 Bb7 Eb D7 Eb
front porch swing, heard a dia - mond ring, I saw a
su - gar bowl, saw the jel - ly roll, I saw a

Bb7 Bb/Ab Eb/G Ebm/Gb Bb7/F Bb7 Eb Eb7#5
pol - ka dot rail - road tie. But I think I will have seen
pick - et fence that's no lie. But I think I will have seen
Ab B9 Eb C7 F7 Bb9 Eb6 Eb7
ev - 'ry - thing when I see an el - e-phant fly.
ev - 'ry - thing when I see an el - e-phant fly.
Ab Abm Eb
I saw a clothes horse rar' up and buck. They tell me that a man made a
I ev - en heard a choc - o - late drop. I went in - to a store, saw a
Eb7 Ab Abm
veg - 'ta - ble "Truck." I did - n't see that, I on - ly heard but
bi - cy - cle shop. You can't de - ny the things that you see, but

E♭ F7 B♭7
just to be soc - ia - ble I'l take their word. ___ I saw a
I know there's cer - tain things that just can't be. ___ The oth - er
Fm7 B♭7 E♭ D7 E♭ B♭7 B♭/A♭
lan - tern slide, ___ saw an old cow - hide, ___ and I just laugh'd till I thought _ I'd
day by chance, _ saw an old barn dance, _ so I'm a gull - i - ble sort ___ of
E♭/G E♭m/G♭ B♭7/F B♭7 E♭ E♭7♯5 A♭ B9
die. ___ But I think I will have seen ev - 'ry - thing __ when
guy. ___ But I think I will have seen ev - 'ry - thing __ when
E♭ C7 F7 B♭7 1 E♭6 Cdim7 B♭7 2 E♭6
I see an el - e-phant fly. ___ I saw a
I see an el - e-phant fly.

Little April Shower

From Walt Disney's *Bambi*

Words by LARRY MOREY
Music by FRANK CHURCHILL

Moderately

C G7 C F C F

mp

Drip, drip, drop, lit - tle A - pril show - er, beat - ing a tune as you
Drip, drip, drop, lit - tle A - pril show - er, beat - ing a tune ev - 'ry -

C G7 C F C F

fall all a-round. Drip, drip, drop, lit - tle A - pril show - er, what can com-pare with your
where that you fall. Drip, drip, drop, lit - tle A - pril show - er, I'm get - ting wet and I

C To Coda E B7 E A

beau - ti - ful sound. Drip, drip, drop, when the sky is cloud - y
don't care at all.

© 1942 Wonderland Music Company, Inc.
Copyright Renewed
All Rights Reserved Used by Permission

E
A
E
B7
your pret - ty mu - sic can bright - en the day. Drip, drip, drop, when the
E
A
E
B
G7
D.C. al Coda
sun says, "How - dy" you say "Good - bye" right a - way.
CODA
F
C
F
C
F
C
Drip! Drop! Drip! Drop! I'll nev - er be a - fraid of a
p
G7
C
good lit - tle gay lit - tle A - pril ser - e - nade.
cresc.

Zip-A-Dee-Doo-Dah

From Walt Disney's *Song Of The South*

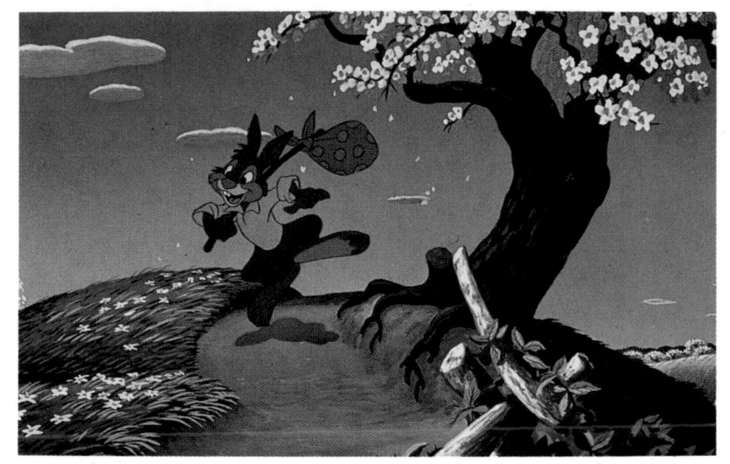

Words by RAY GILBERT
Music by ALLIE WRUBEL

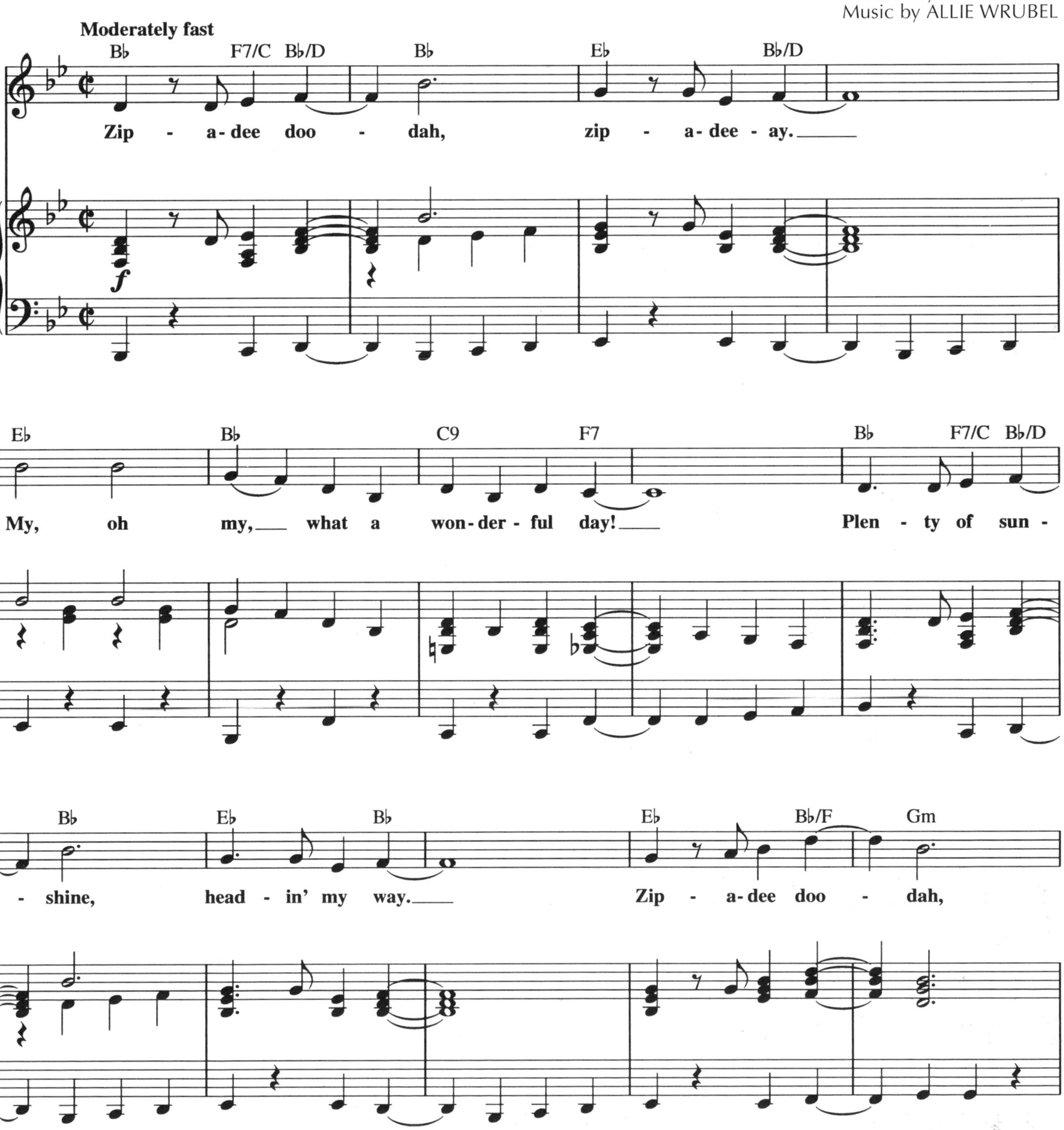

Moderately fast
B♭ F7/C B♭/D B♭ E♭ B♭/D
Zip - a-dee doo - dah, zip - a-dee - ay.
f
E♭ B♭ C9 F7 B♭ F7/C B♭/D
My, oh my, what a won-der - ful day! Plen - ty of sun -
B♭ E♭ B♭ E♭ B♭/F Gm
- shine, head - in' my way. Zip - a-dee doo - dah,

© 1945 Walt Disney Music Company
Copyright Renewed
All Rights Reserved Used by Permission

E♭6 F9 B♭ F7 B♭dim7 B♭
zip a-dee-ay! Mis-ter Blue-bird on my shoul-der.
Gm7 C7 F
It's the truth, it's "act-ch'll." Ev-'ry-thing is
B♭ F7/C B♭/D Cm B♭ E♭ B♭
"sa-tis-fact-ch'll." Zip-a-dee doo-dah, zip-a-dee-ay!
E♭ B♭ Gm C7 F7 B♭ B♭/D D♭dim F7/C
1
2
Won-der-ful feel-ing, won-der-ful day.

Lavender Blue
(Dilly Dilly)
From Walt Disney's *So Dear To My Heart*

Words by LARRY MOREY
Music by ELIOT DANIEL

Moderately

C G Gm7 C9 F

Lav - en - der blue dil - ly, dil - ly, lav - en - der

mf

C F C F D7

green; if {I / you} were king, dil - ly, dil - ly {I'd / you'd} need a

G7 C G Gm7 C9 F

queen. Who told me so, dil - ly, dil - ly, who told me

© 1948 Walt Disney Music Company
Copyright Renewed
All Rights Reserved Used by Permission

C
F
C
F
so? I told my - self, dil - ly, dil - ly,
Dm7
G7
C
F
I told me so. If your dil - ly, dil - ly heart feels a
Em7
A9
Em7
A7
dil - ly, dil - ly way 'n if you'll an - swer, "yes." In a
G
D7
pret - ty lit - tle church on a dil - ly, dil - ly day
you'll
I'll
be wed in a

G7
C
G
Gm7
C9
dil - ly, dil - ly dress of lav - en - der blue dil - ly, dil - ly,
F
C
F
lav - en - der green, then I'll / you'll be
C
F
Dm7
G7
1
C
king, dil - ly, dil - ly and you'll / I'll be my / your queen.
F
D7/F#
Dm7/G
G7
2
C
F/C
Csus
C
queen.

Bibbidi-Bobbidi-Boo
(The Magic Song)
From Walt Disney's *Cinderella*

Words by JERRY LIVINGSTON
Music by MACK DAVID and AL HOFFMAN

Brightly

F

Sa - la - ga - doo - la men - chic - ka boo - la bib - bi - di - bob - bi - di - boo

mp

C7

put 'em to - geth - er and what have you got bib - bi - di - bob - bi - di - boo.

F C7

F

Sa - la - ga - doo - la men - chic - ka boo - la bib - bi - di - bob - bi - di - boo

© 1948 Walt Disney Music Company
Copyright Renewed
All Rights Reserved Used by Permission

C7
it - 'll do mag - ic be - lieve it or not,
bib - bi - di - bob - bi - di - boo.
F
B♭
Sa - la - ga - doo - la means
F
men-chic-ka boo - le-roo,
G7 Dm7 B♭m G7
but the thing-a-ma - bob that does the job is
C7 Gm7 C7
bib - bi - di - bob-bi - di - boo.
F
Sa - la - ga - doo - la men-chic-ka boo la bib - bi - di - bob-bi - di - boo
C7
put 'em to-geth-er and what have you got bib-bi-di - bob-bi-di bib-bi-di - bob-bi-di bib-bi-di - bob-bi-di - boo.
F

A Dream Is A Wish Your Heart Makes

From Walt Disney's *Cinderella*

Words and Music by MACK DAVID, AL HOFFMAN and JERRY LIVINGSTON

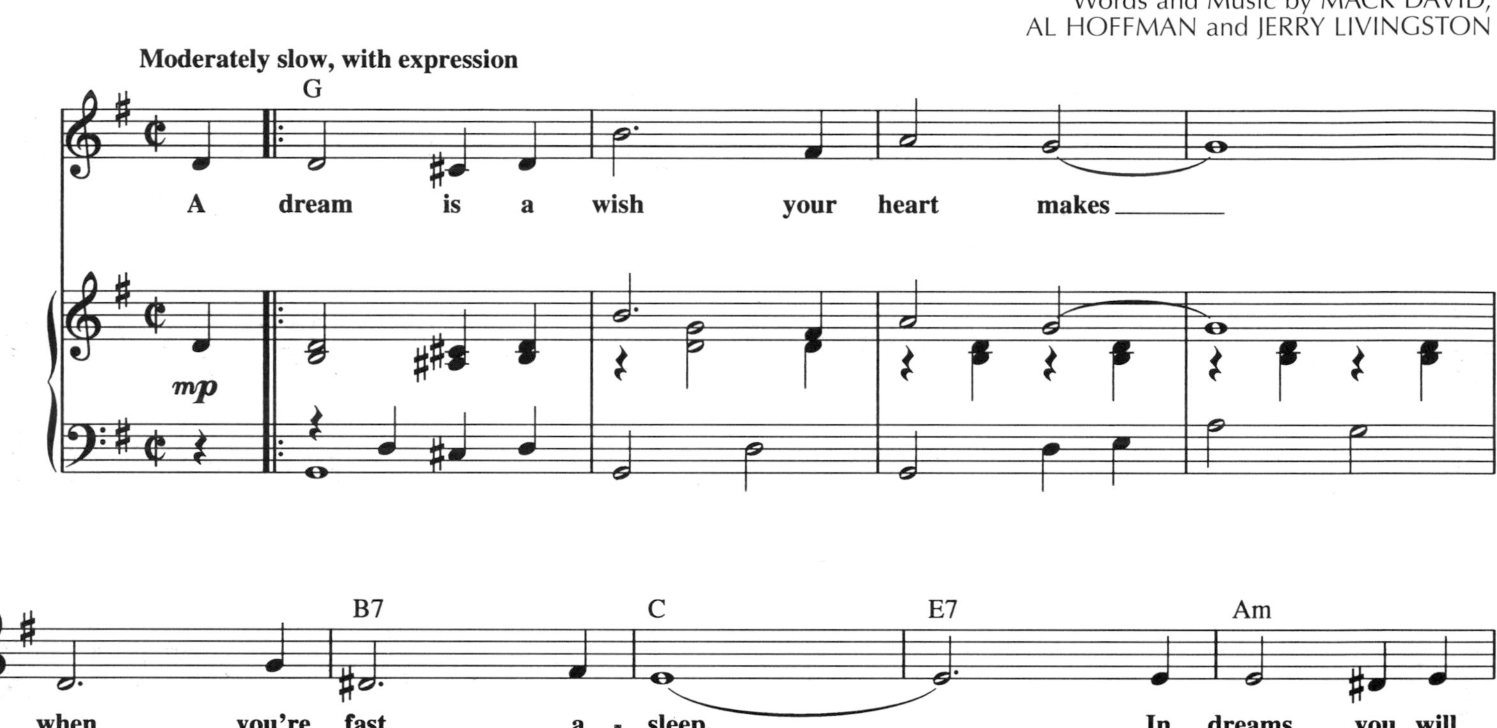
Moderately slow, with expression
G
A dream is a wish your heart makes
mp

B7
C
E7
Am
when you're fast a - sleep.
In dreams you will
3

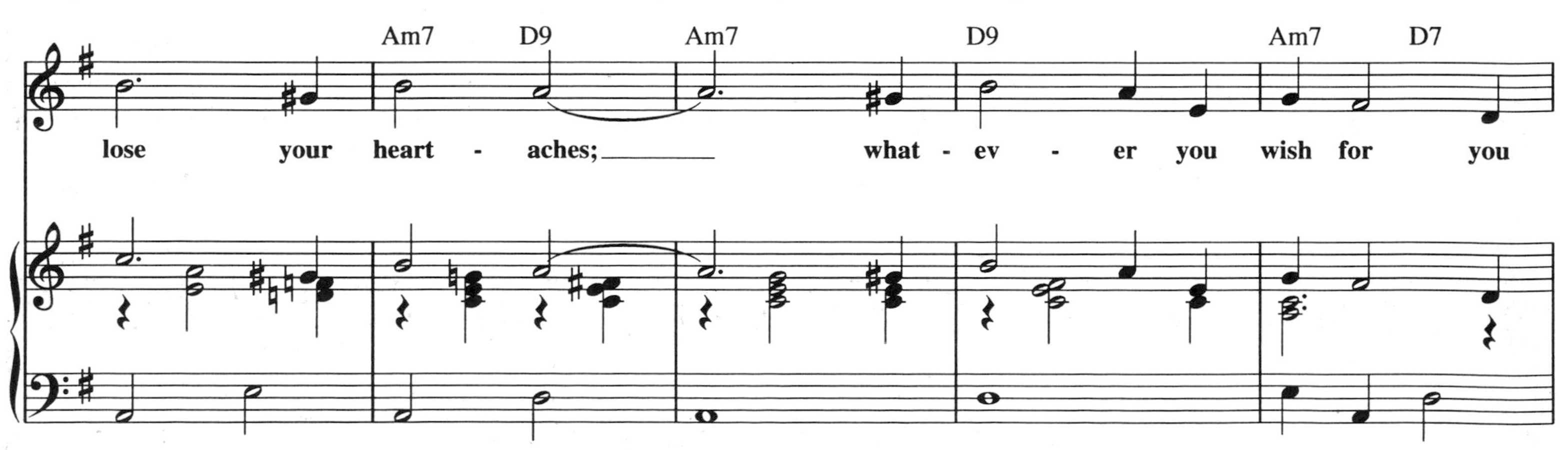
Am7
D9
Am7
D9
Am7
D7
lose your heart - aches;
what - ev - er you wish for you

© 1948 Walt Disney Music Company
Copyright Renewed
All Rights Reserved Used by Permission

G Em7 Am7 D7#5(♭9) G
keep. Have faith in your dreams and some - day
Dm7 G7 G7#5 C
your rain - bow will come smil - ling thru. No mat - ter
Cmaj7 F9 Gsus G A9 Am7 D7 Am7/E
how your heart is griev - ing, if you keep on be - liev - ing, the dream that you
Am7 D9 1 G6 E♭7 D7 2 A♭maj7 G F#/G G
wish will come true. A true.
8va
rit.

I'm Late

From Walt Disney's *Alice In Wonderland*

Words by BOB HILLIARD
Music by SAMMY FAIN

Brightly

Cm

I'm late, I'm late for a ver - y im - por - tant date. No

mp

C G7 C

time to say hel - lo, good - bye, I'm late, I'm late, I'm late, I'm late and

Cm Em

when I wave, I lose the time I save. My fuz - zy ears and

© 1949 Walt Disney Music Company
Copyright Renewed
All Rights Reserved Used by Permission

B7 Em Am Em G7
whis - kers took me too much time to shave. I run and then I
mf
C/G G7 C B7 Em
hop, hop, hop, I wish that I could fly. There's dan - ger if I dare to stop and
D7 G7 Cm
here's the rea - son why, (you see) I'm o - ver - due, I'm in a rab - bit
D7 C G7 C F C
stew. Can't e - ven say good - bye, hel - lo, I'm late, I'm late, I'm late.

The Second Star To The Right

From Walt Disney's *Peter Pan*

Words by SAMMY CAHN
Music by SAMMY FAIN

Moderately slow with expression
E♭
G7
Cm
Gm
The sec - ond star to the right shines in the night for you
mp

A♭
B♭7/A♭
E♭/G
C9
Fm7
A♭/B♭ A♭9
E♭/G
Fm7 B♭7/F
E♭
to tell you that the dreams you plan real - ly can come true. The sec - ond

G7
Cm
Gm
A♭
B♭7/A♭
star to the right shines with a light that's rare and if it's Nev-er

© 1951 Walt Disney Music Company
Copyright Renewed
All Rights Reserved Used by Permission

Eb/G C9 Fm7 Ab/Bb Bb9 Eb Fm7 F#dim Eb/G Ab Bbm7
Land you need, it's light will lead you there. Twin-kle, twin-kle lit - tle star
Ab/C Bbm7 Eb9 Ab G7b9/D Cm
so I'll know where you are, gleam-ing in the skies a - bove, lead me to the
Fm7 Bb9 Bb+ Eb G7 Cm Gm
one who loves me. And when you bring him my way, each time we say "Good - night,"
Ab Bb7/Ab Eb/G C7b9 Fm7 Ab/Bb Bb7#5(b9) Eb Fm7 Fb7 Eb6 Ab6/Eb Eb6
we'll thank the lit - tle star that shines the sec - ond from the right. right.

You Can Fly! You Can Fly! You Can Fly!

From Walt Disney's *Peter Pan*

Words by SAMMY CAHN
Music by SAMMY FAIN

Moderately slow

Eb

Think of the pres-ents you're brought, an - y mer-ry lit - tle thought.

mp

Bb7 Eb Bb7 Eb

Think of Christ - mas, think of snow, think of sleigh bells, here we go! Like

Ab Bb7 Eb

rein-deer in the sky. You can fly! You can

© 1951 Walt Disney Music Company
Copyright Renewed
All Rights Reserved Used by Permission

Fm7
Bb7
Eb
fly! You can fly!
Think of the hap-pi-est things,
that's the way to get your wings.
Bb7
Eb
Now you own a can - dy store.
Bb7
Eb
Ab
Look! You're ris - ing off the floor. Don't won - der how or why.
Bb7
Eb
Fm7
Bb7
Eb
You can fly! You can fly! You can fly!

G
Am7
D7
G
Bm6
G#dim
Soon you'll zoom all a - round the room, all it takes is faith and
Am7
D7
G
G7
C
G
Am7
D7
trust. But the thing that's a pos - i - tive must is a lit - tle bit of Pix - ie
G
Edim
Fm7
B♭7
E♭
Dust. The dust is a pos - i - tive must!
When there's a smile in your heart there's no bet - ter time to start.

B♭7
E♭
B♭7
E♭
It's a ver - y sim - ple plan. You can do what bird - ies can. At
A♭
B♭7
least it's worth a try. You can
E♭
Fm7
B♭7
1
E♭
Fm7
B♭9
2
E♭
fly! You can fly! You can fly! fly!
Fm7
E♭
Fm7
E♭

Bella Notte
(This Is The Night)
From Walt Disney's *Lady And The Tramp*

Words and Music by PEGGY LEE
and SONNY BURKE

Slowly, with expression

G | G/B Bbdim7 | Am7 D7 | Am7/D | D7 | Am7 D7 | C/G G | Dm7

mp

This is the night, it's a beau - ti - ful night and we call it bel - la not - te.
Look at the skies, they have stars in their eyes on this love - ly bel - la not - te.
So take the love of your

© 1952 Walt Disney Music Company
Copyright Renewed
All Rights Reserved Used by Permission

Dm7/G
C
G7#5
Cmaj7
loved one. You'll need it a - bout this time to
Em7
A9
Em7
A9
Am7/D
D7
keep from fall - ing like a star when you make that diz - zy
Am7/D
D7♭9(#5)
G
Bm7♭5
E7#5
climb. For this is the night and the heav- ens are right on this
Am7
D7♭9
1
G
Am7/D
D7#5
2
G
love - ly bel - la not - te. not - te.
L.H.

Once Upon A Dream

From Walt Disney's *Sleeping Beauty*

Words and Music by SAMMY FAIN
and JACK LAWRENCE
Adapted From A Theme By Tchaikovsky

Moderately
F
C9
Gm6
I know you! I walked with you once up -
mp

F#dim7
D7
Gm
C
A♭dim7
Gm7
on a dream. I know you! The

C7
B♭/F
F
Gm7
C9
gleam in your eyes is so fa - mil - iar a gleam. Yet, I

© 1952 Walt Disney Music Company
Copyright Renewed
All Rights Reserved Used by Permission

F
Cdim7
Gm
D7
know it's true that vis - ions are sel - dom all they
Gm
G#dim7
F
D7
Gm
seem. But if I know you, I know what you'll
E7/G#
F/A
F
D7
Gm
Gm7/C
do; you'll love me at once the way you did once up - on
C7
1
F
C7
2
F
a dream. dream.

Cruella De Vil

From Walt Disney's *101 Dalmatians*

Words and Music by
MEL LEVEN

Slow Blues

B♭ B♭9 E♭ E♭9 B♭ B♭9

Cru - el - la De - Vil, Cru - el - la De - Vil, if she does-n't scare you no

mf

E♭ E♭9 B♭ G♭9 A♭9♭5 G9

ev - il thing will. To see her is to take a sud - den chill. Cru-

C7 F9 B♭ B♭9

el - la, Cru - el - la De - Vil. The curl of her lips, the

© 1959 Walt Disney Music Company
Copyright Renewed
All Rights Reserved Used by Permission

E♭
E♭9
B♭
B♭9
E♭
E♭9
ice in her stare; all in - no - cent chil - dren had bet - ter be - ware. She's
B♭
G♭9
A♭9♭5
G9
C7
F7
like a spi - der wait - ing for the kill. Look out for Cru - el - la De -
B♭
D7
Gm
Vil. At first you think Cru - el - la is the dev - il, But
D7
Gm
C7
af - ter time has wore a - way the shock, you come to re - a - lize you've

Gb9
Cm7/F
F9
seen her kind of eyes watch-ing you from un-der-neath a rock. This
Bb
Bb9
Eb
Eb9
Bb
Bb9
vam-pire bat, this in-hu-man beast, she ought to be locked up and
Eb
Eb9
Bb
Gb9
Ab9b5
G9
nev-er re-leased. The world was such a whole-some place un-til Cru-
C7
F7
1
Bb
Dbdim7
F9
2
Bb
el-la, Cru-el-la De-Vil. Cru- Vil.

A Spoonful Of Sugar

From Walt Disney's *Mary Poppins*

Words and Music by RICHARD M. SHERMAN
and ROBERT B. SHERMAN

Brightly

G

In ev-'ry job that must be done there is an el-e-ment of fun. You find the fun and snap the job's a game.

feath-er-ing his nest has ver-y lit-tle time to rest while gath-er-ing his bits of twine and twig.

bees that fetch the nec-tar from the flow-ers to the comb nev-er tire of ev-er buzz-ing to and fro.

mf

Bbdim7 D9 D7b9 D7 C

And ev-'ry task you un-der-take be-comes a piece of cake.

Though quite in-tent in his pur-suit, he has a mer-ry tune to toot.

Be-cause they take a lit-tle nip, from ev-'ry flow-er that they sip.

Eb7 G A7 Am7 Bbdim7 D7 Ddim7

A lark! A spree! It's

He knows a song will

And hence, they find their

f

© 1963 Wonderland Music Company, Inc.
Copyright Renewed
All Rights Reserved Used by Permission

Am7 Ddim7 D7 B♭dim7 D7 G
ver - y clear to see. That a
move the job a - long. For a
task is not a grind. For a
spoon - ful of sug - ar helps the med - i - cine go
mf
D7 Ddim7 D7 D+ G6 F#6 G6 B♭dim7
down, the med - i - cine go dow - wown, med - i - cine go down. Just a
D7 G
spoon - ful of sug-ar helps the med - i - cine go down in a most de -
f
1,2
3
Am7 D7 G B♭dim7 D7/A G
light - ful way. A rob - in way.
The hon - ey
mf

Supercalifragilistic-expialidocious

From Walt Disney's *Mary Poppins*

Words and Music by RICHARD M. SHERMAN
and ROBERT B. SHERMAN

Brightly

C Cmaj7 C6 C#dim7 G7

Mary Poppins:

Sup - er - cal - i - frag - il - is - tic - ex - pi - al - i - do - cious!

Dm7 G7 Dm7 G7 C

E - ven though the sound of it is some - thing quite a - tro - cious.

Cmaj7 C7 F

If you say it loud e - nough, you'll al - ways sound pre - co - cious.

© 1963 Wonderland Music Company, Inc.
Copyright Renewed
All Rights Reserved Used by Permission

F6 F#dim7 C C#dim7 G7 C
Sup - er - cal - i - frag - il - is - tic - ex - pi - al - i - do - cious!
C G7 C
Pearlies:
Um did - dle did - dle did - dle, um did - dle ay! Um did - dle did - dle did - dle,
mp
G7 C Cmaj7
um did - dle ay!
Bert: Be - cause I was a - fraid to speak when
Mary Poppins: He trav - eled all a - round the world and
So when the cat has got your tongue, there's
mf
C6 C#dim7 G7 Dm7 G7
I was just a lad, me fa - ther gave me nose a tweak and
ev - 'ry - where he went he'd use his word and all would say, "There
no need to dis - may, just sum - mon up this word and then you've

Dm7 G7 C Cmaj7
told me I was bad. But then one day I learned a word that
goes a clev - er gent!" Bert: When dukes and ma - 'a - ra - jas pass the
got a lot to say. But bet - ter use it care - ful - ly or
C7 F D7
saved me ach - in' nose. Bert and Mary Poppins: The big - gest word you
time of day with me, I say me spe - cial
it can change your life. Pearlie: One night I said it
G7 C
ev - er 'eard and this is 'ow it goes: All: Oh! 1.,2. Sup - er - cal - i -
word and then they ask me out to tea. Oh!
to me girl and now me girl's me wife. All: She's 3. Sup - er - cal - i -
f
Cmaj7 C6 C#dim7 G7 Dm7
frag - il - is - tic - ex - pi - al - i - do - cious! E - ven though the
frag - il - is - tic - ex - pi - al - i - do - cious! Sup - er - cal - i -

G7 Dm7 G7 C
sound of it is some - thing quite a - tro - cious. If you say it
frag - il - is - tic - ex - pi - al - i - do - cious! Sup - er - cal - i -
Cmaj7 C7 F F6 F#dim7
loud e - nough, you'll al - ways sound pre - co - cious. Sup - er - cal - i -
frag - il - is - tic - ex - pi - al - i - do - cious! Sup - er - cal - i -
C C#dim7 G7 C C
1,2
3
frag - il - is - tic - ex - pi - al - i - do - cious!
frag - il - is - tic - ex - pi - al - i - do - cious!
F6 F#dim7 C C#dim7 G7 C

The Bare Necessities

From Walt Disney's *The Jungle Book*

Words and Music by
TERRY GILKYSON

Bright tempo (with spirit)
F7
Bb
Bbmaj7
Look for the 1.,3. bare ne - ces - si - ties, the sim - ple bare ne -
2. bare ne - ces - si - ties, the sim - ple bare ne -
f
Bb7
F
D7
G7
ces - si - ties; for - get a - bout your wor - ries and your strife.
ces - si - ties; for - get a - bout your wor - ries and your strife.
C7
C7#5
F
F7
Bb
I mean the bare ne - ces - si - ties, or Moth - er Na - ture's
I mean the bare ne - ces - si - ties, that's why a bear can

© 1964 Wonderland Music Company, Inc.
Copyright Renewed
All Rights Reserved Used by Permission

B♭7
F
D7
G7
C7
F
B♭7
re - ci - pes that bring the bare ne - ces - si - ties of life.
rest at ease with just the bare ne - ces - si - ties of life.
F no chord
C7
F
Wher-ev - er I wan - der, wher - ev - er I roam,
When you pick a paw - paw or pric-kl - y pear,
3. So just try to re - lax (Oh yeah!) in my back yard,
no chord
C7
F
I could - n't be fond - er of my big home.
and you prick a raw paw next time be - ware.
if you act like that bee acts you're work-in' too hard.
F7
B♭
B♭m
F
The bees are buzz - in' in the tree to make some hon - ey just for
Don't pick the prick - ly pear by paw, when you pick a pear, try to use the
Don't spend your time just look - in' a - round for some-thing you want that can't be

G7 Dm7 D7 Gm D7
me. You look un-der the rocks and plants and take a glance at the
claw. But you don't need to use the claw when you pick a pear of the
found. When you find out you can live with-out it and go a-long not
Gm G7 C C7 F D7
fan - cy ants, then may - be try a few.
big paw - paw, have I giv - en you a clue?
think-in' a - bout it. I'll tell you some-thing true.
The bare ne -
Gm7 C7 F Dm Gm C7
ces - si - ties of life will come to you, they'll come to
1,2
F Eb9 F no chord
you! 2.,3. Look for the
3
F Eb9 F F6
you!
ff

Trust In Me
(The Python's Song)
From Walt Disney's *The Jungle Book*

Words and Music by RICHARD M. SHERMAN
and ROBERT B. SHERMAN

Moderately

Dm6 — A7 — Dm6 — no chord — Dm6

Trust in me, just in me. Shut your eyes and trust in me. You can sleep safe and sound know - ing

© 1966 Wonderland Music Company, Inc.
Copyright Renewed
All Rights Reserved Used by Permission

A7
Dm6
I am a - round.
F#7
Slip in - to si - lent slum - ber, sail on a sil - ver
Bm
B♭7
mist. Slow - ly and sure - ly your sen - ses will cease to re -
A7
no chord
Dm6
sist. Just re - lax, be at
mp

A7
rest like a bird in a
Dm6
no chord
Dm6
nest. Trust in me, just in
A7
me. Shut your eyes and trust in
Dm6
me.
ppp

Ev'rybody Wants To Be A Cat

From Walt Disney's *The Aristocats*

Words by FLOYD HUDDLESTON
Music by AL RINKER

With a beat

Em Em(maj7) Em7 Em6 Cmaj7 D7

Ev-'ry-bod-y wants to be a cat, be-cause a cat's the on-ly cat who

mf

C7 B7 Em Em(maj7) Em7 Em6

knows where it's at! Ev-'ry-bod-y pick-in' up on the fe-line beat,

Cmaj7 Bm7 Em Bm Em Am Am(maj7) Am7 D7

'cause ev-'ry-thing else is ob-so-lete. Be-ware of a square when he of-fers to share his

© 1968 Walt Disney Music Company
Copyright Renewed
All Rights Reserved Used by Permission

G
milk to sip! _
Am B7
If it has-n't been tried, _
Am B7
I sug - gest you pro - vide _ your
Em Am B7
own cat - nip. _
C B7
I've
Em Em(maj7)
heard some corn - y birds who tried to
Em7 Em6
sing, but still a
Cmaj7 D7
cat's the on-ly cat
C7 B7
who knows how to swing! _ A
Em Em(maj7)
purr be-tween two fur - ry friends may
Em7 Em6
be old hat, _
Cmaj7
But ev - 'ry-bod - y wants to
1
Em Bm7 Em
be a cat! _
To next strain
Am B7
2
Em Bm7 Em
be a cat! _
Fine

F♯m7
B7
F♯m7
B7
E
C7
F♯m
B7
Come on, scat cat, turn me on, I'll take my horn and my best tone, then blow a lit - tle soul in - to the
Emaj7
Amaj7
Emaj7
Gm7
C7
Gm7
C7
tune. Let's take it to an-oth-er key, mod - u-late, then wait for me, I'll
Fmaj7
Gm7
Fmaj7
A♭m7
D♭7
take a few ad libs and pret - ty soon the oth - er cats will all com-mence
D.C. al Fine
A♭m7
D♭7
Am7
D7
Am7
Am7♭5
F♯m7
B7
con - gre-gat-ing on the fence, be - neath the al-ley's on-ly light, where ev -'ry night is out of sight!

Winnie The Pooh

From Walt Disney's
The Many Adventures Of Winnie The Pooh

Words and Music by RICHARD M. SHERMAN
and ROBERT B. SHERMAN

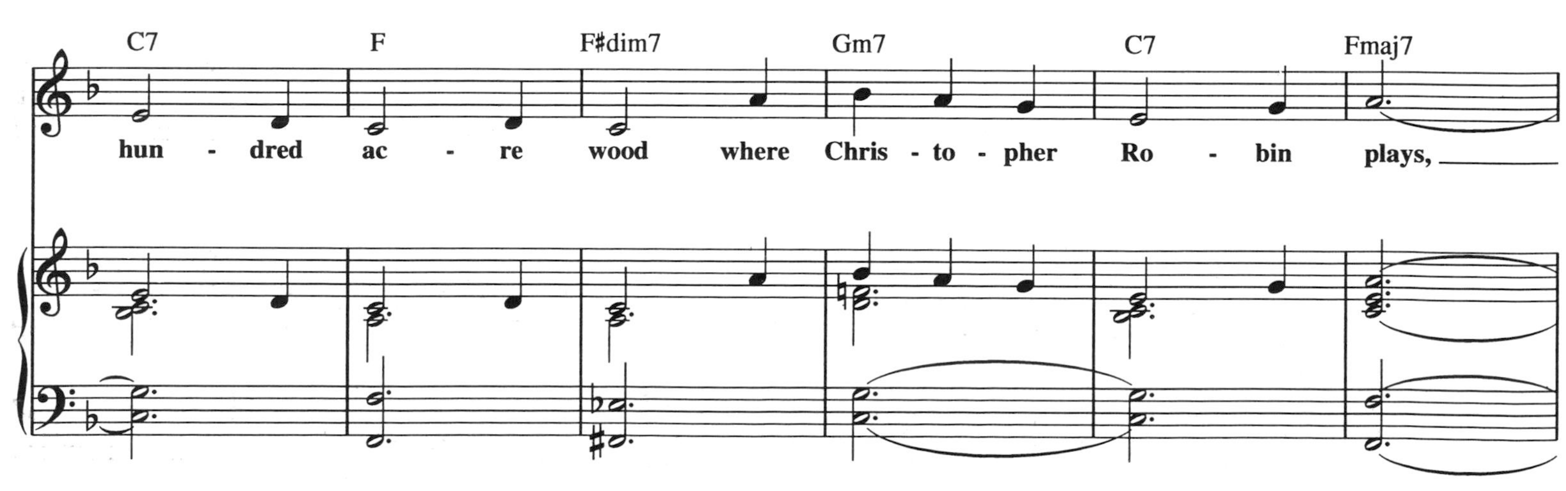

© 1963 Wonderland Music Company, Inc.
Copyright Renewed
All Rights Reserved Used by Permission

F6
Gm7
C7
Am7
Dm
Dm7
G7
you will find the en - chant - ed neigh - bor - hood of Chris - to - pher's
C7
F
Tempo I
Gm7
C7
F
F#dim
Gm7
C7
child - hood days. A don-key named Ee-yore is his friend, and Kang-a and lit - tle
F
Gm7
C7
F
Dm
Dm7
G7
C7
F
D.C. al Coda
Roo. There's Rab-bit and Pig-let and there's Owl but most of all Win-nie-The-Pooh.
CODA
C7
F
C7
F
Wil - ly nil - ly sil - ly ole bear.

The Wonderful Thing About Tiggers

From Walt Disney's
The Many Adventures Of Winnie The Pooh

Words and Music by RICHARD M. SHERMAN
and ROBERT B. SHERMAN

Brightly

C7 F C7 F C7 F C7 F B♭ F B♭ F

mf

1., 3. The won - der - ful thing a - bout Tig - gers is Tig - gers are won - der - ful things! Their tops are made out of rub - ber; their bot - toms are made out of springs! They're boun - cy, troun - cy, floun - cy, poun - cy,

2. won - der - ful thing a - bout Tig - gers is Tig - gers are won - der - ful chaps! They're load - ed with vim and with vig - or; they love to leap in your laps! They're jump - y, bump - y, clump - y, thump - y,

© 1964 Wonderland Music Company, Inc.
Copyright Renewed
All Rights Reserved Used by Permission

G7
C7
F
C7
Dm7
D♭6
Fun! Fun! Fun! Fun! Fun! But the most won - der - ful thing a - bout tig - gers is
C7
1
F
A♭dim
2
To next strain
F
F7
3
Fine
F
I'm the on - ly one! Oh, the one! one!
B♭
F
B♭
F
Tig - gers are cud - di - ly fel - las. Tig - gers are aw - ful - ly sweet.
B♭
F
Dm7
G7
C7
D.S. al Fine
Ev - 'ry - one el - es is jeal - ous. That's why I re - peat and re - peat: The

Candle On The Water

From Walt Disney's *Pete's Dragon*

Words and Music by AL KASHA
and JOEL HIRSCHHORN

Smoothly

C Dm G7 F G C Am F
I'll be your can-dle on the wa - ter, my love for you will al-ways
I'll be your can-dle on the wa - ter, 'til ev-'ry wave is warm and

mp

B♭ G E/G# Am C7/G F C/E
burn. I know you're lost and drift-ing, but the clouds are lift-ing,
bright, my soul is there be-side you, let this can-dle guide you

F G7 C 1 Dm7 G7 2 Dm7 G7
don't give up you have some-where to turn.
soon you'll see a gold-en stream of light.

© 1976 Walt Disney Music Company and Wonderland Music Company, Inc.
All Rights Reserved Used by Permission

Bb
C
C7
Fsus
F
A cold and friend-less tide has found you,
don't let the storm-y dark-ness
F
Gm7
Am7
D7
G
Em/G
pull you down.
I'll paint a ray of hope a-round you,
cir-cling in the air
Bb6/9
G7
Dm
light-ed by a prayer.
I'll be your can-dle on the
Am
E/G#
wa - ter,
this flame in-side of me will grow.
Keep hold-ing

Am C7/G F C/E F G7
on, you'll make it, here's my hand so take it, look for me reach-ing out to
C C7 F Fm C F#m7♭5 F6 G7
show as sure as riv - ers flow, I'll nev - er let you
rit.
a tempo
C G F G7 C G F G7
go, I'll nev-er let you go, I'll nev-er let you
C G/B F/A C/G G C
go.

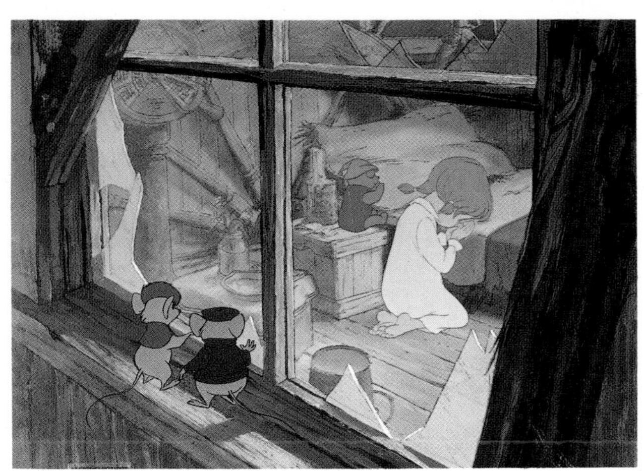

Someone's Waiting For You

From Walt Disney's *The Rescuers*

Words by CAROL CONNORS and AYN ROBBINS
Music by SAMMY FAIN

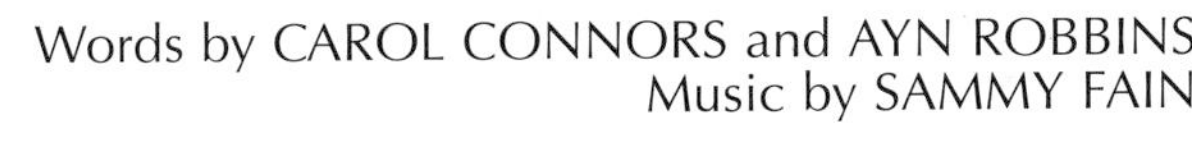

Gently, expressively
D
Em7
G/A
Dmaj7
D6
Be brave lit - tle one.
Make a wish for each sad lit - tle tear.
mf
With pedal throughout
G/A
F#m7
Bm7
E7
Hold your head up though no one is near.
Some-one's wait - ing for
Em/A
G/A
D
Em7
G/A
you.
Don't cry lit - tle one.
There'll be a smile where a

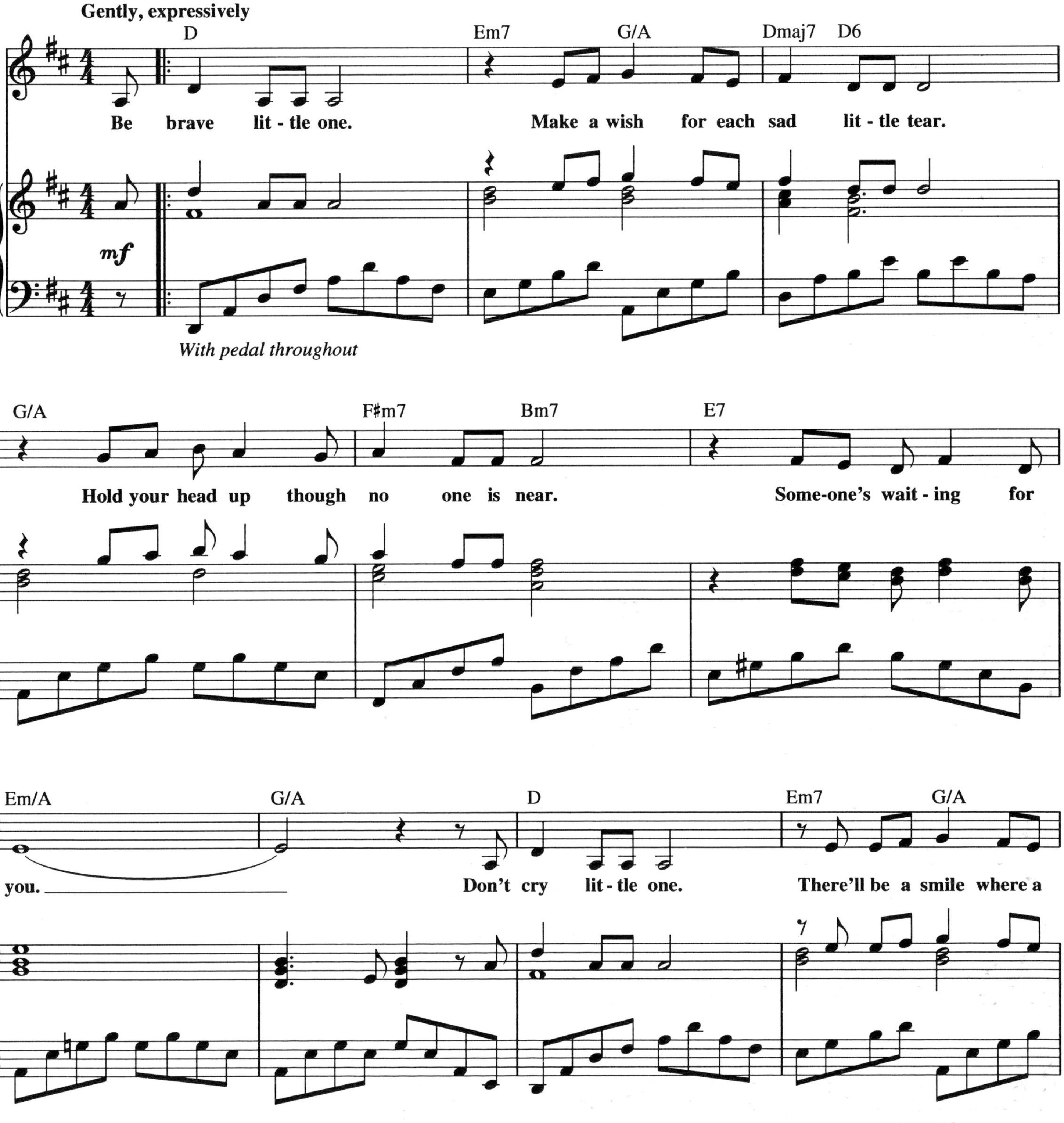

© 1976 Walt Disney Music Company and Sammy Fain Trust
Administered by Walt Disney Music Company
All Rights Reserved Used by Permission

Dmaj7
D6
C#7
F#m
frown used to be.
You'll be part of the love that you see.
C#7
F#m
Some-one's wait - ing for you.
Al - ways
B7
Em
B7
keep a lit - tle prayer in your pock - et and you're sure to see the
Em
C#7
F#m
F#m7♭5
B7
E7
light.
Soon there'll be joy and hap - pi - ness and your lit - tle world will be

G/A
D
Em7
Am
3
bright. Have faith lit-tle one 'til your hopes and your wish-es come true.
3
B7
Em7
Gm6
You must try to be brave lit-tle one. Some - one's
D
Bm
Em7
A7
1
D
Em7
G/A
wait - ing to love you. Be
2
D
G
Gm6
D
D6/9
you.

Under The Sea

From Walt Disney's *The Little Mermaid*

Lyrics by HOWARD ASHMAN
Music by ALAN MENKEN

Brightly

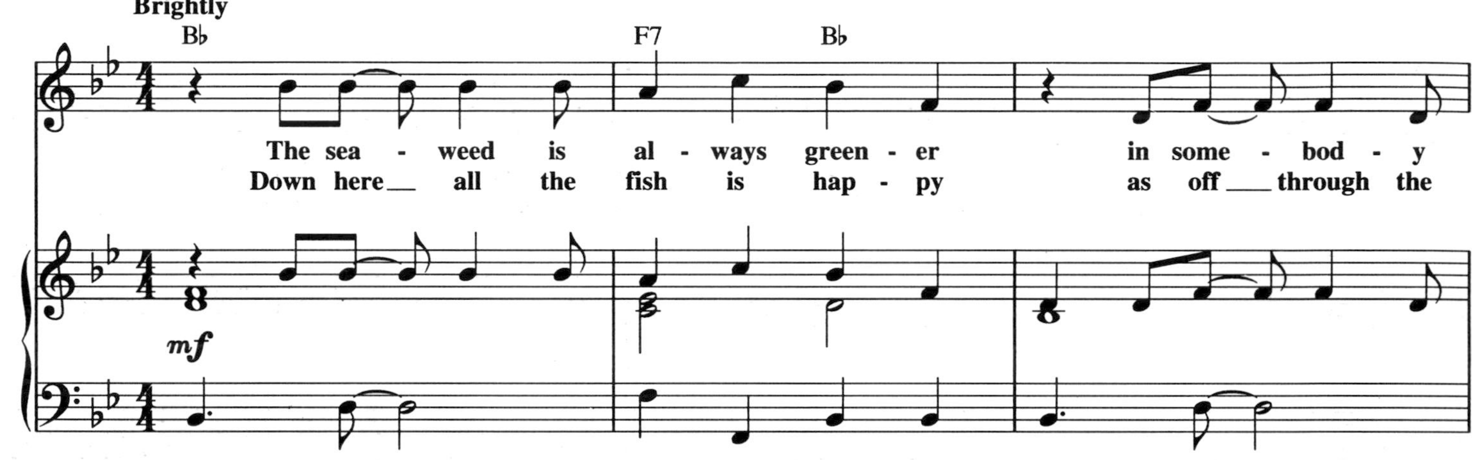
B♭
F7
B♭
The sea - weed is al - ways green - er in some - bod - y
Down here all the fish is hap - py as off through the
mf

F7
B♭
F7
B♭
else - 's lake. You dream a - bout go - ing up there.
waves dey roll. The fish on the land ain't hap - py.

F7
B♭
E♭
But that is a big mis - take. Just look at the
They sad 'cause they in the bowl. But fish in the

© 1988 Walt Disney Music Company and Wonderland Music Company, Inc.
All Rights Reserved Used by Permission

B♭/D B♭ F7 B♭
world a - round you, right here on the o - cean floor.
bowl is luck - y, they in for a wors - er fate.
E♭ B♭/D B♭ F7
Such won - der - ful things sur - round you. What more is you
One day when the boss get hun - gry guess who gon' be
B♭ E♭ B♭
look - in' for?
on the plate.
Un - der the sea, un - der the
F7 B♭ E♭
sea.
Dar - lin' it's bet - ter down where it's
No - bod - y beat us, fry us and

F
Bb
Bb7
Eb
wet-ter. Take_ it from me.
Up_ on the shore they work_ all day.
eat us in_ fri-ca-see.
We_ what the land folks loves_ to cook.
F
Gm
C7
Out_ in the sun they slave_ a-way.
While_ we de-
Un-der the sea we off_ the hook.
We_ got no
Eb
F7
1
Bb
F7
Bb
vo-tin' full-time to float-in' un-der the sea.
trou-bles life_ is the bub-bles un-der the
F7
Bb
2
Eb
Bb
sea.

Under The Sea

From Walt Disney's *The Little Mermaid*

Lyrics by Howard Ashman
Music by Alan Menken

The seaweed is always greener in somebody else's lake.
You dream about going up there.
But that is a big mistake.
Just look at the world around you, right here on the ocean floor.
Such wonderful things surround you.
What more is you lookin' for?
Under the sea, under the sea.
Darlin' it's better down where it's wetter.
Take it from me.
Up on the shore they work all day.
Out in the sun they slave away.
While we devotin' full time to floatin' under the sea.
Down here all the fish is happy as off through the waves they roll.
The fish on the land ain't happy.
They sad 'cause they in the bowl.
But fish in the bowl is lucky, they in for a worser fate.
One day when the boss get hungry guess who gon' be on the plate.
Under the sea, under the sea.
Nobody beat us, fry us and eat us in fricassee.
We what the land folks loves to cook.
Under the sea we off the hook.
We got no troubles life is the bubbles under the sea.
Under the sea.
Since life is sweet here we got the beat here naturally.
Even the sturgeon an' the ray they get the urge 'n' start to play.
We got the spirit, you got to hear it under the sea.
The newt play the flute.
The carp play the harp.
The plaice play the bass.
And they soundin' sharp.
The bass play the brass.
The chub play the tub.
The fluke is the duke of soul.
The ray he can play.
The lings on the strings.
The trout rockin' out.
The blackfish she sings
The smelt and the sprat they know where it's at.
An' oh, that blowfish blow.
Under the sea.
Under the sea.
When the sardine begin the beguine it's music to me.
What do they got, a lot of sand.
We got a hot crustacean band.
Each little clam here know how to jam here under the sea.
Each little slug here cuttin'a rug here under the sea.
Each little snail here know how to wail here.
That's why it's hotter under the water.
Ya we in luck here down in the muck here under the sea.

© 1988 Walt Disney Music Company and Wonderland Music Company, Inc.
All Rights Reserved Used by Permission

Part Of Your World

From Walt Disney's *The Little Mermaid*

Lyrics by HOWARD ASHMAN
Music by ALAN MENKEN

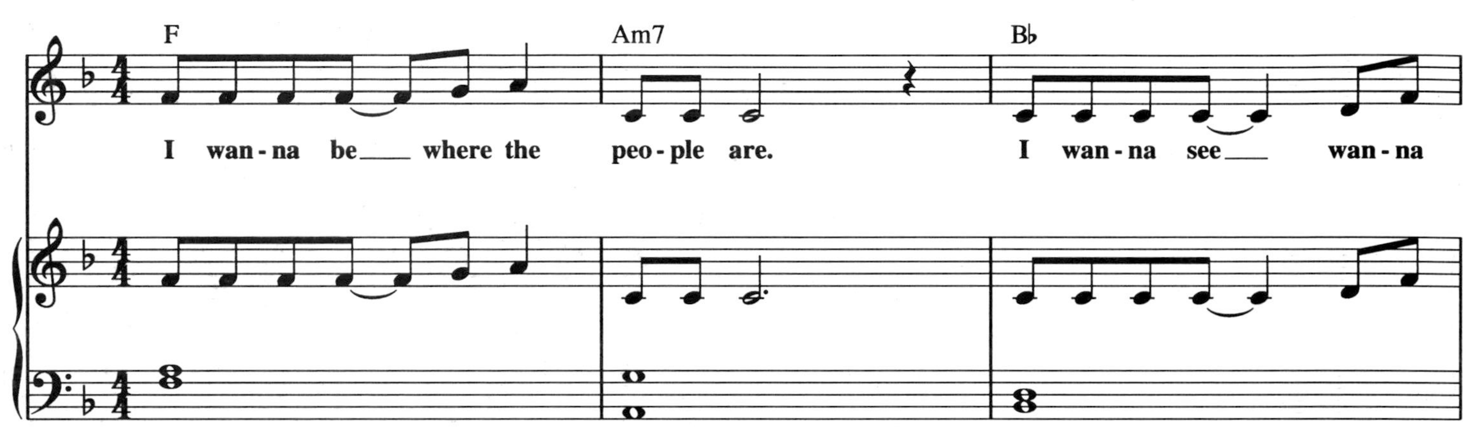
F
Am7
B♭
I wan-na be___ where the peo-ple are. I wan-na see___ wan-na

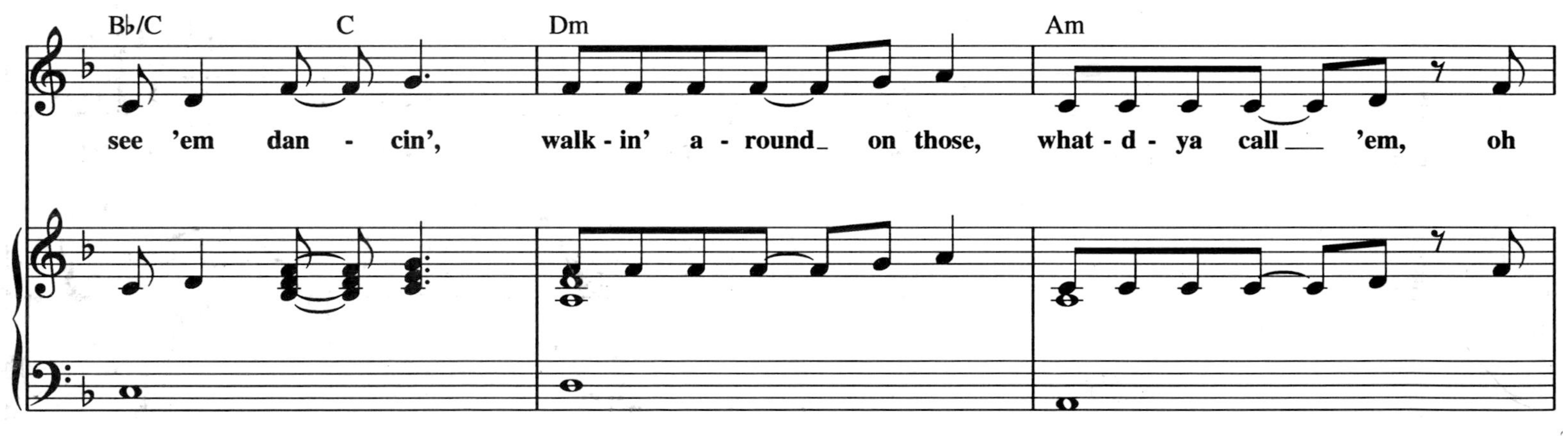
B♭/C
C
Dm
Am
see 'em dan - cin', walk-in' a-round_ on those, what-d-ya call___ 'em, oh

B♭/C
C
C7
F
F/A
feet. Flip-pin' your fins___ you don't get too far.___

© 1988 Walt Disney Music Company and Wonderland Music Company, Inc.
All Rights Reserved Used by Permission

B♭
B♭/C
C
Dm
Am
F/A
Legs are re - quired for jump-in', danc - in'. Stroll-in' a - long down the, what's that word a- gain,
B♭/C
C7
F
F/E♭
street. Up where they walk, up where they run, up where they
B♭/D
B♭m/D♭
F/C
B♭/C
C7
stay all day in the sun. Wan - der - in' free, wish I could be part of that
F
B♭
C/B♭
world. What would I give if I could live out - ta these

Am
Dm
B♭
C/B♭
wa - ters.
What would I pay to spend a day warm on the
Am
F7sus
F7
B♭
C/B♭
sand.
Bet - cha on land they un - der - stand. Bet they don't
A7sus
A7
Dm
Dm/C
F/G
G
F/G
G
re - pri - mand_ their daugh - ters. Bright young wom-en, sick of swim-min', read - y to
rall.
E♭maj7
B♭/C
C
B♭/C
C
F
F/A
stand. ___
And read - y to know_ what the peo - ple know._
a tempo

B♭maj7
B♭/C
C7
Dm
Am
F/A
Ask 'em my ques - tions and get some an - swers. What's a fire, and why does it, what's the word,
Gm7
C7
F
F/E♭
burn. When's it my turn? Would - n't I love, love to ex -
B♭/D
B♭m/D♭
F
plore that shore up a - bove, out of the sea.
slower
B♭/C
C7
F
Wish I could be part of that world.

Part Of Your World

From Walt Disney's *The Little Mermaid*

Lyrics by Howard Ashman
Music by Alan Menken

Look at this stuff.
Isn't it neat?
Wouldn't you think my collection's complete?
Wouldn't you think I'm the girl, the girl who has ev'rything.
Look at this trove, treasures untold.
How many wonders can one cavern hold?
Looking around here you'd think, sure, she's got ev'rything.
I've got gadgets and gizmos aplenty.
I've got whozits and whatzits galore.
You want thingamabobs, I've got twenty.
But who cares?
No big deal. I want more.
I wanna be where the people are.
I wanna see wanna see 'em dancin',
Walkin' around on those, whatdya call 'em, oh feet.
Flippin' your fins you don't get too far.
Legs are required for jumpin', dancin'.
Strollin' along down the, what's that word again, street.
Up where they walk, up where they run, up where they stay all day in the sun.
Wanderin' free, wish I could be part of that world.
What would I give if I could live outta these waters.
What would I pay to spend a day warm on the sand.
Betcha on land they understand.
Bet they don't reprimand their daughters.
Bright young women, sick of swimmin', ready to stand.
And ready to know what the people know.
Ask 'em my questions and get some answers.
What's a fire and why does it, what's the word, burn.
When's it my turn?
Wouldn't I love, love to explore that shore up above, out of the sea.
Wish I could be part of that world.

© 1988 Walt Disney Music Company and Wonderland Music Company, Inc.
All Rights Reserved   Used by Permission

Beauty And The Beast

From Walt Disney's *Beauty And The Beast*

Lyrics by HOWARD ASHMAN
Music by ALAN MENKEN

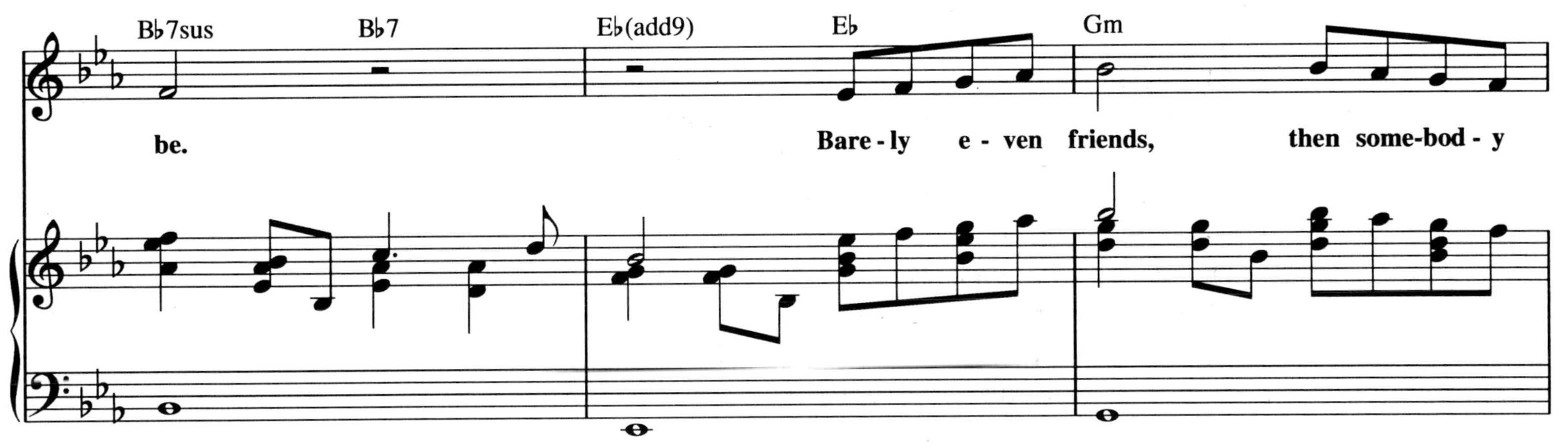

© 1991 Walt Disney Music Company and Wonderland Music Company, Inc.
All Rights Reserved Used by Permission

B♭7sus
B♭7
E♭(add9)
E♭
B♭m7
E♭7
change.
Small, to say the least.
Both a lit - tle
A♭maj7
Gm7
Fm7
B♭7sus
B♭7
E♭(add9)
scared,
nei - ther one pre - pared.
Beau - ty and the Beast.
poco rit.
a tempo
B♭7sus
Gm
A♭(add9)
A♭
Ev - er just the same.
Ev - er a sur -
mf
Gm
A♭(add9)
A♭
Gm7
prise.
Ev - er as be - fore,
ev - er just as

Cm
Cm7
D♭
E♭
F
sure as the sun will rise.
Tale as old as
f
C7sus
C7
F(add9)
F
C7sus
C7
F(add9)
F
time.
Tune as old as song.
Bit-ter-sweet and
Am
B♭(add9)
B♭
B♭/C
C7
strange, find-ing you can change, learn-ing you were wrong.
F(add9)
F
C7sus
F(add9)
F
Cer-tain as the sun
ris-ing in the

Cm F7 B♭maj7 Am7 Gm7 C7sus C7
East. Tale as old as time, song as old as rhyme. Beau-ty and the
poco rit.
F(add9) F/E Dm Am/C B♭ Am
Beast. Tale as old as time, song as old as
dim.
slower
Gm7 C7sus C7 F(add9) Fsus F(add9)
rhyme. Beau-ty and the Beast.
a tempo
Fsus F
rit.
8va

Beauty And The Beast

From Walt Disney's *Beauty And The Beast*

Lyrics by Howard Ashman
Music by Alan Menken

Tale as old as time,
True as it can be.
Barely even friends,
Then somebody bends
Unexpectedly.
Just a little change.
Small to say the least.
Both a little scared,
Neither one prepared.
Beauty and the Beast.
Ever just the same.
Ever a surprise.
Ever as before,
Ever just as sure
As the sun will rise.
Tale as old as time.
Tune as old as song.
Bittersweet and strange,
Finding you can change,
Learning you were wrong.
Certain as the sun
Rising in the East.
Tale as old as time,
Song as old as rhyme.
Beauty and the Beast.
Tale as old as time,
Song as old as rhyme.
Beauty and the Beast.

© 1991 Walt Disney Music Company and Wonderland Music Company, Inc.
All Rights Reserved   Used by Permission

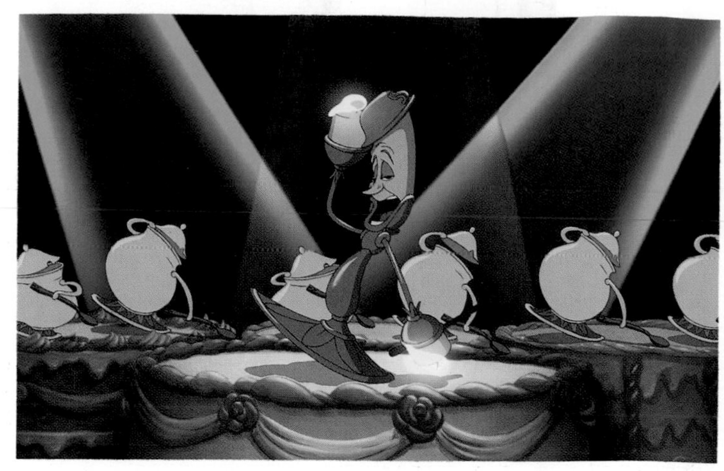

Be Our Guest

From Walt Disney's *Beauty And The Beast*

Lyrics by HOWARD ASHMAN
Music by ALAN MENKEN

Moderate tempo

no chord | G | Gmaj7 | G6

Be our guest! Be our guest! Put our ser - vice to the

G | G#dim | Am7

test. Tie your nap - kin 'round your neck, che - rie and we pro- vide the

D7 | Am | Am(#7) | Am7 | D9

rest. Soup du jour! Hot hors d'oeuvres! Why, we on - ly live to serve. Try the

© 1991 Walt Disney Music Company and Wonderland Music Company, Inc.
All Rights Reserved Used by Permission

Am7
A#dim
Bm7
B♭9#11
Dsus/A
D7
G
grey stuff, it's de - li - cious! Don't be - lieve me? Ask the dish - es! They can sing! They can
Gmaj7
G6
G
Gmaj7
G7
dance! Af - ter all, Miss, this is France! And a din - ner here is nev - er sec - ond
C6
B
C#m7
Ddim
B7/D#
E11
best. Go on, un - fold your men - u, take a glance, and then
A7
Am7
D7
G
you'll be our guest, oui, our guest! Be our guest!

Be Our Guest

From Walt Disney's *Beauty And The Beast*

Lyrics by Howard Ashman
Music by Alan Menken

Lumiere: Ma chere Mademoiselle,
It is with deepest pride and greatest pleasure that we welcome you tonight.
And now, we invite you to relax.
Let us pull up a chair as the dining room proudly presents your dinner!

Be our guest!
Be our guest!
Put our service to the test.

Tie your napkin 'round your neck, cherie,
And we provide the rest.
Soup du jour!
Hot hors d'oeuvres!

Why, we only live to serve.
Try the grey stuff, it's delicious!
Don't believe me?
Ask the dishes!

They can sing!
They can dance!
After all, Miss, this is France!
And a dinner here is never second best.

Go on, unfold your menu,
Take a glance,
And then you'll be our guest,
Oui, our guest!
Be our guest!

Beef ragout!
Cheese souffle!
Pie and pudding "en flambe!"
We'll prepare and serve with flair
A culinary cabaret!

You're alone and you're scared
But the banquet's all prepared.
No one's gloomy or complaining
While the flatware's entertaining.

We tell jokes.
I do tricks with my fellow candlesticks.

Mugs: And it's all in perfect taste.
That you can bet!

All: Come on and lift your glass
You've won your own free pass
To be our guest!

Lumeniere: If you're stressed,
It's fine dining we suggest.

All: Be our guest!
Be our guest!
Be our guest!

Lumeniere: Life is so unnerving for a servant who's not serving.
He's not whole without a soul to wait upon.
Ah, those good old days when we were useful.
Suddenly, those good old days are gone.

Ten years, we've been rusting,
Needing so much more — than dusting.
Needing exercise, a chance to use our skills.

Most days, we just lay around the castle.
Flabby, fat and lazy.
You walked in and oops-a-daisy.

Mrs. Potts: It's a guest!
It's a guest!
Sakes alive,
Well, I'll be blessed!

Wine's been poured and thank the Lord
I've had the napkins freshly pressed.
With dessert she'll want tea.

And my dear, that's fine with me.
While the cups do their soft shoeing,
I'll be bubbling!
I'll be brewing!

I'll get warm, piping hot!
Heaven's sakes!
Is that a spot?
Clean it up!

We want the company impressed!
We've got a lot to do.
Is it one lump or two
For you, our guest?

Chorus: She's our guest!

Mrs. Potts: She's our guest!

Chorus: She's our guest!
Be our guest!
Be our guest!

Our command is your request.
It's ten years since we had anybody here,
And we're obsessed.

With your meal
With your ease,
Yes, indeed,
We aim to please.

While the candlelight's still glowing
Let us help you,
We'll keep going.

Course by course,
One by one!
'Til you shout,
"Enough. I'm done!"

Then we'll sing you off to sleep as you digest.
Tonight you'll prop your feet up!
But for now, let's eat up!

Be our guest!
Be our guest!
Be our guest!
Please, be our guest!

© 1991 Walt Disney Music Company and Wonderland Music Company, Inc.
All Rights Reserved Used by Permission

A Whole New World

From Walt Disney's *Aladdin*

Music by ALAN MENKEN
Lyrics by TIM RICE

Sweetly

D
ALADDIN:

I can show_ you the world, shin - ing, shim - mer - ing,

mf

G/B A/C# Em/G F#7 F#7/A# Bm Bm/A

splen - did. Tell me prin - cess, now when did you last

G D A7 D

let your heart_ de - cide?___ I can o - pen your

© 1992 Wonderland Music Company, Inc. and Walt Disney Music Company
All Rights Reserved Used by Permission

G/B
A/C#
Em/G
F#7
F#7/A#
eyes take you won - der by won - der o - ver, side - ways and
Bm
Bm/A
G
D
un - der on a mag - ic car - pet ride. A whole new
A
D
A
A7/C#
A7
world a new fan - tas - tic point of view.
D(add9)
D
3
G
D/F#
G
D/F#
No - one to tell us no or where to go or
3

Bm7
E7sus
E7
G/A
JASMINE:
A
say we're on - ly dream - ing. A whole new world
D
A
A#dim7
F#7/A#
Bm
D7
a daz - zling place I nev - er knew. But when I'm
G
D/F#
G
D/F#
Bm7
E7sus
E7
way up here it's crys - tal clear that now I'm in a
C
A7sus
A7
D
JASMINE:
whole new world with you.

A Whole New World

From Walt Disney's *Aladdin*

Music by Alan Menken
Lyrics by Tim Rice

Aladdin:	I can show you the world,
	Shining, shimmering, splendid.
	Tell me princess, now
	When did you last let your heart decide?
	I can open your eyes
	Take you wonder by wonder
	Over, sideways and under on a magic carpet ride.
	A whole new world,
	A new fantastic point of view.
	No one to tell us no or where to go
	Or say we're only dreaming.
Jasmine:	A whole new world,
	A dazzling place I never knew.
	But when I'm way up here it's crystal clear
	That now I'm in a whole new world with you.
Aladdin:	Now I'm in a whole new world with you.
Jasmine:	Unbelievable sights, indescribable feeling.
	Soaring, tumbling, free-wheeling
	Through an endless diamond sky.
	A whole new world,
Aladdin:	Don't you dare close your eyes.
Jasmine:	A hundred thousand things to see.
Aladdin:	Hold your breath, it gets better.
Jasmine:	I'm like a shooting star I've come so far
	I can't go back to where I used to be.
Aladdin:	A whole new world.
Jasmine:	Every turn a surprise.
Aladdin:	With new horizons to pursue.
Jasmine:	Ev'ry moment red-letter.
Both:	I'll chase them anywhere. There's time to spare.
	Let me share this whole new world with you.
Aladdin:	A whole new world,
Jasmine:	A whole new world,
Aladdin:	That's where we'll be.
Jasmine:	That's where we'll be.
Aladdin:	A thrilling chase
Jasmine:	A wond'rous place
Both:	For you and me.

© 1992 Wonderland Music Company, Inc. and Walt Disney Music Company
All Rights Reserved Used by Permission

Friend Like Me

From Walt Disney's *Aladdin*

Lyrics by HOWARD ASHMAN
Music by ALAN MENKEN

Bright two-beat

GENIE:

A7 A7/C♯ Dm A7 A7/C♯

Well A - li Ba - ba had them for - ty thieves. Sche - her - a - za - de had a thou - sand tales. _

mf

Dm A7 Dm

_ But, mas - ter, you in luck 'cause up your sleeves _ you got a

E7 A7

brand of mag - ic nev - er fails. _ You got some pow - er in your

© 1992 Walt Disney Music Company and Wonderland Music Company, Inc.
All Rights Reserved Used by Permission

Dm
A7
Dm
cor - ner now, some heav - y am - mu - ni - tion in your camp. You got some
A7
Dm
E7
punch, pi - zazz, ya - hoo and how. See, all you got - ta do is rub that lamp.
A7
no chord
A7
Dm
B♭7
A7
Dm
And I'll say Mis - ter A - lad - din sir, what will your plea - sure be?
B♭7
A7
F
F7/E♭
B♭/D
D♭7
Let me take your or - der, jot it down. You ain't

F/C
A7#5
D(no3rd)
B♭7
A7
Dm
nev - er had a friend like me. No no ___ no. Life is your
B♭7
A7
Dm
C#+
Fm6/C
B♭13
res - tau - rant ___ and I'm your mai - tre d'. ___ C'- mon
F
F/E♭
B♭/D
B♭m/D♭
F/C
A7
whis - per what it is ___ you want. You ain't nev - er had a friend like me.
Dm
B♭7
Dm
A7
Yes, sir, we pride our - selves on ser - vice. You're the boss, the king, the shah. _

Dm
Bb13
Say what you wish. It's yours! True dish how 'bout a
Gm
A7
Dm
lit - tle more bak - la - va?
Have some of
Bb7
A7
Dm
Bb7
A7
F
F/Eb
col - umn "A". Try all of col - umn "B".
I'm in the mood to
Bb/D
Db7
F/C
A7
Dm
help you, dude, you ain't nev - er had a friend like me.

Friend Like Me

From Walt Disney's *Aladdin*

Lyrics by Howard Ashman
Music by Alan Menken

Genie:

Well, Ali Baba had them forty thieves.
Scheherazade had a thousand tales.
But, master, you in luck 'cause up your sleeves
You got a brand of magic never fails.
You got some power in your corner now,
Some heavy ammunition in your camp.
You got some punch, pizazz, yahoo and how.
See, all you gotta do is rub that lamp.
And I'll say, Mister Aladdin, sir,
What will your pleasure be?
Let me take your order, jot it down.
You ain't never had a friend like me. No no no.
Life is your restaurant and I'm your maitre d'.
C'mon whisper what it is you want.
You ain't never had a friend like me.
Yes sir, we pride ourselves on service.
You're the boss, the king, the shah.
Say what you wish. It's yours!
True dish, how 'bout a little more baklava?
Have some of column "A".
Try all of column "B".
I'm in the mood to help you, dude,
You ain't never had a friend like me.
Wa-ah-ah. Oh my.
Wa-ah-ah. No no.
Wah-ah-ah. Na na na.
Can your friends do this?
Can your friends do that?
Can your friends pull this out their little hat?
Can your friends go poof!
(Spoken:) *Well, looky here.*
Can your friends go abracadabra,
Let 'er rip and then make the sucker disappear?
So doncha sit there slack jawed, buggy eyed.
I'm here to answer all your midday prayers.
You got me bonafide certified.
You got a genie for your chargé d'affaires.
I got a powerful urge to help you out.
So whatcha wish I really want to know.
You got a list that's three miles long, no doubt.
Well, all you gotta do is rub like so. And oh.
Mister Aladdin, sir, have a wish or two or three.
I'm on the job, you big nabob.
You ain't never had a friend, never had a friend,
You ain't never had a friend, never had a friend.
You ain't never had a friend like me.
Wa-ah-ah. Wa-ah-ah.
You ain't never had a friend like me. Ha!

© 1992 Walt Disney Music Company and Wonderland Music Company, Inc.
All Rights Reserved Used by Permission

Circle Of Life

From Walt Disney Pictures' *The Lion King*

Music by ELTON JOHN
Lyrics by TIM RICE

© 1994 Wonderland Music Company, Inc.
All Rights Reserved Used by Permission

A♭
F
F7/A
than can ev - er be done.
have to live with the scars.
There's
B♭
Cm/B♭
Some say, "Eat or be eat - en."
Some say,
far too much to take in here,
more to
F7/A
B♭
F/A
"Live and let live."
But
find than can ev - er be found.
But the
Gm7
Cm
all are a - greed as they join the stam - pede,
you should
sun roll - ing high through the sap - phi - re sky
keeps great and
cresc.

A♭
F
never take more ___ than you give ___ in the cir - cle of life. ___
small on the end - less ___ round ___ in the cir - cle of life. ___
B♭
E♭/B♭
B♭
It's the wheel of for -
f
A♭/B♭
- tune.
It's the leap of faith. ___
E♭
A♭/E♭
E♭
F/E♭
It's the band of ___ hope ___

B♭/D
G7
'til we find our place
on the path un-wind-
Cm
G♭(add2)
B♭/F
To Coda
ing
in the cir - cle,
1
F
E♭/B♭
B♭
the cir - cle of life.
2
F
D.S. al Coda
B♭
E♭/B♭
the cir - cle of life!
CODA
F
the cir - cle of life.

E♭/B♭
B♭
Cm/B♭
B♭
dim.
mp
G/B
Cm
G♭(add2)
On the path un - wind - ing in the cir -
B♭/D
Fsus
F
- cle, the cir - cle of life.
E♭/B♭
G♭/B♭
B♭
rall.

Can You Feel The Love Tonight

From Walt Disney Pictures' *The Lion King*

Music by ELTON JOHN
Lyrics by TIM RICE

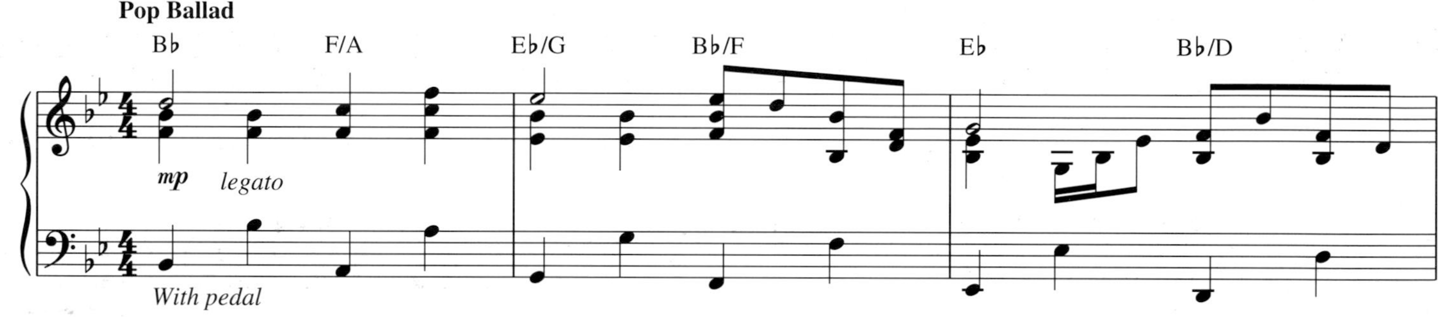
Pop Ballad
B♭ F/A E♭/G B♭/F E♭ B♭/D
mp legato
With pedal

F/A B♭ Cm7 B♭/D E♭ B♭/D E♭ B♭/D
There's a calm_ sur-ren - der to the rush_ of day,_
There's a time_ for ev-'ry-one, if they on - ly learn_

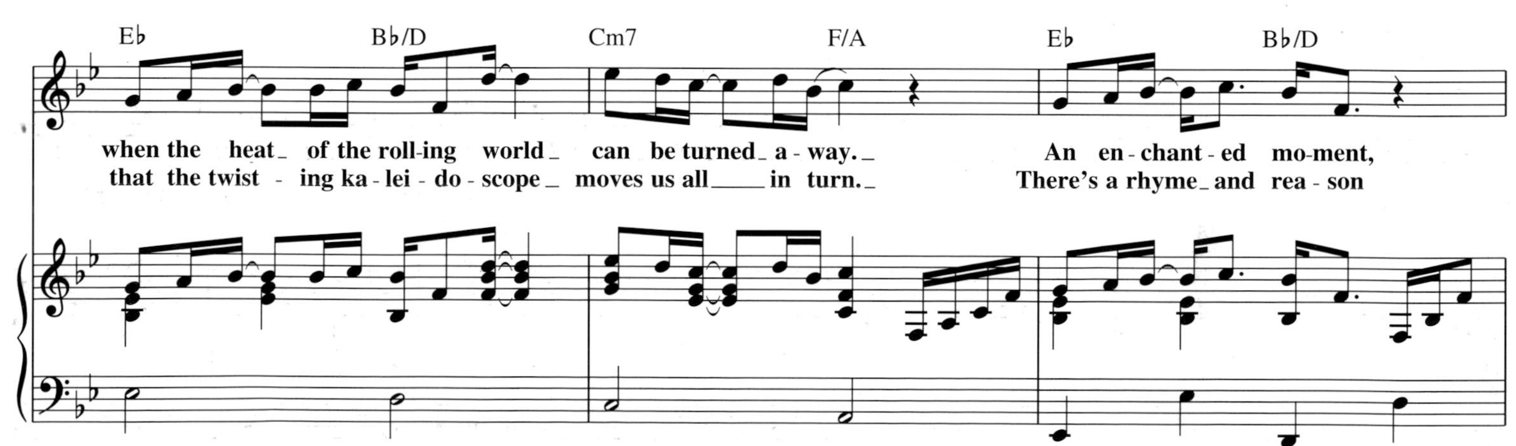
E♭ B♭/D Cm7 F/A E♭ B♭/D
when the heat_ of the roll-ing world_ can be turned_ a - way._ An en-chant-ed mo-ment,
that the twist - ing ka-lei-do-scope_ moves us all___ in turn._ There's a rhyme_and rea-son

© 1994 Wonderland Music Company, Inc.
All Rights Reserved Used by Permission

E♭ B♭/D E♭ Gm
and it sees me through. It's e - nough for this rest - less war - rior
to the wild out - doors when the heart of this star - crossed voy - ag - er
A♭ F B♭ F/A
just to be with you. And can you feel the love
beats in time with yours.
poco cresc.
Gm E♭ B♭ E♭ C/E
to - night? It is where we are.
F E♭ B♭/D
It's e - nough for this

Gm
Gm/F
E♭
wide - eyed wan - der - er
Cm
B♭/D
E♭
C/E
that we got this far.
F
And can
B♭
F/A
you feel the love
Gm
E♭
to - night,
B♭
E♭
C/E
how it's laid to rest?
F
E♭
B♭/D
It's e - nough to make

Gm
Gm/F
E♭
Cm
B♭/D
E♭
F7sus
kings ___ and ___ vag - a - bonds ___ be - lieve the ver - y best. ___
E♭/B♭
B♭
1
F/A
E♭/G
B♭/F
poco dim.
E♭
B♭/D
F/A
B♭
Cm7
B♭/D
2
E♭
B♭/D
It's e - nough ___ to make
Gm
Gm/F
E♭
Cm
B♭/D
E♭
F7sus
E♭/B♭
B♭
kings _ and _ vag - a - bonds _ be - lieve the ver - y best. ___
rall.
molto rit.

Hakuna Matata

From Walt Disney Pictures' *The Lion King*

Music by ELTON JOHN
Lyrics by TIM RICE

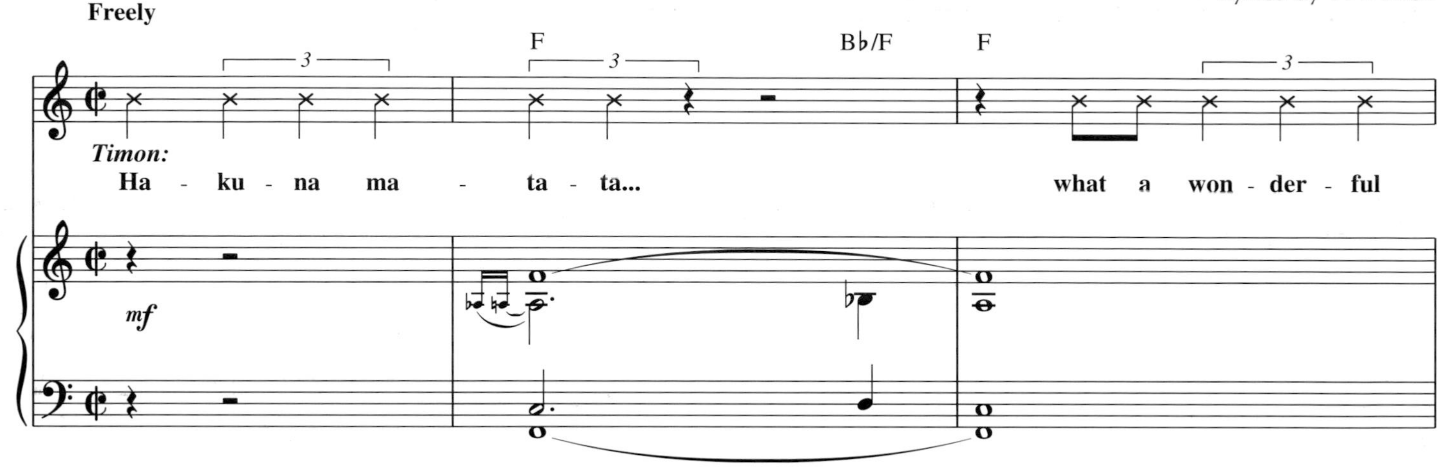

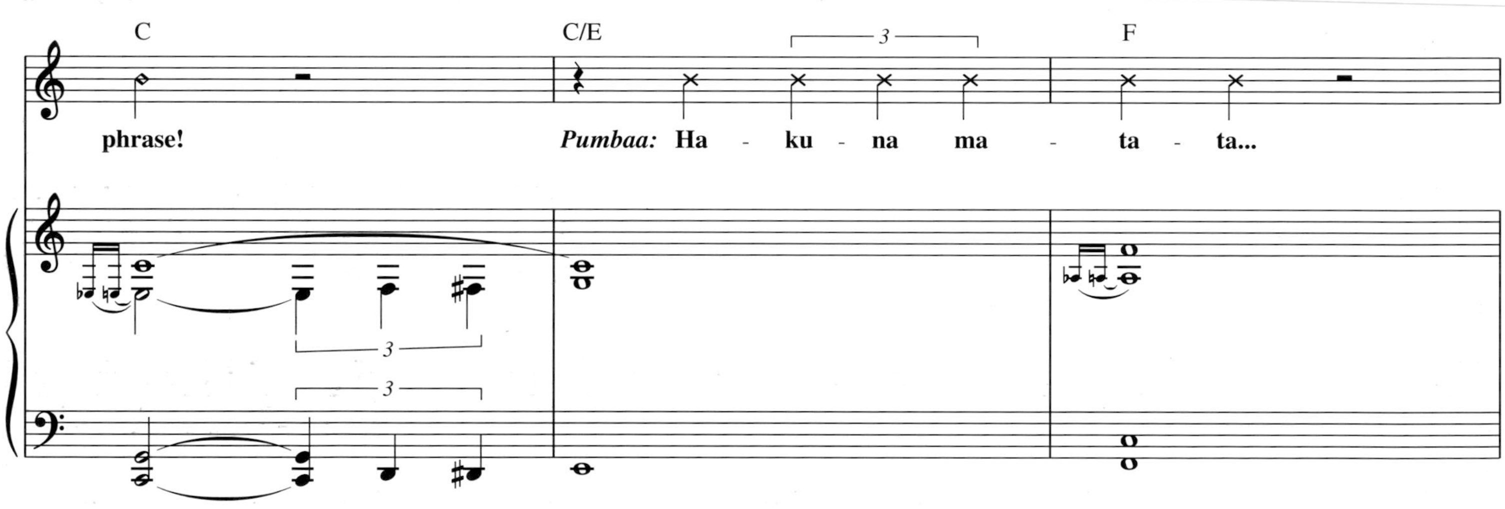

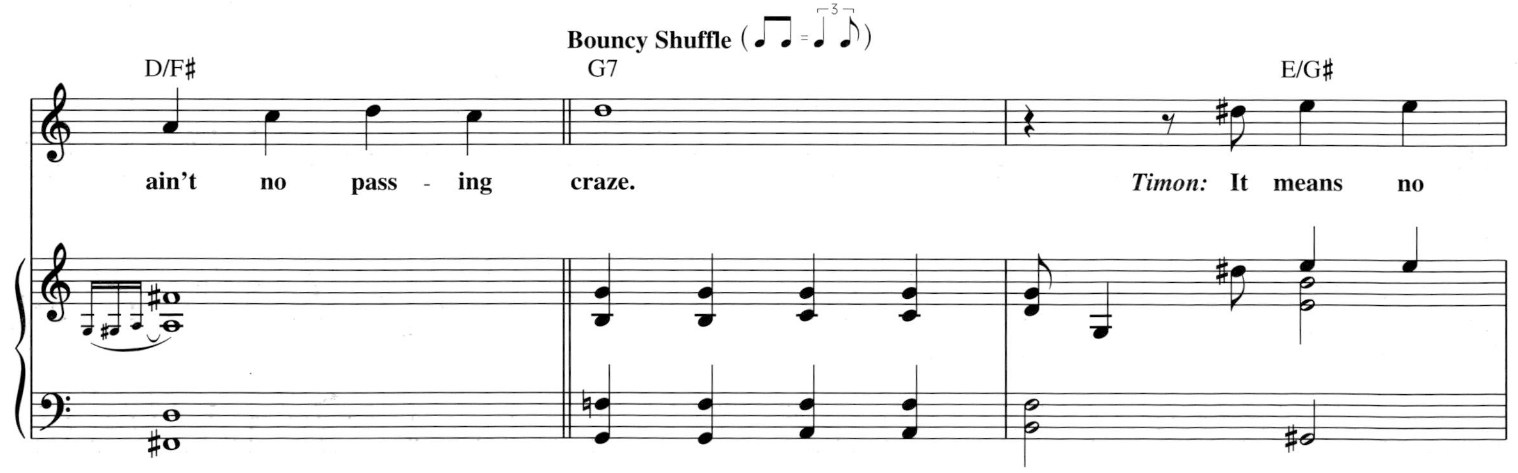

© 1994 Wonderland Music Company, Inc.
All Rights Reserved Used by Permission

Am
C/E
F
D/F#
wor - ries
for the rest of your days.
C/D
Timon & Pumbaa: It's our prob - lem - free phi -
G
C
los - o - phy.
Timon: Ha - ku - na ma - ta - ta.
rall.
freely
Dm
C

G
Dm
Am
G
no chord
Why, when
f
B♭
F
C
B♭
F
he was a young wart - hog... Pumbaa: When I was a young wart -
moving along
ff
dramatically
C
no chord
E♭
(off key)
hog! Timon: Very nice. Pumbaa: Thanks. Timon: He found his a - ro - ma lacked a
rit.
mf
quickly

F
C
G
certain appeal. He could clear the savannah after ev'ry meal!
Pumbaa:
I'm a
Bb
F/A
F
C
sensitive soul, though I seem thick-skinned. And it
rall.
Eb
F
G
hurt that my friends never stood downwind!
accel.
G7sus
C
F/C
C
And, oh, the shame!
Timon:
He was ashamed!
Pumbaa:
Thought of changin' my
rit.
a tempo

G
C/G
G
F/A
B♭
E♭/B♭
B♭
Timon:
name! Oh, what's in a name?
Pumbaa:
And I got down - heart - ed...
Timon:
How did you feel?
no chord
C
Pumbaa:
...ev - 'ry time that I...
Timon:
Hey, Pumbaa, not in front of the kids.
Pumbaa:
Oh, sorry.
Timon & Pumbaa:
Ha - ku - na ma -
a tempo
f
F
3
C
ta - ta... what a won - der - ful phrase.
F
D/F#
Ha - ku - na ma - ta - ta... ain't no pass - ing

G
E/G♯
Am
craze. Simba: It means no wor - ries
C/E
F
D/F♯
for the rest of your days.
Timon: Yeah, sing it kid!
Timon & Simba: It's our
C/G
G
prob - lem - free
Pumbaa: phi - los - o - phy.
C
Timon & Simba:
Ha - ku - na ma - ta - ta.
dim.

Hakuna Matata

From Walt Disney Pictures' *The Lion King*

Music by Elton John
Lyrics by Tim Rice

Timon:	Hakuna matata...what a wonderful phrase!
Pumbaa:	Hakuna matata...ain't no passing craze.
Timon:	It means no worries for the rest of your days.
Timon & Pumbaa:	It's our problem-free philosophy.
Timon:	Hakuna matata.
	Why, when he was a young warthog...
Pumbaa:	When I was a young warthog!
Timon:	(Spoken:) *Very nice.*
Pumbaa:	(Spoken:) *Thanks.*
Timon:	He found his aroma lacked a certain appeal.
	He could clear the savannah after ev'ry meal!
Pumbaa:	I'm a sensitive soul, though I seem thick-skinned.
	And it hurt that my friends never stood downwind!
	And, oh, the shame!
Timon:	He was ashamed!
Pumbaa:	Thought of changin' my name!
Timon:	Oh, what's in a name?
Pumbaa:	And I got downhearted...
Timon:	How did you feel?
Pumbaa:	...ev'ry time that I...
Timon:	(Spoken:) *Hey, Pumbaa, not in front of the kids.*
Pumbaa:	(Spoken:) *Oh, sorry.*
Timon & Pumbaa:	Hakuna matata...what a wonderful phrase.
	Hakuna matata...ain't no passing craze.
Simba:	It means no worries for the rest of your days.
Timon:	(Spoken:) *Yeah, sing it kid!*
Timon & Simba:	It's our problem-free
Pumbaa:	Philosophy.
Timon & Simba:	Hakuna matata.
All:	Hakuna matata. Hakuna matata. Hakuna matata.
	Hakuna matata. Hakuna matata. Hakuna matata.
	Hakuna matata. Hakuna...
Timon:	It means no worries for the rest of your days.
All:	It's our problem-free philosophy.
Timon:	Hakuna matata.
Pumbaa:	Hakuna matata. Hakuna matata.
Timon:	Hakuna matata.
Pumbaa:	Hakuna matata. Hakuna matata.
Timon:	Hakuna matata. Hakuna matata.
	Hakuna matata. Hakuna matata.

© 1994 Wonderland Music Company, Inc.
All Rights Reserved Used by Permission

Colors Of The Wind

From Walt Disney's *Pocahontas*

Music by ALAN MENKEN
Lyrics by STEPHEN SCHWARTZ

Moderately

B♭ Gm E♭(add9) Dm7 Gm F

mf

E♭maj7 E♭maj7/F F9 B♭ Gm

rall. *a tempo*

B♭ Gm B♭

You think you own what-ev-er land you
think the on - ly peo-ple who are

Gm B♭ Dm

land on; the earth is just a dead thing you can claim; but
peo - ple are the peo - ple who look and think like you, but

© 1995 Wonderland Music Company, Inc. and Walt Disney Music Company
All Rights Reserved Used by Permission

Gm Dm Eb6 Bb/D
1
Cm F6
I know ev - 'ry rock and tree and crea - ture has a life, has a spir - it, has a
if you walk the foot - steps of a strang - er you'll learn
Gm F
2
Cm F Eb/F Bb Dm/A
name. You things you nev - er knew you nev - er knew. Have you
Gm Dm Eb Gm
ev - er heard the wolf cry to the blue corn moon or asked the grin - ning bob - cat why he
let the ea - gle tell you where he's
Dm Eb F/Eb Dm7 Gm7
grinned? been? Can you sing with all the voic - es of the moun - tain? Can you

E♭6
B♭/D
Gm7(add4)
Cm7
E♭/F
To Coda
paint with all the col-ors of the wind?
Can you paint with all the col-ors of the
B♭
Gm
F6
E♭
E♭/F
B♭
F
wind?
Come
run the hid-den pine trails of the
rain-storm and the riv - er are my
Gm
E♭(add9)
B♭
Dm7
for - est,
come taste the sun-sweet ber - ries of the earth,
come
broth - ers;
the her - on and the ot - ter are my friends;
and
Gm
F6
E♭6
B♭/D
1
Cm7
B♭/F
F
roll in all the rich - es all a - round you,
and for once
nev-er won-der what they're
we are all con-nect - ed to each oth - er
in a

2
D.S. al Coda
Gm F(add9)/A Cm7 E♭/F B♭ Dm/A
worth. The cir - cle in a hoop that nev - er ends. Have you
CODA
B♭ Dm7 F/E♭ Dm7 Gm7
wind? How high does the syc - a - more grow? If you
A♭maj9 E♭/F F6 E♭/F F
cut it down then you'll nev - er know. And you'll
rall.
Gm Dm7 E♭ F Gm
nev - er hear the wolf cry to the blue corn moon, for wheth - er we are white or cop - per -
a tempo

Dm7
E♭
F(add9)/A
Dm7
Gm7
skinned, we need to sing with all the voic-es of the moun-tain, we need to
Cm7
Dm7
Gm7(add4)
Cm7
paint with all the col-ors of the wind. You can own the earth and still all you'll
Freely
Dm7
E♭maj9
F
Gm7
Dm7
E♭maj9
Cm7/F
B♭
own is earth un-til you can paint with all the col-ors of the wind.
a tempo
Gm
E♭maj7
Gm
F
E♭
E♭/F
no chord
B♭(add9)
rit.

You've Got A Friend In Me

From Walt Disney's *Toy Story*

Music and Lyrics by
RANDY NEWMAN

Easy shuffle (♫ = ♩ ♪ triplet)

Eb G7/D Cm B7 Eb/Bb Ebdim/Bb Bb7

f

Eb D/Bb Db/Bb D/Bb Eb Bb7#5

mf

You've got a friend in me. __
You've got a friend in me. __

Eb9 Ab Adim7 Eb/Bb Eb

You've got a friend in me. __
You've got a friend in me. __

Ab Eb/G G7 Cm

When the road __ looks rough a - head __ and you're miles __
You got trou - bles, then I got 'em too. __

© 1995 Walt Disney Music Company
All Rights Reserved Used by Permission

Ab
Eb/G
G7
Cm
and miles from your nice warm bed,
There is - n't an - y - thing I would - n't do for you.
Ab
D/A
Eb/Bb
G/B
Cm
Ab7
G
Cm
F7
Db7
you just re - mem - ber what your old pal said. Son, you've got a friend in me.
If we stick to - geth - er we can see it through, 'cause you've got a friend in me.
Eb
C7
F7
Bb7
1
G7/D
Yeah, you've got a friend in me.
Yeah, you've got a friend in me.
Cm
B7
Eb/Bb
Ebdim/Bb
Bb7

2
Eb Ebmaj7 Eb7 Ab D
Now, some oth-er folks might be a lit-tle bit smart-er than I am,
Eb6 D7 Eb6 D Em7
big-ger and strong-er too. May-be. But none of them will
Fdim7 D/F# Gm C7 Fm Bb7
ev-er love you the way I do, just me and you, boy.
Eb Bb7#5 Eb7 Ab Adim7
And as the years go by, our friend-ship will nev-er die.

Eb/Bb
Eb
Ab
Adim7
Eb/Bb
G7/B
Cm
You're gon - na see it's our des - ti - ny.
molto rit.
F7
Bb7
Eb
C7
F7
Bb7
You've got a friend in me.
You've got a friend in me.
a tempo
Eb
C7
F7
Bb7
Eb
G7/D
You've got a friend in me.
Cm
B7
Eb/Bb
Ebdim/Bb
Bb7
Eb
rit.

Someday

From Walt Disney's *The Hunchback Of Notre Dame*

Music by ALAN MENKEN
Lyrics by STEPHEN SCHWARTZ

Gently

Ab Dbm6/Ab Ab Dbm6/Ab

mf

Ab Cm/G Db/F Ab7/Eb Bbm/Db Ab/C

Some - day when we are wis - er, when the world's old - er, when we have

Bbm7(add4) Ebsus Eb7 Bbm Eb/G Fm Cm/Eb

learned. I pray some-day we may yet live to

© 1996 Wonderland Music Company, Inc. and Walt Disney Music Company
All Rights Reserved Used by Permission

D♭(add2)
A♭/C
A♭/E♭
E♭7sus
E♭7
live and let live.
A♭
Cm/G
D♭/F
Cm/E♭
Some - day life will be fair - er, need will be
B♭m(add2)/D♭
A♭/C
B♭m7(add4)
E♭7
rar - er, greed will not pay.
B♭m7
E♭/G
E♭7/G
D♭6/A♭
A♭
D♭
God - speed this bright mil - len - ni - um

Bbm6/F Fm Bbm Eb7/Db Db Eb6 Eb Ab Cm/G
on its way. Let it come some - day.
Db/F Ab9/Eb Bbm/Db Ab/C F7sus F7
cresc.
rall.
Broadly
Bb Dm/A Dm7/A Eb/G Dm/F
Some - day our fight will be won then, we'll stand in the
f
Cm/Eb Bb/D Cm7 Cm7/(add4) F7sus F
sun then, that bright af - ter - noon.

Cm
F
Eb6/Bb
Bb
Eb(add9)
Till then, on days when the sun is gone,
Cm6/Gm
Gm
Cm7
F/Eb
Eb
Ebmaj7/F
F#dim7
Gm
Gm7/F
we'll hang on, wish up - on the moon.
Slower
Cm
Bb/D
Eb6
Eb6/F
Eb/F
Ebmaj7/F
F7
Bb
Ebm6/Bb
Change will come one day, some - day soon.
p sub.
a tempo
Bb
Ebm6/Bb
Bb
Ebm6/Bb
Bb
rit.

God Help The Outcasts

From Walt Disney's *The Hunchback Of Notre Dame*

Music by ALAN MENKEN
Lyrics by STEPHEN SCHWARTZ

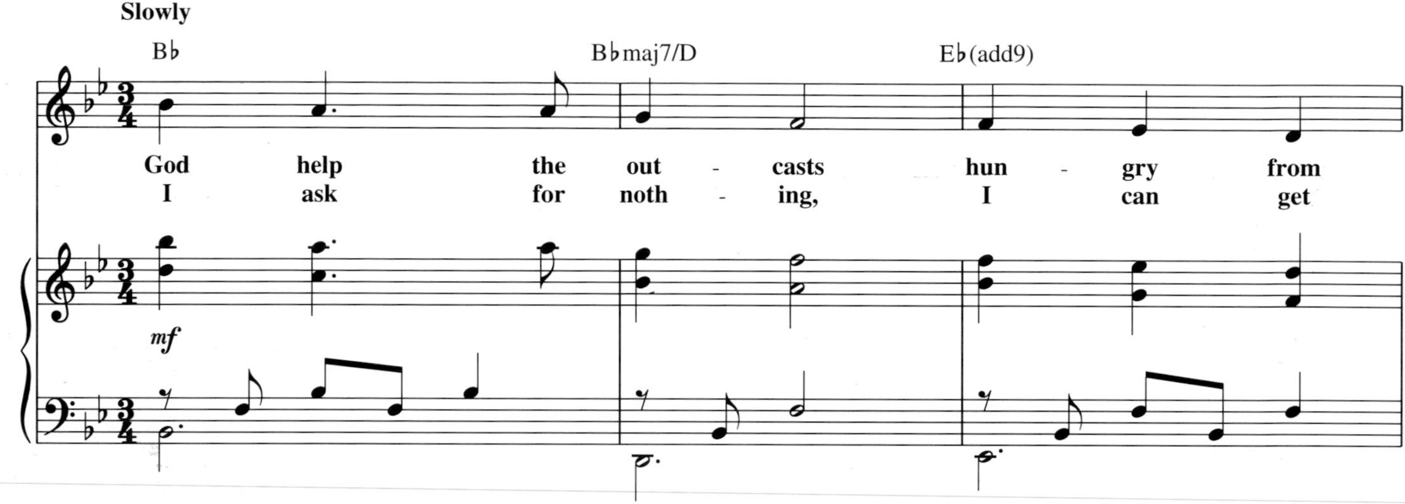

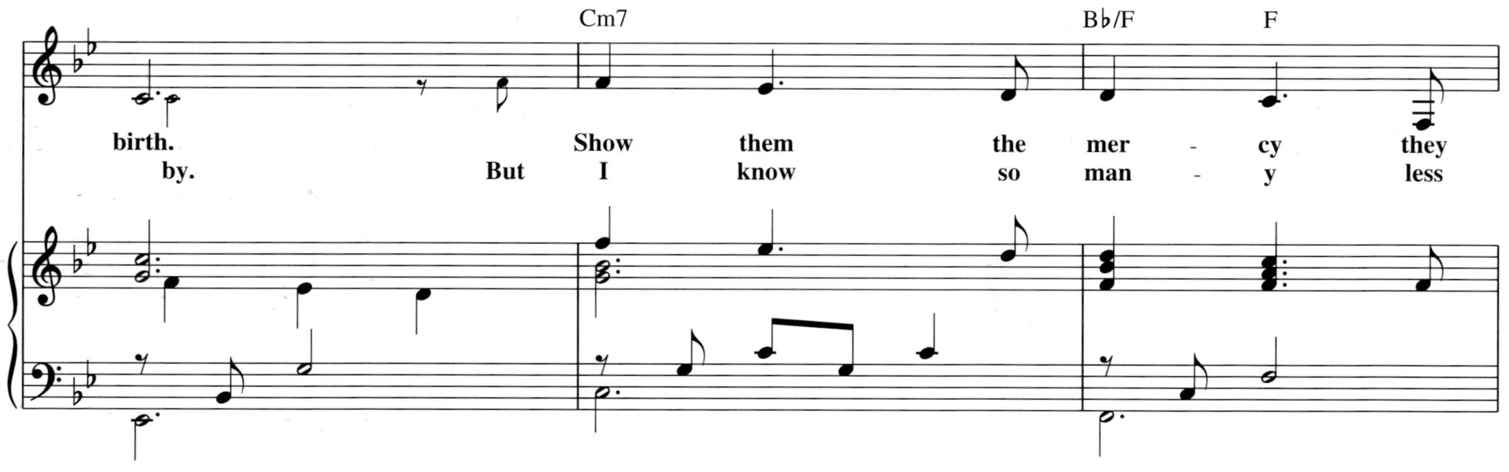

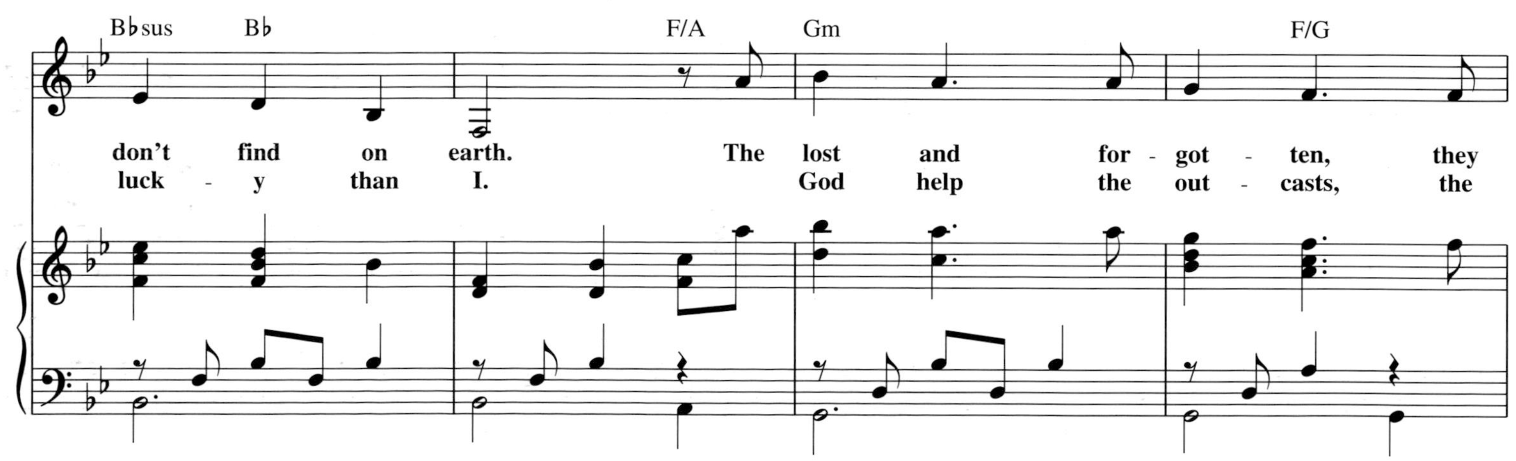

© 1996 Wonderland Music Company, Inc. and Walt Disney Music Company
All Rights Reserved Used by Permission

Cm7
Eb m6
Bb/F
look to You still. God help the out - casts or
poor and down - trod. I thought we all were the
F/b9
1
Bb
Bbmaj7
Eb/Bb
Bb
no - bod - y will.
chil - dren of
F/Bb
Eb/Bb
2
Bb
F/A
Eb/G
God.
I don't know if there's a
Bb/F
Cm/F
Bb
Dm/A
Gm
rea - son why some are blessed, some not.
Why the few You seem to

E♭(add9)
Cm7
B♭/D
fa - vor, they fear us, flee us,
Dm
Gsus
G
C
try not to see us. God help the
f
C/E
F
Dm
out - casts, the tat - tered, the torn, seek - ing an
Gsus
G
Csus
C
G/B
Am
an - swer to why they were born. Winds of mis -

Dm
Fm6
for - tune have blown them a - bout. You made the
dim.
C/G Cmaj7/G G7♭9 Am Cmaj7/G
out - casts; don't cast them out. The
Fm6 C/E Fm6 C/E Fm6 C/E Dm
poor and un - luck - y, the weak and the odd; I thought we
mp
mf poco rall.
C/E G7♭9 C Cmaj7 F/C C
all were the chil - dren of God.
a tempo

God Help The Outcasts

(As Performed by Bette Midler)
From Walt Disney's *The Hunchback Of Notre Dame*

Music by Alan Menken
Lyrics by Stephen Schwartz

I don't know if You can hear me or if You're even there.
I don't know if You will listen to a humble prayer.
They tell me I am just an outcast;
I shouldn't speak to You.
Still I see Your face and wonder:
Were You once an outcast too?
God help the outcasts hungry from birth.
Show them the mercy they don't find on earth.
The lost and forgotten, they look to You still.
God help the outcasts or nobody will.
I ask for nothing, I can get by.
But I know so many less lucky than I.
God help the outcasts, the poor and downtrod.
I thought we all were the children of God.
I don't know if there's a reason why some are blessed, some not.
Why the few You seem to favor, they fear us,
Flee us, try not to see us.
God help the outcasts, the tattered, the torn,
Seeking an answer to why they were born.
Winds of misfortune have blown them about.
You made the outcasts; don't cast them out.
The poor and unlucky, the weak and the odd;
I thought we all were the children of God.

© 1996 Wonderland Music Company, Inc. and Walt Disney Music Company
All Rights Reserved Used by Permission

Go The Distance

From Walt Disney Pictures' *Hercules*

Music by ALAN MENKEN
Lyrics by DAVID ZIPPEL

Slowly

G A D G A D

I have of - ten dreamed of a far - off place where a
un - known road to em - brace my fate, though that

G A Bm7 Gmaj7 Asus A G A D

he - ro's wel - come would be wait - ing for me, where the crowds will cheer when they
road may wan - der, it will lead me to you. And a thou - sand years would be

G A Bm G F♯m Bm D/A G Asus A

see my face, and a voice keeps say - ing this is where I'm meant to be. I'll be
worth the wait. It might take a life-time, but some - how I'll see it through. And I

© 1997 Wonderland Music Company, Inc. and Walt Disney Music Company
All Rights Reserved Used by Permission

D(add9)/F♯ Em/G D/A A A/G D(add9)/F♯ Em/G
there some - day. I can go the dis - tance. I will find my way
won't look back. I can go the dis - tance. And I'll stay on track. No, I
D/A A A/G D(add9)/F♯ G
1
Bm7
if I can be strong. I know ev - 'ry mile will be worth my while.
won't ac - cept de - feat. It's an up - hill slope, but I
Em7 G A D A/C♯ Bm D/A Gmaj7 G/A
When I go the dis - tance, I'll be right where I be -
D A/D G/D D A/D G/D
2
Bm7 Em7
long. Down an won't lose hope till I

G A D A/C♯ Bm D/A G Asus A D A/D G/D
go the dis - tance and my jour - ney is com - plete. Oh, _
D A/D G/D F B♭/D C/E A/C♯
yeah. _ But to look be - yond _ the glo - ry is the hard - est part, _ for a
D G F♯/A♯ E/G♯ F♯/A♯ B
he - ro's strength _ is meas - ured by his heart.
E/G♯ F♯/A♯ B G/B A/C♯ D Bm Em7♭5/B♭
3

D/A
G/A
A7
Like a
rall.
D(add9)/F♯
Em/G
D/A
A
G
D(add9)/F♯
Em/G
shoot - ing star, I will go the dis - tance. I will search the world.
a tempo
D/A
A
G
D(add9)/F♯
E/G♯
F♯/A♯
Bm
I will face its harms. I don't care how far. I can go the dis - tance till I
G
A
D
A/C♯
Bm
D/A
G
Asus
A
G/B
A/C♯
D
find my he-ro's wel-come wait - ing in your arms.
rit.
rit.

Go The Distance

(As Performed by Michael Bolton)
From Walt Disney Pictures' *Hercules*

Music by Alan Menken
Lyrics by David Zippel

I have often dreamed of a far-off place
Where a hero's welcome would be waiting for me,
Where the crowds will cheer when they see my face,
And a voice keeps saying this is where I'm meant to be.
I'll be there someday.
I can go the distance.
I will find my way if I can be strong.
I know ev'ry mile will be worth my while.
When I go the distance, I'll be right where I belong.
Down an unknown road to embrace my fate,
Though that road may wander it will lead me to you.
And a thousand years would be worth the wait.
It might take a lifetime, but somehow I'll see it through.
And I won't look back.
I can go the distance.
And I'll stay on track.
No, I won't accept defeat.
It's an uphill slope, but I won't lose hope
Till I go the distance and my journey is complete.
Oh, yeah.
But to look beyond the glory is the hardest part,
For a hero's strength is measured by his heart.
Like a shooting star, I will go the distance.
I will search the world.
I will face its harms.
I don't care how far.
I can go the distance
Till I find my hero's welcome waiting in your arms.
I will search the world.
I will face its harms
Till I find my hero's welcome waiting in your arms.

© 1997 Wonderland Music Company, Inc. and Walt Disney Music Company
All Rights Reserved Used by Permission

Reflection

From Walt Disney Pictures' *Mulan*

Music by MATTHEW WILDER
Lyrics by DAVID ZIPPEL

Moderately slow
F
Dm7
Look at me, you may think you see who I
mp

Gm
F/C C7
F
really am, but you'll nev-er know me. Ev-'ry day it's

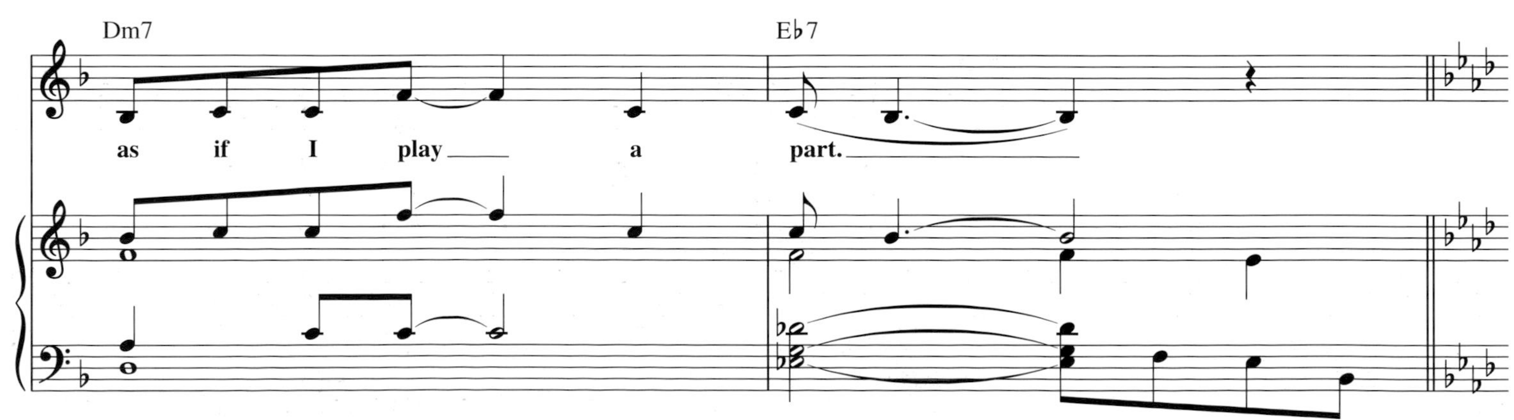
Dm7
Eb7
as if I play a part.

© 1998 Walt Disney Music Company
All Rights Reserved Used by Permission

A♭(add2)
Fm11
Now I see if I wear a mask I can
But some - how I will show the world what's in -

B♭m7
D♭m6/9
A♭
fool the world, but I can - not fool my heart.
side my heart and be loved for who I am.

Who is that
Who is that
(D.S.) Why must we

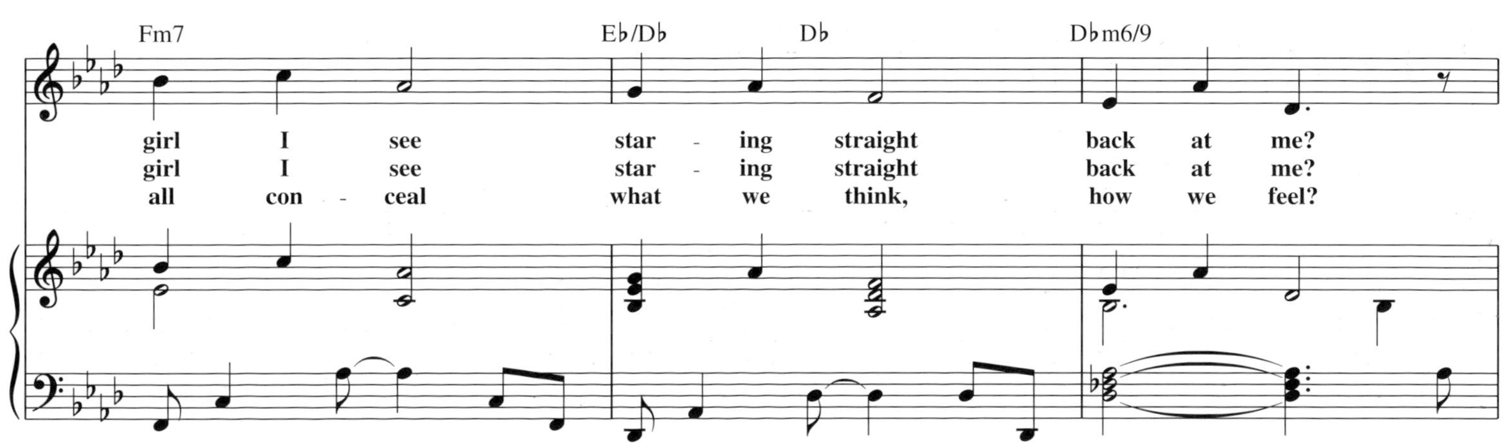
Fm7
E♭/D♭
D♭
D♭m6/9
girl I see star - ing straight back at me?
girl I see star - ing straight back at me?
all con - ceal what we think, how we feel?

Ab Eb/G Fm7 Ab/Eb Dbmaj7 Dbmaj6
1
Dbm6/9
When will my re - flec - tion show who I am in -
Why is my re - flec - tion some - one
Must there be a se - cret me I'm
Ab Fm7 F
side? I am now in a
Dm7 Gm7 C7
world where I have to hide my heart and what I be - lieve in.
2,3
Gb Eb
I don't know?
forced to hide?

Ab
Fm7
Eb/D
Db
Must I pre - tend that I'm some - one else
I won't pre - tend that I'm some - one else

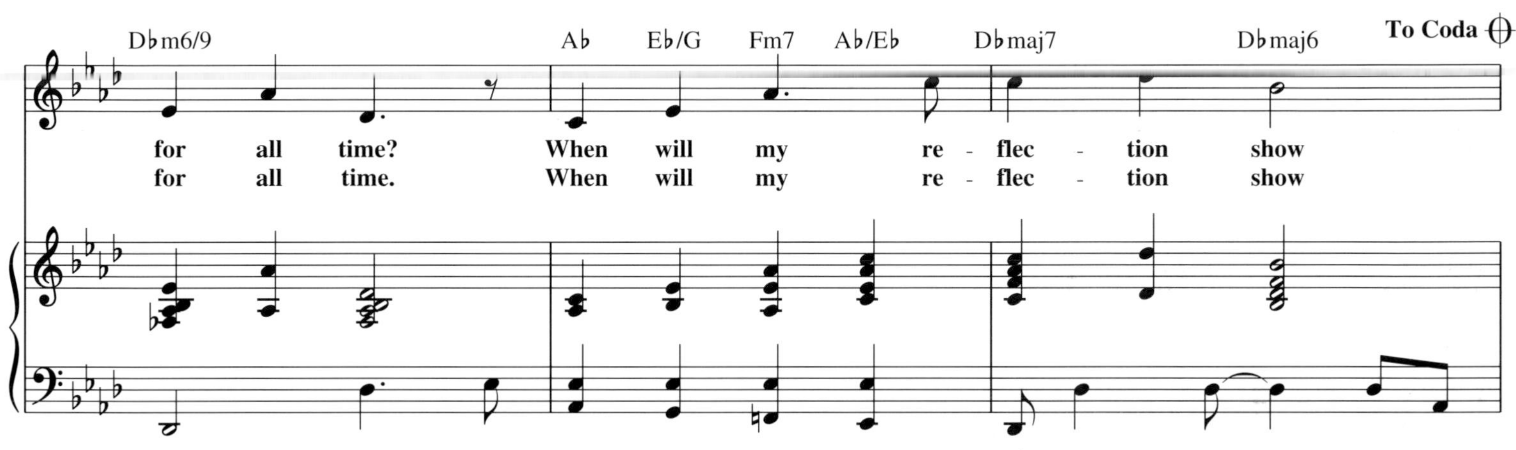
Dbm6/9
Ab
Eb/G
Fm7
Ab/Eb
Dbmaj7
Dbmaj6
To Coda
for all time? When will my re - flec - tion show
for all time. When will my re - flec - tion show

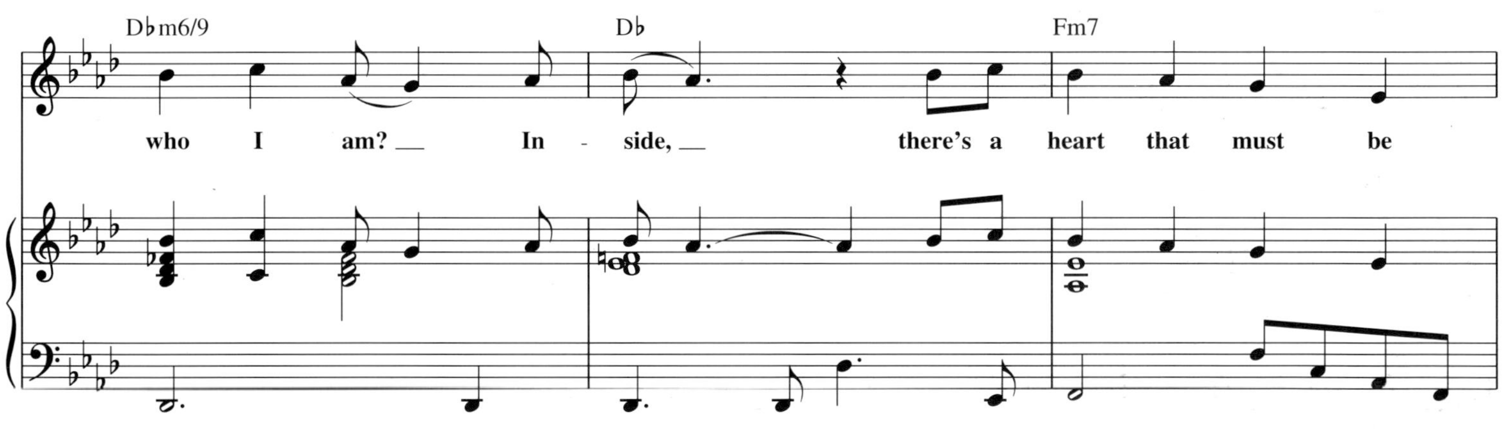
Dbm6/9
Db
Fm7
who I am? In - side, there's a heart that must be

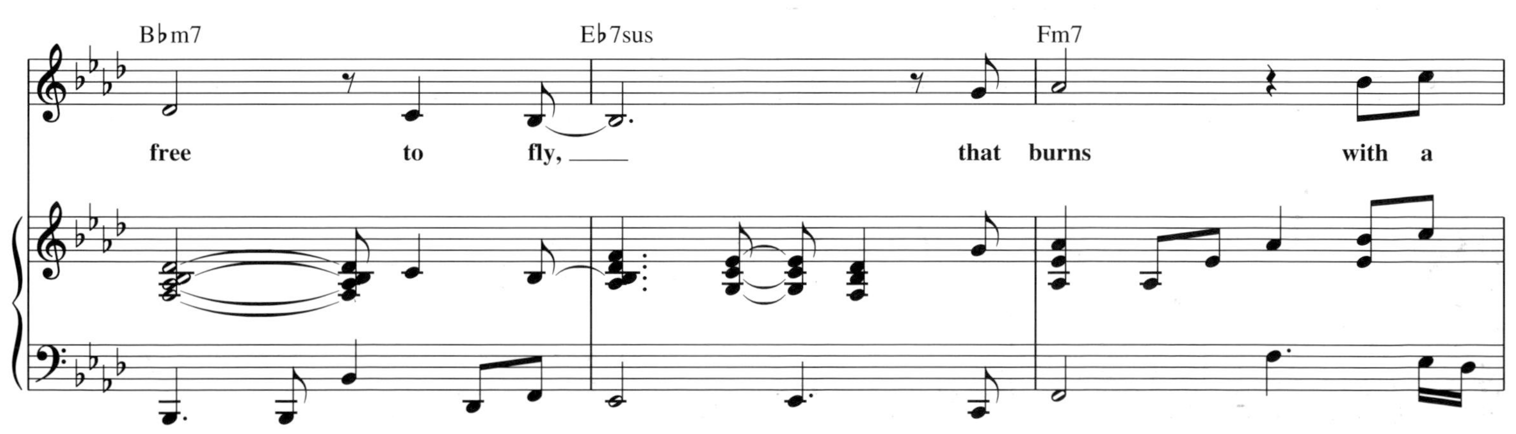
Bbm7
Eb7sus
Fm7
free to fly, that burns with a

D.S. al Coda
(take 2nd ending)
Cm7
Bbm7
Dbm6/9
need to know the rea - son why.
CODA
Dbm6/9
Fm7
Fm/Eb
Dm7b5
Ab
Eb/G
Fm7
Ab/Eb
who I am in - side?
When will my re -
rit.
a tempo
Dbmaj7
Dbmaj6
Dbm6/9
Ab
flec - tion show
who I am in - side?
Fm7
Ab

You'll Be In My Heart
(Pop Version)

As Performed by Phil Collins
From Walt Disney Pictures' *Tarzan™*

Words and Music by
PHIL COLLINS

Moderately
F♯5
Come stop your cry - ing; it will be all right.
Just take my hand,
mf

B5
hold it tight.
I will pro-tect you from all a - round you.

G♯m
C♯
F♯
I will be here; don't you cry.
For one so small you
Why can't they un-der-stand the

© 1998 Edgar Rice Burroughs, Inc. and Walt Disney Music Company
All Rights Reserved Used by Permission

C♯/F♯
F♯
seem so strong.
way we feel?
My arms will hold you, keep you
They just don't trust what they
C♯/F♯
F♯
B(add2)
safe and warm.
can't ex - plain.
This bond be - tween us
I know we're dif - f'rent, but
G♯m
C♯
B♭
can't be bro - ken.
deep in - side us
I will be here; don't you cry.
we're not that dif-fer-ent at all.
'Cause
And
E♭
A♭/E♭
B♭
B♭/A♭
you'll be in my heart,
yes, you'll be in my

Gm7
Cm
A♭
heart from this day on now and for - ev - er -
D♭
To Coda
B♭
E♭
more. You'll be in my
A♭/E♭
B♭
B♭/A♭
Gm7
heart no mat - ter what they say. You'll
Cm
A♭(add2)
D♭
be here in my heart al - ways.

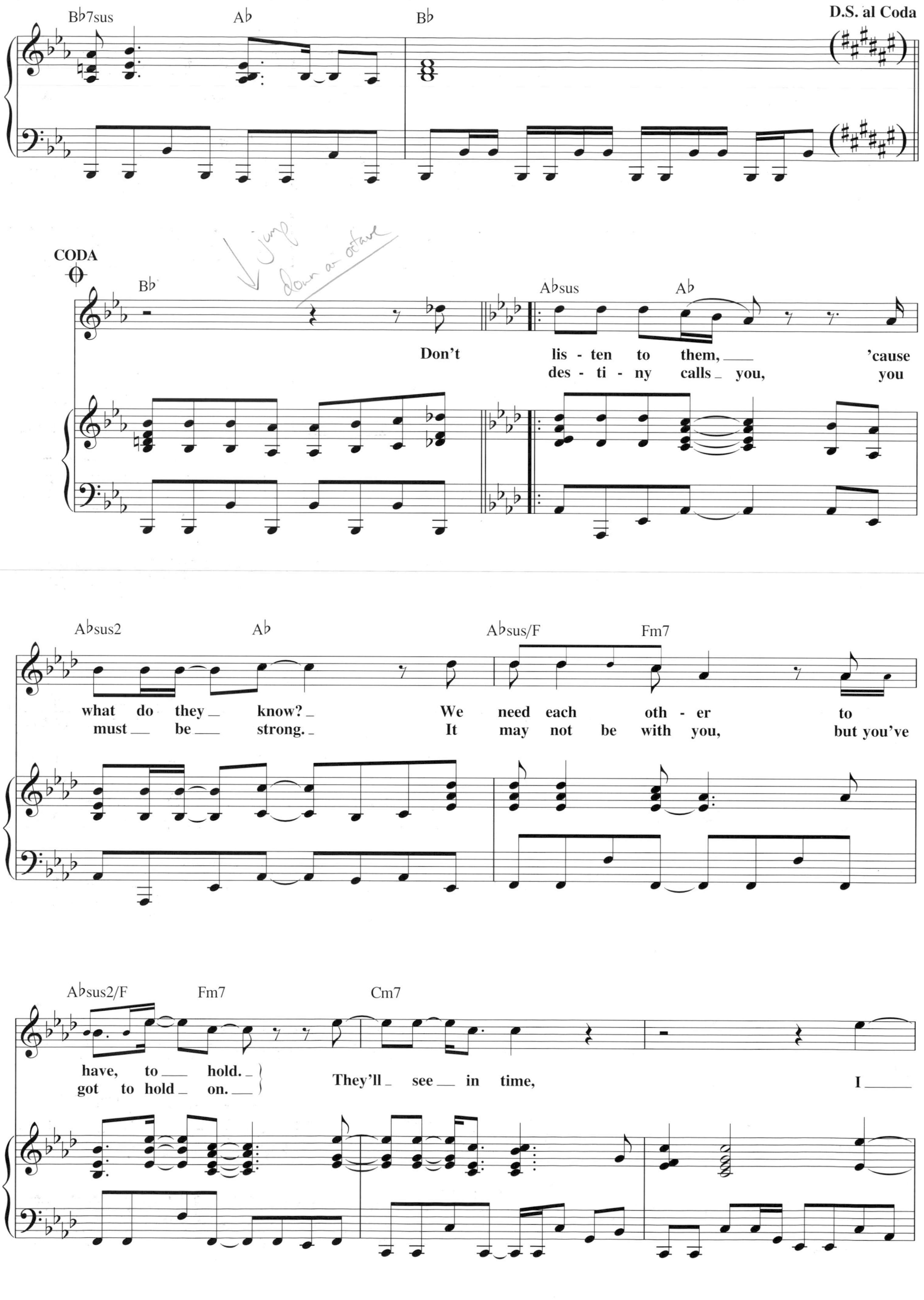

B♭7sus A♭ B♭

D.S. al Coda

CODA

B♭ A♭sus A♭

Don't lis - ten to them, 'cause
des - ti - ny calls you, you

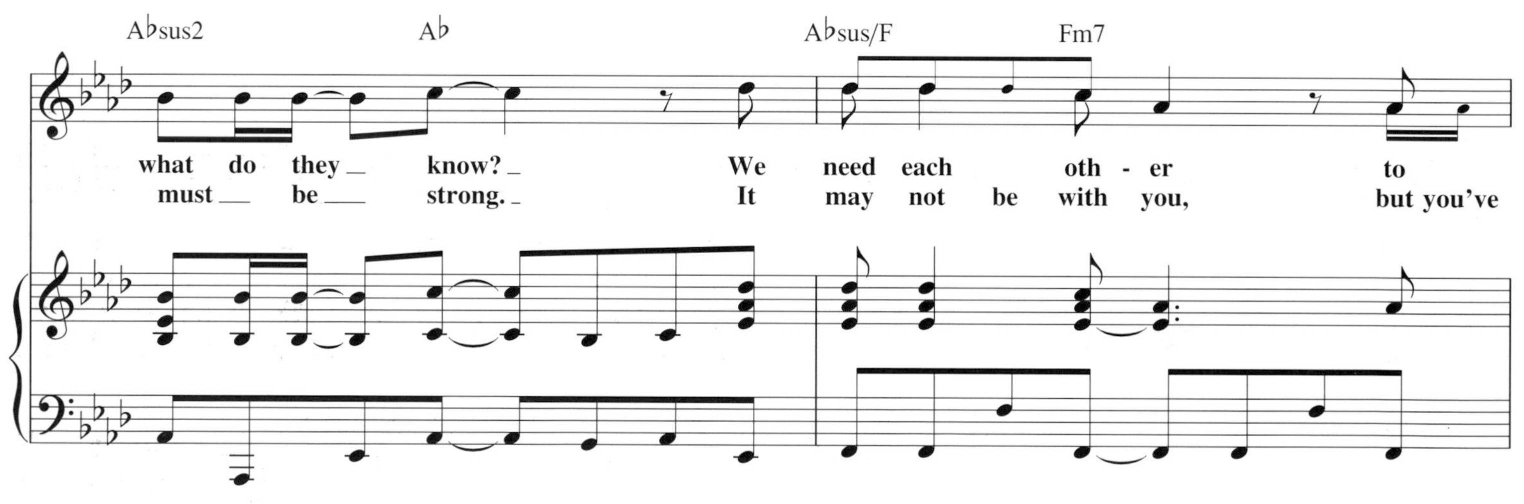

1
2
D♭
know.
When
know.
We'll
E♭
B♭
F
B♭/F
show them to-geth-er, 'cause
you'll be in my heart.
Be-lieve me,
C
C/B♭
Am7
Dm
you'll be in my heart.
I'll be there from this day on, now
B♭
E♭
C
and for-ev-er-more.

F
B♭/F
C
C/B♭
(You'll be here in my heart.)
You'll be in my heart no mat-ter what they
Am
Dm
B♭(add2)
(I'll be with you.)
say. You'll be here in my heart (I'll be there.) al-
E♭
C
B♭maj9
- ways. Al - ways
F(add2)
I'll be with you. I'll be

B♭maj9
F(add2)
there for you al - ways,
al - ways and al - ways.
B♭maj9
Just look o - ver your shoul-der.
Just look o -
F(add2)
B♭maj9
- ver your shoul-der.
Just look o - ver your shoul-der;
F
F(add2)
I'll be there al - ways.

Two Worlds

From Walt Disney Pictures' *Tarzan™*

Words and Music by
PHIL COLLINS

Moderately

B♭sus2 C F B♭sus2

Put your faith in what you most be - lieve_ in. Two worlds,_ one
Soft - ly tread the sand be - low your_ feet_ now. Two worlds,_ one

mf

C F C(add4)/B♭ B♭(add2) E♭sus2

fam - i - ly. Trust your heart,_ let fate de - cide_ to
fam - i - ly. Trust your heart,_ let fate de - cide_ to

Dm Csus C Fm7 E♭/F

guide these_ lives_ we see.____ A par - a - dise_ un - touched_
guide these_ lives_ we see.____ Be-neath the shel - ter_ of ____

© 1998 Edgar Rice Burroughs, Inc. and Walt Disney Music Company
All Rights Reserved Used by Permission

Fm
Fm7
E♭/F
Fm
by man
with-in this world blessed with love.
the trees,
on - ly love can en - ter here.
Fm7
E♭/F
Fm
Fsus
A sim - ple life they live in peace.
A sim - ple life they live in peace.
E♭
A♭
B♭
E♭
Raise your head up; lift high the load. Take strength from those that need
A♭
B♭
E♭
A♭
B♭
you. Build high the walls, build strong the beams. A

E♭
A♭
B♭
new life is wait - ing; but dan - ger's no stran - ger
C5
Fm7
here. No words de - scribe a
E♭sus2/G
E♭/G
Fm/A♭
moth-er's tears. No words can heal a bro -
B♭5
Fm7
E♭/G
Fm/C
Fsus
ken heart. A dream is gone; but where there's hope,

B♭sus2
C
F
B♭sus2
some - where, - some-thing is call - ing for you.
Two worlds, one

C
F
C(add4)/B♭
B♭(add2)
E♭sus2
fam - i - ly.
Trust your heart, let fate de - cide to

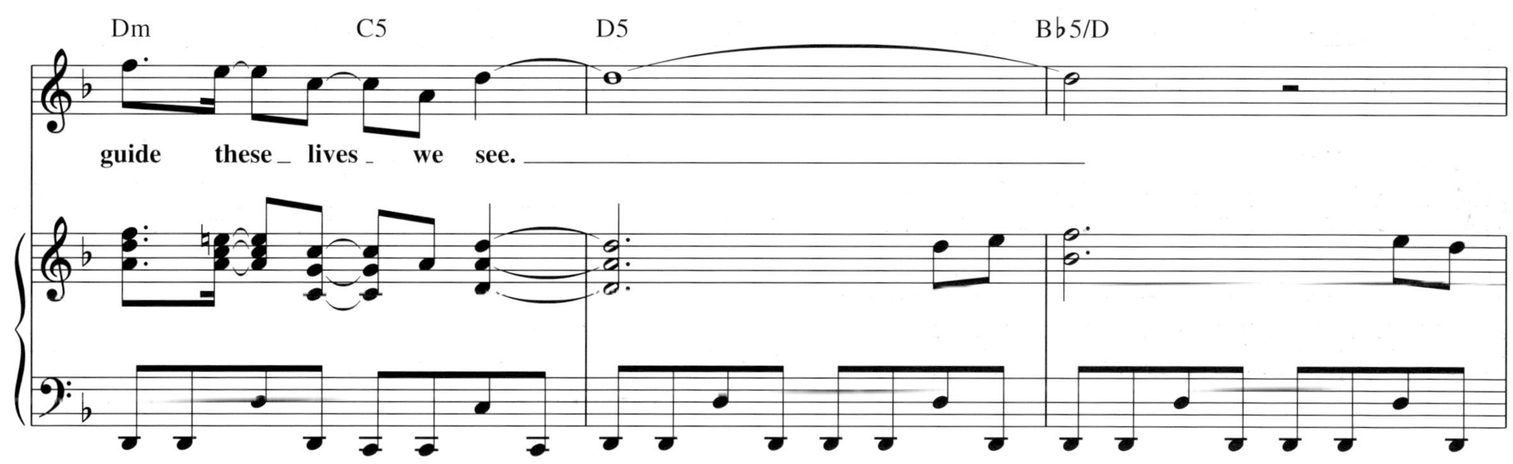
Dm
C5
D5
B♭5/D
guide these lives we see.

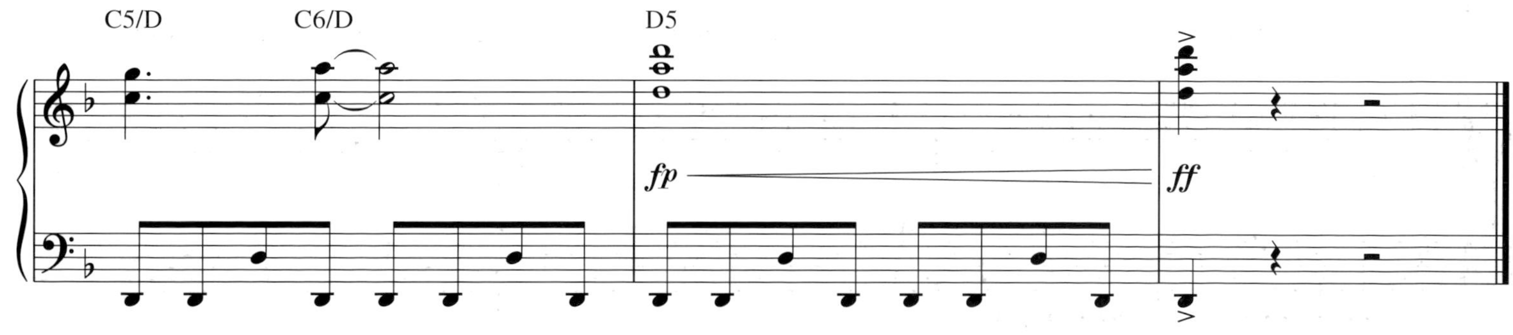
C5/D
C6/D
D5
fp
ff

My Funny Friend And Me

From Walt Disney Pictures'
The Emperor's New Groove

Lyrics by STING
Music by STING and DAVID HARTLEY

Moderately

A(add2) B5/A E/G♯ D/F♯

In the qui - et time of eve - ning, when the stars as-sume their

mp

A/E D(add2) A(add2) E/G♯ F♯m Emaj7

pat - terns _ and the day has made his jour - ney,

Dmaj13 D/E Dmaj7 Bm7 C♯m7

and we won-der just what hap-pened to the life we knew, be-fore the world changed, when not a

© 2000 Wonderland Music Company, Inc.
All Rights Reserved Used by Permission

F♯m
D♯m7
Dmaj7
thing I held _ was true.
But you were kind to me,
D/E
A(add2)
B9/A
E/G♯
and you re-mind-ed me _
that the world is not my play-ground; _
D/F♯
A/E
D(add2)
A(add2)
there are oth-er things that mat - ter; _
what is sim-ple needs pro-
E/G♯
D/F♯
E
Dmaj7
D/E
tect-ing.
My il-lu-sions all would shat - ter, _
but you

Dmaj7
C♯m7
Bm7 C♯m7
F♯m
C♯m7
F♯m
stayed in my cor - ner. The on-ly world I knew was up - side
D♯m7
Dmaj7
Dmaj7/E
down, and now the world and me will know you car - ried me.
A(add2)
E/G♯
F♯m7
E
Dmaj7
E
You see the pat-terns in the big sky; those con-stel-la-tions look like you and I.
F♯m7
C♯m7/E
D♯m7♭5
Just like the pat-terns in the big sky, we could be lost; we could re -

B9
Dmaj7
A/C♯
Bm7 C♯m7
fuse to try. But to have made it through _ in the dark night, _
F♯m
C♯m7
F♯m
D♯m7
Dmaj7
who would those luck-y guys _ turn out to be but that un-us-ual blend _
D/E
A
(add2)
E/G♯
Dmaj9
E7sus
of my fun-ny friend _ and me.
A(add2)
B5/A
E/G♯
D/F♯
I'm not as clev-er as I thought I was. _____ I'm not the boy I used to

A/E D(add2) A(add2) G♯m7 D/F♯ E
be, be - cause_ you showed me some-thing dif-f'rent; you showed _ me some-thing pure. ___
Dmaj7 D/E Dmaj7
I al-ways seemed so cer-tain, but I was real - ly nev-er sure. But you stayed, _ and you
Bm7 C♯m7 F♯m C♯m F♯m D♯m7
called my name __ when oth-ers would have walked out on a lou - sy game.
Dmaj7 D/E A(add2)
And look who made it through but your fun-ny friend_and you.

My Funny Friend and Me

From Walt Disney Pictures' *The Emperor's New Groove*

Lyrics by Sting
Music by Sting and David Hartley

In the quiet time of evening,
When the stars assume their patterns
And the day has made his journey,
And we wonder just what happened
To the life we knew,
Before the world changed,
When not a thing I held was true.
But you were kind to me,
And you reminded me
That the world is not my playground;
There are other things that matter;
What is simple needs protecting.
My illusions all would shatter,
But you stayed in my corner.
The only world I knew was upside down,
And now the world and me will know you carried me.
You see the patterns in the big sky;
Those constellations look like you and I.
Just like the patterns in the big sky,
We could be lost; we could refuse to try.
But to have made it through in the dark night,
Who would those lucky guys turn out to be
But that unusual blend of my funny friend and me.
I'm not as clever as I thought I was.
I'm not the boy I used to be, because
You showed me something different;
You showed me something pure.
I always seemed so certain,
But I was really never sure.
But you stayed, and you called my name
When others would have walked out on a lousy game.
And look who made it through
But your funny friend and you.
You see the patterns in the big sky.
Those constellations look like you and I.
That tiny planet and the bigger guy.
I don't know whether I should laugh or cry.
Just like the patterns in the big sky,
We'll be together 'til the end of time.
Don't know the answer or the reason why.
We'll stick together 'til the day we die.
If I have to do this all a second time,
I won't complain or make a fuss.
Who would the angels send,
But that unlikely blend of these two funny friends?
That's us.

© 2000 Wonderland Music Company, Inc.
All Rights Reserved   Used by Permission

When She Loved Me

From Walt Disney Pictures'
***Toy Story 2*—A Pixar Film**

Music and Lyrics by
RANDY NEWMAN

Tenderly, very freely

F — Gm7 F/A
mp
When some - bod-y loved me,

B♭ G7/B Csus2 C Em7♭5 A/C♯ Dm F(add2)/C B♭(add2) C
ev - 'ry-thing was beau-ti - ful. Ev - 'ry hour we spent to-geth - er lives with-in my heart.

F Gm7 F/A B♭ G7/B Csus2 C Em7♭5 A/C♯ Dm F(add2)/C
And when she was sad, I was there to dry her tears; and when she was hap - py, so — was

© 1999 Walt Disney Music Company and Pixar Talking Pictures
Administered by Walt Disney Music Company
All Rights Reserved Used by Permission

B♭(add2)
F/C
C7
F
I, when she loved me.
B♭
F/C
Cm/B♭
F7/A
B♭
F/C
B♭
F/C
G7/D
Through the sum-mer and the fall, we had each oth-er, that was all. Just she and I to-geth-er, like
G7/B
C
F
Gm7
F/A
B♭
G7/B
Csus2
C
it was meant to be. And when she was lone-ly, I was there to com-fort her, and I
F7/A
B♭
F/C
C7
F
knew that she loved me.

Dm Bbm6/Db F/C
So the years went by; I stayed the same. But
G/B Gdim/Bb F/A Fm6/Ab Eb/Bb A7 Dm Bbm6 C7 Abm/Cb Bb7
she be - gan to drift a - way; I was left a - lone. Still I wait - ed for the day
Gb6/Db Abm/C C7/E
when she'd say, "I will al - ways love you."
rit.
F Gm7 F/A Bb G7/B Csus2 C
Lone - ly and for - got - ten, nev - er thought she'd look my way, and she
a tempo

Em7♭5 A/C♯ Dm F(add2)/C B♭(add2) C F7/A B♭
smiled at me and held me just like she used to do, like she loved me when she
F/C C7sus2 C7 F Gm7 F/A B♭ G7/B Csus2 C
loved me. When some - bod - y loved me, ev - 'ry - thing was beau - ti - ful.
Em7♭5 A/C♯ Dm F(add2)/C B♭(add2) C F/C C7
Ev - 'ry hour we spent to - geth - er lives with - in my heart, when she loved
F
me.

Written In The Stars

From Walt Disney Theatrical Production's *Aida*

Music by ELTON JOHN
Lyrics by TIM RICE

Moderately slow

C G/C F/C C E7 G♯dim7 Am Am/G

(Male:) I am here to tell_ you we can nev-er meet a-gain._ Sim-ple real-ly, is-n't it? A

mf

F C/G G C G/C F/C C Esus E7

word or two and then a life-time of not know-ing where or how or why or when._ You

Am Am/G F C/E Dm7

think of me or speak of me or won-der what be-fell__ the some-one you once loved_ so long a-

© 1999 Wonderland Music Company, Inc., Happenstance Ltd. and Evadon Ltd.
All Rights Reserved Used by Permission

C/G G C G/C F/C
go, so well. (Female:) Nev-er won-der what I'll feel as
(Male:) Noth-ing can be al-tered. Oh, there is
C E7sus E7/G♯ Am Am/G
liv-ing shuf-fles by. You don't have to ask me and
noth-ing to de-cide. No es-cape, no change of heart, nor
F Gsus G/B C G/D F/C
I need not re-ply. Ev-'ry mo-ment of my life from
an-y place to hide. (Female:) You are all I'll ev-er want but
C E7sus E7/G♯ Am Am/G
now un-til I die I will think or dream of you and
this I am de-nied. Some-times in my dark-est thoughts I

F
C/E
Dm7
fail to un - der - stand how a per - fect love can be con - found - ed
wish I nev - er learned what it is to be in love and have that
C/G
G
C
G/B
out of hand.
love re - turned.
(Both:) Is it writ - ten in the stars? Are we
Am
C/G
F
pay - ing for some crime? Is that all that we are good for, just a
Dm7
C/G
G
C
G/B
stretch of mor - tal time? Is this God's ex - per - i - ment in

A
Am/G
F
which we have no say?
In which we're giv - en par - a - dise, but
1
Dm7
C/G
G
C
G/C F/C
C
G/C F/C
on - ly for a day.
2
Dm7
F/G
C/G
C
G/B
on - ly for a day.
Is it writ - ten in the stars?
Are we
Am7
Em/G
F
F/E
pay - ing for some crime?
Is that all that we are good for, just a

Dm7
F/G
C
G/B
stretch of mor - tal time? (Both:) Is this God's ex - per - i - ment (Male:) in
Am
Am/G
F
F/E
which we have no say?
In which we're giv - en par - a - dise
(Female:) In which we have no say, giv - en par - a -
Dm7
F/G
C
G/C F/C
on - ly (Both:) for a day.
dise
C
G/C F/C
G♭(add2)
A♭(add2)
B♭(add2)
C
rall.

If I Didn't Have You

Walt Disney Pictures Presents a Pixar Animation Studios Film *Monsters, Inc.*

Music and Lyrics by
RANDY NEWMAN

Moderately

Eb Eb9 Ab6 Abm6 Eb C7 F9 Bb7 Eb

Sulley: If I were a rich man with a mil-lion or two
Mike: I'd live in a pent-house in a room with a view.
Sulley: And if I were hand-

mf 8vb

© 2001 Walt Disney Music Company and Pixar Talking Pictures
All Rights Reserved Used by Permission

E♭9
A♭6
A♭m6
- some,
(It could happen,)
Sulley: 'cause dreams do come true,
(Spoken:) Mike: No way!
8vb
E♭
C7
F7
B♭7sus
E♭
G♭
I would-n't have
noth-in' if I did-n't have
you.
Would-n't have
8vb
D♭
A♭
G♭
D♭
A♭
noth-in' if I did-n't have,
would-n't have
noth-in' if I did-n't have,
(8vb)
G♭
D♭
B♭
B♭7♯5
E♭
would-n't have
noth - in'.
Mike: For years I have en -
Mike (Spoken): Can I tell you something?

Eb9
Ab6
Abm6
- vied
Mike: your grace and your charm.
Sulley (Spoken): (You're green with it.)
Eb6
C7
F7
Ev - 'ry - one loves you, you know.
Sulley: Yes, I
Bb7
Eb
Eb9
know, I know, I know.
Mike: But I must ad - mit it,
8vb
Ab6
Abm6
Eb
C7
big guy, you al - ways come through.
I would-n't have

F9
Bb7sus
Eb
Bbm7
Eb7
noth-ing if I did-n't have _ you.
Ab
Abmaj7
D7sus
D7
Gm
Gm(maj7)
Gm7
C7
Both: You and me to - geth-er, that's how it al - ways should be.
Fm
Fm(maj7)
Fm7
Bb
Eb6
Bb7#5
One with-out the oth - er don't mean noth - ing to me, noth-ing to me.
rit.
Eb
Eb9
Ab6
Mike: Hey, I n-never told you this,
some-times I get a lit - tle
a tempo
8vb

A♭m6
E♭6
C7
F9
B♭7sus
blue Sulley: Looks good on you.
Mike: but I would-n't have
noth-ing if I did-n't have
E♭
E♭6
E♭9
you.
Sulley: Yes, I would-n't be
noth - in'
8vb
A♭6
A♭m6
E♭
if I did-n't have you.
Mike: I know what you mean, Sulley, because...
Sulley: I would-n't know where to
C7
F9
B♭7sus
go,
Sulley: would-n't know
what to
do.
Mike: Me too, because I...
Mike: Why do you keep singing my part?

E♭6
E♭9
A♭6
A♭m6
Both: I don't have to say it
Both: both know it's true.
Sulley: I'll say it anyway. Mike: 'Cause we
8vb
E♭6
C7
F9
B♭7sus
I would-n't have_ noth-in' if I did-n't have,_
I would-n't have_
8vb
noth-in' if I did-n't have,_
I would-n't have_ noth-in' if I did-n't have_
(8vb)
Much slower
G♭
D♭
A♭
E♭
you. Would-n't have_ noth - in' if I did-n't have_ you.

If I Didn't Have You

Walt Disney Pictures Presents A Pixar Animation Studios Film *Monsters, Inc.*

Music and Lyrics by Randy Newman

Sulley: If I were a rich man with a million or two,
Mike: I'd live in a penthouse in a room with a view.
Sulley: And if I were handsome,
Mike: (Spoken:) *No way!*
Sulley: (Spoken:) *It could happen.*
'Cause dreams do come true,
I wouldn't have nothin' if I didn't have you.
Wouldn't have nothin' if I didn't have,
Wouldn't have nothin' if I didn't have,
Wouldn't have nothin'.
Mike: (Spoken:) *Can I tell you something?*
For years I have envied
Sulley: (Spoken:) *You're green with it.*
Mike: Your grace and your charm.
Everyone loves you, you know.
Sulley: Yes, I know, I know, I know.
Mike: But I must admit it, big guy, you always come through.
I wouldn't have nothing if I didn't have you.
Both: You and me together, that's how it always should be.
One without the other don't mean nothing to me, nothing to me.
Mike: (Spoken:) *Yeah, I wouldn't be nothin' if I didn't have you to serve.*
I'm just a punky little eyeball and a funky optic nerve.
Hey, I never told you this.
Sometimes I get a little blue,
Sulley: (Spoken:) *Looks good on you.*
Mike: But I wouldn't have nothing if I didn't have you.
Sulley: (Spoken:) *Let's dance!*
Mike: (Spoken:) *Look, Ma, I'm dancing! Would you let me lead?*
Look at that! It's true! Big guys are light on their feet.
Don't you dare dip me. Don't you dare dip me.
Don't you dare dip me. Ow! I should have stretched.
Sulley: Yes, I wouldn't be nothin' if I didn't have you.
Mike: (Spoken:) *I know what you mean, Sulley, because...*
Sulley: I wouldn't know where to go,
Mike: (Spoken:) *Me too, because I...*
Sulley: Wouldn't know what to do.
Mike: (Spoken:) *Why do you keep singing my part?*
Both: I don't have to say it
Sulley: (Spoken:) *I'll say it anyway.*
Mike: (Spoken:) *'Cause we...*
Both: ...both know it's true.
I wouldn't have nothin' if I didn't have,
I wouldn't have nothin' if I didn't have,
I wouldn't have nothin' if I didn't have you.
Wouldn't have nothin' if I didn't have you.
Mike: (Spoken:) *One more time. It worked!*
Sulley: Don't have to say it,
Mike: (Spoken:) *Where'd everybody come from?*
Sulley: 'Cause we both know it's true.
Mike: (Spoken:) *Let's take it home, big guy!*
Both: I wouldn't have nothin' if I didn't have,
I wouldn't have nothin' if I didn't have,
I wouldn't have nothin' if I didn't have...
Mike: ...you. You. You. A, E, I, O,
Sulley: That means you. Yeah.

© 2001 Walt Disney Music Company and Pixar Talking Pictures
All Rights Reserved Used by Permission

Hawaiian Roller Coaster Ride

From Walt Disney's *Lilo & Stitch*

Words and Music by ALAN SILVESTRI
and MARK KEALI'I HO'OMALU

Moderately fast

F Gm F

mf

1., 3. *Lead:* There's no __ place I'd rath - er be __ **Chorus:* than on my surf-board out at sea,
2. *All:* There's no __ place I'd rath - er be __ *Chorus:* than on the sea - shore dry, wet, free.

*Children's Chorus

Gm F

Lead: lin - ger - ing __ in the o - cean blue. __ *Chorus:* And if I had one wish come true *Lead:* I'd
All: On gold - en sand is ____ where I'd __ lay, *Chorus:* and if I on - ly had my way *All:* I'd

B♭ F B♭

surf 'til ___ the sun sets __ be - yond the __ ho - ri - zon.
play 'til ___ the sun sets __ be - yond the __ ho - ri - zon.

© 2002 Walt Disney Music Company
All Rights Reserved Used by Permission

F
Gm
F
Chorus: A - wi - ki - wi - ki, mai_ lo hi lo hi. La - we mai i ko pa - pa he-'e na - lu.
Chorus: La - la - la i ka la ha - na - ha - na. Me_ ke kai ho - en e i ka pu-'e o - ne.
C
B♭
All: Fly - ing by on a Ha - wai - ian roll - er coast - er_
All: It's time to try_ the Ha - wai - ian roll - er coast - er_
F
Gm
F
ride.
ride.
B♭6
F
Lead: A - wi - ki - wi - ki, mai_ lo - hi - lo - hi. Chorus: La - we mai i ko pa - pa he-'e na - lu.
All: Hang loose,_ hang ten, how's it shake - a - shak - a. No wor - ry, no_ fear. Ain't_ no big - gy, brah - da.

To Coda
B♭6
F
Lead: Pi' - i na lu - lu la la - ha - la - ha. Chorus: O ka mo - a - na ha - nu - pa - nu - pa.
Put-tin' in, cut - tin' up, cut - tin' back, cut-tin' out. Front side, back side, goof - y - foot-ed wipe out.
1
C
B♭
Lead: La - la - la i ka la ha - na - ha na. Chorus: Me ke kai ho - en - e i ka pu - 'e one.
F
N.C.
Lead: He - le - he - le mai ka - kou e. Chorus: Ha - wai - ian roll - er coast - er ride.
2
C
B♭
Let's go jump - in', surf's up and pump - in'. Coast - in' with the mo - tion of the o - cean.

F
N.C.
Whirl - pools swirl - ing, cas - cad - ing, swirl - ing. Chorus: Ha - wai - ian roll - er coast - er ride.
F
Gm
F
D.C. al Coda
CODA
C
B♭
Lead: La - la - la i ka la ha - na - ha - na. Chorus: Me ke kai ho - en - e i ka pu - 'e one.
F
N.C.
Lead: He - le - he - le mai ka - kou e. Chorus: Ha - wai - ian roll - er coast - er ride.

The Medallion Calls

From Walt Disney's *Pirates of the Caribbean*

Moderately

Music by KLAUS BADELT

f

© 2003 Walt Disney Music Company
All Rights Reserved Used by Permission

8vb
8vb
1
2
8vb

The Incredits

Walt Disney Pictures Presents a Pixar Animation Studios Film *The Incredibles*

Music by MICHAEL GIACCHINO

© 2004 Wonderland Music Company, Inc. and Pixar Music
Administered by Wonderland Music Company, Inc.
All Rights Reserved Used by Permission

1
2
1
2
1

2
1
2
gliss.

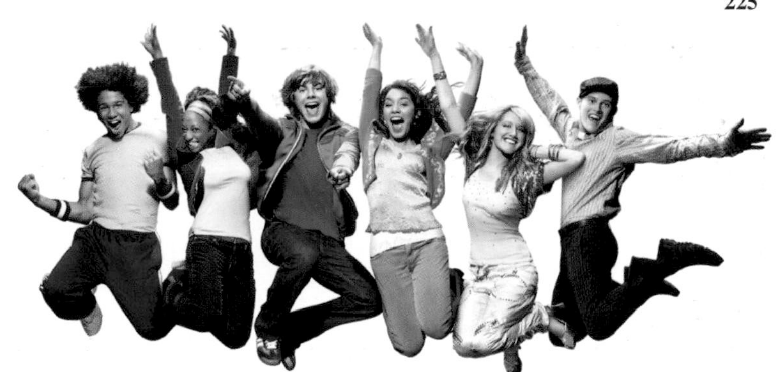

Breaking Free

From Walt Disney's *High School Musical*

Words and Music by
JAMIE HOUSTON

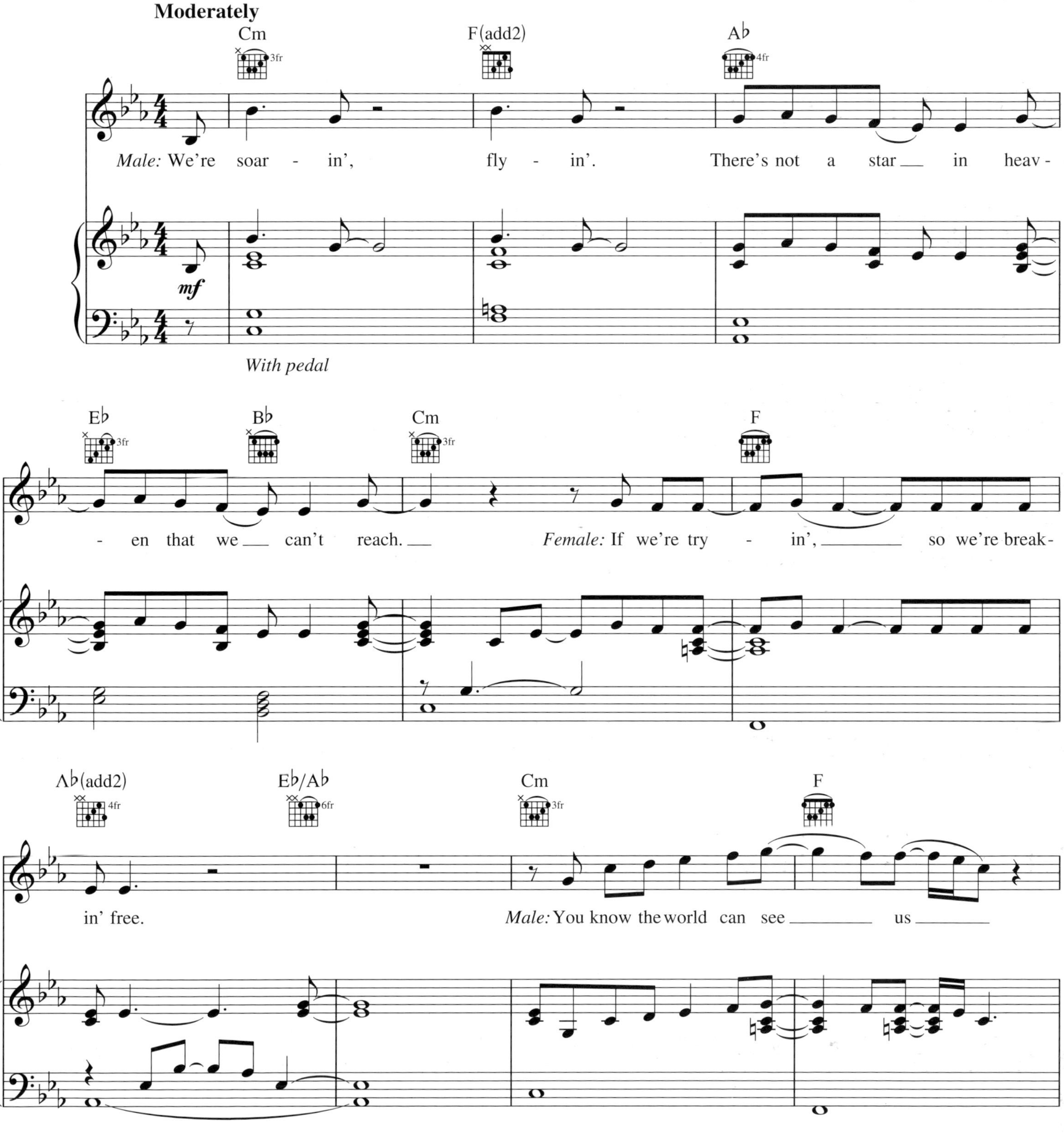

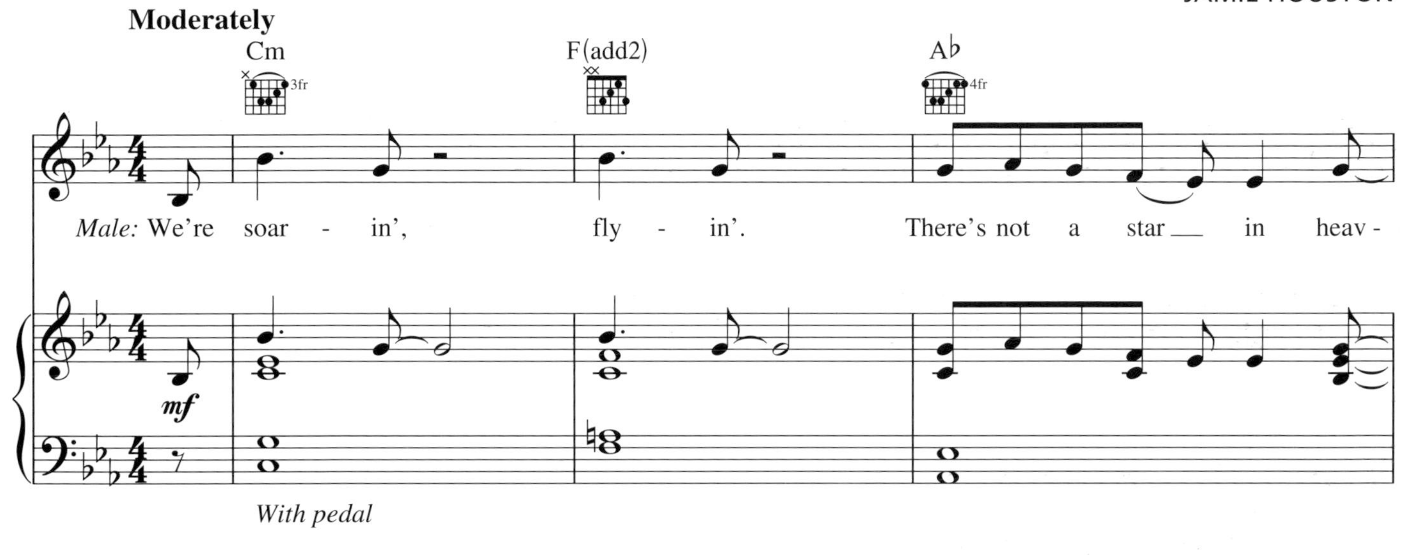

Moderately
Cm
3fr
F(add2)
A♭
4fr
Male: We're soar - in', fly - in'. There's not a star in heav -
mf
With pedal
E♭
3fr
B♭
Cm
3fr
F
- en that we can't reach. Female: If we're try - in', so we're break -
A♭(add2)
4fr
E♭/A♭
6fr
Cm
3fr
F
in' free. Male: You know the world can see us

© 2005 Walt Disney Music Company
All Rights Reserved Used by Permission

A♭
E♭
B♭/D
Cm
in a way that's dif - f'rent from who we are.
Female: Cre - at - ing space be - tween
F
A♭
E♭
B♭/D
A♭
us, till we're sep-'rate hearts.
Both: But your faith, it gives
F7/A
A♭(add2)
E♭/A♭
me strength, strength to be - lieve.
Female: We're
Male: We're break - in' free.
Cm
F
A♭
E♭
B♭/D
soar - in', Male: fly - in'.
Both: There's not a star in heav - en that we can't reach.

Cm
F
A♭ A♭maj7(no3)
A♭ A♭maj7(no3)
3fr
4fr
Male: If we're try - in', Both: yeah, we're break - in' free. Male: Oh, we're break - in' free.
Cm
F
A♭
E♭
B♭/D
Can you feel it build - ing, like a wave the o - cean just can't con - trol,
Cm
F
A♭
Female: con - nect - ed by a feel - in', oh, in our ver - y souls,
E♭
B♭/D
A♭
F7/A
A♭
ris - ing till it lifts us up so ev - 'ry - one can see?

A♭(add2)
Cm
F
4fr
3fr
Female: We're soar - in', Male: fly - in'.
Female: Run - nin', Male: climb - in', Both: to
Male: We're break - in' free.
A♭
E♭
B♭/D
Cm
Both: There's not a star in heav - en that we can't reach.
Male: If we're try -
get to that place to be all that we can be.
Male: Now's the time,
F
A♭
A♭maj7(no3)
To Coda
1
- in', Both: yeah, we're break - in' free.
Male: Oh, we're break - in' free.
Both: so we're break - in' free.
Male: We're break -
2
E♭
B♭/D
A♭
F7/A
in' free.
More than hope, more than faith, Female: this is truth, this is fate;

A♭
4fr
Both:
and to-geth - er, we see it com - in'. Male: More than you, more than me,
F7/A
3fr
A♭
4fr
D.S. al Coda
(verse 1,take repeat)
Female: not a want, but a need: Both: both of us break-in' free.
CODA
A♭
4fr
Cm
3fr
F
in' free. You know the world can see us
A♭(add2)
4fr
E♭
3fr
B♭/D
A♭maj9
3fr
in a way that's dif-f'rent than who we are
8va
rit.

We're All In This Together

From Walt Disney's *High School Musical*

Words and Music by MATTHEW GERRARD
and ROBBIE NEVIL

Moderately

*Recorded a half step lower.

© 2005 Walt Disney Music Company
All Rights Reserved Used by Permission

D♭
E♭
3fr
time for cel - e - bra - tion.
speak - ing out with one voice.
I fi - n'lly fig - ured out,
We're gon - na rock the house,
yeah, yeah,
yeah, yeah.
that all our dreams
The par - ty's on;
have no lim - i - ta - tions;
now ev - 'ry - bod - y, make some noise.
that's what it's all a - bout.
C' - mon and scream and shout.
(C' - mon, now.)
F
N.C.
To Coda
Female: Ev - 'ry - one is spe - cial in their own way;
Female: We've ar - rived be - cause we stuck to - geth - er,

F
E♭
3fr
F
we make each oth - er strong.
We're not the same; we're
E♭
3fr
F
E♭
3fr
dif - f'rent in a good way.
To - geth - er's where we be - long.
F
G
D/F♯
Em
G/D
All: We're all in this to - geth - er; once we know
C
G/B
C/E
D/F♯
G
D/F♯
that we are, we're all stars, and we see that. We're all in this to - geth -

Em G/D C G/B C/E D/F♯
- er; and __ it shows when we stand hand in hand, make our dreams _ come __ true. _
F5 G
Ev-'ry-bod-y now: To-geth - er, to-geth - er,
To-geth - er, we're there _ for
F G
to - geth - er, ev - 'ry - one. To - geth - er, to - geth - er,
each oth - er ev - 'ry time. To - geth - er, to - geth - er,
1 F 2 D.S. al Coda F
c' - mon, __ let's have some fun. c' - mon, __ let's do this right.

CODA
F
E♭
3fr
F
cham - pi - ons one and all.
All: We're
G
D/F♯
Em
G/D
all in this to - geth - er; once we know
all in this to - geth - er; when we reach,
C
G/B
C/E
D/F♯
that we are, we're all stars, and we see that. We're
we can fly, know in - side we can make it. We're
G
D/F♯
Em
G/D
all in this to - geth - er; and it shows
all in this to - geth - er; once we see

C
G/B
1
C/E
D/F♯
when we stand hand in hand, make our dreams come... We're
there's a chance that we have
2
C/E
D/F♯
F
and we take it. Wild cats ev - 'ry - where,
wave your hands up in the air. That's the way we do it; let's get
G
to it, c' - mon ev - 'ry - one!

You Are the Music in Me

From Walt Disney's *High School Musical 2*

Words and Music by
JAMIE HOUSTON

Moderately fast Rock

F(add2) C Bb F C

mf

Kelsi: You know, the words, "once up - on a time" make you lis - ten. There's a rea - son.
we met. Can't ex - plain, there's no name for it.

Kelsi & Gabriella: When you dream, there's a chance you'll find a lit - tle laugh -
T/G: I sang you words I've nev - er said, *Troy:* and it was eas -

© 2007 Walt Disney Music Company
All Rights Reserved Used by Permission

B♭
F
C/E
Gabriella & Troy:
- ter or "hap - py ev - er af - ter." You're a
- y, be - cause you see the real me.
Dm
C/E
har - mo - ny to the mel - o - dy that's
As I Both: am you un - der - stand, and
F
C/E
ech - o - ing in - side my head. A Gabriella: sin -
that's more than I've ev - er known. Gabriella: To
Dm
C/E
- gle voice a - bove the noise, and
hear your voice a - bove the noise, Both: and

B♭
G/T: like a com - mon thread,
Troy: mmm, you're pull - ing me.
know I'm not a - lone.
Gabriella: Oh, you're sing - in' to me.
C
B♭6
Gabriella:
2nd time Both:
When I hear my fav - 'rite song, I know that we
F
B♭(add2)
3fr
be - long.
Troy: Oh, you are the mu - sic in me.
C
B♭6
Yeah, it's liv - ing in all of us,
Gabriella: and it's brought us here

To Coda
F
B♭(add2)
3fr
C
because
Troy & Gabriella: you are the music in me.
All: Na, na, na, na,
B♭6
F
B♭
na, na, na, na, na,
na, na, na, na.
T/G: You are the music in me.
F(add2)
D.S. al Coda
Gabriella: It's like I knew you before
B♭(add2)
CODA
3fr
T/G: you are the music in me.
Dm7
C/E
(Me.)
Together we're gonna sing.
(Sing.)

B♭maj9
5fr
Troy:
We got the pow - er to say what we feel, con - nect - ed and real,
Gabriella: can't keep it all in - side.
C
B♭6
F
All: (Na, na, na, na.) (Na, na, na, na, na.) (Na, na, na, na. You are the mu - sic in me.)
B♭
C
B♭6
All: When I hear my fav - 'rite song, I know that we
(Lead vocals ad lib. to end)

F
B♭(add2)
3fr
C
be - long.
You are the mu - sic in me.
It's liv - in' in all
B♭/D
F
of us, and it's brought us here be - cause you
B♭(add2)
3fr
C
B♭
are the mu - sic in me.
Na, na, na, na.
Na, na, na, na, na.
F
B♭
C/B♭
Na, na, na, na.
You are the mu - sic in me.

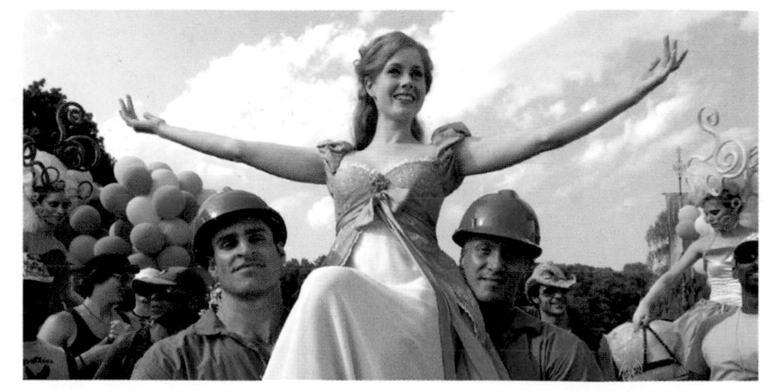

True Love's Kiss

From Walt Disney's *Enchanted*

Music by ALAN MENKEN
Lyrics by STEPHEN SCHWARTZ

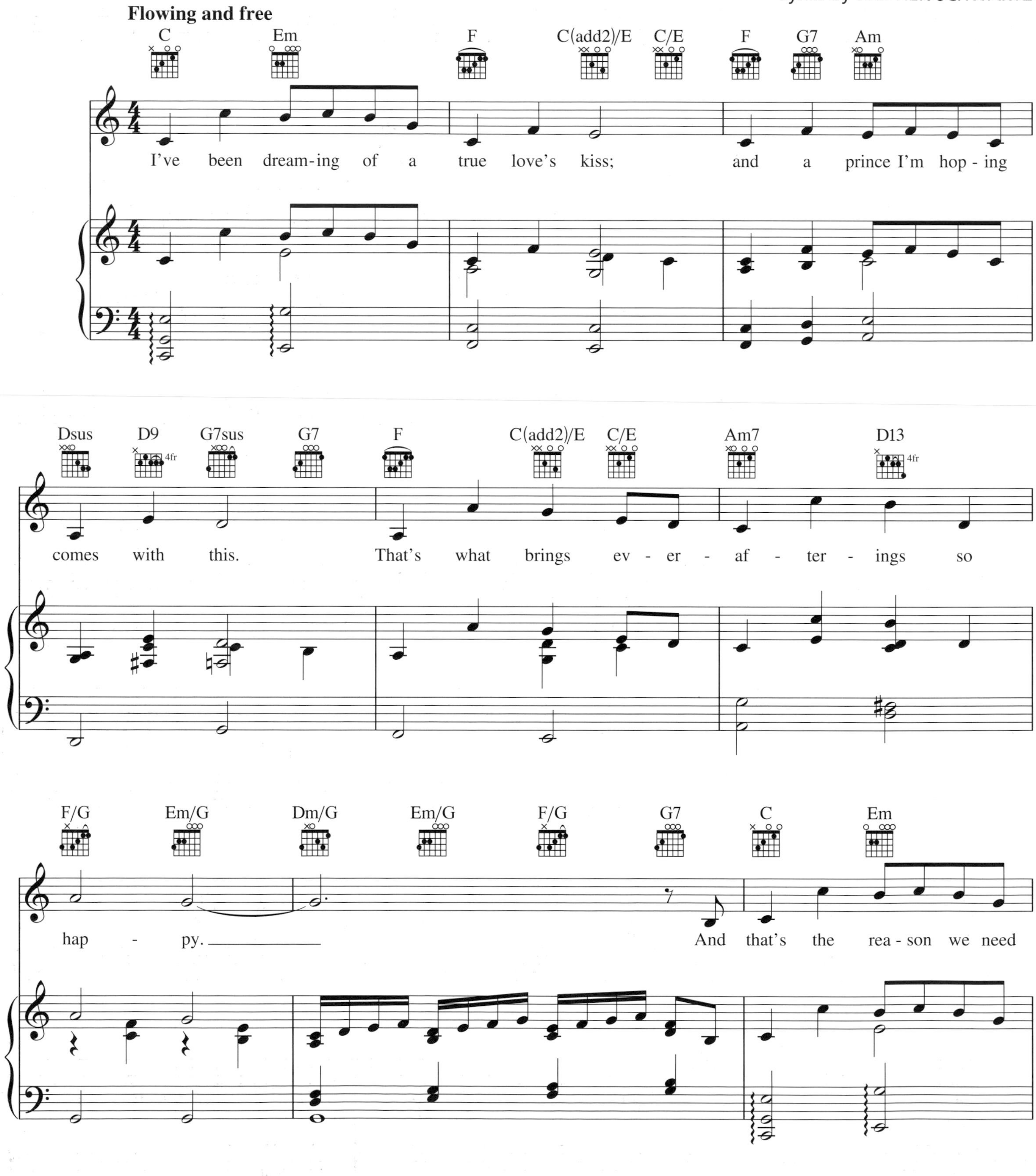

Flowing and free
C Em F C(add2)/E C/E F G7 Am
I've been dream-ing of a true love's kiss; and a prince I'm hop-ing
Dsus D9 G7sus G7 F C(add2)/E C/E Am7 D13
4fr
comes with this. That's what brings ev-er-af-ter-ings so
F/G Em/G Dm/G Em/G F/G G7 C Em
hap-py. And that's the rea-son we need

© 2007 Wonderland Music Company, Inc. and Walt Disney Music Company
All Rights Reserved Used by Permission

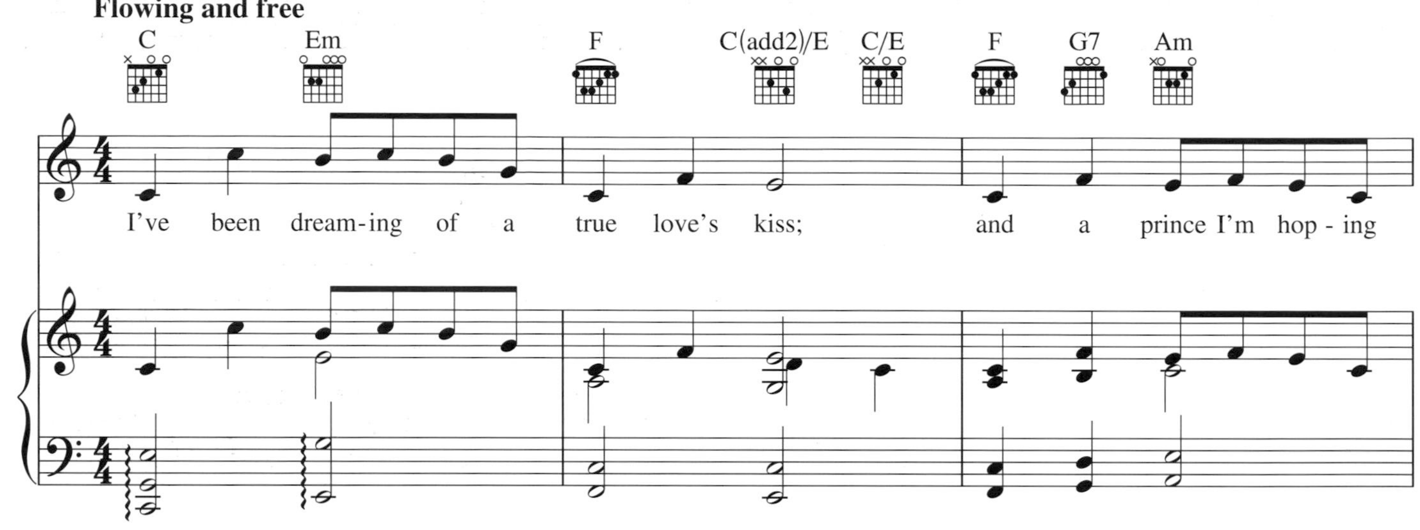

F
C(add2)/E
C/E
F
G7
Am
Dm
E7sus
E7
lips so much, for lips are the on - ly things that touch.
Am
Am/G
F♯m7♭5
Fm6
C/E
So, to spend a life of end - less bliss,
A9
Dm7
Fmaj7/G
G7♭9
just find who you love through true love's
rit.
C
C/E
F
C(add2)/E
C/E
F
G7
Am
kiss.
a tempo

G7
F
C
ma - a - ake the scene to - geth - er.
shar - in' all we got to - geth - er.
1
2
G7
Oh!
G7
F
Oh, I real - ly
think you're swell uh huh,
C
we real - ly ring the bell. Ooh -
D7
ee, and if you stick with me,
G7 Dm7 G7 Dm7
Noth - in' could be great - er. Say,

G7
C
hey, al - li - ga - tor! Let's get to - geth - er. Yea, yea yea! _ Two is twice as nice as
C7
F
C
one. _ Let's get to - geth - er. Right a - way. _ We'll be hav - in' twice the
G7
F
fun, _ and you can al - ways count on me, a groov - y
G7
F
C
two - some we will be. Let's get to - geth - er. _ Yea, yea yea! _

Seize The Day

From Walt Disney's *Newsies*

Music by ALAN MENKEN
Lyrics by JACK FELDMAN

Hymn-like

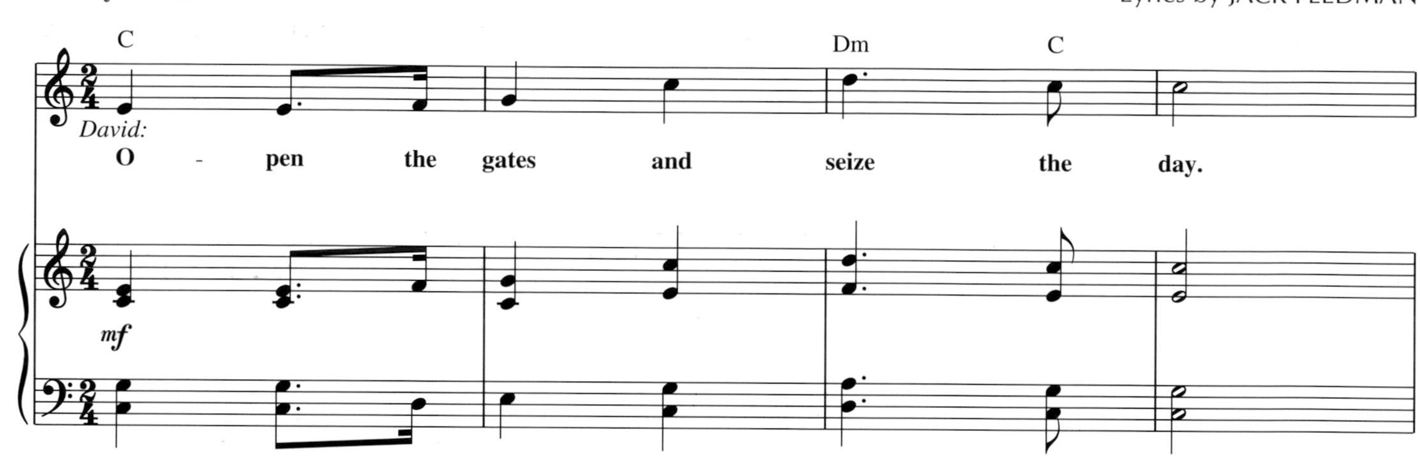

© 1992 Wonderland Music Company, Inc.
All Rights Reserved Used by Permission

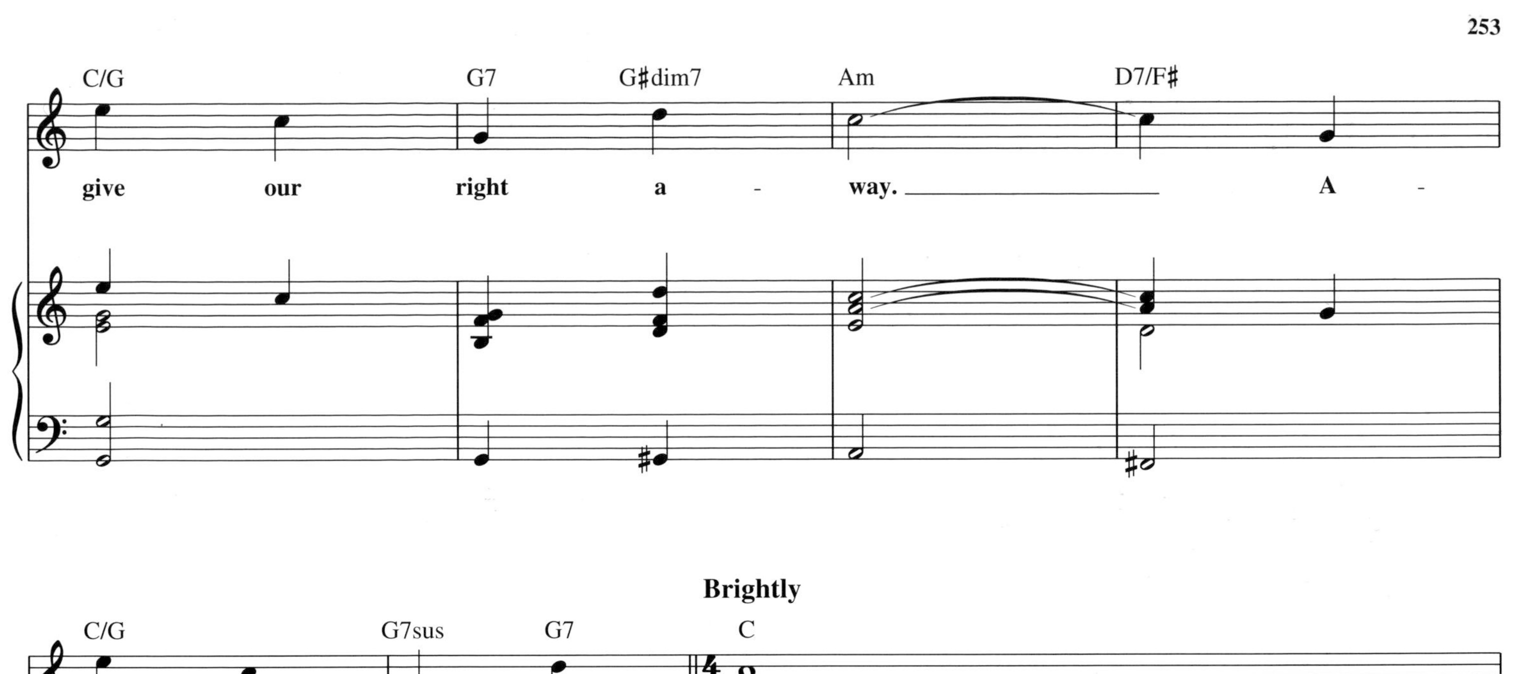
C/G
G7
G#dim7
Am
D7/F#
give our right a - way. A -

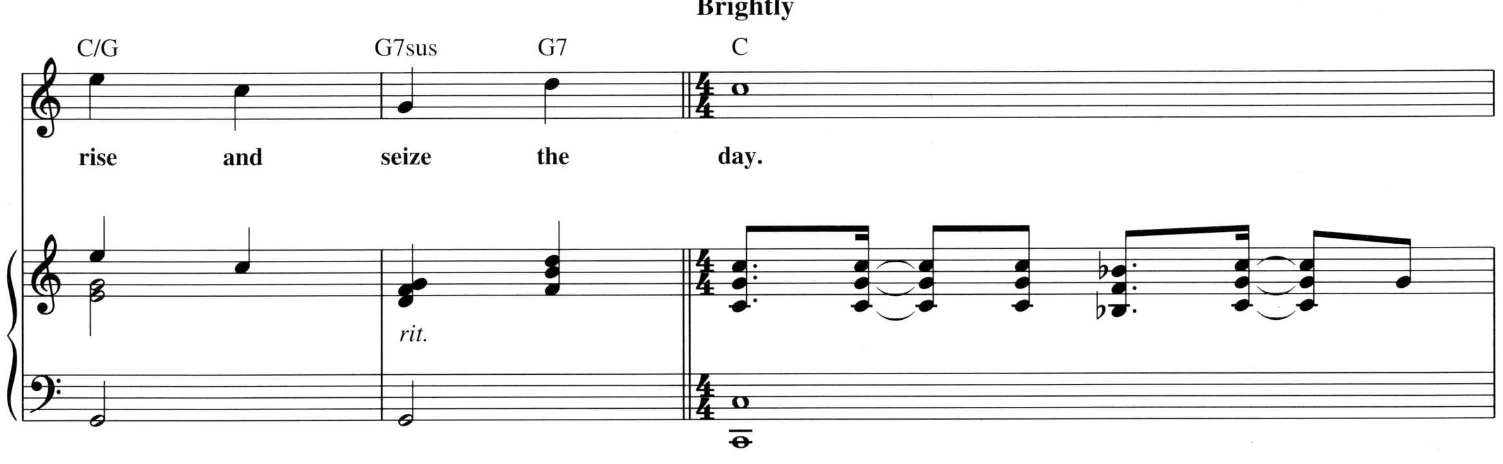
Brightly
C/G
G7sus
G7
C
rise and seize the day.
rit.

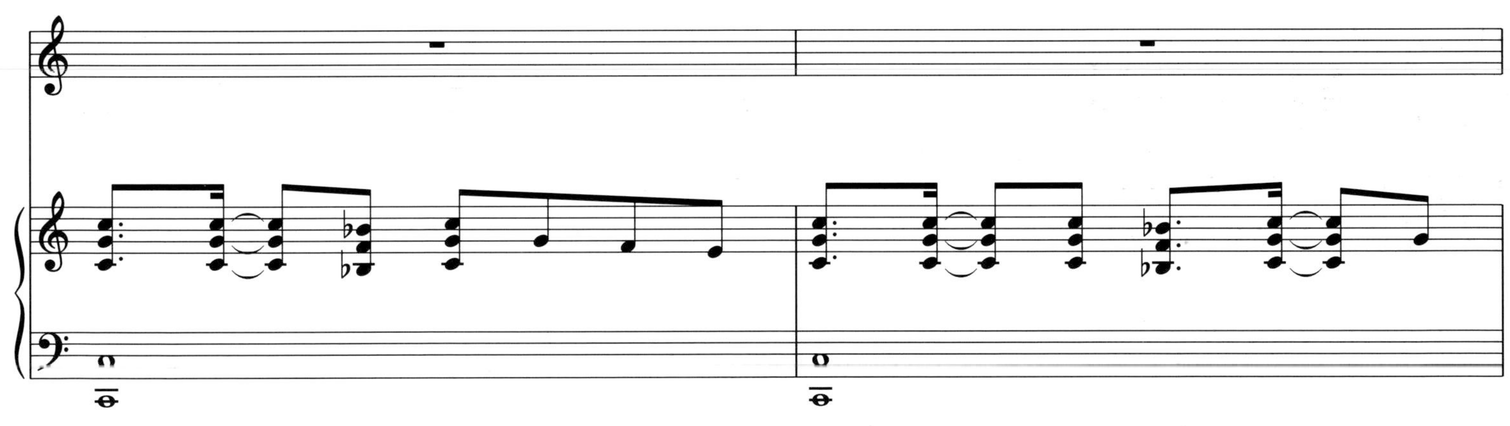

David: Now is the time to seize the day.

B♭
F
Newsies:
(Now is the time to seize the day.)
David:
Send out the call and join the fray.

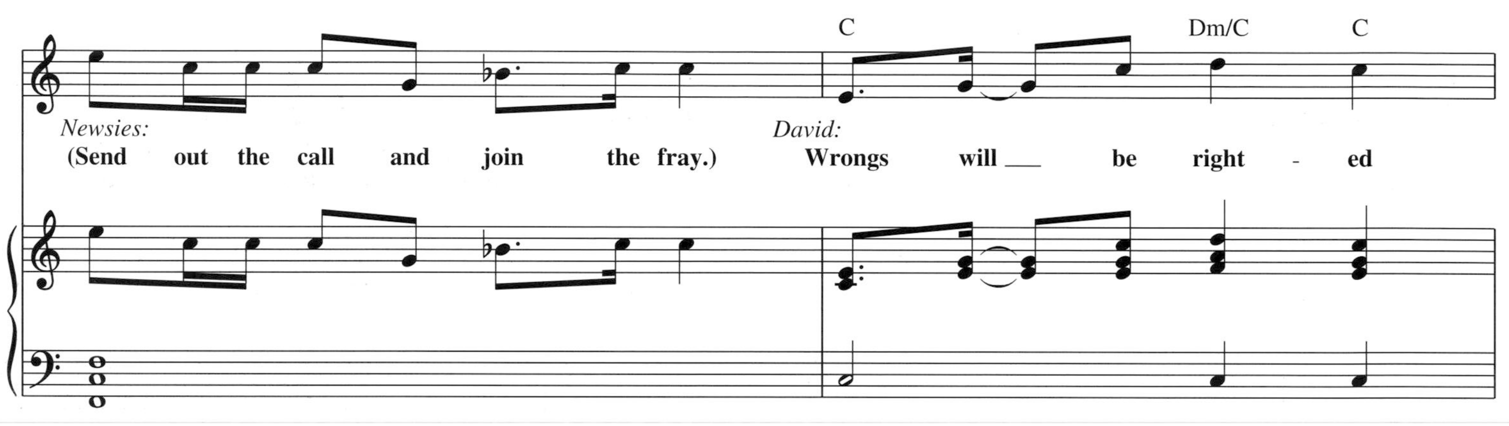
C
Dm/C
C
Newsies:
(Send out the call and join the fray.)
David:
Wrongs will __ be right - ed

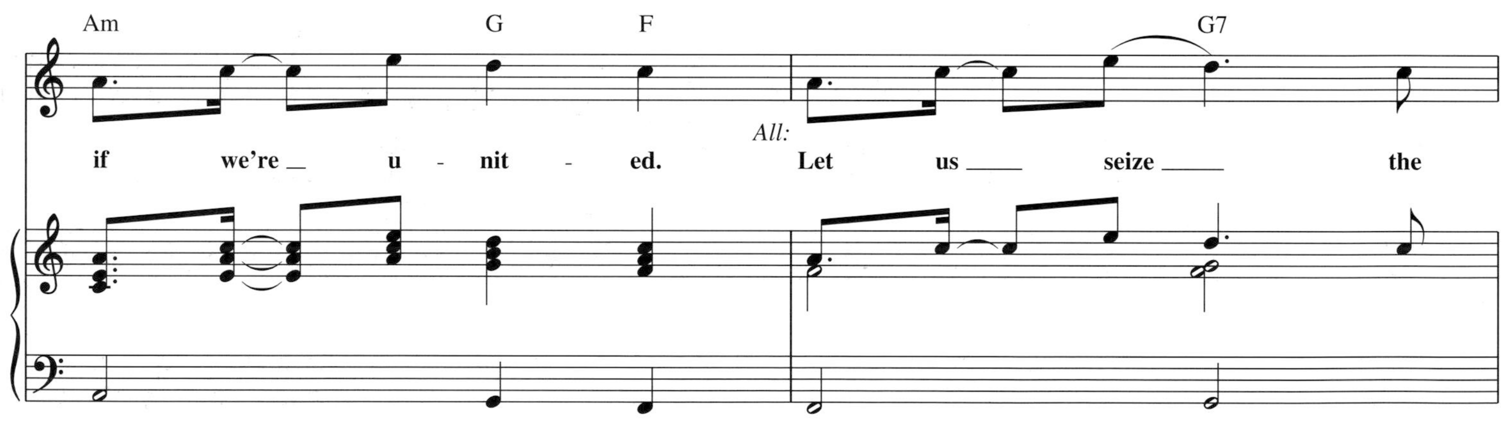
Am
G
F
G7
if we're __ u - nit - ed.
All:
Let us ____ seize ____ the

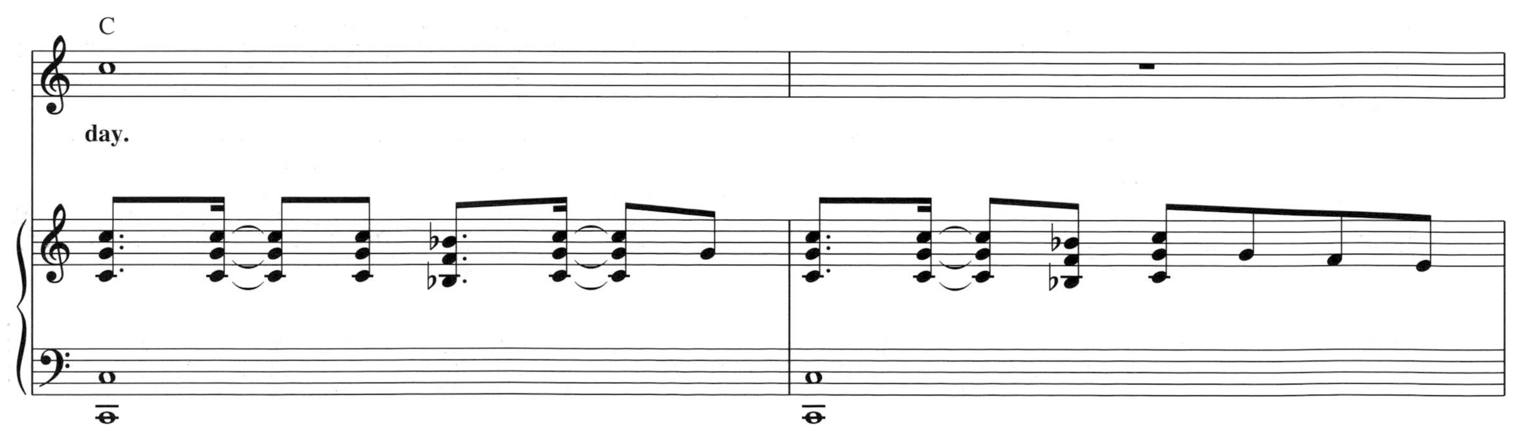
C
day.

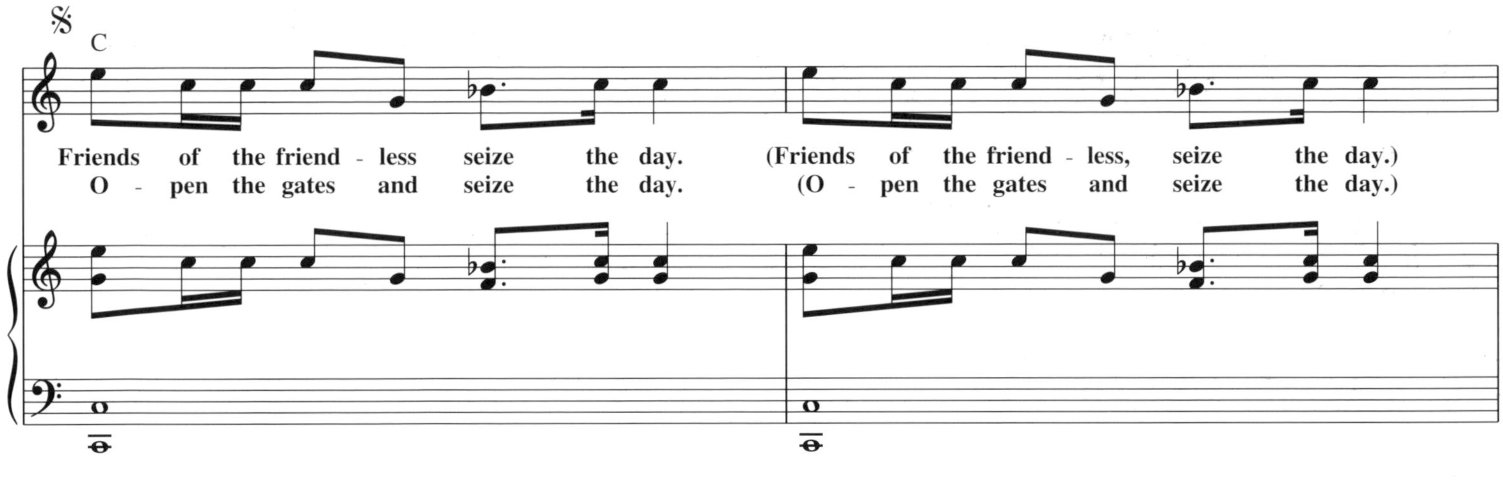
C
Friends of the friend - less seize the day. (Friends of the friend - less, seize the day.)
O - pen the gates and seize the day. (O - pen the gates and seize the day.)

B♭
F
Raise up the torch and light the way. (Raise up the torch and light the way.)
Don't be a - fraid and don't de - lay. (Don't be a - fraid and don't de - lay.)

C
Dm/C
C
Am
G
F
Proud and de - fi - ant we'll slay the gi - ant.
Noth - ing can break us. No one can make us

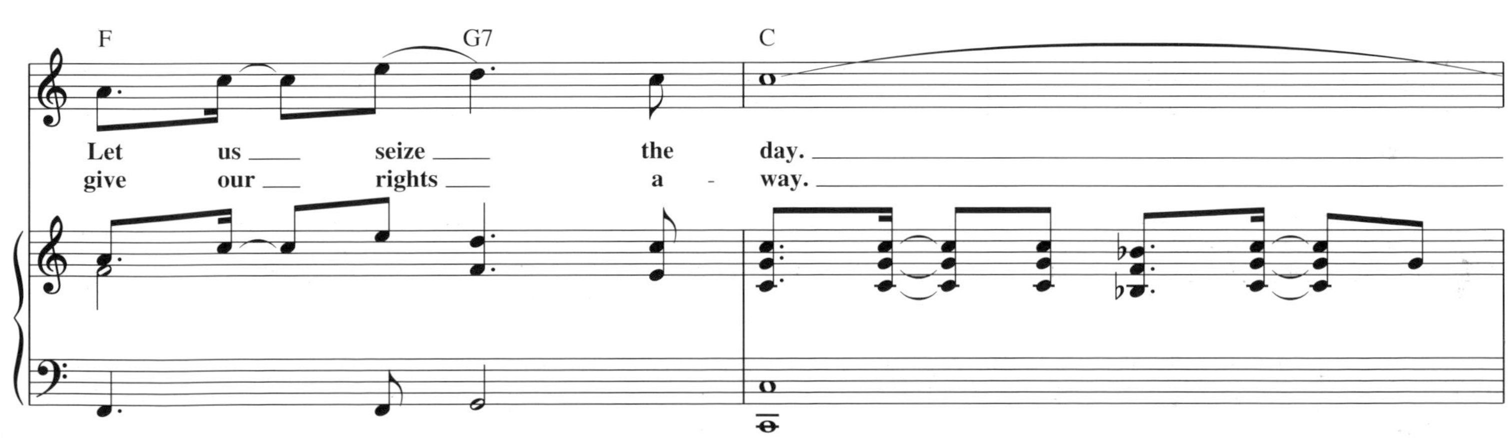
F
G7
C
Let us seize the day.
give our rights a - way.

Am
C7/G
F
G
Neigh - bor to neigh - bor,
fa - ther to
Asus
A/C♯
Dm
C/E
son,
one for
To Coda
F
G
C
all and all for one.
D.S. al Coda
CODA
C
one.

The Ballad Of Davy Crockett

From Walt Disney's *Davy Crockett*

Words by TOM BLACKBURN
Music by GEORGE BRUNS

Moderately

F Bb F C7 F

1. Born on a moun-tain top in Ten - nes - see, green - est state in the
2. eigh - teen - thir - teen the Creeks up - rose, addin' redskin arrows to the
3. Off through the woods _ he's a marchin' a - long, makin' up yarns an' a -
4. - 17. *(See additional lyrics)*

mf

G7 C7 F Bb Gm C7

land of the free, raised in the woods so's he knew ev - 'ry tree, kilt him a b'ar when
coun - try's_ woes. Now, In - jun fightin' is some - thin' he knows, so he should-ers his rifle an'
sing - in' a song, itch - in' fer fightin' an' right - in' a wrong, he's ringy as a b'ar an'

F Bb F C7

he was on - ly three. Da - vy, Da - vy Crock-ett, king of the wild fron -
off he_ goes. Da - vy, Da - vy Crock-ett, the man who_ don't know
twict as_ strong. Da - vy, Da - vy Crock-ett, the buck - skin_ buc - ca -

© 1954 Wonderland Music Company, Inc.
Copyright Renewed
All Rights Reserved Used by Permission

1-16
17
F
F
F C7 F
B♭ F
tier! 2. In fear! 18. When he come home his pol - i - tick - in' done, the
fear! heard of Houston an' Au - stin an' so,
neer! land is biggest an' his land is best, from
C7 F G7 C7 F B♭ Gm
west - ern march had just be - gun. So he packed his gear an' his trust - y gun, an'
to the Texas plains he jest had to go. Where free - dom was fight - in' an - oth - er foe, an'
gras - sy plains to the moun - tain crest. He's a - head of us all meetin' the test,
C7 F B♭ F
lit out grin - nin' to fol - low the sun. Da - vy, Da - vy Crock - ett,
they needed him at the A - la - mo. Da - vy, Da - vy Crock - ett, the
follow - in' his leg - end in - to the West. Da - vy, Da - vy Crock - ett,
C7
1,2
F
3
F
lead - in' the pi - o - neer! 19. He
man who don't know fear! 20. His
king of the wild fron - tier!

Additional Lyrics

4. Andy Jackson is our gen'ral's name,
his reg'lar soldiers we'll put to shame.
Them redskin varmints us Volunteers'll tame,
'cause we got the guns with the sure-fire aim.
Davy—Davy Crockett, the champion of us all!

5. Headed back to war from the ol' home place,
but Red Stick was leadin' a merry chase,
fightin' an' burnin' at a devil's pace
south to the swamps on the Florida Trace.
Davy—Davy Crockett, trackin' the redskins down!

6. Fought single-handed through the Injun War
till the Creeks was whipped an' peace was in store.
An' while he was handlin' this risky chore,
made hisself a legend for evermore.
Davy—Davy Crockett, king of the wild frontier!

7. He give his word an' he give his hand
that his Injun friends could keep their land.
An' the rest of his life he took the stand
that justice was due every redskin band.
Davy—Davy Crockett, holdin' his promise dear!

8. Home fer the winter with his family,
happy as squirrels in the ol' gum tree,
bein' the father he wanted to be,
close to his boys as the pod an' the pea.
Davy—Davy Crockett, holdin' his young 'uns dear!

9. But the ice went out an' the warm winds came
an' the meltin' snow showed tracks of game.
An' the flowers of Spring filled the woods with flame,
an' all of a sudden life got too tame.
Davy—Davy Crockett, headin' on West again!

10. Off through the woods we're ridin' along,
makin' up yarns an' singin' a song.
He's ringy as a b'ar an' twict as strong,
an' knows he's right 'cause he ain' often wrong.
Davy—Davy Crockett, the man who don't know fear!

11. Lookin' fer a place where the air smells clean,
where the trees is tall an' the grass is green,
where the fish is fat in an untouched stream,
an' the teemin' woods is a hunter's dream.
Davy—Davy Crockett, lookin' fer Paradise!

12. Now he's lost his love an' his grief was gall,
in his heart he wanted to leave it all,
an' lose himself in the forests tall,
but he answered instead his country's call.
Davy—Davy Crockett, beginnin' his campaign!

13. Needin' his help they didn't vote blind.
They put in Davy 'cause he was their kind,
sent up to Nashville the best they could find,
a fightin' spirit an' a thinkin' mind.
Davy—Davy Crockett, choice of the whole frontier!

14. The votes were counted an' he won hands down,
so they sent him off to Washin'ton town
with his best dress suit still his buckskins brown,
a livin' legend of growin' renown.
Davy—Davy Crockett, the Canebrake Congressman!

15. He went off to Congress an' served a spell,
fixin' up the Gover'ments an' laws as well,
took over Washin'ton so we heered tell
an' patched up the crack in the Liberty Bell.
Davy—Davy Crockett, seein' his duty clear!

16. Him an' his jokes travelled all through the land,
an' his speeches made him friends to beat the band.
His politickin' was their favorite brand
an' everyone wanted to shake his hand.
Davy—Davy Crockett, helpin' his legend grow!

17. He knew when he spoke he sounded the knell
of his hopes for White House an' fame as well.
But he spoke out strong so hist'ry books tell
an' patched up the crack in the Liberty Bell.
Davy—Davy Crockett, seein' his duty clear!

Mickey Mouse March

From Walt Disney's *The Mickey Mouse Club*

Words and Music by
JIMMIE DODD

Brightly

F Bb C7 F Bb C7

Mick - ey Mouse Club! Mick - ey Mouse Club!

F G7 C7

Who's the lead - er of the club that's made for you and me!
Hey, there! Hi, there! Ho, there! You're as wel - come as can be!

F F7/Eb Bb/D Bbm/Db F/C C7 | 1 F

M - I - C - K - E - Y M - O - U - S - E!

© 1955 Walt Disney Music Company
Copyright Renewed
All Rights Reserved Used by Permission

2
F
B♭ (Shout) Mick - ey Mouse!
F Don - ald
E! Mick - ey Mouse! Mick - ey Mouse.
Duck!
G
G7
C7 (Shout) High!
For - ev - er let us hold our ban - ner high!
cresc.
High! High!
F
G7
Come a - long and sing a song and join the jam - bor -
8va
f
mf
C7
F F7 B♭ B♭m F C7 F
ee! M - I - C - K - E - Y M - O - U - S - E!
8va
rit.

Rock Star

From Walt Disney's *Hannah Montana*

Words and Music by JEANNIE LURIE, ARIS ARCHONTIS and CHEN NEEMAN

Moderately fast

D5
D/F♯
5fr
Some - times I walk a lit - tle fast - er in
Some - times I wish when the phone rings that
f

G5
A5
3fr
5fr
the school hall - way just to get next to you.
it would be you say - in', "Let's hang out,"

D5
D/F♯
5fr
Some days I spend a lit - tle ex - tra time
then you con - fess that there's some - thing spe -

© 2007 Walt Disney Music Company and Wonderland Music Company, Inc.
All Rights Reserved Used by Permission

G5
3fr
A5
5fr
in the morn - ing, dress to im - press you.
- cial be - tween us. Why don't we find out?
Bm
F♯7/A♯
4fr
Guess you don't no - tice, guess you don't need this, sad
You don't e - ven know me. Guess you don't need me. Why
Bm/A
E/G♯
you're not see - in' what you're miss - in'.
you not see - in' what you're miss - in'?
On the
D/G
A5
5fr
out - side, shy - in' a - way;
on the in - side, dy - in' to say...

D5 A5 C5 G5
5fr 5fr 3fr 3fr
I'm un - u - su - al, not so typ - i - cal, way
D5 A5 C5 G5 D5 A5
too smart to be wait - ing a - round. Tai Chi prac - tic - in', snow -
C5 G5 G5
1
A5
N.C.
- board cham - pi - on, I could fix a flat on your car. I might e - ven be a
D5 A5 B5 G5 D5 A5
rock star. I might e - ven be a rock star.

2
B5
G5
3fr
A5
5fr
Bm
I might e - ven be a rock star.
G
A
If you on - ly knew the real me... I might e - ven be a
Bm
G
E
rock star. I'm tell - ing you that we are meant to be,
Gmaj9
that would - n't it be nice if you could see

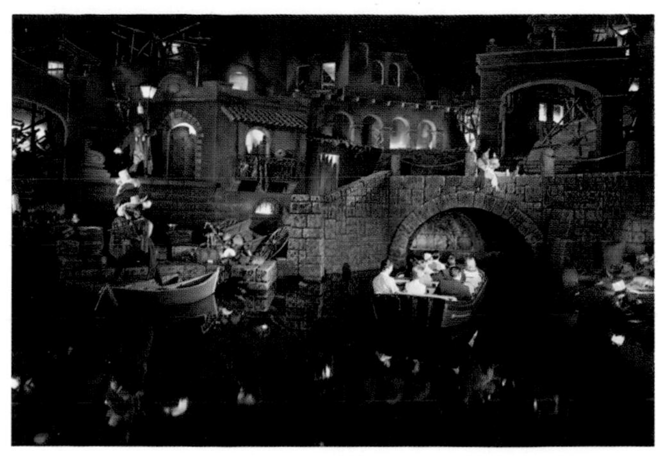

Yo Ho
(A Pirate's Life for Me)
From *Pirates of the Caribbean* at Disneyland Park and Magic Kingdom Park

Words by XAVIER ATENCIO
Music by GEORGE BRUNS

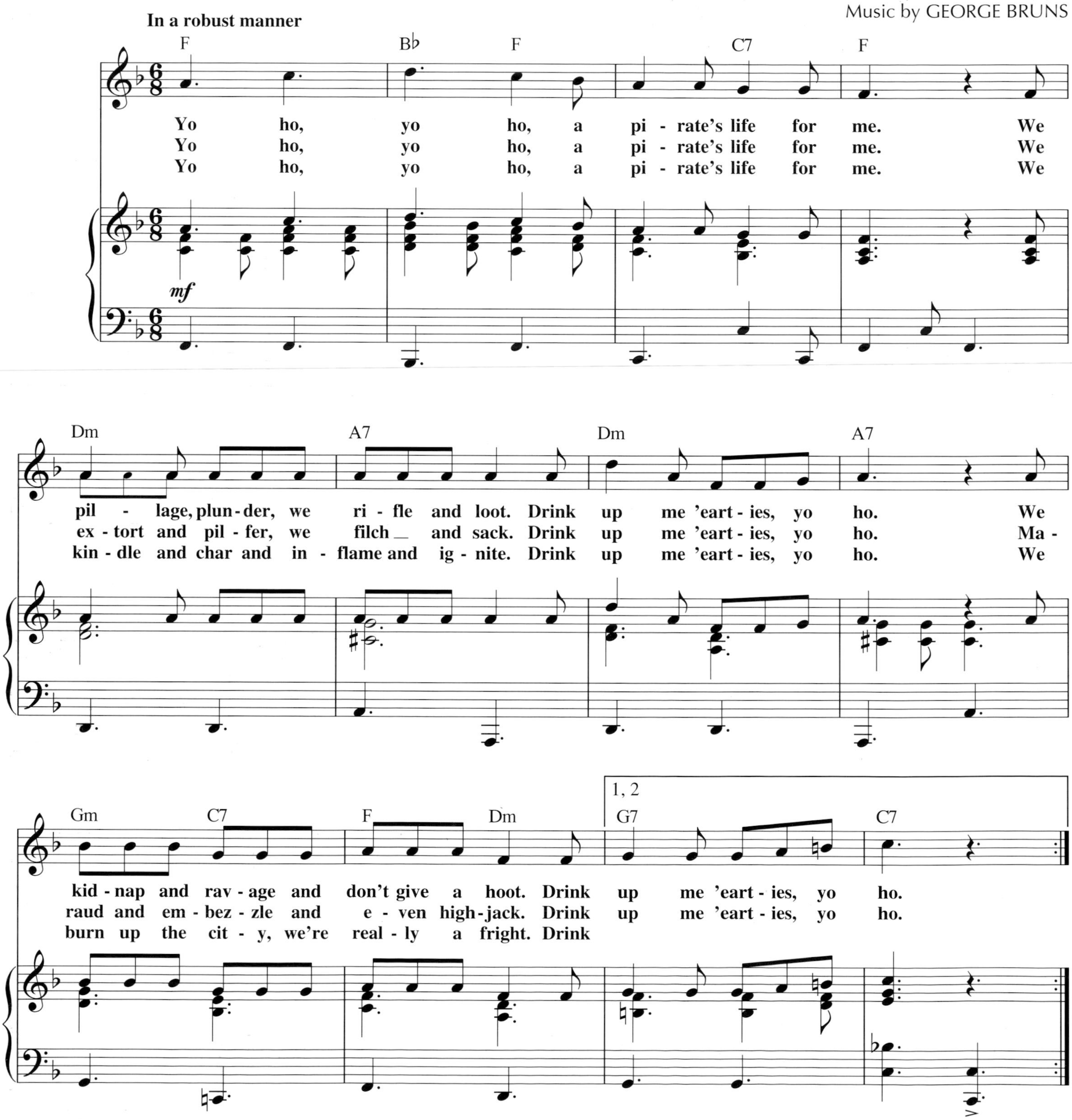

In a robust manner
F Bb F C7 F
Yo ho, yo ho, a pi - rate's life for me. We
Yo ho, yo ho, a pi - rate's life for me. We
Yo ho, yo ho, a pi - rate's life for me. We
mf
Dm A7 Dm A7
pil - lage, plun - der, we ri - fle and loot. Drink up me 'eart - ies, yo ho. We
ex - tort and pil - fer, we filch and sack. Drink up me 'eart - ies, yo ho. Ma -
kin - dle and char and in - flame and ig - nite. Drink up me 'eart - ies, yo ho. We
Gm C7 F Dm
1, 2
G7 C7
kid - nap and rav - age and don't give a hoot. Drink up me 'eart - ies, yo ho.
raud and em - bez - zle and e - ven high - jack. Drink up me 'eart - ies, yo ho.
burn up the cit - y, we're real - ly a fright. Drink

© 1967 Walt Disney Music Company
Copyright Renewed
All Rights Reserved Used by Permission

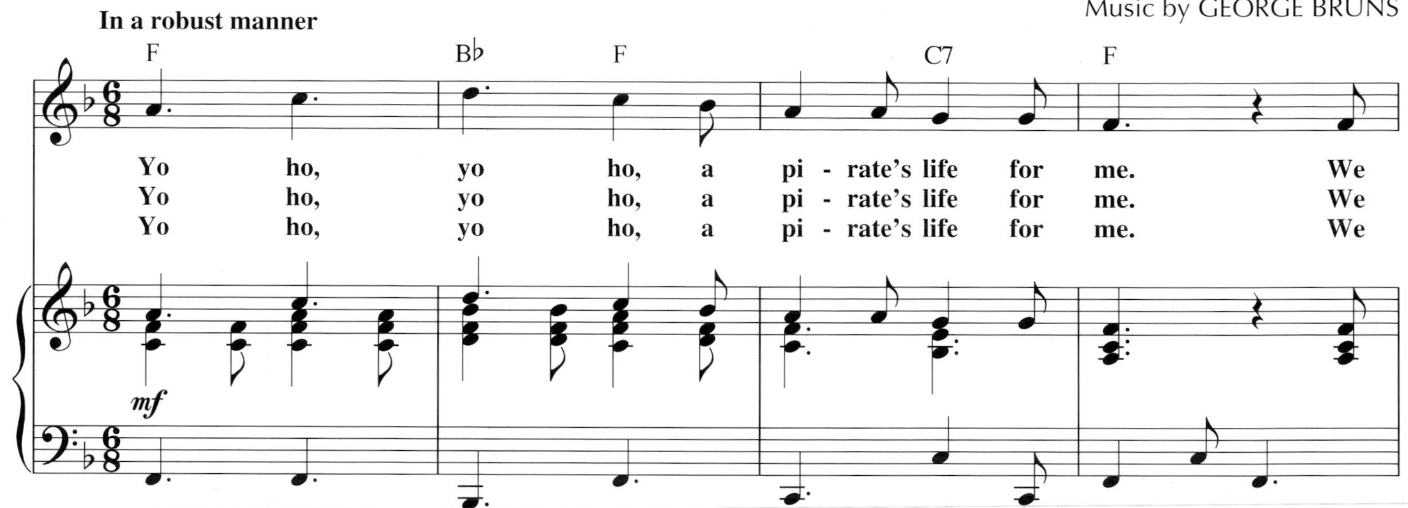

3
G7 C7 A7 Dm
up me 'eart - ies, yo ho. We're ras - cals and scoun - drels, we're
beg - gars and blight - ers and
A7 Dm A7 Gm C7
vil - lains and knaves. Drink up me 'eart - ies, yo ho. We're dev - ils and black sheep, we're
ne'er - do - well cads. Drink up me 'eart - ies, yo ho. Aye, but we're loved by our
F Dm G7 C7 F
real - ly bad eggs. Drink up me 'eart - ies, yo ho. Yo ho,
mom - mies 'n' dads. Drink up me 'eart - ies, yo ho. Yo ho,
B♭ F C7 1 F 2 F
yo ho, a pi - rate's life for me. We're
yo ho, a pi - rate's life for me.
sfz

SONG INDEX

WILEY

IFRS Policies and Procedures

BECOME A SUBSCRIBER!

Did you purchase this product from a bookstore?

If you did, it's important for you to become a subscriber. John Wiley & Sons, Inc. may publish, on a periodic basis, supplements and new editions to reflect the latest changes in the subject matter that you ***need to know*** in order to stay competitive in this ever-changing industry. By contacting the Wiley office nearest you, you'll receive any current update at no additional charge. In addition, you'll receive future updates and revised or related volumes on a 30-day examination review.

If you purchased this product directly from John Wiley & Sons, Inc., we have already recorded your subscription for this update service.

To become a subscriber, please call **1-877-762-2974** or send your name, company name (if applicable), address, and the title of the product to:

mailing address: **Supplement Department**
John Wiley & Sons, Inc.
One Wiley Drive
Somerset, NJ 08875

e-mail: **subscriber@wiley.com**
fax: **1-732-302-2300**
online: **www.wiley.com**

For customers outside the United States, please contact the Wiley office nearest you:

Professional & Reference Division
John Wiley & Sons Canada, Ltd.
22 Worcester Road
Etobicoke, Ontario M9W 1L1
CANADA
Phone: 416-236-4433
Phone: 1-800-567-4797
Fax: 416-236-4447
Email: canada@jwiley.com

John Wiley & Sons, Ltd.
The Atrium
Southern Gate, Chichester
West Sussex, PO19 8SQ
ENGLAND
Phone: 44-1243-779777
Fax: 44-1243-775878
Email: customer@wiley.co.uk

John Wiley & Sons Australia, Ltd.
33 Park Road
P.O. Box 1226
Milton, Queensland 4064
AUSTRALIA
Phone: 61-7-3859-9755
Fax: 61-7-3859-9715
Email: brisbane@johnwiley.com.au

John Wiley & Sons (Asia) Pte. Ltd.
2 Clementi Loop #02-01
SINGAPORE 129809
Phone: 65-64632400
Fax: 65-64634604/5/6
Customer Service: 65-64604280
Email: enquiry@wiley.com.sg

WILEY

IFRS Policies and Procedures

Barry J. Epstein
Eva K. Jermakowicz

WILEY
JOHN WILEY & SONS, INC.

Coventry University Library

This book is printed on acid-free paper. ♾

Copyright © 2008 by John Wiley & Sons, Inc. All rights reserved.
Published by John Wiley & Sons, Inc., Hoboken, New Jersey
Published simultaneously in Canada

No part of this publication may be reproduced, stored in a retrieval system or transmitted in any form or by any means, electronic, mechanical, photocopying, recording, scanning or otherwise, except as permitted under Section 107 or 108 of the 1976 United States Copyright Act, without either the prior written permission of the Publisher, or authorization through payment of the appropriate per-copy fee to the Copyright Clearance Center, 222 Rosewood Drive, Danvers, MA 01923, 978-750-8400, fax 978-646-8600, or on the Web at www.copyright.com. Requests to the Publisher for permission should be addressed to the Permissions Department, John Wiley & Sons, Inc., 111 River Street, Hoboken, NJ 07030, 201-748-6011, fax: 201-748-6008, or online at http://www.wiley.com/go/permissions.

Limit of Liability/Disclaimer of Warranty: While the publisher and author have used their best efforts in preparing this book, they make no representations or warranties with respect to the accuracy or completeness of the contents of this book and specifically disclaim any implied warranties of merchantability or fitness for a particular purpose. No warranty may be created or extended by sales representatives or written sales materials. The advice and strategies contained herein may not be suitable for your situation. You should consult with a professional where appropriate. Neither the publisher nor author shall be liable for any loss of profit or any other commercial damages, including but not limited to special, incidental, consequential, or other damages.

For general information on our other products and services, please contact our Customer Care Department within the United States at 800-762-2974, outside the United States at 317-572-3993 or fax 317-572-4002.

Wiley also publishes its books in a variety of electronic formats. Some content that appears in print may not be available in electronic books.

For more information about Wiley products, visit our Web site at www.wiley.com.

Library of Congress Cataloging-in-Publication Data

Epstein, Barry Jay, 1946 –

Wiley IFRS : policies and procedures / Barry J. Epstein, Eva K. Jermakowicz.

p. cm.

Intended as a companion volume to Wiley IFRS 2005 : interpretation and application of international accounting and financial reporting standards / Barry J. Epstein, Abbas Ali Mirza. c2005. It provides advice on controls, policies and procedures, forms, reports, and archiving requirements not included in the previous volume.

Includes index.

ISBN 978-0-471-69958-3 (pbk.)

1. Accounting – Standards. 2. International business enterprises – Accounting. I. Jermakowicz, Eva K. II. Epstein, Barry Jay, 1946 – Wiley IFRS 2005. III. Title. IV. Title: Wiley International accounting and financial reporting standards: policies and procedures.

HF5626.E673 2005

657.02'18—dc22 2007039471

Printed in the United States of America

10 9 8 7 6 5 4 3 2 1

CONTENTS

PREFACE

International Financial Reporting Standards (IFRS), while in wide use around the world for many years, are receiving vastly more attention currently for several reasons. First, IFRS acceptance has reached "critical mass" with endorsement for use by European Union–based publicly held companies and announced intentions by standard-setting authorities of major nations (including Canada, China, and Russia) to adopt IFRS as national generally accepted accounting principles (GAAP) over the next few years. Australia and several other countries adopted national equivalents to IFRS and other jurisdictions use IFRS as a benchmark for their own accounting standards or permit the use of IFRS. Thus, there will be a substantially increasing number of reporting entities, as well as entities doing business as vendors to or customers of companies domiciled in IFRS-reporting nations, which will need to be at least conversant with IFRS. Second, the securities regulator in the United States, the Securities and Exchange Commission, recently has adopted a new rule permitting foreign private issuers of securities to register in the United States without the need to present financial statements in compliance with US GAAP or the need to reconcile to US GAAP, *if* those financial statements are prepared in accordance with IFRS. This likely will increase the number of foreign companies registered on US stock exchanges, increasing exposure of US companies to IFRS financial reporting. Third, the SEC currently is contemplating granting US registrants the same right, that is, to elect to report under IFRS without any reconciliation to US GAAP.

While IFRS represents a comprehensive set of financial reporting standards, the body of guidance is vastly smaller than under US GAAP for several reasons. The standard setter—the International Accounting Standards Board—is philosophically committed to "principles-based" standards, which implies less detailed guidance than is found under, for example, US GAAP. The authors of this book have provided that guidance to IFRS users in their book, *Wiley IFRS: Interpretation and Application of International Financial Reporting Standards* (2008). However, that book does not provide advice on how to *implement* IFRS—that is, it does not purport to address controls, policies and procedures, forms, reports, or archiving requirements that should be put into place by the reporting entity. This book fills that void.

Each chapter of this book briefly summarizes relevant IFRS, but the primary intent of this book is to add new categories of information designed to assist accountants in properly applying IFRS. Some of these major sections are found in each chapter:

Definitions of Terms. Contains the terms most commonly used in the *Concepts and Examples* section that follows.

Concepts and Examples. A summary of the requirements under the relevant standards, which has been derived from the far more extensive coverage in the *Wiley IFRS* book.

Decision Trees. Illustrations of the decision factors required to interpret multiple options under IFRS requirements.

Policies. Identifies specific accounting policies the reporting entity can adopt in order to comply with IFRS, particularly relating to creation of controls that mesh with IFRS reporting needs.

Procedures. Lists specific procedures for the most common accounting transactions, adapted to be workable within the IFRS framework. These procedures can be modified readily, as necessary, for inclusion within the entity's accounting procedures manual (or equivalent).

Controls. Itemization of specific accounting controls that further the internal control goals of a well-managed enterprise whose financial statements are to conform to IFRS.

Forms and Reports. Provides templates for forms and reports that can be adapted readily for use in an IFRS-compliant accounting system.

Footnotes. Provides numerous examples of footnotes (informative disclosures) that can be used to describe and expand on IFRS-compliant financial statements.

Journal Entries. Shows hundreds of IFRS-compliant journal entries for most accounting transactions.

Recordkeeping. Notes the types of reports and other information to be retained as part of a comprehensive accounting system.

Chapters are sequenced in the same manner as in *Wiley IFRS* addressing topics such as receivables, inventories, revenue recognition, liabilities, leases, stockholders' equity, and foreign currency translation. *Wiley IFRS Policies and Procedures* is an ideal companion volume for *Wiley IFRS,* providing practical application information needed to ensure that the reporting entity's accounting system and procedures are capable of producing fully IFRS-compliant financial reports.

Barry J. Epstein, Ph.D., CPA
Eva K. Jermakowicz, Ph.D, CPA
Chicago, Illinois
November 2007

ABOUT THE AUTHORS

Barry J. Epstein, PhD, CPA, a partner in the firm Russell Novak & Company, has 40 years' experience in the public accounting profession as auditor, technical director/partner for several national and local firms, and a consulting and testifying accounting and auditing expert on over 100 litigation matters to date. His current practice is concentrated on providing technical consultations to CPA firms and corporations on US GAAP and IFRS accounting and financial reporting matters; on US and international auditing standards; matters involving financial analysis; forensic accounting investigations; and on corporate governance matters. He regularly serves as an accounting, auditing, financial reporting, and financial analysis expert in litigation matters, including assignments for both the private sector entities and governmental agencies.

Dr. Epstein is a widely published authority on accounting and auditing. His current publications include *Wiley GAAP*, now in its 24th edition, for which he is the lead coauthor. He has also appeared on over a dozen national radio and television programs discussing the crises in corporate financial reporting and corporate governance, and has presented hundreds of educational programs to professional and corporate groups in the United States and internationally. He previously chaired the Audit Committee of the AICPA's Board of Examiners, responsible for the Uniform CPA Examination, and has served on other professional panels at state and national levels.

Dr. Epstein holds degrees from DePaul University (Chicago—BSC, accounting and finance, 1967) University of Chicago (MBA, economics and industrial relations, 1969), and University of Pittsburgh (PhD, information systems and finance, 1979). He is a member of the American Institute of Certified Public Accountants, the Illinois CPA Society, and the American Accounting Association.

Eva K. Jermakowicz, PhD., CPA, has taught accounting for 25 years and has served as a consultant to international organizations and businesses. She is currently a Professor of Accounting and Chair of the Accounting and Business Law Department at Tennessee State University. Her previous positions were on the faculties of the University of Southern Indiana and Warsaw Tech University in Poland, and she has taught accounting courses in several additional countries. Dr. Jermakowicz was a Fulbright scholar under the European Union Affairs Research Program in Brussels, Belgium, for the academic year 2003—2004, where her project was "Convergence of National Accounting Standards with International Financial Reporting Standards." She was also a Fulbright scholar in Poland in 1997. Dr. Jermakowicz has consulted on international projects under the auspices of the World Bank, United Nations, and Nicom Consulting, Ltd. Her primary areas of interest are international accounting and finance.

Dr. Jermakowicz has had numerous articles published in academic journals and proceedings, including *Abacus,* the *Journal of International Accounting, Auditing & Taxation, Journal of International Financial Management & Accounting, Multinational Finance Journal, Journal of Accounting and Finance Research, Bank Accounting & Finance, Financial Executive*, and *Strategic Finance*. She is a member of many professional organizations, including the American Accounting Association, the European Accounting Association, the American Institute of Certified Public Accountants, the Tennessee Society of CPAs, and the Institute of Management Accountants.

1 RESEARCHING IFRS IMPLEMENTATION PROBLEMS

OVERVIEW

This book is designed to provide readers with guidance regarding the application of international financial reporting standards that extends beyond that which is immediately obvious from an understanding of the IFRS concepts. Although there are Concepts and Examples sections in each of the chapters that provide summarized versions of the relevant IFRS issues, the primary focus of this book is to provide information about ancillary topics that allow one to implement IFRS, such as accounting policies and procedures, controls, and the construction of financial reporting footnotes. Presently, there are few or no authoritative sources for these IFRS implementation topics. Instead, the sections of this chapter devoted to each implementation topic list some organizations that can provide additional information, as well as key publications that summarize or discuss related topics, including identification of each cited book's author, publisher, and date of publication. But first, we address the IFRS hierarchy of accounting standards and rules, followed by the general approach for researching IFRS-related issues.

The IFRS Hierarchy

International financial reporting standards (IFRS) are standards and rules for reporting financial information, as established and approved by the Financial Accounting Standards Board (IASB). IASB succeeded the International Accounting Standards Committee (IASC), which promulgated International Accounting Standards (IAS), in 2001. The extant IAS have the same status as the more recently issued IFRS and, in this book, all will be referred to as IFRS, for simplicity. Interpretive literature (SIC and IFRIC) issued by bodies of IASB and its predecessor are also considered in the discussions in this book.

The IASB inherited the IASC's *Framework for the Preparation and Presentation of Financial Statements* (the *Framework*). Like the other current conceptual frameworks established by Anglo-Saxon standard setters, this derives from the US GAAP conceptual framework, or at least those parts completed in the 1970s. The

Framework states that "the objective of financial statements is to provide information about the financial position, performance and changes in financial position of an enterprise that is useful to a wide range of users in making economic decisions." The information needs of investors are deemed to be a paramount concern, and if financial statements meet their needs, it is presumed, and likely, that other users' needs would generally also be satisfied.

The *Framework* holds that financial statement users need to evaluate the reporting entity's ability to generate cash as well as the timing and certainty of its generation. The financial position is affected by the economic resources controlled by the entity, its financial structure, its liquidity and solvency, and its capacity to adapt to changes in the environment in which it operates.

The qualitative characteristics of financial statements are *understandability, relevance, reliability,* and *comparability.* Reliability comprises representational *faithfulness, substance over form, completeness, neutrality,* and *prudence.* It suggests that these are subject to a cost/benefit constraint and that, in practice, there will often be a trade-off between characteristics. The *Framework* does not specifically include a "true and fair" requirement, but says that application of the specified qualitative characteristics should result in statements that present fairly or are true and fair. IAS 1, *Presentation of Financial Statements,* states that financial statements are to present fairly the financial position, financial performance, and cash flows of the reporting entity and that the achievement of a fair presentation requires the faithful representation of the effects of the reporting entity's transactions, other events and conditions. IAS 1 most recently has been substantially revised in 2007, for mandatory application by 2009. Among the changes imposed are the elimination of the term "balance sheet" (replaced by statement of financial position), and the adoption of a requirement for presentation of a statement of comprehensive income, largely modeled on the approach long in use under US GAAP.

Of great importance are the definitions of assets and liabilities. According to IASB, "an asset is a resource controlled by the enterprise as a result of past events and from which future economic benefits are expected to flow to the enterprise." A liability is a "present obligation of the enterprise arising from past events, the settlement of which is expected to result in an outflow from the enterprise of resources embodying future benefits." Equity is simply a residual arrived at by deducting the liabilities from assets. Neither asset nor liability is recognized in the financial statements unless they have a cost or value that can be measured reliably—which, as the *Framework* acknowledges, means that some assets and liabilities may remain unrecognized. However, with the ever-expanding use of fair value measurements, and the greatly expanded availability of information from a wide array of sources, including that found via the Internet, there will be a continuing decline in the incidence of "off-balance-sheet" transactions or events, and of those recognized at other-than-current fair values.

The asset and liability definitions have, in the past, not been central to financial reporting standards, many of which were instead guided by a "performance" view of the financial statements. For example, IAS 20 on government grants has been severely criticized, and has been targeted for either revision or elimination, in part because it allows government grants to be treated as a deferred credit and amortized to earnings. Deferred credits do not meet the *Framework* definition of a liability. Similarly, IFRS 3 requires that, where negative goodwill is identified in a business combination, this should be released to the income statement immediately; IAS 22 treated it as a deferred credit, which does not meet the criterion for recognition as a liability.

Both FASB and IASB now intend to analyze solutions to reporting issues in terms of whether they cause any changes in assets or liabilities. The revenue recognition project that both are pursuing is perhaps the ultimate example of this new and rigorous financial position perspective. This project has tentatively embraced the view that where an entity receives an order and has a legally enforceable contract to supply goods or services, the entity has both an asset (the right to receive future revenue) and a liability (the obligation to fulfill the order) and it thus follows that, depending on the measurement of the asset and the liability, some earnings could be recognized at that point. This would be a sharp departure from existing IFRS, under which executory contracts are almost never formally recognized, and never can be the basis for recognition of earnings.

The IASB *Framework,* in its current incarnation, is relatively silent on measurement issues. The three paragraphs that address this matter merely mention that several different measurement bases are available and that historical cost is the most common. Revaluation of tangible fixed assets is, for example, perfectly acceptable under IFRS. In practice, IFRS employs a mixed-attribute model, based mainly in historical cost, but requiring reference to value in use (the present value of expected future cash flows from the use of the asset within the entity) for impairment and the utilization of fair value (market value) for some financial instruments, biological assets, business combinations, and investment properties.

FASB and IASB currently are revisiting their respective conceptual frameworks, the objective of which is to refine and update them and develop them into a common framework that both can use in developing accounting standards. With concurrent IASB and FASB deliberations and a single integrated staff team, this is truly an international project. A joint discussion paper on certain of these matters was issued in mid-2006, stressing the qualitative characteristics of financial statement information. Other aspects of the multiphase conceptual framework project have since been addressed. An Exposure Draft of the first phase is promised for late 2007, with early-stage exposure literature addressing subsequent parts of this project likely to be forthcoming over the next several years.

The existing *Framework* is used by IASB members and staff in their debate, and they expect that those commenting on exposure drafts will articulate their arguments in terms of the *Framework.* However, it is not intended that the *Framework* can be used directly by preparers and auditors in determining all of their accounting methods. In its 2003 revision of IAS 8, IASB introduced a hierarchy of accounting rules that should be followed by preparers in seeking solutions to accounting problems. This hierarchy says that the most authoritative guidance is IFRS, and the preparer should seek guidance in this way:

1. First, by reference to IAS/IFRS and SIC/IFRIC Interpretations, when these specifically apply to a transaction or condition.
2. In the absence of such a directly applicable standard, judgment is to be used to develop and apply an accounting policy that is relevant to the economic decision-making needs of the users, and is reliable in that the financial statements: represent faithfully the financial position, financial performance and cash flows of the reporting entity; reflect the economic substance of transactions, events and conditions, rather than merely the legal forms thereof; are neutral; are prudent; and are complete in all material respects.
3. If this is not possible, the preparer should then look to recent pronouncements of other standard setters that use a similar conceptual framework to develop its standards, as well as other accounting literature and industry practices that do not conflict with higher-level guidance. US GAAP would be the most useful source for such assistance, in the authors' opinion, since it has the largest volume of detailed applications guidance, and since IFRS were heavily influenced, in their development, by US GAAP standards.
4. Only if that also fails should the preparer look to the IASB *Framework* directly, and attempt to draw inferences regarding specific applications that have not been formally addressed in promulgated standards.

In effect, therefore, if IFRS do not cover a subject, the preparer should look to national GAAP, and the most obvious choice is US GAAP, partly because that is the most complete set of standards and partly because, in the global capital market, US GAAP is the alternative best understood (and use of US GAAP removes reconciliation items on the Form 20-F for foreign SEC registrants, although it is now highly likely that the reconciliation requirement will be dropped by the SEC, assuming foreign private issuers adhere to full IFRS as established by IASB). In any event, given the professed intention that IFRS and US GAAP converge, it would make little sense to seek guidance in any other set of standards, unless US GAAP were also silent on the matter needing clarification.

Researching IFRS

The simplest approach to researching IFRS is to review the Concepts and Examples sections in this book. If this does not yield a sufficiently detailed answer, a more comprehensive source of summarized IFRS information is *Wiley IFRS 2008. Wiley IFRS 2008* contains a more comprehensive Concepts section than this book and also begins with a list of authoritative pronouncements as well as the applicable page reference leading to a more complete discussion of the issues within the text. If this approach still does not yield a clear answer to an IFRS problem, readers are invited to review selected IFRS source documents. If these still do not yield a clear answer, it is suggested that readers can inquire of other entities in the same industry how they are handling the issue (if only to identify alternative solutions). If all else fails, use basic accounting theory to resolve the issue, or consult with a technical expert at a public accounting firm.

Researching Accounting Controls

The issue of adequacy of accounting controls is distinct from that of IFRS, but in practice, unless a minimum threshold of control effectiveness has been achieved, there can be no real assurance that IFRS are being applied correctly and consistently.

There is no standard source document itemizing the key control areas related to all types of IFRS. Instead, controls are either described in general terms through the reports issued by various accounting review committees (see discussion of the *COSO Implementation Guide* below) or else entities must infer the correct types of controls to use based on various types of fraud that may occur (several examples are noted below). A good source for controls-related publications is the Institute of Internal Auditors (Web site: www.theiia.org). Several reference books related to this topic are

COSO Implementation Guide

Author: James P. Roth
Publisher: Institute of Internal Auditors
Publication Date: 1995

Financial Crime Investigation and Control

Authors: K.H. Spencer Pickett, Jennifer M. Pickett
Publisher: John Wiley & Sons, Inc.
Publication Date: 2002

Financial Reporting Fraud

Author: Charles Lundelius Jr.
Publisher: AICPA
Publication Date: 2003

Financial Statement Fraud

Author: Zabihollah Rezaee
Publisher: John Wiley & Sons, Inc.
Publication Date: 2002

Fraud 101

Author: Howard Davia
Publisher: John Wiley & Sons, Inc.
Publication Date: 2000

Internal Control Integrated Frameworks

Authors: Coopers & Lybrand
Publisher: AICPA
Publication Date: 1994

Process Development Life Cycle

Author: Albert Marcella Jr.
Publisher: Institute of Internal Auditors
Publication Date: 2001

Researching Accounting Forms and Reports

There is no single book or periodical containing a comprehensive set of forms or reports linked to IFRS. Suggestions for useful forms and reports are presented within this book. An alternative is to review publications describing how to construct these documents. Such information can then be used to design forms and reports based on the specific accounting structures unique to a company. This source book provides information about constructing forms and reports:

Design and Maintenance of Accounting Manuals

Authors: Steven M. Bragg and Harry L. Brown
Publisher: John Wiley & Sons, Inc.
Publication Date: 2007

Some examples of forms and reports can be found in certain of the larger accounting "how to" books, such as

Controllership: The Work of the Managerial Accountant, 7th Edition

Authors: Janice M. Roehl-Anderson and Steven M. Bragg
Publisher: John Wiley & Sons, Inc.
Publication Date: 2004

Researching Accounting Footnotes

Source documents for IFRS will describe the general contents of footnotes to financial statements but rarely give more than a few limited examples. Expanded discussions of disclosures can be found in *Wiley IFRS 2008*. Another option is to access the Web site of the Securities and Exchange Commission at www.sec.gov and review the individual filings of various public companies, which can be accessed through the "Search for Company Filings" option on that Web page. Several hundred foreign private issuers file with the SEC, and most of these present financial statements in conformity with IFRS.

Researching Accounting Journal Entries

Examples of journal entry formats are listed in the Journal Entry sections of each chapter in this book. In addition, you can consult *Wiley IFRS 2008* for the most recent year, which may include different examples of journal entries for a specific topic.

Researching Accounting Recordkeeping

Information about the proper time period over which to retain accounting documents is difficult to find, as are procedures and documentation for organizing and destroying documents. The principal organization concerning itself with these issues is the Association for Information Management Professionals (Web site: www.arma.org), headquartered in Lenexa, Kansas. Its Web site cites a number of books related to records retention.

APPENDIX A

Current International Financial Reporting Standards (IAS/IFRS) and Interpretations (SIC/IFRIC)

(Recent revisions noted parenthetically)

IAS 1	Presentation of Financial Statements (revised 2007, effective 2009)
IAS 2	Inventories (revised 2003, effective 2005)
IAS 7	Cash Flow Statements
IAS 8	Accounting Policies, Changes in Accounting Estimates and Errors (revised 2003, effective 2005)
IAS 10	Events After the Balance Sheet Date (revised 2003, effective 2005)
IAS 11	Construction Contracts
IAS 12	Income Taxes
IAS 14	Segment Reporting (superseded by IFRS 8, effective 2009)
IAS 16	Property, Plant, and Equipment (revised 2003, effective 2005)
IAS 17	Accounting for Leases (revised 2003, effective 2005)
IAS 18	Revenue
IAS 19	Employee Benefits (revised 2004)
IAS 20	Accounting for Government Grants and Disclosure of Government Assistance
IAS 21	The Effects of Changes in Foreign Exchange Rates (revised 2003, effective 2005; minor further amendment 2005)
IAS 23	Borrowing Costs (revised 2007, effective 2009)
IAS 24	Related-Party Disclosures (revised 2003, effective 2005)
IAS 26	Accounting and Reporting by Retirement Benefit Plans
IAS 27	Consolidated and Separate Financial Statements (revised 2003, effective 2005)
IAS 28	Accounting for Investments in Associates (revised 2003, effective 2005)
IAS 29	Financial Reporting in Hyperinflationary Economies
IAS 31	Financial Reporting of Interests in Joint Ventures (revised 2003, effective 2005)
IAS 32	Financial Instruments: Presentation (revised 2003, effective 2005; disclosure requirements removed to IFRS 7 effective 2007)
IAS 33	Earnings Per Share (revised 2003, effective 2005)
IAS 34	Interim Financial Reporting
IAS 36	Impairments of Assets (revised 2004)

IAS 37	Provisions, Contingent Liabilities, and Contingent Assets
IAS 38	Intangible Assets (revised 2004)
IAS 39	Financial Instruments: Recognition and Measurement (amended 2005)
IAS 40	Investment Property (revised 2003, effective 2005)
IAS 41	Agriculture
IFRS 1	First-Time Adoption of IFRS (minor amendment 2005)
IFRS 2	Share-Based Payment
IFRS 3	Business Combinations
IFRS 4	Insurance Contracts
IFRS 5	Noncurrent Assets Held for Sale and Discontinued Operations
IFRS 6	Exploration for and Evaluation of Mineral Resources
IFRS 7	Financial Instruments: Disclosures
IFRS 8	Operating Segments
SIC 7	Introduction of the Euro
SIC 10	Government Assistance–No Specific Relation to Operating Activities
SIC 12	Consolidation—Special-Purpose Entities
SIC 13	Jointly Controlled Entities—Nonmonetary Contributions by Venturers
SIC 15	Operating Leases—Incentives
SIC 21	Income Taxes—Recovery of Revalued Nondepreciable Assets
SIC 25	Income Taxes—Changes in the Tax Status of an Enterprise or Its Shareholders
SIC 27	Evaluating the Substance of Transactions Involving the Legal Form of a Lease
SIC 29	Disclosure—Service Concession Arrangements
SIC 31	Revenue—Barter Transactions Involving Advertising Services
SIC 32	Intangible Assets—Web Site Costs
IFRIC 1	Changes in Existing Decommissioning, Restoration and Similar Liabilities
IFRIC 2	Members' Shares in Cooperative Entities and Similar Instruments
IFRIC 4	Determining Whether an Arrangement Contains a Lease
IFRIC 5	Rights to Interest Arising from Decommissioning, Restoration and Environmental Rehabilitation Funds

IFRIC 6	Liabilities Arising from Participating in a Specific Market—Waste Electrical and Electronic Equipment
IFRIC 7	Applying the Restatement Approach under IAS 29, *Financial Reporting in Hyperinflationary Economies*
IFRIC 8	Scope of IFRS 2
IFRIC 9	Reassessment of Embedded Derivatives
IFRIC 10	Interim Financial Reporting and Impairment
IFRIC 11	IFRS 2: Group and Treasury Share Transactions
IFRIC 12	Service Concession Arrangements
IFRIC 13	Customer Loyalty Programs
IFRIC 14	IAS 19: The Limit on a Defined Benefit Asset, Minimum Funding Requirements, and Their Interaction

2 CASH, RECEIVABLES, AND PREPAID EXPENSES

DEFINITIONS OF TERMS

Accounts receivable. A current asset on the statement of financial position, representing short-term amounts due from customers who have purchased goods or services on account.

Assignment. Creating a loan using accounts receivable as the collateral. If the debtor is unable to repay the loan, the creditor can collect the accounts receivable and retain the proceeds. The borrower retains risk of loss on the receivables, and customers are generally not notified of the assignment.

Cash. All petty cash, currency, held checks, certificates of deposit, traveler's checks, money orders, letters of credit, bank drafts, cashier's checks, and demand deposits that are held by a company without restriction, and that are readily available on demand.

Collateral. Assets that have been pledged to secure debtor repayment of a loan. If it cannot repay the loan, the creditor can sell the assets and retain the proceeds.

Factoring. The sale of accounts receivable to a third party, which then assumes the risk of loss if the accounts receivable cannot be collected.

Factor's holdback. That portion of the payment for an accounts receivable sale retained by the factor in expectation of product returns by, or other credits granted to, customers.

Net realizable value. The expected revenue to be gained from the sale of an item or service, less the costs of the sale transaction.

Pledging. Assigning accounts receivable as collateral on company debt.

Recourse. The right of a creditor under a factoring arrangement to be paid by the debtor for any uncollectible accounts receivable sold to the creditor.

CONCEPTS AND EXAMPLES[1]

Cash

If there is a short-term restriction on cash, such as a requirement that it be held in a sinking fund in anticipation of the payment of a corresponding debt within a year, then it should still be itemized as a current asset, but as a separate line item. If there is a long-term restriction on cash, such as a compensating balance agreement that is linked to debt that will not be paid off within the current year, then the cash must be reported as a long-term asset. Alternatively, if a compensating balance agreement is tied to a loan that matures within the current period, then it may be recorded separately as a current asset.

If a company issues checks for which there are not sufficient funds on hand, it will find itself in a negative cash situation as reported on its statement of financial position. Rather than show a negative cash balance among assets, it is more appropriate to shift the amount of the excess checks back into the accounts payable liability account, thereby leaving the reported cash balance at or near zero. Note that an overdraft condition exists for financial reporting purposes if there is a negative *book* balance for the cash account, whether the financial institution is aware of the condition or not (due to timing of check clearances and deposits in transit, these generally will not correspond).

---

[1] *Some portions of this section are adapted with permission from Chapters 14 and 16 of Steven M. Bragg,* ***Ultimate Accountants' Reference*** *(Hoboken, NJ: John Wiley & Sons, Inc., 2006).*

Cash held in foreign currencies should be included in the cash account on the statement of financial position, subject to two restrictions. First, it must be converted to local currency units at the prevailing exchange rate as of the date of the statement of financial position. Second, the funds must actually be readily convertible into local currency units; if not (perhaps due to currency restrictions by the foreign government), the cash cannot properly be classified as a current asset and instead must be classified as a long-term asset. This latter item may be a key issue for those organizations that want to report the highest possible current ratio but which find foreign deposits subject to exchange restrictions.

Prepaid Expenses

Prepaid expenses are itemized as current assets on the statement of financial position, and should include advance payments for any expenditures that would have otherwise been made during the next 12 months. For example, prepayments on key man life insurance, rent, or association fees would be charged to this account. There should be a supporting schedule for this account, detailing each line item charged to it and the amortization schedule over which each item will be ratably charged to expense (see the sample report in the Recordkeeping section).

The prepaid expense account does *not* include deposits, since they are typically not converted back to cash until the ends of the associated agreements, which are often more than one year beyond the date of the statement of financial position. For example, the usual one-month rent deposit required with a building lease agreement cannot be recovered until the lease term has expired. Instead, deposits are usually recorded in the Other Assets or Deposits accounts, which are listed as noncurrent assets on the statement of financial position. If the related agreement is to expire within one year, however, deposits are to be included in current assets.

Receivables—Presentation

The items captioned as accounts receivable in the statement of financial position is sometimes found to include a variety of amounts owed to the reporting entity that are not strictly accounts receivable, so it is useful to define what should be included in this account. An account receivable is a claim that is payable in cash and is in exchange for the services or goods provided by the company. This definition *excludes* a note receivable—essentially a return of loaned funds—for which a signed note is usually available as documentary evidence. A note receivable should be set forth in the financial statements as a separate item. It also excludes any short-term funds loaned to employees (such as employee advances) or employee or officer loans of any type that may be due over a longer term. These items may be more appropriately reported in an Other Receivable or Receivable from Employees account.

Receivables—Collateral, Assignments, and Factoring

If a company uses its accounts receivable as collateral for a loan, then no accounting entry is required, although disclosure is necessary either on the face of the statement of financial position or in the footnotes. An *assignment* of accounts receivable, where specific receivables are pledged as collateral on a loan and where customer payments are generally forwarded to the lender by the reporting entity, also requires no accounting entry. If a company actually sells some or all of its accounts receivable, without retaining any continuing involvement in their collection, and with no requirement to repay the transferee in the event that a customer defaults on its payment of a receivable, this is called *factoring*. In this case, a sale transaction must be recorded (see the Decision Tree section for more information). This typically involves a credit to the Accounts Receivable account, a debit to the Cash account for the amount of the buyer's payment, and a Factoring Expense entry to reflect extra charges made by the factor on the transaction. The amount of cash received from the factor will also be reduced by an interest charge that is based on the amount of cash issued to the company for the period when the factor has not yet received cash from the factored accounts receivable. This is often an estimated amount based on the due dates of the individual customer obligations. It results in a debit to the Interest Expense account and a further credit to the Accounts Receivable account.

A variation on this transaction is if the company draws cash from the factor only when needed, rather than at the time when the accounts receivable are sold to the factor. This arrangement results in a smaller interest charge by the factor for the period when it is awaiting payment on the accounts receivable. In this instance, a new receivable is created that can be labeled "Due from Factor."

Another variation occurs when the factor holds back payment of some portion of the net cash due for the accounts receivable, generally on the grounds that there may be inventory returns from customers that will need to be charged back to the company. In this case, the proper entry is to offset the account receivable being transferred to the factor with a holdback receivable account. Once all cash receipt transactions have been cleared by the factor, any amounts left in the holdback account are eliminated with a debit to Cash (being remitted by the factor) and a credit to the Holdback account.

A sample journal entry that includes all of the preceding factoring issues is shown in Exhibit 2.1. In this case, a company has sold €100,000 of accounts receivable to a factor, which includes a 10% holdback provision. The factor expects to incur €4,800 in bad debts that it must absorb as a result of the transaction. As a result, the factor pays the company €4,800 less than the face value of the accounts receivable, which forces the company to recognize an additional expense of €4,800 on the transaction. Also, the company does not elect to receive all funds allowed by the factor. In order to save interest costs, in fact, it only takes delivery of €15,000 to meet its immediate cash needs. Finally, the factor charges 18% interest (annual rate) for the 30-day period that is expected to elapse, on average, before it collects the factored accounts receivable, resulting in an interest charge of €225 on the €15,000 of delivered funds.

Exhibit 2.1: Sample Factoring Journal Entry

Cash	14,775	
Accounts receivable—factoring holdback	10,000	
Factoring expense	4,800	
Interest expense	225	
Due from factor	70,200	
Accounts receivable		100,000

If the company factors its accounts receivable, but the factor has recourse against the company for uncollectible amounts (an alternative arrangement, called *factoring with recourse,* which typically reduces the factoring fee since risk is not assumed), or if the company agrees to service the receivables subsequent to the factoring arrangement, then the company still can be construed as having retained control over the receivables. In this case, the factoring arrangement is considered to be a secured loan rather than a sale of receivables, resulting in the retention of the accounts receivable on the company's statement of financial position as well as the addition of a loan liability. When receivables are sold with recourse, one should shift the expected amount of bad debts to be incurred from the Allowance for Bad Debts account to a Recourse Obligation account, from which bad debts will be subtracted as incurred.

Receivables—Sales Returns

When a customer returns goods to a company, the accountant should set up an offsetting sales contra account, rather than reversing the original sale transaction. The resulting transaction would be a credit to the Accounts Receivable account and a debit to the Contra-revenue account. There are two reasons for using this approach. First, a direct reduction of the original sale would impact the financial reporting in a prior period, if the sale originated in a prior period. Second, a large number of sales returns charged directly against the sales account would be essentially invisible on the financial statements, with management seeing only a reduced sales volume, which might be interpreted differently than a surge in product returns after the sales were made. Only by using (and reporting) an offsetting contra account can management gain some knowledge of the extent of any sales returns. If a company ships products on approval (i.e., customers have the right of return) and there is a history of significant returns, then it should create a reserve for sales returns based on historical rates of return. The offsetting sale returns expense account should be categorized as part of the cost of goods sold.

Example of reserve for sales made on approval

The Black Forest Company issues new versions of its books to a subscriber list that has purchased previous editions. Historically, it has experienced a 22% rate of return from these sales. In the current month, it shipped €440,000 of books to its subscriber list. Given the historical rate of return, Black Forest's controller expects to see €96,800 worth of books returned to the company. Accordingly, she records this entry:

Sale return expense	96,800	
Allowance for sales returns		96,800

Receivables—Early Payment Discounts

Unless a company offers an exceedingly large early payment discount, it is unlikely that the total amount of the discount taken will have a material impact on the financial statements. Consequently, some variation in the standard treatment of this transaction can be used. The most theoretically accurate approach is to initially record the account receivable at its discounted value, which assumes that all customers will take the early payment discount. Any cash discounts that are not taken will then be recorded as additional revenue. This method results in an appropriately conservative view of the amount of funds that one can expect to receive from collections of the accounts receivable. An alternative that results in a slightly higher initial revenue figure is to record the full, undiscounted amount of each sale in accounts receivable and then record any discounts later taken in a sales contra account. One objection to this second approach is that the discount taken will be recognized only in an accounting period that is later than the one in which the sale was initially recorded (given the time delay usually associated with accounts receivable payments), which is an inappropriate revenue recognition technique. An alternative approach that avoids this problem is to set up a reserve for cash discounts taken in the period in which the sales occur and offset actual discounts against it as they occur.

Receivables—Long-Term

If an account receivable is not due to be collected for more than one year, then for financial reporting purposes it should be discounted at an interest rate that fairly reflects the rate that would have been charged to the debtor under a normal lending situation. An alternative is to use whatever interest rate that may be noted in the sale agreement, but this should not be less than the prevailing market rate at the time when the receivable was originated. The result of this calculation will be the display of a smaller receivable balance than is indicated by its face amount. The difference should be gradually accrued as interest income over the life of the receivable.

Example of a long-term accounts receivable transaction

The Bavaria Furniture Company (BFC) sells a large block of office furniture in exchange for a receivable of €82,000 payable by the customer in two years. There is no stated interest rate on the receivable, so the BFC controller uses the current market rate of 6% to derive a present value discount rate factor of 0.8900. She multiplies the €82,000 receivable by the discount rate factor of 0.8900 to arrive at a present value of €72,980 and makes this entry:

Notes receivable	82,000	
Furniture revenue		72,980
Discount on notes receivable		9,020

In succeeding months, the BFC controller ratably debits the discount on the notes receivable account and credits interest income, so that the discount is entirely eliminated by the time the note receivable is collected. Also, note that the initial debit is to a notes receivable account, *not* accounts receivable, since this is considered neither an account receivable nor a current asset.

Receivables—Bad Debts

The accountant must recognize a bad debt as soon as it is reasonably certain that a loss is likely to occur and the amount in question can be estimated with a resonable degree of accuracy. For IFRS financial reporting purposes, the only allowable method for recognizing bad debts is to establish a bad debt reserve (allowance for doubtful accounts) as a contra account to the Accounts Receivable account. Under this approach, one should estimate a long-term average ratio of bad debt to sales, debit the Bad Debt Expense (which is most commonly reported in the selling expenses section of the income statement) for this percentage of the period-end accounts receivable balance, and credit the Bad Debt Reserve contra account. When an actual bad debt is recognized, the accountant credits the Accounts Receivable account and debits the reserve. No reduction is made to the Sales account. If there is an unusually large bad debt to be recognized, and it will more than offset the existing bad debt reserve, then the reserve should be increased sufficiently to ensure that the remaining balance in the reserve is not negative.

There are several ways to determine the long-term estimated ratio of bad debts for the preceding calculation. One is to determine the historical average bad debt as a proportion of the total credit sales for the past 12 months. Another option that results in a more accurate estimate is to calculate a different historical bad debt percentage based on the relative age of the accounts receivable at the end of the reporting period. For example, accounts aged greater than 90 days may have a historical bad debt experience of 50%, whereas those over 30 days have a loss percentage of 20% and those below 30 days are at only 4%. This type of experience percentage is more difficult to calculate but can result in a more precise bad debt allowance, and hence more accurate periodic financial reports.

It is also possible to estimate the bad debt level based on an analysis of customer types. For example, one could make the case that government entities never go out of business and so have a much lower bad debt rate than other types of customers. Whichever approach is used, it must be fully documented so that an auditor can trace through the calculations to ensure that a sufficient bad debt reserve has been provided.

Example of a bad debt reserve calculation

The Granny Clock Company has €120,000 of outstanding accounts receivable. Of that amount, €20,000 is more than 90 days old, while €41,000 is in the 60-to-90 day category. The company has historically experienced a loss rate of 25% on receivables more than 90 days old, a loss rate of 10% on receivables in the 60-to-90 day category, and 2% on all other receivables. Based on this information, the controller calculates a reserve of €1,180 on the current receivables (€59,000 × 2%), €4,100 for receivables in the 60-to-90 day category (€41,000 × 10%), and €5,000 for receivables older than 90 days (€20,000 × 25%), which totals €10,280. The company already has a reserve of €2,000 left over from the previous month, so the new entry is a debit to bad debt expense and a credit to the reserve for bad debts of €8,280 (€10,280 required reserve less the existing balance).

If an account receivable has been already written off as a bad debt and is subsequently collected, the receipt may be credited to the bad debt reserve or to earnings. The incorrect treatment would be to record a new sale and charge the receipt against that, since this would improperly suggest a higher level of sales activity than really occurred.

DECISION TREES

Receivables—Ownership Decision

The main issue involving the use of accounts receivable as collateral—or for assignment or factoring—is how to report these transactions in the financial statements. The illustration in Exhibit 2.2 may be of some assistance. As shown in the exhibit, if receivables are pledged as collateral on a loan, if they are assigned with recourse, or if the company has some means of forcing their return, then the company essentially has control over the receivables and should continue to record them as such on its statement of financial position. However, if the receivables purchaser has assumed the risk of loss, *and* can pledge or exchange the receivables to a third party, *and* the company or its creditors can no longer access the receivables for any reason, then the purchaser has control over the assets, and the selling company must record the sale of the receivables and remove them from its statement of financial position. Thus, if there is any evidence that the selling company retains any aspect of control over the receivables, they must continue to be reported on the selling company's statement of financial position, with additional footnote disclosure of their status as collateral for a loan.

Exhibit 2-2: Reporting Status of Accounts Receivable

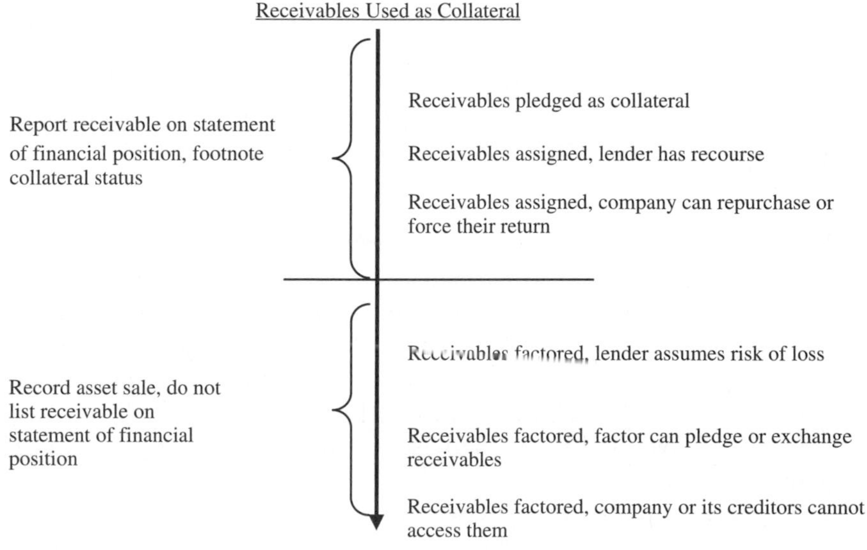

POLICIES

Cash

- **No accounts payable personnel shall be authorized to sign checks or approve money transfers.** This policy is designed to separate the preparation of accounts payable documents from their approval, thereby keeping a single person from falsely creating a payable and authorizing its payment to himself.
- **All check or money transfers exceeding €_____ shall be countersigned by the _____ position.** This policy provides for a second review of very large payments to ensure that they are appropriate and to reduce the incidence of fraudulent transfers. Unfortunately, many banks do not review the existence of a required second signature on a check, making such a requirement a less effective policy.
- **All check signers shall be adequately bonded.** This policy requires a company to retain an adequate level of bonding on its check signers to ensure that it will suffer no loss if a signer commits fraud. Bonding companies usually conduct a background review on check signers before agreeing to provide bond, which may give a company warning of previously unknown fraudulent employee activities, thereby allowing it to remove check-signing authority from someone before they have the opportunity to commit fraud again.

Prepaid Expenses

- **All advances to employees must be repaid within three months.** This policy keeps a company from becoming a bank for employees. In addition, it rapidly draws down the balances due from employees, so there is a minimal risk of loss to the company if an employee quits work without having paid off the entire balance of an advance.
- **Employee advances shall be limited to __% of their annual pay.** This policy is designed to reduce the amount of money a company can have due from its employees, which mitigates its risk of nonpayment in the event of an employee departure.

Receivables

- **Allow the accounting staff to write off accounts receivable balances under €___ without management approval.** Though one could require management approval of all receivable write-offs in order to reduce the risk of false write-offs, this is not an efficient control point for very small balances. Instead, it is common to allow the write-off of small balances by the accounting staff, thereby avoiding time otherwise wasted by the management staff investigating these write-offs.
- **Require credit manager approval for all prospective sales exceeding customer credit limits.** A common problem for the credit department is to be rushed into granting credit when a salesperson lands a large sale, which tends to result in excessively large credit limits being granted. A better approach is to require an advance review of prospective sales by the credit manager, who

can then tell the sales staff the maximum amount of credit the company is willing to grant before any sale is finalized.

- **Require formal annual reviews of all customer credit limits exceeding €______.** Customer financial situations change over time, making the initial credit limits granted to them incorrect. This is a particular problem when a customer is spiraling down toward bankruptcy, while the company blithely continues to grant it large amounts of credit. Annual reviews of large credit limits can mitigate this problem, though feedback from the collections staff will warn of possible customer problems well before any formal annual review would do so.
- **No factoring arrangements are allowed when receivables are used as collateral for other debts.** This policy prevents a company from violating the terms of a loan agreement under which it must retain its receivables as collateral, rather than reduce them through sale to a factor. Otherwise, the company could be seen as selling assets to the detriment of a secured lender, which would then have the right to call its loan to the company.

PROCEDURES

Cash—Apply Cash to Accounts Receivable

Use this procedure to apply cash received from customers to open accounts receivable balances:

1. Add up all daily cash receipts and match the paper tape of the summarization to the individual payments to ensure that the total is correct.
2. Go to the accounting software and access the cash application screen. At the top of the screen, enter today's date and the total amount to be applied.
3. For each customer payment, enter the customer number, individual check amount, as well as the check number and date. Then tab to the detail section of the screen where the list of all open invoices for the customer will appear. Click on each invoice being paid and enter any discounts taken. After identifying all invoices paid by each customer, complete the transaction and move to the next customer from whom a check was received. Continue in this fashion until all receipts have been entered.
4. Print a daily cash receipts report and verify that the total on the report matches the total amount of cash received on the initial paper tape. Compare the remittance advices attached to individual checks to the daily cash receipts report to find the error, and correct it.
5. Press the "post cash" button to transfer all the receipts' information to the general ledger.
6. Photocopy all checks received, staple the cash receipts report to the photocopies, and file the set of documents in the applied cash filing cabinet.

Cash—Receive and Deposit Cash

Use this procedure to receive cash from a variety of sources and deposit it into the company bank account.

1. Summarize all cash on an adding machine tape.
2. Enter all checks and cash received on a deposit slip. Verify that the deposit slip total and the adding machine tape total are the same. If not, recount the cash and checks.
3. Give the deposit slip and attached cash and checks to a second cash clerk, who compares the check total to the summary sheet forwarded from the mailroom. Reconcile any differences.
4. Photocopy all checks, including attached remittance advices, as well as the deposit slip. Verify that this packet of information matches the total to be sent to the bank in the deposit. Then send the photocopies to the accounts receivable staff, which will apply these payments to outstanding accounts receivable.
5. Send the completed deposit to the bank by courier.

Cash—Process Credit Card Payments

This procedure is useful for processing credit card payments through an Internet-based processing site.

1. Verify that the customer has supplied all information required for the credit card processing: name on the card, credit card number, expiration date, and billing address. Also retain the customer's phone number in case the payment is not accepted, so corrected information can be obtained.
2. Access the Internet credit card processing site and log in.
3. Enter all customer-supplied information on the Web screen, as well as the invoice number, amount to be billed, and a brief description of the billing.
4. If the transaction is not accepted, call the customer and review all supplied information to determine its accuracy. As an alternative, obtain information for a different credit card from the customer.
5. If the transaction is accepted, go to the accounting computer system and log in the cash receipt associated with the transaction. Date the transaction one day forward, since this more closely corresponds to the settlement date and corresponding receipt of cash.
6. Copy the invoice, stamp it with a "Paid in Full" stamp, and initial the stamp. Mail it to the person whose name was on the credit card (*not* the person listed on the invoice, if any), since this person will need it as a receipt.

Cash—Reconcile Petty Cash

Use this procedure to conduct a manual reconciliation of the petty cash balance in any petty cash box.

1. Access the general ledger account for the petty cash box and determine the amount of cash it should contain as of the last reconciliation.

2. Go to the petty cash box and add up all cash contained in the box. Subtract this amount from the box balance as of the last reconciliation and add any amounts deposited into the box during the interval since the last reconciliation. This calculation reveals the amount of missing cash that should be accounted for by expense vouchers.
3. Add up all vouchers in the box and compare this amount to the predetermined amount of missing cash. If they do not match, review petty cash procedures with the person responsible for it.
4. Create a journal entry summarizing the expenses represented by all vouchers in the box, as well as the amount of any shortfalls or overages. Staple the vouchers to this journal entry and give the packet to the general ledger accountant for entry into the general ledger.
5. Calculate the amount of cash that should be added to the petty cash box, based on usage levels, and recommend to the assistant controller in charge of accounts payable that this amount of cash be forwarded to the person responsible for the petty cash box.

Cash—Reconcile Bank Account

Use this procedure to reconcile any differences between the bank and company records of cash transactions. This procedure assumes that a computerized reconciliation module is available through the accounting software.

1. Verify that the beginning bank balance matches the beginning adjusted book record, net of reconciling items. If not, go back and fix the bank reconciliations for earlier periods.
2. Enter the ending bank balance on the computer screen.
3. Check off all company records of deposits in the computer system if they match the bank record of receipts. As one progresses through this list, one should check off the deposit records on the bank statement that have also been checked off in the computer system. If there are any deposits that cannot be immediately reconciled, pull out the detailed deposit records for the days in question and determine which deposits are in error. Fix any deposit record differences and verify that the total book record of deposits matches the total bank record of deposits.
4. Scan the bank statement for any special charges levied by the bank that have not already been recorded in the company books. Enter these adjustments as a journal entry, and check off all recorded expenses of this type on the bank statement.
5. Check off all company checks in the computer system if they match the amount of checks recorded as having cleared on the bank statement. *It is not good enough to just match check numbers!* One must also verify the amount of each cleared check on the bank statement, since this can be a source of discrepancy.
6. If there are checks still listed on the bank statement that do not appear in the company records, then these are most likely manual checks that were not initially recorded in the company records. Also review these unrecorded

checks to see if any were fraudulently created. Enter these items in the computer system as manual checks.

7. If the bank statement reveals transfers between bank accounts, verify that these entries have been recorded in the computer system. If not, make journal entries to match the bank transaction record.
8. Verify that the bank ending balance now matches the company's records, net of any deposits or checks in transit. If not, repeat the preceding steps. Then print two copies of the reconciliation report; file one copy in the journal entry binder for the applicable month, and file one copy in the bank statement binder next to the applicable bank statement.

Receivables—Print and Issue Invoices

Use this procedure to verify shipment of goods and to create invoices based on the shipments. This procedure assumes that the shipping department, rather than the accounting staff, is logging out shipped goods from the computer system and tracking back orders.

1. Locate the shipping paperwork in the "shippers" box in the mailroom. The paperwork should include a copy of the shipping log and a copy of the bill of lading.
2. Verify that there is a bill of lading for every order listed on the shipping log and also that all bills of lading are listed on the log. Then put the bills of lading in order, first by customer number and then by order number (if there is more than one order per customer). Next check the "carrier" column on the shipping log—some will indicate shipment pickups by customers. For all other deliveries, the shipping department should have turned in a freight worksheet containing the cost of additional freight for each shipment. Locate these sheets, which will be used to determine the freight charge on each invoice.
3. Locate on each freight sheet the method of delivery as well as the weight of the order. Cross-reference this information against the standard freight charge table, and write on the freight sheet the price of the freight to be billed to the customer.
4. Locate the signed customer order that contains the pricing for the items shipped, the customer name and address, and the name of the salesperson to whom a commission will be paid.
5. Go to the computer system and access the customer information screen. Call up the customer name and verify that the invoice-to address and contact name are correct. If not, either change the existing information or add a new invoice-to address for the customer.
6. Go to the invoicing screen in the computer system and enter the customer name verified in the last step. Verify that the default salesperson listed on the screen is correct, or change it to match the salesperson name listed on the signed customer order. Enter the part numbers and quantities shipped that are listed on the shipping log as well as the prices noted on the customer order. Enter the freight charge listed on the freight sheet.

7. Print two copies of the invoice and mail one to the customer. If the order is complete, then also file the bill of lading, invoice, customer order, and freight sheet in the customer file. If the order is not complete, store the customer order form in a pending orders file for cross-referencing purposes when back-ordered items are shipped at a later date.

Receivables—Calculate the Bad Debt Reserve

Use this procedure to alter the bad debt reserve to reflect new billing and bad debt activity in a reporting period.

1. Print the accounts receivable aging report and review all invoices on the report that are at least 60 days old with the collections staff.
2. If the collections staff deems a reviewed invoice to be uncollectible, complete a bad debt authorization form for it and charge it off to the bad debt reserve account (see following procedure).
3. Once all receivables designated as bad debts have been cleared from the aging report, summarize the total amount written off during the reporting period, which can be obtained from the list of written-off invoices listed in the bad debt reserve account in the general ledger.
4. Enter the period's bad debt total as a running balance in an electronic spreadsheet alongside the remaining accounts receivable balance for the reporting period. Calculate the rolling three-month bad debt percentage of accounts receivable on this spreadsheet.
5. Multiply the rolling three-month bad debt percentage calculated from the spreadsheet by the remaining accounts receivable balance to determine the estimated amount of bad debt reserve required.
6. If the amount of estimated bad debt reserve is greater than the actual amount listed in the general ledger, make an entry crediting the bad debt reserve account for the difference, with the offsetting debit going to the bad debt expense account.

Receivables—Authorize Bad Debt Write-Offs

Use this procedure to formalize the process of writing off bad debts from the accounts receivable aging report.

1. At least once a month, review all outstanding accounts receivable on the accounts receivable aging report with the collections staff to see which invoices or portions of invoices must be written off, taking into account customer bankruptcy, history of collection problems, and the size of the amounts owed.
2. Complete the Bad Debt Write-Off Approval Form (see the Forms section). In particular, note on the form the reason for the write-off. If there is a systemic problem that is causing the write-off to occur, forward a copy of the completed form to the appropriate department for review.

3. Forward the form to the general ledger accountant, who will create a credit based on the information in the form and offset the credit against the outstanding customer invoice.
4. Summarize all completed bad debt forms at the end of each month and send the results to the general manager, showing the total write-off amounts attributable to each type of systemic problem.
5. Store the completed bad debt write-off forms in a separate binder and store them in the archives after year-end.

CONTROLS

Cash

The controls that follow can be used to reduce the risk of asset theft through the unauthorized transfer of cash.

- **Control check stock.** This is a key control. All check stock must be secured when not in use. Otherwise, it is a simple matter for someone to take a check from the bottom of a check stack (where its loss will not be noticed for some time), forge a signature on it, and cash it. Be sure to keep the key or combination to the lock in a safe place, or else this control will be worthless.
- **Control signature plates.** This is another key control. Many companies use either signature plates or stamps to imprint an authorized signature on a check, thereby saving the time otherwise required of a manager to sign checks. If someone obtains access to a signature plate and some check stock, that person can easily pay himself the contents of the entire corporate bank account. The best control is to lock up signature plates in a different storage location than the check stock, so a perpetrator would be required to break into two separate locations in order to carry out a thorough check fraud.
- **Separate responsibility for the cash receipt and cash disbursement functions.** If a person has access to both the cash receipt and disbursement functions, it is much easier to commit fraud by altering the amount of incoming receipts and then pocket the difference. To avoid this, each function should be handled by different people within the organization.
- **Perform bank reconciliations.** Though widely practiced and certainly necessary, this is not a preventive control, and so it should be implemented *after* the control of check stock and signature plates. Bank reconciliations are most effective when completed each day; this can be done by accessing the daily log of cash transactions through the company bank's Internet site. By staying up-to-date on reconciliations, evidence of fraudulent check activity can be discovered more quickly, allowing for faster remedial action. Note that the so-called "four column" bank reconciliation (more formally, the reconciliation of receipts, disbursements and bank accounts) is a much more effective tool than is the more commonly encountered bank-to-book reconciliation.
- **Reconcile petty cash.** There tends to be a high incidence of fraud related to petty cash boxes, since money can be removed from them more easily. To reduce the incidence of these occurrences, initiate unscheduled petty cash box

reconciliations, which can catch perpetrators before they have covered their actions with a false paper trail. This control can be strengthened by targeting those petty cash boxes that have experienced unusually high levels of cash replenishment requests.

- **Require that bank reconciliations be completed by people independent of the cash receipts and disbursement functions.** The bank reconciliation is intended to be a check on the activities of those accounting personnel handling incoming and outgoing cash, so it makes little sense to have the same people review their own activities by completing the reconciliation. Instead, it should be done by someone in an entirely different part of the department, and preferably by a senior person with a proven record of reliability.
- **Require that petty cash vouchers be filled out in ink.** Anyone maintaining a petty cash box can easily alter a voucher previously submitted as part of a legitimate transaction and remove cash from the petty cash box to match the altered voucher. To avoid this, one should require that all vouchers be completed in ink. To be extra careful, one can even require users to write the amount of any cash transactions on vouchers in words instead of numbers (e.g., "fifty-two euros" instead of €52.00"), since numbers can be modified more easily.
- **Compare the check register to the actual check number sequence.** If checks are prenumbered, one can compare the check numbers listed in the computer's check register to those on the checks. If a check were to be removed from the check stock, then this action would become apparent when the check number on the check stock no longer matches the check number in the computer system.

  If the check stock is on a continuous sheet, as is used for sheet-fed dot matrix printers, then the more likely way for a perpetrator to steal checks would be to detach them from the top or bottom of the stack of check stock. In this case, one can detect the problem by keeping separate track of the last check number used as well as of the last check number on the bottom of the stack. Unfortunately, many accounting clerks like to keep this list of check numbers used with the check stock, so a perpetrator could easily alter the last number listed on the sheet while stealing checks at the same time. Consequently, the list of check numbers used should be kept in a separate location.
- **Review uncashed checks.** Review all checks that have not been cashed within 90 days of their check dates. In a few cases, it may be possible to cancel the checks, thereby increasing the available cash balance. This review can also highlight checks that have gone astray. By placing stop payment orders on these checks, one can keep them from being incorrectly cashed by other parties, while new checks can be issued to the proper recipients.
- **Route incoming cash payments through a lockbox.** When customers are told to send payments directly to a bank lockbox, this eliminates a number of control points within a company, since it no longer has to physically handle any forms of cash. Some payments will inevitably still be mailed directly to

the company, but the proportion of these payments will drop if customers are promptly asked to send future payments to the lockbox address.

- **Verify amount of cash discounts taken.** A cash receipts person can falsely report that customers are taking the maximum amount of early payment discounts when they have not actually done so, and pocket the amount of the false discount. This can be detected by requiring that photocopies of all incoming checks be made and then tracing payments on which discounts have been taken back to the copies of the checks. This is a less common problem area, since it requires a perpetrator to have access to both the receipts and payments aspects of the accounting operation, and so is a less necessary control point.

Prepaid Expenses

The largest problem with prepaid expenses is that they tend to turn into a holding area for payments that should have been converted into expenses at some point in the past. There is also a potential for advances to be parked in this area that should have been collected. The controls that follow address these problems.

- **Reconcile all prepaid expense accounts as part of the month-end closing process.** By conducting a careful review of all prepaid accounts once a month, it becomes readily apparent which prepaid items should now be converted to an expense. The result of this review should be a spreadsheet that itemizes the nature of each prepaid item in each account. Since this can be a time-consuming process involving some investigative work, it is best to review prepaid expense accounts shortly before the end of the month, so that a thorough review can be conducted without being cut short by the time pressures imposed by the usual closing process.
- **Review all employee advances with the payroll and payables staffs at least once a month.** A common occurrence is for an employee to claim hardship prior to a company-required trip and request a travel advance. Alternatively, an advance may be paid when an employee claims that he or she cannot make it to the next payroll check. For whatever the reason, these advances will be recorded in an employee advances account, where they can sometimes be forgotten. The best way to ensure repayment is a continual periodic review, either with the accounts payable staff that process employee expense reports (against which travel advances should be netted) or the payroll staff (which deducts pay advances from future paychecks).
- **Require approval of all advance payments to employees.** The simplest way to reduce the burden of tracking employee advances is not to make them in the first place. The best approach is to require management approval of any advances, no matter how small they may be.

Receivables

- **Confirm payment terms with customers.** Receivable collections can be particularly difficult when the sales staff has established side agreements with customers that alter payment terms—especially when the sales staff does not communicate these new terms to the collections department. One can discover the existence of these deals by confirming payment terms at the time of invoice creation with selected customers and then working with the sales manager to reprimand the sales staff that authorized special terms without notifying anyone else in the company.

- **Require approval of bad debt write-offs.** A common form of fraud is for a collections person to write off an invoice as a bad debt and then pocket the customer payment when it arrives. This can be avoided by requiring management approval of all bad debt write-offs (though staffs are usually allowed to write off small balances as an efficiency measure). Management should be particularly wary when a large proportion of bad debt requests come from the same collections person, indicating a possible fraud pattern.
- **Require approval of credits.** Credits against invoices can be required for other reasons than bad debts: incorrect pricing, incorrect quantities delivered, incorrect payment terms, and so on. In these cases, management approval should be required not only to detect the presence of false credit claims, but also to spot patterns indicating some underlying problem requiring correction, such as inaccurate order picking in the warehouse.
- **Match invoiced quantities to the shipping log.** It is useful to spot-check the quantities invoiced to the quantities listed on the shipping log. By doing so, one can detect fraud in the billing department caused by invoicing for too many units, with the accounting staff pocketing the difference when it arrives. This is a rare form of fraud, since it generally requires collaboration between the billing and cash receipts staff, and so the control is needed only where the fraud risk clearly exists.
- **Verify invoice pricing.** The billing department can commit fraud by issuing fake invoices to customers at improperly high prices and then pocketing the difference between the regular and inflated prices when the customer check arrives. Having someone compare the pricing on invoices to a standard price list before invoices are mailed can spot this issue. As was the case for the last control, this form of fraud is possible only when there is a risk of collaboration between the billing and cash receipts staff, so the control is needed only when the fraud risk is present.

FORMS AND REPORTS

Cash—Mailroom Remittance Receipt

In larger companies, all incoming checks are recorded in the mailroom, which summarizes all receipts on a worksheet such as the one shown in Exhibit 2.3. This sheet can then be matched against cash receipts recorded by the accounting department, thereby indicating if any checks were fraudulently removed from the mail delivered by the mailroom staff. The "City and State (or Province)" column on the report is used to identify which branch of customer has sent in a check, since payments may be received from multiple customer locations. For companies with a smaller number of customers, this column can be omitted.

Exhibit 2-3: Mailroom Remittance Sheet

Company Name
Mailroom Remittance Sheet
Receipts of [Month/Day/Year]

Check Number	Source If Not Check	Remitter	Location	Amount
1602		The Rush Airplane Company	Birmingham, UK	€ 126.12
	Cash	Rental Air Service	Paris, France	€ 19.50
2402		Automatic Service Company	Los Angeles, CA	€ 316.00
1613		Voe Parts Dealer	Toledo, Spain	€ 2.90
9865		Brush Electric Company	London, UK	€ 25.50
2915		Ajax Manufacturing Company	Helsingborg, Sweden	€1,002.60
8512		Apex Machine Tool Co.	Glasgow, Scotland	€ 18.60
			Total Receipts	€1,511.22
			Prepared by:	
			Date:	

SOURCE: Adapted with permission from Willson et al., ***Controllership, 6th ed.*** *(New York: John Wiley & Sons, Inc., 1999), p. 617.*

Cash—Bank Reconciliation

The bank reconciliation identifies the differences between a company's record of cash on hand and that of its bank. Preparing the report frequently results in the identification of errors in recorded cash transactions, and the report can be used as a control to spot fraudulent activities. It should be completed at least once a month but can be done each day if online bank records are available through the Internet. Many accounting computer systems include a partially automated reconciliation module, along with a bank reconciliation report. If not, the format in Exhibit 2.4 can be used as a model.

Exhibit 2.4: Bank Reconciliation Report

Company Name
Bank Reconciliation
Bank: ____________________ Account No: ____________________
As of ____________________________

	Balance 11/30/XX	Receipts	Disbursements	Balance 12/31/XX
Per bank..................	€126,312.50	€92,420.00	€85,119.00	€133,613.50
Add:				
Deposits in transit				
11/30 per book	€ 5,600.00	€ (5,600.00)		
12/31 per book		€12,500.00		€ 12,500.00
Deduct				
Outstanding checks				
November (see list)	€ 4,320.00		€ (4,115.00)	€ 205.00
December (see list)			€ 6,110.00	€ 6,110.00
Other Items:				
Bank charges not recorded			-5.01	5.01
Per books................	€127,592.50	€99,320.00	€87,108.99	€139,803.51

Prepared by __________
Date __________

SOURCE: Adapted with permission from Willson et al., ***Controllership, 6th ed.*** *(New York: John Wiley & Sons, Inc., 1999), p. 623.*

Cash—Cash Forecasting Model

The cash forecasting model is the most important report in the controller's arsenal of cash reports because it gives a detailed forward-looking view of when excess cash can be invested or when new cash inflows are required. A good working model is shown in Exhibit 2.5. The report shows weekly cash flows for each week of the next two months, which are usually fairly predictable in most businesses. The model then switches to monthly forecasts for the next three months; these forcasts tend to be increasingly inaccurate for the later months. The first block of information is receipts from sales projections, which is drawn for the corporate sales funnel report. The next block is uncollected invoices, listing larger invoices by customer name and smaller ones at a summary level in a Cash, Minor Invoices category. The collections staff can itemize the weeks when individual collections are most likely to arise, based on their experience with individual customers. The third block contains the most common categories of expenses, such as payroll, rent, and capital purchases, with all other expenses summarized under the Other Expenses category. By combining cash inflows from the first two blocks with the cash outflows listed in the third block, one can obtain a reasonably accurate picture of cash flows in the near term. These projections can be compared to budgeted cash levels, which are noted at the bottom of the report, in order to gain some idea of the accuracy of the budgeting process.

Exhibit 2.5: Cash Forecasting Model

Cash Forecast

Date Last Updated 3/9/2008

	For the Week Beginning on									(partial)		
	3/9/2008	3/16/2008	3/23/2008	3/30/2008	4/6/2008	4/13/2008	4/20/2008	4/27/2008	5/4/2008	May-07	Jun-07	Jul-07
Beginning Cash Balance	**€1,037,191**	€ 1,034,369	€ 968,336	€ 367,918	€ 918,082	€ 932,850	€ 918,747	€ 829,959	€ 834,924	€ 754,124	€808,592	€ 798,554
Receipts from Sales Projections:												
Coal Bed Drilling Corp.										€ 16,937		€ 174,525
Oil Patch Kids Corp.								€ 12,965		€ 45,521		€ 28,775
Overfault & Sons Inc.									€ 2,500		€129,000	
Platte River Drillers									€ 3,000	€ 53,000		
Powder River Supplies Inc.									€ 8,700		€ 18,500	€ 14,500
Submersible Drillers Ltd.										€ 2,500	€ 16,250	€ 16,250
Commercial, Various											€ 25,000	€ 25,000
Uncollected Invoices:												
Canadian Drillers Ltd			€ 9,975									
Coastal Mudlogging Co.			€ 6,686									
Dept. of the Interior	€ 1,823			€ 11,629		€ 2,897				€ 18,510		
Drill Tip Repair Co.				€ 5,575								
Overfault & Sons Inc.			€ 9,229									
Submersible Drillers Ltd.				€ 4,245								
U.S. Forest Service		€ 2,967	€ 812	€ 8,715								
Cash, Minor Invoices	€ 2,355	€ --	€ 3,668	€ --	€ 21,768							
Total Cash In	€ 4,178	€ 2,967	€ 30,370	€ 30,164	€ 21,768	€ 2,897	€ --	€ 12,965	€ 14,200	€ 139,468	€ 188,750	€ 259,050
Cash Out:												
Payroll + Payroll Taxes		€ 62,000		€ 65,000			€ 68,000		€ 71,000	€ 71,000	€ 138,000	€ 138,000
Commissions				€ 7,000					€ 7,000		€ 8,000	€ 9,000
Rent			€ 10,788				€ 10,788				€ 10,788	€ 10,788
Capital Purchases			€ 10,000			€ 10,000			€ 10,000		€ 10,000	€ 10,000
Other Expenses	€ 7,000	€ 7,000	€ 10,000	€ 8,000	€ 7,000	€ 7,000	€ 10,000	€ 8,000	€ 7,000	€ 14,000	€ 32,000	€ 32,000
Total Cash Out	€ 7,000	€ 69,000	€ 30,788	€ 80,000	€ 7,000	€ 17,000	€ 88,788	€ 8,000	€ 95,000	€ 85,000	€ 198,788	€ 199,788
Net Change in Cash	€ (2,822)	€ (66,033)	€ (418)	€ (49,836)	€ 14,768	€ (14,103)	€ (88,788)	€ 4,965	€ (80,800)	€ 54,468	€ (10,038)	€ 59,262
Ending Cash	€1,034,369	€ 968,336	€ 967,918	€ 918,082	€ 932,850	€ 918,747	€ 829,959	€ 834,924	€ 754,124	€ 808,592	€ 798,554	€ 857,816
Budgeted Cash Balance:				**€ 897,636**				**€ 833,352**		**€ 800,439**	**€ 815,040**	**€ 857,113**

SOURCE: Adapted with permission from Steven Bragg, ***Ultimate Accountants' Reference*** *(Hoboken, NJ: John Wiley & Sons, Inc., 2006), p. 600*

Receivables—Bad Debt Authorization Form

The bad debt authorization form is used to itemize the specific invoice to be written off and the reason for doing so, and to obtain management permission for the write-off. Of considerable importance, from an operational perspective, is the list of reasons used on the form for writing off an invoice; this information can be summarized and used to improve company systems to ensure that write-offs are reduced in the future. For example, if there are many incidents of "customer unable to pay," then there is a probable need for more intensive credit reviews prior to the acceptance of customer orders. Consequently, the form format shown in Exhibit 2.6 can and should be modified to match the types of bad debt problems being encountered by a business.

Exhibit 2.6: Bad Debt Authorization Form

Company Name

Bad Debt Write-Off Approval Form

Customer Name: ____________________ Invoice Number: ____________

Customer Code: ____________________ Invoice Amount: ____________

Reason for Write-Off

☐ Customer unable to pay

☐ Damaged goods

☐ Incorrect pricing

☐ Incorrect shipment quantity

☐ Product quality not acceptable

Other nonstandard reasons for a write-off: ________________________

____

____

Requested Write-Off Amount: ________________________

Name of Requesting Clerk: ________________________

Signature of Requesting Clerk: ________________________ Date: __________

Name of Approving Manager: ________________________

Signature of Approving Manager: ________________________ Date: __________

Receivables—Collection Actions Taken

Any reasonably organized collections staff should make notes about the status of their collection activities with each customer account, including the dates of contact, representations made by customers, and when the next collection contact is scheduled to be made. This information may be just handwritten notes, in which case it is quite difficult to summarize into a report. A better approach is to have the entire collections staff use a centralized collections database from which a variety of reports can be printed. With such a system, the report shown in Exhibit 2.7 can be easily printed whenever necessary. It can be sorted by the dollar amount of overdue balances to bring attention to the largest items, or by invoice date in order to focus attention on the oldest collection problems, or by collection staff so that problems with collection techniques can be highlighted.

Exhibit 2.7: Collection Actions Report

Collections Contact	*Customer*	*Invoice Number*	*Amount*	*Next Contact Date*	*Comments*
Jones	Alpha Labs	5418	€500.25	5/04	Waiting on controller approval
Jones	Blue Moon	5009	250.00	5/09	Sent bill of lading
Jones	White Ice	5200	375.15	5/03	Sent replacement part
Jones	Zora Inc.	5302	1,005.00	5/12	Meeting in person to discuss
Smith	Chai Tea	5400	2,709.15	5/01	Issued credit for price change
Smith	Deal Time	5417	5,010.00	5/13	Sent claim to bankruptcy court
Smith	Energy Ltd.	5304	128.45	5/08	Faxed new invoice copy
Smith	Foo & Sons	5215	495.31	5/07	Waiting for call back
Smith	Green Way	5450	95.97	5/05	Offered 25% discount to pay

Receivables—Aging Report

The single most used receivables report is the aging report, which divides outstanding invoices into 30-day time groupings. It is heavily used by the collections staff as their key source of information about old unpaid invoices. The report is standard with all accounting packages and so would be constructed only if a manual accounting system were used. An example is shown in Exhibit 2.8. The main modification worth considering is shifting the date range on the time groupings to match the terms of company invoices, plus a few days to allow for mail float. For example, altering the current time grouping to contain all invoices issued within the past 35 days instead of the usual 30 days would cover all invoices issued under "net 30" terms as well as any invoices already paid by customers that are in transit to the company. This approach does not bring invoices to the attention of the collections staff until collection activities are truly required.

Exhibit 2.8: Accounts Receivable Aging Report

Customer	*Invoice no.*	*Current*	*+30 Days*	*+60 Days*	*+90 Days*
Alpha Labs	5418			€500.25	
	5603		€1,042.75		
	5916	€639.50			
Chai Tea Inc.	5400				€2,709.15
	5511			€25.19	
	5618		€842.68		
	5900	€100.00			
Totals		€739.50	€1,885.43	€525.44	€2,709.15

Receivables—Loan Collateralization Report

Receivables are the most common asset used as loan collateral, since they can be liquidated more easily than other assets. Typically, a lender requires that a loan collateralization report such as the one shown in Exhibit 2.9 be completed at the end of each month. The agreement usually requires that old receivables be stripped from the reported balance to arrive at a core set of receivables most likely to be collected by the lender in the event of default. In addition, each category of assets used as collateral is multiplied by a reduction percentage (shown in bold in the exhibit), reflecting the amount of cash the lender believes it can collect if it were to sell each type of asset. The reduced amount of all asset types is then summarized and compared to the outstanding loan balance; if the collateral amount has dropped below the loan balance, then the company must pay back the difference. The report typically is signed by a company officer.

Exhibit 2.9: Loan Collateralization Report

Company Name
Loan Collateralization Report

For the month ended: ___________

Accounts receivable balance	€1,800,000	
Less receivables > 90 days old	(€42,500)	
Net accounts receivable	€1,757,500	
80% of net accounts receivable balance		€1,406,000
Raw materials inventory balance	€2,020,000	
40% of raw materials inventory balance		€1,010,000
Finished goods inventory balance	€515,000	
70% of finished goods inventory balance		€360,500
Total collateral		€2,776,500
Total loan balance		€2,000,000
Total collateral available for use		€776,500

I assert that the above calculation is correct, and that all bad debts, work in process, and obsolete inventory have been removed from the above balances.

CFO Signature: ____________________ Date: __________

FOOTNOTES

Cash—Restrictions on Use

Any restriction on a company's use of its cash should be disclosed in a footnote. An example follows:

Contributors to the organization have specified that their contributions be restricted to one of three funds: conservation, trail maintenance, and mountain properties. As of year-end, approximately €875,000 was restricted in the conservation fund, €520,000 in the trail maintenance fund, and €1,209,000 in the mountain properties fund. This left approximately €2,041,000 in unrestricted cash.

Cash—Restrictions Caused by Compensating Balance Agreements

If there are restrictions on a company's cash balances caused by compensating balance agreements, a footnote should detail the terms of the agreement as well as the amount of cash restricted by the agreement. An example follows:

> As part of the company's loan arrangement with the Second National Bank of Boise, it must maintain a compensating balance at the bank of no less than €200,000 at all times. The bank segregates this amount and does not allow drawdowns from it unless the balance of the associated line of credit is less than €500,000. Also, the bank requires an additional compensating balance of 10% of the loan balance; there is no restriction on use of this additional compensating balance, but the company must pay an additional 2% interest on the loan balance whenever its average cash balance drops below the required compensating balance. During the past year, this resulted in an average 0.4% increase in the average interest rate paid on the line of credit.

Cash—Excessive Concentration in Uninsured Accounts

If there is a significant amount of credit risk resulting from the excessive concentration of cash in bank accounts that exceeds federally insured limits, the excess amounts should be revealed in a footnote. An example follows:

> The company concentrates the bulk of its cash at the Second National Bank of Boise for cash management purposes. This typically results in cash investments exceeding Federal Deposit Insurance Corporation (FDIC) insurance limits. As of the statement of financial position date, €2,045,000 held as cash reserves at this bank exceeded the FDIC insurance limits.

Receivables—Bad Debt Recognition

The method by which a company derives its bad debt reserves should be noted in a footnote, including the amount of the reserve contained within the statement of financial position, and its method for recognizing bad debts. Any factors influencing the judgment of management in calculating the reserves also should be noted. An example follows:

> The company calculates a bad debt reserve based on a rolling average of actual bad debt losses over the past three months, divided by the average amount of accounts receivable outstanding during that period. It calculates separate loss percentages for its government and commercial receivables, since government receivables have a significantly lower loss rate. Given the current recession, management has elected to increase this calculated reserve by an additional 1.5%. As of the date of the statement of financial position, the loss reserve percentage for government receivables was 1.1%, while the reserve for commercial receivables was 2.9%. This resulted in a total loss reserve of €329,000 on outstanding accounts receivable of €18,275,000. The company recognizes all receivables as bad debts that have been unpaid for more than 90 days past their due dates, or earlier upon the joint agreement of management and the collections staff, or immediately if a customer declares bankruptcy.

Receivables—Separation of Types

Though different types of receivables may be clustered into a single line item on the statement of financial position, one should describe the different types of receivables in a footnote, describing each general category of receivable and the approximate amount of each type. An example follows:

> The ABC Truck Company had approximately €12,525,000 in accounts receivable as of the statement of financial position date. Of this amount, €485,000 was a short-term note due from a distributor, while €48,000 was for a cash advance to a company officer and €9,000 was for cash advances to non-key employees. The company expects all cash advances to be paid within 90 days, except for the advance to the company officer, which will be paid back as a single balloon payment in six months.

Receivables—Used as Collateral

When accounts receivable are pledged to a lender as collateral on a loan, the terms of the agreement should be described in the footnotes, as well as the carrying amount of the receivables so pledged. An example follows:

> The XYZ Scuba Supplies Company has entered into a loan agreement with the International Credit Consortium. Under the terms of the agreement, XYZ has pledged the full amount of its trade receivables as collateral on a revolving line of credit carrying a floating interest rate 2% above the prime rate. The amount loaned cannot exceed 80% of all outstanding accounts receivable billed within the past 90 days. As of the date of the statement of financial position, the total amount of accounts receivable subject to this agreement was €2,500,000.

JOURNAL ENTRIES

Cash

Bank reconciliation. To adjust the accounting records to reflect differences between the book and bank records. The cash entry is listed as a credit, on the assumption that bank-related expenses outweigh the interest income.

Bank charges	xxx	
Credit card charges	xxx	
Interest income		xxx
Cash		xxx

Receivables

Accounts receivable, initial entry. To record the creation of a receivable at the point when a sale is made. The entry includes the creation of a liability account for a sales tax. The second entry records the elimination of the account receivable when cash is received from the customer, while the third entry records the payment of sales taxes payable to the relevant government authority.

Accounts receivable	xxx	
Sales		xxx
Sales taxes payable		xxx
Cash	xxx	
Accounts receivable		xxx
Sales taxes payable	xxx	
Cash		xxx

Accounts receivable, recording of long-term payment terms. To record any accounts receivable not due for payment for at least one year. The receivable is discounted at no less than the market rate of interest. The first journal entry shows the initial record of sale, while the second entry shows the gradual recognition of interest income associated with the receivable.

Notes receivable	xxx	
Revenue		xxx
Discount on notes receivable		xxx
Discount on notes receivable	xxx	
Interest income		xxx

Accounts receivable, sale of. To record the outright sale of an account receivable, including the recognition of interest expense and any loss on the transaction due to the expected incurrence of bad debt losses by the factor on the purchased receivables.

Cash	xxx	
Factoring expense	xxx	
Loss on sale of receivables	xxx	
Interest expense	xxx	
Accounts receivable		xxx

Accounts receivable, payment due from factor. To record the outright sale of accounts receivable to a factor, but without taking payment until the due date of the underlying receivables, thereby avoiding interest expenses. The second entry records the eventual payment by the factor for the transferred receivables.

Receivable due from factor	xxx	
Factoring expense	xxx	
Loss on sale of receivables	xxx	
Accounts receivable		xxx
Cash	xxx	
Receivable due from factor		xxx

Accounts receivable, establishment of recourse obligation. To record an obligation to repay the factor for any bad debts experienced among the receivables sold to the factor for which the company is liable under a factoring with recourse arrangement. The second entry shows the recourse obligation being reduced as bad debts are incurred and the company pays back the factor for the receivables written off as bad debts.

Allowance for bad debts	xxx	
Recourse obligation		xxx
Recourse obligation	xxx	
Cash		xxx

Accounts receivable, write-off. To cancel an account receivable by offsetting it against the reserve for bad debts located in the bad debt accrual account.

Bad debt accrual	xxx	
Accounts receivable		xxx

Accrue bad debt expense. To accrue for projected bad debts, based on historical experience.

Bad debt expense	xxx	
Bad debt accrual		xxx

Account for receipt of written-off receivable. To record the receipt of cash on a sale that had previously been written off as uncollectible.

Cash	xxx	
Bad debt accrual		xxx

Accrue for sales returns. To accrue for expected sales returns from sales made on approval, based on historical experience.

Sales returns expense	xxx	
Reserve for sales returns		xxx

Early payment discounts, record receipt of. To record the amount of early payment discounts taken by customers as part of their payments for accounts receivable.

Cash	xxx	
Sales: Discounts taken	xxx	
Accounts receivable		xxx

RECORDKEEPING

Detailed and well-organized cash records are needed by all external auditors. Accordingly, all bank statements should be stored in a binder by account number and by date within each account number. In addition, a copy of the bank reconciliation for each month should be stored alongside each bank statement. If canceled checks are returned by the bank, they can be stored separately and labeled by month of receipt. If canceled checks are stored, one should pay the bank a small additional amount to sort the checks by check number prior to returning them to the company, which makes it much easier to locate checks in the archives.

Prepaid expenses should be reconciled as part of the month-end closing process, so there is no risk of an item continuing to be carried on the books as an asset when it should really have been written off as an expense. This is a common problem that can have serious ramifications at the end of the reporting year if large amounts of prepaid items have been ignored, resulting in large write-offs that drive profits below predicted levels. The best approach is to list not only the detail in the prepaid expense account, but also the date by which it is to be written off (if any) and the calculation method used to write it off over time. The spreadsheet should be retained in the journal entry file for each month in which a balance is maintained in the prepaid expense account. An example of such a reporting format is shown in Exhibit 2.10.

Exhibit 2.10: Itemization of Prepaid Expenses

Origination date	*Payee*	*Description*	*Termination date*	*Remaining amount*
1/07	MESE LLC	Employers' council annual dues (expense at 1/12 per month)	12/07	€3,200.00
7/07	LifeConcepts	Key man life insurance (expense at 1/6 per month)	12/07	5,800.00
8/07	CSE Software	Software maintenance fee (expense at 1/12 per month)	7/08	29,500.00
10/07	Halley & Burns	Annual audit fee (expense at 1/12 per month)	9/08	24,000.00
			Total	€62,500.00

Auditors reviewing a company's accounts receivable balances are interested primarily in an accounts receivable aging report that they can trace back to individual invoices and supporting documents. They show evidence of product shipment or services rendered, such as shipping logs, bills of lading, and employee time sheets showing evidence of time billed to customer projects. Thus, recordkeeping for accounts receivable should include a complete aging as of the fiscal year-end date, while invoices should be stored in order either by customer name or invoice number, so they can be easily traced back from the receivables aging document. The packet of information used to create each invoice, such as freight billing information, time sheets, bills of lading, customers, or shipping logs, should be stapled to each invoice, so that proof of delivery is easily accessible.

Accounts receivable information must also be stored for sales tax auditors. They will want to determine which invoices were billed within their state. Therefore, it is useful to have access to a report that sorts invoices by state, though a detailed sales journal is usually acceptable. In addition, one can regularly archive a report listing customer addresses, which government auditors can then use to trace back to the sales journal for those customers whose addresses are in the state for which sales tax remittances are being investigated. These auditors will trace back from the sales journal to individual invoices in order to test sales tax calculations; thus the same packets of invoice information described in the previous paragraph must be retained for this purpose too. Sales tax remittance forms must also be retained, since auditors will want to compare them to the records in the sales tax payable account in the general ledger to ensure that all liabilities are being properly paid to the applicable state sales tax revenue department.

Completed bad debt write-off forms should be sorted by date and stored in a separate binder in the archives. This information is particularly useful in situations where fraud by a collections person is suspected, and evidence is needed detailing the amounts of write-offs requested, the reasons given, and who approved the forms. Given the sensitive nature of this information, the binder should be stored in a secure location.

3 SHORT-TERM INVESTMENTS AND FINANCIAL INSTRUMENTS

DEFINITIONS OF TERMS

Cash flow hedge. A hedge, using a derivative or other financial instrument, of the exposure to variability in cash flows that is attributable to a particular risk associated with a recognized asset or liability (such as all or a portion of future interest payments on variable-rate debt) or a forecasted transaction (such as an anticipated purchase or sale) that will affect reported income or loss.

Comprehensive income. The change in the equity of an entity during a period resulting from transactions and other events and circumstances from nonowner sources. It includes all changes in net assets during a period, except those resulting from investments by owners and distributions to owners. It comprises all components of both "profit or loss" and "other comprehensive income."

Derivative. A financial instrument or other contract with all of three characteristics: (1) its value changes in response to changes in a specified interest rate, security price, commodity price, foreign exchange rate, index of prices or rates, a credit rating or credit index, or other variable, provided in the case of a nonfinancial variable that the variable is not specific to a party to the contract (sometimes called the "underlying"), (2) it requires little or no initial net investment relative to other types of contracts that have a similar response to changes in market conditions, and (3) it is settled at a future date. Examples of derivatives are interest rate caps and floors, option contracts, letters of credit, swaps, and futures.

Fair value hedge. A hedge, using a derivative or other financial instrument, of the exposure to changes in the fair value of a recognized asset or liability or an unrecognized firm commitment, or an identified portion of such an asset, liability, or firm commitment, that is attributable to a particular risk and will affect reported profit or loss (net income).

Financial instrument. Any contract that gives rise to both a financial asset of one entity and a financial liability or equity instrument of another entity.

Forecasted transaction. An expected transaction that has not yet occurred, and for which there is no final commitment.

Foreign currency hedge. A hedge designed to protect against future fluctuations in the value of an investment denominated in a foreign currency.

Hedge. Designating one or more hedging instruments such that the change in fair value is an offset, in whole or in part, to the change in the fair value or the cash flows of a hedged item.

Net investment hedge. A hedge of a net investment in a foreign operation.

Other comprehensive income. Items of income and expense (including reclassification adjustments) that are not recognized in profit or loss as required or permitted by other IFRS. The components of other recognized income include: (1) changes in revaluation surplus (IAS 38); (2) actuarial gains and losses on defined benefit plans (IAS 19); (3) translation gains and losses (IAS 21); (4) gains and losses on remeasuring available-for-sale financial assets (IAS 39); and (5) the effective portion of gains and losses on hedging instruments in a cash flow hedge (IAS 39).

Profit or loss. The total of income less expenses, excluding the components of other comprehensive income.

Reclassification adjustments. Amounts reclassified to profit or loss in the current period that were recognized in other comprehensive income in the current or previous periods.

CONCEPTS AND EXAMPLES

IAS 39 defines three types of hedging relationships: fair value hedges, cash flow hedges, and hedges of net investment in a foreign entity.

A hedge of the foreign currency risk of a firm commitment can be accounted for as a fair value hedge or as a cash flow hedge.

Fair Value Hedges

A hedging transaction qualifies as a fair value hedge only if both the hedging instrument and the hedged item qualify under all of these criteria:

- **Documentation.** At hedge inception, there is documentation of the relationship between the hedging instrument and the hedged item, the risk management objectives of the hedging transaction, how the hedge is to be undertaken, the method to be used for gain or loss recognition, identification of the instrument used for the hedge, and how the effectiveness calculation is measured.
- **Effectiveness.** There is a high level of expected effectiveness for the transaction to regularly create offsetting fair value changes that are attributable to the hedged risk, and consistent with the originally documented risk management strategy for that hedging relationship.
- **Assessment of effectiveness.** The hedge should be assessed on an ongoing basis and determined to have been effective throughout the financial reporting period. Under IAS 39, hedge accounting is permitted only when the hedge is

effective, which is defined by the degree of correlation of value changes in the hedging and hedged instruments.

A financial asset or liability is considered a hedged item to which a hedging instrument can be matched only if it qualifies under all of these criteria:

- It is not a held-to-maturity debt security, however; a held-to-maturity investment can be a hedged item with respect to risks from changes in foreign currency exchange rates and credit risk.
- It is exposed to fair value changes that can impact profit or loss.
- The documented hedge risk is comprised of fair value changes in the market interest rates, the total hedged item, foreign currency rates, or the obligor's creditworthiness.
- It is not an equity method investment, minority interest, or firm commitment to acquire or dispose of a business.
- It must be specifically associated with a fair value risk—changes in the fair value of a total hedged item (or a percentage thereof), specific contractual cash flows, the residual value of a lessor's net investment in a direct financing or sales-type lease, or a call, put, floor, or cap not qualifying as an embedded derivative.
- In a fair value hedge of the interest rate exposure of a portfolio of financial assets or financial liabilities (and only in such a hedge), the amount designated must be an amount of assets or an amount of liabilities. Designation of a net amount including assets and liabilities is not permitted.
- A nonfinancial asset, or a nonfinancial liability, should be designated as a hedged item (1) for foreign currency risks, or (2) in its entirety for all risks because of the difficulty of insolating and measuring the appropriate portion of the fair value changes attributable to specific risks.

Gains and losses on from remeasuring the hedging instrument at fair value are recognized in profit or loss. Gains and losses on the hedged item attributable to the hedged risk should adjust the carrying amount of the hedged item and be recognized in profit or loss. The impact of any ineffective amounts or factors excluded from a hedging relationship in its initial documentation is recognized in profit or loss. This accounting can continue until as the criteria for the hedge are no longer met, the hedging designation is canceled, or the derivative instruments used in the hedge are terminated. If any of these circumstances arise, a new hedging relationship can be documented with a different derivative instrument.

Macrohedging. As amended, IAS 39 permits the next eight rules to apply for purposes of accounting for a fair value hedge of a portfolio of interest rate risk:

1. The reporting entity identifies a portfolio of items whose interest rate risk it wishes to hedge. The portfolio may include both assets and liabilities, or could include only assets or only liabilities.
2. The reporting entity analyzes the portfolio into repricing time periods based on *expected*, rather than contractual, repricing dates.
3. The reporting entity then designates the hedged item as a percentage of the amount of assets (or liabilities) in each time period. All of the assets from

which the hedged amount is drawn have to be items (a) whose fair value changes in response to the risk being hedged and (b) that could have qualified for fair value hedge accounting under the original IAS 39 had they been hedged individually. The time periods have to be sufficiently narrow to ensure that all assets (or liabilities) in a time period are homogeneous with respect to the hedged risk—that is, the fair value of each item moves proportionately to, and in the same direction as, changes in the hedged interest rate risk.

4. The reporting entity designates what interest rate risk it is hedging. The risk may be a portion of the interest rate risk in each of the items in the portfolio, such as a benchmark interest rate like LIBOR or the US prime bank rate.
5. The reporting entity designates a hedging instrument for each time period. The hedging instrument may be a portfolio of derivatives (e.g., interest rate swaps) containing offsetting risk positions.
6. The reporting entity measures the change in the fair value of the hedged item that is attributable to the hedged risk. The result is then recognized in profit or loss and in one of two separate line items in the statement of financial position. The statement of financial position line item depends on whether the hedged item is an asset (in which case the change in fair value would be reported in a separate line item within assets) or is a liability (in which case the value change would be reported in a separate line item within liabilities). In either case, this separate statement of financial position line item is to be presented on the face of the statement of financial position adjacent to the related hedged item—but it is not permissible to allocate it to individual assets or liabilities, or to separate classes of assets or liabilities (i.e., it is not acceptable to employ "basis adjustment").
7. The reporting entity measures the change in the fair value of the hedging instrument and recognizes this as a gain or loss in profit or loss. It recognizes the fair value of the hedging instrument as an asset or liability in the statement of financial position.
8. Ineffectiveness will be given as the difference in profit or loss between the amounts determined in steps 6. and 7.

A change in the amounts that are expected to be repaid or mature in a time period will result in ineffectiveness, measured as the difference between (1) the initial hedge ratio applied to the initially estimated amount in a time period and (2) that same ratio applied to the revised estimate of the amount.

Under the provisions of IAS 39, assuming other conditions are also met, hedge accounting may be applied as long as, and to the extent that, the hedge is effective. A hedge is regarded as highly effective only if both of two conditions are met: (1) At the inception of the hedge and in subsequent periods, the hedge is expected to be highly effective in achieving offsetting changes in fair value or cash flows attributable to the hedged risk during the period for which the hedge is designated. By *effective*, the standard is alluding to the degree to which offsetting changes in fair values or cash flows attributable to the hedged risk are achieved by the hedging instrument. (2) A hedge is generally deemed effective if, at inception and throughout the period of the hedge, the ratio of changes in value of the underlying to changes in value of the hedging instrument are in a range of 80% to 125%. That is, changes in the value of the hedging instrument must be highly correlated with (but opposite in direction to) changes in value of the underlying (hedged) item.

The periodic determination of hedging effectiveness first requires the establishment of the method to be used to make the assessment, as well as the designation of what type of fair value change in the derivative instrument will be used to assess the hedge effectiveness. The method used depends on an entity's risk management strategy. Hedge effectiveness, at the very least, must be evaluated at the time an entity prepares its annual or interim financial statements. It must include an assessment of both the retrospective and prospective ability of the hedging instrument to manage the designated risk. Both assessments can be accomplished through statistical analysis.

Cash Flow Hedges

A cash flow hedge is designed to cope with uncertain future cash flows. To establish a valid cash flow hedge, one must document the relationship between the hedging instrument and an asset, liability, or forecasted transaction (including expected date of occurrence and amount). The documentation must also describe the hedging strategy, risk management objectives, and how the effectiveness of the transaction is to be measured.

In addition, the hedging relationship must be expected to be highly effective, and, at a minimum, must be evaluated at the time an entity prepares its annual or interim financial statements.

It is possible to match a forecasted transaction with a hedging instrument, but only under certain circumstances: If the forecasted transaction is *probable* of occurrence, it will not be a held-to-maturity debt security; it is specifically identified; it could affect earnings; it will be with an external counterparty; and it does not involve a business combination or any equity investment.

One must discontinue a cash flow hedge when the hedge criteria are no longer met, the hedging designation is canceled, or the derivative instruments used in the hedge are terminated. If any of these circumstances arise, a new hedging relationship can be documented with a different derivative instrument.

When reporting derivative gains and losses for a cash flow hedge, the portion of the gains or losses on the hedging instrument determined to be effective should be recognized in other comprehensive income. Any gains or losses attributable to the ineffective portion of the hedge are recognized currently in profit or loss.

According to IAS 39, the separate component of equity associated with the hedged item is to be adjusted to the *lesser* of two amounts: (1) the cumulative gain or loss on the hedging instrument needed to offset the cumulative change in expected future cash flows on the hedged item from inception of the hedge, less the portion associated with the ineffective component, or (2) the fair value of the cumulative change in expected future cash flows on the hedged item from inception of the hedge. Any remaining gain or loss (i.e., the ineffective portion of the hedge) is either taken to profit or loss or other comprehensive income as described earlier.

Revised IAS 39 requires that when a hedged forecasted transaction occurs and results in the recognition of a *financial asset* or a *financial liability*, the gain or loss recognized in other comprehensive income does not adjust the initial carrying amount of the asset or liability; thus, the formerly acceptable method of basis adjustment has now been prohibited. This remains in other comprehensive income and is reclassified from equity to profit or loss as a reclassification adjustment (see IAS 1 [revised 2007]). However, for hedges of forecast transactions that result in the recognition of a *nonfinancial asset* or a *nonfinancial liability*, the entity may elect whether to apply basis adjustment or retain the hedging gain or loss in other comprehensive income and report it in profit or loss when the asset or liability affects profit or loss.

In the case of other cash flow hedges (i.e., those not resulting in recognition of assets or liabilities), the amounts reflected in other comprehensive income will be reclassified from equity to profit or loss as a reclassification adjustment in the same period or periods when the hedged firm forecast transaction (or commitment) affects profit or loss.

Hedge accounting is to be discontinued when the hedging instrument is sold, expires, is terminated or exercised. If the gain or loss was accumulated in other comprehensive income, it should remain there until such time as the forecasted transaction occurs, when it is added to the asset or liability recorded, or when it is reclassified to profit or loss as a reclassification adjustment at the time the transaction impacts profit or loss. Hedge accounting is also discontinued prospectively when the hedge ceases meeting the criteria for qualification of hedge accounting. The accumulated gain or loss remains in other comprehensive income until the forecasted (or committed) transaction occurs, whereupon it will be accounted for as discussed earlier.

Finally, if the forecasted transaction is no longer expected to occur, hedge accounting is prospectively discontinued. In this case, the accumulated gain or loss must be reclassified from equity to profit or loss immediately.

A hedge is generally deemed effective if, at inception and throughout the period of the hedge, the ratio of changes in value of the underlying to changes in value of the hedging instrument are in a range of 80% to 125%.

Hedge effectiveness will be heavily impacted by the nature of the instruments used for hedging. For example, interest rate swaps will be almost completely effective if the notional and principal amounts match and the terms, repricing dates, interest and principal payment dates, and basis for measurement are the same. However, if the hedged and hedging instruments are denominated in different currencies, effectiveness will most likely not be 100%. Also, if the rate change is due partially to changes in perceived credit risk, there will be a lack of perfect correlation.

Net Investment Hedge

Hedges of a net investment in a foreign entity are accounted for similarly to those of cash flows. To the extent it is determined to be effective, accumulated gains or losses are reflected in other comprehensive income. The ineffective portion is reported in profit or loss.

In terms of financial reporting, the gain or loss on the effective portion of these hedges should be classified in the same manner as the foreign currency translation gain or loss. According to IAS 21, revised in 2007, translation gains and losses are not reported in profit or loss but instead are reported in other comprehensive income (as part of total comprehensive income for the year) with allocation being made to minority interest when the foreign entity is not wholly owned by the reporting entity. Likewise, any hedging gain or loss would be reported in other comprehensive income. When the foreign entity is disposed of, the accumulated translation gain or loss would be reclassified from equity to profit or loss as a reclassification adjustment, as would any related deferred hedging gain or loss.

When a hedge does not qualify for special hedge accounting (due to failure to properly document, ineffectiveness, etc.), any gains or losses are to be accounted for based on the nature of the hedging instrument. If the item is a derivative financial instrument, the gains or losses must be reported in profit or loss.

Foreign Currency Hedges

In brief, the accounting for various types of foreign currency hedges is described next.

- **Available-for-sale security hedge.** One can designate a derivative instrument as a fair value hedge for an available-for-sale *equity* security only if all fair value hedge criteria are met, the payments to equity holders are denominated in the same currency to be received upon sale of the security, and the security is not publicly traded in the investor's functional currency. These restrictions do not apply if the available-for-sale security is a debt security.
- **Debt-for-equity swaps.** If a company's foreign debt is legally required to be reinvested in that country, one must first determine the difference between the values of the debt and the equity in which it is invested. The difference must first be used to reduce the basis of acquired long-term assets and then to reduce the basis of existing long-term assets, with any remaining variance being treated as negative goodwill.
- **Forecasted transaction in foreign currency denomination.** One can designate a derivative instrument as a cash flow hedge of a forecasted transaction denominated in a foreign currency. Cash flow hedge accounting can be used only if the transaction is not denominated in the functional currency, all cash flow hedge criteria are met, foreign currency inflows and outflows are not included in the same groups of transactions, and one party to the transaction is an operating unit with foreign currency exposure.
- **Net investment hedge.** One can designate a derivative or financial instrument as a foreign currency hedge for an investment in a foreign operation. Any effective gain or loss is reported in other comprehensive income as exchange differences (translation adjustment).
- **Unrecognized firm commitment hedge.** One can designate a derivative or financial instrument as a fair value hedge of an unrecognized firm commitment in a foreign currency. A hedge of foreign currency risk arising from a

firm commitment may be accounted for as a fair value hedge or as a cash flow hedge.

POLICIES

Hedges—General

- **The determination of hedge effectiveness will always use the same method for similar types of hedges.** IFRS allows one to use different assessment techniques in determining whether a hedge is highly effective. The method an entity adopts for assessing hedge effectiveness depends on its risk management strategy. However, changing methods, even when justified, allows the accounting staff to alter effectiveness designations, which can yield variations in the reported profit or loss. This can create a negative impression of earning manipulation and is suggestive of poor controls. Consequently, creating and consistently using a standard assessment method for each type of hedge eliminates the risk of assessment manipulation.
- **A hedge will be considered highly effective if the fair values of the hedging instrument and hedged item are at least ___% offset.** A hedge is generally deemed effective if, at inception and throughout the period of the hedge, the ratio of changes in value of the underlying to changes in value of the hedging instrument are in a range of 80% to 125%. A company should create a policy defining the numbers, but no more liberally than the limits set forth under IFRS. A different hedging range can be used for different types of hedges, if doing so is warranted by the facts and circumstances and not varied for earnings management purposes.

CONTROLS

Hedges—General

- **Include in the hedging procedure a requirement for full documentation of each hedge.** Hedging accounting is allowed under IFRS only if transactions are fully documented at the inception of the hedge. One can ensure compliance by including the documentation requirement in an accounting procedure for creating hedges.

Fair Value Hedges

- **Include in the closing procedure a requirement to review the effectiveness of any fair value hedges.** IFRS requires that hedging transactions be accounted for as fair value hedges only if a hedging relationship regularly produces offsets to fair value changes. Since this review must be conducted, at a minimum, at the time an entity prepares its annual or interim financial statements, including the requirement in the closing procedure is an effective way to ensure compliance with IFRS.
- **Compare hedging effectiveness assessments to what is prescribed by the corporate policy setting forth effectiveness ranges.** The actual results of the

hedge should be within a range of 80% to 125%, and hedged items must offset each other in order to be deemed highly effective; therefore a corporate policy should be established (see the Policies section) to create such a standard. This control is intended to ensure that the policy is followed when making effectiveness assessments. Comparison to the corporate policy should be included in the assessment procedure.

Cash Flow Hedges

- **Include in the monthly financial statement preparation procedure a review of the recoverability of cash flow hedge losses.** IFRS requires that a nonrecoverable cash flow hedge loss be reclassified in the current period from equity to profit or loss. Since this can only result in a reduced level of earnings, accounting personnel tend not to conduct the review. Including the step in the monthly procedure is a good way to ensure prompt loss recognition.
- **Include in the monthly financial statement procedure a review of the likely occurrence of forecasted cash flow transactions.** IFRS requires that any accumulated gain or loss recorded in other comprehensive income be shifted into profit or loss as soon as the forecasted cash flow transaction is no longer expected to occur. Including a standard periodic review of forecasted transactions in the monthly procedure is a good way to ensure prompt inclusion of accumulated gains or losses in profit or loss.
- **Compare hedging effectiveness assessments to the corporate policy setting forth effectiveness ranges.** Although under IFRS the actual results of the hedge should be within a range of 80% to 125%, a corporate policy should be established (see the Policies section) to create such a standard. This control is intended to ensure that the policy is followed when making effectiveness assessments. Comparison to the corporate policy should be included in the assessment procedure.

FOOTNOTES

Short-Term Investments

A company should disclose the types of investments it makes on a short-term basis as well as their usual term and how they are recorded in the financial records. An example follows.

> The company invests all excess cash over €1 million in marketable [illegible]ks and bonds. All stocks held are required by company policy to be of companies [illegible] on the Euronex, while all bonds must be of investment grade. Given the company's high tax bracket, it keeps at least 50% of all excess cash invested in investm[illegible]de tax-free municipal bonds. These investments are carried at cost, which ap[illegible]ates market pricing.

Restricted Short-Term Investments

If there is a restriction on the ability of a company to access its invested funds, this information should be disclosed, along with the reason for the restriction, the amount restricted, and the duration of the restriction period. An example follows.

> The company is required by the terms of its building term loan with the First National Bank of Australia to restrict all investments related to its loan for the construction of a new corporate headquarters. Accordingly, the First National Bank has custody over these funds, which are invested in short-term Australian Treasury funds yielding approximately 3.25%. The restricted amount is AUD 4,525,000 as of the statement of financial position date and is expected to be eliminated as of year-end, when the headquarters building will be completed and all contractors paid.

Disclosure of Objectives for Derivative Use

If a company is party to a derivative financial instrument, it should state its objective, the related strategies for using such an instrument, and what specific risks are being hedged with its use. Additional disclosures required for fair value and cash flow hedges follow.

- **Fair value hedge.** One must disclose the net gain or loss recognized in profit or loss during the period stemming from the ineffective portion of a fair value hedge, as well as any derivative instrument's gain or loss excluded from the assessment of hedge effectiveness. If a hedged firm commitment no longer qualifies as a fair value hedge, then disclosure must also include the resulting gain or loss shown in profit or loss.
- **Cash flow hedge.** One must disclose the net gain or loss recognized in profit or loss during the period stemming from the ineffective portion of a cash flow hedge, as well as any derivative instrument's gain or loss excluded from the assessment of hedge effectiveness. One also must note the future events that will result in the reclassification of gains or losses from other equity into profit or loss, as well as the net amount expected to be reclassified in the next year.

  Further, one must itemize the maximum time period over which the company hedges its exposure to cash flows from forecasted transactions (if any). Finally, if forecasted transactions are no longer expected to occur, one must note the amount of gains or losses reclassified from equity to profit or loss as a result of canceling the hedge.

[illegible] first footnote sample is for a fair value hedge, while the second addresses a cash [illegible]w hedge.

1.

> [illegible]e Company designates certain futures contracts as fair value hedges of firm com[illegible]ments to purchase coal for electricity generation. Changes in the fair value of a [illegible]tive that is highly effective and that is designated and qualifies as a fair value [illegible] along with the loss or gain on the hedged asset or liability that is attributable [illegible]dged risk are recorded in current period profit or loss. Ineffectiveness re[illegible] the change in the fair value of the hedge instruments differs from the [illegible]ir value of the hedged item. Ineffectiveness recorded related to the [illegible]ir value hedges was not significant during fiscal 20[illegible].

2. If a derivative instrument used by the Company in a cash flow hedge is sold, terminated, or exercised, the net gain or loss remains in equity and is reclassified into profit or loss in the same period when the hedged transaction affects earnings. Accordingly, accumulated other comprehensive income reported in equity at September 30, 2008, includes €6.5 million of the loss realized upon termination of derivative instruments that will be reclassified into profit or loss over the original term of the derivative instruments, which extend through December 2012. As of September 30, 2008, the Company had entered into contracts for derivative instruments, designated as cash flow hedges, covering 200,000 tons of coal with a floor price of €58 per ton and a ceiling price of €69 per ton, resulting in other current assets of €0.7 million and €0.7 million of accumulated other comprehensive income representing the effective portion of unrealized hedge gains associated with these derivative instruments.

Valuation of Financial Instruments

If a reporting entity has outstanding financial instruments, it must describe the method and assumptions used to estimate their fair value. If it is impossible to determine fair value, then it must disclose the carrying amount, effective interest rate, and maturity of the instruments, as well as why it is not possible to determine their fair value.

> The Company's significant financial instruments include cash and cash equivalents, investments and debt. In evaluating the fair value of significant financial instruments, the Company generally uses quoted market prices of the same or similar instruments or calculates an estimated fair value on a discounted cash flow basis using the rates available for instruments with the same remaining maturities. As of December 31, 2008, the fair value of financial instruments held by the Company approximated the recorded value except for long-term debt. Fair value of long-term debt was €2.9 billion on December 31, 2008.

Hedging of Foreign Operation Investment

When a company hedges its investment in a foreign operation, it must disclose the net gain or loss incorporated within the cumulative translation adjustment. This applies to any derivative or hedging instruments that may cause foreign currency gains or losses. An example follows.

> The company has invested €40 million in a manufacturing facility in Dubai. It has entered into certain foreign currency derivative instruments that are designed to hedge its investment in this facility. The cumulative exchange differences account includes a net loss of €1,240,000 from these derivative instruments.

RECORDKEEPING

At the inception of a fair value hedge, IFRS requires documentation of the relationship between the hedging instrument and the hedged item, the hedging strategy, the risk management objectives of the hedging transaction, how the hedge is to be undertaken, the method to be used for gain or loss recognition, the identification of the instrument used for the hedge, and how the effectiveness calculation is measured. Since hedge accounting cannot be used unless this documentation exists, it is important to store a complete set of documentations for each hedge for the duration not only of the hedge, but also through the audit following the hedge termination. It can then be included in the archives with accounting documentation for the year in which the transaction terminated.

4 INVENTORY

DEF[INITIONS OF TERMS]

Book invent[ory] … pany's accountin[g] … cost of any rece[ived] … cantly different … odically.

Consignm[ent] … a third party b…

to the consignee. The inventory continues to be recorded on the books of the owning entity until it has been sold.

Cycle counting. The ongoing incremental counting of perpetual inventory records, with the intent of correcting record inaccuracies and determining the underlying causes of those errors.

Finished goods. Completed manufactured goods that have not yet been sold.

First-in, first-out. A process costing methodology that assigns the earliest cost of production and materials to units being sold, while the latest costs of production and materials are assigned to units still retained in inventory.

Inventory. Assets held for sale in the normal course of business, that are in the process of production for such sale, or that are in the form of materials or supplies to be consumed in the production process or in the rendering of services.

Last-in, first-out. An inventory costing methodology that bases the recognized cost of sales on the most recent costs incurred, while the cost of ending inventory is based on the earliest costs incurred. Formerly permitted by IFRS, the use of LIFO has now been banned.

Lower of cost and net realizable value. Inventories must be valued at lower of cost or realizable value.

Periodic. Inventory system where quantities are determined only periodically by physical count.

Perpetual. Inventory system where up-to-date records of inventory quantities are kept.

Raw materials. For a manufacturing firm, materials on hand awaiting entry into the production process.

Scrap. The excess unusable material left over after a product has been manufactured.

Specific identification. Inventory system where the seller identifies which specific items are sold and which remain in ending inventory.

Spoilage, abnormal. Spoilage arising from the production process that exceeds ...l or expected rate of spoilage. Since it is not a recurring or expected cost ...roduction, its expensed to the current period.

...ormal. The amount of spoilage that naturally arises as part of a pro... matter how efficient the process may be.

... For a manufacturing firm, the inventory of partially com-

...EPTS AND EXAMPLES

... continues to be owned by the seller as ...portation costs. If the seller is paying ...s to a third-party shipper, then its ... buyer.

... transit, preferring instead not ...in the case of the seller) or have not yet arrived at the facility (in the case of the buyer). The reason for avoiding this task is the difficulty in determining the amount of goods in transit that belong to the company, especially when the accounting staff is trying to close the books very quickly and does not want to keep the books open long enough to make a proper determination. This avoidance has minimal impact on the receiving company's recordkeeping, since a missing inventory item would have required both a debit to an inventory account and a credit to a liability account, which cancel each other out. This is more of an issue for the shipping firm, since it is probably recognizing revenue at the point of shipment, rather than at some later point in transit, which can potentially overstate revenue if this occurs near the end of the reporting period and is not mitigated or fully offset by a similar situation at the beginning of the reporting period.

Examples of different types of transit scenarios

- If goods are shipped under a cost, insurance and freight (C&F) contract, the buyer is paying for all delivery costs and so acquires title to the goods as soon as they leave the seller's location.
- If goods are shipped Free Alongside (FAS), the seller is paying for delivery of the goods to the side of the ship that will transport the goods to the buyer. If so, it retains ownership of the goods until they are alongside the ship, at which point the buyer acquires title to the goods.
- If goods are shipped Free on Board (FOB) destination, then transport costs are paid by the seller, and ownership will not pass to the buyer until the carrier delivers the goods to the buyer.
- As indicated by the name, an Ex-Ship delivery means that the seller pays for a delivery until it has departed the ship, so it retains title to the goods until that point.
- If goods are shipped FOB shipping point, then transport costs are paid by the buyer, and ownership passes to the buyer as soon as the carrier takes possession of the delivery from the seller.
- If goods are shipped FOB a specific point, such as Nashville, then the seller retains title until the goods reach Nashville, at which point ownership transfers to the buyer.

Accounting for Inventories

The type and quantity of items stored in inventory can be accounted for on a periodic basis by using the *periodic inventory system,* which requires one to conduct a complete count of the physical inventory in order to obtain a calculation of the inventory cost. A more advanced method that does not require a complete inventory count is the perpetual inventory system; under this approach, one incrementally adds or subtracts inventory transactions to or from a beginning database of inventory records in order to maintain an ongoing balance of inventory quantities. The accuracy of the inventory records under this latter approach will likely degrade over time, so an ongoing cycle counting program is needed to maintain its accuracy level.

The **perpetual inventory system** is highly recommended, because it avoids expensive periodic inventory counts, which also tend not to yield accurate results. Also, it allows the purchasing staff to have greater confidence in what inventory is on hand for purchasing planning purposes. Further, accountants can complete period-end financial statements more quickly, without having to guess at ending inventory levels.

Perpetual inventory example

A company wishes to install a perpetual inventory system, but it has not established tight control over the warehouse area with fencing or gate control. Accordingly, production employees are able to enter the warehouse and remove items from the shelf for use in the manufacturing process. Because of this issue, inventory balances in the perpetual inventory system are chronically higher than is the really the case, since removed items are not being logged out of the system.

The scenario changes to one where the company has not assigned responsibility for inventory accuracy to anyone in the company but still creates a perpetual inventory system. As a result, the employees charged with entering inventory transactions into the computer system have no reason to do so, and no one enforces high accuracy levels. In this case, inventory accuracy levels rapidly worsen, especially for those items being used on a regular basis, since they are most subject to transactional inaccuracies. Only the inventory of slow-moving items remains relatively accurate.

The scenario changes to one where transactional procedures have not been clearly established, and employees entering inventory transactions have not been properly trained. This results in the worst accuracy levels of the three scenarios, since employees are not even certain if they should be adding or subtracting quantities, what units of measure to enter, or what special transactions call for what types of computer entries.

Consigned inventory is any inventory shipped by a company to a reseller while retaining ownership until the product is sold by the reseller. Until it is sold, the inventory remains on the books of the originating company, and it is not on the books of the reseller. A common cause of inventory valuation problems is the improper recording of consignment inventory on the books of a reseller. Inventory that has been sold with a *right of return* receives treatment similar to consignment inventory if the amount of future inventory returns cannot be reasonably estimated. Until the probability of returns is unlikely, the inventory must remain on the books of the selling company, even though legal title to the goods has passed to the buyer.

Right of return example

A company has sold a large shipment of refrigerators to a new customer. Included in the sales agreement is a provision allowing the customer to return one-third of the refrigerators within the next 90 days. Since the company has no experience with this customer, it cannot record the full amount of the sale. Instead, it records that portion of the sale associated with the refrigerators for which there is no right of return, and waits 90 days until the right of return has expired before recording the remainder of the sale.

Valuation of Inventories

Overhead costs allocable to inventory. All costs can be assigned to inventory that are incurred to put goods in a salable condition. For raw materials, this includes the purchase price, inbound transportation costs, insurance, and handling costs. If inventory is in the work-in-process or finished goods stages, then an allocation of the overhead costs shown in Exhibit 4.1 must be added.

Exhibit 4.1 Costs to Allocate to Overhead

Depreciation of factory equipment	Quality control and inspection
Factory administration expenses	Rent, facility and equipment
Indirect labor and production supervisory wages	Repair expenses
Indirect materials and supplies	Rework labor, scrap and spoilage
Maintenance, factory and production equipment	Taxes related to production assets
Officer salaries related to production	Uncapitalized tools and equipment
Production employees' benefits	Utilities

Allocation of overhead costs can be made by any reasonable measure, but it must be applied consistently across reporting periods. Common bases for overhead allocation are direct labor hours or machine hours used during the production of a product.

Overhead allocation example

A company manufactures and sells Product A and Product B. Both require considerable machining to complete, so it is appropriate to allocate overhead costs to them based on total hours of standard machine time used. In March, Product A manufacturing required a total of 4,375 hours of machine time. During the same month, all units of Product B manufactured required 2,615 hours of machine time. Thus, 63% of the overhead cost pool was allocated to Product A and 37% was allocated to Product B. This example results in a reasonably accurate allocation of overhead to products—especially if the bulk of expenses in the overhead pool relate to the machining equipment used to complete the products. However, if a significant proportion of expenses in the overhead cost pool could be reasonably assigned to some other allocation measure, then these costs could be stored in a separate cost pool and allocated in a different manner. For example, if Product A was quite bulky and required 90% of the storage space in the warehouse, as opposed to 10% for Product B, then 90% of the warehouse-related overhead costs could be reasonably allocated to Product A.

Lower of cost or net realizable value. In accordance with IAS 2, inventories are measured at the lower of cost or net realizable value. Net realizable value is the net amount that an entity expects to realize from the sale of inventory in the ordinary course of business. It is defined in IAS 2 as the estimated selling price in the ordinary course of business, less the estimated costs of completion and the estimated costs necessary to make the sale. Estimates of net realizable value should be made at least at the date of the statement of financial position, or earlier during the reporting period when management becomes aware that goods or services can no longer be sold at a price above cost.

The next example illustrates the application of lower of cost or net realizable value (NRV) measurement rule.

Item	*Quantity*	*Selling price*	–	*Completion/ selling cost*	=	*NRV per unit*	*Cost per unit*	*Lowest of cost and NRV per unit*	*Inventory at lower of cost and NRV*
A	246	€15.00		€4.00		€11.00	€8.50	€8.50	€2091.00
B	100	40.15		6.00		34.15	35.00	34.15	3415.00
C	178	20.00		6.50		13.50	17.00	13.50	2403.00
D	254	10.50		2.35		8.15	8.00	8.00	2667.00
Inventory at the lower of cost and net realizable value									€10,576.00

Using this information, the lower of cost and net realizable value (NRV) calculation for each of the listed products is

- **Product A, NRV higher than existing inventory cost.** The NRV of €11.00 is higher than the existing inventory cost of €8.50. Thus, the lower of cost and NRV is the same as the existing inventory cost.
- **Product B, NRV lower than existing inventory cost.** The NRV of €34.15 is lower than the existing inventory cost of €35.00, so the lower of cost and NRV becomes €34.15.
- **Product C, NRV lower than existing inventory cost.** The NRV of €13.50 is lower than the existing inventory cost of €17.00, so the lower of cost and NRV becomes €13.50.
- **Product D, NRV higher than existing inventory cost.** The NRV of €8.15 is higher than the existing inventory cost of €8.00, so the lower of cost and NRV becomes €8.00.

Revised IAS 2 states that estimates of net realizable value should be applied on an item-by-item basis in most instances, although it makes an exception for those situations where there are groups of related products or similar items that can be properly valued in the aggregate.

A company is required to write down—and recognize an additional expense in its cost of goods sold in the current period—any of its inventory whose net realizable value has declined below its carrying cost, as a result of a falling selling price, physical deterioration, obsolescence, and so on. If the net realizable value of the inventory subsequently rises back to or above its original carrying cost, the amount of a previous write-down can be reversed—but not in excess of the original write-down. As a result, the recorded value of the inventory after the reversal of prior write-down to net realizable value cannot exceed the original carrying amount.

Specific identification inventory valuation method. When each individual item of inventory can be clearly identified, it is possible to create inventory costing records for each one, rather than summarizing costs by general inventory type. This approach is rarely used, since the amount of paperwork and effort associated with developing unit costs is far greater than under all other valuation techniques. It is most applicable in businesses like home construction, where there are very few units of inventory to track and where each item is truly unique.

Under the current IFRS on inventories, revised IAS 2, there are two acceptable cost flow assumptions: (1) first-in, first-out (FIFO) method and (2) weighted-average method. In certain jurisdictions, other costing methods, such as the last-in, first-out (LIFO) method and the base stock method, continue to be permitted (e.g., in the United States, LIFO costing remains popular, since it provides tax advantages during periods of rising prices). The LIFO method was an allowed alternative method of costing inventories under IAS 2 until its most recent revision, in 2003 (effective 2005), at which time it was banned.

First-in, first-out (FIFO) inventory valuation method. A computer manufacturer knows that the component parts it purchases are subject to extremely rapid rates of obsolescence, sometimes rendering a part worthless in a month or two. Accordingly, it will be sure to use up the oldest items in stock first, rather than running the risk of scrapping them a short way into the future. For this type of environment, the first-in, first-out (FIFO) method is the ideal way to deal with the flow of costs. This method assumes that the oldest parts in stock are always used first, which means that their associated old costs are used first as well.

The concept is best illustrated with an example, which is set forth in Exhibit 4.2. In the first row, a single layer of inventory results in 50 units of inventory, at a per-unit cost of €10.00. In the second row of data, monthly inventory usage of 350 units is recorded, which FIFO assumes will use the entire stock of 50 inventory units that were left over at the end of the preceding month, as well as 300 units that were purchased in the current month. This eliminates the first cost layer of inventory, leaving a single new layer that is composed of 700 units at a cost of €9.58 per unit. In the third row, 400 units of usage is reflected, which comes from the new first inventory layer, shrinking it down to just 300 units. However, since extra stock was purchased in the same period, we now have an extra inventory layer that is comprised of 250 units, at a cost of €10.65 per unit. The rest of the exhibit proceeds using the same FIFO layering assumptions.

Exhibit 4.2 FIFO Valuation Example

Part Number BK0043

Col. 1	Col. 2	Col. 3	Col. 4	Col. 5	Col. 6	Col. 7	Col. 8	Col. 9
Date purchased	*Quantity purchased*	*Cost per unit*	*Monthly usage*	*Net inventory remaining*	*Cost of 1st inventory layer*	*Cost of 2nd inventory layer*	*Cost of 3rd inventory layer*	*Extended inventory cost*
05/03/08	500	€10.00	450	50	(50 × €10.00)	--	--	€500
06/04/08	1,000	9.58	350	700	(700 × €9.58)	--	--	6,706
07/11/08	250	10.65	400	550	(300 × €9.58)	(250 × €0.65)	--	5,537
08/01/08	475	10.25	350	675	(200 × €10.65)	(475 × €0.25)	--	6,999
08/30/08	375	10.40	400	650	(275 × €10.40)	(375 × €0.40)	--	6,760
09/09/08	850	9.50	700	800	(800 × €9.50)	--	--	7,600
12/12/08	700	9.75	900	600	(600 × €9.75)	--	--	5,850
02/08/09	650	9.85	800	450	(450 × €9.85)	--	--	4,433
05/07/09	200	10.80	0	650	(450 × €9.85)	(200 × €0.80)	--	6,593
09/23/09	600	9.85	750	500	(500 × €9.85)	--	--	4,925

There are some factors to consider before implementing a FIFO costing system.

- **Reduces taxes payable in periods of declining costs.** The it is unusual in recent decades to see declining inventory costs, it sometimes occurs in industries where there is aggressive price competition among suppliers or extremely high rates of innovation that in turn lead to cost reductions. In such cases, using the earliest costs first will result in the immediate recognition of the highest inventory costs being charged to expense, reducing the reported profit level and reducing the taxes payable.
- **Shows higher profits in periods of rising costs.** Since it charges off the earliest costs first, any very recent increase in costs will be stored in inventory rather than being immediately recognized. This will result in higher levels of reported profits, although the attendant income tax liability will also be higher.
- **Less risk of outdated costs in inventory.** Because earliest costs are used first in a FIFO system, there is no way for old and outdated costs to accumu-

late in inventory. This prevents the management group from having to worry about the adverse impact of inventory reductions on reported levels of profit, either with excessively high or excessively low charges to the cost of goods sold. Invasion of lower-cost inventory layers was a common problem under LIFO costing, but that method has now been banned under IFRS.

In short, the FIFO cost layering system tends to result in the inclusion of the most recently incurred costs in inventory and thus in higher levels of reported profits. It is most useful for those companies whose main concern is reporting high profits rather than reducing income taxes.

Weighted-average inventory valuation method. The weighted-average costing method is calculated in accordance with its name—it is a weighted-average of the costs in inventory. The advantage of this method is its simplicity, since it does not require a database that itemizes the many potential layers of inventory at the different costs at which they were acquired. Instead, the weighted-average of all units in stock is determined, at which point *all* of the units in stock are accorded that weighted-average value. When parts are used from stock, they are all issued at the same weighted-average cost. If new units are added to stock, then the cost of the additions are added to the weighted-average of all existing items in stock. This will result in a new, slightly modified weighted average for *all* of the parts in inventory (both the old and new ones).

This system is easy to apply and well suited to homogeneous inventory items. It is also useful for very small inventory valuations, where there would not be any significant change in the reported level of income, even if the FIFO method were to be used.

Exhibit 4.3 illustrates the weighted-average calculation for inventory valuations, using a series of 10 purchases of inventory. There is a maximum of one purchase per month, with usage (reductions from stock) also occurring in most months. Each of the columns in the exhibit shows how the average cost is calculated after each purchase and usage transaction.

Exhibit 4.3 FIFO Weighted-Average Costing Valuation Example

Part Number BK0043

Col. 1	Col.2	Col.3	Col.4	Col.5	Col.6	Col.7	Col.8	Col.9
Date purchased	*Quantity purchased*	*Cost per unit*	*Monthly usage*	*Net inventory remaining*	*Net change in inventory during period*	*Extended cost of new inventory layer*	*Extended inventory cost*	*Average inventory cost/unit*
05/03/08	500	€10.00	450	50	50	€500	€500	€10.00
06/04/08	1,000	9.58	350	700	650	6,227	6,727	9.61
07/11/08	250	10.65	400	550	(150)	0	5,286	9.61
08/01/08	475	10.25	350	675	125	1,281	6,567	9.73
08/30/08	375	10.40	400	650	(25)	0	6,324	9.73
09/09/08	850	9.50	700	800	150	1,425	7,749	9.69
12/12/08	700	9.75	900	600	(200)	0	5,811	9.69
02/08/09	650	9.85	800	450	(150)	0	4,359	9.69
05/07/09	200	10.80	0	650	200	2,160	6,519	10.03
09/23/09	600	9.85	750	500	(150)	0	5,014	10.03

We begin the illustration with the first row of calculations, which shows that we have purchased 500 units of item BK0043 on May 3, 2008. These units cost €10.00 per unit. During the month in which the units were purchased, 450 units were sent to production, leaving 50 units in stock. Since there has been only one purchase thus far, we can easily calculate, as shown in column 7, that the total inventory valuation is €500, by multiplying the unit cost of €10.00 (in column 3) by the number of units left in stock (in column 5). So far, we have a per-unit valuation of €10.00.

Next we proceed to the second row of the exhibit, where we have purchased another 1,000 units of BK0043 on June 4, 2008. This purchase was less expensive, since the purchasing volume was larger, so the per-unit cost for this purchase is only €9.58. Only 350 units are sent to production during the month, so we now have 700 units in stock, of which 650 are added from the most recent purchase. To determine the new weighted-average cost of the total inventory, we first determine the extended cost of this newest addition to the inventory. As noted in column 7, we arrive at €6,227 by multiplying the value in column 3 by the value in column 6. We then add this amount to the existing total inventory valuation (€6,227 plus €500) to arrive at the new extended inventory cost of €6,727, as noted in column 8. Finally, we divide this new extended cost in column 8 by the total number of units now in stock, as shown in column 5, to arrive at our new per-unit cost of €9.61.

The third row reveals an additional inventory purchase of 250 units on July 11, 2008, but more units are sent to production during that month than were bought, so the total number of units in inventory drops to 550 (column 5). This inventory reduction requires no review of inventory layers, as was the case for the FIFO calculations. Instead, we simply charge off the 150-unit reduction at the average per-unit cost of €9.61. As a result, the ending inventory valuation drops to €5,286, with the same per-unit cost of €9.61. Thus, reductions in inventory quantities under the average costing method require little calculation—just charge off the requisite number of units at the current average cost.

The remaining rows of the exhibit repeat the concepts just noted, alternatively adding units to and deleting them from stock. Though there are a number of columns to examine in this exhibit, the concept is simple to understand and work with. The typical computerized accounting system will perform all of the calculations automatically.

DECISION TREES

The decision tree in Exhibit 4.4 shows how to determine which entity owns inventory that is in transit. The "ex-ship" transportation noted in the tree refers to the practice of the seller paying for delivery up to the point when the product is removed from a ship on its way to the buyer.

Exhibit 4.4 Decision Tree for Ownership of Inventory in Transit

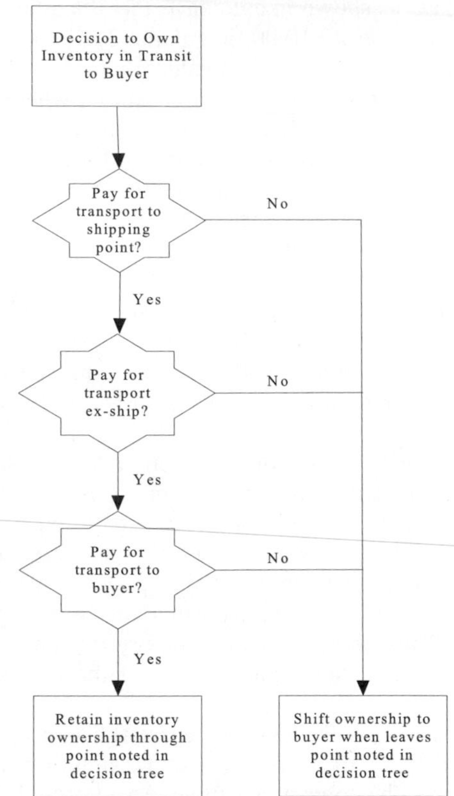

The decision tree in Exhibit 4.5 assists in determining which inventory tracking system to install, based on the presence of several items that are required to achieve an accurate perpetual inventory system.

Exhibit 4.5 Decision Tree for Type of Inventory Tracking System to Use

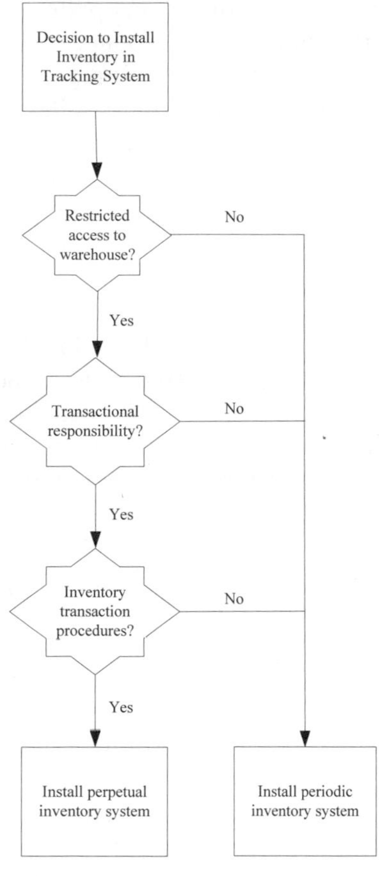

POLICIES

This section lists the policies that should be used in relation to the handling, accounting for, and valuation of inventory. Though some are mutually exclusive, most can be copied directly into a company's policy manual.

Goods in Transit

- **Revenue shall be recognized on goods in transit based on the point when the company no longer has title to the goods.** This policy ensures that there is a consistent cutoff at the point at which a company records revenue on shipments of finished goods to customers.
- **Incoming inventory shall be recorded after it has been received and inspected.** This policy ensures that the quantity and quality of incoming inventory have been verified prior to recording the inventory in the inventory database, thereby avoiding later problems with having incorrect usable quantities on hand.

- **Goods received on consignment shall be identified and stored separately from company-owned inventory.** This policy keeps a company from artificially inflating its inventory by the amount of incoming consignment inventory; otherwise, they would increase their reported profits.
- **Consignment inventory shipped to reseller locations shall be clearly identified as such, both in the shipping log in and the inventory tracking system.** This policy keeps a company from inflating its sales through the recognition of shipments sent to resellers that are actually still owned by the company.

Accounting for Inventories

- **A complete physical inventory count shall be conducted at the end of each reporting period.** This policy ensures that an accurate record of the inventory is used as the basis for a cost-of-goods-sold calculation.
- **The materials manager is responsible for inventory accuracy.** This policy centralizes control over inventory accuracy, thereby increasing the odds of it being kept at a high level.
- **Cycle counters shall continually review inventory accuracy and identify related problems.** This policy is intended for perpetual inventory systems, resulting in a much higher level of inventory accuracy and attention to the underlying problems that cause inventory errors.
- **No access to the inventory is allowed by unauthorized personnel.** This policy generally leads to the lockdown of the warehouse, yielding much greater control over the accurate recording of inventory issuance transactions.
- **No inventory transaction shall occur without being immediately recorded in the perpetual inventory database.** This policy keeps the inventory database accurate at all times, preventing errors from arising when employees adjust the database on the incorrect assumption that the current record is correct.
- **Only designated personnel shall have access to the inventory database and item master file.** This policy not only ensures that only trained employees adjust inventory records, but also that the responsibility for their accuracy can be traced to designated people.

Valuation of Inventories

- **Only designated personnel shall have access to the labor routing and bill of materials databases.** This policy ensures that untrained employees are kept away from the critical computer files needed to value inventory quantities.
- **Standard cost records shall be updated at least annually.** This policy ensures that standard costs used in inventory valuations do not stray too far from actual costs.
- **Lower of cost or net realizable value calculations shall be conducted at least annually.** This policy ensures that excessively high inventory costs are stripped out of the inventory before they can become an excessively large pro-

portion of it. This policy may be modified to require more frequent reviews, based on the variability of market rates for various inventory items.

- **Formal inventory obsolescence reviews shall be conducted at least annually.** This policy requires an inventory review team to scan the inventory periodically for obsolete items. This not only removes the cost of such items from stock, but also gives management a chance to profitably dispose of older inventory items before they become worthless.
- **Management shall actively seek out, identify, and dispose of scrap as soon as possible.** This policy requires the production team to remove scrap from the manufacturing process immediately, keeping it from being recorded in the inventory records and artificially inflating profits.
- **Changes in production processes shall be immediately reflected in labor routings.** This policy ensures that the costs assigned to products through labor routings accurately reflect the actual production process, equipment usage, and production staffing.
- **Changes in product components shall be immediately reflected in the associated bills of material.** This policy ensures that the costs assigned to a product through a bill of materials accurately reflect the current product configuration as designed by the engineering staff.

PROCEDURES

Goods in Transit—Receiving Procedure

Take these five steps to ensure that received goods are properly inspected and recorded in the accounting system.

1. When the shipper arrives, compare the shipment to the description on the bill of lading and the authorizing purchase order. If there are significant discrepancies, reject the shipment.
2. Sign a copy of the bill of lading to accept the delivery.
3. Access the authorizing purchase order on the corporate computer system and record both the received quantity and the warehouse location in which they will be stored. If portable bar code scanners are used, then record this transaction at the time the warehouse move is made.
4. Store a copy of the bill of lading in an indexed file.
5. Forward a copy of the bill of lading to the accounting department or digitize the image in a scanner and enter the document into the corporate accounting system.

NOTE: If items are received during a physical inventory count, clearly mark them as not being available for counting and segregate them. Either wait to enter the transaction in the corporate accounting system after the count has been completed, or make the entry but list the received goods as being unavailable for counting in the database.

Accounting for Inventories—Physical Count Procedure for Periodic Inventory

Take the next six steps one week before the physical count.

1. Contact the printing company and order a sufficient number of sequentially numbered count tags. The first tag number should always be "1000." The tags should include fields for the product number, description, quantity count, location, and the counter's signature.
2. Review the inventory and mark all items lacking a part number with a brightly colored piece of paper. Inform the warehouse manager that these items must be marked with a proper part number immediately.
3. Clearly mark the quantity on all sealed packages.
4. Count all partial packages, seal them, and mark the quantity on the tape.
5. Prepare "Do Not Inventory" tags and use them to mark all items that should not be included in the physical inventory count.
6. Issue a list of count team members, with a notice regarding where and when they should appear for the inventory count.

Take these six steps one day before the physical count.

1. Remind all participants that they are expected to be counting the next day.
2. Notify the warehouse manager that all items received during the two days of physical counts must be segregated and marked with "Do Not Inventory" tags.
3. Notify the manager that no shipments are allowed for the duration of the physical count.
4. Notify the warehouse manager that all shipments with paperwork that has not been sent to accounting by that evening will be included in the inventory count on the following day.
5. Notify the warehouse manager that all shipping and receiving documentation from the day before the count must be forwarded to the accounting department that day, for immediate data entry. Likewise, any pick information must be forwarded at the same time.
6. Notify all outside storage locations to fax in their inventory counts.

Take these eight steps on the morning of the physical count.

1. Enter all transactions from the previous day.
2. Assemble the count teams. Then issue counting instructions to them, as well as blocks of tags to sign. Give each team a map of the warehouse with a section highlighted on it that they are responsible for counting. Those teams with forklift experience will be assigned to count the top racks; those without this experience will be assigned the lower racks.
3. Call all outside storage warehouses and ask them to fax in their counts of company-owned inventory.
4. The count supervisor assigns additional count areas to those teams that finish counting their areas first.
5. The tag coordinator assigns blocks of tags to those count teams that run out of tags, tracks the receipt of tags, and follows up on missing tags. All tags should be accounted for by the end of the day.

6. The data entry person enters the information on the tags into a spreadsheet, summarizes the quantities for each item, and pencils the totals into the cycle count report that was run earlier in the day.
7. The count supervisor reviews any unusual variances with the count teams to ensure that the correct amounts were entered.
8. Review the test count with an auditor, if necessary. Give the auditor a complete printout of all tags, as well as the cycle counting spreadsheet, showing all variances.

The next job descriptions apply to the inventory counting procedure.

- The **count supervisor** is responsible for supervising the count, including the assignment of count teams to specific areas and ensuring that all areas have been counted and tagged. This person also waits until all count tags have been compared to the quantities listed in the computer and then checks the counts on any items that appear to be incorrect.
- The **tag coordinator** is responsible for tracking the blocks of count tags that have been issued, as well as for accounting for all tags that have been returned. When distributing tags, the coordinator marks down the beginning and ending numbers of each block of tags on a tracking sheet and obtains the signature of the person who receives the tags. When the tags are returned, the coordinator puts them in numerical order and verifies that all tags are accounted for. Once that is done, this person checks off the tags on the tracking sheet as having been received. When the returned tags have been properly accounted for, they are forwarded to the extension calculation clerk.
- The **extension calculation clerk** is responsible for summarizing the amounts on the tags (if there are multiple quantities listed) to arrive at a total quantity count on each tag. This person also compares the part numbers and descriptions on each tag to see if there are any potential identification problems and forwards all the completed tags to the data entry person upon completion.
- The **data entry person** is responsible for entering the information on all count tags into the computer spreadsheet. When doing so, this person must make sure to enter all the information on each tag into a spreadsheet. After a group of tags has been entered, this person stamps them as having been enter d, clips them together, and stores them separately. Once all tags are enter d in the spreadsheet, the data entry person sorts the data by part number a prints it. Next, this person summarizes the quantities by part number and ansfers the total quantities by part number to the cycle count report. If th are any significant variances between the counted and cycle count qua es, they must be brought to the attention of the count supervisor for revie

Accounting for Inventories—Cycle Counting Procedure for petual Inventory

Take the next seven steps to ensure that a perpetual i ory database is properly cycle counted.

1. Print a portion of the inventory report, sorted by location. Block out a portion of the physical inventory locations shown on the report for cycle counting purposes.
2. Go to the first physical inventory location to be cycle counted and compare the quantity, location, and part number of each inventory item to what is described for that location in the inventory report. Mark on the report any discrepancies between the on-hand quantity, location, and description for each item.
3. Use the reverse process to ensure that the same information listed for all items on the report matches the items physically appearing in the warehouse location. Note any discrepancies on the report.
4. Verify that the noted discrepancies are not caused by recent inventory transactions that have not yet been logged into the computer system.
5. Correct the inventory database for all remaining errors noted.
6. Calculate the inventory error rate and post it in the warehouse.
7. Call up a history of inventory transactions for each of the items for which errors were noted, and try to determine the cause of the underlying problem. Investigate each issue and recommend corrective action to the warehouse manager, to make sure that the problems do not arise again.

Accounting for Inventories—Part Logging Procedure for Perpetual Inventory

Use these six steps to ensure that all transactions associated with the use of inventory are properly logged into the inventory database, thereby ensuring the ongoing existence of accurate perpetual inventory records.

1. The materials management department will issue a parts request form to the warehouse for each new job to be produced. Upon arrival, the warehouse staff should set up a pallet on which to store the requested items.
2. The warehouse staff collects the requested items from the warehouse, checking off each completed part number on the list and noting the quantity removed and the location from which they were removed.
3. The warehouse staff accesses the inventory database record for each removed item and logs out the quantities taken from the appropriate warehouse locations.
4. The warehouse staff delivers the filled pallet to the production floor.
5. If any parts remain after the production job is complete, the warehouse staff accepts them at the warehouse gate, logs them back into the computer system, and notifies the materials management department of the overage, so they can adjust the bill of material for the products being produced.
6. If any parts are returned in a damaged condition, the warehouse staff logs them in with a damaged code and stores them in the review area where the materials review board can easily access them. The warehouse staff periodically prints a report listing all items stored in this area and forwards it to the materials review board, so they will be aware that items require their attention.

Accounting for Inventories—Inbound Consignment Inventory

Use these four steps to track consignment inventory owned by other parties but stored in the company's warehouse.

1. When consigned inventory arrives in the warehouse, prominently label the inventory with a colored tag, clearly denoting its status.
2. Record the inventory in the computer system using a unique part number to which no valuation is assigned. If a consignment flag is available in the database, flag the part number as being a consignment item.
3. Store the item in a part of the warehouse set aside for consigned inventory.
4. Include the consigned inventory in a review by the materials review board (see next procedure), which should regularly determine the status of this inventory and arrange for its return if there are no prospects for its use in the near future.

Accounting for Inventories—Obsolete Inventory Review

Use these seven steps to periodically review the inventory for obsolete items and account for items considered to be obsolete.

1. Schedule a meeting of the materials review board, to meet in the warehouse.
2. Prior to the meeting, print enough copies of the Inventory Obsolescence Review Report (see the Forms and Reports section) for all members of the committee.
3. Personally review all items on the report for which there appear to be excessive quantities on hand.
4. Determine the proper disposal of each item judged to be obsolete, including possible returns to suppliers, donations, inclusion in existing products, or scrap.
5. Have the warehouse staff mark each item as obsolete in the inventory database.
6. Have the accounting staff write down the value of each obsolete item to its disposal value.
7. Issue a memo to the materials review board, summarizing the results of its actions.

Valuation of Inventories—Period-End Inventory Valuation

Take these seven steps to ensure that the inventory valuation created by a computerized accounting system is accurate and up to date with the latest overhead costs.

1. Following the end of the accounting period, print out and review the computer change log for all bills of material and labor routings. Review the log with the materials manager and production engineer to ensure its accuracy. Revise any changes made in error.
2. Go to the warehouse and manually compare the period-end counts recorded on the inventory report for the most expensive items in the warehouse to

what is in the warehouse racks. If there are any variances, adjust them for any transactions that occurred between the end of the period and the date of the review. If there are still variances, adjust for them in the inventory database.

3. Print a report that sorts the inventory in declining extended dollar order and review it for reasonableness. Be sure to review not only the most expensive items on the list but also the least expensive, since this is where costing errors are most likely to be found. Adjust for any issues found.
4. Review all entries in the general ledger during the reporting period for costs added to the cost pool, verifying that only approved costs have been included. Also investigate any unusually large overhead entries.
5. Verify that the overhead allocation calculation conforms to the standard allocation used in previous reporting periods or that it matches any changes approved by management.
6. Verify that the journal entry for overhead allocation matches the standard journal entry listed in the accounting procedures manual.
7. Print out the inventory valuation report and compare its results by major category to those of the previous reporting period, both in terms of dollars and proportions. Investigate any major differences.

Valuation of Inventories—Lower of Cost or Net Realizable Value Calculation

Use these six steps to periodically adjust the inventory valuation for those items whose net realizable value has dropped below their recorded cost.

1. Export the extended inventory valuation report to an electronic spreadsheet. Sort it by declining extended dollar cost, and delete the 80% of inventory items that do not comprise the top 20% of inventory valuation. Sort the remaining 20% of inventory items by either part number or item description. Print the report.
2. Send a copy of the report to the materials manager, with instructions to compare unit costs for each item on the list to market prices. Be sure to mutually agree on a due date for completion of the review.
3. When the materials management staff has completed its review, meet with the materials manager to go over its results and discuss any major adjustments. Have the materials management staff write down the valuation of selected items in the inventory database whose cost exceeds their net realizable value.
4. Have the accounting staff expense the value of the write-down in the accounting records.
5. Write a memo detailing the results of the lower of cost and net realizable value calculation. Attach one copy to the journal entry used to write down the valuation, and issue another copy to the materials manager.
6. If a new assessment confirms that net realizable value of inventory previously written down below cost has subsequently increased, the amount of a previous write-down can be reversed (but not in excess of the original write-down).

CONTROLS

Goods in Transit

These controls should be installed to ensure that goods in transit are properly accounted for.

- **Audit shipment terms.** Certain types of shipment terms will require that a company shipping goods must retain inventory on its books for some period of time after the goods have physically left the company or that a receiving company record inventory on its books prior to its arrival at the receiving dock. Though in practice most companies will record inventory only when it is physically present, this is technically incorrect under certain shipment terms. Consequently, a company should perform a periodic audit of shipment terms used to see if there are any deliveries requiring different inventory treatment. The simplest approach is to mandate no delivery terms under which a company is financially responsible for transportation costs.
- **Audit the receiving dock.** A significant problem from a recordkeeping perspective is that the receiving staff may not have time to enter a newly received delivery into the corporate computer system, so the accounting and purchasing staffs have no idea that the items have been received. Accordingly, one should regularly compare items sitting in the receiving area to the inventory database to see if they have been recorded. One can also compare supplier billings to the inventory database to see if items billed by suppliers are not listed as having been received.
- **Reject all purchases that are not preapproved.** A major flaw in the purchasing systems of many companies is that all supplier deliveries are accepted at the receiving dock, irrespective of the presence of authorizing paperwork. Many of these deliveries are verbally authorized orders from employees throughout the company, many of whom either are not authorized to make such purchases or are not aware that they are buying items at high prices. This problem can be eliminated by enforcing a rule that all items received must have a corresponding purchase order on file that has been authorized by the purchasing department. By doing so, the purchasing staff can verify that there is a need for each item requisitioned and that it is bought at a reasonable price from a certified supplier.

Accounting for Inventories

These controls should be installed to ensure that inventories are properly accounted for.

- **Conduct inventory audits.** If no one ever checks the accuracy of the inventory, it will gradually vary from the book inventory, as an accumulation of errors builds up over time. To counteract this problem, one can schedule either a complete recount of the inventory from time to time or else an ongoing cycle count of small portions of the inventory each day. Whichever method is used, it is important to conduct research in regard to why errors are occurring and to attempt to fix the underlying problems.

- **Control access to bill of material and inventory records.** The security levels assigned to the files containing bill of material and inventory records should allow access to only a very small number of well-trained employees. By doing so, the risk of inadvertent or deliberate changes to these valuable records will be minimized. The security system should also store the keystrokes and user access codes for anyone who has accessed these records, in case evidence is needed to prove that fraudulent activities have occurred.
- **Keep bill of material accuracy levels at a minimum of 98%.** For manufacturing concerns, the bills of material are critical for determining the value of inventory as it moves through the work-in-process stages of production. Eventually the bills arrive in the finished goods area, since they itemize every possible component that comprises each product. These records should be regularly compared to actual product components to verify that they are correct. Many major management decisions, including product pricing, may be affected by the accuracy of bills of materials, so attention to this step is crucial.
- **Pick from stock based on bills of material.** A way to maintain control over material costs is to require the use of bills of material for each item manufactured and require that parts be picked from the raw materials stock for the production of these items based on the quantities listed in the bills of material. Doing this, a reviewer can hone in on those warehouse issuances that were *not* authorized through a bill of material, given that there appears to be no objective reason why these issuances should have taken place.
- **Require approval to sign out inventory beyond amounts on pick list.** If there is a standard pick list used to take raw materials from the warehouse for production purposes, then this should be the standard authorization for inventory removal. If the production staff requires any additional inventory, they should go to the warehouse gate and request it, and the resulting distribution should be logged out of the warehouse. Furthermore, any inventory that is left over after production is completed should be sent back to the warehouse and logged in. By using this approach, the cost accountant can tell if there are errors in the bills of material that are used to create pick lists, because any extra inventory requisitions or warehouse returns probably represent errors in the bills.
- **Require transaction forms for scrap and rework transactions.** A startling amount of materials and associated direct labor can be lost through the scrapping of production or its occasional rework. This tends to be a difficult item to control, since scrap and rework can occur at many points in the production process. Nonetheless, the manufacturing staff should be well trained in the use of transaction forms that record these actions, so that the inventory records will remain accurate.
- **Restrict warehouse access to designated personnel.** Without access restrictions, the company warehouse is like a large store with no prices—just take all

you want. This does not necessarily mean that employees are taking items from stock for personal use, but they may be removing excessive inventory quantities for production purposes, which leads to a cluttered production floor. Also, this leaves the purchasing staff with the almost impossible chore of trying to determine what is in stock and what needs to be bought for immediate manufacturing needs. Consequently, a mandatory control over inventory is to fence it in and closely restrict access to it.

- **Segregate customer-owned inventory.** If customers supply a company with some parts that are used when constructing products for them, it becomes very easy for this inventory to be mingled with the company's own inventory, resulting in a false increase in its inventory valuation. Though it is certainly possible to assign customer-specific inventory codes to these inventory items in order to clearly identify them, a more easily discernible control is to physically segregate these goods in a different part of the warehouse.

Valuation of Inventories

The next controls should be installed to ensure that the correct costs are assigned to inventory items.

- **Audit inventory material costs.** Inventory costs usually are assigned either through a standard costing procedure or as part of some inventory layering concept such as FIFO. In the case of standard costs, one should regularly compare assigned costs to the actual cost of materials purchased to see if any standard costs should be updated to bring them more in line with actual costs incurred. If it is company policy to update standard costs only at lengthy intervals, then one should verify that the variance between actual and standard costs is being written off to the cost of goods sold.

  If inventory layering is used to store inventory costs, then one should periodically audit the costs in the most recently used layers, tracing inventory costs back to specific supplier invoices.
- **Audit production setup cost calculations.** If production setup costs are included in inventory unit costs, there is a possibility of substantial costing errors if the assumed number of units produced in a production run is incorrect. For example, if the cost of a production setup is €1,000 and the production run is 1,000 units, then the setup cost should be €1 per unit. However, if someone wanted to artificially increase the cost of inventory in order to create a jump in profits, the assumed production run size could be reduced. In the example, if the production run assumption were dropped to 100 units, the cost per unit would increase tenfold to €10. A reasonable control over this problem is to review setup cost calculations regularly. An early warning indicator of this problem is to run a report comparing setup costs over time for each product to see if there are any sudden changes. Also, assure that access to the computer file storing this information is strictly limited.
- **Compare unextended product costs to those for prior periods.** Product costs of all types can change for a variety of reasons. An easy way to spot

these changes is to create and regularly review a report that compares the unextended cost of each product to its cost in a prior period. Any significant changes can then be traced back to the underlying costing information to see exactly what caused each change. The main problem with this control is that many less expensive accounting systems do not retain historical inventory records. If this is the case the information should be exported to an electronic spreadsheet or separate database once a month, where historical records can then be kept.

- **Review sorted list of extended product costs in declining dollar order.** This report is more commonly available than the historical tracking report noted in the previous bullet point, but contains less information. The report lists the extended cost of all inventories on hand for each inventory item, sorted in declining order of cost. By scanning the report, one can readily spot items that have unusually large or unusually small valuations. Finding these items, however, does require some knowledge of what costs were in previous periods. Not only that, but a lengthy inventory list makes the efficient location of costing problems difficult. Thus, this report is inferior to the unextended historical cost comparison report from a control perspective.
- **Control updates to bill of material and labor routing costs.** The key sources of costing information are the bill of material and labor routing records for each product. One can easily make a few modifications to these records in order to substantially alter inventory costs. To prevent such changes from occurring, one should impose strict security access to these records. If the accounting software has a change-tracking feature that stores data about who made changes and what changes were made, this feature should be used. If it is used, one should periodically print a report (if available) detailing all changes made to the records and scan it for evidence of unauthorized access.
- **Review inventory for obsolete items.** The single largest cause of inventory valuation errors is the presence of large amounts of obsolete inventory. To avoid this problem, periodically one should print a report that lists which inventory items have *not* been used recently—including the extended cost of these items. A more accurate variation is to print a report itemizing all inventory items for which there are no current production requirements (possible only if a material requirements planning system is in place). Alternatively, one can use a report that compares the amount of inventory on hand to annual historical usage of each item. With this information in hand, one should then schedule regular meetings with the materials manager to determine what inventory items should be scrapped, sold off, or returned to suppliers.
- **Review inventory layering calculations.** Most inventory layering systems are maintained automatically through a computer system and cannot be altered. In these cases, there is no need to verify the layering calculations. However, if the layering information is maintained manually, one should schedule periodic reviews of the underlying calculations to ensure proper cost layering. This usually involves tracing costs back to specific supplier invoices; however, one should also trace supplier invoices forward to the layer-

ing calculations, because it is quite possible that invoices have been excluded from the calculations. Also one should verify consistency in the allocation of freight costs to inventory items in the layering calculations.

- **Verify the calculation and allocation of overhead cost pools.** Overhead costs usually are assigned to inventory as the result of a manually derived summarization and allocation of overhead costs. This can be a lengthy calculation, subject to error. The best control over this process is a standard procedure that clearly defines which costs to include in the pools and precisely how these costs are to be allocated. In addition, one should regularly review the types of costs included in the calculations, verify that the correct proportions of these costs are included, and ensure that the costs are being correctly allocated to inventory. A further control is to track the total amount of overhead accumulated in each reporting period—any sudden change in the amount may indicate an error in the overhead cost summarization.

FORMS AND REPORTS

Goods in Transit

If a company has a fully integrated computer system where the receiving staff can directly enter all receipts, there will be no forms required for goods in transit. If not, a receiving log will be used, like the one shown in Exhibit 4.6. The report may contain additional room for notations by the receiving staff, such as the condition of the items received.

Exhibit 4.6 Receiving Log

Date	*Supplier*	*Item*	*Quantity shipped*	*Quantity received*
9/10/07	Acme Acorn Co.	Pistachio Nuts	3 barrels	3 barrels
9/10/07	Acme Acorn Co.	Pine Nuts	2 barrels	2 barrels
9/10/07	Durango Nut Co.	Pine Cones	100 pounds	98 pounds

The same information is commonly used in receiving reports, which are sorted by date, supplier, part number, or part description.

Accounting for Inventories

A physical inventory count usually is taken by using a tag to be affixed to each lot. The tags are numbered serially in advance, and since a portion of the tag is left on the stock, it serves as a means of ensuring that all lots are counted. A sample inventory tag is shown in Exhibit 4.7. This is a two-part tag, with the lower section being collected for summarization. Space is provided on the reverse side for noting movements so that slow-moving items can be counted in advance of the regular count.

Exhibit 4.7 Inventory Tag

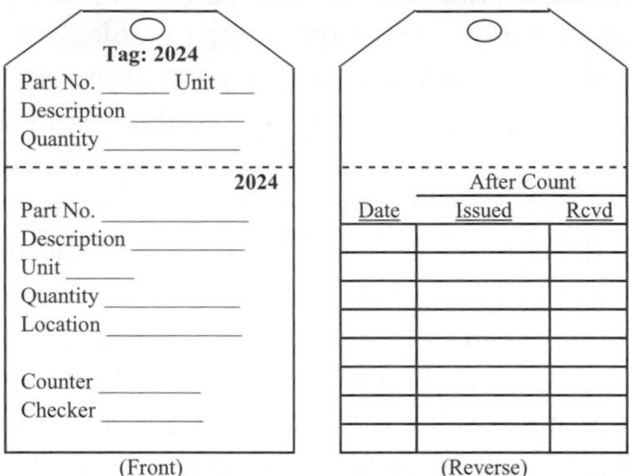

Tag: 2024
Part No. ______ Unit ___
Description __________
Quantity ____________

2024
Part No. ____________
Description __________
Unit ______
Quantity ____________
Location ____________

Counter _________
Checker _________

(Front)

	After Count	
Date	Issued	Rcvd

(Reverse)

A cycle counting report is used by cycle counters to compare inventory records from the accounting database to physical counts in the warehouse. The sample report in Exhibit 4.8 usually is sorted by warehouse location code, so that counters can verify all items within a small area—the most efficient accounting method. Although the report has space on it to record physical inventory counts, one can also write in any adjustments to part descriptions or units of measure.

Exhibit 4.8 Cycle Counting Report

Location	*Item no.*	*Description*	*U/M*	*Quantity*
A-10-C	Q1458	Switch, 120V, 20A	EA	
A-10-C	U1010	Bolt, Zinc, 3 × 1/4	EA	
A-10-C	M1458	Screw, Stainless Steel, 2 × 3/8	EA	

Once cycle counting information has been collected, accuracy levels for each part of the inventory should be recorded on a trend line, preferably on a wall-mounted display board. By doing so, management makes a statement that this information is extremely important and that it wishes to see improvement in the accuracy statistics. An example of an inventory accuracy report is shown in Exhibit 4.9.

Exhibit 4.9 Inventory Accuracy Report

Aisles	*Responsible person*	*2 Months ago*	*Last month*	*Week 1*	*Week 2*	*Week 3*	*Week 4*
A-B	Fred P.	82%	86%	85%	84%	82%	87%
C-D	Alain Q.	70%	72%	74%	76%	78%	80%
E-F	Davis L.	61%	64%	67%	70%	73%	76%
G-H	Jeff R.	54%	58%	62%	66%	70%	74%
I-J	Alice R.	12%	17%	22%	27%	32%	37%
K-L	George W.	81%	80%	79%	78%	77%	76%
M-N	Robert T.	50%	60%	65%	70%	80%	90%

Most inventory to be used on the production floor is kitted by the warehouse staff based on bills of material and issued on pallets to the production floor. If the amount listed on the bill of materials is too low, however, more inventory will be requested from the warehouse. Alternatively, if the bill of materials is too high, some inventory will be returned. More inventory may also be requested if parts are damaged on the production floor. When any of these issues arise, the warehouse staff should record all related transactions on an inventory sign-out and return a form such as the one shown in Exhibit 4.10. It is useful not only as a written record of transactions that must be entered into the inventory database, but also as a record of prospective adjustments to erroneous bills of material.

Exhibit 4.10 Inventory Sign-Out and Return Form

Description	Part no.	Quantity issued	Quantity returned	Job no.	Date

Production operations frequently result in either scrapped inventory or inventory that must be reworked in some manner before it can be completed. The accounting department needs to know as soon as scrap is created, so it can charge off the related cost to the cost of goods sold. Many companies give the same treatment to items requiring rework, reassigning a cost to them only once they are fixed and sent back into production. The two-part form shown in Exhibit 4.11 can be filled out by the production or materials management staffs whenever scrap or rework occurs, with one copy being attached to the inventory and the other being forwarded to accounting. The form is prenumbered, in case the accounting staff wants to verify that all forms are submitted. If the "Scrapped" block is filled out, accounting charges off the inventory cost to the cost of goods sold. If the "Sent to Rework" block is filled out, accounting must also shift the related inventory to a rework inventory category in the inventory database, where it will stay until rework activities are completed. The form can be sent later to the production or engineering managers, in case they wish to review the reasons why scrap or rework occurred.

Exhibit 4.11 Scrap/Rework Transaction Form

7403

Date: ______________

Item Number: ______________________

Description: ___________________________________

Scrapped	Sent to Rework
Quantity Scrapped: ______________	Quantity to Rework: ______________
Reason: ______________	Reason: ______________
______________	______________
______________	______________
Signature: ______________	Signature: ______________

Valuation of Inventories

When standard costs are used to create an inventory valuation, there will inevitably be some differences between standard and actual costs that will create variances that appear in the cost of goods sold. The report shown in Exhibit 4.14 itemizes these variances.

Exhibit 4.12 Standard to Actual Cost Comparison Report

Part description	Standard cost (€)	Actual cost (€)	Variance (€)	Unit volume	Extended variance (€)
Antenna	1.20	2.00	(0.80)	500	(400.00)
Speaker	0.50	0.70	(0.20)	375	(75.00)
Battery	2.80	3.10	(0.30)	201	(60.30)
Plastic case, top	0.41	0.50	(0.09)	14,000	(1,260.00)
Plastic case, bottom	0.23	0.41	(0.18)	11,000	(1,980.00)
Base unit	4.00	4.25	(0.25)	820	(205.00)
Cord	0.90	0.91	(0.01)	571	(5.71)
Circuit board	5.78	4.00	1.78	1,804	3,211.12
Total	--	--	--	--	(774.89)

Standard costs will be altered from time to time in order to bring them more in line with actual costs. When this happens, it is useful to show the changes on a report, along with the reasons why costs were changed. If management is particularly sensitive about altering standard costs, one could also add a manager sign-off section to the report in order to record formal approval of the changes. An example of this report is shown in Exhibit 4.13.

Exhibit 4.13 Standard Cost Changes Report

Part description	Beginning standard cost	Cost changes	Ending standard costs	Remarks
Power unit	820.00	30.00	850.00	Price increase
Fabric	142.60		142.60	
Paint	127.54	(22.54)	105.00	Modified paint type
Instruments	93.14	(1.14)	92.00	New altimeter
Exhaust stock	34.17		34.17	
Rubber grommet	19.06	(.06)	19.00	New material
Aluminum forging	32.14	(2.00)	30.14	Substitute forging
Cushion	14.70		14.70	
Total	1,283.35	4.26	1,287.61	

More parts than are normally needed may be taken from stock to complete various items in production, which will unexpectedly reduce inventory levels and increase the cost of goods sold. Given its potentially large impact on inventory valuation, this issue may require a separate report such as the one shown in Exhibit 4.16. If excess parts usage continues over time, the report can also be used as proof of a need for changes to an item's underlying bill of materials.

Exhibit 4.14 Excess Material Usage Report

Material used	Standard usage (units)	Actual usage (units)	Excess usage (units)	Unit cost	Total excess cost	Comments
A	3,960	4,110	150	€4.75	€712.50	(a)
B	15,840	15,960	120	2.00	240.00	(b)
C	3,960	4,000	40	21.50	860.00	(c)
D	3,960	3,970	10	65.40	654.00	(d)
E	15,840	15,920	80	3.25	260.00	(e)
Total	--	--	--	--	€2,726.50	

(a) Parts defective
(b) Careless workmanship

(c) Power down
(d) Wrong speed drilling
(e) Maintenance technician dropped case

One of the easiest ways to detect obsolete inventory is to create a list of inventory items for which there has been no usage activity. The version shown in Exhibit 4.15 compares total inventory withdrawals to the amount on hand, which by itself may be sufficient information to conduct an obsolescence review. It also lists planned usage, calling for information from a material requirements planning system and informing one of any upcoming requirements that might keep one from otherwise disposing of an inventory item. An extended cost for each item is also listed, in order to give report users some idea of the write-off that might occur if an item is declared obsolete. In the exhibit, the subwoofer, the speaker bracket, and the wall bracket appear to be obsolete based on prior usage, but the planned use of more wall brackets would keep that item from being disposed of.

Exhibit 4.15 Inventory Obsolescence Review Report

Description	*Item no.*	*Location*	*Quantity on hand*	*Last year usage*	*Planned usage*	*Extended cost*
Subwoofer case	0421	A-04-C	872	520	180	€9,053
Speaker case	1098	A-06-D	148	240	120	1,020
Subwoofer	3421	D-12-A	293	14	0	24,724
Circuit board	3600	B-01-A	500	5,090	1,580	2,500
Speaker, bass	4280	C-10-C	621	2,480	578	49,200
Speaker bracket	5391	C-10-C	14	0	0	92
Wall bracket	5080	B-03-B	400	0	120	2,800
Gold connection	6233	C-04-A	3,025	8,042	5,900	9,725
Tweeter	7552	C-05-B	725	6,740	2,040	5,630

FOOTNOTES

Disclosure of Inventory

If a company uses both the FIFO and weighted cost valuation methods, the extent to which each method is used should be described. Also, irrespective of the type of valuation method used, a company must reveal whether it is using the lower of cost and net realizable adjustment (and the extent of any losses and recovery gains), whether any inventories are recorded at costs above their acquisition costs, whether any inventory is pledged as part of a debt arrangement, and the method of valuation being used. An example follows.

> The company uses the FIFO valuation method for approximately 65% of the total dollar value of its inventories, with the weighted-average method being used for all remaining inventories. The company lost €.74 per share during the period as a result of a write-down of inventory costs to net realizable value. The company records no inventories above their acquisition costs. As of the date of the statement of financial position, the company had pledged €540,000 of its inventory.

JOURNAL ENTRIES

This section describes the most common inventory-related journal entries. The first block of entries are for goods in transit, beginning with the receipt of raw material, and progressing through the various types of inventory to their eventual sale to customers. The next block of entries lists common adjustments to inventory: this includes obsolescence, physical count adjustments, and abnormal scrap. The final block of entries shows how to shift indirect costs of various kinds into the overhead cost pool and then to allocate these costs back out to either the cost of goods sold or inventory. For each journal entry, there is a sample description as well as the most likely debit and credit for each account used within the entry.

Goods in Transit

Record received goods. To increase inventory levels as a result of a supplier delivery.

Raw materials inventory	xxx	
Accounts payable		xxx

Move inventory to work-in-process. To shift the cost of inventory to the work-in-process category once production work begins on converting it from raw materials to finished goods.

Work-in-process inventory	xxx	
Raw materials inventory		xxx

Move inventory to finished goods. To shift the cost of completed inventory from work-in-process inventory to finished goods inventory.

Finished goods inventory	xxx	
Work-in-process inventory		xxx

Sell inventory. To record the elimination of the inventory asset as a result of a product sale, shifting the asset to an expense and also recording the creation of an accounts receivable asset to reflect an unpaid balance from the customer on sale of the product.

Cost of goods sold	xxx	
Finished goods inventory		xxx
Accounts receivable	xxx	
Revenues		xxx
Overhead cost pool		xxx

Accounting for Inventories

Adjust inventory for obsolete items. To charge an ongoing expense to the cost of goods sold that increases the balance in a reserve against which obsolete inventory can be charged (first entry). The second entry charges off specific inventory items against the reserve.

Cost of goods sold	xxx	
Obsolescence reserve		xxx
Obsolescence reserve	xxx	
Raw materials inventory		xxx
Work-in-process inventory		xxx
Finished goods inventory		xxx

Adjust inventory to lower of cost and net realizable value. To reduce the value of inventory to a net realizable value that is lower than the cost recorded in the company records.

Loss on inventory valuation	xxx	
Raw materials inventory		xxx
Work-in-process inventory		xxx
Finished goods inventory		xxx

Adjust inventory to physical count. To adjust inventory balances, either up or down, as a result of changes in the inventory quantities that are noted during a physical count. The entries shown assume that there are increases in inventory balances. If there are declines in the inventory balances, the debits and credits are reversed.

Raw materials inventory	xxx	
Work-in-process inventory	xxx	
Finished goods inventory	xxx	
Cost of goods sold		xxx

Write off abnormal scrap/spoilage. To shift unexpected, one-time scrap or spoilage costs directly to the cost of goods sold, effectively writing off this amount in the current period.

Cost of goods sold	xxx	
Work-in-process inventory		xxx

Valuation of Inventories

Record indirect expenses incurred. To add the amount of indirect expenses related to the production process to the overhead cost pool.

Overhead cost pool	xxx	
Accounts payable		xxx

Record indirect wages incurred. To add the amount of indirect wages related to the production process to the overhead cost pool.

Overhead cost pool	xxx	
Wages payable		xxx

Record receipt of supplies. To add the cost of incidental manufacturing supplies to the overhead cost pool for eventual allocation to inventory.

Overhead cost pool	xxx	
Accounts payable		xxx

Record normal scrap/spoilage. To shift the normal, expected amount of scrap or spoilage cost to the overhead cost pool, where it is allocated as a part of overhead to inventory.

Overhead cost pool	xxx	
Work-in-process inventory		xxx

Allocate overhead costs to inventory. To shift the amount of costs built up in the overhead cost pool to the work-in-process and finished goods inventory categories, as well as to the cost of goods sold for any inventory sold during the period.

Cost of goods sold	xxx	
Work-in-process inventory		xxx
Finished goods inventory		xxx

RECORDKEEPING

Goods in Transit

A company receiving inventory typically records it as soon as it arrives. This way both the inventory and liability accounts increase at the same time, thereby resulting in no net change in the statement of financial position and no impact on profit or loss. Consequently, there is no particular need for recordkeeping.

The situation is different for companies shipping goods for which they retain title until some point in the shipment process. Shipping documents, such as a shipping log or bill of lading, should be stored that indicate the date of shipment from the facility, as well as a notification form from the shipping entity that describes the date on which title passed to the buyer. The shipping log or bill of lading can be used to estimate the date on which title passes by adding a standard number of days to the ship date, based on the distance of the buyer from the shipper's facility; thus it is a critical document for affirming the timing of any revenue transactions.

A particular problem for adequate recordkeeping is the tracking of consignment inventory. A company receiving such inventory should make a notation in its computer system at the time of receipt that clearly identifies this inventory. Preferably, there should also be a flag in the software that prevents the consignment inventory from being assigned a value. If the consignment inventory matches company-owned inventory, then it will be particularly difficult to segregate it; therefore one should create a unique inventory number for the item. For example, a wash basin might normally be inventory number 11478, so an identical item received on consignment could be given the number 11478-C.

If a company has sent inventory on consignment to a third-party location, then the inventory tracking system in its software should contain an *off-site* inventory location code clearly identifying where it has been sent. A reasonable location code would be the name of the company to which it was sent, truncated to match the size of the inventory location field in the computer system.

Accounting for Inventories

Recordkeeping for perpetual inventory systems is accomplished most easily by having the computer system store a transaction log that shows what transactions were entered, who made the entries, and the date they were made. This log can be subdivided into a variety of reports that reveal only certain types of transactions or only transactions for particular inventory items. If the perpetual records are stored on paper, these documents should be kept for at least one year following year-end, so inventory levels can be reconstructed manually at a later date. Also, tax regulations in most countries require at least one physical inventory count per year; thus, these records should be stored in the event of a tax audit. If continuous cycle counting is used instead of a single physical inventory count, then these records must also be stored.

Recordkeeping for periodic systems is more complex, since the systems usually are manual ones. First, the counting records for each physical inventory count must be stored. Also, all purchasing records for the year should be retained, which can be as minimal as the general ledger detail for the purchasing account. However, this approach reveals nothing about who ordered goods, what goods were ordered, and from whom they were bought. Accordingly, one should also retain the purchase order and the receiving documentation, which can be quite voluminous. The reason for this much document retention is that the calculation of the cost of goods sold requires one to add purchases to the beginning inventory and then subtract out the ending inventory, calling for backup information on all three parts of the calculation.

If inventory is tracked using the specific identification method, then the computer system should contain a unique identifying number for each item tracked, such as a serial number. This identification number should be included in the standard inventory valuation report, which should be printed at the fiscal year-end and stored.

Valuation of Inventories

There are a number of recordkeeping issues related to the valuation of inventory. In all cases, the main issue is creating a paper trail that can be traced back to the source documents at any point in the future, so that anyone (especially an auditor) can easily determine the reason why a specific cost was assigned to an inventory item. The discussion that follows covers recordkeeping issues for the standard costing of work-in-process and finished goods inventory, as well as inventory layering, spoilage, and the cost reductions for the lower of cost or net realizable value rule. In all cases, it is crucial to maintain accurate records of these transactions because they have a major impact on corporate expenses.

When auditors review the raw material costs listed on the statement of financial position, their first source of evidentiary material for affirming this cost will be the invoices received from suppliers. These are normally stored in the accounts payable files, so no additional recordkeeping is necessary. The main point is to ensure that the supplier name and invoice number are recorded in the raw materials valuation report, or easily traced from there, so the auditors have a clear documentation path from the inventory valuation report to the backup materials.

Many manufactured goods move through the production process so fast that there is no reason to track their progress from workstation to workstation, since they arrive in finished goods inventory so quickly. In other cases, materials may plod through the production process for weeks or months, traveling from workstation to workstation. In these latter cases, their recorded work-in-process (WIP) cost will gradually increase as value is added to them. If so, there must be a way to record the stage of completion of all WIP inventory at the end of a reporting period and to consistently assign a value to each stage of completion. This is done through a labor cost assignment routine—usually a computer record assigned to each product in the computer system's item master file, itemizing the work processes that must be performed on the product and the cost of those processes. When a reporting period ends, the accounting staff must itemize in the computer system the last workstation through which work has been completed on each inventory item; the computer then increases the cost of the inventory by the incremental production work completed, based on the standard costs used in the labor routings. Accordingly, one must store copies of the labor cost assignments used for the period-end report, either in the computer system or as printed copies. If they are to be stored on the computer, there should be an archiving function or a change-tracking feature, so that one can find the correct version of a routing.

Once completed units of production are shifted into finished goods inventory, they are assigned a cost that usually is based on a bill of materials, which is a list of standard parts included in each product. Given its importance in the valuation process, one should keep a record of the bill of materials as proof of how costs were derived at the end of each accounting period. The bills can be printed and kept separately or stored in the computer under an appropriate archiving or change control methodology. That way, one can scroll back in time through various changes to the bills in order to find the version used to calculate the cost of inventory on a specific date.

Both labor cost assignments and bills of materials assign a standard amount of cost to either WIP or finished goods inventories, using a standard list of work centers and parts that are comprised of standard costs. Actual costs may vary somewhat from the standard costs used, due to variations in the market prices of parts, changing labor rates, different parts or work center configurations, and so on. The standard costs used in a labor routing and a bill of materials are always incrementally varying from actual costs, requiring periodic adjustments to the standards in order to bring them more in line with actual costs. Whenever this happens, one should create and store a record of the changes made or use a computer system that stores this information whenever changes are made.

When the actual amount of material scrap used to create a product varies substantially from the amount included in a bill of materials, it is considered abnormal scrap, and it will drop directly into the cost of goods sold in the current period. There is no need from an accounting perspective to track the exact items lost to scrap, since they are no longer stored in inventory. Nonetheless, it may be useful for operational reasons to know where this scrap is occurring, which products are most likely to generate scrap, or what workstations in which scrap is most likely to occur. By tracking this information on a trend line, one can direct the attention of production engineers to those areas of the production process where their efforts can result in the greatest decrease in scrap costs. There is no further need to retain records in this area, however.

Overhead is a major component of inventory cost, in some cases comprising far more than the cost of labor or materials in a product. The overhead rate is compiled in one or more cost pools within the general ledger and then allocated to work in process, finished goods, or the cost of goods sold using some sort of activity measure—such as the amount of direct labor or machine time used by a product, or perhaps a combination of several activity measures. Given the large amount of money being allocated, this is an extremely important area in which to have accurate recordkeeping. Records should itemize what costs are included in the overhead cost pool and the exact derivation of the allocation methodology. The method by which the allocated costs are assigned to inventory, such as through a journal entry or an alteration in the standard overhead rate used in the bills of material, should also be noted.

If the FIFO method is used to value inventory, the computer system should maintain a database of all cost layers used to derive the inventory valuation. Unless the inventory is very small, maintaining this information manually usually is very labor intensive; thus, it is not recommended. However, computer databases typically store data for only a few years into the past, so adequate recordkeeping in this area will require one to print out the layering records when old computer files are about to be deleted from the system.

If a lower of cost or net realizable value review is made that results in a reduction in the recorded cost of inventory, then the adjustment typically is made as a journal entry that reduces the cost of inventory in a single lump sum. If so, there is no way to tell which costs were reduced or what calculation was used to determine the reduction. Consequently, the journal entry records should include complete documentation of the comparison of standard costs to market costs, unfavorable variances between the two, and the total cost of these variances incorporated into the journal entry.

If the purchasing department has entered into any material long-term purchasing commitments with suppliers, the amount of these commitments must be included in the footnotes to the financial statements. Accordingly, the purchasing staff should be recording all of its purchase orders in the corporate computer system, while all receipts against those purchase orders should be logged into the system by the receiving staff. By netting out the receipts against the purchase orders, one can easily determine the total amount of long-term purchasing commitments. This report should be printed and stored at the fiscal year-end.

The one problem with this recordkeeping approach is when long-term commitments are contained within legal agreements only and they have not yet been converted into purchase orders. Though some companies have stored this information in separate computer databases, many more keep legal agreements only in paper format, which makes them much more difficult to summarize (or even locate). If this is the case, the accounting staff should either maintain the master file of legal contracts or at least be given access to it, and schedule regular reviews of new or modified contracts in order to determine the amount of purchase commitments. Notes from these reviews should be stored as supporting documentation for the footnote disclosure.

5 REVENUE RECOGNITION

DEFINITIONS OF TERMS

Construction in progress. An inventory account in which costs are accumulated for ongoing work related to separately identifiable construction projects. For the percentage-of-completion method, this account also includes the gross profit earned to date.

Cost recovery method. The most conservative method for accounting for installment sales, where the recognition of all gross profit is deferred until the entire cost of sales has first been recognized.

Cost-to-cost method. The division of cost incurred to date on a project by the total estimated project cost to derive the overall project percentage of completion for incremental billing and income recognition purposes.

Deferred gross profit. The gross profit associated with a sale whose recognition is deferred due to the uncertainty of final cash collection.

Fair value. The amount for which an asset could be exchanged, or a liability settled, between knowledgeable, willing parties in an arm's-length transaction.

Initiation fee. An up-front fee charged as part of a service or membership agreement, entitling the customer to specific services or if additional periodic payments are made.

Installation fee. An up-front fee required to install equipment.

Installment method. A method for recognizing the profit on an installment sale when cash is received.

Installment transaction. When a customer pays for a purchase through a series of periodic payments.

Percentage-of-completion method. Method of accounting that recognizes income on a contract as work progresses by matching contract revenue with contract costs incurred based on the proportion of work completed. Any expected loss, which is the excess of total incurred and expected contract costs over the total contract revenue, is recognized immediately, irrespective of the stage of completion of the contract.

Revenue. Gross inflow of economic benefits (e.g., cash, accounts receivable, or barter) resulting from an entity's ordinary activities is considered "revenue," provided those inflows result in increases in equity, other than increases relating to contributions from owners or equity participants. Revenue refers to the gross amount (of revenue) and excludes amounts collected on behalf of third parties.

Right of return. The right of a customer to return goods to the seller within a specific time period.

Substantial completion. The point at which essentially all work has been completed and major risks incurred in relation to a project.

Unearned revenue. A payment from a customer that cannot yet be recognized as earned revenue because the offsetting services or products for which the money was paid have not yet been delivered.

CONCEPTS AND EXAMPLES[1]

The IASB's *Framework* defines "income" to include both revenue and gains; IAS 18, however, deals only with revenue. Revenue is defined as income arising from the ordinary activities of an entity and may be referred to by a variety of names including sales, fees, interest, dividends, and royalties. Revenue encompasses only the gross inflow of economic benefits received or receivable by the entity, on its own account, net of amounts collected on behalf of third parties.

Revenue should be measured at the fair value of the consideration received or receivable, net of any trade discounts and volume rebates allowed by the entity. The determination of the point in time when a reporting entity is considered to have transferred the significant risks and rewards of ownership in goods to the buyer is critical to the recognition of revenue from the sale of goods.

The accountant should not recognize revenue until it has been earned. There are a number of rules regarding exactly when revenue can be recognized, but the key concept is that revenue occurs at the point when substantially all services and deliveries related to the sale transaction have been completed. Within this broad requirement are a number of more precise rules regarding revenue recognition:

- **Recognition at point of delivery.** One should recognize revenue when the product is delivered to the customer. For example, revenue is recognized in a retail store when a customer pays for a product and walks out of the store with it in hand. Alternatively, a manufacturer recognizes revenue when its products are placed onboard a conveyance owned by a common carrier for delivery to a customer; however, this point of delivery can change if the company owns the method of conveyance, since the product is still under company control until it reaches the customer's receiving dock.
- **Recognition at time of payment.** If payment by the customer is not assured, even after delivery of the product or service has been completed, then the most appropriate time to recognize revenue is upon receipt of cash. For example, if a book publisher issues new editions of books to the buyers of the previous

---

[1] *Some portions of this section are adapted with permission from Chapter 20 of Steven Bragg,* ***Accounting Reference Desktop*** *(Hoboken, NJ: John Wiley & Sons, Inc. 2002).*

edition without any indication that they will accept the new shipments, then waiting for the receipt of cash is the most prudent approach to the recognition of revenue.

- **Other rules.** In addition to the preceding rules, a few others are applicable in all instances. The first is that the seller should have no obligation to assist the buyer in reselling the product to a third party; if this were the case, it would imply that the initial sale had not yet been completed. The second is that any damage to the product subsequent to the point of sale will have no impact on the buyer's obligation to pay the seller for the full price of the product; if this were the case, one would reasonably assume that at least some portion of the sale price either includes a paid warranty that should be separated from the initial sale price and recognized at some later date, or that the sale cannot be recognized until the implied warranty period has been completed. The third rule is that the buying and selling entities cannot be the same entity or so closely related that the transaction might be construed as an intercompany sale; if this were the case, the intercompany sale would have to be eliminated from the financial statements of both the buyer and the seller for reporting purposes, since the presumption would be that no sale had occurred.

Revenue Recognition Scenarios

The most common revenue recognition system is based on the *accrual method.* Under this approach, if the revenue recognition rules presented in the previous section have been met, then revenue may be recognized in full. In addition, expenses related to that revenue—even if supplier invoices have not yet been received—should be recognized and matched against the revenue.

Example of revenue recognition

If the Mediterranean Dive Company sells a set of face masks for €500 and recognizes the revenue at the point of shipment, then it must also recognize at the same time the €325 cost of those masks, even if it has not yet received a billing from the supplier that sold it the masks. In the absence of the billing, the cost can be accrued based on a purchase order value, net realizable value, or supplier price list.

The **installment method** is used when there is a long string of expected payments from a customer that are related to a sale, and for which the level of collectibility of individual payments cannot be reasonably estimated. This approach is particularly applicable in the case of multiyear payments by a customer; however, revenue is recognized only in the amount of each cash receipt, and for as long as cash is received. Expenses can be proportionally recognized to match the amount of each cash receipt, creating a small profit or loss at the time of each receipt.

An alternative approach, called the *cost recovery method,* uses the same revenue recognition criterion as the installment sales method, but the amount of revenue recognized is exactly offset by the cost of the product or service until all related costs have been recognized. All remaining revenues then have no offsetting cost, which effectively pushes all profit recognition out until near the end of the installment sale contract.

It is generally not allowable to record inventory at net realizable values (selling price less costs to complete and sale) at the time when production has been completed (but mandated exceptions exist under IFRS, most notably for biological assets). This is allowed, however, in the few cases where the item produced is a commodity, has a ready market, and can be sold easily at the market price. Examples of such items are gold, silver, and wheat. In these cases, the producer can mark up the cost of the item to the selling price at the point when production has been completed. However, this amount must then be reduced by the estimated amount of any remaining selling costs, such as would be incurred to transport the commodity to market. In practice, most companies prefer to recognize revenue at the point of sale. Consequently, this practice tends to be limited to those companies that produce commodities but have difficulty in calculating an internal cost that they can record the cost of their production (and so are forced to use the market price instead).

When property is sold on a conditional basis, where the buyer has the right to cancel the contract and receive a refund up until a prespecified date, the seller cannot recognize any revenue until the date when cancellation is no longer allowed. Until that time, all funds are recorded as a deposit liability. If only portions of the contract can be canceled by the buyer, then revenue can be recognized at once by the seller for just those portions not subject to cancellation.

Bill and Hold Revenue Transactions

When a company is striving to reach difficult revenue goals, it sometimes will resort to bill and hold transactions. In this case, it completes a product and bills the customer, but then it stores the product rather than sending it to the customer (who may not want it yet). Though there are a limited number of situations where this treatment is legitimate (perhaps the customer has no storage space available), there have also been a number of cases where bill and hold transactions subsequently have been proven to be a fraudulent method for recognizing revenue. Consequently, these rules must now be met before a bill and hold transaction will be considered valid:

- **Origination.** The *buyer* must have requested that the bill and hold transaction be completed, and have a good reason for doing so.
- **Completion.** The product being stored under the agreement must be ready for shipment. This means that the seller cannot have production staff in the storage area, making changes to the product subsequent to the billing date.
- **Delivery schedule.** The products cannot be stored indefinitely. Instead, there must be a schedule in place for the eventual delivery of the goods to the customer.
- **Documentation.** The buyer must have signed a document in advance clearly stating that it is buying the products being stored by the seller.
- **Ownership.** The buyer must have taken on all risks of ownership, so the seller is now simply the provider of storage space.

- **Performance.** The terms of the sales agreement must not state that there are any unfulfilled obligations on the part of the seller at the time when revenue is recognized.
- **Segregation.** The products involved in the transaction must have been split away from all other inventory and stored separately. They also must not be made available for the filling of orders from other customers.

Recording Revenues at Gross or Net

Some companies that act as brokers will overreport their revenue by recognizing not just the commission they earn on brokered sales, but also the revenue earned by their clients. For example, if a brokered transaction for an airline ticket involves a £1,000 ticket and a £20 brokerage fee, the company will claim that it has earned revenue of £1,000, rather than the £20 commission. This results in the appearance of enormous revenue (albeit with very small gross margins), which can be quite misleading. Consequently, one should apply these rules to see if the full amount of brokered sales can be recognized as revenue:

- **Principal.** The broker must act as the principal who is originating the transaction.
- **Risks.** The broker must take on the risks of ownership, such as bearing the risk of loss on product delivery, returns, and bad debts from customers.
- **Title.** The broker must obtain title to the product being sold at some point during the sale transaction.

Several key indicators in a transaction reveal whether it should be recorded at gross or net. It should be recorded at gross if these indicators are present:

- The company adds value to products sold, perhaps through alteration or added services.
- The company can establish a selling price to the customer.
- The company is responsible to the customer for order fulfillment.
- The company takes title to inventory before shipping it to the customer.

The transaction should be recorded at net if the answer to any of the preceding indicators is no. In addition, it should be recorded at net if these indicators are present:

- The company earns a fixed fee (such as a commission payment) from a transaction.
- The company has only one source of supplier for the product it sells.
- The supplier cannot obtain payment from the company if the customer does not pay. If a specific transaction contains indicators pointing in either direction, the decision to record at gross or net should be based on the preponderance of evidence pointing in a particular direction.

Example of recording revenues at gross or net

The Ulm Travel Agency (UTA), which sells trips to Australia, purchases blocks of tickets from the airlines and resells them to customers as part of its package deals. If it cannot find purchasers for the tickets, it must absorb the cost of the tickets. In this case,

UTA should record as revenues the entire amount of the airline tickets, since it has taken title to the tickets, bears the risk of loss, and is originating the transaction.

UTA also reserves airline seats on behalf of its clients, charging a €30 fee for this service. Since it is acting only as an agent for these transactions, it can record only the €30 fee as revenue, not the price of the airline tickets.

Reducing Revenue by Cash Paid to Customers

If a company pays cash consideration to its customers, this is presumed to be a reduction in the company's revenue. The only exception is when a clearly identifiable benefit is being passed from the customer to the company, and the fair value of that benefit can be estimated. If the fair value of the benefit is less than the amount of cash paid, the difference must be deducted from revenue. This approach is designed to keep companies from inflating their reported revenue levels through delayed cash-back payments to customers as part of sales deals. Alternatively, if the company pays its customers with goods or services, the transaction should be recorded as an expense.

Example of revenue reduction based on cash payments to customers

An international customer of the ABC Widget Company has operations in a country that has imposed foreign exchange controls. As part of an agreement to sell widgets to this customer, ABC agrees to overbill the customer by 10% and rebate this amount to a customer location in a third country. Whenever this transaction occurs, ABC should credit its cash account and debit its revenue account by the amount of the overbilling.

Example of expense incurrence based on noncash payments to customers

The XYZ Technology Company sells a variety of software packages to its customers and offers free training classes at its in-house university to purchasers. In a recent sale, the company promised 10 days of free training, which equated to 20 days of instructor time at a payroll cost of £7,000. Accordingly, this cost was shifted from the training department's payroll expense and charged to the sale as a cost of goods sold.

Long-Term Construction Contracts

The principal concern of accounting for long-term construction contracts involves the timing of revenue (and thus profit) recognition.

Construction contract revenue may be recognized during construction rather than at the completion of the contract. This "as-earned" approach to revenue recognition is justified because under most long-term construction contracts, both the buyer and the seller (contractor) obtain enforceable rights. The buyer has the legal right to require specific performance from the contractor and, in effect, has an ownership claim to the contractor's work in progress. The contractor, under most long-term contracts, has the right to require the buyer to make progress payments during the construction period. The substance of this business activity is that a continuous sale occurs as the work progresses.

Under the percentage-of-completion method, a percentage of the income associated with a project is recognized in proportion to the estimated percentage of completion of the project. An approach under the completed-contract method is to wait until a construction project has been completed in all respects before recognizing any related revenue. The completed-contract method is not in accordance with IFRS, but this is an allowable method of accounting for long-term construction contracts in the United States, Canada, and Japan—and the only method permitted in Germany.

The completed-contract method makes the most sense when the costs and revenues associated with a project cannot be reasonably tracked, or when there is some uncertainty regarding either the addition of costs to the project or the receipt of payments from the customer. This approach does not, however, reveal the earning of any revenue on the financial statements of a construction company until its projects are substantially complete, giving the reader of its financial statements very poor information about its ability to generate a continuing stream of revenues (except for projects of such short duration that they will be initiated and completed within the same accounting period). Consequently, the percentage-of-completion method is the preferred method in jurisdictions that allow the use of both methods.

IAS recognizes the *percentage-of-completion* method as the only valid method of accounting for construction contracts. Under an earlier version of IAS 11, both the percentage-of-completion method and the completed-contract method were recognized as being acceptable alternative methods of accounting for long-term construction activities.

Under the percentage-of-completion method, accounting must be performed for each project, in which the entity accumulates all project-related expenses. At the end of each reporting period, the budgeted gross margin associated with each project is added to the total expenses accumulated in each account and subtracted from the accumulated billings to date. If the amount of expenses and gross profit exceeds the billings figure, then the company recognizes revenue, matching the difference between the two figures. If the expenses and gross profit figure are less than the amount of billings, the difference is stored in a liability account.

Under the percentage-of-completion method, the accounting staff creates a new asset construction-in-progress (CIP) account to accumulate costs and recognize income. When the CIP exceeds billings, the difference is reported as a current asset. If billings exceed CIP, the difference is reported as a current liability. Where more than one contract exists, the excess cost or liability should be determined on a project-by-project basis, with the accumulated costs and liabilities being stated separately on the statement of financial position. Assets and liabilities may not be offset unless a right of offset exists. Thus, the net debit balances for certain contracts should not ordinarily be offset against net credit balances for other contracts. An exception may exist if the balances relate to contracts that meet the criteria for combining.

Under the percentage-of-completion method, income should not be based on advances (cash collections) or progress (interim) billings. Cash collections and interim billings are based on contract terms that do not necessarily measure contract performance.

Costs and estimated earnings in excess of billings should be classified as an asset. If billings exceed costs and estimated earnings, the difference should be classified as a liability.

Contract costs are comprised of costs that are identifiable with a specific contract, those that are attributable to contracting activity in general—and can be allocated to the contract—and those that are contractually chargeable to a customer. Generally, contract costs would include all direct costs, such as direct materials, direct labor, and direct expenses, as well as any construction overhead that could specifically be allocated to specific contracts.

Contract costs can be broken down into two categories: costs incurred to date and estimated costs to complete. The *costs incurred to date* include precontract costs and costs incurred after contract acceptance. *Precontract costs are costs* incurred before a contract has been entered into, with the expectation that the contract will be accepted and these costs will thereby be recoverable through billings.

Precontract costs include costs of architectural designs, costs of learning a new process, cost of securing the contract, and any other costs that are expected to be recovered if the contract is accepted. Contract costs incurred after the acceptance of the contract are put toward the completion of the project, and are capitalized in the construction-in-progress (CIP) account. The contract does not have to be identified before the capitalization decision is made; it is only necessary that there be an expectation of the recovery of the costs. Once the contract has been accepted, the precontract costs become contract costs incurred to date. Nevertheless, if the precontract costs are already recognized as an expense in the period in which they are incurred, they are not included in contract costs when the contract is obtained in a subsequent period.

Estimated costs to complete are the anticipated costs required to complete a project at a scheduled time. They would be comprised of the same elements as the original total estimated contract costs and would be based on prices expected to be in effect when the costs are incurred. The latest estimates should be used to determine the progress toward completion.

Under the percentage-of-completion method, revenues are recognized based on the stage of completion of a contract. The standard recognizes that the stage of completion of a contract may be determined in many ways and that an entity uses the method that measures reliably the work performed. The standard further stipulates that depending on the nature of the contract, one of these three methods may be chosen:

1. The proportion that contract costs incurred bears to estimated total contract cost (also referred to as the cost-to-cost method)
2. Survey of work performed method
3. Completion of a physical proportion of contract work (also called units-of-work-performed) method

NOTE: Progress payments and advances received from customers often do not reflect the work performed.

Each of these methods of measuring progress on a contract can be identified as being either an input or an output measure. The *input measures* attempt to identify progress in a contract in terms of the efforts devoted to it. The cost-to-cost method is an example of an input measure. Under the cost-to-cost method, the percentage of completion would be estimated by comparing total costs incurred to date to total costs expected for the entire job. *Output measures* are made in terms of results by attempting to identify progress toward completion by physical measures. The units-of-work-performed method is an example of an output measure. Under this method, an estimate of completion is made in terms of achievements to date, but it is not considered to be as reliable as input measures.

When the stage of completion is determined by reference to the contract costs incurred to date, the standard specifically refers to certain costs that are to be excluded from contract costs. Examples of such costs are

- Contract costs that relate to future activity (e.g., construction materials supplied to the site but not yet consumed during construction)
- Payments made in advance to subcontractors prior to performance of the work by the subcontractor

Under the *cost-to-cost method,* we measure the percentage of completion by dividing the total amount of costs incurred to date by the total estimated project cost. This method works well only if the total estimated project cost is revised regularly to reflect the most accurate cost information. Also, it tends to result in proportionately greater amounts of revenue recognition early in a project, since this is when most of the material-related costs are incurred. A more accurate way to calculate the percentage of completion when there are large up-front materials costs is to include the materials costs only when the aspects of the project in which they are used are completed.

Example of the cost-to-cost method

The Brisbane Construction Company (BCC) is building a hotel and has elected to purchase the materials for the air-conditioning system, costing €A200,000, at the beginning of the project. The total estimated project cost is €2 million and the amount billable to the customer is €A2.5 million. After one month, BCC has incurred a total of €A400,000 in costs, including the air conditioning equipment. This is 20% of the total project cost, and would entitle BCC to recognize €A500,000 of revenue (20% of $A2.5 million). However, because the air-conditioning equipment has not yet been installed, a more accurate approach would be to exclude the cost of this equipment from the calculation, resulting in a project completion percentage of 10% and recognizable revenue of €A250,000. The resulting journal entry would be

Costs and estimated earnings in excess of billings	125,000	
Contract revenues earned		125,000

The trouble with these methods is that one must have good cost tracking and project planning systems in order to ensure that all related costs are being properly accumulated for each project, and that cost overruns are accounted for when deriving the percentage of completion. For example, if poor management results in a doubling of the costs incurred at the halfway point of a construction project—from €A5,000 up to €A10,000—this means that the total estimated cost for the entire project (of €A10,000) would already have been reached when half of the project had not yet been completed. In such a case, one should review the remaining costs left to be incurred and change this estimate to ensure that the resulting percentage of completion is accurate.

If the percentage-of-completion calculation appears suspect when based on costs incurred, one can also use a percentage of completion that is based on a Gantt chart or some other planning tool that reveals how much of the project has actually been completed. For example, if a Microsoft Project plan reveals that a construction project has reached the 60% milestone, then one can reasonably assume that 60% of the project has been completed, even if the proportion of costs incurred may result in a different calculation.

Costs that may be included in the construction-in-progress account include direct labor, materials, and overhead related to the project. Expenses included in overhead should be consistently applied across multiple projects, as should the method of applying overhead to jobs; this keeps one from arbitrarily shifting overhead expenses between project accounts.

If the estimate of costs left to be incurred plus actual costs already incurred exceeds the total revenue to be expected from a contract, then the full amount of the difference should be recognized in the current period as a loss, and it should be presented on the statement of financial position as a current liability. If the percentage-of-completion method has been used on the project, then the amount recognized will be the total estimated loss on the project plus all project profits previously recognized. If, after the loss estimate has been made, the actual loss turns out to be a smaller number, the difference can be recognized in the current period as a gain.

Example of project loss recognition

The BCC Construction Company's cost accountant has determined that its construction of a new office building will probably result in a loss of €A80,000, based on his most recent cost estimates. The company uses the percentage-of-completion method, under which it had previously recorded gross profits of €A35,000 for the project. Thus, the company must record a loss of €A115,000 in the current period, both to record the total estimated loss and to back out the formerly recognized profit. The entry is

Loss on uncompleted project	115,000	
Estimated loss on uncompleted contract		115,000

If costs are incurred prior to the signing of a project contract, these costs must be charged to expense at once rather than storing them in the construction-in-progress account as an asset. It is not allowable to shift these costs retroactively from an expense account into the construction-in-progress account.

Service Revenues

Service revenues differ from product sales in that revenue recognition is generally based on the performance of specific activities rather than on the shipment of a product. The recognition of revenue should be with reference to the stage of completion of the transaction at the date of the statement of financial position. The outcome of a transaction can be estimated reliably when each of the four conditions set out next is met.

1. The amount of revenue can be measured reliably.
2. The probability that the economic benefits related to this transaction will flow to the entity exists.
3. The stage of completion of the transaction at the statement of financial position date can be measured reliably.
4. The costs incurred for the transaction and the costs to complete the transaction can be measured reliably.

This manner of recognition of revenue, based on the stage of completion, is often referred to as the percentage-of-completion method. IAS 11 also mandates recognition of revenue on this basis. Revenue is recognized only when it is probable that the economic benefits related to the transaction will flow to the reporting entity. If there is uncertainty with regard to the collectibility of an amount already included in revenue, though, the uncollectible amount should be recognized as an expense instead of adjusting it against the amount of revenue originally recognized.

In order to be able to make reliable estimates, an entity should agree with the other party to these points:

- Each other's enforceable rights with respect to the services provided
- The consideration to be exchanged
- The manner and terms of settlement

It is important that the entity has in place an effective internal financial budgeting and reporting system. This ensures that the entity can promptly review and revise the estimates of revenue as the service is being performed. It should be noted, however, that merely because there is a later need for revisions does not by itself make an estimate of the outcome of the transaction unreliable.

Progress payments and advances received from customers are emphatically *not* a measure of stage of completion. The stage of completion of a transaction may be determined in a number of ways. Depending on the nature of the transaction, the method used may include

- Surveys of work performed
- Services performed to date as a percentage of total services to be performed
- The proportion that costs incurred to date bear to the estimated total costs of the transaction (Only costs that reflect services performed or to be performed are included in costs incurred to date or in estimated total costs.)

In certain cases, services are performed by an indeterminable number of acts over a specified period of time. Revenue in such a case should be recognized on a straight-line basis unless it is possible to estimate the stage of completion more reliably by some other method. Similarly, when in a series of acts to be performed in rendering a service a specific act is much more significant than other acts, the recognition is postponed until the significant act is performed.

During the early stages of the transaction, it may not be possible to estimate the outcome of the transaction reliably. In all such cases, where the outcome of the transaction involving the rendering of services cannot be estimated reliably, revenue should be recognized only to the extent of the expenses recognized that are recoverable. In a later period, when the uncertainly that precluded the reliable estimation of the outcome no longer exists, revenue is recognized as usual.

Under the percentage-of-completion (or proportional performance) method, the amount of revenue recognized is based on the proportional amount of direct costs incurred for each action to the estimated total amount of direct costs required to complete the entire service. If the service involves many identical actions (such as delivering the newspaper for a year), then revenue can be based on the proportion of actions completed thus far under the contract. Alternatively, if the service period is fixed but the amount of service provided cannot be determined (such as annual customer support for a software package), then service revenue can be ratably recognized over the service period.

Example of the percentage-of-completion method using direct costs

If a service contract for €100,000 involved the completion of a single step that required €8,000 of direct costs to complete, and the total direct cost estimate for the entire job were €52,000, then the amount of revenue that could be recognized at the completion of that one action would be €15,385 = (€8,000/€52,000) × €100,000.

Example of the percentage-of-completion method using a fixed period

A software company sells annual support agreements along with its software packages. A typical support agreement costs €2,400 per year. The company has no obligation other than to respond to customer calls, whose timing, duration, and frequency cannot be predicted. Accordingly, it ratably recognizes €200 of revenue per month for each agreement, which is 1/12 of the total amount.

Recognition of Losses on Service Contracts

If the amount of direct costs incurred on a services project plus the estimate of remaining costs to be incurred exceeds the net revenue estimate for a project, the excess cost should be charged to expense, with the offsetting credit first being used to eliminate any deferred costs and any remainder being stored in a liability account.

Example of loss recognition on a services contract

The ABC Software Development Company expects to earn €100,000 in revenues from the sale of a new computer game it is developing. Unfortunately, its incurred direct expenses of €64,000 and estimated remaining costs of €50,000 exceed projected revenues by €14,000. The company had stored an additional €3,500 of incurred costs related to the project in an asset account. The next entry records the initial loss transaction:

	Debit	Credit
Loss on service contract	14,000	
Unrecognized contract costs		3,500
Estimated loss on service contracts		10,500

As actual losses are incurred in later periods, the Estimated Loss on Service Contracts account is debited to reduce the outstanding liability.

Recording Initiation Fees as Service Revenue

A company may charge an initiation fee as part of a service contract, such as the up-front fee that many health clubs charge to new members. This fee should be recognized immediately as revenue only if there is a discernible value associated with it that can be separated from the services provided from ongoing fees that may be charged at a later date. If the initiation fee does not yield any specific value to the purchaser, however, then revenue from it can be recognized only over the term of the agreement to which the fee is attached. For example, if a health club membership agreement were to last for two years, then the revenue associated with the initiation fee should be spread over two years.

Recording Out-of-Pocket Expense Reimbursements

It is a common occurrence for service companies to bill their customers for any out-of-pocket expenses incurred, such as photocopying and delivery charges. It is not acceptable to record customer reimbursement of these expenses as a reduction in expenses. Instead, revenue must be credited for the amount of any reimbursements made.

Example of treatment of out-of-pocket expense reimbursements

The ABC Legal Services LLP entity charges a client for €552.00 in document delivery charges. It incorporates this charge into its standard monthly customer billing, crediting revenues for €552.00 and debiting receivables for €552.00.

Sales When Collection Is Uncertain

Two methods are used to record sales when the collection of those sales is uncertain. The first approach is the *installment method,* under which both revenue and the associated cost of goods sold are recognized at the time of the initial sale, but gross profit recognition is deferred until cash payments are received. This method requires one to track the gross margin percentage for each reporting period, so the correct percentage can be recognized when the associated cash receipts arrive at a later date. The second approach is the *cost recovery method,* under which the recognition of all gross profit is delayed until cash payments have been received that equal the entire cost of goods sold. The cost recovery method is the more conservative method and should be used only when the collection of sales is highly uncertain.

For both recognition methods, installment accounts receivable are recognized as current assets, since the full term of the installment sale represents the normal operating cycle of the company. If installment sales are not a part of normal company operations, then the receivables are classified as long-term assets. In either case, installment accounts receivable should be itemized on the statement of financial position by year. For example, all outstanding receivables due for payment in 2008 would be listed next to the title "Installment Receivables Due in 2008" in the statement of financial position.

A typical component of installment sales is interest income, which is included in the periodic installment payments. Since installment payments typically are designed to be in equal amounts, the interest income component of these billings will comprise a gradually decreasing amount as more of the installment receivable is paid off. In order to properly account for the interest income component of installment sales, interest income must be stripped out of each payment made and credited to the interest income account, leaving the remaining balance of the payment subject to accounting under either the installment or cost recovery method. For the cost recovery method, interest income related to any long-term installment sales increases the unrecognized gross profit until the aggregate customer payments exceed the asset cost, after which the interest income is recognized.

Example of the installment method

The Debussy Music Company sells musical instruments in bulk to school districts. Under one recent deal, it sold €10,000 of instruments to a district in Brittany at a gross profit of 30%. The district paid for the instruments in four annual installments that included 8% interest. The next table illustrates the recognition of both interest income and gross profit under the deal. Equal cash payments of €3,019.21 were made at the end of each year (column 1), from which interest income was separated and recognized (column 2), leaving an annual net receivable reduction (column 3). The gross profit on the deal (column 5) was recognized in proportion to the amount of accounts receivable reduction each year, which was 30% of column 3.

Date	*(1)* *Cash payment*	*(2)* *Interest @ 8%*	*(3)* *Receivable reduction*	*(4)* *Receivable balance*	*(5)* *Profit realized*
1/1/2008				€10,000.00	
12/31/2009	€3,019.21	€ 800.00	€2,219.21	€7,780.79	€ 665.76
12/31/2010	3,019.21	622.46	2,396.75	5,384.04	719.02
12/31/2011	3,019.21	430.72	2,588.49	2,795.56	776.55
12/31/2012	3,019.20	223.64	2,795.56	0.00	838.67
		€2,076.83			€3,000.00

In short, Debussy recognized 30% of the deferred gross profit contained within each cash payment, net of interest income. As an example of the journal entry made with each cash receipt, the company made this entry to record the cash payment received on 12/31/2008:

	Debit	Credit
Cash	3,019.21	
Interest income		800.00
Accounts receivable		2,219.21
Deferred gross profit	665.76	
Recognized gross profit		665.76

Example of the cost recovery method

We use the same assumptions for the Debussy Music Company under the cost recovery method. Cash payments are the same, as are the interest charges and beginning balance. However, no gross profit or interest income is realized until all €7,000 of product costs have been recovered through cash payments net of interest income. Instead, interest income is shifted to a deferred account. To reflect these changes, column 5 shows a declining balance of unrecovered costs that are eliminated when the third periodic payment arrives. This allows Debussy's controller to recognize a small amount of deferred interest income in the third year, representing the net amount of cash payment left over after all costs have been recovered. In the final year, all remaining deferred interest income can be recognized, leaving the deferred gross margin as the last item to be recognized.

Date	(1) Cash payment	(2) Interest @ 8%	(3) Receivable reduction	(4) Receivable balance	(5) Unrecovered cost	(6) Profit realized	(7) Interest realized
1/1/2008				€10,000.00	€7,000.00		
12/31/2008	€3,019.21	€ 800.00	€2,219.21	7,780.79	€4,780.79		
12/31/2009	3,019.21	622.46	$2,396.75	5,384.04	€2,384.04		
12/31/2010	3,019.21	430.72	$2,588.49	2,795.56	€ --		€ 204.43
12/31/2011	3,019.20	223.64	$2,795.56	0.00	€ --	€3,000.00	€1,872.40
		€2,076.83				€3,000.00	€2,076.83

Repossession of Goods under Installment Sales

It is acceptable to recognize bad debts only under installment sales, since the seller can usually repossess the underlying goods. When the goods are repossessed, however, their value must be adjusted to their net realizable value, which in most cases calls for the recognition of a loss.

Example of goods repossession

The Xian Trailer Company has repossessed a construction trailer, for which €40,000 of accounts receivable is still outstanding, as well as €10,000 of deferred gross profit. The trailer has a fair market value of €28,000, so the company records the next entry to eliminate the receivable and deferred gross profit, while recognizing a loss of €2,000 on the write-down of the construction trailer:

Deferred gross margin	10,000	
Finished goods inventory	28,000	
Loss on inventory write-down	2,000	
Accounts receivable		40,000

Revenue Recognition When Right of Return Exists

If a sale transaction allows the buyer to return goods to the seller within a stated time period, then the transaction should be recognized only when one can reasonably estimate the amount of returns. If so, a sales return allowance should be established at the time of the sale, and it should coincide with the recognition of the sale. In practice, many companies do not record a returns allowance because the amount of sales returns is so small.

If the amount of sales returns cannot be reasonably estimated, then revenue recognition must be delayed until the expiration date of the return privilege has passed.

Revenue Recognition for Multiple Deliverables

Arrangements between vendors and their customers often include the sale of multiple products and services (deliverables). A multiple deliverable arrangement (MDA) can be structured using fixed, variable, or contingent pricing or a combinations thereof. Product delivery and service performance can occur at different times and in different locations, and customer acceptance can be subject to various return privileges or performance guarantees.

The accounting for multiple-element revenue arrangements is not currently addressed under IFRS, but the IASB's ongoing project on revenue recognition does deal with this increasingly common phenomenon. As part of its current project, it has examined the application of an assets and liabilities (statement of financial position) approach to revenue recognition against the cases involving multiple-element revenue arrangements. Afterward, it contrasted the impact of such an approach to the positions taken by the FASB's Emerging Issues Task Force's *Accounting for Revenue Arrangements with Multiple Deliverables*—EITF Issue 00-21 (2002), focusing on when revenue is earned (income statement approach). The IASB noted that the EITF's approach was consistent with, but more extensive than, the revenue recognition criteria in IAS 18. It tentatively agreed that from the case studies examined, similar outcomes would result in many cases from applying either approach.

Three steps must be followed when determining revenue recognition for an MDA arrangement under EITF 00-21:

1. Separate the components of the MDA into separate units of accounting; this can occur only if each component to be tracked separately has stand-alone value to the customer and there is objective evidence of its fair value.
2. Allocate proceeds from the total sale arrangement to the separate units of accounting based on their relative fair values.
3. Apply revenue recognition criteria separately to each unit of accounting.

When determining the fair value of each of the units of accounting in an MDA, it is best to use vendor-specific objective evidence (VSOE), the price at which the vendor has sold these units elsewhere in the marketplace on a stand-alone basis.

Example of multiple deliverable revenue recognition

Peach Company sells an MP3 player, which it calls the Nectarine. Peach prefers to sell the Nectarine with a bundled annual support package, which sells for €320. Without the service package, the Nectarine retails for €250, and Peach sells the servicing package separately for €120 per year.

Peach splits apart the two revenue elements of the bundled annual support package by allocating revenue to the Nectarine, based on the fair values of the Nectarine and its support package, which it calculates as:

$$\frac{(\text{€250 product price})}{(\text{€250 product price} + \text{€120 servicing price})} \times \text{€320 bundled price} = \text{€216.22}$$

Peach also allocates revenue to the support package in the same manner with this calculation:

$$\frac{(\text{€120 servicing price})}{(\text{€250 product price} + \text{€120 servicing price})} \times \text{€320 bundled price} = \text{€103.78}$$

Based on these calculations, Peach can recognize €216.22 of revenue every time it sells the bundled Nectarine support package. However, because Peach must provide one year of service under the support package, the remaining €103.78 of revenue associated with the servicing contract can be recognized only incrementally on a monthly basis over the 12-month life of the service contract, which is €8.65 per month.

Franchise Sales

Franchise operations are generally subject to the same accounting principles as other commercial enterprises. Special issues arise out of franchise agreements, however, which require the application of special accounting rules.

Revenue is recognized, with an appropriate provision for bad debts, when the franchisor has substantially performed all material services or conditions. Only when revenue is collected over an extended period of time and collectibility cannot be predicted in advance would the use of the cost recovery or installment methods of revenue recognition be appropriate. Substantial performance means

- The franchisor has no remaining obligation to either refund cash or forgive any unpaid balance due.
- Substantially all initial services required by the agreement have been performed.
- No material obligations or conditions remain.

Even if the contract does not require initial services, the pattern of performance by the franchisor in other franchise sales will impact the time period of revenue recognition. This can delay such recognition until services either are performed or it can reasonably be assured they will not be performed. The franchisee operations will be considered as started when such substantial performance has occurred.

If initial franchise fees are large compared to services rendered, and if continuing franchise fees are small compared to services to be rendered, then a portion of the initial fee is deferred in an amount sufficient to cover the costs of future services plus a reasonable profit—after considering the impact of the continuing franchise fee.

Example of initial franchise fee revenue recognition

Shanghai Oriental Cuisine sells a Quack's Roast Duck franchise to Toledo Restaurants. The franchise is renewable after two years. The initial franchise fee is €50,000, plus a fixed fee of €500 per month. In exchange, Shanghai provides staff training, vendor relations support, and site selection consulting. Each month thereafter, Shanghai provides €1,000 of free local advertising. Shanghai's typical gross margin on franchise start-up sales is 25%.

Because the monthly fee does not cover the cost of monthly services provided, Shanghai defers a portion of the initial franchise fee and amortizes it over the two-year life of the franchise agreement, using this calculation:

	Cost of monthly services provided €1,000 × 24 months	=	€24,000
÷	Markup to equal standard 25% gross margin	=	.75
=	Estimated revenue required to offset monthly services provided	=	32,000
	Less: Monthly billing to franchise €500 × 24 months	–	12,000
=	Amount of initial franchise fee to be deferred	=	€20,000

Shanghai's entry to record the franchise fee deferral is

Franchise fee revenue	20,000	
Unearned franchise fees (liability)		20,000

Shanghai recognizes 1/24th of the unearned franchise fee liability during each month of the franchise period on a straight-line basis, which amounts to €833.33 per month.

Motion Picture Revenues

An entity recognizes revenue from a sale or licensing arrangement only when all of these five conditions are met:

1. Persuasive evidence exists of a sale or licensing arrangement with a customer. This requires documented evidence of the license period, films covered by the agreement, the rights transferred, and the payment terms.
2. The film is complete and, in accordance with the terms of the arrangement, has been delivered or is available for immediate and unconditional delivery. This requirement is not fulfilled if the customer requires significant changes to the film.
3. The license period for the arrangement has started and the customer can begin exploitation, exhibition, or sale.
4. The arrangement fee is fixed or determinable. If there are multiple films in the agreement, this may require allocation of the fee to each film based on the relative fair values of the rights to exploit each film. If relative fair values cannot be determined, then the company cannot recognize revenue until those determinations can be made.
5. Collection of the arrangement fee is reasonably assured.

If any of these conditions has not been met, the company defers revenue recognition until all of the conditions are met. In some cases, whether a license fee or royalty will be received or not is contingent on the occurrence of a future event. In such cases, revenue is recognized only when it is probable that the fee or royalty will be received, which is normally when the event has occurred.

DECISION TREE

Recording Revenues at Gross or Net

Given the large company valuations that can be achieved by recording the largest possible amount of revenue, it is no surprise that companies have a tendency to record revenue even when they are only acting as brokers rather than the initiators of revenue transactions. The decision tree in Exhibit 5.1 is designed to show the criteria that a company must pass before it can record revenue at the gross amount; all three criteria must be satisfied; otherwise only the commission or broker fee associated with the sale can be recorded as revenue.

Exhibit 5.1 Decision Tree for Recording Revenue at Gross or Net

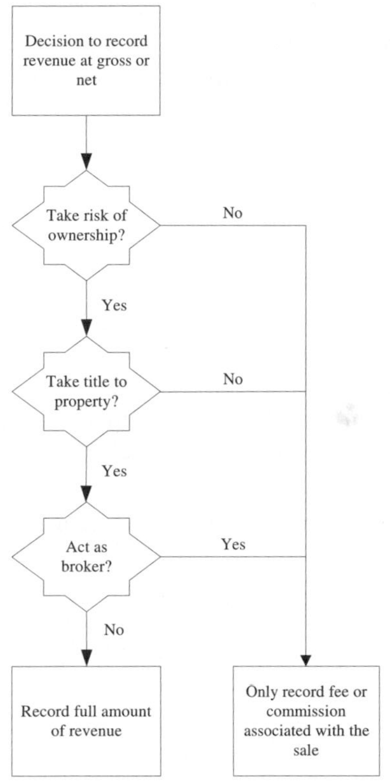

POLICIES

Revenue—General

- **Preliminary revenue summaries shall be issued no later than one day following the close of an accounting period.** This policy is designed to prevent the accounting staff from artificially keeping the books open past the end of the reporting period, since it must commit to a specific revenue figure within a day of closing.
- **Extended rights of return shall not be allowed.** This policy limits the ability of the sales staff to engage in "channel stuffing," because it cannot offer special rights of return to customers in exchange for early sales. The policy keeps a company from vacillating between large swings in sales caused by channel stuffing.
- **Special sale discounts shall not be allowed without senior management approval.** This policy prevents large bursts in sales caused by special price discounts that can stuff a company's distribution channels, causing rapid sales declines in subsequent periods.
- **The company shall not use bill and hold transactions.** Though bill and hold transactions are allowable under clearly defined and closely restricted circumstances, they are subject to abuse and so should generally be avoided.

This policy ensures that bill and hold transactions would require board approval before being used.

- **Estimated profits on service contracts shall be reviewed monthly.** This policy ensures that estimated losses on service contracts are identified and recognized promptly, rather than being delayed until the contracts are closed.

Barter Revenues

- **The company shall not engage in barter transactions whose sole purpose is the creation of revenue.** This policy informs the accounting staff that it is unacceptable to create barter swap transactions, the sole purpose of which are to create additional revenues without the presence of any economic reason for the transaction. An exchange of similar advertising services is not a transaction that generates revenue under IAS 18.
- **All expenses associated with barter transactions shall be recognized in the same proportions as related revenues.** This policy is designed to keep expenses associated with barter swap transactions from being significantly delayed, while revenues are recognized up front. The policy will keep profits from being recorded incorrectly in advance.

Long-Term Construction Contracts

- **Construction contract revenue shall be calculated using the percentage-of-completion method.** This policy allows a company to calculate all construction revenues using a consistent methodology; that way, there is no question of using one method over another to gain a short-term advantage in reporting the amount of revenue.
- **Accounts used in overhead pools shall be reviewed annually and altered only with management approval.** This policy keeps the accounting staff from arbitrarily altering the contents of overhead cost pools. Overhead pool alterations are a classic approach for shifting expenses out of the current period and into construction-in-process asset accounts.

Sales When Collection Is Uncertain

- **A single revenue recognition method shall be used for all installment sales.** This policy keeps an accounting department from switching back and forth between the installment method and cost recovery method for recognizing this type of revenue; otherwise it would be able to manipulate reported levels of profitability.

Revenue Recognition When Right of Return Exists

- **A sales return allowance shall be maintained for all goods sold with a right of return.** This policy ensures that profits are not overstated initially by the amount of any potential returns by requiring an initial reserve to be established.

Franchising Revenues

- **The initial franchise fee shall not be recognized as revenue until all start-up services to be provided by the franchisor have been substantially completed (or equipment and other tangible assets are delivered or title passes).** This policy keeps the accounting staff from recognizing revenue prematurely.
- **The estimated number of total franchise locations shall be regularly reviewed and updated.** Under an area franchise sale agreement, the franchisor typically recognizes initial fee revenue based on the proportion of actual franchise locations completed within the area as a proportion of the total estimated number to be completed. Thus, the number of estimated locations directly impacts revenue recognition, and should be kept as accurate as possible.
- **Deferred franchise costs shall be matched against franchise fees as part of the monthly closing process.** If deferred costs related to a franchise exceed the amount of the franchise fee, then the excess costs must be recognized at once. This policy ensures that any excess costs will be found and charged to expense in a timely manner.

PROCEDURES[2]

Issue a Customer Credit Rating

Follow these eight steps to both create and adjust a customer's credit rating.

1. Pull the standard credit references form (see the Customer Credit Application in the Forms and Reports section) and fax it to the customer requesting credit.
2. Once the completed form is returned, verify with each customer reference the maximum and average amounts of credit granted and used, as well as any issues with slow payment.
3. Obtain the names of other credit references from these references, if possible, and record the answers to the same questions from them.
4. Contact Dun & Bradstreet's automated credit reporting system (or other system available), enter the customer's contact information, and specify that you want to receive the Business Information Report.
5. To determine an appropriate credit level, ignore any exceedingly high credit amounts granted by other companies, and pick the average level of the remainder. Then reduce this amount by 5% for every additional day of late payments as reported for the customer by Dun & Bradstreet.
6. If there has been some sales experience with a customer, consult with the collections staff to obtain their opinion of the most appropriate credit level. Also review the Dun & Bradstreet bankruptcy early warning notification

---

[2] *Many of the procedures in this section are reprinted with permission from Chapter 5 of Steven Bragg, **Design and Maintenance of Accounting Manuals** (Hoboken, NJ: John Wiley & Sons, Inc. 2003).*

system to see if there are any recent customer problems. Revise the credit level based on this information.

7. Enter the credit level in the accounting system's customer file.
8. Notify the sales staff of the credit level granted.

Process a Shipment

Use this 11-step procedure to ensure that the proper paperwork and computer transactions are completed when a product is shipped to a customer.

1. Access the daily schedule of shipments in the computer system and print the report.
2. Verify that all finished goods listed on the daily schedule are on hand and available for shipment.
3. If the required quantities are not available, contact the customer service staff to ascertain customer wishes regarding partial orders, or contact the production scheduling staff to ensure that the production department will complete the missing products as soon as possible.
4. Mark all other items on the daily schedule as being ready for delivery.
5. Using the daily schedule, remove all targeted items from the warehouse bins and relocate them to the shipping area.
6. Contact freight carriers regarding scheduled pickup times.
7. Prepare bills of lading and packing slips for all shipments.
8. Load shipments on trucks for delivery.
9. Complete the shipping log.
10. Send copies of the bills of lading and packing slips to the accounting department by interoffice mail. Include a copy of the day's shipping log; it should match all other documentation sent.
11. Access the computer system and enter the customer, ship date, part number, and quantity shipped for each shipment sent out that day.

Create an Invoice

Follow these eight steps to create invoices based on shipping and pricing information.

1. Receive the daily packet of shipping information from the warehouse manager. The paperwork should include a handwritten shipping log as well as two copies of the bills of lading. Print the customer order from the computer system. Separate these documents into different piles.
2. Verify that there is a bill of lading for every order listed on the shipping log and also that *all* bills of lading are listed on the log. Then put the bills of lading in order, first by customer name and then by order number (if there is more than one order per customer), and match the order forms to them.
3. Check the "carrier" column on the shipping log. There is no shipping charge if "customer pickup" is noted. Otherwise, if a carrier name is listed, calculate a freight rate based on the standard freight rate schedule. Note the amount of the freight charge on the order form.

4. Go to the invoicing module in the accounting software and access the invoicing screen. Enter the customer name and verify that the "Bill To" name in the system is correct. If not, change it to match the name listed on the order. Then enter the part number, the quantity, and the price listed on the order form; add the freight rate to the bottom of the invoice. Also verify that the sales tax code is correct. Save the invoice record and repeat until all invoices have been entered.
5. Verify that the invoice form is correctly positioned in the printer. Run a test invoice, if necessary, to ensure that the form is properly aligned. Then print the daily invoice batch.
6. Burst all printed invoices, with the pink copies going to the alphabetical filing bin, the white copies going to customers, and the goldenrod copies going to the numerical filing bin.
7. Stuff the white invoice copies into envelopes and mail them to customers.
8. Attach the pink invoice copies to the bills of lading, packing slip, and customer orders, and file them by customer name. File the goldenrod copies in numerical order.

Compare Billings to the Shipping Log

Use this five step procedure to verify that shipments are matched by the same number of invoices, thereby ensuring that no invoices are missing or duplicated.

1. Go to the warehouse and make a copy of the shipping log for the previous week. Alternatively (if available), access this information on-line through the receiving system and print out the shipping log.
2. Match the shipments listed on the shipping log to invoices issued during the same period. Note all exceptions in the shipping log for missing billings. Also, note on invoices any incorrect quantities that were billed as well as "leftover" invoices for which there is no shipping record.
3. Using the list of shipments for which there are no corresponding invoices, go to the shipping department and obtain bills of lading for the unbilled shipments. If these are not available, determine which freight carrier shipped the items and obtain shipping traces on them. Then create invoices, mail a copy to the customer, and attach proof of delivery to the company's copy of the invoice. File the company's copy in the accounting files.
4. Using the list of invoices for which no corresponding shipment is recorded in the shipping log, go back to the company's copy of these invoices and see if there is any bill of lading or other proof of delivery attached to the invoice. If not, call the shipping department to verify that no such documentation exists there. If not, issue a credit to eliminate these invoices.
5. Using the list of invoices for which the quantity of product billed is different from the quantity shipped, go back to the company's copy of the invoice and check the attached bill of lading to determine the actual quantity shipped. If the quantity is different, verify this with the shipping department and then either issue a credit (if the quantity billed was too high) or an additional invoice (if the quantity billed was too low).

Review Pricing Errors

Use this seven-step procedure to locate all invoice pricing errors occurring during a fixed time period, determine underlying problems, and report on the results to management.

1. Go to the accounting software and access the invoice register for the past month.
2. Convert the invoice register to an Excel file. Open the Excel file and sort the invoice list by dollar order. Delete all invoices from the list that do not have a credit balance.
3. Search the description field for each credit for wording regarding corrections of pricing errors. Retain these records and delete all others. Print the spreadsheet.
4. Transfer this information to a separate spreadsheet report: credit number, credit amount, customer name, correct price, actual price charged, the quantity of product to which the correction applies, the grand total pricing error, and the initials of the customer service person who processed the credit.
5. Go to the customer service person who processed the credit and determine the cause of the pricing error. Include this information on the spreadsheet.
6. Print the spreadsheet and distribute it to the sales manager, controller, and chief operating officer.
7. Enter the total number of pricing errors and the total dollar error in the monthly corporate statistics report.

Process Bill and Hold Transactions

Although bill and hold transactions are generally to be discouraged, as noted under the Policies section, they can be used under very specific circumstances. When this occurs, a separate procedure is needed because invoices are not triggered by a shipping transaction. The next six steps show the proper approach.

1. Access the warehouse database on a specific recurring date and call up the report listing all bill and hold items currently in stock. Take the report to the warehouse and verify that all items listed on the report match what is in stock alternately, trace all items in stock back to the report. Investigate any variances.
2. If the invoice number associated with each bill and hold item is not already listed in the report, retrieve this information from the file containing the last period's bill and hold transactions. Compare this information to the validated warehouse report and note any items that have not yet been billed.
3. For all items not yet billed, print the Acknowledgment of Bill and Hold Transaction form (see the Forms and Reports section for a sample version) and fax it to the authorized customer representative with a request that it be signed and sent back.
4. Once the signed form has been received, verify that all signature spots have been signed, attach a copy of the customer's purchase order to the form,

copy both, and send them to the billing staff for invoicing. Meanwhile, put the originals in a pending file.

5. Once the accounting staff creates the invoice, an invoice copy will be returned. Attach this copy to the signed form and customer purchase order, staple them together, and file them by customer name.
6. When bill and hold items are eventually shipped to the customer, the warehouse staff removes them from the inventory database and sends the bill of lading to the accounting person handling the bill and hold transactions. This person removes the transaction's previously filed invoice packet from the files, attaches to it the bill of lading, and forwards the complete package to the billings staff, which then files the packet in the completed invoices file.

Process Sales Returns

Use this procedure to issue a sales return authorization number to a customer, log the authorization into the accounting system, and record the receipt upon arrival.

1. **Customer service staff.** When a customer calls to ask for a return authorization number, call up the return authorization screen in the computer system and verify that the part numbers and quantities to be returned were previously ordered and received by the customer. If not, deny return authorization; if it was, enter the part numbers and quantities to be returned into the system and issue a return authorization number.
2. **Receiving staff.** When products are returned from a customer, verify the existence of a return authorization number on the delivery. If not, the attempted delivery should be rejected. If so, enter it into the computer system and verify that the items included in the delivery were authorized. If not, reject the order. If so, enter the amounts actually received into the computer, and close the authorization if all items received match the amounts authorized.
3. **Accounting staff.** The computer system will create a credit based on the amount of product returned. Offset this amount against the relevant outstanding accounts receivable. If the computer system does not automatically create credits for sales returns, then calculate the credit due, net of any return and restocking charges, and enter the amount in the sales journal. All related documentation should be retained in the customer file.
4. **Warehouse staff.** Move all returned merchandise to the returned goods section of the warehouse. Open and test all returned items, replacing them in new packaging. Log them into the inventory database and move them to the finished goods section of the warehouse.

Collect Overdue Accounts

Use this eight-step procedure to manage the collections process as well as to determine the causes of collection problems and correct them.

1. Go to the accounting database and access the accounts receivable module. Print the accounts receivable aging report.

2. Review the printed report and circle all invoices more than forty days old.
3. Return to the accounts receivable module and print the customer master file, showing contact information for each customer.
4. Using the contact information on the customer master file, use the next four-step sequence of escalating contacts to ensure that customers are aware of nonpayment situations:
    a. Send a fax to the customer noting a payment problem, including a copy of the invoice.
    b. Send an e-mail to the customer noting a payment problem, including an Adobe Acrobat PDF version of the invoice.
    c. Call the customer and verify receipt of the prior information. If no one answers, then leave a message.
    d. If there was no direct contact during the last step, send an overnight delivery package containing the same information.
5. Upon making contact with a customer, determine why payment has not been made. If a customer states that a payment is on the way, verify exactly what invoices are being paid and then inquire about any overdue invoices that will continue to be open after the payment.
6. Go to the customer contact log and enter the date of each customer contact, who was contacted, and what information was gained. Use this information as a reference whenever calling the customer again in the future. Also, if there is new customer contact information as a result of the most recent customer contact, update the customer file with this information.
7. If it is necessary to adjust a customer's credit limit to more properly reflect its ability to pay, go to the credit department and review the credit status with the credit manager. If new credit terms are agreed on, contact the customer with this information.
8. If customer contacts reveal that internal problems are causing collection difficulties, then assign a problem code to each collection issue in the collections database as well as a brief description of the issue. Periodically run a summary report sorted by problem code and send this information to the controller or chief financial officer for further action.

Long-Term Construction Contracts—Percentage-of-Completion Calculation

Use this six-step procedure to determine the amount of revenue to be recognized on a construction project.

1. Access the approved project bid file and determine the estimated gross profit percentage for the project.
2. Discuss the estimated gross margin with the project manager to verify that the percentage is still valid; if it is not, use the project manager's revised estimate.
3. Access the general ledger and note the total amount of expenses accumulated to date in the project's construction-in-progress account.

4. Divide the total project expenses by one, minus the estimated gross profit percentage resulting in the total expenses plus the estimated gross profit.
5. Access the project billing records and determine the total amount of billings made to the customer thus far.
6. Subtract the total expenses and estimated gross profit from the billings figure. If the amount of expenses and gross profits is larger than the billed amount, debit the Unbilled Contract Receivables account and credit the Contract Revenues Earned account for the difference. If the amount of expenses and gross profits is less than the billed amount, debit the Contract Revenues Earned account and credit the Billings Exceeding Project Costs and Margin account for the difference.

Service Revenues—Advance Recognition of Losses

Use this five-step procedure to review service contracts periodically to determine the existence of any projected contract losses.

1. Summarize all project-to-date direct costs from the relevant general ledger account.
2. Go to the project manager and review the amount of estimated costs that have yet to be incurred on the project. Compare this amount to the estimated completion cost from the last review to see if there are any unusual changes, and discuss the differences. Also verify the cost estimated against any project planning database, such as a Gantt or critical path method (CPM) chart.
3. Summarize all project billings to date, and verify the amount of remaining billings, adjusted for any contract modifications.
4. Combine the actual and estimated costs and subtract them from the total expected project revenues. If the costs exceed revenues, notify the controller of the difference with a memo, outlining the reasons for the loss.
5. Debit the Loss on Contracts account for the amount of the estimated loss. Use the offsetting credit to eliminate any unrecognized costs stored in an asset account, and credit the remaining loss to the Estimated Loss on Service Contracts account.

Sales When Collection Is Uncertain—Goods Repossession

Use this three-step procedure to process back into inventory any goods received as part of a repossession from an installment sale when the customer failed to make payments.

1. Upon the return of goods, the warehouse staff segregates the inventory and contacts the materials review board for an evaluation.
2. The materials review board periodically examines all returned goods to determine if they can be returned directly to finished goods inventory at full valuation, refurbished, or donated.
   a. If the goods are returned to finished goods stock, they are entered into inventory at full cost, and the accounting department is notified of the

transaction so it can record the inventory valuation as an offset to the receivable being canceled as part of the repossession.

b. If the goods are to be refurbished, they are entered into inventory at their current fair value, and the accounting department is notified of the reduced valuation so it can record the reduced inventory valuation as a smaller offset to the receivable being canceled as part of the repossession.

c. If the inventory is donated, the warehouse manager fills out the Asset Donation form and sends the original to the accounting department, which retains it for use by the tax department in determining charitable donations. The accounting staff also records a full loss on the returned inventory.

3. Based on the treatment of the returned inventory, the accounting staff credits the accounts receivable account to eliminate the no-longer-due balance, debits the Finished Goods account for the fair value of the returned inventory, debits the Deferred Gross Profit account to eliminate the unpaid balance of unearned gross profit on the transaction, and debits the Loss on Repossessed Inventory account to charge off any difference between these entries.

Revenue Recognition When Right of Return Exists

Use this four-step procedure to determine the amount of sales returns to record at the end of each reporting period.

1. Summarize all sales occurring during the period for which a right of return exists, using subcategories if there are significant differences in sales returns for different products.
2. Calculate the sales return percentage for each category of products on a one-year rolling basis.
3. Multiply the sales return percentage by sales in each category to arrive at the required sales return allowance.
4. Debit the revenue account for the amount of the allowance to be added, while crediting the associated cost of goods sold and deferred gross profit accounts.

CONTROLS

General

- **Investigate all journal entries increasing the size of revenue.** Any time a journal entry is used to increase a sales account, this should be a red flag indicating the potential presence of revenues that were not created through a normal sales journal transaction. These transactions can be legitimate cases of incremental revenue recognition associated with prepaid services, but can also be barter swap transactions or fake transactions whose sole purpose is to increase revenues.

It is especially important to review all sales transactions where the offsetting debit to the sales credit is *not* accounts receivable or cash. This is a prime indicator of unusual transactions that may not really qualify as sales. For example, a gain on an asset sale may be incorrectly credited to a sales account, misleading the reader of a company's financial statements into thinking that its operating revenues have increased.

- **Compare the shipping log and shipping documents to invoices issued at period-end.** This control is designed to spot billings on transactions not completed until after the reporting period had closed. An invoice dated within a reporting period when the associated shipping documentation shows the transaction as having occurred later is clear evidence of improper revenue reporting. If invoices are based on services instead of goods provided, then invoices can be matched to service reports or timesheets instead.
- **Issue financial statements within one day of the period-end.** By eliminating the gap between the end of the reporting period and the issuance of financial statements, it is impossible for anyone to create additional invoices for goods shipping subsequent to the period-end, thereby automatically eliminating any cutoff problems.
- **Compare customer-requested delivery dates to actual shipment dates.** If customer order information is loaded into the accounting computer system, run a comparison of the dates on which customers have requested delivery to the dates on which orders were actually shipped. If there is an ongoing tendency to make shipments substantially early, there may be a problem with trying to create revenue by making early shipments. Pay particular attention for a surge of early shipments in months when revenues would otherwise have been low, indicating a clear intention to increase revenues by avoiding customer-mandated shipment dates. It may be possible to program the computer system to not allow the recording of deliveries if the entered delivery date is prior to the customer-requested delivery date, thereby effectively blocking early revenue recognition.
- **Compare invoice dates to the recurring revenue database.** In cases where a company obtains recurring revenue stream by billing customers periodically for maintenance or subscription services, there can be a temptation to create early billings in order to record revenue somewhat sooner. For example, a billing on a 12-month subscription could be issued after 11 months, thereby accelerating revenue recognition by one month. This issue can be spotted by comparing the total of recurring billings in a month to the total amount of recurring revenue for that period as compiled from the corporate database of customers with recurring revenue. Alternatively, one can compare the recurring billing dates for a small sample of customers to the dates on which invoices were actually issued.
- **Identify shipments of product samples in the shipping log.** A product that is shipped with no intention of being billed is probably a product sample being sent to a prospective customer, marketing agency, and so on. These should be noted as product samples in the shipping log, and the internal audit staff

should verify that each of them was properly authorized—preferably with a signed document.

- **Verify that a signed Acknowledgment of Bill and Hold Transaction has been received for every related transaction.** If a company uses bill and hold transactions, then this control is absolutely mandatory. By ensuring that customers have agreed in advance to be billed for items to be kept in the company's warehouse, one can be assured of being in compliance with the strict rules applying to these transactions. Also, a continual verification of this paperwork (as shown in the Forms and Reports section) will keep managers from incorrectly inflating revenues by issuing false bill and hold transactions.
- **Confirm signed Acknowledgment of Bill and Hold Transactions with customers.** If a company begins to match bill and hold acknowledgment letters to invoices issued to customers (see previous control), the logical reaction of any person who wants to fraudulently continue issuing bill and hold invoices is to create dummy acknowledgments. Consequently, it is useful to contact the persons who allegedly signed the acknowledgments to verify that they actually did so.
- **Do not accept any product returns without an authorization number.** Customers sometimes will try to return products if there is no justification required, clearing out their inventories at the expense of the company. This can be avoided by requiring a return authorization number, which must be provided by the company in advance and prominently noted on any returned goods. If the number is not shown, the receiving department is required to reject the shipment.
- **Compare related company addresses and names to customer list.** By comparing the list of company subsidiaries to the customer list, it can be determined if any intercompany sales have occurred, and if these transactions have all been appropriately backed out of the financial statements. Since employees at one subsidiary may conceal this relationship by using a false company name or address, the same information can be verified at all the other subsidiaries by matching subsidiary names and addresses to their supplier lists; after all it is possible that the receiving companies are *not* trying to hide the intercompany sales information.

Barter Revenues

- **Require a written business case for all barter transactions.** Require the creation of a business case detailing why a barter transaction is required and what type of accounting should be used for it. The case should be approved by a senior-level manager before any associated entry is made in the general ledger, attached to the associated journal entry, and filed. This approach makes it less likely that sham barter swap transactions will be created.

Cash Payments to Customers

- **Verify that cash-back payments to customers are charged to sales.** Compare the customer list to the cash disbursements register to highlight all cash payments made to customers. Investigate each one and verify that the revenue account was debited in those instances where cash-back payments were made. This should not apply to the return of overpayments made by customers to the company.

Recording Revenues at Gross or Net

- **Create a revenue accounting procedure to specify the treatment of gross or net transactions.** When a company deals with both gross and net revenue transactions on a regular basis, there should be a procedure that clearly defines the situations under which revenues shall be treated on a gross or net basis. This reduces the need for internal audit reviews (see next control) to detect revenue accounting problems after the fact.
- **Review the revenue accounting for potential pass-through transactions.** In situations where there is an extremely high cost of goods sold (indicating a possible pass-through transaction) or where there is no clear evidence of the company acting as principal, taking title to goods, or accepting risk of ownership, the internal audit staff should review the appropriateness of the transaction.
- **Trace commission payments back to underlying sale transactions.** One can keep a list of all business partners who pay the company commissions, and run a periodic search on all payments made by them to the company. The internal audit staff can then trace these payments back to the underlying sales made by the company and verify that they were recorded at net rather than at gross.

Long-Term Construction Contracts

- **Compare declared percentage of completion to estimated work required to complete projects.** A very common way to record excessive revenue on a construction project is to falsely claim that the percentage of completion is greater than the actual figure, thereby allowing the company to record a greater proportion of revenues in the current reporting period. Though difficult to verify with any precision, a reasonable control is to match the declared percentage of completion to a percentage of the actual hours worked, divided by the total estimated number of hours worked. The two percentages should match.
- **Ensure that project expenses are charged to the correct account.** A common problem with revenue recognition under the percentage-of-completion method is that extra expenses may be erroneously or falsely loaded into a project's general ledger account, which can then be used as the justification for the recognition of additional revenue related to that project. Auditing expenses in active project accounts can spot these problems.
- **Promptly close project accounts once projects are completed.** It is easy to store project-related expenses in the wrong accounts, and it may be done fraudulently in order to avoid recognizing losses related to excessive amounts of expenses being incurred on specific projects. This problem can be resolved

by promptly closing general ledger project accounts once the related projects are complete; because they can be included in the month-end closing procedure, it will ensure that this problem will be addressed on a regular basis.

- **Control access to general ledger accounts.** Employees are less likely to shift expenses between general ledger construction accounts either if they are unable to access the accounts or if they have no way of reopening closed accounts. This can be achieved by tightly restricting account access, and especially access to the closed or open status flag for each account.
- **Compare the dates on supplier invoices in the construction-in-progress account to the project start date.** Since precontract costs must be charged to expense, there is a temptation to hold these supplier invoices until after the project contract has been signed; as such, they can be stored in the construction-in-progress account instead as an asset. To detect this problem, examine a selection of invoiced expenses in the account to see if any are dated prior to the project's contract date.
- **Review journal entries shifting expenses into construction-in-progress accounts.** Since precontract costs must be charged to expense, there is a temptation to increase short-term profits by shifting these expenses into the construction-in-progress account with a journal entry. To spot this problem, review all journal entries adding expenses to the construction-in-progress account.
- **Consistently aggregate expenses into overhead accounts and charge them to individual projects.** One could charge different overhead expenses to various projects, or apply the same pool of overhead costs inconsistently to the accounts, thereby effectively shifting expenses to those projects that would result in the greatest revenue increase under the percentage-of-completion revenue recognition method. To avoid this problem, periodically verify that the same expenses are being charged consistently to overhead cost pools over time and that the same allocation method is used to shift these expenses from the overhead cost pools to project accounts.
- **Exclude the cost of unused materials from cost-to-cost percentage-of-completion calculations.** Typically more materials than are initially needed are purchased at the beginning of a project. This increases the amount of recognizable revenue early in a project when the cost-to-cost percentage-of-completion method is used. To avoid this problem, remove all unused materials from the calculation.
- **Compare the percentage of revenues recognized to expenses recognized.** When revenues associated with a project are recognized, one must also make a second entry to shift costs from the construction-in-progress account to the cost of goods sold. If this second entry is missed for any reason, profits will be unusually high. To spot this problem, compare the amount of recognized revenue to recognized expenses for each project and verify that it matches the most recent gross profit estimate for the project. If the percentage is higher, some expenses probably have not been recognized.

- **Review prospective project issues with the construction manager.** A common fraud involving project accounting is to shift the timing and amount of recognized losses on projects. These losses can be delayed in order to make the current period's results look better, or made excessively large or small in order to meet reporting targets. Though it is quite difficult to ascertain if the size of a loss is correct, it is possible to guess *when* a loss should be recognized. By having regular discussions with a project's construction manager regarding ongoing and upcoming project-related issues, it is possible to see when significant unbudgeted costs are to be incurred, thereby giving some insight into the need for loss recognition.
- **Watch for expense loading on cost-plus contracts.** When a company is guaranteed by the customer to pay for all expenses incurred, there is a temptation to load extra expenses into an account. These expense additions can be spotted by looking for charges from suppliers whose costs are not normally charged to a specific type of contract, by looking for expense types that increase significantly over expenses incurred in previous periods, and by investigating any journal entries that increase expense levels.

Service Revenues

- **Review underlying contract terms for all percentage-of-completion revenue calculations.** For this control, trace each revenue-creation journal entry back to the related service contract and verify that collection is reasonably assured and that billings are not tied to specific actions. If either of these cases holds true, other more conservative revenue recognition methods must be used that may reduce the amount of revenue recognized.
- **Regularly review service contracts for potential losses.** Losses on service contracts must be recognized as expenses immediately, even if the losses are only estimated. Since there is a natural reluctance to recognize losses in advance of the actual event, a good control is to include a standard review of estimated losses on service contracts as part of the monthly closing process.

Sales When Collection Is Uncertain

- **Verify that the correct gross margin percentage is used for the recognition of gross margins upon the receipt of cash.** The gross margins associated with installment sales should be deferred until the related cash payments are received from customers. This margin is typically aggregated for all sales within a specific time period and used for all receipts related to that time period. If the gross margin percentage for a different period were to be incorrectly used to recognize gross margin dollars, there would be an impact on the reported level of profitability. The best control over this issue is a procedure clearly stating how to calculate, track, and apply gross margins when cash is received. A secondary control is a regular review of all calculations made to recognize gross margins.

Revenue Recognition When Right of Return Exists

- **Include a sales return allowance calculation in the standard closing procedure.** By requiring someone to address the issue of return allowances as part of every period-end close, there is a much greater chance that the allowance amount will be verified against actual returns, resulting in an accurate return allowance.
- **Verify the amount of the return allowance against actual experience.** One can examine the basis for a specific returns allowance amount being recorded, comparing it to actual experience with the same or similar products in the recent past. Conversely this is an after-the-fact control that must be repeated regularly to ensure that allowance levels are reasonable.
- **Review the condition of returned inventory.** Sales returns tend not to be in pristine condition, so a company must record a write-down to their net realizable value at the time of the return. However, the warehouse staff tends to place returned inventory back in stock without any consideration of condition, resulting in the overstatement of finished goods inventory. A good control is to have all sales returns set to one side for review, after which they are either shifted back to stock at full value, thrown away, donated, or reclassified as used stock and assigned a reduced inventory value.

Multiple Deliverable Arrangements (MDAs)

- **Review clusters of invoices issued to individual customers.** A company can circumvent the MDA rules by issuing separate contracts for each element of a sale that normally would be considered to have multiple deliverables. One way to spot this issue is to conduct a periodic audit that searches for clusters of contracts entered into with a single customer within a short period of time. The audit program should include a review of these contracts to determine if they are in fact associated with a single sale transaction.
- **Review definitions of units of accounting.** If a company has multiple sale arrangements that include multiple deliverables, it is possible that it will not separate the various elements into separate units of accounting in a consistent manner. To guard against this issue, a periodic audit should compare the documentation of the various MDAs to locate any inconsistencies in the definition of units of accounting.
- **Compare billings to unbilled costs.** A control problem is indicated when a company records a combination of revenue and "costs and estimated earnings in excess of billings" that exceed the total amount a customer has agreed to pay. A billing procedure should require the accounting staff to compare the combination of billings and unbilled costs to the customer's contractual agreement to pay and to record a loss for any costs incurred that exceed this amount.

Franchise Revenues

- **Compare gross margins earned on initial and ongoing franchise fees.** To ensure that revenue recognition is not accelerated through the use of an excessively high initial franchise fee in proportion to services generated, a periodic audit could calculate and compare the gross margins earned on initial and ongoing franchise fees.
- **Compare completion of services to fee recognition.** It is also possible that revenue could be recognized on an initial franchise fee before all related services have been completed, falsely accelerating revenue recognition. To detect this problem, a periodic audit could compare the completion of services to the recognition of initial franchise fee revenue for each franchise agreement.
- **Compare actual to estimated franchise locations.** It is possible to incorrectly accelerate the recognition of initial franchise fees when area franchise sales have been made, simply by underestimating the number of franchise locations to be situated within the area franchise. A periodic audit can investigate the number of actual and estimated franchise locations used in the revenue recognition calculation to determine if improperly low estimates have been used.
- **Review the timing of franchise revenue recognition.** The franchisor may recognize ongoing franchise fees automatically, without regard to whether related services have been provided at the same time. This is most likely to occur when certain activities, such as advertising campaigns, are conducted only at long intervals and therefore do not coincide with the receipt of franchisee payments. As a result, revenue is incorrectly recognized prior to the completion of all related services by the franchisor. To detect this issue, a periodic audit should review the calculations used to recognize ongoing franchise revenue and whether some revenue recognition is withheld pending the completion of such services.

FORMS AND REPORTS

Customer Credit Application

A key control point over the granting of customer credit is a formal credit application, which the treasury department's credit staff then evaluates to determine an appropriate credit level. An example of this form is shown in Exhibit 5.2. The form contains three blocks of information: the contact block requires the customer to list its address information, which allows the credit staff to run a credit report on the customer through a third-party credit analysis agency; the credit block reveals the customer's general financial status; and the references block contains information about the customer's trade references, as well as who can be contacted for further information.

Exhibit 5.2 Customer Credit Application

Customer Credit Application

Contact

Company Name: ______________________

Address: ______________________

Address: ______________________

City: ____________ State: ___ Zip: ________

Date Started: ________ State of Incorporation: ____________

For Company Use	
Customer No:	
Credit Limit:	
Date Approved:	
Approved By:	

Parent Company Name and Address: ______________________

Contact Name: ______________ Phone: ______________

Web Site: ______________ Fax: ______________

Credit

Credit Requested: € __________ Annual Sales: € __________

Annual Profit: € __________ Total Cash: € __________

Total Debt: € __________ Retained Earnings: € __________

Bank Name: __________ Bank Contact: __________

Bank Address: ______________________

Checking Account Number: __________ Savings Account Number: __________

References

Reference Name: ______________ Phone: __________

Reference Address: ______________________

Reference Name: ______________ Phone: __________

Reference Address: ______________________

Reference Name: ______________ Phone: __________

Reference Address: ______________________

I hereby authorize the above-referenced bank and trading partners to release credit information to the Company for use in reviewing this credit application.

Officer Signature: ______________________

Print Officer Name: ______________ Officer Title: __________

Return to The Company
Address
City State, Zip Code

Acknowledgment of Bill and Hold Transaction

External auditors frown upon the use of bill and hold transactions, since there is a high probability of improper revenue recording associated with them. To anticipate their heightened level of investigation, it is best to have customers initial and sign the form in Exhibit 5.3, indicating customer acknowledgment of all aspects of each bill and hold transaction. Please note that the form is designed for individual purchase orders—it is not sufficient to have a customer sign a blanket acknowledgment covering all transactions over a long time period.

Exhibit 5.3 Acknowledgment of Bill and Hold Transaction Form

Acknowledgment of
Bill and Hold Transaction

Customer Name: ____________________

This document indicates your acknowledgment that a bill and hold transaction exists in regard to purchase order number _________, which you ordered from [company name]. Please indicate your acknowledgment of this transaction by initialing next to each of the following statements and signing at the bottom of the page. If you disagree with any of the statements, please indicate your concerns at the bottom of the page. Thank you!

________ I agree that I ordered the items noted in the purchase order.
(initial)

________ I agree that [company name] is storing the items noted in the purchase order on my behalf.
(initial)

________ I acknowledge that I have taken on all risks of ownership related to this purchase order.
(initial)

________ I agree that I requested the bill and hold transaction, and my reason for doing so is as
(initial) follows:

____

____

________ I agree that all performance issues related to this purchase order were completed no
(initial) later than ___________.

________ I agree that the held goods will be delivered to me no later than __________.
(initial)

I disagree with some or all of the statements on this page. My concerns are as follows:

____

____

____

______________________________ ________________
Signature Date

______________________________ ________________
Name (Please Print) Title

Sales Return Authorization Form

Requiring customers to complete a sales return authorization form, or to at least obtain a sales return authorization number prior to returning goods, is an effective approach for reducing the number of returns. It also assists with the categorization of reasons why sales returns are being made; otherwise, sales returns would appear at the company receiving dock with no explanation for the return, making it difficult to determine what problems are causing the returns. An example of a sales return authorization form is shown in Exhibit 5.4. The standard list of reasons for product returns listed on the sample form should be regularly reviewed and revised to reflect changes in product-related problems.

Exhibit 5.4 Sales Return Authorization Form

Company Name
Sales Return Authorization Form

Customer Name: ____________________ Date: ___________

Sales Return Authorization Number: _______________ **(Required)**

Product Being Returned			Reason for
Number	Quantity	Description	Return
________	________	________________	________
________	________	________________	________
________	________	________________	________
________	________	________________	________

Standard Reason Codes:
1 = Product damaged in transit
2 = Product quality below required level
3 = Incorrect product shipped
4 = Incorrect quantity shipped
5 = Shipment made to wrong location
6 = Other (describe below)

Other reasons for return: ____

____

____

Sales Return Credit Calculation Form

Companies rarely take back prior sales at full credit. Instead, they charge restocking fees, transaction processing charges, damage credits, or some combination of them in order to give customers an incentive to keep what they have bought. Because some of these calculations can be difficult to follow, it is best to categorize the information neatly in a credit calculation form. This is an invaluable document when discussing the proper amount of receivables still owed by a customer after a return has been made. The customer needs to see the calculation before paying whatever net amount is left on the related receivable. An example is shown in Exhibit 5.5.

Exhibit 5.5 Sales Return Credit Calculation Form

Company Name
Sales Return Credit Calculation Form

Customer Name: ________________ Date: __________

Sales Return Authorization Number: ________________

Product Number	Quantity	Description	Unit Price	Extended Price	Damage Credit
			Totals		

Less:

20% Restocking Fee	
Total Damage Credit	
€25 Transaction Fee	€ 25
Net Credit Granted	

_______________ Clerk Signature

_______________ Clerk Name

FOOTNOTES

Disclosure of Revenue Recognition Policy

The general principles followed by company management in recognizing revenue should be stated in a footnote. An entity should disclose

- The accounting policies adopted for the recognition of revenue, including the methods adopted to determine the stage of completion of transactions involving the rendering of services.
- The sale of goods; the rendering of services; interest; royalties; dividends.
- The amount of revenue arising from exchange of goods or services included in each significant category of revenue.

An entity also must disclose in accordance with IAS 37 any contingent liabilities and contingent assets that may arise from items such as warranty costs, claims, penalties, or possible losses.

Footnotes can include the time span over which revenue from maintenance agreements is to be recognized, how the company handles different types of products and services bundled into the same pricing packages, and at what point revenues are to be recognized. Here are two sample footnotes.

1. The company sells maintenance agreements along with its home air conditioning units. Maintenance revenue is recognized ratably over the term specified within each agreement, which can range from 12 to 60 months. In cases where maintenance agreements are offered to customers at a discount, the company assumes that the discounts really apply to the complete package of air conditioning products and related maintenance agreements, and so recalculates the discount as a percentage of the entire package. This results in approximately 65% of the discounts being assigned to product sales and the remaining 35% to maintenance sales. The adjusted maintenance revenues are then recognized ratably over the term specified within each agreement. As of the statement of financial position date, €1,389,000 of maintenance revenues had not been recognized.
2. The company sells electrical appliance monitoring devices to large industrial manufacturers. It charges a nominal amount for each unit sold, and takes 5% of the electricity savings generated from the use of each unit for the first three years after each unit is installed, up to a maximum of €5,000 per quarter. Given the uncertainty of the savings to be generated from electricity cost savings, the company does not feel that it can reasonably recognize any revenue until after cost savings have been determined at the end of each quarter. Also, since cost savings tend to be disputed by recipients, making cash receipts problematic, management has elected to further delay revenue recognition until after cash has been received from each customer.

In the case of service-related revenues, disclosures should also include information about unearned revenues, such as the amount billed but not earned, and where it is placed on the statement of financial position. Related expenses that have been deferred should also be described, including their amount and where they are itemized on the statement of financial position. Two examples follow:

1. The company recognizes revenue under the proportional performance method, whereby revenue is recognized based on the hours charged to a project as a percentage of the total hours required to complete the job. Billings occur at quarterly intervals on most contracts, resulting in recognized but unbilled revenue. At the end of 2009, there was €1,895,000 of recognized but unbilled revenue, as compared to €2,905,000 in 2008. This asset is listed in the Unbilled Revenue current asset account.
2. The company recognizes revenue under the specific performance method, whereby revenue is recognized only after specific project milestones have been approved by customers. When costs are incurred prior to a revenue recognition event, they are stored in the Unrecognized Project Expense current asset account. At the end of 2009, there was €1,505,000 of unrecognized project expense, as compared to €1,759,000 in 2008.

Disclosure of Bill and Hold Transactions

Bill and hold transactions are generally frowned on, given the risk of abuse by companies that can use this technique to inflate their current period revenues, although there are no specific rules under IFRS at this time. Consequently, if any bill and hold transactions are used, put this information in a footnote, clearly stating that the company follows all IFRS requirements for these and all other revenue transactions. Also note the monetary amount and percentage of revenues involved and any change in the level of bill and hold revenue from the preceding year. For example

> During the past year, the company sold €172,000 of stoves to its restaurant customers under "bill and hold" transactions. Under these arrangements, restaurant owners asked the company to retain stoves in its warehouse facilities until new restaurants had been built to accommodate them. All these customers acknowledged in writing that they had ordered the inventory, that the company was storing the stoves on their behalf, that they had taken on all risks of ownership, and that the stoves would be delivered in no more than three months. Total bill and hold transactions were €15,000 lower than the €187,000 in similar transactions that occurred in the preceding year. In both years, bill and hold transactions comprised 14% of total company revenues.

Disclosure of Contract Revenue Recognition

If a company recognizes revenue based on the percentage-of-completion method, it should state how it makes this calculation, how it is recorded on the statement of financial position, when claims against customers are recognized, and how changes in estimates can impact reported profits or losses on contracts. If there is a change in the method of contract revenue recognition, an explanation and the net effect of the change should be included. Three examples follow.

1. The company recognizes all revenue in its construction division using the percentage-of-completion method, under which it ascertains the completion percentage by dividing costs incurred to date by total estimated project costs. It not only revises estimated project costs regularly, but it also alters the reported level of project profitability. If project losses are calculated under this method, they are recognized in the current reporting period. Claims against customers are recorded in the period when payment is received; if billings exceed recognized revenue, the difference is recorded as a current liability, while any recognized revenues exceeding billings are recorded as a current asset.
2. The company recognizes claims against customers when a cash receipt is probable, the claim is legally justified, and the amount of the claim can be proven. If any of these factors cannot be reasonably proven, then claims are recognized only upon the receipt of cash. Since claims involve the use of estimates, it is reasonable to record some changes to the initially reported revenue figure upon the eventual receipt of cash—or sooner if there is a firm basis for this information.
3. The company has switched to the percentage-of-completion method from the completed-contract method for recording the results of its construction projects. Management authorized the change due to the increasingly long-term nature of its contracts, which have increased from single-month to multimonth durations. The net impact of this change was an increase in profits of €218,000 in 2008. The

change was carried back to 2007, resulting in a profit increase of €12,000 in that period.

Disclosure of Barter Revenue

Barter transactions should be recognized at the fair market value of the assets received in an exchange. The nature of any such transactions, the approximate value of the transactions, and how they are recorded in the financial statements should all be noted in a footnote. An example follows.

The company provides aerial traffic reports to a number of radio stations; in return, air time is given to the company. The company then obtains advertising to run on these free minutes and collects the proceeds. The company recognizes revenue from these barter transactions only after advertisements have been obtained and have been run on the participating radio stations. No asset is recorded on the company statement of financial position when air time is received from radio stations, since there is still significant uncertainty that the company will be able to convert the air time into paid advertisements. In 2008, the revenue recognized from these transactions was €1,745,000.

Disclosure of Consignment Revenue

Shipments made to a distributor on consignment are not truly sales until they are sold by the distributor. The exact method of revenue recognition should be clearly stated in a footnote, so readers can be sure that revenue is not recognized too soon in the sales process. Not only that, but inventory may be shipped to a company by its customers on a consignment basis, to be included in custom products that are then sold back to the customers; however, only the value added to these custom products should be recognized as revenue. The next two footnotes show proper disclosure of these situations.

1. The company ships its eyewear products to a number of distributors, having no direct sales function of its own. All shipments to distributors continue to be recorded as inventory by the company until notification of shipment is received from distributors. In selected cases where there has been a problematic payment history by distributors, the company does not record revenue until cash has been received.
2. The company produces custom rockets for its payload launch customers. Several customers prefer to supply rocket engines to be incorporated into the company's rockets. Accordingly, these engines are recorded as consignment inventory when they are received and assigned a zero cost. When the completed rockets are shipped to customers, the price of the consigned engines is not included in the amount billed, thereby reducing the total revenue recognized by the company.

Disclosure of Gain or Loss on Asset Sale

When a company recognizes a material gain or loss on the sale of an asset or a group of assets, it should disclose in a footnote the general transaction, its date, the gross amount of the sale, the amount of the gain or loss, and its presentation in the financial statements. An example follows.

The company sold its printing press in August 2008 for €5.3 million as part of a plan to reduce the capacity of its printing facilities in the United States. Net of its original cost, less depreciation and tax effects, this resulted in a net gain of €420,000, which is itemized as a Gain on Sale of Assets in the financial statements.

Disclosure of Life Insurance Proceeds

If a company receives a payout from a life insurance policy, it should disclose in a footnote the amount of the payout, the event that caused the payout to be earned, and how the transaction was presented in the financial statements. An example follows.

> The company received a payout of €20 million upon the death of a major shareholder in May 2008. The payout is recognized in the income statement under the Life Insurance Receipts line item. Under the terms of a stock buyback agreement with this shareholder, the company intends to use the proceeds to purchase all company shares held by the shareholder's estate.

Disclosure of Research and Development Revenue

Research and development contracts typically are accounted for in the same manner as any other construction project, though sometimes product profit-sharing terms will require a company to incur an up-front loss against the promise of future earnings. The primary disclosure is the method used to recognize revenue. A sample footnote follows.

> The company's research division enters into research and development contracts with a variety of organizations, typically on a fixed-fee basis. The company recognizes revenue from these contracts on a percentage-of-completion basis. In some instances, customers offer profit-sharing agreements from future product proceeds rather than up-front payments. In these cases, the company recognizes a loss when contracts begin, (based on anticipated costs) and updates this loss information as projects progress. The company records revenue from these profit-sharing arrangements only when profit-sharing payments are received from customers.

Disclosure of Warranty Revenue Recognition

In the case of any long-term service revenue contract, the period over which warranty revenues are calculated should be described if there is a significant proportion of revenues. For many companies, this is a small revenue component not requiring separate disclosure. If it is disclosed, note the term over which warranty revenues are recognized and the amount of unrecognized warranty revenues. A sample footnote follows.

> The company sells a one-year warranty agreement with its kitchen appliances; warranty revenues comprise approximately 8% of total revenues. These revenues are recognized ratably over their service periods, with the unrecognized balance listed as a short-term liability in the Unrecognized Warranty Revenues account. The unrecognized balance of these sales was €850,000 as of the statement of financial position date.

Disclosure of Membership Fee Recognition

A membership organization should describe the types of membership fees charged and the method used to recognize revenue. The footnote can also reveal the amount of unrecognized revenue currently listed as a liability. Two examples follow.

1. The club charges a onetime nonrefundable membership fee of €10,000 as well as monthly dues of €300. Since members have no right to the return of the initial fee, the club recognizes this amount in its entirety when paid. Monthly dues are recognized when billed. There is no liability associated with unrecognized revenue shown on the statement of financial position.
2. The club charges a onetime membership fee of €10,000, which can be repaid to members if they choose to resign from the club, less a €500 termination fee. The club holds all membership fees in escrow and recognizes the termination fee only when members resign from the club. The total amount of membership fees currently held in escrow is €1,620,000, and is listed under the Membership Fees Held in Reserve liability account. The club also charges €300 monthly dues, which are recognized when billed.

Disclosure of Sales Return Allowance

There is no specific IFRS requirement that a company state its policy regarding the use of an allowance for sales returns. However, if a reserve has been created, then a footnote should detail how the amount of the reserve was derived. An example follows.

> The company recorded an allowance for sales returns of €148,000. This amount is based on a historical average rate of return of 12% of the company's subscription book sale business.

Disclosure of Warranty Expense Allowance

If there is a history or expectation of significant warranty expenses, one should accrue an appropriate amount when related revenues are recognized. The footnote should describe the basis for the warranty expense calculation, as well as the current amount of the reserve. An example follows.

> The company recognizes a warranty expense when it recognizes the sale of its amusement park bumper cars. This expense is based on the most recent one year of actual warranty claims, which is currently 1.9% of sales. The current warranty expense reserve, as listed in the Warranty Reserve liability account on the statement of financial position, is €302,000.
>
> The company has just released a completely reengineered bumper car, containing 90% new parts. Given the large number of changes in this new product, there is considerable uncertainty in regard to probable future warranty claims; they could be materially larger than the amount previously reserved, and they could have a material impact on the company's financial results in the near term.

Disclosure of Computer Software Sales

When a company sells computer software, the sale should be split into product and service components and the service portion of the sale should be recognized ratably over the maintenance period covered by the sales contract; this information should be included in a footnote. An example follows.

Approximately 80% of the company's sales are from computer software and related maintenance agreements. The company splits these sales into their software and maintenance components and recognizes the software portion of the sales at once. The maintenance portion of the sales are initially recorded in an Unrecognized Maintenance Service Agreements liability account and recognized ratably over the term of the agreements—either 3 or 12 months. In cases where the software and maintenance components of a sale are not clearly differentiated in a sale contract, the company estimates the relative price of each component based on its separate retail price. As of the statement of financial position date, there was approximately €725,000 of unrecognized maintenance sales in the Unrecognized Maintenance Service Agreements account.

Disclosure of Customers

If a company has revenues from individual customers that amount to at least 10% of total revenues, then it must report the amount of revenues from each of these customers, as well as the name of the business segment with which these customers are doing business. An example follows.

The company does a significant amount of its total business with two customers. One customer, comprising 15% of total revenues for the entire company, also comprises 52% of the revenues of the Appliances segment. The second customer, comprising 28% of total revenues for the entire company, also comprises 63% of the revenues of the Government segment.

Disclosure of Foreign Customers

If sales are concentrated in foreign locations where there are risks of sales reductions due to political issues, then the extent of these sales and the types of risks should be disclosed. An example follows.

The company sells 55% of its customer relationship management software through a distributor in Iran. Given the large proportion of company sales attributable to this supplier, any unrest in the region, such as wars, terrorist activity, or an enforced shutdown in business activities by the Iranian government would have a material impact on the company's financial results.

Disclosure of Installment Sales

If installment sales comprise a significant proportion of corporate sales, a footnote should be written to include the revenue recognition policy used, the amounts of gross profit recognized from the current and prior years, the total amount of deferred gross profit, and its placement in the statement of financial position. An example follows:

The company sells kitchen appliances on various installment payment plans. Given the extreme uncertainty associated with the collection of receivables under this plan, the company uses the cost recovery method to recognize profits, under which it recognizes no gross profit until all costs of goods sold have been paid back through cash receipts. In 2008, the company recognized €397,000 of gross profit earned in the current year, as well as €791,000 deferred from prior years. An additional €2,907,000 of deferred gross profits is classified as a current liability in the Unrecognized Gross Profit on Installment Sales account.

Disclosure of Sales with Significant Rights of Return

If there is considerable uncertainty regarding the amount of potential sales returns, such as may be caused by a new product, potential product obsolescence, or heightened competition, then a company may be forced to not recognize any revenue at all until the right of product return has passed. This can cause a substantial reduction in recognized revenue; thus, a footnote describing the reason for the recognition delay is necessary. The information in the next two footnotes illustrates a sufficient level of disclosure.

1. The company is in the beta testing phase of its new crop planting system, resulting in the decision to grant an unconditional right of return to the first 10 customers who have agreed to purchase the product. The right of return privilege extends for six months from the shipment date. Since there is no return history for this new product, the company has recorded the total amount of all 10 sales in an Unearned Sales liability account, and will not recognize the revenue until the right of return period has expired. The total amount in this account is €328,000. Of this amount, €275,000 will be recognizable in March 2008 and the remaining €53,000 in May 2008, assuming that no products are returned in the interim.
2. The company's light saber product is entirely new and is being introduced into a new market, so management feels that it cannot estimate potential levels of product returns. Consequently, the company has not recognized any revenues related to recent shipments of the product until the three-month right of return period has passed. The company plans to reevaluate this policy after a sufficient amount of time has passed for it to make a better estimate of potential sales returns. The initial amount of light saber revenues that would otherwise have been recognized in the first month of shipments was €1,750,000.

Disclosure of Multiple Deliverables

IFRS has not yet dealt definitively with the accounting for transactions (such as software sales) having multiple deliverable elements. However, the authors suggest that until this is addressed (perhaps as part of the ongoing revenue recognition project being conducted jointly with FASB), existing guidance under US GAAP be consulted and, as appropriate, followed. The financial statements of a vendor are to include two disclosures, when applicable:

1. The nature of the vendor's MDAs, including provisions relative to performance, cancellation, termination, or refund
2. The vendor's accounting policy with respect to the recognition of revenue from MDAs (e.g., whether deliverables are separable into units of accounting)

An example of this disclosure follows.

The company enters into multiple-element revenue arrangements, which may include any combination of services, software, hardware, and/or financing. A multiple-element arrangement is separated into more than one unit of accounting if all of these criteria are met: (1) the delivered item has value to the client on a stand-alone basis; (2) there is no objective and reliable evidence of the fair value of the undelivered item; (3) if the arrangement includes a right of return relative to the delivered item, delivery is considered probable and is under the company's control. If these criteria are met for each element and there is objective and reliable evidence of fair value for all units of accounting in an arrangement, the arrangement consideration is allocated to the separate units of accounting based on each unit's relative fair value. There may be cases, however, when there is objective and reliable evidence of fair value of the undelivered item but no such evidence for the delivered item. In those cases, the residual method is used to allocate the arrangement consideration, meaning the amount of consideration allocated to the delivered item equals the total arrangement consideration less the aggregate fair value of the undelivered item. The revenue policies described below are then applied to each unit of accounting, as applicable. If the allocation of consideration in a profitable arrangement results in a loss on an element, that loss is recognized at the earlier of (1) delivery of that element, (2) when the first dollar of revenue is recognized on that element, or (3) when there are no remaining profitable elements in the arrangement to be delivered.

Disclosure of Franchise Revenues

Disclosures for franchise fee transactions should include

- The types of significant commitments resulting from franchising arrangements, as well as franchisor services not yet performed
- The franchise sale price
- The amount of deferred revenue and costs
- The periods when fees become payable by the franchisee
- The amounts of revenue initially deferred due to collectibility uncertainties, but then recognized due to resolution of the uncertainties
- The number of franchises sold, purchased, and in operation during the period (which shall segregate the number of franchisor-owned outlets in operation from the number of franchisee-owned operations)
- Segregating the reporting of initial franchise fees from other franchise fee revenue, if they are significant
- Segregating the revenues and costs of franchisor-owned outlets from those of franchisees, when practicable
- If there is no reasonable basis for estimating the ability of the franchisor to collect franchise fees, the type of accounting method used to recognize franchise fee revenue (either the installment or cost recovery method) must be disclosed
- If initial franchise fee revenue is likely to decline because of market saturation, this issue should be disclosed

Here are three examples of company disclosures that follow some of the preceding reporting requirements.

1. The Company's revenues consist of sales by Company-operated restaurants and fees from restaurants operated by franchisees and affiliates. Sales by Company-operated restaurants are recognized on a cash basis. Fees from franchised and affiliated restaurants include continuing rent, service fees, initial fees, royalties received from foreign affiliates, and developmental licensees. Continuing fees and royalties are recognized in the period earned. Initial fees are recognized upon opening of a

restaurant, which is when the Company has performed substantially all initial services required by the franchise arrangement.

2. The Company enters into franchise agreements committing to provide franchisees with various marketing services and limited rights to utilize the Company's registered trademarks. These agreements typically have an initial term of 10 years with provisions permitting franchisees to terminate after 5 years under certain circumstances. In most instances, initial franchise fees are recognized upon execution of the franchise agreement because the initial franchise fee is nonrefundable and the Company has no continuing obligations related to the franchisee. The initial franchise fee related to executed franchise agreements, which include incentives such as future potential rebates, are deferred and recognized when the incentive criteria are met or the agreement is terminated, whichever occurs first.
3. The following are changes in the Company's franchised locations for each of the fiscal years 2007 through 2009:

	2009	2008	2007
Franchises in operation—beginning of year	7,958	7,637	7,322
Franchises opened	355	425	470
Franchises closed	(121)	(122)	(104)
Net transfers within the system	(1)	18	(51)
Franchises in operation—end of year	8,191	7,958	7,637
Company-owned stores	1,758	1,748	1,672
Total system-wide stores	9,949	9,706	9,309

Disclosure of Motion Picture Revenues

IFRS does not explicitly address this industry's financial reporting requirements, but guidance is available under US GAAP, which is the basis for the recommendations here. A company should disclose its methods of accounting for revenue. Three sample disclosures follow.

1. Revenue from the sales of home video units is recognized at the later of when product is made available for retail sale or when video sales to customers are reported by third parties, such as fulfillment service providers or distributors. Management calculates an estimate of future returns of product by analyzing a combination of historical returns, current economic trends, projections of consumer demand for the Company's product, and point-of-sale data available from certain retailers. Based on this information, a percentage of each sale is reserved, provided that the customer has the right of return. Actual returns are charged against the reserve.
2. Long-term noninterest-bearing receivables arising from television licensing agreements are discounted to present value, net of an allowance for doubtful accounts.
3. The Company recognizes revenues from its films net of reserves for returns, rebates, and other incentives after it has retained a distribution fee of ___% and recovered all of its distribution and marketing costs on a title-by-title basis.

JOURNAL ENTRIES

Revenue—General

Record sales return allowance. To create a reserve for expected sales returns. This entry is not normally made unless there is an expectation of an appreciable amount of returns. The second entry records the actual return of products by eliminating the related account receivable and charging this amount to the allowance for sales returns.

Sales returns expense	xxx	
Allowance for sales returns		xxx
Allowance for sales returns	xxx	
Accounts receivable		xxx

Bill and Hold Transactions

A common problem with bill and hold transactions is that while the sale is recorded, the subtraction from inventory of the items sold is not, resulting in a sale with a 100% gross margin. To avoid this, use the second part of the next journal entry to shift the sold inventory items into a special cost of goods sold account that clearly identifies the items sold. When the items eventually are shipped to the customer, the third journal entry is used to shift the expense into the regular cost of goods sold account. By using this approach, one can monitor the "Cost of Goods Sold—Bill and Hold" account to determine which billed inventory items have not yet been shipped.

Accounts receivable	xxx	
Sales		xxx
Cost of goods sold—bill and hold	xxx	
Inventory		xxx
Cost of goods sold	xxx	
Cost of goods sold—bill and hold		xxx

Cash Payments to Customers

When cash-back payments are made to customers, the offset to the cash reduction should correspond in the revenue earned from that customer, as is recorded in the first of the next two entries. If the company receives some benefit back from the customer, then only the difference between the fair value of the benefit and the cash payment shall be charged against the revenue account. This later scenario is covered in the second journal entry.

Revenue	xxx	
Cash		xxx
Revenue	xxx	
Expense account (various)	xxx	
Cash		xxx

Long-Term Construction Contracts

Record additional revenues under percentage-of-completion method. To record the amount of extra revenues thus far not recognized, computed as the difference between project expenses and the estimated gross profit margin, without any prior billings. The second entry is the recording of a proportional amount of offsetting cost of goods sold, so that the principle of matching revenues to expenses is observed.

Unbilled contract receivables	xxx	
Contract revenues earned		xxx
Cost of recognized revenues	xxx	
Construction-in-progress		xxx

Record excessive billings under percentage-of-completion method in a liability account. To record the amount of excess billings over the amount of project expenses and the estimated gross profit margin in a liability account.

Contract revenues earned	xxx	
Billings exceeding project costs and margin		xxx

Record amount of costs exceeding the total project billing. To record the estimated amount of expenses incurred on a project that will exceed the total billable amount of the contract. This is a loss recognizable in the current period.

Loss on uncompleted project	xxx	
Estimated loss on uncompleted contract		xxx

Service Revenues

Record unearned service revenue. To record a liability when a sales transaction for unearned services work is recorded. The first entry records the offset to an account receivable in a liability account, whereas the second entry records incremental revenue recognition from the liability account as services are completed.

Accounts receivable	xxx	
Unearned service contracts		xxx
Unearned service contracts	xxx	
Service revenue		xxx

Record earned revenue under the percentage-of-completion method. Under the percentage-of-completion method, revenue can be recognized in proportion to the amount of direct cost incurred on a service job. The first entry is the simplest, showing a basic sale transaction under which the customer is billed for the same amount of proportional revenue recognized by the company. The second entry assumes there is no customer billing yet to match the revenue recognized, so the sales offset is stored in an asset account. The third entry shows the reduction of the asset account when a customer billing eventually occurs.

Accounts receivable	xxx	
Sales		xxx
Earned revenue asset account	xxx	
Sales		xxx
Accounts receivable	xxx	
Earned revenue asset account		xxx

Recognize a loss on a service contract. This entry is used when it becomes apparent that actual and estimated expenses on a service contract will exceed related revenue. An estimated loss is recognized, while the offsetting credit is used first to eliminate any unrecognized contract costs, with the remainder being credited to an estimated loss account that is later drawn down as actual losses are incurred.

Account	Debit	Credit
Loss on service contract	xxx	
Unrecognized contract costs		xxx
Estimated loss on service contracts		xxx

Installment Revenues

Revenue (installment basis). To record the initial installment sale, as noted in the first entry. As cash is received over time in payment of installment accounts receivable, the second entry is used to recognize portions of the gross profit and interest income from the installment sale.

Account	Debit	Credit
Installment receivables collectible in (year)	xxx	
Inventory		xxx
Deferred gross profit		xxx
Cash	xxx	
Deferred gross profit	xxx	
Installment receivables collectible in (year)		xxx
Interest income		xxx
Recognized gross profit		xxx

Repossession of goods sold under installment plans. When goods are repossessed due to lack of payment under an installment sales plan, the deferred gross profit associated with the initial sale must be reversed, while the repossessed goods should be transferred back into inventory at their fair value. If there is a difference between the book value and fair value of the goods, then a gain or loss should be recognized on the difference. The next entry illustrates the transaction.

Account	Debit	Credit
Finished goods inventory	xxx	
Loss on repossessed inventory	xxx	
Deferred gross profit	xxx	
Accounts receivable		xxx

Revenue Recognition When Right of Return Exists

To record predictable amounts of sales returns. When the amount of sales returns can be estimated reasonably, one should record an estimate of returns—evidenced in the first journal entry. Meanwhile, the second entry shows the offsetting of an actual return against the sales return reserve, and the third entry notes the elimination of any remaining amount left in the reserve after the right of return has expired.

NOTE: In the case of sales where the amount of sales returns is not predictable, the same entries are used, but they will apply to the entire amount of sales made, rather than just an estimated amount of returns.

Account	Debit	Credit
Revenue	xxx	
Cost of goods sold		xxx
Deferred gross profit		xxx
Finished goods inventory	xxx	
Deferred gross profit	xxx	
Loss on returned inventory	xxx	
Accounts receivable		xxx

Cost of goods sold	xxx	
Deferred gross profit	xxx	
Revenue		xxx

RECORDKEEPING

When a company engages in barter swap transactions, there is a strong likelihood that auditors will want to review the transactions to see if any related revenue recognition is reasonable; consequently, business cases should be written for each such transaction and then filed for later review. A copy of the business case should be attached to the journal entry used to record each of these transactions. It may also be useful to store a second copy of each business case in the legal department, given that the legal staff may need to monitor the progress of each transaction to ensure that it is properly completed.

If credits are calculated manually for sales returns from customers, this information should be retained in the customer file because it may be subject to dispute by the customer. The documentation should include the amounts of any return-related charges, such as restocking fees. It is best to use a formal credit calculation worksheet (see, the Forms and Reports section so it) can be better understood by customers.

Any journal entries increasing the reported level of sales should be stored in the journal entries binder, explaining why specific entries were made. Auditors are very likely to examine these when they review the suitability of any journal entries that increase sales. This is especially common for service revenues recognized under the percentage-of-completion method, since the amount of revenue recognized may be higher than the amount billed to the customer. In this case, the specific percentage-of-completion calculation should be retained for each service contract on which revenue is recognized.

If a company engages in bill and hold transactions, then it should have its customers sign the Acknowledgment of Bill and Hold Transaction form (see the Forms and Reports section). External auditors will review these completed forms as part of their auditing of the revenue portion of the income statement; therefore the forms should be sorted by date and stored in a binder in the accounting archives.

When long-term installment sales cover multiple years, all information regarding the annual calculation of the gross margin percentage should be retained until all collections related to that year have been made. Similarly, records for cash receipts, repossessions, and the recognition of bad debts should be retained for the duration of all installment sales.

If repossessed goods from installment sales are not considered to be worth reconditioning for resale, they may be donated. That being the case, all asset donation forms should be given to the taxation department for consideration in the creation of the annual corporate income tax return, and the forms should be archived with all other source documents used to create the tax returns.

6 LONG-LIVED ASSETS

DEFINITIONS OF TERMS

Amortization. The expensing of an asset over the period of time when the asset is to be used. This term is applied most commonly to the gradual write-down of intangible items (e.g., goodwill or organizational costs).

Asset retirement obligation. A legal requirement to retire assets at a certain date, such as leasehold improvements as of the termination date of the lease.

Book value. An asset's original cost, net of any depreciation that has been incurred through the financial reporting date.

Boot. The monetary portion of an exchange involving similar assets.

Capitalization limit. The minimum threshold of expenditure; if exceeded, a purchased asset will be recorded as a fixed asset, but if it is below this limit, the expenditure will be recorded as an expense.

Carrying amount. The amount where an asset is recognized after deducting any accumulated depreciation (amortization) and accumulated impairment losses.

Cash-generating unit. The smallest identifiable group of assets that generates cash inflows from continued use, largely independent of the cash inflows associated with other assets or groups of assets.

Comprehensive income. The change in equity of an entity during a period resulting from transactions and other events and circumstances from nonowner sources. It includes all changes in net assets during a period, except those resulting from investments by owners and distributions to owners. It comprises all components of "profit or loss" and "other comprehensive income."

Corporate assets. Assets, excluding goodwill, that contribute to future cash flows of both the cash-generating unit under review for impairment and other cash-generating units.

Cost. Amount of cash or cash equivalent paid, the fair value of the other consideration given to acquire an asset at the time of its acquisition or construction, or (where applicable) the amount attributed to that asset when initially recognized in accordance with the specific requirements of other IFRS—for example, IFRS 2, *Share-Based Payment*.

Depreciable amount. Cost of an asset, or another amount that has been substituted for cost, minus the residual value of the asset.

Depreciation. Both the decline in value of an asset over time as well as the systematic allocation of the depreciable amount of an asset over its useful life.

Development. The application of research findings or other knowledge to a plan or design for the production of new or substantially improved materials, devices, products, processes, systems, or services before the start of commercial production or use. Under IFRS, developments costs are differentiated from research costs, with the former being capitalized and then amortized, while the latter being expensed as incurred.

Entity-specific value. Present value of the cash flows an entity expects to be derived from the continuing use of an asset and from its disposal at the end of its useful life, or that it expects to incur when settling a liability.

Exchange. Reciprocal transfer between the reporting entity and another entity that results in the acquisition of assets or services, or the satisfaction of liabilities, through a transfer of other assets, services, or other obligations.

Fair value. Amount that would be obtained for an asset in an arm's-length exchange transaction between knowledgeable, willing parties.

Fixed assets. Assets used in a productive capacity that have physical substance, are relatively long-lived, and provide a future benefit that is readily measurable. Also referred to as property, plant, and equipment.

Goodwill. The future economic benefits arising from assets that are not individually identified and separately recognized; measured as the excess of the cost of a business combination over the fair value of the identifiable assets and liabilities acquired at the date of combination.

Impairment loss. The excess of the carrying amount of an asset over its recoverable amount.

Intangible assets. Identifiable nonmonetary assets, not having physical substance.

Leasehold improvements. Improvements made by a reporting entity to properties it leases rather than owns.

Monetary assets. Money held and assets to be received in fixed or determinable amounts of money. Some examples include cash, accounts receivable, and notes receivable.

Net selling price. The amount that could be realized from the sale of an asset by means of an arm's-length transaction, net of the costs of disposal.

Nonmonetary assets. Assets other than monetary assets (e.g., inventories, investments in common stock, and property, plant, and equipment).

Nonmonetary transactions. Exchanges and nonreciprocal transfers that involve little or no monetary assets or liabilities.

Nonreciprocal transfer. Transfer of assets or services in one direction, from the reporting entity, either to its owners or to another entity or from owners or another entity to the enterprise. An entity's reacquisition of its outstanding stock is a nonreciprocal transfer.

Other comprehensive income. Items of income and expense (including reclassification adjustments) that are not recognized in profit or loss as required or permitted by other IFRS. The components of other recognized income include: (1) changes in revaluation surplus (IAS 38); (2) actuarial gains and losses on defined benefit plans (IAS 19); (3) translation gains and losses (IAS 21); (4) gains and losses on remeasuring available-for-sale financial assets (IAS 39); and (5) the effective portion of gains and losses on hedging instruments in a cash flow hedge (IAS 39).

Profit or loss. The total of income less expenses, excluding the components of other comprehensive income.

Property, plant, and equipment. Tangible assets with an expected useful life of more than one year that are held for use in the process of producing goods or services for sale, that are held for rental to others, or that are held for administrative purposes; also referred to commonly as fixed assets.

Provision. A liability established to recognize a probable outflow of resources, whose timing or value is uncertain, where the reporting entity has a present obligation arising out of a past event.

Recoverable amount. The greater of an asset's net selling price or its value in use.

Research. The original and planned investigation undertaken with the prospect of gaining new scientific or technical knowledge and understanding. Research costs are expensed as incurred, not capitalized.

Residual value. Estimated amount of what the entity would currently obtain upon disposal of the asset, net of estimated costs of disposal, if the asset were already of the age and in the condition expected at the end of its useful life.

Retirement. The permanent cessation of regular use of a fixed asset. This is typically followed by the idling, disposal, or sale of the asset.

Similar productive assets. Productive assets that are of the same general type, that perform the same function, or that are employed in the same line of business.

Useful life. Period over which an asset is expected to be available for use by an entity; or the number of production, or similar units, expected to be obtained from the asset by an entity.

Value in use. The present value of the future cash flows expected to be received from an asset or cash-generating unit.

CONCEPTS AND EXAMPLES[1]

Property, Plant, and Equipment (PP&E)—Purchases

When a company purchases an item of property, plant, and equipment (hereinafter referred to as PP&E), there may be additional expenditures (so-called directly attributable costs) that are allowed or required to include in the capitalized cost of the asset, in addition to the asset's actual purchase price. These costs include the sales tax and ownership registration fees (if any). Also, the cost of all freight, insurance, and duties required to bring the asset to the location where it will be placed into service are added to the capitalized cost. The cost to install the asset will be included, although if the asset is later relocated, care must be taken to not have multiple installation (and moving) costs included in its book value. Installation costs are broadly defined, and comprise the cost to test and break in the asset as well as the cost of test materials. The capitalized costs of plant assets also include the initial estimate of the costs of dismantling and removing the item, restoring the site where it was located, and any other obligations incurred either when the item is acquired or as a consequence of having used the item should be included in the cost. For example, if site restoration is contractually or statutorily required when the asset ultimately is disposed of, the present value of that future cost is a part of the purchase cost of the asset.

If an item of PP&E is acquired for only cash, its recorded cost is simply the amount of cash paid. If, however, the asset is acquired by taking on a payable—such as a stream of debt payments, or taking over the payments that were initially to be made by the seller of the asset—then the present value of all future payments yet to be made must also be included in the recorded asset cost. If the stream of future payments contains no explicit interest charges, then interest must be imputed reflecting the pertinent current market rates. If the amount of the payable is not clearly evident at the time of purchase, then it is also admissible to record the asset at its fair market value.

---

[1] *Much of the information in this section is adapted with permission from Chapter 17 of Steven Bragg,* ***Ultimate Accountant's Reference*** *(Hoboken, NJ: John Wiley & Sons, 2006).*

If an asset is purchased fully or partially using the reporting entity's capital stock, a value may be assigned to the acquired asset based on the fair market value of either the stock or the asset, whichever is easier to determine. In general, the value of the asset received is the preferred measure.

Example of an asset acquired in exchange for capital stock

The Shanghai Motor Car Company issues 500 shares of its stock to acquire a sheet metal bender. This is a publicly held company, and on the day of the acquisition, its shares were trading for €13.25 each. Since this is an easily determinable value, the cost assigned to the equipment is €6,625 (= 500 shares × €13.25/share). A year later, the company has gone private, and chooses to issue another 750 shares of its stock to acquire a router. In this case, the value of the shares is no longer easily determined. The company asks an appraiser to determine the router's fair value, and it is subsequently set at €12,000. In the first transaction, the journal entry was a debit of €6,625 to the fixed asset equipment account and a credit of €6,625 to paid-in capital accounts, while the second transaction required entries to the same accounts, but for €12,000.

If a company obtains an asset through an exchange involving a dissimilar asset, the acquired asset should be recorded at fair market value. This almost always will differ from the book value of the outgoing asset, and thus a gain or loss on the exchange will be recognized. If no fair market value is readily obtainable for either asset, then the net book value of the relinquished asset can be used; this is expected to be necessary only rarely, however, since in arm's-length transactions the reporting entity should know the value of the asset being obtained.

Under IFRS, a company should record an item of PP&E acquired in exchange for a nonmonetary asset, or a combination of monetary and nonmonetary assets, at fair value—unless the exchange transaction lacks commercial substance. Under the previous version of IAS 16, an entity measured this type of acquired asset at fair value unless the exchanged assets were similar. Book value exchanges are now expected to be extremely infrequent.

Commercial substance is defined under IFRS as the event or transaction causing the cash flows of the entity to change. In other words, if the expected cash flows after the exchange differ from what would have been expected absent the exchange (which is likely to be the case, since improved future cash flows generally will be the motive for the exchange transaction) , the exchange has commercial substance and is to be accounted for at fair value. In assessing whether this has occurred, the entity has to consider if the amount, timing, and uncertainty of the cash flows from the new asset are different from the one given up, or if the entity-specific portion of the company's operations will be different. If either of these is significant, then the transaction has commercial substance and fair value accounting will be required.

Example of an exchange for a dissimilar asset

The Akita Motor Company exchanges an automobile with a book value of €6,500 (net of accumulated depreciation of €4,000) with Jinan Motor Company for a tooling machine with a fair value of €7,400. No boot (the term used to denote a cash component of what is otherwise is a nonmonetary transaction) is exchanged in the transaction. The fair value of the automobile is not readily determinable. Akita recognizes a gain of €900 on the transaction, as noted in the next entry:

Machine	7,400	
Accumulated depreciation	4,000	
Automobile		10,500
Gain on exchange of plant asset		900

If the transaction does not have commercial substance, or if the fair value of *neither* the asset received nor the asset given up can be measured reliably, then the asset acquired is valued at the carrying amount of the asset given up. Such situations are expected to be very rare in practice, and assertions that values cannot be ascertained should be vigorously challenged.

In a *nonreciprocal transfer*, one party gives or receives property without the other party reciprocating. Most often these transfers involve an entity and the owners of the entity. Examples of nonreciprocal transfers with owners include dividends paid in kind, nonmonetary assets exchanged for common stock, split-ups, and spin-offs. An example of a nonreciprocal transaction between an entity and parties other than owners would be a donation of property either by or to the enterprise. For example, if a governmental unit grants a factory building to an entity in order to promote local job creation, this would be deemed a nonreciprocal exchange.

The accounting for most nonreciprocal transfers should be based on the fair value of the asset given (or received, if the fair value of the nonmonetary asset is both objectively measurable and would be clearly recognizable under IFRS). Conversely, nonmonetary assets distributed to owners of an enterprise in a spin-off or other form of reorganization or liquidation should be based on the recorded amount. Where no asset is given, the valuation of the transaction should be based on the fair value of the asset received.

Example of accounting for a nonreciprocal transfer

The Salaam Manufacturing Company donated property having a book value of €10,000 to a charity during the current year. The property had a fair market value of €17,000 at the date of the transfer. The transaction is to be accounted for by reference to the fair value of the property transferred, and any gain or loss is to be recognized. Thus, Salaam should recognize a gain of €7,000 (= €17,000 – €10,000) in the determination of the current period's net income. The entry to record the transaction would be

Charitable donations	17,000	
Property (net of accumulated depreciation)		10,000
Gain on transfer of property		7,000

If a group of assets is acquired through a single purchase transaction (often called a bulk purchase), the cost should be allocated based on the proportional share of the assets' total fair market values. The fair market value may be difficult to ascertain in many instances, in which case an appraisal value or tax assessment value can be used. It may also be possible to use the present value of estimated cash flows for each asset as the basis for the allocation, though this measure can be subject to considerable variability in the foundation data and requires a great deal of analysis to obtain. Note that goodwill cannot be recognized as part of a bulk asset purchase;

goodwill arises only from certain purchases of businesses, not from purchases of assets.

Example of a group asset acquisition

The Akita Motor Company acquires three machines for €80,000 as part of the liquidation auction of a competitor. Because there is no ready market for the machines, Akita hires an appraiser to determine their value. Machines A and B are judged to be worth €42,000 and €18,000, respectively; however, no basis can be found in comparison to Machine C, and an appraisal is passed. Akita's production manager thinks the net present value of cash flows arising from the use of Machine C will be about €35,000. Based on this information, these costs are allocated to the machines:

Machine Description	*Value*	*Proportions*	*Allocated Costs*
Machine A	€42,000	44%	€35,200
Machine B	18,000	23%	18,400
Machine C	35,000	33%	26,400
Totals	€95,000	100%	€80,000

PP&E—Improvements

Costs that are incurred after the purchase or construction of the long-lived asset, such as those for repairs, maintenance, or betterments, may either involve an adjustment to the carrying value or be subject to mandatory immediate expensing, depending on the facts and circumstances.

To be subject to capitalization, costs must be associated with incremental benefits. Costs can be added to the carrying value of the related asset only when it is *probable* that future economic benefits (in general, defined as expected cash flows) beyond those originally anticipated for the asset will be received by the entity. For example, modifications to the asset made to extend its useful life (measured either in years or in units of potential production) or to increase its capacity (e.g., as measured by units of output per hour) would be capitalized. Similarly, if the expenditure results in an improved quality of output or permits a reduction in other cost inputs (e.g., it would result in labor savings), it is a candidate for capitalization.

As with self-constructed assets, if the costs incurred exceed the defined recoverable value threshold, they must be expensed currently. That is, the asset cannot be carried at an amount in excess of fair value, even if costs actually are incurred in making improvements.

Where a modification involves changing part of the asset (e.g., substituting a more powerful power source), the undepreciated cost of the original component part that is removed should be treated as a disposal.

For example, roofs of commercial buildings, linings of blast furnaces used for steel making, and engines of commercial aircraft all need to be replaced or overhauled before the related buildings, furnaces, or airframes themselves can be replaced. If componentized deprecation was employed properly, building elements such as the roofs, linings, and engines would have been depreciated over their respectively shorter useful lives, and when the replacements or overhauls are performed, on average, these will have been fully depreciated. The undepreciated costs of these components would have to be removed from the account (i.e., charged to expense in the period of replacement or overhaul) as the newly incurred replacement or overhaul costs are added to the asset accounts; this way, reporting "two roofs on one building" is avoided.

For the most part, it can be assumed that ordinary maintenance and repair expenditures will occur on a ratable basis over the life of the asset and, as a result, should be charged to expense as incurred. Thus, if the purpose of the expenditure is either to maintain the productive capacity anticipated when the asset was acquired or constructed, or to restore it to that level, the costs are not subject to capitalization.

A partial exception can occur if an asset is acquired in a condition or at a location that needs certain expenditures in order to put it into the appropriate state, or at the correct location, for its intended use. For example, a deteriorated building may be purchased with the intention that it be restored and then utilized as a factory or office facility. In such cases, costs that otherwise would be categorized as ordinary maintenance items might be subject to capitalization and to the constraint that the asset not be presented at a value that exceeds its recoverable amount. Once the restoration is completed, further expenditures of similar type would be viewed as being ordinary repairs or maintenance, and thus expensed as incurred.

Costs associated with required inspections (e.g., of aircraft), however, could be capitalized and depreciated. These costs would be amortized over the expected period of benefit (i.e., the estimated time to the next inspection). As with the cost of physical assets, removal of any undepreciated costs of previous inspections would be required. The capitalized inspection cost would have to be treated as a separate component of the asset.

PP&E—Capitalization of Interest

IFRS previously permitted either capitalization or immediate expensing of financing costs associated with asset construction. In revised IAS 23, which was issued in March 2007 as a part of the Short-Term Convergence project with the FASB, IASB removed the option of immediately recognizing as an expense borrowing costs that relate to assets that take a substantial period of time to get ready for use or sale. An entity is required to capitalize such borrowing costs as part of the cost of the qualifying asset. A qualifying asset is an asset that takes a substantial period of time to get ready for use or sale, including manufacturing plants, power generation facilities, and properties that will become self-constructed investment properties once their construction or development is complete and investment properties measured at cost that are being redeveloped.

The revised Standard does not require the capitalization of borrowing costs relating to assets measured at fair value (e.g., biological assets, or investment property if fair value accounting is elected) and inventories that are manufactured or produced in large quantities on a repetitive basis, even if they take substantial period of time to get ready for use or sale. The revised IAS 23 applies to borrowing costs relating to qualifying assets for which the commencement date for capitalization is on or after January 1, 2009, with earlier application permitted.

Capitalized interest expenses are calculated based on the interest rate of the debt used to construct the asset or, if there was no new debt, at the weighted-average interest rate the company pays on its total debt. The interest rate is multiplied by the average capital expenditures acquired to construct the targeted asset. The capitalized amount of interest is limited to an amount less than or equal to the total interest expense actually incurred by the company during the period of asset construction.

Example of an interest capitalization transaction

The Carolina Astronautics Corporation (CAC) is constructing a new launch pad for its suborbital rocket launching business. It pays a contractor €5,000,000 at project inception and €2,500,000 after the project completion six months later. At the beginning of the project, it issued €15,000,000 in bonds at 9% interest to finance the project as well as other capital needs. The calculation of interest expense to be capitalized is

Investment amount	*Months to be capitalized*	*Interest rate*	*Interest to be capitalized*
€5,000,000	6	9%	€225,000
2,500,000	0	N/A	0
		Total	€225,000

There is no interest expense to be capitalized on the final payment of €2,500,000, since it was incurred at the very end of the construction period. CAC accrued €675,000 in total interest expenses during the period when the launch pad was built (€15,000,000 × 9%/12 × 6 months). Because the total expense incurred by the company greatly exceeds the amount of interest to be capitalized for the launch pad, there is no need to reduce the amount of capitalized interest to the level of actual interest expense incurred. Accordingly, CAC's controller makes this journal entry to record the capitalization of interest:

Assets (launch pad)	225,000	
Interest expense		225,000

PP&E—Dispositions

When a company disposes of an item of PP&E, it should completely eliminate all record of it from the accumulated depreciation accounts. Not only that, it should recognize a gain or loss on the difference between the net book value of the asset and the price it was sold at. For example, Company ABC is selling a machine originally purchased for €10,000, with €9,000 of depreciation recorded, and a used sale price of €1,500. The proper journal entry is to credit the asset account for €10,000 (thereby removing the machine from the plant asset journal), debit the accumulated depreciation account for €9,000 (thereby removing all related depreciation from the accumulated depreciation account), debit the cash account for €1,500 (to reflect the receipt of cash from the asset sale), and credit the gain on sale of assets account for €500.

As part of its ongoing efforts to converge IFRS with U.S. GAAP, IASB issued IFRS 5, *Noncurrent Assets Held for Sale and Discontinued Operations*. This has introduced new and substantially revised guidance for the accounting for long-lived tangible (and other) assets that have been identified for disposal. IFRS 5 states that where management has decided to sell an asset, or group of assets, these should be classified in the statement of financial position as "held-for-sale" and should be measured at the lower of carrying value or fair value less cost to sell. After reclassification, these assets will no longer be subject to systematic deprecation.

IFRS 5 states that assets and liabilities that are to be disposed of together in a single transaction are to be treated as a *disposal group.* The measurement basis for noncurrent assets classified as held-for-sale is to be applied to the group as a whole, and any resulting impairment loss will reduce the carrying amount of the noncurrent assets in the disposal group.

The reporting entity would classify a noncurrent asset (or disposal group) as held-for-sale if its carrying amount will be recovered principally through a sale transaction rather than through continuing use. The six criteria are that

1. Management, of an appropriate seniority to approve the action, commits itself to a plan to sell.
2. The asset (or disposal group) is available for immediate sale in its present condition subject only to terms that are usual and customary for sales of such assets (or disposal groups).
3. An active program to locate a buyer and other actions required to complete the plan to sell the asset (or disposal group) are initiated.
4. The sale is *highly probable,* and is expected to qualify for recognition as a completed sale, within one year from the date of classification as held-for-sale (with limited exceptions, set out in Appendix B to the Standard).
5. The asset (or disposal group) is being actively marketed for sale at a price that is reasonable in relation to its current fair value.
6. Actions required to complete the plan indicate that it is unlikely that significant changes to the plan will be made or that the plan will be withdrawn.

Assets that are classified as being held for disposal are measured differently and presented separately from other noncurrent assets. IFRS 5 requires that noncurrent assets classified as held-for-sale to be measured at the *lower* of carrying amount or fair value less costs to sell. If a newly acquired asset is intended for immediate disposal (e.g., when it has been acquired as part of a larger transaction, but is not needed in operations), it should be initially measured at fair value less cost to sell upon acquisition. The *present value* would be recorded if the sale is expected to occur more than a year after acquisition.

If an individual asset or liability is removed from a disposal group classified as held-for-sale, the remaining assets and liabilities still to be sold will continue to be measured as a group only if they meet the criteria for categorization as held-for-sale. In other circumstances, the remaining noncurrent assets of the group that individually meet the criteria to be classified as held-for-sale will need to be measured individually at the lower of their carrying amounts or fair values less costs to sell at that date.

There may be identifiable costs associated with a dismantled asset ("decommissioning costs"), required by a legal agreement; that is, the cost of the asset is "grossed up" for these estimated disposal costs, with the offsetting credit being posted to a liability account. Under IAS 37 a liability can be recognized only when (1) the reporting entity has a *present* obligation, whether legal or constructive, as a result of a *past* event; (2) it is *probable* that an outflow of resources embodying economic benefits will be required to settle the obligation; and (3) a reliable estimate can be made of the amount of the obligation.

For example, a building lease may require the lessee to remove all equipment by the termination date of the lease; the cost of this obligation should be recognized at the time the lease is signed. As another example, the passage of legislation requiring the cleanup of hazardous waste sites would require the recognition of these costs as soon as the legislation is passed.

The costs of dismantlement, removal, restoration, and similar legal or constructive obligations are included in the cost of the asset and allocated over the life of the asset through the depreciation process. Each period, the discounting of the liability should be "unwound" so that interest cost is accreted each period. If this is done at the expected date on which the expenditure is to be incurred, it will be stated appropriately. The increase in the carrying value of the liability should be reported as interest expense or a similar financing cost.

PP&E—Inbound Donations

If an asset is donated to a company (common only in the case of a not-for-profit corporation), the receiving company can record the asset at its fair value, which can be derived from market rates on similar assets, an appraisal, or the net present value of its estimated cash flows.

PP&E—Outbound Donations

When a company donates an asset to another company, it must recognize the fair value of the asset donated, netted against its net book value. The difference between the asset's fair value and its net book value is recognized as either a gain or loss.

Example of an outbound donation

The Bartok Company has donated to the local orchestra a portable violin repair workbench from its manufacturing department. The workbench was originally purchased for €15,000, and €6,000 of depreciation has since been charged against it. The workbench can be purchased on the eBay auction site for €8,000, which establishes its fair market value. The company uses this journal entry to record the transaction:

Charitable donations	8,000	
Accumulated depreciation	6,000	
Loss on property donation	1,000	
Machinery asset account		15,000

PP&E—Construction In Progress

If a company constructs its own fixed assets, it should capitalize all direct labor, materials, and overhead costs that are clearly associated with the construction project. Meanwhile, the fixed overhead costs considered to have "discernible future benefits" should be charged to the capital account; this makes it unlikely that a significant amount of fixed overhead costs should be charged to a capital project.

If a company constructs its own assets, it should compile all costs associated with it into an account or journal, commonly known as the construction-in-progress

(CIP) account. There should be a separate account or journal for each project that is currently under way, so there is no risk of commingling expenses among multiple projects. The costs that can be included in the CIP account include all costs normally associated with the purchase of a fixed asset as well as the direct materials and direct labor used to construct the asset. Additionally, all overhead costs that are reasonably apportioned to the project may be charged to it as well as the depreciation expense associated with any other assets that are used during the construction process.

One may also charge to the CIP account the interest cost of any funds that have been loaned to the company for the express purpose of completing the project. That being the case, either the interest rate associated with a specific loan that was procured to fund the project or the weighted-average rate for a number of company loans can be used. The amount of interest charged in any period should be based on the cumulative amount of expenditures thus far incurred for the project, but the amount charged for the project should not exceed the interest incurred for all associated loans through the same time period.

Once the project has been completed, all costs should be carried over from the CIP account into one of the established fixed asset accounts, where the new asset is recorded on a summary basis. All of the detail-level costs should be stored for future review. The asset should be depreciated beginning on the day when it is officially completed; under no circumstances should depreciation begin prior to this point.

PP&E—Land

Land cannot be depreciated; as a result, companies tend to avoid charging expenses to this account on the grounds that they cannot recognize taxable depreciation expenses. Nonetheless, those costs reasonably associated with the procurement of land, such as real estate commissions, title examination fees, escrow fees, and accrued property taxes paid by the purchaser, should all be charged to the fixed asset account for land; this should also include the cost of an option to purchase land. All subsequent costs associated with the improvement of the land, such as draining, clearing, and grading, should be added to the land account, whereas the cost of interest that is associated with the development of land should be capitalized. Property taxes incurred during the land development process need to be charged to the asset account, but they should be charged to current expenses once the development process has been completed.

PP&E—Leasehold Improvements

When a lessee makes improvements to a property that is being leased from another entity, it can still capitalize the cost of the improvements (subject to the amount of the capitalization limit). The time period over which these costs can be amortized, however, must be limited to the lesser of the useful life of the improvements or the length of the lease.

If the lease has an extension option that would allow the lessee to increase the time period over which it can potentially lease the property, the total period over which the leasehold improvements can be depreciated must still be limited to the initial lease term, on the grounds that there is no certainty that the lessee will accept the lease extension option. This limitation is waived for depreciation purposes only if there is either a bargain renewal option or extensive penalties in the lease contract that would make it highly likely that the lessee would renew the lease.

PP&E—Depreciable Amount

The depreciable amount of an asset, equal to its capitalized cost net of any residual value that the company expects to receive at the time when the asset is expected to be taken out of active use, should be allocated on a systematic basis over its useful life. The residual value and the useful life of an asset should be reviewed at least at each financial year-end and, if expectations differ from previous estimates, the change should be accounted for as a change in an accounting estimate.

The residual value can be difficult to determine, for several reasons. First, there may be a removal cost associated with the asset, which will reduce the net residual value that will be realized. If the equipment is especially large (such as a printing press) or if it involves environmental hazards (such as any equipment involving the use of radioactive substances), then the removal cost may exceed the residual value. In this latter instance, the residual value may be negative; in that case, it should be ignored for depreciation purposes. It is important to note that asset obsolescence is so rapid in some industries (especially in relation to computer equipment) that a reasonable appraisal of salvage value at the time an asset is put into service may require drastic revision shortly thereafter. Another difficulty is the lack of a ready market for the sale of used assets in many instances. Finally, the cost of conducting an appraisal in order to determine a net residual value may be excessive in relation to the cost of the equipment being appraised. For all these reasons, a company should certainly attempt to set a net residual value in order to arrive at a cost base for depreciation purposes, but it will probably be necessary to make regular revisions in a cost-effective manner to reflect the ongoing realities of asset resale values.

In the case of low-cost assets, it is rarely worth the effort to derive residual values for depreciation purposes; as a result, typically these items are fully depreciated on the assumption that they have no residual value.

PP&E—Depreciation

IAS 16 states that the depreciation method should reflect the pattern in which the asset's future economic benefits are expected to be consumed by the entity and that appropriateness of the method should be reviewed at least annually in case there has been a change in the expected pattern. Beyond that, the standard leaves the choice of method to the entity, even though it does cite straight-line, diminishing balance, and units of production methods.

Depreciation is designed to spread an asset's cost over its entire useful service life. The service life is the period of time over which the product is anticipated to be used, after which it is expected to have been worn out. At the end of the service life, the asset is no longer expected to be economically usable (or at least not usable without extensive overhaul), or when it no longer has a sufficient productive capacity for ongoing company production needs, thus rendering it essentially obsolete.

Anything can be depreciated that has a business purpose, has a productive life of more than one year, gradually wears out over time, and whose cost exceeds the corporate capitalization limit. Since land does not wear out, it cannot be depreciated.

There are a variety of depreciation methods, as outlined in the next sections. Straight-line depreciation provides for a depreciation rate that is the same amount in every year of an asset's life, whereas diminishing balance depreciation methods are oriented toward the more rapid recognition of depreciation expenses, on the grounds that an asset is used most intensively when it is first acquired. Perhaps the most accurate depreciation methods are those that are tied to actual asset usage (such as the units of production method), though they require much more extensive recordkeeping in relation to units of usage. There are also depreciation methods based on compound interest factors, resulting in delayed depreciation recognition; since these methods are rarely used, however, they are not presented here.

If an asset is present but is temporarily idle, then its depreciation should be continued using the existing assumptions for the usable life of the asset. Only if it is permanently idled should the accountant review the need to recognize impairment of the asset. (See the later section discussing impairment.)

An asset is rarely purchased or sold precisely on the first or last day of the fiscal year, which brings up the issue of how depreciation is to be calculated in these first and last partial years of use. Although IAS 16 is silent on the matter, when an asset is either acquired or disposed of during the year, the full-year depreciation calculation should be prorated between the accounting periods involved; this is necessary to achieve proper matching. It may so happen that individual assets in a relatively homogeneous group are regularly acquired and disposed of; in this case, there are a number of alternatives available, all of which are valid as long as they are consistently applied. One option is to record a full year of depreciation in the year of acquisition and no depreciation in the year of sale. It is also possible to record a half-year of depreciation in the first year and a half-year of depreciation in the last year. One can even prorate the depreciation more precisely, making it accurate to within the nearest month (or even the nearest day) of when an acquisition or sale transaction occurs.

PP&E—Straight-Line Depreciation

The straight-line depreciation method is the simplest method available, it is the most popular one when a company has no particular need to recognize depreciation costs at an accelerated rate (as would be the case when it wants to match the book value of its depreciation to the accelerated depreciation used for income tax calculation purposes), and it is used for all amortization calculations.

This method is calculated by subtracting an asset's expected residual value from its capitalized cost and then dividing this amount by the estimated useful life of the asset. For example, a candy wrapper machine has a cost of £40,000 and an expected residual value of £8,000. It is expected to be in service for eight years. Given these assumptions, its annual depreciation expense is

= (Cost – residual value) / number of years in service
= (£40,000 – £8,000) / 8 years
= £32,000 / 8 years
= £4,000 depreciation per year

PP&E—Accelerated Depreciation Methods

Under accelerated methods, depreciation expense is higher in the early years of the asset's useful life and lower in the later years. IAS 16 mentions only one accelerated method, the diminishing balance method, but other methods have been employed in various national GAAP under earlier or contemporary accounting standards.

1. Diminishing balance—the depreciation rate is applied to the net book value of the asset, resulting in a diminishing annual charge. There are various ways to compute the percentage to be applied. The next formula provides a mathematically correct allocation over useful life.

$$\text{Rate } \% = \left(1 - \sqrt[n]{\text{residual value/cost}}\right) \times 100$$

where n is the expected useful life in years.

For example, a printing machine costing £20,000 is estimated to have a residual value of £1,000, and a useful life of four years. The depreciation rate under the diminishing balance, applying the preceding formula, is approximately 44%. Consequently, the depreciation expense during each of the four years is

Year 1 = 44% × £10,000 =£4,400

Year 2 = 44% × £5,600 = £2,464

Year 3 = 44% × £3,136 = £1,380

Year 4 = £10,000 – £4,400 – £2,464 – £1,380 – £1,000 = £756

However, companies generally use approximations or conventions influenced by tax practice, such as a multiple of the straight-line rate times the net carrying value at the beginning of the year.

$$\text{Straight-line rate} = \frac{1}{\text{Estimated useful life}}$$

Example

Double-declining balance depreciation (if residual value is to be recognized, stop when book value = estimated residual value)

Depreciation = 2 × Straight-line rate × Book value at beginning of year

For example, a dry cleaning machine costing £20,000 is estimated to have a useful life of six years. Under the straight-line method, it would have depreciation of £3,333 per year. Consequently, the first year of depreciation under the 200% DDB method would be double that amount, or £6,667. The calculation for all six years of depreciation is noted in the next table.

Year	*Beginning cost basis*	*Straight-line depreciation*	*200% DDB depreciation*	*Ending cost basis*
1	£24,000	£3,333	£6,667	£17,333
2	17,333	2,889	5,778	11,555
3	11,555	1,926	3,852	7,703
4	7,703	1,284	2,568	5,135
5	5,135	856	1,712	3,423
6	3,423	571	1,142	2,281

Note that there is still some cost left at the end of the sixth year that has not been depreciated. This is usually handled by converting over from the DDB method to the straight-line method in the year in which the straight-line method would result in a higher amount of depreciation; then the straight-line method is used until all of the available depreciation has been recognized.

2. Another method to accomplish a diminishing charge for depreciation is the sum-of-the-years' digits method, which is commonly employed in the United States and certain other venues.

   Sum-of-the-years' digits (SYD) depreciation =

   (Cost less salvage value) × Applicable fraction

$$\text{where applicable fraction} = \frac{\text{number of years of estimated life remaining as of the beginning of the year}}{\text{SYD}}$$

$$\text{and SYD} = \frac{n(n+1)}{2} \quad \text{and } n = \text{estimated useful life}$$

This depreciation method is designed to recognize the bulk of all depreciation within the first few years of an asset's depreciable period, but does not do so quite as rapidly as the double-declining balance method described in the previous section. Its calculation can be surmised from its name. For the first year of depreciation, one adds up the number of years over which an asset is scheduled to be depreciated and then divides this into the total number of years remaining. The resulting percentage is used as the depreciation rate. In succeeding years, simply divide the reduced number of years left into the same total number of years remaining.

For example, a punch press costing £24,000 is scheduled to be depreciated over five years. The sum-of-the-years' digits is 15 (Year 1 + Year 2 + Year 3 + Year 4 + Year 5). The depreciation calculation in each of the five years is

Year 1	=	(5/15)	×	£24,000	=	£8,000
Year 2	=	(4/15)	×	£24,000	=	£6,400
Year 3	=	(3/15)	×	£24,000	=	£4,800
Year 4	=	(2/15)	×	£24,000	=	£3,200
Year 5	=	(1/15)	×	£24,000	=	£1,600
						£24,000

In practice, unless there are tax reasons to employ accelerated methods, large companies tend to use straight-line depreciation. This has the merit that it is simple to apply, and where a company has a large pool of similar assets, some of which are replaced each year, the aggregate annual depreciation charge is likely to be the same, irrespective of the method chosen. (Consider a trucking company that has 10 trucks, each costing £200,000, one of which is replaced each year. The aggregate annual depreciation charge will be £200,000 under any mathematically accurate depreciation method.)

PP&E—Units of Production Depreciation Method

The units of production depreciation method can result in the most accurate matching of actual asset usage to the related amount of depreciation that is recognized in the accounting records. Its use is limited to those assets for which some estimate of production can be attached, but it is a particular favorite of those who use activity-based costing systems because it closely relates asset cost to actual activity.

To calculate it, estimate the total number of units of production that are likely to result from the use of an asset. Then divide the total capitalized asset cost (less residual value, if this is known) by the total estimated production to arrive at the depreciation cost per unit of production. The recognized depreciation is derived by multiplying the number of units of actual production during the period by the depreciation cost per unit. If there is a significant divergence of actual production activity from the original estimate, the depreciation cost per unit of production can be altered to reflect the realities of actual production volumes.

An example of this method's use would be if an oil derrick is constructed at a cost of £350,000. It is expected to be used in the extraction of 1 million barrels of oil, which results in an anticipated depreciation rate of £0.35 per barrel. During the first month, 23,500 barrels of oil are extracted. Using this method, the depreciation cost is

= (Cost per unit of production) × (Number of units of production)
= (£0.35 per barrel) × (23,500 barrels)
= £8,225

This calculation also can be used with service hours as its basis rather than units of production. When used in this manner, the method can be applied to a larger number of assets for which production volumes would not be otherwise available.

PP&E—Cost Model versus Revaluation Model

IAS 16 provides for two acceptable alternative approaches to accounting for long-lived tangible assets. The first of these is the cost model, under which an item of PP&E is carried at its cost net of any accumulated depreciation and any accumulated impairment losses. In many jurisdictions this is the only method permitted by statute; however, a number of jurisdictions, particularly those with significant rates of inflation, do permit either full or selective revaluation. IAS 16 acknowledges this fact by also mandating what it calls the "revaluation model."

Using the revaluation model, an item of PP&E whose fair value can be measured reliably is carried at a revalued amount, which is its fair value at the date of the revaluation net of any subsequent accumulated depreciation and accumulated impairment losses. IAS 16 requires that revaluations be made with sufficient regularity to ensure that the carrying amount does not differ materially from that which would be determined using fair value at the date of the statement of financial position. If an item of PP&E is revalued, the entire class of the assets to which that item belongs has to be revalued.

The fair value of land and buildings should be appraised professionally based on the market; similarly, the fair value of items of plant and equipment is also determined by appraisal. IAS 16 states that if there is no market-based evidence of fair value because of the specialized nature of the item, an entity may need to estimate fair value using an income or a depreciated replacement cost approach.

Example of depreciated replacement cost (sound value) as a valuation approach

An asset acquired January 1, 2004, at a cost of €40,000 was expected to have a useful economic life of 10 years. On January 1, 2007, it is appraised as having a gross replacement cost of €50,000. The sound value, or depreciated replacement cost, would be 7/10 × €50,000, or €35,000. This compares with a book, or carrying, value of €28,000 at that same date. Mechanically, to accomplish a revaluation at January1, 2006, the asset should be written up by €10,000 (i.e., from €40,000 to €50,000 gross cost) and the accumulated depreciation should be proportionally written up by €3,000 (from €12,000 to €15,000). Under IAS 16, the net amount of the revaluation adjustment, €7,000, would be credited to revaluation surplus, and reported in other comprehensive income.

An alternative accounting procedure is also permitted under the standard, whereby accumulated depreciation at the date of the revaluation is written off against the gross carrying value of the asset. In the previous example, this would mean that the €12,000 of accumulated depreciation at January 1, 2006, immediately prior to the revaluation, would be credited to the gross asset amount, €40,000, thereby reducing it to €28,000. Then the asset account would be adjusted to reflect the valuation of €35,000 by increasing the asset account by €7,000 (€35,000 – €28,000), with the offset again in other comprehensive income. In terms of total assets reported in the statement of financial position, this has exactly the same effect as the first method.

Nevertheless, many users of financial statements, including credit grantors and prospective investors, pay heed to the ratio of net property and equipment as a fraction of the related gross amounts. This is done to assess the relative age of the enterprise's productive assets and, indirectly, to estimate the timing and amounts of cash needed for asset replacements. There is a significant diminution of information under the second method. Accordingly, the first approach described, preserving the relationship between gross and net asset amounts after the revaluation, is recommended as being the preferable alternative if the goal is meaningful financial reporting.

Although IAS 16 requires revaluation of all assets in a given class, the Standard recognizes that it may be more practical to accomplish this on a rolling, or cycle, basis. This could be done by revaluing one-third of the assets in a given asset category (such as machinery) in each year, so that as of the date of any statement of financial position, one-third of the group is valued at current fair value, another one-third is valued at amounts that are one year obsolete, and another one-third are valued at amounts that are two years obsolete. Unless values are changing rapidly, it is likely that the statement of financial position would not be materially distorted.

Therefore, this approach would be a reasonable means to facilitate the revaluation process.

In accordance with IAS 1 (as revised in 2007), if an asset's carrying value increased as a result of revaluation, the increase should be recognized in other comprehensive income and accumulated in equity as revaluation surplus. If a revalued asset subsequently is found to be impaired, the impairment provision is offset against the revaluation surplus first; only when that has been exhausted is it expensed. Equally, if an asset carried at historical cost had been impaired but was subsequently revalued above historical cost because of some dramatic change in economic circumstances, the previous impairment provision would flow back through income and only the increase above historical cost would be reported in other comprehensive income.

Under the provisions of IAS 16, the amount credited to revaluation surplus either can be amortized to retained earnings (but *not* through the income statement!) as the asset is being depreciated, or can be held in the surplus account until such time as the asset is disposed of or retired from service. Any amortization is limited to an amount equal to the difference between the historical cost amortization and that charged in the income statement, based on the revalued amount.

Deferred tax effects of revaluations must be provided in the financial statements. Where plant assets are depreciated over longer lives for financial reporting purposes than for tax reporting purposes, a deferred tax liability will be created in the early years and then drawn down in later years. Generally the deferred tax provided will be measured by the expected future tax rate applied to the temporary difference at the time it reverses; unless future tax rate changes have already been enacted, the current rate structure is used as an unbiased estimator of those future effects.

In the case of a revaluation of plant assets, it may be that taxing authorities will not permit the higher revalued amounts to be depreciated for purposes of computing tax liabilities; instead, only the actual cost incurred can be used to offset tax obligations. However, since revaluations reflect a holding gain, this gain could be taxable if realized. Accordingly, a deferred tax liability still is required to be recognized, even though it does not relate to temporary differences arising from periodic depreciation charges.

SIC 21 confirms that measurement of the deferred tax effects relating to the revaluation of nondepreciable assets must be made with reference to the tax consequences that would follow from recovery of the carrying amount of that asset through an eventual sale. This is necessary because the asset will not be depreciated; hence, no part of its carrying amount is considered to be recovered through use. As a practical matter, this means that if there are differential capital gain and ordinary income tax rates, deferred taxes will be computed with reference to the former.

PP&E—Asset Impairment

A company is allowed to write down its remaining investment in an asset if it can be proven that the asset is impaired. The impairment test should be applied to the smallest group of assets for which the entity has identifiable cash flows, which is called a cash-generating unit. The carrying amount of the asset or assets in the cash-generating unit is compared with the fair value and the present value of the cash flows expected to be generated by using the asset ("value in use"). If the higher of these future values is lower than the carrying amount, impairment is recognized for the difference.

IAS 36 defines impairment as the excess of carrying value over recoverable amount and defines recoverable amount as the greater of two alternative measures: net selling price and value in use. The objective is to recognize impairment when the economic value of an asset (or cash-generating unit comprised of a group of assets) is truly below its book (carrying) value.

The determination of the fair value less costs to sell (i.e., net selling price) and the value in use of the asset being evaluated will typically present some difficulties. For actively traded assets, fair value can be ascertained by reference to publicly available information (e.g., from price lists or dealer quotations), and costs of disposal will be either implicitly factored into those amounts (such as when a dealer quote includes pick-up, shipping, etc.) or readily estimated. Most common productive tangible assets, such as machinery and equipment, will not be priced easily, however, since active markets for used items will either not exist or be relatively illiquid. Often it will be necessary to reason by analogy (i.e., to draw inferences from recent transactions in similar assets), making adjustments for age, condition, productive capacity, and other variables.

For example, a five-year-old machine having an output rate (for a given component) of 2,000 units per day, and an estimated useful life of eight years, might be valued at 30% (= 3/8 × .8) of the cost of a new replacement machine having a capacity of 2,500 units per day. In many industries, trade publications and other data sources can provide a great deal of insight into the market value of key assets.

The computation of value in use involves a two-step process: (1) estimate future cash flows, and (2) calculate the present value of these cash flows by application of an appropriate discount rate. Projection of future cash flows must be based on reasonable assumptions. Exaggerated revenue growth rates, significant anticipated cost reductions, or unreasonable useful lives for plant assets must be avoided if meaningful results are to be obtained.

In general, recent past experience is a fair guide to the near-term future, but a recent sudden growth spurt should not be extrapolated to more than the very near-term future. For example, if growth over the past five years averaged 5% but in the latest year equaled 15%, unless the recent rate of growth can be identified with factors that demonstrate it as being sustainable, a future growth rate of 5%, or slightly higher, would be more supportable.

There is no requirement for the periodic testing of asset impairment. Instead, it should be done if there is a major drop in asset usage, if there is a downgrade of its physical condition, or if government regulations or business conditions likely will result in a major drop in usage. For example, if new government regulations are imposed that are likely to significantly reduce a company's ability to use the asset, such as may be the case for a coal-fired electricity-generating facility that is subject to pollution controls, then an asset impairment test would be necessary. The test also can be conducted if there are major cost overruns during the construction of an asset or if there is a history or future expectation of operating losses associated with an asset. An expectation of early asset disposition also can trigger the test.

In general, IAS 36 requires that the entity tests for impairment when there is an indication that an asset might be impaired (but annually for intangible assets having an indefinite useful life). At a minimum, these external and internal signs of possible impairment are to be given consideration on an annual basis:

- There have been market value declines for specific assets or cash-generating units, beyond the declines expected as a function of asset aging and use.
- Significant changes have occurred in the technological, market, economic, or legal environments in which the enterprise operates or the specific market to which the asset is dedicated.
- There have been increases in the market interest rate or other market-oriented rate of return such that increases in the discount rate to be employed in determining value in use can be anticipated, with a resultant enhanced likelihood that impairments will emerge.
- Declines in the (publicly owned) entity's market capitalization suggest that the aggregate carrying value of assets exceeds the perceived value of the enterprise taken as a whole.
- There is specific evidence of obsolescence or of physical damage to an asset or group of assets.
- There have been significant internal changes to the organization or its operations, such as product discontinuation decisions or restructurings, so that the expected remaining useful life or utility of the asset has seemingly been reduced.
- Internal reporting data suggest that the economic performance of the asset or group of assets is, or will become, worse than previously anticipated.

When an asset is no longer in use and there is no prospect for it to be used at any point in the future, then it must be written down to its net realizable value. All depreciation stops at the time of the write-down because there will be no remaining asset value to depreciate and because the purpose for depreciation (allocation of cost to period of productive use) is no longer present.

Intangible Assets

At the time an intangible asset is purchased, it should be capitalized on the company books at the amount of cash that was paid for it. If another asset was given in exchange for the intangible, then the cost should be set at the fair market value of the asset given up. Another alternative would be to use the present value of any liability that is assumed in exchange for the intangible asset. Of course, it is also possible to create an intangible asset internally (such as the creation of a customer list), as long as the detail for all costs incurred in the creation of the intangible asset is tracked and summarized adequately.

The four key criteria for determining whether intangible assets are to be recognized are

1. Whether the intangible asset can be identified separately from other aspects of the business enterprise
2. Whether the use of the intangible asset is controlled by the enterprise as a result of its past actions and events
3. Whether future economic benefits can be expected to flow to the enterprise
4. Whether the cost of the asset can be measured reliably

IAS 38 says an intangible meets the identifiability requirement if

1. It is separable (i.e., is capable of being separated or divided from the entity and sold, transferred, licensed, rented or exchanged, either individually or together with a related contract, asset, or liability); or
2. It arises from contractual or other legal rights, regardless of whether those rights are transferable or separable from the entity or from other rights and obligations.

IAS 38 offers a fairly comprehensive listing of seven possible separate classes of intangibles. These are

1. Brand names
2. Mastheads and publishing titles
3. Computer software
4. Licenses and franchises
5. Copyrights, patents, and other industrial property rights, service and operating rights
6. Recipes, formulas, models, designs and prototypes
7. Intangible assets under development

IAS 38 incorporates two alternative measurement bases: the cost model and the revaluation model. This is entirely comparable to what is prescribed under IAS 16 relative to tangible long-lived assets.

Under the *cost model*, after initial recognition, an intangible asset should be carried at its cost less any accumulated amortization and any accumulated impairment losses.

Under the *revaluation model*, as with tangible assets, the standard for intangibles permits revaluation subsequent to original acquisition, with the asset being written up to fair value. The two unique features of IAS 38 as applied to intangibles assets are

1. If the intangibles were not initially recognized (i.e., they were expensed rather than capitalized), it would not be possible to later recognize them at fair value.
2. Deriving fair value by applying a present value concept to projected cash flows (a technique that can be used in the case of tangible assets under IAS 16) is deemed to be too unreliable in the realm of intangibles, primarily because it would tend to commingle the impact of identifiable assets and goodwill. Accordingly, fair value of an intangible asset should be determined *only* by reference to an active market in that type of intangible asset. Active markets providing meaningful data are not expected to exist for such

unique assets as patents and trademarks, and thus it is presumed that revaluation will not be applied to these types of assets in the normal course of business. As a consequence, the standard effectively restricts revaluation of intangible assets to freely tradable intangible assets.

As with the rules pertaining to PP&E under IAS 16, if some intangible assets in a given class are subjected to revaluation, all the assets in that class should be consistently accounted for unless fair value information is not or ceases to be available. Not only that, but IAS 38 requires that revaluations be recognized in other comprehensive income and accumulated in equity through the use of a revaluation surplus account, except to the extent that previous impairments had been recognized by a charge against income.

If an intangible asset has an indefinite life, as demonstrated by clearly traceable cash flows well into the future, then it is not amortized. Instead, it is subject to an annual impairment test, resulting in the recognition of an impairment loss for the excess of carrying value over greater of net selling price and value in use. If an intangible asset in this category no longer has a demonstrably indefinite life, then it would convert to a normal amortization schedule based on its newly defined economic life.

Where an asset is determined to have an indefinite useful life, the entity must conduct impairment tests annually as well as whenever there is an indication that the intangible may be impaired. Furthermore, the presumption that the asset has an indefinite life must also be reviewed.

The impairment of intangible assets other than goodwill (such as patents, copyrights, trade names, customer lists, and franchise rights) should be considered in precisely the same way as long-lived tangible assets are considered. Carrying amounts must be compared to the greater of net selling price or value in use when there are indications that an impairment of the asset may have been suffered. Reversals of impairment losses under defined conditions also are recognized. The effects of impairment recognitions and reversals will be reflected in current period operating results, if the intangible assets in question are being accounted for in accordance with the cost method.

If the revaluation method of accounting for intangible assets is followed, however (use of which is possible only if strict criteria can be met), impairments will normally be charged to other comprehensive income to the extent of any credit balance in the revaluation surplus of that asset, and only to the extent that the loss exceeds previously recognized valuation surplus will the impairment loss be reported as a charge against profit. Recoveries are handled consistently with the method that impairments were reported, in a manner entirely analogous to impairments of PP&E.

Example of intangible amortization

Mr. Mel Acorn purchases cab license #512 from the city of St. Moriz for CHF100,000. The license term is for five years, after which he can renew it with no anticipated difficulties. The cash flows from the cab license can be reasonably shown to extend into the indefinite future, so there is no amortization requirement. The city council then changes the renewal process to a lottery where the odds of obtaining a renewal are poor. Mr. Acorn must now assume that the economic life of his cab license will end in five years, so he initiates amortization to coincide with the license renewal date.

Example of an intangible asset purchase

To purchase a competitor, an acquirer spends €1 million more than the book value. The acquirer decides to assign €400,000 of this excess amount to the patent formerly owned by the competitor, which amortizes over the remaining life of the patent. If the acquirer assigns the remaining €600,000 to a customer list asset, and the customer loss rate is 20% per year, then it can reasonably amortize the €600,000 over five years to match the gradual reduction in value of the customer list asset.

Example of revaluation of intangible assets

A patent right is acquired July 1, 2005, for €250,000; while it has a legal life of 15 years, due to rapidly changing technology, management estimates a useful life of only five years. In this case, straight-line amortization will be used. On January 1, 2006, management is uncertain that the process actually can be made economically feasible, and decides to write down the patent to an estimated market value of €75,000, and amortization will be taken over three years from that point. On January 1, 2008, having perfected the related production process, the asset is now appraised at a sound value of €300,000. Furthermore, the estimated useful life is now believed to be six more years. The entries to reflect these events are

7/1/05	Patent	250,000	
	Cash, etc.		250,000
12/31/05	Amortization expense	25,000	
	Patent		25,000
1/1/06	Loss from asset impairment	150,000	
	Patent		150,000
12/31/06	Amortization expense	25,000	
	Patent		25,000
12/31/07	Amortization expense	25,000	
	Patent		25,000
1/1/08	Patent	275,000	
	Gain on asset value recovery		100,000
	Revaluation surplus		175,000

Certain of the entries in this example will be explained further. The entry at year-end 2005 is to record amortization based on original cost, since there had been no revaluations through that time; only a half-year amortization is provided [(€250,000/5) × 1/2]. On January 1, 2006, the impairment is recorded by writing down the asset to the estimated value of €75,000, which necessitates a €150,000 charge to income (carrying value, €225,000, less fair value, €75,000).

In 2006 and 2007, amortization must be provided on the new lower value recorded at the beginning of 2006; moreover, since the new estimated life was three years from January 2006, annual amortization will be €25,000.

As of January 1, 2008, the carrying value of the patent is €25,000; had the January 2006 revaluation not been made, the carrying value would have been €125,000 (€250,000 original cost, less two-and-one-half-years' amortization versus an original estimated life of five years). The new appraised value is €300,000, which will fully recover the earlier write-down and add even more asset value than the originally recognized cost. Under the guidance of IAS 38, the recovery of €100,000 that had been charged to expense should be taken into income; the excess will be credited to shareholders' equity.

Goodwill

Goodwill is recognized only if it is acquired in a business combination. When a company acquires another company or its assets, any excess of the purchase price over the fair value of tangible net assets should be allocated to intangible assets to the greatest degree possible. Examples of such assets include customer lists, patents, trademarks, and brand names. When some value is assigned to these intangible assets, they will then be amortized over a reasonable time period. If the excess purchase price cannot be fully allocated to intangible assets, however, the remainder is added to the goodwill account.

Goodwill cannot be amortized. Instead, it is subject to annual impairment testing, or more frequently if circumstances indicate that impairment is likely. The impairment test is based on the lowest level of identifiable group of assets that generates cash inflows from continuing use (cash-generating unit) to which the goodwill can be assigned. For example, if Company A purchases another business and renames it as an operating division of Company A, then the impairment test will be conducted on the results of only that division. Alternatively, if the purchased business is merged into the operations of Company A in such a manner that its cash flows no longer can be tracked, then the impairment test will be conducted on the results of all of Company A.

Goodwill impairment testing is conducted by comparing the net carrying value (including goodwill) of the subject *cash-generating unit* to its recoverable value. If the recoverable value is greater, then no adjustment is required; however, if the recoverable value figure is lower than the net carrying value, take these three steps:

1. Determine the implied value of goodwill, which is the difference between recoverable value of the cash-generating unit less the net fair value of the identifiable assets (assets minus liabilities and contingent liabilities).
2. Compare the carrying value of goodwill on the company books with the implied value of goodwill.
3. Recognize goodwill impairment loss for any excess of the carrying value of goodwill over the implied value of goodwill.

Example

At the end of 2006 entity A acquired entity Z, and goodwill of €50,000 was recognized on the company books. At the end of 2007 the recoverable value of entity A (cash-generating unit) is €385,000 and the net fair value of the identifiable assets is €350,000. As the carrying amount of the goodwill of €50,000 exceeds the implied value of €35,000 (= €385,000 – €350,000), there is an impairment loss for goodwill of €15,000.

If the carrying amount of the cash-generating unit exceeds the recoverable amount, the impairment loss is recognized and must be allocated to reduce: (1) the carrying amount of any goodwill assigned to this unit; and (2) the other assets of the unit pro rata on the basis of the carrying amount of each asset in the unit.

In general, under IFRS, reversal of an impairment identified with a cash-generating unit is permitted. Due to the special character of this asset, however, IAS 36 has imposed a requirement that reversals may not be recognized for previous write-downs in goodwill. Thus, a later recovery in value of the cash-generating unit will be allocated to assets other than goodwill. (The adjustments to those assets cannot be for amounts greater than would be needed to restore them to the carrying amounts at which they currently would be stated had the earlier impairment not been recognized—that is, at the former carrying values less the depreciation that would have been recorded during the intervening period.)

In certain purchase business combination transactions, the purchase price is less than the fair value of the net assets acquired; these are often identified as being "bargain purchases." The difference between fair value and cost traditionally has been referred to as "negative goodwill." IFRS 3 requires that, before negative goodwill is recognized, the allocation of fair values is to be revisited and all liabilities—including contingencies—be reviewed. After this is completed, if indeed the fair values of identifiable assets acquired net of all liabilities assumed exceeds the total cost of the transaction, then negative goodwill will be acknowledged. Under IFRS 3, negative goodwill is taken immediately into income. Essentially, this is regarded, for financial reporting purposes, as a gain realized upon the acquisition transaction, and it is accounted for accordingly.

Research and Development (R&D) Costs

IAS 38 provided that an expenditure incurred for nonfinancial intangible assets should be recognized as an expense unless

1. It relates to an intangible asset dealt with in another IAS;
2. The cost forms part of the cost of an intangible asset that meets the recognition criteria prescribed by IAS 38; or
3. It is acquired in a business combination and cannot be recognized as an identifiable intangible asset. In this case, this expenditure should form part of the amount attributable to goodwill as at the date of acquisition.

As a consequence of applying these three criteria, these costs are expensed as they are incurred:

- Research costs
- Preopening costs for a new facility or business, and plant start-up costs incurred during a period prior to full-scale production or operation, unless these costs are capitalized as part of the cost of an item of PP&E
- Organization costs, such as legal and secretarial costs, which are typically incurred in establishing a legal entity
- Training costs involved in operating a business or a product line
- Advertising and related costs
- Relocation, restructuring, and other costs involved in organizing a business or product line
- Customer lists, brands, mastheads, and publishing titles that are internally generated

The criteria for recognition of intangible assets as provided in IAS 38 are rather stringent, and many enterprises will find that expenditures either to acquire or to develop intangible assets will fail the test for capitalization. In such instances, all these costs must be expensed currently as incurred. Furthermore, once expensed, these costs cannot be resurrected and capitalized in a later period, even if the conditions for such treatment are later met. This is not meant, however, to preclude correction of an error made in an earlier period if the conditions for capitalization were met but interpreted incorrectly by the reporting entity at that time.

IAS 38 provides a list of criteria, all of which must be met in order for a development cost to be capitalized. In order to capitalize development costs, an entity must be able to demonstrate all of these points:

- The technical feasibility of completing the intangible asset so that it will be available for use or sale
- Its intention to complete the intangible asset and use or sell it
- Its ability to use or sell the intangible asset
- How the intangible asset will generate probable future economic benefits
- The availability of adequate technical, financial, and other resources to complete the development and to use or sell the intangible asset
- Its ability to measure reliably the expenditure attributable to the intangible asset during its development

Example

An enterprise is developing a new product. Costs incurred by the R&D department in 2007 on the "research phase" amounted to €200,000. In 2008, technical and commercial feasibility of the product was established. Costs incurred in 2008 were €20,000 personnel costs and €15,000 legal fees to register the patent. In 2009, the enterprise incurred €30,000 to successfully defend a legal suit to protect the patent. The enterprise would account for these costs in this way:

- Research costs incurred in 2007, amounting to €200,000, should be expensed, as they do not meet the recognition criteria for intangible assets. The costs do not result in an identifiable asset capable of generating future economic benefits.
- Personnel and legal costs incurred in 2008, amounting to €35,000, would be capitalized as patents. The company has established technical and commercial feasibility of the product as well as obtained control over the use of the asset. The standard specifically prohibits the reinstatement of costs previously recognized as an expense. Thus €200,000, recognized as an expense in the previous financial statements, cannot be reinstated and capitalized.
- Legal costs of €30,000 incurred in 2009 to defend the enterprise in a patent lawsuit should be expensed. Under US GAAP, legal fees and other costs incurred in successfully defending a patent lawsuit can be capitalized in the patents account, to the extent that value is evident, because such costs are incurred to establish the legal rights of the owner of the patent. However, in view of the stringent conditions imposed by IAS 38 concerning the recognition of subsequent costs, only such subsequent costs should be capitalized that would enable the asset to generate future economic benefits *in excess of the originally assessed standards of performance*. This represents, in most instances, a very high, possibly insurmountable, hurdle. Thus, legal costs incurred in connection with defending the

patent, which could be considered as expenses incurred to maintain the asset at its originally assessed standard of performance, would not meet the recognition criteria under IAS 38.

- Alternatively, if the enterprise were to lose the patent lawsuit, then the useful life and the recoverable amount of the intangible asset would be in question. The enterprise would be required to provide for any impairment loss and, in all probability, even to fully write off the intangible asset. What is required must be determined by the facts of the specific situation.

Development costs pose a special problem in terms of the application of the revaluation method under IAS 38. In general, it will not be possible to obtain fair value data from active markets, as is required by IAS 38. Accordingly, it is expected that the cost method will be applied for development costs almost universally.

Example of development cost capitalization

Assume that Creative, Incorporated incurs substantial research and development costs for the invention of new products, many of which are brought to market successfully. In particular, Creative has incurred costs during 2007 amounting to €750,000, relative to a new manufacturing process. Of these costs, €600,000 was incurred prior to December 1, 2005. As of December 31, the viability of the new process was still not known, although testing had been conducted on December 1. In fact, results were not conclusively known until February 15, 2006, after another €75,000 in costs were incurred post–January 1. Creative, Incorporated's financial statements for 2005 were issued February 10, 2006, and the full €750,000 in research and development costs was expensed, since it was not yet known whether a portion of these qualified as development costs under IAS 38. When it is learned that feasibility had, in fact, been shown as of December 1, Creative management asks to restore the €150,000 of post–December 1 costs as a development asset. Under IAS 38 this is prohibited; however, the 2006 costs (€75,000 thus far) would qualify for capitalization, in all likelihood, based on the facts known.

If it is determined that fair value information derived from active markets is indeed available, and the enterprise desires to apply the revaluation method of accounting to development costs, then it will be necessary to perform revaluations on a regular basis, such that at any reporting date the carrying amounts are not materially different from the current fair values.

DECISION TREE

There are a variety of decision points involved in the determination of how to treat an expenditure related to PP&E. The decision tree shown in Exhibit 6.1 can be used to determine the correct accounting treatment of these expenditures. There may be some uncertainty about whether an expenditure adds to an asset's future value and whether the entity expects future economic benefits from this expenditure. When this situation arises, choose the decision point corresponding to the most dominant impact of the expenditure. For example, switching to a concrete roof from a wooden one may extend the life of a structure, but its dominant impact is to increase the building's future value.

Exhibit 6.1 Asset Acquisition Capitalization or Expense Decision

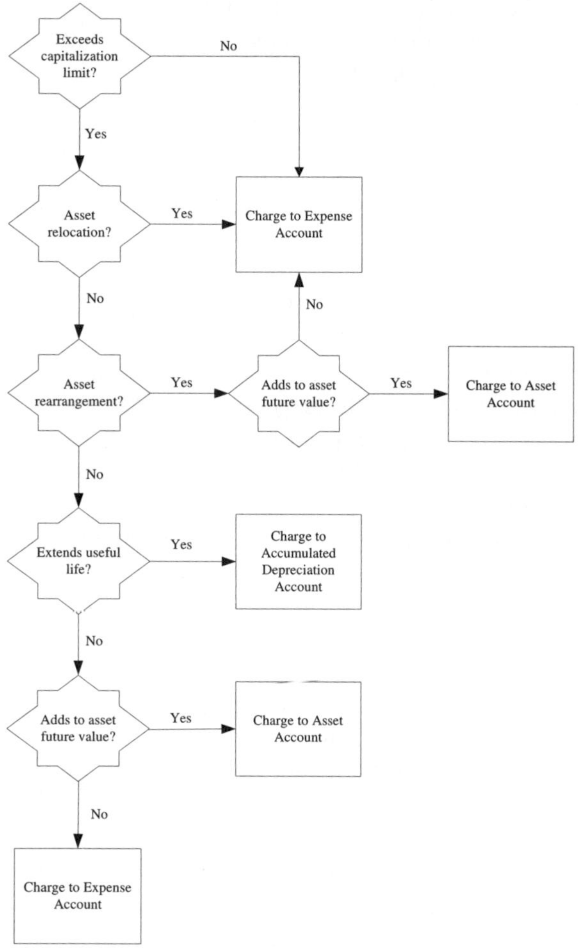

POLICIES

PP&E

- **Management must approve all asset additions through a formal review process.** This policy requires the management team to follow a formal review process, preferably using a capital investment proposal form, such as the one shown in the Forms and Reports section that requires both the use of cash flow analysis and a hierarchy of approvals depending on the size of the proposed expenditure.
- **All assets with a purchase price exceeding €1,000 shall be recorded as PP&E.** This policy reduces the amount of paperwork associated with fixed asset tracking by shifting smaller assets into the expense category.

- **The capitalization limit shall be reviewed annually.** This policy requires the controller to verify that the existing capitalization limit represents a reasonable balance of minimized recordkeeping for PP&E, and not an excessive amount of charges to expense for lower-cost assets.
- **Capital investment results shall be reviewed annually.** This policy requires a company to compare the actual results of a capital investment to what was predicted in its capital investment proposal form (see the Forms and Reports section). The intent is to highlight incorrect assumptions that still may be used for other capital investment proposals, which then can be corrected to ensure better ongoing capital investment decisions.
- **Conduct an annual inventory of all items of PP&E.** This policy requires the accounting staff to compare the record of fixed assets to their actual locations, typically resulting not only in adjustments to their recorded locations but also a determination of the need to dispose of selected assets.
- **A detailed record shall be maintained of each item of PP&E.** This policy centralizes the recordkeeping for each asset, making it much easier to identify, locate, cost, and determine the warranty provisions associated with each one.
- **All asset valuations associated with dissimilar asset exchanges shall be reviewed by an outside appraiser.** This policy prevents the accounting staff from intentionally creating gains or losses on asset exchange transactions by assuming incorrect asset fair values.
- **Copies of property records shall be maintained in an off-site location.** This policy reduces the risk of lost records by requiring a periodic shifting of record copies to a secure outside location.
- **All asset transfers and disposals require management approval.** This policy brings any asset movements to the attention of the accounting department, which then can record the revised asset locations in the accounting records. The policy also allows one to review the proposed prices to be obtained from the sale or disposal of assets.
- **Conduct revaluations with sufficient regularity when the revaluation model is applied to a class of assets.** This policy confirms that the carrying value does not differ materially from that which would be determined using fair value at the date of the statement of financial position.
- **Periodically review all items for impairment.** This policy ensures that the accounting staff will regularly compare the carrying value of all items of PP&E to their fair (recoverable) value and write down the carrying value to the fair value if this is the lower amount. Record the reversal of the impairment loss if needed.

Intangible Assets

- **All transactions involving the recording of intangible assets must be approved by the external auditors in advance.** Intangible assets are subject to a considerable degree of scrutiny by auditors. By gaining advance approval of these transactions, it is much less likely that there will be significant audit adjustments related to them after the end of the fiscal year.

- **Periodically review all intangible assets for impairment.** This policy ensures that the accounting staff will regularly compare the carrying value of all intangible assets to their recoverable value and write down the carrying value to the recoverable value if this is the lower amount. Record the reversal of the impairment loss if needed.

Research and Development Costs

- **All research and development costs must be recorded under unique general ledger account codes.** Under IFRS, research costs are charged to expense in the current period, and it is imperative to ascertain that development costs, which are capitalized, meet all the criteria for capitalization. Otherwise, it is likely that some development costs not meeting the criteria are capitalized, thereby incorrectly increasing reported profits.

PROCEDURES

PP&E—Calculate Depreciation

Use these seven steps to ensure that the correct depreciation type and period is used for each capitalized asset.

1. Compare the type of asset to the company policy statement on asset types in the accounting policy manual.
2. Go to the PP&E register in the computer database and enter the asset under the correct asset category.
3. When adding the asset to the database, set the number of years of depreciation in accordance with the standard listed in the company policy statement on asset types.
4. Set the first-year depreciation at the half-year convention (if this is the practice).
5. Set the depreciation method as the _______ method.
6. Print the transaction and store it in the PP&E records manual.
7. Print the depreciation register and verify that the system has correctly calculated the depreciation expense for the newly added asset.

PP&E—Conduct Inventory of Assets

Use these eight steps to periodically verify the existence of PP&E items in the locations listed in the computer system.

1. Obtain a list of all assets in a company location that is scheduled to be reviewed.
2. Check off all assets on the list as they are found and their tag numbers are matched to the list.
3. Make note of the tag numbers of all physical assets found that are not on the computer list for this location.

4. Inquire of the staff in the target location as to where the missing assets might be located. Enter these notes in the computer database, to be included in subsequent physical counts.
5. Go to the computer database and enter the correct physical location code for those assets found at the review location that were not listed on the report.
6. Go to the computer database and reset the location code to "Pending" for those assets not found in the location that were listed on the report.
7. If inquiries indicate that assets have been disposed of or transferred, refer the matter to the internal audit staff for review of potential control problems.
8. If assets have been disposed of or transferred, record a gain or loss based on the remaining net carrying value of the assets in question, and retire them from the PP&E assets register.

PP&E—Enter Asset Payments

Follow these four steps to process PP&E transactions by the accounts payable clerk.

1. Determine if an asset purchase exceeds the corporate capitalization limit. If so, code the purchase into the appropriate asset account. If not, contact the assistant controller to verify which expense account is to be charged for the purchase.
2. Open the purchasing module and create a purchase transaction. Include in the asset account all expenses required to bring the asset to the company and install it. In the case of the current invoice in question, this means including the listed sales tax, delivery charges, and shipping insurance in the asset account.
3. Open the PP&E register and enter the asset's name, account type, and location within the company. Also enter the asset tag number, if available. The system automatically will assign a depreciation calculation method, and period to the asset based on the account type to which it was assigned.
4. Verify that the amount listed in the PP&E register matches the amount entered for the purchase transaction.

PP&E—Evaluate Capital Purchase Proposals

Use these eight steps to verify the assumptions, cash flows, and net present value of all capital proposals.

1. Review each submitted capital expenditure form to ensure that all fields have been completed. If not, return the form to the sender with a note regarding the missing information.
2. Review all assumptions, which are noted at the bottom of the form. If these vary significantly from assumptions used for previous approved capital budgets, or if there are reasonable grounds for doubt, review them with the originating person, and modify them, if necessary, as well as all underlying numerical data.

3. Review all itemized cash flows with the project manager, purchasing staff, sales staff, and anyone else with a reasonable degree of knowledge regarding the amount or timing of the cash flows.
4. Adjust the amount or timing of cash flows in the capital expenditure analysis based on the preceding cash flow review.
5. Obtain the cost of capital from the controller, and use this to discount the stream of cash flows noted in the capital expenditure proposal.
6. If the project seems unusually risky, also recalculate the net present value using a higher discount rate, to be determined by the controller.
7. If the net present value is positive, then issue a favorable project recommendation to the controller and project sponsor.
8. If the net present value is negative, state the amount by which it is negative and the internal rate of return, so that the project sponsor can rework the assumptions and perhaps arrive at a positive net present value.

PP&E—Record Gain/Loss on Sale of an Asset

Use this procedure to calculate the gain or loss on the sale or disposal of any capital assets.

1. Receive documentation from the purchasing department regarding the sale of assets. This should include a signed Asset Disposition form that authorized someone to sell an asset. If the document is not signed by an authorized person, return it with a note asking for the appropriate signature. The document should be accompanied by a copy of the bill of sale and a copy of the check or other document that shows proof of the amount paid.
2. Once the sale documentation is complete, go to the PP&E database and call up the record for the asset being sold. The easiest way is to conduct a search based on the name of the asset, though the documentation may contain the asset number, which also can be used to find the correct record.
3. Write down the original asset cost and total accumulated depreciation, which is located in the record in the fixed asset database.
4. Subtract the sale amount and accumulated depreciation from the original asset cost. If there is a positive amount left over, this is a loss on the sale of the asset; if there is a negative amount left over, this is a gain on the sale of the asset.
5. Obtain a journal entry form and complete it for the gain or loss transaction. The asset's original cost goes in the "Credit Column," while the accumulated depreciation amount goes in the "Debit Column." The sale amount is a debit to cash. If there is a gain, it is recorded as a credit, but a loss is recorded as a debit.
6. Access the PP&E database and record the sale of the asset. Print the fixed asset database after the transaction is recorded, and compare the total of the account to the general ledger to ensure that the information is recorded in the same amounts in both locations.
7. File a copy of the gain or loss calculation in the journal entry book and also in the permanent file documenting the addition or removal of these assets.

PP&E—Testing Assets for Impairment

Follow these seven steps to determine if the recoverable amount of an item of PP&E has dropped below its carrying value and to adjust the carrying value down to the recoverable value if this is the case. Most assets have carrying values clustered near the corporate capitalization limit, making them so small that impairment testing would not result in significant asset valuation changes. Regardless, this procedure is designed to test the values of only the largest assets.

1. Sort the items of the PP&E register by declining net carrying value (e.g., original purchase price less accumulated depreciation).
2. For impairment testing, select those 20% of the listed assets containing 80% of the total carrying value of the asset register.
3. Determine the recoverable amounts for each of the selected assets—defined as the greater of net selling price and value in use, where value in use is equal to the total discounted cash flows expected to be generated—and list this amount next to their net carrying values.
4. Compare the net carrying value figure to the recoverable amount figure, and highlight those assets for which the carrying value is higher.
5. For the highlighted assets, determine the amount of the variance between the net carrying value and the recoverable value figure, and record an adjustment in the general ledger for this amount. (See the Journal Entries section for the entry format.)
6. Reduce the net carrying values of all adjusted assets in the PP&E register to match the amount of their recoverable values.
7. Calculate depreciation based on the new reduced carrying value figures, and adjust any recurring depreciation journal entries to include these changes.

Intangible Assets—Test Assets for Impairment

Follow these four steps to determine if the recoverable value of an intangible asset is less than its carrying value and to adjust its carrying value downward if this is the case. As opposed to the impairment testing on PP&E assets, impairment testing should be conducted on all intangible assets.

1. Print the asset register, selected only for intangible assets.
2. Determine the recoverable amounts for each of the selected assets—defined as the greater of net selling price and value in use, where value in use is equal to the total discounted cash flows expected to be generated—and list this amount next to their net carrying values. If intangible assets can be grouped by cash-generating unit, this information may be obtained by reviewing the budget for that unit.
3. Compare the carrying value figure for each intangible asset or related group of assets to its expected recoverable value figure.
4. Reduce the carrying values of all adjusted intangible assets in the intangible asset register to match the value of their recoverable amounts.

CONTROLS

PP&E

These controls[2] should be installed to ensure that all assets are properly accounted for.

- **Ensure that asset purchases have appropriate prior authorization.** A company with a capital-intensive infrastructure may find that its most important controls are over the authorization of funds for new or replacement capital projects. Depending on the potential amount of funding involved, these controls may include a complete net present value (NPV) review of the cash flows associated with each prospective investment as well as multilayered approvals that reach all the way up to the board of directors. A truly comprehensive control system will also include a postcompletion review that compares the original cash flow estimates to those actually achieved. This is beneficial not only to see if a better estimation process can be used in the future, but also to see if any deliberate misrepresentation of estimates was initially made.
- **Compare capital investment projections to actual results.** Managers have been known to make overly optimistic projections in order to make favorable cases for asset acquisitions. This issue can be mitigated by conducting regular reviews of the asset acquisitions, comparing them to the initial predictions, and tracing the findings back to the initial managers. This approach also can be used at various points during the asset construction to ensure that costs incurred match original projections.
- **Verify that correct depreciation calculations are being made.** Although there is no potential loss of assets if incorrect depreciation calculations are being made, it can result in an embarrassing adjustment to the previously reported financial results at some point in the future. This control should include a comparison of capitalized items to the official corporate capitalization limit in order to ensure that items are not being inappropriately capitalized and depreciated. It would also be helpful to include a review of the asset categories in which each individual asset has been recorded, to ensure that an asset has not been misclassified and therefore incorrectly depreciated.
- **Verify the fair value assumptions on asset exchanges.** Accounting rules allow one to record a gain or loss on the exchange of items of PP&E for nonmonetary assets or a combination of monetary and nonmonetary assets. It is important to note that this calculation is based on the fair value of the assets involved (which is not already clearly stated in the accounting records); therefore, there is a possibility for someone to artificially create an asset fair value that will result in a gain or loss. This situation can be avoided by having an outside appraiser review the fair value assumptions used in this type of transaction.

---

[2] *Selected controls for fixed assets have been copied with permission from Bragg,* ***Ultimate Accountants' Reference****, pp. 463–465.*

- **Ensure that capital construction projects are not delayed for accounting reasons.** Accounting rules require the interest expense associated with the construction of certain types of assets to be capitalized. By artificially delaying the completion date of an asset, for accounting purposes or otherwise, one can improperly extend the time period over which interest expenses can be ascribed to a project and capitalized as part of its cost, thereby reducing the overall corporate interest expense and increasing profits. This problem can be avoided by personally reviewing the physical status of construction projects in relation to planning documents (such as Gantt charts) and determining the validity of reasons for delays in completion.
- **Verify that asset disposals are properly authorized.** A company does not want to have a fire sale of its assets taking place without any member of the management team knowing about it. Consequently, the sale of assets should be properly authorized prior to any sale transaction being initiated—even if only to ensure that the eventual price paid by the buyer is verified as being a reasonable one.
- **Verify that all changes in asset retirement obligation assumptions are authorized.** A company can artificially increase its short-term potential for profit by altering the assumed amount of future cash flows associated with its obligations for the costs of dismantling and removing the asset. Since downward revisions to these assumptions will be reflected in the current period's income statement as a gain, any changes to these assumptions should be approved prior to implementation.
- **Verify that cash receipts from asset sales are properly handled.** Employees may sell a company's assets, pocket the proceeds, and report to the company that the asset actually was scrapped. This control issue can be reduced by requiring that a bill of sale or receipt from a scrapping company accompany the file for every asset that has been disposed of.
- **Verify that assets are being utilized.** Many fixed assets are parked in a corner and neglected, with no thought to their being profitably sold off. To see if this problem is occurring, the accounting staff should conduct a periodic review of all items of PP&E, including a visual inspection and discussion with employees to see if assets are no longer in use.
- **Test for asset impairment.** There are a variety of circumstances for the net carrying value of an asset to be reduced to its recoverable value, which can result in significant reductions in the recorded value of an asset. This test requires significant knowledge of the types of markets in which the company operates, the regulations it is subject to, and the demand for its products. Consequently, only a knowledgeable person who is at least at the level of a controller should be relied on to detect the presence of assets whose values are likely to have been impaired.

Intangible Assets

- **Verify that excess acquisition purchase costs are fully allocated to intangible assets.** Companies have a major incentive to allocate the amount of acquisition purchase costs in excess of the fair values of the tangible assets purchased in the goodwill account. Doing so not only avoids extra depreciation or amortization expenses (subject to periodic impairment tests), but also avoids IFRS rules to shift this excess amount to other types of intangible assets that can be amortized. Thus, the main result is that all intangible assets acquired as part of an acquisition are fully valued, leaving the minimum possible amount to be charged to the goodwill account.

Research and Development Costs

- **Preconfigure account codes for R&D suppliers to expense accounts, except for those development costs that are capitalized.** When setting up the account codes for suppliers of R&D services and products to a company, configure the records to an expense account; this reduces the chance that an R&D expense will find its way into an asset account and be capitalized, without meeting the stringent criteria for capitalization.
- **Compare R&D expenses over multiple periods to spot expense changes.** Create a multiperiod report that tracks all R&D expenses by cost category; this makes it visible when expenses suddenly drop, indicative of an incorrect charge to an asset account.
- **Compare capitalized R&D expenses over multiple periods (and as a percentage of total R&D costs) to spot changes in the asset account.** By creating a multiperiod report that tracks all capitalized R&D expenses by cost category, it can be seen when charges to an asset account suddenly increase; this is indicative of an incorrect capitalization of R&D costs in the asset account, instead of recording them in the expense account, resulting in an incorrect increase in reported profits.

FORMS AND REPORTS

PP&E

When a company is considering the purchase or construction of an expensive asset, it typically summarizes all relevant cash flow information pertaining to it on a form such as the one shown in Exhibit 6.2. This form clearly reveals the ability of an asset to generate a return to the company. Moreover, if the asset is required for other reasons than the generation of cash flow, it is noted in the lower left corner. Finally, the form requires an increasing number of management approvals, depending on its size. The approval matrix is noted in the lower right corner of the form.

Exhibit 6.2 Capital Investment Proposal Form

Name of Project Sponsor: *H. Henderson* **Submission Date:** *Date*

Investment Description:
Additional press for newsprint

Cash Flows:

Year	*Equipment*	*Working Capital*	*Maintenance*	*Tax Effect of Annual Depreciation*	*Residual Value*	*Revenue*	*Taxes*	*Total*
0	(5,000,000)	(400,000)		800,000				(5,400,000)
1			(100,000)	320,000		1,650,000	(700,000)	1,170,000
2			(100,000)	320,000		1,650,000	(700,000)	1,170,000
3			(100,000)	320,000		1,650,000	(700,000)	1,170,000
4			(100,000)	320,000		1,650,000	(700,000)	1,170,000
5		400,000	(100,000)	320,000	1,000,000	1,650,000	(700,000)	1,170,000
Totals	(5,000,000)		(500,000)	2,400,000	1,000,000	8,250,000		1,850,000

Tax Rate:	**40%**
Hurdle Rate:	**10%**
Payback Period:	4.28%
Net Present Value:	(86,809)
Internal Rate of Return:	9.4%

Type of Project (check one):

Legal requirement	
New product-related	
Old product extension	Yes
Repair/replacement	
Safety issue	

Approvals:

Amount	Approver	Signature
<€5,000	Supervisor	
€5–19,999	General Manager	
€20–49,999	President	
€50,000+	Board	

SOURCE: Adapted with permission from Steven Bragg, ***Financial Analysis: A Controller's Guide*** *(Hoboken, NJ:,John Wiley & Sons, 2000), p. 24.*

If a company has a large project under construction that will result in a fixed asset (such as a new headquarters building), it must accumulate all information pertaining to it on a project cost sheet, as noted in Exhibit 6.3. Though some of this information could be accumulated solely in a separate general ledger account, that approach results in less storage of detailed information about a project. Overall, the larger the project, the more need for a form of this type.

Exhibit 6.3 Project Cost Sheet

Form 2-520

PROJECT COST SHEET

Balance Sheet Account No. ________ Project No. ________

Project Name: ________________

Project Description: ____

Start Date: ________________ Budgeted Total €: ___________

Item	Date	Invoice No.	Supplier or Payroll	Item or Service	Amount	
Materials						
Direct Labor						
Contractors						

Project Completion Date ______________

Transferred to Balance Sheet Account No. __________

Total Materials Total Direct Labor Total Contractors		
Total Project		

Whenever a company acquires land, it should record all pertinent information on a land record form such as the one shown in Exhibit 6.4. Any title or surveying information should be attached to this form for easy reference. By consolidating this information, one will have easy access to zoning, assessment, easement, and other information critical for taxation and subsequent construction purposes.

Exhibit 6.4 Land Record Form

Form 2-530

LAND RECORD

Property number: ______________

1. General description: ____

2. Cost: ______________ Date purchased: ______________
3. Address: ____
4. City, State, Zip Code: ____
5. Township: ______________ County: ______________

6. Approximate size: ______________
7. Legal description: ____

8. Zoning classification: ____
9. Easements: ____

10. Restrictions on use: ____

11. Assessed valuation: Year: ________ Amount: ______________
Year: ________ Amount: ______________
Year: ________ Amount: ______________
Year: ________ Amount: ______________

12. Land improvements: ____

13. Buildings on property: ____

Whenever there are land improvements, such as septic systems or landscaping, it should be recorded on a separate land improvement form (see Exhibit 6.5). By clearly stating the size, cost, and type of constructions installed, a company not only has a better chance of defending itself from adverse tax valuations, but it also can compile a reasonable land value for resale purposes.

Exhibit 6.5 Land Improvement Form

Form 2-540

LAND IMPROVEMENT RECORD

Property number: ___________

1. General description: ____
2. Cost: ________________
3. Date put in use: _________________
4. Approximate size: ______________________
5. Construction materials: ______________________________________
6. Useful life: ___________________
7. Assessed valuation: Year: ________ Amount: _____________

   Year: ________ Amount: _____________

   Year: ________ Amount: _____________

   Year: ________ Amount: _____________

Often the documentation of the expenses associated with the construction of company-owned buildings and later upgrades to them are disorganized; sometimes it is nonexistent. This becomes problematic when the accounting staff attempts to determine which expenses can be shifted into a fixed asset account, or when to begin depreciation of the asset, or to determine trends in assessed values for property tax purposes. It can be avoided, though, with the use of a building record form, such as the one shown in Exhibit 6.6.

Exhibit 6.6 Building Form

Form 2-550

BUILDING RECORD

Property number: __________

1. Building name/number: ______________________________
2. General description: ______________________________
3. Type of construction: ______________________________
4. General use of building: ______________________________
5. Cost: __________ Date put in use: __________ Useful life: ________
6. Approximate size: Length: ________ Width: __________
   Number of floors: ___________
   Square footage: ____________
7. Assessed valuation: Year: ______ Amount: __________
   Year: ______ Amount: __________
   Year: ______ Amount: __________
   Year: ______ Amount: __________

Of all company assets, equipment suffers from having the least amount of documentation; this can include factory, office, or computer equipment. The usual approach is to keep a copy of the purchase invoice in a separate file for the external auditors to peruse and to keep no other records besides a depreciation calculation. Problems arise, however, when someone attempts to locate the equipment, determine what period is covered by its warranty, when it was first put into use, and so on. This information should be summarized on an equipment record form, exemplified in Exhibit 6.7. The form should be the lead document in separate files to maintained for each piece of equipment, which should also contain all warranty and related maintenance information.

Exhibit 6.7 Equipment Form

Form 2-560

EQUIPMENT RECORD

Property number: __________

1. General description: ______________________________
2. Purpose of equipment: ______________________________
3. Fixed or portable: __________
4. Location, building and room: ______________________________
5. Cost: __________ Date put in use: __________ Useful life: __________
6. Model: ______________ Serial number: ________________
7. Supplier name: ______________________________
   Supplier address: ______________________________
7. Warranty coverage period: ______________________________
   Warranty provisions: ______________________________
8. Property tag number: ______________

Leases frequently appear in the accounting records as nothing more than a series of monthly payments; it says nothing about any required maintenance by the lessor, the term of the lease, or any bargain purchase options. This information should be stored on a lease record form, as illustrated in Exhibit 6.8. The form should be the lead document in a separate file on each lease that also contains a copy of the lease. If a company also maintains a contracts database, lease terms should be noted there, so the legal department can plan for lease expirations and renewals.

Exhibit 6.8 Lease Record

Form 2-570

LEASE RECORD

Number: __________

1. Description of leased property: ______________________________

2. Serial number: __________________________

3. Location of property: ____________________________________

4. Lessor name: ____

   Lessor address: ____

5. Lease begin date: ___________________

   Lease end date: ____________________

6. Monthly rental amount: ________________

   Annual rental amount: _________________

7. Maintenance by lessee: ___________________________________
   (type and frequency)

8. Lease renewal/extension terms: ______________________________

9. Lease termination terms: ___________________________________

Nearly all computerized accounting systems contain a standard PP&E asset report itemizing the asset type, cost, and periodic and accumulated depreciation for each asset. A typical format is shown in Exhibit 6.9, but more detailed formats also can include the date in which an asset was put into service, the type of depreciation method used, the depreciation duration, and assumed salvage value. Most accounting systems will allow this format to be presented in a variety of different data sorts, such as asset type, general ledger account, or asset carrying value. This basic report format is useful for verifying recurring depreciation calculations, and external auditors require this format as part of their review of financial statements.

Exhibit 6.9 PP&E—Asset Depreciation Report

Account no.	*Asset type*	*Description*	*Net cost*	*Periodic depreciation*	*Accumulated depreciation*	*Net book value*
13000	Computers	Dell laptop	€3,500	€97.22	€ 291.66	€ 3,208.34
	Computers	HP laptop	3,000	83.33	749.97	2,250.03
	Computers	Compaq server	10,000	277.78	4,166.70	5,833.30
	Computers	IBM server	42,000	1,166.67	19,833.39	22,166.61
14000	Software	Quark license	3,800	105.56	2,744.56	1,055.44
	Software	Office license	1,000	27.78	833.40	166.60
	Software	Windows license	2,500	69.44	2,360.96	139.04
15000	Equipment	50-ton press	45,000	375.00	14,250.00	30,750
	Equipment	150-ton press	220,000	1,833.33	76,999.86	143,000.14

When the accounting staff is conducting a periodic audit of PP&E assets, it is useful to print a report of assets by location, identifying information such as model and serial numbers, and adding a notation field for notes about changes in fixed asset locations. In Exhibit 6.10, the location code begins with a letter to identify the building, followed by the floor and room numbers in which an asset is located.

Exhibit 6.10 PP&E—Asset Audit Report

Location	*Tag number*	*Description*	*Model no.*	*Serial no.*	*Notes*
A-02-13	05432	Dell laptop	Dim 43	IE75J	
A-02-01	05021	HP laptop	HP 312	06M14	
A-02-14	04996	Compaq server	CQ 007	MK14J	
A-02-07	04985	IBM server	A31	A09J5	
A-02-11	04900	Quark license	Ver 4.0	MM047	
A-02-15	04730	Office license	Ver. 2004	F4KQW	
A-02-08	04619	Windows license	Ver. XP	9M4G7	
C-01-01	01038	50-ton press	G42	Z9G2K	
C-01-01	01004	150-ton press	G90	V12L9	

FOOTNOTES

Disclosure of Asset Impairments

If a company writes down the value of impaired assets, the accountant should take these steps:

1. Describe the assets.
2. Note which segment of the business is impacted by the loss.
3. Disclose the amount of the loss, how fair value was determined, where the loss is reported in the income statement, the remaining cost assigned to the assets, and the date by which the company expects to have disposed of them (if it is expected to do so).

See the next scenario for an example.

The company has written down the value of its server farm, on the grounds that this equipment has a vastly reduced resale value as a result of the introduction of a new generation of microprocessor chips. The services of an appraiser were used to obtain a net selling price, which was greater than value in use. The resulting impairment loss of €439,500 was charged to the application service provider segment of the company and is contained within the "Other Gains and Losses" line item on the income statement. The remaining valuation ascribed to these assets as of the statement of financial position date is €2,450,000. There are no immediate expectations to dispose of these assets.

Disclosure of Goodwill

If a company elects to immediately write down some or all of the goodwill recorded on its books, it must explain its reasons for doing so. The footnote should specify why an impairment of goodwill has occurred, the events that have caused the impairment to take place, those portions of the business to which the impaired goodwill is associated, and how the company measured the amount of the loss. Any calculation assumptions used in determining the amount of the write-down should be noted. An example follows.

> The company has taken a write-down of €1.2 million in its goodwill account. It is specifically tied to the expected increase in competition due to the approval of a competing patent given to Westmoreland Steel Company. The write-down will allow them to produce steel much more efficiently than the company's Arbuthnot Foundry, to which the €1.2 million in goodwill is associated. This write-down is based on the assumption that the Arbuthnot Foundry will not be able to compete with Westmoreland Steel for longer than four years. Consequently, the present value of all goodwill that will remain on the company's books four years from the date of these financial statements has been written off.

Disclosure of Intangibles

If a company has a material amount of intangible assets on its books, the accountant should describe the types of intangibles, the amortization period and method used to offset their value, and the amount of accumulated amortization. An example follows.

> The company has €1.5 million of intangible assets on its books, comprised solely of the estimated fair value of patents—a direct result of the company's acquisition of the R.C. Goodnough Company, which was reported under the purchase method of accounting. This intangible asset is being amortized over 15 years, which is the remaining term of the acquired patents. The accumulated amortization through the reporting period is €300,000.

JOURNAL ENTRIES

PP&E

Depreciation. To record the depreciation incurred during the month. The amortization account is used to write off intangible assets.

Depreciation, computer equipment	xxx	
Depreciation, computer software	xxx	
Depreciation, furniture and fixtures	xxx	
Depreciation, leasehold improvements	xxx	
Depreciation, manufacturing equipment	xxx	
Amortization expense	xxx	
Accumulated depreciation, computer equipment		xxx
Accumulated depreciation, computer software		xxx
Accumulated depreciation, furniture and fixtures		xxx
Accumulated depreciation, leasehold improvements		xxx
Accumulated depreciation, manufacturing equipment		xxx
Intangible assets		xxx

PP&E (capitalization of interest). To capitalize interest expense associated with the construction of a qualified asset.

Asset account	xxx	
Interest expense		xxx

PP&E (impairment of). To record the reduction in carrying value when an asset's recoverable value is less than its carrying value.

Impairment loss	xxx	
Accumulated depreciation		xxx

PP&E (retirement obligation). To record legally mandated costs of dismantling and removing the item and restoring the site on which it is located (asset retirement costs). The first entry records the initial liability for these costs. The second entry shows ongoing adjustments to the present value of the asset retirement obligation (ARO) as the termination date of the liability approaches and its present value increases. The third entry records a gradual reduction in the asset retirement liability account as actual expenses are incurred to remove an asset. The fourth entry records the final settlement of the liability; a loss will be incurred if the actual expense exceeds the amount of the initial liability, while a gain will be recorded if the reverse is true.

Asset account	xxx	
Asset retirement obligation		xxx
Accretion expense	xxx	
Asset retirement obligation		xxx
Asset retirement obligation	xxx	
Accounts payable		xxx
Asset retirement obligation	xxx	
Loss on settlement of ARO liability	xxx	
Gain on settlement of ARO liability		xxx

PP&E (sale of). To record the cash received from the sale of an asset as well as any gain or loss in its sale. This entry also eliminates all associated accumulated depreciation that has built up over the term of the company's ownership of the asset.

Cash	xxx	
Accumulated depreciation	xxx	
Loss on sale of assets	xxx	
(Various fixed asset accounts)		xxx
Gain on sale of assets		xxx

PP&E (outbound donation). To record the donation of a company asset to a charitable organization. This entry clears the original asset and depreciation entries from the company's records and records a gain or loss on the transaction in relation to the asset's fair value after being netted against the asset's net carrying value.

Charitable donations	xxx	
Accumulated depreciation	xxx	
Loss on property donation	xxx	
Gain on property donation		xxx
Asset account		xxx

PP&E (purchase with stock). To record the acquisition of an asset with company stock. The amount of the stock paid out must be split between the par value and paid-in capital accounts, depending on the predetermined par value of each share issued.

Asset account	xxx	
Stock, par value		xxx
Stock, additional paid-in capital		xxx

PP&E (exchange for a dissimilar asset). To record the trade of a company asset for a different type of asset, including a cash payment. Any loss on this transaction is caused by the remaining net carrying value of the asset being relinquished being greater than its fair value. If the fair value is greater than carrying value, a gain is recognized. The debit to accumulated depreciation is used to clear from the accounting records the accumulated depreciation associated with the asset being traded away.

Asset account for new asset	xxx	
Accumulated depreciation	xxx	
Loss on asset exchange	xxx	
Gain on asset exchange		xxx
Asset account for asset traded away		xxx
Cash		xxx

PP&E (write-off). To record the unreimbursed disposal of an asset. This entry also eliminates all associated accumulated depreciation that has built up over the term of the company's ownership of the asset.

Accumulated depreciation	xxx	
Loss on disposal of assets	xxx	
(Various fixed asset accounts)		xxx

Intangible Assets

Goodwill, write-down. To record a reduction in the amount of recorded goodwill caused by impairment of the asset value.

Loss due to goodwill impairment	xxx	
Goodwill (asset account)		xxx

RECORDKEEPING[3]

The amount of recordkeeping recommended here may appear voluminous, but it is necessary to maintain sufficient information about the warranties, maintenance, vendor contact information, and other items about each asset. Nevertheless, it is possible to reduce the amount of recordkeeping by using a relatively high capitalization limit, below which assets are immediately charged to expense rather than being recorded as an asset.

Depreciation records used to be calculated manually for each of the records noted in this chapter, and stored with them. The advent of inexpensive computerized

---

[3] *Much of the information in this section and the Forms and Reports section is adapted with permission from Steven Bragg, **Design and Maintenance of Accounting Manuals**, 4th ed.(Hoboken, NJ: John Wiley & Sons, 2003), Chapter 8.*

depreciation software, however, has rendered this approach inefficient. Instead, a central database is used to record all depreciable asset information, where depreciation calculations can easily be made.

Retain fixed asset records for as long as the company retains the asset (e.g., purchasing documents, title records, related warranties, and the detailed records noted in the next paragraphs). The records may be archived once the assets have been disposed of and may be destroyed on the same schedule used for other accounting records. The calculation of capitalized interest associated with the construction of qualified assets should be fully documented and included with these records.

If capital assets acquired or constructed need additional work before being placed into service, a project cost sheet should be used to accumulate the additional charges. To complete the form for each asset, enter the descriptive heading information (such as the name of the project or asset), assign a project number with a prefix letter to indicate the asset category (*L*and, *B*uilding, *F*actory, *E*quipment, etc.), put the statement of financial position account where the item will be recorded, and write a brief description of the project. The form also should include

- Date project is initiated
- Budget approval amount
- Asset serial number
- Materials used, including description, supplier, and cost
- Labor used, including date incurred and cost
- Contractors, including date incurred and cost
- Date of project completion
- Account number to which accumulated costs were transferred
- Summary totals for all cost categories

Maintain a record of the purchase price of land, including tax stamps, recording fees, surveys, title insurance, and any state fees; do not include property taxes or the cost of land improvements. Information about each land purchase should be maintained on a separate property accounting record containing this information:

- General description of the land site
- Purchase cost
- Postal address of the location
- Township (if in a western state) and county location
- Approximate size
- Legal description
- Zoning classification, such as residential single or multiple unit, commercial retail, or light or heavy industry
- Easements for electricity, water, sewers, or gas lines
- Use restrictions
- Year of valuation and assessed value

Land improvements are depreciable. Examples of land improvements are fences and gates, parking lots, roads, sewage ponds, and signs. Information about each land improvement should be maintained on a separate property accounting record, containing this information:

- General description
- Purchase cost
- Date put into use
- Approximate size
- Construction materials used
- Useful life
- Assessed valuation

Under the "construction materials used" category, the description for fences and gates should note whether they are constructed of wood, brick, or chain link. The description for roads or parking lots should note the use of gravel, asphalt, or concrete.

Maintain a record of each company-owned building, and use a sufficiently high capitalization limit to ensure that small additions—such as a small wall or shed attachment—do not become part of the building asset. Each building should have a name or number for reference purposes, but information about each building should be maintained on a separate property accounting record containing this information:

- Building name or number
- General description
- Type of construction
- Intended use
- Cost, date put into use, and useful life
- Approximate size
- Assessed valuation

In a manufacturing environment, the factory equipment will be the largest-dollar asset category, therefore requiring special attention—especially in regard to asset warranty information that may very well be used. Information about each piece of factory equipment should be maintained on a separate property accounting record containing this information:

- General description
- Purpose of the equipment
- Fixed or portable equipment designation
- Location by building and room number
- Cost, date put into use, and useful life
- Model and serial number
- Vendor name and address
- Warranty provisions and the period covered
- Property tag number

The increasing uses of technology in the modern office mean that the volume of office equipment can make this the largest asset category, especially in service industries where all staff members have computers. Examples of office equipment include personal computers, video presentation equipment, fax machines, and copiers. Information about each piece of office equipment should be maintained on a separate property accounting record containing this information:

- General description
- Purpose of the equipment
- Fixed or portable equipment designation
- Location by building and room number
- Cost, date put into use, and useful life
- Model and serial number
- Vendor name and address
- Warranty provisions and the period covered
- Property tag number

Anything that is portable and can serve as a means of conveyance for a person is defined as a vehicle. A car, truck, trailer, motorcycle, boat, airplane, lift truck, snowmobile, riding lawnmower, construction equipment, and so forth are all vehicles. Information about each vehicle should be maintained on a separate property accounting record containing this information:

- General description
- Serial or vehicle identification number
- Purpose of equipment
- Location where stored
- Cost
- Vendor name and address
- Warranty provisions and period covered
- Property tag number
- Person assigned to

Leasehold improvements are additions to leased land and buildings. Examples include storage cabinets, shelves, counters, refrigeration units, drapes, air conditioning, parking lots, roads, signs, fences and gates, and anything else that will be abandoned when the lease contract expires. The amortization of these improvements is recorded over the time period of the lease agreement, unless the lease term exceeds the useful life; in this case, calculate depreciation only through the useful life of the asset. Information about each leasehold improvement should be maintained on a separate property accounting record containing this information:

- General description
- Serial number (if available)
- Purpose of improvement
- Location where stored
- Cost, date put into use, and useful life
- Vendor name and address
- Warranty provisions and period covered
- Property tag number
- Lease record number

Maintain a separate record for each lease entered into by the organization. All leasehold improvements recorded elsewhere are tied to these lease records by the item number of the lease. If the company is required to have annual financial statements prepared by a certified public accountant, the lease information will be needed to develop footnote disclosure in the financial statements, itemizing the future lease payments for each of the following five years. Information about each lease should be maintained on a separate property accounting record containing this information:

- Description of the leased property
- Serial number (if available)
- Location of property
- Name and address of lessor
- Beginning and ending dates of the lease
- Lease amount
- Required maintenance by the lessee
- Lease renewal provisions
- Termination provisions

7 INVESTMENTS

DEFINITIONS OF TERMS

Associate. An entity, including an unincorporated entity such as a partnership, over which an investor has significant influence but which is neither a subsidiary nor a joint venture of the investor company.

Available-for-sale financial assets. Those financial assets that are not held for trading or held to maturity, and are not loans and receivables originated by the entity.

Carrying amount. The amount at which an asset is recognized in the statement of financial position.

Comprehensive income. The change in equity of an entity during a period from transactions and other events and circumstances from nonowner sources. It includes all changes in net assets during a period, except those resulting from investments by owners and distributions to owners. It comprises all components of "profit or loss" and "other comprehensive income."

Consolidated financial statements. Financial statements of a group presented as those of a single economic entity.

Control. The power to govern the financial and operating policies of an economic activity so as to obtain benefits from it.

Cost. The amount of cash, or cash equivalents paid, the fair value of other consideration given to acquire an asset at the time of its acquisition or construction, or (where applicable) the amount attributed to that asset when initially recognized in accordance with the specific requirements of other IFRS, for example, IFRS 2, *Share-Based Payment.*

Cost method. A method of accounting for investment whereby the investment is recorded at cost; the income statement reflects income from the investment only to the extent that the investor receives distributions from the investee's accumulated net profits arising after the date of acquisition. Distributions received in excess of accumulated profits are regarded as a recovery of investment and are recognized as a reduction of the cost of the investment.

Current investment. An investment that is, by its nature, readily realizable and is intended to be held for not more than one year.

Derecognize. Remove a financial asset or liability, or a portion thereof, from the entity's statement of financial position.

Differential. The difference between the investment cost and the carrying value of underlying net assets of the investee; this should be allocated to restate net assets acquired to fair value (excess or deficiency of fair value over or under carrying value of net assets). Goodwill is recognized for the investment cost in excess of fair value of net assets acquired.

Equity method. A method of accounting whereby the investment is initially recorded at cost and subsequently adjusted for the postacquisition change in the investor's share of net assets of the investee. The investor's profit or loss includes the investor's share of the investee's results of operations.

Fair value. The amount for which an asset could be exchanged between a knowledgeable, willing buyer and seller in an arm's-length transaction.

Firm commitment. A binding agreement for the exchange of a specific quantity of resources, at a specified price, and on a specified future date or dates.

Forecast transaction. An uncommitted but anticipated future transaction.

Goodwill. The excess of the cost of the acquired entity over the fair value of net identifiable assets acquired (identifiable assets acquired net of any liabilities assumed, including contingent liabilities).

Held-for-trading investments. A financial asset that is acquired principally for the purpose of generating a profit from short-term fluctuations in price or dealer's margin. Regardless of why acquired, a financial asset should be denoted as held-for-trading if there is a pattern of short-term profit taking by the entity. Derivative financial assets are always deemed held-for-trading unless designated and effective as hedging instruments.

Held-to-maturity investments. Financial assets with fixed or determinable payments and fixed maturities, that the entity has positive intent and ability to hold to maturity, except for loans and receivables originated by the entity.

Investee. An entity that issued voting stock that is held by an investor.

Investee capital transaction. The purchase or sale by the investee of its own common shares, which alters the investor's ownership interest and is accounted for by the investor as if the investee were a consolidated subsidiary.

Investment. An asset held by an entity for the accumulation of wealth through distributions of interest, royalties, dividends, and rentals, or for capital appreciation or other benefits to be obtained.

Investment property. Property (land or a building, or part of a building, or both) held (by the owner or by the lessee under a finance lease) to earn rentals or for capital appreciation purposes or both, as opposed to being held as

- An owner-occupied property (i.e., for use in the production or supply of goods or services or for administrative purposes); or
- Property held for sale in the ordinary course of business (i.e., as inventory).

Investor. A business entity that holds an investment in the voting stock of another entity.

Joint control. The contractual agreement entailing joint control over the operations and/or assets of an economic activity; this exists only when the strategic financial and operating decisions relating to the activity require the unanimous consent of the parties sharing control (the venturers).

Joint venture. A contractual arrangement whereby two or more parties undertake an economic activity subject to their joint control.

Long-term investment. An investment other than a current investment.

Market value. The amount obtainable from the sale of an investment in an active market.

Marketable. Assets for which there are active markets and from which market values, or other indicators that permit determination thereof, are available.

Marketable security. An easily traded investment, such as Treasury bills, that is easily convertible into cash. It is recorded as a current asset.

Other comprehensive income. Items of income and expense (including reclassification adjustments) that are not recognized in profit or loss as required or permitted by other IFRS. The components of other recognized income include: (1) changes in revaluation surplus (IAS 38); (2) actuarial gains and losses on defined benefit plans (IAS 19); (3) translation gains and losses (IAS 21); (4) gains and losses on remeasuring available-for-sale financial assets (IAS 39); and (5) the effective portion of gains and losses on hedging instruments in a cash flow hedge (IAS 39).

Owner-occupied property. Property held by the owner (i.e., the entity itself) or by a lessee under a finance lease, for use in the production or supply of goods or services or for administrative purposes.

Proportional consolidation. A method of accounting whereby an investor's share of each of the assets, liabilities, income, and expenses of the investee is combined line by line with similar items in the investor's financial statements or reported as separate line items in the investor's financial statements.

Reclassification adjustments. Amounts reclassified to profit or loss in the current period that were recognized in other comprehensive income in the current or previous periods.

Separate financial statements. Financial statements presented by a parent, an investor in an associate, or a venturer in a jointly controlled entity, in which the investments are accounted for on the basis of the direct equity interest rather than on the basis of the reported results and net assets of the investees.

Significant influence. The power of the investor to participate in the financial and operating policy decisions of the investee; this is not, however, a method of providing for full control over those policies.

Subsidiary. An entity, including an unincorporated entity such as a partnership, that is controlled by another entity (its parent).

Trading securities. Either debt or equity securities bought with the express intention of being sold in the short term for a profit.

Undistributed investee earnings. The investor's share of investee earnings in excess of dividends paid.

Venturer. A party to a joint venture and has control over that joint venture.

CONCEPTS AND EXAMPLES[1]

Accounting for Marketable Equity Securities

Marketable securities are investments that can be easily liquidated through an organized exchange, such as the New York, Tokyo, London, Euronext, or Hong Kong stock exchanges. If a company also holds securities that are intended for the control of another entity, then these securities should be segregated as a long-term investment. Marketable securities must be grouped into one of three categories at the time of purchase and reevaluated periodically to see if they still belong in the designated categories:

1. **Available-for-sale.** This category includes both debt and equity securities, and it contains those securities that do not readily fall into either of the next two categories. More specifically, it can include investments in other companies that comprise less than 20% of total ownership. These securities are reported on the statement of financial position at their fair value, while unrealized gains and losses are recognized in the other comprehensive income section of the statement of comprehensive income in the current period (and the cumulative amount in equity), until the financial asset is derecognized. At that time the cumulative gain or loss previously recognized in other comprehensive income should be reclassified from equity to profit or loss as a reclassification adjustment (IAS 1, *Presentation of Financial Statements,* as revised in 2007). Consequently, the balance in the equity account is eliminated only upon sale of the underlying securities. If a permanent reduction in the value of an individual security occurs, impairment losses are recognized in profit or loss, resulting in a new and lower cost basis in the remaining investment. Any subsequent increase in the value of such an investment above the new cost basis, if the increase can be objectively related to an event occurring after the impairment loss was recognized in profit or

[1] *Much of the information in this section is adapted with permission from Chapter 14 of Steven Bragg,* ***Ultimate Accountants' Reference*** *(Hoboken, NJ: John Wiley & Sons, 2006).*

loss, can be accounted for as a reversal, with the amount of the reversal recognized in profit or loss.

All interest, realized gains or losses, and debt amortization are recognized within the continuing operations section of the income statement (statement of profit or loss). The listing of these securities on the statement of financial position under either current or long-term assets is dependent on their ability to be liquidated in the short term and to be available for disposition within that time frame, unencumbered by any obligations.

2. **Held to maturity.** This category includes only debt securities that the company has both the intent and ability to hold until their time of maturity. These securities should be measured at amortized cost using the effective interest method, and are likely to be listed on the statement of financial position as noncurrent assets.

   If marketable securities are reclassified from the available-for-sale category into the held-to-maturity category, their fair value carrying amount on that date becomes their new cost, or amortized cost (if applicable). Any previous unrealized holding gain or loss on these assets that has been recognized in other comprehensive income (and the cumulative amount in equity) should continue to be stored in the equity section while being gradually amortized down to zero over the remaining life of each security in the case of a financial asset with a fixed maturity. If a financial asset does not have a fixed maturity, then the gain or loss should remain in equity until the asset is sold, at which point it is reclassified from equity to profit or loss as a reclassification adjustment.

3. **Trading securities.** This category includes both debt and equity securities that the company intends to sell in the short term for a profit. Not only that, but it can include investments in other companies comprising less than 20% of total ownership. They are recorded on the statement of financial position at their fair value, with gains and losses recognized in profit or loss. This type of marketable security is always positioned in the statement of financial position as a current asset.

   No matter how an investment is categorized, a material decline in its fair value subsequent to the statement of financial position date but prior to the release of the financial statements should be disclosed. Further, clear evidence of permanent impairment in the value of available-for-sale securities prior to the release date of the financial statements is grounds for restatement to recognize permanent impairment of the investment.

Examples of available-for-sale transactions

The Arabian Knights Security Company has purchased €100,000 of equity securities, which it does not intend to sell in the short term for profit, and therefore designates as available-for-sale. Its initial entry to record the transaction is

Investments—available-for-sale	100,000	
Cash		100,000

After a month, the fair market value of the securities drops by €15,000, but management considers the loss to be a temporary decline and does not record a loss in current earnings. Still, it must alter the value of the investment on the statement of financial position to show its fair value and report the loss in equity, which requires this entry:

Unrealized loss on available-for-sale investments (reported in other comprehensive income)	15,000	
Investments—available-for-sale		15,000

Management then obtains additional information indicating that the loss is likely to be a permanent one, so it recognizes the loss with this entry:

Loss on security investments	15,000	
Unrealized loss on available-for-sale investment (reported in other comprehensive income)		15,000

Another month passes and the fair value of the investment rises by €3,500. Since the amount of the impairment loss decreases and the decrease can be related objectively to an event occurring after the impairment was recognized, the previously recognized impairment loss should be reversed either directly or by adjusting an allowance account — but only to the extent of previously recognized impairment losses. The amount of the reversal should be recognized in profit or loss.

Investments—available-for-sale	3,500	
Gain on security investments		3,500

Examples of trading transactions

The Arabian Knights Security Company purchases €50,000 of equity securities that it intends to trade for a profit in the short term. Given its intentions, these securities are added to the corporate portfolio of trading securities with this entry:

Investments—held-for-trading	50,000	
Cash		50,000

After two months, the fair value of these trading securities declines by €3,500. The company recognizes the change in current earnings with this entry:

Loss on security investment	3,500	
Investments—held-for-trading		3,500

Later in the year, the fair value of the securities experiences a sudden surge, resulting in a value increase of €5,750. The company records the change with this entry:

Investments—held-for-trading	5,750	
Gain on security investments		5,750

Transfers between Available-for-Sale and Trading Investments

An investment designated as a trading security can be shifted into the available-for-sale portfolio of investments with no recognition of a gain or loss on the value of the investment—this type of investment should have been adjusted to its fair value in each reporting period already. If a gain or loss has arisen since the last adjustment to fair value, this amount should be recognized at the time of the designation change. An investment designated as an available-for-sale security may be shifted into the trading portfolio of investments; as a result, any gain or loss is required to be immediately adjusted from its value to fair value. In the entry, include an adjustment from any prior write-down in value that may have occurred when securities were classified as available-for-sale.

Example of transfer from the trading portfolio to the available-for-sale portfolio

The Arabian Knights Security Company owns €17,500 of equity securities that it had originally intended to sell for a profit in the short term and so had classified the investment in its trading portfolio. Its intent has now changed, and it wishes to hold the securities for a considerably longer period, so it must shift the securities into the available-for-sale account. It had marked the securities to market one month previously, but now the securities have lost €350 of value. The company records this entry to reclassify the security and recognize the additional loss:

Investments—available-for-sale	17,150	
Loss on equity securities	350	
Investments—held-for-trading		17,500

Example of transfer from the available-for-sale portfolio to the trading portfolio

The Arabian Knights Security Company finds that it must liquidate €250,000 of its available-for-sale portfolio in the short term. This investment had previously been marked down to €250,000 from an initial investment value of €275,000, and its value has since risen by €12,000. The incremental gain must now be recognized in current income. The entry is:

Investments—held-for-trading	262,000	
Investments—available-for-sale		250,000
Gain on security investments		12,000

Accounting for Investments in Debt Securities

A debt security can be classified as held-for-trading, available-for-sale (as previously defined for equity securities), or as held-to-maturity. The held-to-maturity portfolio is intended for any debt securities for which a company has the intent and ability to retain the security for its full term, until maturity is reached. An investment held in the held-to-maturity portfolio is recorded at its historical cost and is measured at amortized cost using the effective interest method; this is not changed at any time during the holding period, unless it is shifted into a different investment portfolio. The only exceptions to the historical cost rule are (1) the periodic amortization of any discount or premium from the face value of a debt instrument, depending on the initial purchase price, and (2) clear evidence of a permanent reduction in the value of the investment.

Examples of held-to-maturity transactions

The Arabian Knights Security Company purchases €82,000 of debt securities at face value. The company has both the intent and ability to hold the securities to maturity. Given its intentions, these securities are added to the corporate portfolio of held-to-maturity securities with this entry:

Investment in debt securities—held-to-maturity	82,000	
Cash		82,000

The fair value of the investment subsequently declines by €11,000. There is no entry to be made, since the investment is recorded at its historical cost, but the company receives additional information that the debt issuer has filed for bankruptcy and intends to repay debt holders at 50 cents on the euro. Since management considers this to be a permanent reduction, a charge of €41,000 is recorded in profit or loss with this entry:

Loss on debt investments	41,000	
Investment in debt securities—held-to-maturity		41,000

The company subsequently learns that the debt issuer is instead able to pay 75 cents on the euro. This increase in value of €20,500, and the amount of the reversal is recorded in profit with this entry:

Investment in debt securities—held-to-maturity	41,000	
Gain on debt investments		41,000

Transfers of Debt Securities among Portfolios

The accounting for transfers between debt securities portfolios varies based on the portfolio from which the accounts are being shifted, with the basic principle that transfers are recorded at the fair value of the security on the date of the transfer. The treatment of gains or losses on all possible transfers is noted in Exhibit 7.1.

Exhibit 7.1 Accounting Treatment of Debt Transfers between Portfolios

"From" portfolio	*"To" portfolio*	*Accounting treatment*
Trading	Available-for-sale	No entry (assumes gains and losses have already been recorded)
Trading	Held-to-maturity	No entry (assumes gains and losses have already been recorded)
Available-for-sale	Trading	Reclassify any previously recorded gain or loss shown in other comprehensive income (and the cumulative amount in equity) to profit or loss
Available-for-sale	Held-to-maturity	Amortize to profit or loss over the remaining period to debt maturity any previously recognized gain or loss in other comprehensive income (and the cumulative amount in equity) to profit or loss, using the effective interest method
Held-to-maturity	Trading	Record the unrealized gain or loss in profit or loss
Held-to-maturity	Available-for-sale	Record the unrealized gain or loss in other comprehensive income (and the cumulative amount in equity)

The offsetting entry for any gain or loss reported in the other comprehensive income section of the statement of comprehensive income goes to a contra account; this is used to offset the investment account on the statement of financial position, thereby revealing the extent of changes in the value of securities from their purchased cost.

Recognition of Deferred Tax Effects on Changes in Investment Valuations

A deferred tax benefit or tax liability needs to be recognized alongside the recognition of any change in the fair value of an investment listed in either a trading or an available-for-sale portfolio or of a permanent decline in the value of a debt security being held to maturity. The tax impact varies by investment type and is noted as

- **Gains or losses on the trading portfolio.** The deferred tax effect is recognized in profit or loss. If there is a loss in value, debit the Deferred Tax Benefit account and credit the Provision for Income Taxes account; however, if there is a gain in value, then debit the Provision for Income Taxes account and credit the Deferred Tax Liability account.

- **Gains or losses on the available-for-sale portfolio.** Use the same treatment noted for gains or losses on the trading portfolio, except that taxes are noted in other comprehensive income on the statement of comprehensive income).
- **Gains or losses on the held-to-maturity portfolio.** There is no tax recognition if changes in value are considered to be temporary. With a permanent reduction in value, however, the treatment is identical to the treatment of losses in the trading portfolio, as just noted.

The Equity Method of Investment Accounting

There are three ways to account for an investment: (1) report the investment at its fair value, (2) report it under the "equity method," and (3) fully consolidate the results of the investee in the investing company's financial statements. The rules under which each of these methods is applied are noted in Exhibit 7.2.

Exhibit 7.2 Accounting Treatment of Significant Equity Investments

Investment method	Proportion of ownership	Notes
Fair Value	Less than 20% ownership or no significant influence over investee	Record gains or losses based on fair value of shares held
Equity Method	20% to 50% ownership and significant influence over the investee	Record proportionate share of investee earnings, less dividends received
Consolidation	50%+ ownership of the investee	Fully consolidate results of the investor and investee

IAS 28, *Investments in Associates,* requires that investments in associates over which the investor has significant influence must be accounted for using the equity method—whether the investor also has investments in subsidiaries or not—and must prepare consolidated financial statements. The presence of "significant influence" over an investee is assumed if the investor owns at least 20% of its common stock. Nevertheless, this is not the case if there is clear evidence of not having influence, such as being unable to obtain financial information from the investee, not being able to place a representative on its board of directors, clear opposition to the investor by the investee, loss of voting rights, or proof of a majority voting block that does not include the investor.

Income taxes are recognized only when dividends are received from an investee or the investment is liquidated. Deferred income taxes, however, are recognized when a company records its share of investee income and are then shifted from the deferred income tax account to income taxes payable when dividends are received. A key issue is the assumed income tax rate used, since it can vary based on an assumption of investment liquidation via dividends (which is usually at a lower tax rate) or sale of the investment (which is usually at a higher tax rate).

As just noted in Exhibit 7.2, the equity method of accounting requires one to record the investor's proportionate share of investee earnings, less any dividends received. What if, however, the investee records such a large loss that the investor's share of the loss results in a negative investment? In this case, the correct treatment is to limit the investment to zero and ignore subsequent losses. Use of the equity method should be resumed only if subsequent investee earnings completely offset the losses that had previously been ignored. The main exception to this rule is when the investor has committed to fund investee operations or indemnify other creditors or investors for losses incurred.

Example of the equity method of accounting

The Arabian Knights Security Company purchases 35% of the common stock of the Night Patrollers Security Company for €500,000. At the end of a year, Night Patrollers has earned €80,000 and issued €20,000 in dividends. Under the equity method, Arabian Knights reports a gain in its investment of €28,000 (35% investment × €80,000 in earnings), less dividends of €7,000 (35% investment × €20,000 in dividends) for a total investment change of €21,000. The two entries required to record these changes are

Investment in Night Patrollers	28,000	
Equity in Night Patrollers		28,000
Cash	7,000	
Investment in Night Patrollers		7,000

In addition, Arabian Knights' controller assumes that the investment will eventually be sold, which requires a full corporate tax rate of 34%. Accordingly, the next entry records a deferred income tax on the €28,000 share of Night Patrollers income while the second entry records the shifting of a portion of this deferred tax to income taxes payable to reflect the company's short-term tax liability for the dividends received (assuming a 34% tax rate for dividend income):

Income tax expense	9,520	
Deferred taxes		9,520
Deferred taxes	2,380	
Taxes payable		2,380

It is quite common for the investor to pay a premium over the carrying value of the investee's common stock. When this happens under the equity method, one should informally (i.e., without the use of journal entries) assign the difference in value (the so-called differential) to other assets and liabilities of the investee to the extent that the fair value of those assets differs from their net carrying value. Any changes in these assumed assets should be amortized, resulting in a periodic journal entry to reduce the value of the investor's recorded investment.

Example of the amortization of assigned asset valuations

To continue with the last example, 35% of the carrying value of Night Patrollers Security Company was €350,000, as compared to the €500,000 paid by Arabian for 35% of Night Patrollers. Arabian's controller must assign this differential to the excess fair value of any Night Patrollers assets or liabilities over their carrying value. The only undervalued Night Patrollers asset category is its fixed assets, to which the controller can assign €30,000. The remaining unassigned €120,000 is designated as goodwill. Given the nature of the underlying assets, the €30,000 assigned to fixed assets should be amortized over five years, resulting in a monthly amortization charge of €500. The monthly journal entry is

Equity in Night Patrollers income	500	
Investment in Night Patrollers		500

Any remaining unassigned excess value is considered to be goodwill and is subject to annual impairment testing that may result in an additional reduction in the recorded level of investment. An impairment test requires a periodic comparison of the fair value (the recoverable amount) of the investment to the current carrying value of the investment as recorded by the investor. If the fair value is less than the recorded carrying value, goodwill is reduced until the recorded investment value matches the new fair value. If the amount of the reduction is greater than the informal goodwill associated with the transaction, however, then the excess is used to proportionally reduce any amounts previously assigned to the investee's assets. In effect, a large enough reduction in the fair value of its investment will result in an immediate write-down of the recorded investment rather than a gradual reduction due to amortization.

Example of investment impairment

To continue with the last example, Night Patrollers loses several large security contracts, resulting in a significant reduction in the value of the business. Arabian's controller estimates this loss in value to be €130,000, which requires her to eliminate the entire €120,000 goodwill portion of the initial investment, as well as €10,000 that had been assigned to the fixed assets category. This later reduction results in a decrease in the monthly amortization charge by €166.66 (€10,000 / 60 months).

If a company *reduces* its investment in an investee to the point where its investment comprises less than 20% of the investee's common stock, it should discontinue use of the equity method of accounting and instead record the investment at its fair value, most likely tracking it as part of the company's available-for-sale portfolio. When the transition occurs from the equity method to the fair value method, no retroactive adjustment in the investment account is required—the investor simply begins using the ending investment balance it had derived under the equity method.

If a company *increases* its investment in an investee to the 20% to 50% range from a lesser figure, it must convert to the equity method of accounting on a retroactive basis. This means the investor must go back to the initial investment date and recalculate its investment using the equity method of accounting. The offset to any resulting adjustment in the investment account must then be charged to the Retained Earnings account as a prior period adjustment. This also requires restatement of prior financial statements in which the fair value method was used to record this investment.

Accounting for Investments in Joint Ventures

IFRS addresses accounting for interests in joint ventures as a topic separate from accounting for other investments. Joint ventures share many characteristics with investments that are accounted for by the equity method: The investor clearly has significant influence over the investee but does not have absolute control—hence full consolidation typically is unwarranted. According to the provisions of IAS 31, two different methods of accounting are possible, although not as true alternatives for the same fact situations: the proportionate consolidation method and the equity method.

Joint ventures can take many forms and structures. In fact, joint ventures may be created as partnerships, as corporations, or as unincorporated associations. The

Standard identifies three distinct types, referred to as jointly controlled operations, jointly controlled assets, and jointly controlled entities. Notwithstanding the formal structure, all joint ventures are characterized by certain features: having two or more venturers that are bound by a contractual arrangement and by the fact that the contractual agreement establishes joint control of the entity. The contractual provision(s) establishing joint control most clearly differentiates joint ventures from other investment scenarios in which the investor has significant influence over the investee.

Specific accounting guidance is dependent on whether the entity represents jointly controlled operations, jointly controlled assets, or a jointly controlled entity.

The first of three types of joint ventures, *jointly controlled operations*, is characterized by the assigned use of certain assets or other resources, in contrast to an establishment of a new entity, whether it is a corporation or partnership. Thus, from a formal or legal perspective, this variety of joint venture may not have an existence separate from its sponsors; from an economic point of view, however, the joint venture can still be said to exist, which means that it may exist as an accounting entity.

IAS 31 is concerned with the accounting not by the entity conducting the jointly controlled operations but by the venturers having an interest in the entity. Each venturer should recognize in its separate financial statements all assets of the venture that it controls, all liabilities that it incurs, all expenses that it incurs, and its share of any revenues produced by the venture. Often, since the assets are already owned by the venturers, they would be included in their respective financial statements in any event; similarly, any debt incurred will be reported by the partner even absent this special rule. Perhaps the only real challenge, from a measurement and disclosure perspective, would be the revenues attributable to each venture's efforts, which will be determined by reference to the joint venture agreement and other documents.

Note that joint control may be precluded when an investee is in legal reorganization or in bankruptcy, or operates under severe long-term restrictions on its ability to transfer funds to the venturer; in such cases, application of IAS 31 would not be appropriate.

In certain industries, such as oil and gas exploration and transmission and mineral extraction, *jointly controlled assets* are employed frequently. For example, oil pipelines may be controlled jointly by a number of oil producers, each of which uses the facilities and shares in its costs of operation. Certain informal real estate partnerships may also function in this fashion.

IAS 31 stipulates that in the case of jointly controlled assets, each venturer must report in its own financial statements its share of all jointly controlled assets, appropriately classified according to their natures. It must also report any liabilities that it has incurred on behalf of these jointly controlled assets as well as its share of any jointly incurred liabilities. Each venturer will report any income earned from the use of its share of the jointly controlled assets, along with the pro rata expenses and any other expenses it has incurred directly.

The major type of joint venture is the *jointly controlled entity*, which is really a form of partnership (although it may well be structured legally as a corporation), where each partner has a form of control as opposed to significant influence alone. The classic example is an equal partnership of two venturers; obviously, neither has a majority, and either can block any important action, so the two partners must effectively agree on each key decision. Although this may be the model for a jointly controlled entity, it may in practice have more than two venturers, and, depending on the partnership or shareholders' agreement, even minority owners may have joint control. For example, a partnership whose partners have 30%, 30%, 30%, and 10% interests, respectively, may have entered into a contractual agreement that stipulates that investment or financing actions may be taken only if there is unanimity among the partners.

Jointly controlled entities control the assets of the joint venture and may incur liabilities and expenses on its behalf. As a legal entity, it may enter into contracts and borrow funds, among other activities. In general, each venturer will share the net results in proportion to its ownership interest. As an entity with a distinct and separate legal and economic identity, the jointly controlled entity normally will produce its own financial statements and other tax and legal reports.

IAS 31 provides alternative accounting treatments that may be applied by the venture partners to reflect the operations and financial position of the venture. The objective is to report economic substance, rather than mere form, but there is no universal agreement on how this may best be achieved.

The benchmark treatment under the Standard is the use of proportionate consolidation, which requires that the venture partner reflect its share of all assets, liabilities, revenues, and expenses on its financial statements as if these were incurred or held directly. In fact, this technique is very effective at conveying the true scope of an entity's operations, when those operations include interests in one or more jointly controlled entities.

If the venturer employs the proportionate consolidation method, it will have a choice between two presentation formats that are equally acceptable. First, the venture partner may include its share of the assets, liabilities, revenues, and expenses of the jointly controlled entity with similar items under its sole control. Thus, under this method, its share of the venture's receivables would be added to its own accounts receivable and presented as a single total on its statement of financial position. Alternatively, the items that are undivided interests in the venture's assets, and so on, may be shown on separate lines of the venture's financial statements, although still placed within the correct grouping. For example, the venture's receivables might be shown immediately below the partner's individually owned accounts receivable. In either case, the same category totals (aggregate current assets, etc.) will be presented; the only distinction is whether the venture-owned items are given separate recognition. Even if presented on a combined basis, however, the appropriate detail still can be shown in the financial statement footnotes. Indeed, to achieve a fair presentation, this might be needed.

The proportionate consolidation method should be discontinued when the partner no longer has the ability to control the entity jointly. This may occur when the interest is held for disposal within 12 months from acquisition date or when external restrictions are placed on the ability to exercise control. In some cases a partner will waive its right to control the entity, possibly in exchange for other economic advantages, such as a larger interest in the operating results. In such instances, IAS 39 should be used to guide the accounting for the investment.

Under the provisions of IAS 31, a second accounting method, the equity method, is also considered to be acceptable. As with the proportionate consolidation method, use of the equity method must be discontinued when the venturer no longer has joint control or significant influence over the jointly controlled entity. In such a case, IAS 39 would be the relevant accounting requirement.

Example: Proportionate consolidation versus equity method

On January 1, 2007, ULM GmbH signed a joint venture agreement with two other venturers for the production of bottled mineral water. A Partnership ABC was established for that purpose. ULM invests €200,000 for a 40% share of initial capital of ABC Partnership and a 40% share of the profits and losses. For the year 2007, ULM reports these results, excluding its investment in ABC Partnership:

Assets	€2,000,000
Liabilities	600,000
Revenues, 2007	800,000
Expenses	500,000

Statement of Financial Position

ULM GmbH Statement of Financial Position			
€	*ABC Partnership*	*Proportionate Consolidation*	*Equity Method*
Assets	800,000	2,320,000[a]	2,000,000
Investment in ABC Partnership			240,000[b]
Total assets	800,000	2,320,000	2,240,000
Liabilities	200,000	680,000[c]	600,000
Equity	600,000[d]	1,640,000[e]	1,640,000[f]
Total	800,000	2,320,000	2,240,000

[a]€2,320,000 = €2,000,000 + (€800,000 ×.40)
[b]€240,000 = €200,000 + (€100,000 × .40)
[c]€680,000 = €600,000 + (€200,000 × .40)
[d]€600,000 = €500,000 + €100,000
[e]Capital, ULM €240,000
Capital, Outside Partners €360,000
€1,640,000 = €1,400,000 + (€600,000 ×.40)

Income Statement

ULM GmbH Income Statement			
€	*ABC Partnership*	*Proportionate Consolidation*	*...thod*
Revenues	300,000	920,000[a]	...00
Expenses	(200,000)	(580,000)[b]	...,000)
Income from Partnership			...0,000[c]
Net income	100,000[d]	340,000	340,000

[a]€920,000 = €800,000 + (€300,000 × .40)
[b]€580,000 = €500,000 + (€200,000 × .40)
[c]€40,000 = €100,000 x .40
[d]Allocation of income:

ULM (40%)	€40,000
Other Partners (60%)	€60,000

A proportionate consolidation of a partnership involves combining the investor's proportionate share of the partnership's assets, liabilities, revenues, and expenses with those of the investee. This method provides the same overall results as the equity method concerning the amount of net assets and net income, but individual items within the financial statements differ.

Although the expectation is that investments in jointly controlled entities will be accounted for by the proportionate consolidation or equity method (the benchmark and allowed alternative treatments, respectively), in certain circumstances the venturer should account for its interest following the guidelines of IAS 39 (i.e., as a *passive investment*). This would be the prescription when the investment has been acquired and is being held with a view toward disposition within 12 months of the acquisition, or when the investee is operating under severe long-term restrictions that severely impair its ability to transfer funds to its venturer owners.

The venturers' interest in the jointly controlled entity may be increased, whether by an acquisition of some or all of another of the venturers' interest, or by action of a contractual provision of the venture agreement (resulting from a failure to perform by another venturer, etc.); if so, then the proportionate consolidation method of accounting ceases to be appropriate and full consolidation will become necessary. Guidance on preparation of consolidated financial statements is provided by IAS 27 and is discussed fully in Chapter 8.

Accounting for transactions between venture partner and jointly controlled entity. IAS 31 stipulates that when a venturer sells or transfers assets to a jointly controlled entity, it may recognize profit only to the extent that the venture is owned by the other venture partners, and then only to the extent that the risks and rewards of ownership have indeed been transferred to the jointly controlled entity. The logic is that a portion of the profit has in fact been realized, to the extent that the purchase was agreed on by unrelated parties that jointly control the entity making the acquisi-tion.

xample of transfers at a gain to the transferor

Assume that venturers A, B, and C jointly control venture ABC (each having a one-
f terest), and A sells equipment having a carrying value of €40,000 to the venture
re 000, only two-thirds of the apparent gain of €60,000, or €40,000, may be
wo its statement of financial position immediately after this transaction, A
ABC its share of the asset reflected in the statement of financial position of
€13,3 100,000 = €33,333, minus the unrealized gain of €20,000, for a net of
of the identical to A's remaining one-third interest in the pretransaction basis
the pro €40,000 = €13,333). Thus, there is no step-up in the carrying value of
position. If the share of the asset reflected in the transferor's statement of financial
€60,000 =
the venture, ject to depreciation, the deferred gain on the transfer (1/3 ×
would have d be amortized in proportion to the depreciation reflected by
epreciated balance of the asset reported by A is the same as
the transfer not taken place. For example, assume that the

asset has a useful economic life of five years after the date of transfer to venture. The deferred gain (€20,000) would be amortized to income at a rate of €4,000 per year. At the end of the first posttransfer year, ABC would report a net carrying value of €100,000 – €20,000 = €80,000; A's proportionate interest is 1/3 × €80,000 = €26,667. The unamortized balance of the deferred gain is €20,000 – €4,000 = €16,000. Thus the net reported amount of A's share of the jointly controlled entity's asset is €26,667 – €16,000 = €10,667. This amount is precisely what A would have reported the remaining share of its asset at on this date: 1/3 × (€40,000 – €8,000) = €10,667.

Of course, A has also reported a gain of €40,000 as of the date of the transfer of its asset to joint venture, but this represents the gain that has been realized through the sale of two-thirds of the asset to unrelated parties B and C, the coventurers in ABC. In short, two-thirds of the asset has been sold at a gain while one-third has been retained and is continuing to be used and depreciated over its remaining economic life and is reported on the cost basis in A's financial statements.

The situation where a transfer to the jointly controlled entity is at an amount below the transferor's carrying value is not analogous; rather, such a transfer is deemed to be confirmation of a permanent decline in value, which must be recognized by the transferor immediately rather than being deferred. This reflects the conservative bias in accounting: unrealized losses are often recognized while unrealized gains are deferred.

Example of transfers of assets at a loss

Assume that venturer C (a one-third owner of ABC, as described above) transfers an asset it had been carrying at €150,000 to jointly controlled entity ABC at a price of €120,000. If the decline is deemed to be other than temporary in nature (that presumptively it is, since C would not normally have been willing to engage in this transaction if the decline were expected to be reversed in the near term), C must recognize the full €30,000 at the time of the transfer. Subsequently, C will pick up its one-third interest in the asset held by ABC (1/3 × €120,000 = €40,000) as its own asset in its statement of financial position, before considering any depreciation, and so on.

A similar situation arises when a venture partner acquires an asset from a jointly controlled entity: The venturer cannot reflect the gain recognized by the joint venture, to the extent that this represents its share in the results of the venture's operations.

Example of transfers at a gain to the transferor

Assume that A, B, and C jointly own ABC and an asset having a carrying value of €200,000 is transferred by ABC to B for a price of €275,000. Since B has a one-third interest in ABC, B will record the asset at its cost, €275,000, less the deferred gain, €25,000, for a net carrying value of €250,000, which represents the transferor's basis, €200,000, plus the increase in value realized by unrelated parties (A and C) in the amount of €50,000.

If the asset was acquired by B at a loss to ABC, however, and the decline was deemed to be indicative of an other-than-temporary diminution in value, B should recognize its share of this decline. This contrasts with the gain scenario discussed immediately above, and it is entirely consistent with the accounting treatment for transfers from the venture partner to the jointly controlled venture.

Example of transfers at a loss to the transferor

Assume that A, B, and C jointly own ABC and ABC sells an asset carried at €50,000 to B for €44,000, and the reason for this discount is an other than temporary decline in the value of said asset. In this example, the venture ABC records a loss of €6,000 and each venture partner will in turn recognize a €2,000 loss. B would report the asset at its acquisition cost of €44,000 and will also report its share of the loss, €2,000. This loss will not be deferred and will not be added to the carrying value of the asset in B's hands (as would have been the case if B treated only the €4,000 loss realized by unrelated parties A and C as being recognizable).

Accounting for Investment Property

An investment in land or a building, part of a building, or both, if held by the owner (or a lessee under a finance lease) with the intention of earning rentals or for capital appreciation or both, is defined by IAS 40 as an investment property. An investment property is capable of generating cash flows independently of other assets held by the entity. Investment property sometimes is referred to as being "passive" investments, to distinguish it from actively managed property, such as plant assets, the use of which is integrated with the rest of the entity's operations. This characteristic is what distinguishes investment property from owner-occupied property, which is property held by the entity or a lessee under a finance lease, for use in its business (i.e., for use in production or supply of goods or services or for administrative purposes).

Revised IAS 40 permits property interests held in the form of operating leases to be classified and accounted for as investment property. This may be done if

1. The other elements of the definition of investment property (see below) are met;
2. The operating lease is accounted for as if it were a finance lease in accordance with IAS 17 (that is, it is capitalized); and
3. The lessee uses the fair value model set out in IAS 40 for the asset recognized.

This classification option—to report the lessee's property interest as investment property—is available on a property-by-property basis. IAS 40 requires that all investment property should be consistently accounted for, however, employing either the fair value or the cost model. Given these requirements, it is held that once the investment alternative is selected for one leased property, all property classified as investment property must be accounted for consistently, on the fair value basis.

The best way to understand what investment property constitutes is to look at examples of investments that are considered by the Standard as investment properties and contrast these with those investments that do not qualify for this categorization.

According to the Standard, examples of investment property are

- Land held for long-term capital appreciation as opposed to short-term purposes like land held for sale in the ordinary course of business
- Land held for an undetermined future use

- Building owned by the reporting entity (or held by the reporting entity under a finance lease) and leased out under one or more operating leases
- Vacant building held by an entity to be leased out under one or more operating leases

According to IAS 40, investment property does *not* include

- Property employed in the business (i.e., held for use in production or supply of goods or services or for administrative purposes, the accounting for which is governed by IAS 16)
- Property being constructed or developed on behalf of others, the accounting for which is outlined in IAS 11
- Property held for sale in the ordinary course of the business, the accounting for which is specified by IAS 2
- Property under construction or being developed for future use as investment property. IAS 16 is applied to such property until the construction or development is completed, at which time IAS 40 governs. However, existing investment property that is being redeveloped for continued future use would qualify as investment property

Certain properties are not held entirely for rental purposes or for capital appreciation purposes. For example, portions of these properties might be used by the entity for manufacturing or for administrative purposes. If these portions, earmarked for different purposes, could be sold separately, then the entity is required to account for them separately; however, if the portions cannot be sold separately, the property would be deemed as investment property if an insignificant portion is held by the entity for business use.

Ancillary services can be provided by the entity, in which case they are a relatively insignificant component of the arrangement—as when the owner of a residential building provides maintenance and security services to the tenants—the entity treats such an investment as investment property. If the service provided is a comparatively significant component of the arrangement, however, then the investment would be considered as an owner-occupied property.

For instance, an entity that owns and operates a motel and also provides services to the guests of the motel would be unable to argue that it is an investment property as that term is used by IAS 40. Rather, such an investment would be classified as an owner-occupied property. Judgment is therefore required in determining whether a property qualifies as investment property. It is so important a factor that if an entity develops criteria for determining when to classify a property as an investment property, it is required by this Standard to disclose these criteria in the context of difficult or controversial classifications.

Property leased to a subsidiary or its parent company is considered an investment property from the perspective of the entity. For the purposes of consolidated financial statements, however, and from the perspective of the group as a whole, it will not qualify as an investment property because it is an owner-occupied property when viewed from the parent company level.

Investment property will be recognized when it becomes probable that the entity will enjoy the future economic benefits that are attributable to it, and when the cost or fair value can be measured reliably. In general, this will occur when the property is first acquired or constructed by the reporting entity.

Initial measurement will be at cost, which is equivalent to fair value, assuming that the acquisition was the result of an arm's-length exchange transaction. Included in the purchase cost will be such directly attributable expenditure as legal fees and property transfer taxes, if incurred in the transaction. If the asset is self-constructed, cost will include not only direct expenditures on product or services consumed but also overhead charges that can be allocated on a reasonable and consistent basis, in the same manner as these are allocated to inventories under the guidelines of IAS 2. To the extent that the acquisition cost includes an interest charge, if the payment is deferred, the amount to be recognized as an investment asset should not include the interest charges. Furthermore, start-up costs (unless they are essential in bringing the property to its working condition), initial operating losses (incurred prior to the investment property achieving planned level of occupancy), or abnormal waste (in construction or development) do not constitute part of the capitalized cost of an investment property. If an investment property is acquired in exchange for equity instruments of the reporting entity, the cost of the investment property is the fair value of the equity instruments issued, although the fair value of the investment property received is used to measure its cost if it is more clearly evident than the fair value of the equity instruments issued.

In some instances there may be further expenditure incurred on the investment property after the date of initial recognition. Consistent with similar situations arising in connection with plant, property, and equipment (dealt with under IAS 16), if it can be demonstrated that the subsequent expenditure will enhance the generation of future economic benefits to the entity, then those costs may be added to the carrying value of the investment property. That is, the cost can be capitalized only when it is probable that it increases the future economic benefits in excess of its standard of performance assessed immediately before the expenditure was made. By implication, all other subsequent expenditure should be expensed in the periods they are incurred.

Sometimes the appropriate accounting treatment for subsequent expenditure would depend on the circumstances that were considered in the initial measurement and recognition of the investment property. For example, if a property (e.g., an office building) is acquired for investment purposes in a condition that makes it incumbent upon the entity to perform significant renovations thereafter, then such renovation costs (which would constitute subsequent expenditures) will be added to the carrying value of the investment property when incurred later.

Analogous to the financial reporting of plant and equipment under IAS 16, IAS 40 provides that investment property may be reported at either fair value or at depreciated (historical) cost less accumulated impairment. The cost model is the benchmark treatment prescribed by IAS 16 for plant assets. The fair value approach under IAS 40 more closely resembles that used for financial instruments than it does the allowed alternative (revaluation) method for plant assets, however. Also, under

IAS 40, if the cost method is used, fair value information must nonetheless be disclosed.

When investment property is carried at fair value, the carrying amount must be adjusted to the then-current fair value at each subsequent financial reporting date, with the adjustment being reported in the net profit or loss for the period in which it arises. Any decrease in the carrying amount of the property is recognized in profit or loss and only to the extent that an amount is included in revaluation surplus for the property, the decrease is recognized in other comprehensive income and reduces the revaluation surplus within equity. Any increase in the carrying value of the property is recognized in profit or loss to the extent that this amount does not exceed the amount needed to restore the carrying amount to what it would have been, net of depreciation, had the earlier impairment loss not occurred. Any remaining part of the increase is recorded in other comprehensive income and increases the revaluation surplus within equity.

The inclusion of the value adjustments in profit or loss—in contrast to the revaluation approach under IAS 16, whereby adjustments are generally reported in other comprehensive income—is a reflection of the different roles played by plant assets and by other investment property. The former are used, or consumed, in the operation of the business, which is often centered on the production of goods and services for sale to customers. The latter are held for possible appreciation in value, and hence those value changes are highly germane to the assessment of periodic operating performance. With this distinction in mind, the decision was made not only to permit fair value reporting, but to require value changes to be included in profit or loss.

Transfers to or from investment property should be made only when there is a demonstrated "change in use," as contemplated by the Standard. A change in use takes place when there is a transfer:

- From investment property to owner-occupied property, when owner-occupation commences
- From investment property to inventories, on commencement of development with a view to sale
- From an owner-occupied property to investment property, when owner-occupation ends
- Of inventories to investment property, when an operating lease to a third party commences
- Of property in the course of development or construction to investment property, at end of the construction or development

In the case of an entity that employs the cost model, transfers between investment property, owner-occupied property, and inventories do not change the carrying amount of the property transferred and thus do not change the cost of that property for measurement or disclosure purposes. When the investment property is carried under the fair value model, vastly different results follow as far as recognition and measurement is concerned. These results are explained next.

- **Transfers from (or to) investment property to (or from) plant and equipment (in the case of investment property carried under the fair value model).** In some instances, property that at first is classified appropriately as investment property under IAS 40 may later become plant, property, and equipment as defined under IAS 16. For example, a building is obtained and leased to unrelated parties, but at a later date the entity expands its own operations to the extent that it now chooses to utilize the building formerly held as a passive investment for its own purposes, such as for the corporate executive offices. The amount reflected in the accounting records as the fair value of the property as of the date of change in status would become the cost basis for subsequent accounting purposes. Previously recognized changes in value, if any, would not be reversed.

  Similarly, if property first classified as owner-occupied property and treated as plant and equipment under the benchmark treatment of IAS 16 is later redeployed as investment property, it is to be measured at fair value at the date of the change in its usage. If the value is lower than the carrying amount (i.e., if there is a previously unrecognized decline in its fair value), then this will be reflected in profit or loss in the period of redeployment as an investment property. If there has been an unrecognized increase in value, however, the accounting will depend on whether this is a reversal of previously recognized value impairment. If the increase is a reversal of a decline in value, the increase should be recognized currently in earnings; the amount reported, however, should not exceed the amount needed to restore the carrying amount to what it would have been, net of depreciation, had the earlier impairment loss not occurred.

  If, however, there was no previously recognized impairment that the current value increase is effectively reversing (or, to the extent that the current increase exceeds the earlier decline), then the increase should be recognized in other comprehensive income and increases the revaluation surplus within equity. If the investment property is later disposed of, any resultant gain or loss computation should *not* include the effect of the amount reported directly in other comprehensive income.
- **Transfers from inventory to investment property (in the case of investment property carried under the fair value model).** It may also happen that property originally classified as inventory, held for sale in the normal course of the business, is later redeployed as investment property. When reclassified, the initial carrying amount should be fair value as of that date. Any gain or loss resulting from this reclassification would be reported in current period's profit or loss. IAS 40 does not contemplate reclassification from investment property to inventory, however. When the entity determines that property held as investment property is to be disposed of, that property should be retained as investment property until actually sold. It should not be derecognized (eliminated from the statement of financial position) or transferred to an inventory classification.

- **Transfer on completion of construction or development of self-constructed investment property (to be carried at fair value).** On completion of construction or development of self-constructed investment property that will be carried at fair value, any difference between the fair value of the property at that date and its previous carrying amount should be recognized in the net profit or loss for the period.

An investment property should be derecognized (i.e., eliminated from the statement of financial position of the entity) on disposal or when it is permanently withdrawn from use and no future economic benefits are expected from its disposal. The word "disposal" has been used in the Standard to mean not only a sale but also the entering into of a finance lease by the entity. Any gains or losses on disposal or retirement of an investment property should be determined as the difference between the net disposal proceeds and the carrying amount of the asset and should be recognized in profit or loss for the period.

DECISION TREE

Accounting for Gains or Losses on Securities

The flowchart shown in Exhibit 7.3 shows how gains and losses are handled for different types of securities portfolios. The decision flow begins in the upper left corner. For example, if a security is designated as available-for-sale and there is a change in its fair value, then the decision tree moves to the right, asking if there is a permanent value impairment. If so, the proper treatment matches that of a loss for a held-for-trading security; if not, the proper treatment is listed as being reported in the other comprehensive income section of the statement of comprehensive income.

7.3 Accounting for Gains or Losses on Securities

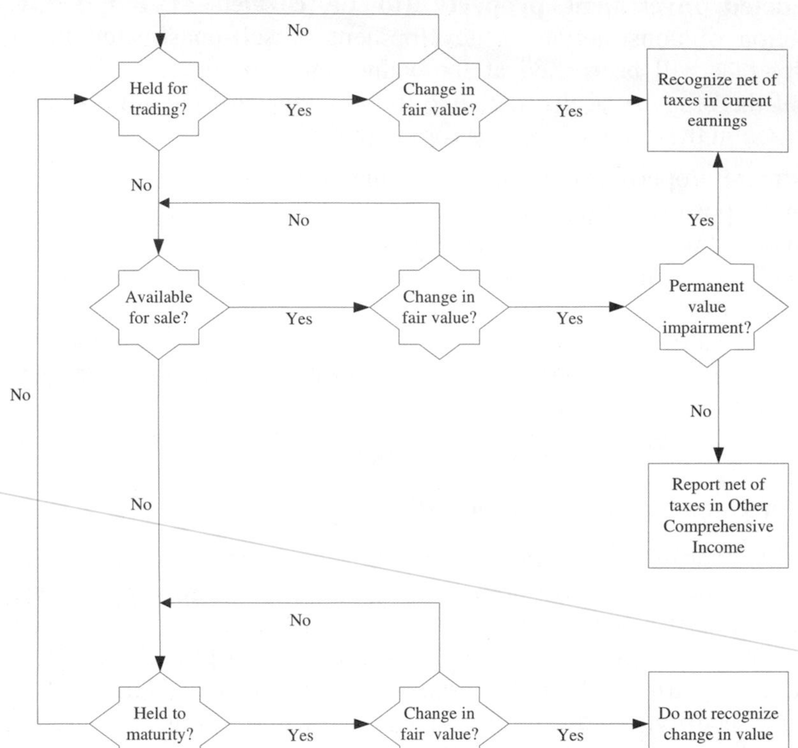

POLICIES

Funds Investment Policies

- **At least €____ shall be invested in overnight investments and in negotiable marketable obligations of major issuers.** This policy forces the treasury staff to attain a minimum level of liquidity. The fixed dollar amount used in the policy should be reviewed regularly to match upcoming budgeted working capital requirements.
- **No more than ____% of the total portfolio shall be invested in time deposits or other investments with a lack of liquidity.** This policy is similar to the preceding one, except that it ignores a fixed liquidity requirement. Instead, it focuses on a maximum proportion of the total portfolio that must be retained for short-term requirements, requiring less periodic updating.
- **The average maturity of the investment portfolio shall be limited to ____ years.** This policy is designed to keep a company from investing in excessively long maturities. It can be broken down into more specific maturity limitations for different types of investments, such as five years for any government obligations, one year for bank certificates of deposit, and 270 days for commercial paper.

- **Investments in foreign commercial paper shall be limited to those unconditionally guaranteed by a prime issuer and fully hedged.** This policy is designed to lower the risk of default on investments in securities issued by foreign entities.
- **Investments in commercial paper shall be limited to those of companies having long-term senior debt ratings of Aa or better.** This policy is designed to limit the risk of default on commercial paper investments by focusing investments on only the highest-grade commercial paper.
- **Investments in bank certificates of deposit shall be limited to those banks with capital accounts exceeding €1 billion.** This policy is designed to limit the risk of default on certificates of deposit, on the assumption that large capital accounts equate to minimal risk of bank failure.
- **Investments shall be made only in investments backed by government debt obligations.** This policy can be used in place of the preceding ones that specify allowable investments in nongovernmental investments, and it tends to be used by highly risk-averse companies that place less emphasis on the return generated from their investments.

Accounting for Marketable Equity Securities

- **All securities purchases shall be designated as trading securities at the time of purchase.** This policy is intended to avoid the designation of an investment as "available for sale," which would allow management to avoid recording short-term changes in the fair value of the investment in reported earnings. It removes the ability of management to alter financial results by shifting the designation of an investment.
- **All losses on securities designated as available-for-sale shall be considered permanent.** Accounting rules allow one to avoid recognizing losses on available-for-sale securities by assuming that the losses are temporary. By using this policy to require an immediate write-down on all losses, management no longer has the ability to manipulate earnings by making assumptions that losses are temporary in nature.
- **Available-for-sale securities shall not be sold solely to recognize related gains in their fair market value.** Accounting rules do not allow ongoing recognition of gains in the value of available-for-sale securities in earnings until they have been sold, so there is a natural temptation to manage earnings by timing their sale. This policy is designed to set an ethical standard for management to prevent such actions from taking place. In reality, this is a difficult policy to enforce, since management can find reasonable excuses for selling securities when their unrecognized gains are needed for bookkeeping purposes.

Transfers between Investment Portfolios

- **The board of directors shall be notified of the reasons for any significant shift in the designation of securities between the held-to-maturity, available-for-sale, and trading portfolios, and the approximate impact on different categories of income.** This policy is designed to require management to justify its actions in shifting securities between portfolios (which is likely to reduce the amount of shifting) while also keeping the board informed of any likely movements of gains or losses between the operating income and Other Comprehensive Income parts of the income statement.

Accounting for Investments in Debt Securities

- **The unrecognized amount of gains or losses on held-to-maturity securities shall be regularly reported to the board of directors.** Management may designate poorly performing debt securities as held-to-maturity, in which case any changes in their fair value will not be recognized. This policy is designed to reveal any gains or losses that would be recognized if these securities were to have any other portfolio designation, so the board is aware of any "hanging" gains or losses.
- **Debt securities shall not be classified as held-to-maturity unless sufficient investments are already on hand to cover all budgeted short-term cash requirements.** IFRS already requires that debt securities not be classified as held-to-maturity if a company does not have the ability to hold the securities for the required time period—this policy is more specific in stating that all anticipated cash flows be fully covered by other investments before any debt securities receive the held-to-maturity classification. The policy makes it more likely that a company will not be forced to prematurely liquidate its held-to-maturity debt portfolio.

Transfers of Debt Securities among Portfolios

- **The board of directors must authorize all shifts in investment designation out of the held-to-maturity portfolio.** There are specific accounting instances where the transfer of securities out of the held-to-maturity portfolio will preclude a company's subsequent use of the held-to-maturity portfolio. Accordingly, the board of directors should be notified of the reasons for such a designation and give its formal approval before the designation change can be made.

The Equity Method of Accounting for Investments

- **The chief financial officer shall regularly review with the board of directors the existing assumptions of significant influence over all entities of whose voting common stock the company owns between 20% and 50%.** Evidence of significant influence requires a company to use the equity method in reporting the financial results of an investee, whereas a lack of influence would require it to record the investment in an investment portfolio category.

Regularly reviewing the level of influence over an investee will ensure that the appropriate accounting treatment is used.

- **The tax rate used to recognize taxes under equity method gains shall be the higher of the rates paid on dividend income or sale of the investment.** The income tax rate used to record equity method transactions can be the tax rate either on dividends or from sale of the investment, depending on the investor's intent to eventually dispose of the method. Always using the higher tax rate goes against IFRS to some extent but keeps the accounting staff from inflating income by using the more conservative tax rate.

PROCEDURES

Funds Investment Procedure

Use the next procedure to invest excess funds in accordance with the corporate investment policy.

1. Review the short-term cash forecast with the treasury staff and determine the amount of funds that are not needed immediately for operations.
2. Using the corporate investment policy and the size of the investable cash balance as guidelines, select the appropriate investment vehicle. For short-term cash investments, select the most liquid investments on the investing policy.
3. Extract a copy of the investment form from the forms cabinet and fill it out, entering the investment initiation date, the type of investment, the broker or bank used to fulfill the order, and the amount of the investment.
4. Have an authorized signer sign the investment form.
5. Fax this form to the company's third-party broker or bank for fulfillment.
6. Call the firm to verify receipt of the fax.
7. Send a copy of the investment form to the general ledger accountant for proper recording in the general ledger.
8. File the original completed investment form, sequenced by date.

Transfers between the Available-for-Sale and Trading Portfolios

Use this procedure not only to specify the correct accounting transactions for a shift between the available-for-sale and trading portfolios, but also to ensure that justification for the change has been documented and approved.

1. Document the reason for the shift between portfolios, and summarize the total impact of gains or losses to be recognized in current income as a result of the change, including the tax impact.
2. If the impact on current earnings is significant, notify the board of directors of the prospective change, if required by company policy.
3. Create a journal entry to shift funds between the available-for-sale and trading portfolios, including the recognition of any gains or losses required to bring the recorded value of the securities to their fair value as of the transaction date.

4. Send the journal entry, documentation of the shift in portfolios, and documentation of board notification to the general ledger accountant, with instructions to log the journal entry into the general ledger and store the related documentation in the journal entry binder.

The Equity Method of Accounting for Investments

Use this procedure to record an investment under the equity method of accounting.

1. Determine the proper type of accounting methodology to use. If the cumulative investment in the investee is less than 20%, or the investment is less than 50% and there is no significant control over the investee, record the transaction at its fair value. If the cumulative investment in the investment is between 20% and 50% and there is significant control over the investee, use the equity method of accounting. If the investment exceeds 50% of the investee, use consolidated reporting. The remainder of this procedure assumes that the equity method will be used.
2. Multiply the investor's cumulative proportion of ownership in the investee by the investee's carrying value, and then subtract this amount from the amount paid by the investor.
3. On an electronic spreadsheet, itemize the major categories of investee assets and liabilities, and record in adjacent columns the carrying and fair values of each category.
4. Create a column in the spreadsheet that calculates the difference between the carrying and fair values of each asset and liability category.
5. Allocate any difference calculated in step 2 to the investor's share of any excess in fair value over carrying, as calculated in step 4.
6. If there remains any unallocated excess purchase price after the allocation in step 5 is completed, record the excess as goodwill.
7. Note in another column in the spreadsheet a reasonable amortization period for each asset or liability category to which an allocation was made.
8. Calculate the current period amortization for each asset or liability category to which an allocation was made.
9. Record the initial investment transaction as a debit to Investment in [company name] account and a credit to the Cash account.
10. Record an amortization entry for the current period based on the calculation in step 8, using a debit to the Equity in [company name] account and a credit to the Investment in [company name] account (if the fair values of assets exceeded carrying values).
11. Send the proposed transaction and all supporting documentation to the company auditors, with a request to review the transaction for errors and conformance with IFRS.
12. Upon auditor approval, send the journal entry to the general ledger accountant for entry in the general ledger.

13. The general ledger accountant attaches all backup materials related to the transaction to the journal entry and stores the entire packet in the journal entry file.

CONTROLS

Transfers between Available-for-Sale and Trading Investments

- **Require board approval of substantial changes in investment account designations.** Management can modify the amount of reported gains or losses on investments by shifting investment designations from the "available-for-sale" investment portfolio to the "trading" portfolio. If the gain or loss on such a change in designation is significant, the board of directors should be notified in advance of the reason for the change and its impact on the level of profit or loss.

Transfers of Debt Securities among Portfolios

- **Impose investment limits.** When investing its excess funds, a company should have a policy that requires it to invest only certain amounts in particular investment categories or vehicles. For example, only the first €100,000 of funds is insured through a bank account, so excess funding beyond this amount can be shifted elsewhere. As another example, the board of directors may feel that there is too much risk in junk bond investments, and so will place a general prohibition on this type of investment. These sorts of policies can be programmed into a treasury workstation, so that the system will automatically flag investments that fall outside a company's preset investment parameters.
- **Require authorizations to shift funds among accounts.** A person who is attempting to fraudulently shift funds out of a company's accounts must have approval authorization on file with one of the company's investment banks to transfer money out to a noncompany account. This type of authorization can be controlled strictly through signatory agreements with the banks. It is also possible to impose strict controls over the transfer of funds *between* company accounts, since a fraudulent person may uncover a loophole in the control system whereby a particular bank has not been warned *not* to allow fund transfers outside of a preset range of company accounts, and then shift all funds to that account and thence to an outside account.

The Equity Method of Accounting for Investments

- **Verify consistent use of the same income tax rate for equity method transactions.** IFRS allows the assumed use of tax rates for either dividend payments or capital gains to record gains from equity method transactions. This can result in improperly switching between different tax rates on successive equity method transactions in order to meet short-term profitability goals. A simple control over this problem is to review the calculation of journal entries in the income tax expense account periodically to see if tax rate usage has been consistent.

- **Require approval of the assumed tax rate used for equity method transactions.** As noted in the preceding control, IFRS allows one to use a range of possible tax rates for equity method transactions, which can result in improperly altering tax rates to meet profitability goals. To avoid this problem, the general ledger accountant should be required to obtain management approval of any journal entries involving the income tax expense account.
- **Require auditor review and approval of excess purchase price allocations to investee assets.** If the amount of an investment exceeds the investee's book value, IFRS requires that as much of the excess investment as possible be allocated to any investee assets for which the fair value exceeds the carrying value. When this occurs, one must also amortize the incremental value assigned, which will reduce the recorded amount of the investment. Thus, the investor will have an incentive to allocate the minimum amount to assets, if not entirely forgo the allocation process. By having independent auditors review and approve informal asset allocations as well as the related amortization calculations, one can ensure that a reasonable valuation and resulting amortization of asset values will occur.
- **Add to the monthly closing schedule the amortization of purchase price allocations to investee assets.** If the purchase price of an investment exceeds the carrying value of the investee and the equity method of accounting is being used, an informal amortization calculation usually is kept that is not integrated into the usual asset depreciation schedule. Because it is maintained separately, there is a strong possibility that this additional amortization will be forgotten and not periodically included in the financial statements. To avoid the problem, the amortization entry should be noted in the formal closing procedure. Also, the amortization should be set up as a recurring journal entry in the general ledger, though inclusion in the procedure is still necessary to ensure that the recurring amortization entry continues to be checked for accuracy.
- **Obtain independent verification of the fair value of investee land assets to which investor goodwill has been allocated.** IFRS requires that the maximum possible amount of excess investment over an investee's carrying value be assigned to identifiable assets, which are then amortized. By assigning an excessive amount of the investment to land assets, which are not amortized, a company can incorrectly retain a high reported level of investment. Requiring independent verification of the fair value of the land assets is an effective method for ensuring that the correct amount of amortization is entered in the general ledger each month. It is also useful to include in the month-end closing procedure a requirement to obtain a fair value estimate of any new allocation to investee land and compare it to the amount of excess investment informally assigned to the land asset group, thereby formalizing the process.

FORMS AND REPORTS

Investment Approval Form

The investment approval form is a critical document for controlling the types of investments made as well as how they are designated in the accounting records. The form shown in Exhibit 7.4 contains four blocks that cover key investment information. The first block contains check-off boxes for the various types of approved investments, as noted in the corporate investments policy. The user enters additional information about each type of investment in the "Investment Description" field, followed by the amount to be invested and the maturity date (if any) of the investment. The next block contains check-off boxes for the investment designation to be used in the accounting records while the third block contains fields for special permissions required for certain types of investments and investment designations. Finally, the fourth block reveals the proper document routing and includes signature fields to indicate that each step in the process has been completed.

Exhibit 7.4 Investment Approval Form

INVESTMENT APPROVAL FORM

Investment Type:

	Investment Description	Amount	Maturity Date
☐ Bank Demand Deposit			
☐ Certificate of Deposit			
☐ Short term Government debt			
☐ Commercial Paper			
☐ Other			

Investment Designation:

☐ Trading ☐ Available-for-Sale ☐ Held-to-Maturity

Special Approvals:

Held-to-Maturity Designation ______ Chief Financial Officer ______ Date

"Other" Investments ______ Chief Financial Officer ______ Date

Routings:

Investment Approval → Investment Transaction → G/L Entry

Treasurer Signature	Investment Clerk Signature	G/L Clerk Signature
Date	Date	Date

Bond Ledger Sheet

A considerable amount of information must be retained and tracked for each bond in which a company invests, not only to ensure that profits and losses are properly calculated and recorded but also to maintain a history of all transactions related to it. The Bond Ledger Sheet shown in Exhibit 7.5 is a good example of a computer report that should be printed for each bond purchased and sold. It lists all descriptive information in the header section while noting individual transactions, such as premium amortization, bond purchase and sale, and interest payments in the detail section at the bottom of the report. The report is also useful for auditors, who will have all needed review information about a bond summarized onto one page.

Exhibit 7.5 Bond Ledger Sheet

Bond Name:________Intergalactic Coal Mining Co.___________											
Purchased Through____ABC Bond Sales________					Nominal Rate___10%___ Actual Rate____9.3%___						
Description: Numbers:________B1676,B1677________ Denomination:____€5,000______________ Where Payable:___Third Trust, London___ Trustee:_________Third Trust, London___					Dated:_________1/1/2008________ When Due:_____12/31/2028______ Interest Payable:_6/30, 12/31______ Redeemable:____Yes____________						
Date	Pieces	Memo	Price	Debit	Credit	Balance	Profit or Loss	Due Date	Interest Amount	Paid Date	
4/1/06	2	ABC Bond	€ 07.5	€10,750		€10,750		6/60/08	€500	6/30/08	
6/30/06		Premium			€50	€10,700		12/31/08	€500	12/31/08	
12/31/06		Premium			€100	€10,600		6/30/09	€500	6/30/09	
6/30/07		Premium			€100	€10,500	€100				
7/1/07	1	Denver National	€107.0		€5,200	€5,250					

SOURCE: Adapted with permission from Willson et al., ***Controllership,*** *6th ed. (New York: John Wiley & Sons, 1999), p. 693.*

Stock Ledger Sheet

Just as information must be retained for bonds, information must also be retained for any stock investments. In the Stock Ledger Sheet shown in Exhibit 7.6, the details of all buy and sell transactions can be listed for each stock investment made. The report leaves separate blocks of columns for entries related to stock buys and sells while showing stock balances on the far right side.

Exhibit 7.6 Stock Ledger Sheet

Stock Ledger Report

Issued by:_____Intergalactic Coal Mining Co.__________

Class:_____Common_____ Par Value:_____ €1.00_______

Bought				Sold					Balance		
Date	No. of Shares	Price	Cost*	Date	No. of Shares	Price	Total Received*	Profit or Loss	No. of Shares	Average Price	Cost
1/30/2008	100	€30	€3,020						100	€30.20	€3,020
				9/30/2008	25	€36	€890	€135	75	€30.20	€2,265
10/3/2008	50	€35	€1,770						125	€32.28	€4,035
				11/15/2008	25	€38	€940	€133	100	€32.28	€3,228

* *Includes commission*

SOURCE: Adapted with permission from Willson et al., ***Controllership,*** *6th ed. (New York: John Wiley & Sons, 1999), p. 693.*

Report on Investment Position

An alternative to the level of detail shown in the Bond Ledger Sheet and Stock Ledger Sheet is a more summary-level report itemizing the investment, current market value, and return on investment for each investment made. As is shown in

Exhibit 7.7, this approach yields a quick view of a company's overall level of investment and the results thereof.

Exhibit 7.7 Report on Investment Position

	Security	Number of shares	Market value	Purchase price	Rate of return	Total dividends Y-T-D
1.	ABC Corporation	500	€37,000	€31,000	5.2%	€800
2.	Atlas Construction	100	2,400	2,400	6.3	75
3.	National Co.	1,000	30,000	31,000	6.5	1,000
4.	USA Corporation	1,000	65,500	64,000	7.8	2,000
5.	JPC Corporation	100	1,900	1,875	7.5	70
6.	Security Co.	500	42,000	38,000	5.3	1,000
	Total or average		€178,800	€168,275	6.5%	€4,945

SOURCE: Adapted with permission from Willson et al., ***Controllership,*** *6th ed. (New York: John Wiley & Sons, 1999), p. 693.*

Report on Amortization of Allocated Asset Valuation

If the equity method of accounting is being used for an investment, some portion of any excess amount of the investment price over the investee's carrying value must be informally allocated to the investee's assets and liabilities. Since the financial presentation of an investment under the equity method is only a single line item, these adjustments must be tracked informally outside the general ledger. An example of such a tracking spreadsheet is shown in Exhibit 7.8, which itemizes the amount of the excess purchase price allocated, the amortization period to be used, and the amortization calculation for each year.

Exhibit 7.8: Report on Amortization of Allocated Asset Valuation

Asset type	Investment allocation	Amortization period	2008	2009	2010
Receivables	€20,000	1 year	€20,000	€ 0	€ 0
Fixed assets	82,000	5 years	16,400	16,400	16,400
Intangibles	150,000	10 years	15,000	15,000	15,000
Totals	€252,000		€51,400	€31,400	€31,400

FOOTNOTES

Disclosure of Cash Deposits in Excess of FDIC Insurance Limits

If a company concentrates its cash holdings in accounts exceeding the FDIC insurance limit of €100,000, it should disclose the amount exceeding the limit. An example follows.

> For cash management purposes, the company concentrates its cash holdings in a single account at the Third National Bank of Rotterdam. The balance in this account may exceed the llmit of €100,000 insured by a Government fund in case of bank failure. At December 31, 2007, the company had €829,000 in excess of the insurance limit at this bank.

Disclosure of Change in Reported Method of Investment

If a company changes from the cost method to the equity method of accounting or vice versa, a footnote should disclose the change in the level of investment that required the change in method. It should also note the general accounting treatment required by each method as well as the impact of the change on net income and any change in retained earnings resulting from the retroactive application of the new method. An example follows.

The company increased its investment in the Alhambra Boutiques Company (ABC) in May 2008 from 18% to 35%. Consequently, the company changed from the cost method of accounting for this investment to the equity method. Instead of recording its investment at cost and treating dividends as income, as was the case under the cost method, the company now records its proportionate share of all ABC earnings. The change reduced the company's earnings in 2008 by €109,000 while retained earnings as of the beginning of 2008 were adjusted downward by €128,000 to reflect the retroactive application of the equity method to this investment.

Disclosure of Investments

If a company holds any investments, the accountant must disclose the existence of any unrealized valuation accounts in the equity section of the statement of financial position as well as any realized gains or losses that have been recognized through the income statement. The classification of any material investments should also be noted (i.e., as available-for-sale or held-to-maturity).

Investments accounted for under the equity method need the name of the entity in which the investment is made, the company's percentage of ownership, the total value based on the market price of the shares held, and the total amount of any unrealized appreciation or depreciation to all be noted, with a discussion of how these amounts are amortized. The amount of any goodwill associated with the investment should be noted as well as the method and specifications of the related amortization. If this method of accounting is used for an investment in which the company's share of investee ownership is less than 20%, then the reason should be noted; similarly, if the method is not used in cases where the percentage of ownership is greater than 20%, then the reasoning also should be discussed. Finally, the accountant should reveal the existence of any contingent issuances of stock by the investee that could result in a material change in the company's share of the investee's reported earnings. The first entry gives a general overview of a company's security classification policies, the second entry reveals the breakdown of security types within its available-for-sale portfolio, and the third entry describes gains and losses resulting from both the sale of securities and transfers between security portfolios.

1. The company classifies its investments when purchased and reviews their status at the end of each reporting period. The company classifies those marketable securities bought and intended for sale in the short term as Trading Securities and records them at fair value. The company classifies those debt securities it intends to hold to maturity, and has the intent to do so, as Held-to-Maturity Securities. All remaining securities are classified as Available-for-Sale and are recorded at fair value. Unrealized gains and losses on Trading Securities are recognized in earnings, while they are included in comprehensive income for Available-for-Sale securities.
2. The company's available-for-sale portfolio is recorded at a total value of €1,150,000, of which €650,000 is equity securities and €500,000 is debt securities. The aggregate fair value of investments in this portfolio is €1,050,000, plus

€100,000 of gross unrealized holding losses. The contractual maturity dates of €500,000 in debt securities fall into these categories:

Maturity date range	*Debt reaching maturity*
Less than 1 year	€ 72,000
1–5 years	109,000
6–10 years	201,000
10+ years	118,000
Totals	€500,000

3. The company recognized €42,000 in gains from the sale of its securities during the period, which was calculated using the specific identification method. It also recognized a loss of €36,000 when it transferred securities from its available-for-sale portfolio to its trading portfolio, due to a change in the intent of management to sell the securities in the short term.
4. The company recorded €1,050,000 of debt securities classified as held-to-maturity. The next table summarizes the debt by type of issuer and also notes the historical cost at which the debt is recorded on the statement of financial position, its fair value, and the gross amount of unrealized gains and losses as of the statement of financial position date.

Security issuer	*Historical cost*	*Fair value*	*Gross unrealized gain*	*Gross unrealized loss*
Government debt	€ 450,000	€400,000	--	€(50,000)
Mortgage-backed loans	275,000	285,000	€10,000	--
Corporate debt	325,000	310,000	--	(15,000)
Totals	€1,050,000	€995,000	€10,000	€(65,000)

The contractual maturities of the €1,050,000 in debt securities recorded in the held-to-maturity portfolio fall into these date ranges:

Maturity date range	*Debt reaching maturity*
Less than 1 year	€275,000
1–5 years	409,000
6–10 years	348,000
10+ years	18,000
Totals	€1,050,000

Disclosure of Reduction in Market Value of Equity Investments

If management is of the opinion that a permanent decline in an equity investment has occurred, it should note the amount and date of a write-down in the investment valuation as well as its presentation in the financial statements. An example follows.

The company wrote down the value of several investments in equity instruments held in its available-for-sale portfolio during August 2008 by €193,000. The write-down was based on management's judgment that the equity instruments have experienced a permanent reduction in value. The write-down is itemized as a Loss on Investments in the operating section of the income statement.

Disclosure of Increase in Value of a Written-Down Held-to-Maturity Investment

If a company writes down the value of a held-to-maturity investment, it cannot record any subsequent recovery of the written-down value in the financial statements but should do so in the footnotes. A disclosure should note the amount of the initial write-down and the amount of any subsequent value recovery. An example follows.

> The company wrote down the value of its €850,000 held-to-maturity investment in ABC Corporation in July 2008 by €288,000, based on ABC's bankruptcy filing in that month. Subsequently, ABC emerged from bankruptcy with the commitment to pay off its debt at 92% of face value and on the existing payment schedule. This resulted in an increase in the value of the company's ABC holdings of €220,000, which is not reflected in the attached financial statements.

Disclosure of Sale of Held-to-Maturity Investments

If a debt security classified as held-to-maturity is sold, a footnote should disclose the reason for the sale as well as the amount of any gains or losses recognized and the amount of any as-yet unamortized premiums or discounts. An example follows.

> The company liquidated €2,800,000 of its held-to-maturity portfolio in order to pay for an acquisition. The transaction resulted in the recognition of a gain of €145,000. Also, a previously unamortized discount of €16,500 on the original debt purchase was written off as part of the transaction.

Disclosure of Changes in Investment Fair Value After the Reporting Period

If there is a significant change in the value of a company's investments after the statement of financial position date but before the issuance of financial statements, the amount of the change should be described in a footnote. Two examples follow.

1. Subsequent to the statement of financial position date, the fair value of the company's trading portfolio declined by €98,000, or 17% of the total portfolio value. In addition, the continuing decline of the fair value of the available-for-sale portfolio by an additional €43,000 after the reporting period confirms management's opinion that the decline in value of this portfolio has been permanently impaired. For this reason, management recognized a permanent loss of €109,000 in the value of the available-for-sale portfolio subsequent to the statement of financial position date.
2. The fair value of the company's available-for-sale portfolio declined by €89,000 subsequent to the statement of financial position date. Because the decline is caused by the expected bankruptcy of an investee, management now considers the investment to be permanently impaired. Fair value declines prior to the statement of financial position date had not been considered permanently impaired, since the investee had not announced its bankruptcy intentions at that time. The company plans to record the losses in the available-for-sale account as permanent impairments in the next quarterly financial statements.

Disclosure of Shifts between Securities Accounts

If company management feels that the purpose of various investments has changed, it can shift the funds between its held-to-maturity and available-for-sale categories. That being the case, it should disclose in a footnote the reason for the change, the aggregate amount of securities shifted between accounts, and any related unrealized gain or loss, net of income taxes. An example follows.

The company shifted approximately half of its securities recorded as held-to-maturity securities to the held-for-trading account during the last quarter of 2008. These securities had a net carrying value of €42 million at the time of the transfer, including unrealized losses net of income taxes of €2.5 million. Management authorized this change in order to reflect its increased need for additional cash in the short term as part of its general upgrade of production facilities.

Disclosure of Nonstandard Reported Method of Investment

If a company chooses to account for an investment in a nonstandard manner, such as using the equity method for a minor investment that normally would require the cost method, then it should disclose in a footnote that it exercises a sufficient degree of control over the investee's operating and financial activities to warrant the change (or vice versa for a larger investment recorded under the cost method). Two examples follow.

1. The company owns a 35% interest in the Vienna Botox Clinics Company (VBC), which normally would be accounted for under the equity method of accounting. However, due to the considerable resistance of the VBC management to the company's investment, the company's management feels that it has minimal control over VBC's financial and operating activities, and so has chosen to record the investment under the cost method, whereby it records its investment at cost and only records income on the investment when dividends are received.
2. The company owns a 12% interest in the Russian Bear Company (RBC), which normally would be accounted for under the cost method of accounting. However, because the company's CEO is also president of RBC, the company's management feels that it has financial and operating control over RBC, and so has chosen to record the investment under the equity method, whereby it records its proportionate share of RBC's net earnings.

Disclosure of Reduced Equity Method Investment

If an investee has acted to increase its pool of issued shares, or there is a possibility of this occurring through the conversion of convertible securities, options, or warrants, then a footnote should disclose the aggregate amount of the potential reduction in a company's investment as well as the potential impact on its reported share of the investee's earnings. An example follows.

As of December 31, 2008, the company had a 39% ownership interest in General Navigation, Inc. (GNI). On that date, GNI issued 1,000,000 options to its employees, which can be exercised at any time at an exercise price of €14.00. If these options were to be converted to common stock, the company's ownership interest in GNI would have been diluted by 4%, resulting in a reduced ownership level of 35%. The potential ownership reduction would have reduced the company's reported share of GNI's 2008 earnings by €355,000.

Disclosure of Reduction in Equity Method Investment

If a company's investment in another entity is accounted for under the equity method, any losses recorded under that method should be adequately described in a footnote, which can include the company's percentage ownership in the entity, the amount of any loss by the entity that is recorded on the company's financial records, and the resulting impact on the company's recorded investment in the entity. The footnote should also disclose any requirement for the company to fund further entity losses, if any. If the reported investment has dropped to zero, the footnote should state that the equity method of accounting will not be used in order to avoid recording a negative investment. Three examples follow.

1. The company has a 35% interest in the Dusseldorf Electric Company, which operates the power grid in the greater Dusseldorf metropolitan area. This investment has been accounted for under the equity method of accounting since 2005. The company's financial results include a loss of €5.3 million, representing its share of Dusseldorf's loss due to a write-down in goodwill on a failed subsidiary. The loss reduced the company's investment balance in Dusseldorf to €4.0 million. The company has no obligation to fund any additional losses reported by Dusseldorf.
2. The company has a 29% interest in the Bogota Power Company, which operates all hydroelectric facilities in Colombia. This investment has been accounted for under the equity method of accounting since 1992. The company's financial results include a loss of €22.8 million, representing its share of Bogota's loss due to reduced maintenance fees paid by the Colombian government. The loss reduced the company's investment balance in Bogota to zero. The company is contractually obligated to provide an additional €100 million in funding if Bogota's losses continue. Given the current regulatory environment, management feels that the additional funds will be required, so a loss contingency of €100 million has been recognized on the statement of financial position.
3. The company has a 40% investment in the Euclid Power Company. This investment has been accounted for under the equity method of accounting since 2005. The company's financial results include a loss of €21 million, representing its share of Euclid's losses. Recognition of this loss has resulted in a reported investment in Euclid of €0. Since the company cannot report a negative investment in Euclid under the equity method, it will not record its share of future Euclid losses until such time as future Euclid profits offset any subsequent losses that would otherwise have resulted in the reporting of a negative investment by the company.

Disclosure of Joint Venture

A venture partner is required to disclose in the notes to the financial statements its ownership interests in all significant joint ventures, including its ownership percentage and other relevant data. If the venturer uses proportionate consolidation and merges its share of the assets, liabilities, revenues, and expenses of the jointly controlled entity with its own assets, liabilities, revenues, and expenses, or if the venturer uses the equity method, the notes should disclose the amounts of the current and long-term assets, current and long-term liabilities, revenues, and expenses related to its interests in jointly controlled ventures.

Furthermore, the joint venture partner should disclose the aggregate amount of various contingent liabilities, unless the probability of loss is remote, separately from the amount of other contingent liabilities. Additionally, the aggregate amount of various capital commitments should be disclosed. Included are any capital commitments the partner has and the partner's share of any joint commitments he or she may have incurred with other venture partners, as well as this partner's share of the capital commitments of the joint ventures themselves, if any. An example follows.

> The company has included nine joint ventures by proportionate consolidation in compliance with IAS 31, *Financial Reporting of Interests in Joint Ventures*, which involves recognizing a proportionate share, on a line-by-line basis, of each of joint venture's assets, liabilities, income, and expenses in the consolidated financial statements. A listing and description of interests in significant joint ventures and the proportion of ownership interest held in jointly controlled entities is provided in Note 11, *Interests in Associates and Joint Ventures*. The effect of joint ventures on the Group statement of financial position and income statement is as follows:

€ million			
Noncurrent assets	225	Revenues	411
Current assets	74	Other income	98
Pension provisions	(9)	Expenses	(480)
Other provisions	(11)		
Financial liabilities	(59)		
Remaining liabilities	(99)		
Net assets	121	Income after taxes	29

Disclosure of Investment Property

Disclosures applicable to all investment properties:

- When classification is difficult, an entity that holds an investment property will need to disclose the criteria used to distinguish investment property from owner-occupied property and from property held for sale in the ordinary course of business.
- The methods and any significant assumptions that were used in ascertaining the fair values of the investment properties are to be disclosed as well. Such disclosure also includes a statement about whether the determination of fair value was supported by market evidence or relied heavily on other factors (which the entity needs to disclose as well) due to the nature of the property and the absence of comparable market data.
- If investment property has been revalued by an independent appraiser, who has recognized and relevant qualifications and who has recent experience with properties having similar characteristics of location and type, the extent to which the fair value of investment property (either used in case the fair value model is used or disclosed in case the cost model is used) is based on valuation by such an independent valuer. If there is no such valuation, that fact should be disclosed as well.
- These points should be disclosed in the income statement:

- The amount of rental income derived from investment property
- Direct operating expenses (including repairs and maintenance) arising from investment property that generated rental income
- Direct operating expenses (including repairs and maintenance) arising from investment property that did not generate rental income
- The existence and the amount of any restrictions that may potentially affect the realizability of investment property or the remittance of income and proceeds from disposal to be received
- Material contractual obligations to purchase or build investment property or for repairs, maintenance, or improvements thereto

In addition to the disclosures just outlined, an entity that uses the fair value model should also present a reconciliation of the carrying amounts of the investment property, from the beginning to the end of the reporting period. An entity that applies the cost model should also disclose: the depreciation methods used, the useful lives or the depreciation rates used, and the gross carrying amount and the accumulated depreciation (aggregated with accumulated impairment losses) at the beginning and end of the period. It should also disclose a reconciliation of the carrying amount of investment property at the beginning and the end of the period as well as the fair value of investment property carried under the cost model.

JOURNAL ENTRIES

Accounting for Marketable Equity Securities

Initial investment designated as held-for-trading. To record an investment that management intends to trade for a profit in the short term.

Investment in equity securities—held-for-trading	xxx	
Cash		xxx

Initial investment designated as available-for-sale. To record an investment that management intends to hold as a long-term investment.

Investment in equity securities—available-for-sale	xxx	
Cash		xxx

Gain or loss on investment designated as held-for-trading. The first entry shows the immediate recognition in the current period of a loss due to a drop in the value of an investment designated as a trading security as well as the related tax effect. The second entry shows the immediate recognition in the current period of a gain due to an increase in the value of an investment designated as a trading security as well as the related tax effect.

Loss on equity security investment	xxx	
Deferred tax benefit	xxx	
Investment in equity securities—held-for-trading		xxx
Provision for income taxes		xxx

Investment in equity securities—held-for-trading	xxx	
Provision for income taxes	xxx	
Gain on equity security investments		xxx
Deferred tax liability		xxx

Gain or loss on investment designated as available-for-sale. The first entry shows an unrealized loss in the Other Comprehensive Income account on an investment designated as available-for-sale as well as the related tax effect. The second entry shows an unrealized gain in the Other Comprehensive Income account on an investment designated as available-for-sale as well as the related tax effect. In both cases, the tax effect is netted against the Investment account rather than against a Provision for Income Taxes account.

Unrealized loss on equity security investment	xxx	
Deferred tax benefit	xxx	
Investment in equity securities—available-for-sale		xxx

Investment in equity securities—available-for-sale	xxx	
Unrealized gain on equity security investment		xxx
Deferred tax liability		xxx

Impairment in value of equity investments classified as available-for-sale. When a drop in the value of an available-for-sale investment is judged to be other than temporary, the first journal entry should be used to recognize the drop in value. The entry includes the initial recognition of a related income tax benefit on the transaction. If one had previously recognized an income tax benefit associated with the loss but prior to its classification as a permanent decline in value, the offset to the deferred tax benefit would have been the investment account itself. If so, one should shift the offset from the investment account to an income tax liability account, as shown in the second journal entry.

Loss on equity securities	xxx	
Deferred tax benefit	xxx	
Unrealized loss on available-for-sale securities		xxx
Provision for income taxes		xxx

Loss on equity securities	xxx	
Unrealized loss on available-for-sale securities		xxx
Provision for income taxes		xxx

Transfers of Equity Securities between Available-for-Sale and Trading Portfolios

Shift investment designation from a trading security to an available-for-sale security. To shift the designation of a security currently recorded as a trading security to that of an available-for-sale security. The journal entry includes provisions for the recognition of any gains or losses on the fair value of the securities transferred since they were last marked to market.

Investments—available-for-sale	xxx	
Loss on equity securities	xxx	
Investments—held-for-trading		xxx
Gain on equity securities		xxx

Shift investment designation from an available-for-sale security to a trading security. To shift the designation of a security currently recorded as an available-for-sale security to that of a trading security, which requires the recognition of all unrealized gains or losses. The first entry assumes the recognition of unrealized losses on securities, while the second entry assumes the recognition of unrealized gains.

Investments—held-for-trading	xxx	
Loss on equity securities	xxx	
Investments—available-for-sale		xxx
Unrealized loss on available-for-sale securities		xxx

Investments—held-for-trading	xxx	
Unrealized gain on available-for-sale securities	xxx	
Investments—available-for-sale		xxx
Gain on equity securities		xxx

Accounting for Investments in Debt Securities

Initial investment designated as held-for-trading. To record an investment in debt securities that management intends to trade for a profit in the short term.

Investment in debt securities—held-for-trading	xxx	
Cash		xxx

Initial investment designated as available-for-sale. To record an investment in debt securities that management intends to hold as a long-term investment.

Investment in debt securities—available-for-sale	xxx	
Cash		xxx

Initial investment designated as held-to-maturity. To record an investment in debt securities that management has the intent and ability to hold to the debt maturity date.

Investment in debt securities—held-to-maturity	xxx	
Cash		xxx

Gain or loss on debt investment designated as held-for-trading. The first journal entry records the immediate recognition in the current period of a loss due to a drop in the value of a debt investment designated as a trading security. The second journal entry records the immediate recognition of a gain due to an increase in the value of a debt investment designated as a trading security.

Loss on debt security investment	xxx	
Investment in debt securities—held-for-trading		xxx

Investment in debt securities—held-for-trading	xxx	
Gain on debt securities—held-for-trading		xxx

Gain or loss on debt investment designated as available-for-sale. The first journal entry records the immediate recognition in the current period of a loss due to a drop in the value of a debt investment designated as an available-for-sale security, which is reported in the Other Comprehensive Income section of the income statement. The second journal entry records the immediate recognition of a gain due to an increase in the value of a debt investment designated as an available-for-sale security.

Unrealized loss on debt security investment	xxx	
Deferred tax benefit	xxx	
Investment in debt securities—available-for-sale		xxx

Investment in debt securities—available-for-sale	xxx	
Unrealized gain on debt security investment		xxx
Deferred tax liability		xxx

Impairment in value of debt investments classified as held-to-maturity. To record a loss on a held-to-maturity debt investment, which occurs only when management considers a drop in value to be permanent in nature.

Loss on debt investment	xxx	
Investment in debt securities—held-to-maturity		xxx

Transfers of Debt Securities among Portfolios

Shift investment designation from the available-for-sale debt security portfolio to the trading debt security portfolio. Any debt security shifted from the available-for-sale portfolio to the trading portfolio must be recorded at its fair value on the date of the transfer. The first journal entry records the recognition of a loss on the transfer date while the second entry records a gain.

Investment in debt securities—held-for-trading	xxx	
Loss on debt securities	xxx	
Investment in debt securities—available-for-sale		xxx
Unrealized loss on debt securities—available-for-sale		xxx

Investment in debt securities—held-for-trading	xxx	
Unrealized gain on debt securities—available-for-sale	xxx	
Investment in debt securities—available-for-sale		xxx
Gain on holding debt securities		xxx

Shift investment designation from the available-for-sale debt security portfolio to the held-to-maturity debt security portfolio. Any debt security shifted from the available-for-sale portfolio to the held-to-maturity portfolio must be recorded at its fair value on the date of the transfer. The first journal entry records the recognition of a loss on the transfer date while the second entry records a gain.

Investment in debt securities—held-to-maturity	xxx	
Loss on debt securities	xxx	
Investment in debt securities—available-for-sale		xxx
Unrealized loss on debt securities—available-for-sale		xxx

Investments in debt securities—held-to-maturity	xxx	
Unrealized gain on debt securities—available-for-sale	xxx	
Investment in debt securities—available-for-sale		xxx
Gain on holding debt securities		xxx

Shift investment designation from the held-to-maturity debt security portfolio to the available-for-sale debt security portfolio. To record any accumulated gain or loss on a held to-maturity debt security being transferred into the available-for-sale portfolio, which is recorded in Other Comprehensive Income. The first entry records a loss on the transaction while the second entry records a gain.

Investment in debt securities—available-for-sale	xxx	
Unrealized loss on holding debt securities	xxx	
Investment in debt securities—held-to-maturity		xxx

Investment in debt securities—available-for-sale	xxx	
Investment in debt securities—held-to-maturity		xxx
Unrealized gain on holding debt securities		xxx

Shift investment designation from the held-to-maturity debt security portfolio to the held-for-trading debt security portfolio. To record any accumulated gain or loss on a held-to-maturity debt security being transferred into the held-for-trading portfolio. The first entry records a loss on the transaction while the second entry records a gain. There are no unrealized gains or losses to recognize, since no gains or losses are recognized for held-to-maturity debt investments.

Investment in debt securities—held-for-trading	xxx	
Loss on holding debt securities	xxx	
Investment in debt securities—held-to-maturity		xxx

Investment in debt securities—held-for-trading	xxx	
Investment in debt securities—held-to-maturity		xxx
Gain on holding debt securities		xxx

The Equity Method of Accounting for Investments

Investment (equity method). To record the company's cash or loan investment in another business entity.

Investment in [company name]	xxx	
Cash		xxx
Notes payable		xxx

Investment (equity method), record share of investee income. To record the company's proportional share of the income reported by [name of company in which investment was made]. The second entry records in a Deferred Taxes account the amount of income taxes related to the investor's share of investee income.

Investment in [company name]	xxx	
Income from equity share in investment		xxx

Income tax expense	xxx	
Deferred tax liability		xxx

Investment (equity method), record dividends from investee. To reduce the amount of the original investment by the cash value of dividends received. In the second entry, we assume that a deferred income tax was already recognized when the investor recorded a share of investee income and now shift the portion of the deferred taxes related to dividends received to the Taxes Payable account.

Cash	xxx	
Investment in [company name]		xxx

Deferred tax liability	xxx	
Taxes payable		xxx

Investment (equity method), record periodic amortization of incremental increase in investee assets due to allocation of excess purchase price. To reduce the equity in the investee's income as recorded by the investor, based on the periodic amortization of any investee assets to which value was assigned as a result of the apportionment of an investment cost exceeding the carrying value of the investee.

Equity in [company name] income	xxx	
Investment in [company name]		xxx

Investment (equity method), sale of investment at a gain. To record a cash payment in exchange for liquidation of an investment, including the recordation of a gain on the transaction. The second entry recognizes an income tax on the investment gain above any income tax previously deferred, and also shifts any previously deferred income tax into a current Taxes Payable account.

	Debit	Credit
Cash	xxx	
Investment in [company name]		xxx
Gain on sale of investment		xxx

	Debit	Credit
Income tax expense	xxx	
Deferred tax liability	xxx	
Taxes payable		xxx

Investment (equity method), sale of investment at a loss. To record a cash payment in exchange for liquidation of an investment, including the recordation of a loss on the transaction. The second entry eliminates any previously deferred income tax.

	Debit	Credit
Cash	xxx	
Loss on sale of investment	xxx	
Investment in [company name]		xxx

	Debit	Credit
Deferred tax liability	xxx	
Income tax expense		xxx

RECORDKEEPING

When the designation of securities is changed between the trading account and available-for-sale account, there is an impact on the recognition of unrealized gains on available-for-sale securities. Since a simple designation change can impact reported income, one should sufficiently document the reason for the change to the point where the altered designation is highly credible. This documentation should be attached to the journal entry used to shift securities into a different account.

The bond ledger sheet and the stock ledger sheet described in the Forms and Reports section should be retained in the accounting archives, since they will be needed as evidentiary material for any type of financial or income tax audit. Given the potentially large sums tracked through these sheets, it is best to store them in a locked area, or at least to retain duplicate copies in separate locations. If they are stored in the computer system, be sure to print them out for archiving purposes whenever a year of computer data is being purged from the computer system.

The investment approval form is the primary form of evidence showing that an investment has been approved and recorded properly in the correct investment portfolio. Accordingly, it should be stored as part of the accounting records. Typically, the general ledger accountant will attach a copy of the completed form to the journal entry form used to make the initial investment entry. The treasury staff should also retain a copy of the form, usually filed by date.

When recording investments under the equity method of accounting, make sure to record an associated income tax expense using the tax rate at which the company eventually intends to liquidate its investment (e.g., the rates applying either to the receipt of dividends or from sale of the underlying stock). The assumption of eventual disposition should be documented clearly in all journal entries recording the income tax expense and changes in the expense.

Under the equity method of accounting, if there is a difference between the amount paid by the investor and the carrying value of the investee, at least some portion of the difference must be assigned informally to the assets of the investee and amortized, with an amortization entry regularly being made by the investor. A spreadsheet documenting the allocation to assets and the associated amortization must be created and retained in order to provide sufficient evidence for how the amortization entry was derived. A copy of the amortization spreadsheet should be attached to every amortization journal entry.

8 BUSINESS COMBINATIONS AND CONSOLIDATED FINANCIAL STATEMENTS

DEFINITIONS OF TERMS

Acquiree. The business or businesses the acquirer obtains control of in a business combination.

Acquirer. The entity that obtains control of the acquiree.

Acquisition. An entity pays cash, stock, and/or debt to acquire some portion of the voting stock of another entity, and the acquired entity continues to exist as a separate legal entity.

Accounting consolidation. The process of combining the financial statements of a parent company and one or more legally separate and distinct subsidiaries as if they were a single economic entity.

Business Combination. A transaction or other event in which an acquirer obtains control of one or more businesses.

Cash-generating unit. The smallest identifiable group of assets that generates cash inflows from continuing use, largely independent of the cash inflows associated with other assets or groups of assets.

Controlling financial interest. Equity investors have voting rights to make decisions about an entity's activities, must absorb the entity's expected losses, and are entitled to the entity's expected residual returns.

Consolidated financial statements. The financial statements of a group presented as those of a single economic entity.

Fair value less costs to sell. The amount that can be obtained from the sale of an asset or cash-generating unit in an arm's-length transaction between knowledgeable, willing parties, less the costs of disposal.

Goodwill. The future economic benefits arising from assets that are not individually identified and separately recognized; measured as the excess of the cost of a business combination over the fair value of the identifiable assets and liabilities acquired, including contingent liabilities, at the date of combination.

Impairment loss. The amount by which the carrying value of an asset or a cash-generating unit exceeds its recoverable amount.

Noncontrolling interest. The portion of the profit or loss and net assets of a subsidiary attributable to equity interests that are not owned, directly or indirectly through subsidiaries, by the parent.

Recoverable amount. The amount of an asset or a cash-generating unit that is the higher of its fair value less costs to sell and its value in use.

Reverse acquisition. Transaction in which the acquiring entity issues such a large proportion of its shares to the owners of the entity being acquired that the owners of the nominal acquiree become the majority owners of the acquiring entity.

Value in use. The present value of the future cash flows expected to be received from an asset or cash-generating unit.

CONCEPTS AND EXAMPLES[1]

General Concepts

The key issue in a business combination is how to account for the purchase price. In essence, the acquiring entity records the acquiree's assets and liabilities at their fair values as of the date of the transaction and then amortizes these fair values over the useful economic lives of the underlying assets. If the purchase price exceeds the fair values of all acquired assets and liabilities, as is often the case, the excess amount is recorded by the acquiring entity as goodwill.

It is also possible for a business combination to be completed where the acquisition price is less than the fair value of the acquiree's assets and liabilities, which often is referred to as a bargain purchase, creating what is called *negative goodwill*. IFRS 3 requires that, before negative goodwill is recognized, the allocation of fair values is to be revisited, and that all liabilities—including contingencies—be reviewed. After this is completed, if indeed the fair values of identifiable assets acquired net of all liabilities assumed exceeds the total cost of the transaction, then negative goodwill is recognized immediately, as a gain. However, if the business combination includes a purchase price that is contingent on future events, then any excess negative goodwill is recorded as a deferred credit (to be used as an offset against any additional payments to the acquiree's shareholders) until the contingent

[1] *Some portions of this section are adapted with permission from Chapters 14 and 16 of Steven Bragg,* ***Ultimate Accountants' Reference*** *(Hoboken, NJ: John Wiley & Sons, 2006).*

conditions are resolved, after which the balance is recognized as a gain from the acquisition.

Goodwill is not subject to amortization. Instead, companies must conduct periodic impairment testing, as noted in the Goodwill Impairment Testing discussion.

Determining the Fair Value of Acquiree Assets

When a business combination is completed, the acquiring entity must determine the fair value of all acquiree assets and liabilities and record them on its books at their fair values, subject to the goodwill provisions noted in the last section. The next list itemizes how these 11 assets and liabilities are to be valued (Appendix B of IFRS 3).

1. **Financial instruments traded in an active market**—Current market values.
2. **Financial instruments not traded in an active market**—Estimated fair values, determined on a basis consistent with relevant price-earnings ratios, dividend yields, and expected growth rates of comparable securities of entities having similar characteristics.
3. **Receivables**—Present values of amounts to be received determined by using current interest rates, less allowances for uncollectible accounts.
4. **Inventories**
   a. Finished goods and merchandise inventories—Estimated selling prices less the sum of the costs of disposal and a reasonable profit.
   b. Work in process inventories—Estimated selling prices of finished goods less the sum of the costs of completion, costs of disposal, and a reasonable profit.
   c. Raw material inventories—Current replacement costs.
5. **Plant and equipment**—At market value as determined by appraisal; in the absence of market values, use depreciated replacement cost. Land and building are to be valued at market value.
6. **Identifiable intangible assets** (such as patents and licenses)—Fair values determined primarily with reference to active markets as per IAS 38. In the absence of market data, use the best available information, with discounted cash flows being useful only when information about cash flows which are directly attributable to the asset, and which are largely independent of cash flows from other assets, can be developed.
7. **Net employee benefit assets or obligations for defined benefit plans**—The actuarial present value of promised benefits, net of the fair value of related assets. (Note that an asset can be recognized only to the extent that it would be available to the enterprise as refunds or reductions in future contributions.)
8. **Tax assets and liabilities**—The amount of tax benefits arising from tax losses or the taxes payable in respect to net earnings or loss. The amount to be recorded is net of the tax effect of restating other identifiable assets and liabilities at fair values.

9. **Liabilities** (such as notes and accounts payable, long-term debt, warranties, claims payable)—Present value of amounts to be paid determined at appropriate current interest rates; discounting is not required for short-term liabilities where the effect is immaterial.
10. **Onerous contract obligations and other identifiable liabilities**—The present value of the amounts to be disbursed.
11. **Contingent liabilities**—The amount that a third party would charge to assume those liabilities. The amount must reflect expectations about cash flows rather than the single most likely outcome. (Note that the subsequent measurement should fall under IAS 37 and in many cases would call for derecognition. IFRS 3 provides an exception for such contingent liabilities, in that subsequent measurement is to be at the higher of the amount recognized under IFRS 3 or the amount mandated by IAS 37.)

Often, in business combinations, part of the consideration paid is in recognition of ongoing product development efforts by the acquiree. IFRS requires immediate expensing of research costs incurred but capitalization and amortization of development expenditures. In a slight departure from this general principle, purchased in-process research and development (IPR&D) acquired as part of a business combination should generally be recorded as an intangible asset. This asset is separate and distinct from goodwill. Thus costs ineligible for recognition when incurred internally by the acquirer may need to be recognized when acquired in a business purchase transaction.

To qualify for capitalization, IPR&D must meet all these criteria:

- It must be separately identifiable.
- It must be a resource that is controlled.
- It must be a probable source of future economic benefits.
- It must have a reliably measurable fair value.

IPR&D is separately identifiable if it arises from contractual or other legal rights. If the IPR&D is not contractual or separable, it would form part of the amount attributable to goodwill.

Subsequent expenditure on IPR&D acquired in a business combination, if recognized as an asset separate from goodwill, would be accounted for in accordance with the requirements in IAS 38. If the subsequent expenditure is properly characterized as research, the expenditure would be recognized as an expense when it is incurred; but if it is in the nature of development, and assuming that the entity can satisfy all of the criteria for deferral in IAS 38, then the expenditure would be capitalized.

If some acquired assets will be redundant with those of the acquiring entity and are therefore to be disposed of, the cost allocated to these assets should equal their estimated net residual value. If the acquirer plans to dispose of an entire subsidiary of the acquiree, then the expected cash flows from the subsidiary through the expected disposition date are used to assign a value to it. When the subsidiary is sold, any difference between the subsidiary's carrying value on the disposition date and sale proceeds is reapportioned to other company assets. If the difference is caused by events occurring after the business combination date, however, then the difference is reported as a gain or loss.

It may not be possible to determine precisely the fair values of some assets, estimated liabilities, or contingent liabilities as of the date of the business combination. IFRS 3 states that the amounts initially recognized may be changed subsequently only if an error occurred (or where the agreement has contingent aspects). In such a case, in compliance with IAS 8, the adjustment is made retrospectively to the financial statements so that, as revised, they appear as if the error had never happened. Where there is a change in estimate, however, this is to be accounted for prospectively, and the adjustment will flow through income for the current and, if appropriate, future periods. The only exception to this rule is in the case of an adjustment to deferred taxes. Where a deferred tax asset did not qualify for recognition originally but subsequently is realized, the benefit is treated as income but an adjustment is also made to the originally recorded goodwill, also through income.

Identification and Evaluation of Intangible Assets

One item on the preceding list of assets and liabilities is intangible assets. As part of a business combination, the acquiring entity must identify all of the acquiree's intangible assets, valuing them separately from goodwill. Examples of intangibles that should be separately recognized include

Computer software	Licensing agreements
Construction permits	Noncompetition agreements
Customer lists and relationships	Operating or use rights
Databases	Order backlog
Employment contracts	Patented and unpatented technology
Franchise agreements	Servicing contracts
Internet domain names	Trade secrets
Lease agreements	Trademarks and service marks

These intangible assets are to be recognized at their fair values and amortized by the acquiring entity during the period over which they are expected to directly or indirectly generate cash flows for the entity. Intangible assets may be assigned a considerable proportion of the purchase price of an acquiree, so a large amount of attention should be paid to the proper valuation of these assets.

Example of a purchase transaction

The Arabian Knights Security Company acquires the Templar Security Agency for €800,000 cash. Templar's statement of financial position as of the acquisition date, is listed next, showing both the carrying value and fair value of each item.

	Carrying value	*Fair value*
Cash	€48,000	€48,000
Accounts receivable, net of bad debts	240,000	230,000
Inventory	50,000	20,000
Equipment, net of depreciation	190,000	170,000
Intangible assets—databases	--	80,000
Intangible assets—licensing agreements	--	70,000
Total assets	€528,000	€618,000
Current liabilities	€90,000	€90,000
Long-term debt	400,000	380,000
Shareholders' equity	38,000	148,000
Total liabilities and equity	€528,000	€618,000

The fair value of Templar's long-term debt has declined, since the debt is at a fixed interest rate, and the current market rate at the time of the acquisition has increased from that fixed rate. Independent appraisals are used to determine the decline in the fair value of Templar's equipment and inventory, though these appraisals also indicate that significant value can be assigned to several intangible assets.

The computation of goodwill resulting from the acquisition is

Purchase price		€800,000
Cash	€48,000	
Accounts receivable, net of bad debts	230,000	
Inventory	20,000	
Equipment, net of depreciation	170,000	
Intangible assets—databases	80,000	
Intangible assets—licensing agreements	70,000	
Current liabilities	(90,000)	
Long-term debt	(380,000)	148,000
Goodwill (excess of purchase price over fair value)		€652,000

The journal entry format used to record a purchase transaction is shown later in the Journal Entries section.

When the acquiring entity records the assets subject to depreciation of the acquired entity, it does so using the fair value of those assets as of the acquisition date. None of the depreciation formerly recognized by the acquired entity carries forward to the books of the acquirer.

Goodwill Impairment Testing

The amount of goodwill that a company maintains on its books as an asset must be tested at least annually to see if it has been impaired (though more frequent testing is needed if adverse events arise). If so, any impaired goodwill must be charged to expense in the current reporting period.

For the purpose of impairment testing, goodwill acquired in a business combination should, from the acquisition date, be allocated to each of the acquirer's cash-generating units, or groups of cash-generating units, that are expected to benefit from the synergies of the combination (irrespective of whether other assets or liabilities of the acquiree are assigned to those units). A cash-generating unit is the smallest level of identifiable group of assets that generates cash inflows that are largely independent of the cash inflows from other assets or groups of assets.

Each cash-generating unit, or groups of cash-generating units, to which goodwill is allocated and tested for impairment should

- Represent the lowest level within the entity at which the goodwill is monitored for internal management purposes; and
- Not be larger than an operating segment determined in accordance with IFRS 8, *Operating Segments.*

Three steps are required for goodwill impairment testing. First, determine the recoverable amount of a cash-generating unit which is the higher of the cash-generating unit's fair value less costs to sell (net selling price) and its value in use, which is the present value of the estimated future cash flows expected to be derived from the cash-generating unit. Second, compare the recoverable amount of the cash-generating unit to its carrying value. If the recoverable value exceeds the carrying value, then there is no goodwill impairment, and the third testing step is not required.

However, if the carrying value exceeds the recoverable value of the cash-generating unit, then a third step is required. In this third step, allocate the recoverable value of the cash-generating unit as of the testing date to its assets (including intangible assets) and liabilities, with the remainder (if any) being assigned to goodwill. If the amount of goodwill resulting from this calculation is less than the carrying amount of goodwill, then the difference is impaired goodwill and must be charged to expense in the current period.

IAS 36 has imposed a requirement that reversals may not be recognized for previous write-downs in goodwill. Conversely, a later recovery in value of the cash-generating unit will be allocated to assets other than goodwill.

Example of goodwill impairment testing

The Arabian Knights Security Company acquired the Templar Security Agency (Templar) and operates it as a cash-generating unit. For the most recent year of operations, Templar had annual revenues of €900,000 and carrying values of assets and liabilities that are

Cash	€32,000
Accounts receivable, net of bad debts	250,000
Inventory	15,000
Equipment, net of depreciation	190,000
Intangible assets	135,000
Goodwill	652,000
Current liabilities	(110,000)
Long-term debt	(390,000)
Total	€774,000

In order to determine the fair (recoverable) value of Templar, Arabian locates several companies whose operations are similar to those of Templar. The management of Arabian believes that the recoverable value of Templar is €720,000 (the greater of the net selling price of €720,000 and the present value of estimated future cash flows of €711,000) and so uses this amount in this assessment:

Recoverable value of the Templar cash-generating unit	€720,000
Carrying amount of cash-generating unit, including goodwill	774,000
Recoverable value above or below carrying value	€(54,000)

Templar's carrying amount exceeds its recoverable value, so additional testing is required to determine the extent of goodwill impairment. To do so, Arabian Knight's accounting staff compares the carrying value of the cash-generating unit and fair value of Templar's assets and liabilities (excluding goodwill) in the next table to compute the implied value of goodwill and the extent of goodwill impairment.

	Carrying value	*Fair value*
Cash	€32,000	€32,000
Accounts receivable, net of bad debts	250,000	230,000
Inventory	15,000	10,000
Equipment, net of depreciation	190,000	200,000
Intangible assets	135,000	100,000
Goodwill	652,000	--
Current liabilities	(110,000)	(110,000)
Long-term debt	(390,000)	(370,000)
Totals	€774,000	€ 92,000
Recoverable value of Templar cash-generating unit		€720,000
Implied fair value of goodwill		628,000
Carrying value of goodwill		652,000
Impairment loss		€(24,000)

Based on this analysis, goodwill impairment loss is €24,000 and Templar must charge €24,000 of its goodwill asset to expense in the current period.

A company can select any date for impairment testing, but once selected, the same date must be used every year.

The aggregate amount of goodwill impairment losses should be reported as a separate line item in the operating section of the income statement.

Contingent Consideration

In many business combinations, the purchase price is not completely fixed at the time of the exchange; instead, it is dependent on the outcome of future events. The accounting for contingent consideration is handled differently depending on the reason for the payment. Two major types of future events commonly might be used to modify the purchase price: the performance of the acquired entity (acquiree) and the market value of the consideration given for the acquisition.

The most frequently encountered contingency involves the postacquisition performance of the purchased entity or operations. The contractual agreement dealing with this often is referred to as an "earn-out" provision. It typically calls for additional payments to be made to the former owners of the acquiree if defined revenue or earnings thresholds are met or exceeded. These may extend for several years after the acquisition date, and may define varying thresholds for different years. For example, if the acquiree, during its final pretransaction year, generated revenues of €4 million, there might be additional sums due if the acquired operations produced €4.5 million or greater revenues in year one after the acquisition, €5 million or greater in year two, and €6 million in year three.

The contingent consideration may be deemed likely to become payable and may be measured reliably at the date of the acquisition; if this is the case, an estimate should be included in the cost of the acquisition. If all or some of the accrued contingent consideration is not later earned and paid, an adjustment has to be made to the cost of the acquisition. Since the inclusion of the contingent payment most likely resulted in initial or increased recognition of goodwill, the revision for nonpayment normally will cause an adjustment to be made to goodwill.

The less often observed type of postacquisition adjustment that can occur is where the acquirer has guaranteed the value of the consideration given. For example, if €3 million of shares were issued to effect the purchase, the acquiring entity might warrant that the market price would not fall below, say, €2.8 million over a defined time horizon, generally no longer than one or two years. If the value of the consideration given declines below this threshold level, and the acquirer is obliged to make a further payment of shares, this is not accounted for as an additional cost of the business combination. Rather, the newly increased number of shares issued is adjusted against the value of the equity originally issued, not against the purchase price of the acquiree. Thus, the acquirer's capital accounts would be adjusted, typically by increasing the aggregate par or stated value of shares issued (since more shares will now be given) and decreasing additional paid-in capital.

Noncontrolling Interests

An acquiring company may sometimes acquire less than 100% of the acquiree's stock. When this happens, the acquiring entity presents the entire amount of the acquiree's assets, liabilities, revenue, and expenses as well as offsetting line items for the proportion of each of these items that the acquiring entity does not own. In the income statement, the noncontrolling interest in the profit or loss of a subsidiary is deducted from or added to consolidated profit or loss. The format of this offset in the statement of financial position is a credit in the shareholders' equity section, based on preacquisition carrying values.

If the acquiring company increases its ownership share of another entity through the purchase of additional shares of its stock, this additional investment is recorded as an increase in the Investment in Subsidiary account.

Leveraged Buyouts

When a change in control arises in a leveraged buyout (LBO), then it is necessary to step up the reported value of all assets and liabilities of the entity being purchased. If there is no change in control, then the transaction is essentially a recapitalization, in which case the original asset and liability values shall continue to be reported. The determination of a change in control is addressed by a flowchart in the Decision Trees section. In all cases, control of the holding company must be substantive, genuine, and not intended to be merely temporary.

The normal structure of an LBO transaction is that a holding company is formed that acquires an operating company. If the holding company is owned by the current owners of the operating company, then there should be no revaluation of the existing assets and liabilities of the operating company, since the substance of the LBO is that the operating company has not really been sold to a new owner. This is a significant issue, since revaluation can result in significantly different operating results because of changes in depreciation and amortization.

Reverse Acquisitions

A reverse acquisition occurs when the acquiring entity issues such a large proportion of its subsequently outstanding shares to the owners of the acquiree that control passes to the acquiree due to the number of additional shares issued by the acquirer, and the owners of the acquiree effectively become the majority owners of the acquiring entity. A reverse acquisition is most commonly used when a public shell corporation nominally acquires a nonpublic operating company, which uses the transaction to transform itself into a publicly held entity without an initial public offering (IPO).

IFRS 3 acknowledges the possibility of reverse acquisitions, where the acquirer becomes a subsidiary of the acquired company. In such cases, notwithstanding the nominal or legal identification of the acquirer and acquiree, for accounting purposes, the enterprise whose shareholders now control the combined entity is the acquirer.

Because the substance of a reverse transaction is that the owners of the acquiree own the majority of the entire company, the financial statements should show the historical financial results of the acquiree, with the results of the acquiring entity added as of the reverse acquisition date. The financial statements would show the acquiring company's assets and liabilities at fair value and those of the acquiree at historical cost. In addition, the retained earnings of only the acquiree will appear in the consolidated financial statements.

When a nonpublic company is, in substance, buying a public shell company, the valuation of the transaction should be based on the fair value of the net assets acquired, since there may be so little trading in the shell's shares that those shares cannot be accurately valued. Thus, it is very unlikely that goodwill will be recognized in such a transaction.

Business Combinations Achieved in Stages

In many instances, control over another entity is not achieved in a single transaction but instead as the culmination of a series of transactions. For example, one enterprise may acquire a 25% interest in another entity, followed by another 20% some time later, and then followed by another 10% at yet a later date. The last step gives the acquirer a 55% interest and, thus, control. The accounting issue is to determine at what point in time the business combination took place and how to measure the cost of the acquisition.

IFRS 3 stipulates that the cost of the acquisition is measured with reference to the cost and fair value data as of that exchange transaction. In the foregoing example, therefore, it would be necessary to look to the consideration given for each of the three separate purchases of stock. If one or more of these transactions were noncash, they would have to be valued as described earlier in this section. To the extent that the value of the consideration given differed from the fair value of the underlying net assets, measured at the date of the respective exchange, goodwill or negative goodwill would have to be computed and accounted for as stipulated under IFRS. Conceivably, some of these purchases could be made at premiums over fair value and others could be consummated at discounts from fair values.

In the example just mentioned, the first acquisition results in a 25% holding in the investee, which is over the threshold where significant influence is assumed to be exerted by the investor. Thus, the equity method should be employed beginning at the time of the first exchange and continuing through the second exchange (when a 45% ownership interest is achieved). The difference between cost and the fair value of the underlying interest in the net assets of the investee is to be treated as goodwill or negative goodwill and accounted for consistent with the provisions of IFRS 3. The amount of goodwill (or negative goodwill) at the date of the first exchange transaction should not be merged into the next step transaction computation of goodwill. In other words, each step in the transaction sequence should be accounted for as a separate acquisition.

When control is achieved, the fair value of the subsidiary's net assets will be represented by a blending of fair values computed at different points in time. In the example, the fair value of net assets is determined 25% by the first purchase transaction, another 20% by the second transaction, and the final 10% by the third transaction, at the time control is achieved. Since values will vary and will be dependent on the dates of the respective transactions, it is possible that both goodwill and negative goodwill might be present simultaneously.

Business Combinations in Which the Acquirer Holds Less than 100% of the Equity Interests in the Acquiree at the Acquisition Date

When an acquirer obtains a majority interest, but not 100% ownership, in another entity, the portion of the acquired operation not owned by the acquirer but claimed (in an economic sense) by outside interests, is referred to as *noncontrolling interest.* In such situations, IFRS 3 specifies that identifiable assets and liabilities are valued entirely at fair value, and the noncontrolling interest is correspondingly adjusted to reflect the relevant proportion of the net assets.

Under IFRS 3, all identifiable (i.e., excluding goodwill) assets and liabilities are recognized at their respective fair values, including those corresponding to the noncontrolling's ownership interest. This means that there is a step-up in recorded amounts to reflect the valuation being placed on the enterprise indirectly by the new majority owner.

If the acquiring company purchases less than 100% of an acquiree, then

- The controlling interest in the acquiree's net assets recognized is equal to the sum of the controlling interest's proportional interest in the fair values of identifiable assets acquired and liabilities assumed plus goodwill, if any.
- The noncontrolling interest in the acquiree's net assets recognized is equal to the sum of the noncontrolling interest's proportional interest in the fair values of identifiable assets acquired and liabilities assumed.

The Exposure Draft (ED), *Proposed Amendments to IFRS 3*, issued in June 2005, proposed that even if the acquirer obtains less than 100% of the acquiree, goodwill attributable to the noncontrolling interest will be recognized, contrary to current practice. It is anticipated that this change (described as applying full fair value accounting to business combinations) will occur by late 2008.

Spin-Off Transactions

A spin-off transaction occurs when a company unilaterally transfers a subsidiary to its shareholders. If the company owns a small percentage of the subsidiary, then the spin-off is essentially a property dividend and is recorded at the fair value of the subsidiary.

If the company owns a majority of the shares of the subsidiary, then the transaction is recorded at the carrying value of the subsidiary's assets and liabilities. If the subsidiary has a positive net carrying value, this net worth is recorded as a reduction of the parent company's retained earnings. If the subsidiary has a negative net carrying value, this is recorded as an addition to the parent company's additional paid-in capital account. These transactions are shown later in the Journal Entries section.

It is also possible to have a reverse spin-off, where the subsidiary being transferred to shareholders has larger assets, revenues, earnings, and fair value than the parent company, and usually retains its senior management. In this case, the proper accounting treatment is to follow the substance of the transaction and treat the spun-off subsidiary as the parent company.

Disposal of a Business Segment

If a company disposes of some portion of a business segment that is a significant proportion of a cash-generating unit and that constitutes a separate business, then it should allocate to the disposed segment some portion of the goodwill assigned to the cash-generating unit. This allocation should be based on the relative fair values of the disposed segment and the remainder of the cash-generating unit. When this occurs, the company should conduct a goodwill impairment test for the remaining cash-generating unit, to verify that there is no goodwill impairment.

Consolidation Requirements

Under IAS 27, a parent entity must present consolidated financial statements, unless *all* of these four conditions apply:

1. The reporting entity is a wholly owned subsidiary, or if the owners of the noncontrolling interests, including those not otherwise entitled to vote, unanimously agree that the parent need not present consolidated financial statements;
2. Its securities are not publicly traded;
3. It is not in the process of issuing securities in public securities markets; and
4. The immediate or ultimate parent publishes consolidated financial statements that comply with IFRS.

Consolidated financial statements are to consolidate a parent and all of its subsidiaries, foreign and domestic, when those entities are controlled by the parent. For making this determination, control is presumed to exist when the parent owns, directly or indirectly through subsidiaries, more than one-half of the voting power of an entity—unless, in exceptional circumstances, it can be clearly demonstrated that this ownership does not connote control. Control also exists when the parent owns one-half or less of the voting power of an entity, when there is

1. Power over more than one-half of the voting rights by virtue of an agreement with other investors (e.g., a voting trust);
2. Power to govern the financial and operating policies of the entity under a statute or an agreement;
3. Power to appoint or remove the majority of the members of the board of directors or equivalent governing body and control of the entity is by that board or body; or
4. Power to cast the majority of votes at meetings of the board of directors or equivalent governing body and control of the entity is by that board or body.

If a subsidiary has its own majority-owned subsidiaries, then it should consolidate the results of these lower-tier subsidiaries into its own financial statements, which will in turn be consolidated into the results of the parent company.

DECISION TREE

Determination of Control in a Leveraged Buyout

When an operating company is acquired by a holding company as part of an LBO, and if control over the operating company has not changed since the LBO, then the transaction is accounted for as a recapitalization. Conversely, its assets and liabilities must be recorded at their fair value if control actually has changed. The decision tree shown in Exhibit 8.1 shows the LBO control criteria needed to determine the presence or absence of a change of control.

Exhibit 8.1 Determination of Control in a Leveraged Buyout Transaction

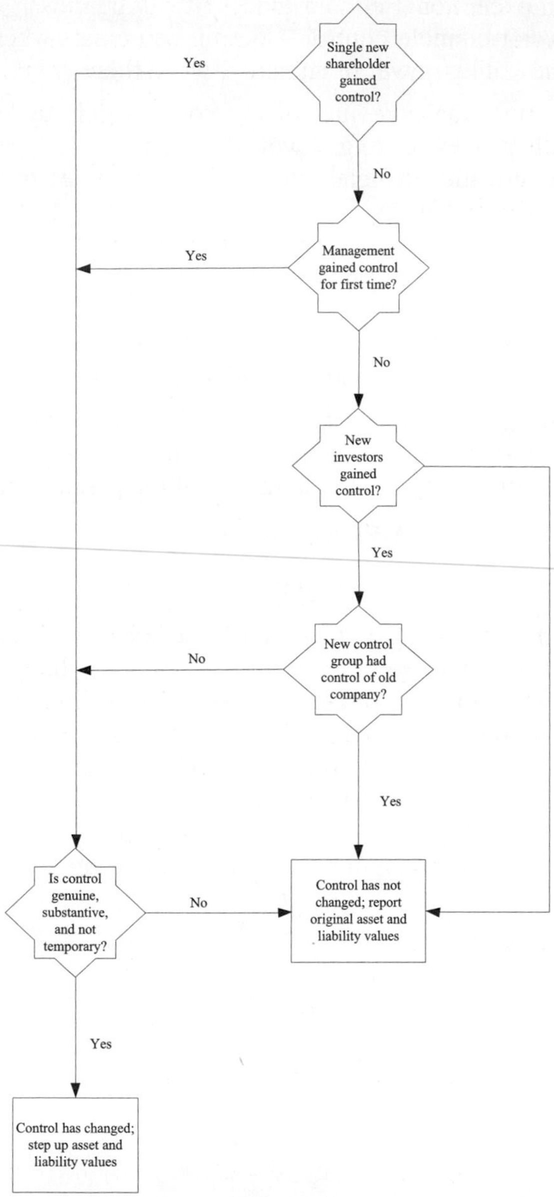

Single new shareholder gained control?
Yes
No
Management gained control for first time?
Yes
No
New investors gained control?
Yes
No
New control group had control of old company?
No
Yes
Is control genuine, substantive, and not temporary?
No
Control has not changed; report original asset and liability values
Yes
Control has changed; step up asset and liability values

POLICIES

- **The allocation of the acquisition purchase price to an acquiree's in-process research and development (IPR&D) activities shall not exceed the estimated fair value of those activities.** This policy is designed to keep the accounting staff from assigning an excessive proportion of the purchase price to R&D activities, a portion of which then may be charged to expense immediately, allowing for the recognition of greater levels of profitability in the future. Under IFRS, the purchased IPR&D acquired as part of a business combination generally should be recorded as an intangible asset, subject to the limitation that this cannot exceed fair value. In practice, the valuation of R&D is extremely difficult, so this policy is designed primarily to stop egregious allocations from occurring.

- **The amortization period of newly acquired assets will be limited to the depreciation periods used for the same asset classes by the acquiring company.** IFRS allows acquired assets to be amortized over their useful economic lives. This guidance could be construed as allowing for longer amortization periods than the acquiring company uses for similar assets that it acquires by other means, thereby spreading the amortization expense over more periods than normal and inflating reported profits. To avoid this, the acquiring entity should use its standard amortization periods for similar classes of assets as the maximum cap for the amortization periods of acquired assets.
- **Goodwill impairment testing shall be conducted on the same date in every year.** It is possible that a cash-generating unit's financial results could vary substantially over several reporting periods. If so, the accounting department could be tempted to conduct goodwill impairment testing following a month having excellent reporting results, in an effort to obtain the highest possible recoverable value for the cash-generating unit, and thereby avoid any goodwill impairment. This policy is designed to ensure a consistent application of the goodwill impairment methodology on the same date of every year, thereby eliminating the cherry-picking of testing dates.

PROCEDURES

Use this six-step procedure to test for goodwill impairment.

1. Use valuation methods to calculate the recoverable value of the cash-generating unit, which is defined as the higher of the cash-generating unit's fair value less costs to sell (net selling price) and its value in use. If there are publicly held comparable entities, then determine the average multiple of their fair values to revenues, and apply this multiple to the trailing 12-month revenues of the cash-generating unit (less estimated selling costs) to estimate its net selling price. Determine the expected present value of cash flows from the cash-generating unit for the next five years (using the form shown in the Forms and Reports section) to calculate its value in use. The recoverable value is the higher of the net selling price and value in use.
2. Compile the carrying value of all identifiable assets and liabilities of the cash-generating unit as of the impairment measurement date.
3. Compare the cash-generating unit's recoverable value to the carrying value of its assets and liabilities. If the recoverable value exceeds the carrying value, then there is no impairment, and no further testing is required.

4. If the carrying value exceeds the recoverable value, then goodwill has been impaired. Proceed to the next step.
5. Allocate the recoverable value of the cash-generating unit to its assets (including intangible assets, except for goodwill) and liabilities. After this allocation is completed, any excess recoverable value should be assigned to goodwill.
6. Compare the newly assigned goodwill value to the previously booked goodwill value. If the previously booked goodwill is higher than the newly assigned goodwill value, then charge the difference to expense in the current period.

CONTROLS

- **Verify that the amount of the purchase price allocated to research and development is not excessive.** A common ploy is for the acquiring entity to allocate an excessive proportion of the purchase price to an acquiree's R&D activities and then to charge most of this allocation to expense in the current period, thereby enhancing reported profits in later periods, on the basis that the allocated amount exceeds fair value or recoverable amount. A recurring internal audit program could require the examination of these allocated amounts for any new acquisitions, comparing them to industry benchmarks or past practice or requiring the use of an independent appraisal. This is an extremely difficult area in which to determine fair value, so the methods used may vary or require the use and comparison of multiple valuation techniques.
- **Verify that all intangible assets were identified properly and that adequate values were assigned to them.** The single largest problem with accounting for business combinations is that companies can avoid amortization of the purchase price by parking a large proportion of the purchase price in the goodwill asset account. Though an excessive quantity of goodwill eventually may be written off through goodwill impairment testing, this may not take place for some time. Until a write-down occurs, the acquiring company will report excessively high profit levels. To avoid this issue, the acquisition accounting procedure should include the use of an independent appraiser and an outside audit firm to properly designate all intangible assets and ensure that adequate values are assigned to them. In addition, a recurring internal audit program should call for the verification that this procedure is being followed and that the independent appraiser is truly independent. The result should be a reduction in the proportion of acquisition prices that are allocated to goodwill.
- **Verify the reason for contingent payments.** There is a substantial incentive for the accounting staff to treat a contingent payment as one mandated by a decline in the value of the original purchase package, since this does not call for the creation of an offsetting asset, such as higher fixed asset or goodwill values (as would be the case if the payment were treated as an earn-out). Accordingly, a recurring internal audit program should require the internal audit staff to review the acquisition documents to ensure that the transaction is being treated correctly.

FORMS AND REPORTS

Impairment Testing with Expected Present Value Form

One way to conduct goodwill impairment testing is to compare periodically the carrying value of the assets and liabilities of a cash-generating unit to the cash flow expected to be generated by that cash-generating unit. A sample form that can be used for this analysis is shown in Exhibit 8.2. To use the form, enter three scenarios for revenues, expenses, and profits, along with their associated probabilities of occurrence, in the appropriate columns for each of the next five years. Then multiply the cash flow (assumed here to be the earnings before interest, taxes, and depreciation [EBITDA]) for each scenario by its probability to arrive at the expected cash flow by period. Next, use the risk-free interest rate to calculate the present value of the expected cash flows for all five years. Then enter the carrying values of all the assets and liabilities listed in the lower left corner of the form and total them. Compare the expected present value (EPV) of all cash flows to the estimated net selling price to determine the recoverable value. Finally, compare recoverable value with total carrying value of all assets and liabilities. If the carrying values are higher than the cash flows, then goodwill impairment has occurred.

FOOTNOTES

When a business combination is completed, the acquiring entity should disclose the name and a brief description of the acquiree as well as the percentage of voting shares acquired. It should also note the period for which the results of the acquiree are included in the income statement of the acquiring entity. The disclosure should also note the cost of the acquisition, the number of shares issued, and the value of those shares as well as the basis for determining the share value. Contingent payments also must be noted. An example follows.

> In September 2007, the Company completed the acquisition of Superior Night Vision Corporation ("Night"), acquiring all of the issued outstanding shares of Night through a cash tender offer, which was completed at a purchase price of €13.50 per share. Night provides portable night vision equipment to the security and military industries. The transaction was valued at approximately €12 million plus related transaction costs and was funded from borrowings under the Company's credit facility. The purchase price was allocated to assets acquired and liabilities assumed based on estimated fair value as of the date of acquisition. The Company acquired assets of €18 million and assumed liabilities of €7 million. The Company recorded €200,000 in goodwill, which is not deductible for income tax purposes, and intangible assets of €800,000. The €800,000 of intangible assets is attributable to customer relationships and noncompete agreements with useful lives of five years. The operating results of the acquired business are included in the Company's financial statements in the Commercial segment from the effective date of the acquisition, September 2007.

Exhibit 8-2: Form for Impairment Testing with Expected Present Value

Impairment Testing with Recoverable Value (RV) Analysis

	Year 1			Year 2			Year 3			Year 4			Year 5		
	Scenario 1	Scenario 2	Scenario 3	Scenario 1	Scenario 2	Scenario 3	Scenario 1	Scenario 2	Scenario 3	Scenario 1	Scenario 2	Scenario 3	Scenario 1	Scenario 2	Scenario 3
Probabilty (sum to 100%)															
Revenue:															
Expenses:															
Cost of goods sold															
Salaries & wages															
Depreciation															
Interest															
Taxes															
Other expenses															
Total expenses:															
Net profit															
EBITDA															

Expected cash flow by period

Interest Rate ______

Present value of cash flows ______

Carrying Value Analysis:	Current period
Cash	
Accounts receivable	
Inventories	
Fixed assets	
Identifiable intangibles	
Goodwill	
Accounts payable	( )
Debt	( )
Total carrying value	
Present value of cash flows	
Net selling price Recoverable Value (RV)	
RV over/under carrying value	

If an acquiring entity acquires a number of other business entities that are individually immaterial but are material in aggregate, then disclosure must be made of the number of entities acquired and a brief description of their activities. Disclosure also must be made in aggregate of the acquisition cost, the number of shares issued, and the value assigned to those shares. Furthermore, the amounts of acquired goodwill related to each business segment should be noted. An example follows.

During 2007, the Company acquired these three entities for a total of €4,900,000 in cash:

- Squelch, Inc., based in Silence, Montana, the developer and patent owner of a technology to reduce the sound emitted by noisy children.
- ThinKid, Inc., based in LowCal, Mexico, a producer of appetite reduction supplements for children.
- WhereRU, Inc., based in Area 51, New Mexico, a producer of child-tracking GPS wristwatches.

The goodwill recognized in these transactions totaled €3,250,000 and that amount is expected to be fully deductible for tax purposes. All of the goodwill was assigned to the Child Monitoring business segment.

When contingent payments are made by the acquiring entity to shareholders of the acquiree subsequent to the business combination date, the amount of these payments should be disclosed as well as the nature of the contingent event that caused the payments to be made. Two examples follow.

1. The acquiree's shareholders arc eligible to receive contingent consideration in each of the four successive annual periods commencing on January 1, 2008, based on the acquiree's operating results in each period. The contingent consideration in each period consists of a payment equal to 10% of the net income of the acquiree for that period, provided that the cumulative sum of all such contingent consideration does not exceed €2 million. At December 31, 2008, the Company has accrued €92,000 in consideration payable for the first annual period.
2. On June 30, 2008, the Company paid €410,000 to the acquiree's shareholders. Of that amount, €392,000 represented the additional consideration due on the first anniversary and €92,000 represented contingent consideration based on net incomc.

When intangible assets are acquired as part of business combination, disclosure must include the total amount assigned to each major intangible asset class, the amount of any major class of intangible assets. In subsequent periods, disclosure must be made of the gross carrying amount and accumulated amortization for each class of intangible asset, the aggregate amortization expense for the period, and the estimated amortization expense for each of the next five fiscal years. An example follows.

Other intangible assets consisted of these assets as of December 31, 2008:

	Gross carrying value	*Accumulated amortization*	*Net carrying value*
Long-term contracts	€320,000	€(180,000)	€140,000
Customer relationships	680,000	(200,000)	480,000
Noncompete agreements	40,000	(35,000)	5,000
Trade names	108,000	(32,000)	76,000
Totals	€1,148,000	€(447,000)	€701,000

Amortization expense was €149,000 for the year ended December 31, 2008. Based on the Company's amortizable intangible assets as of December 31, 2008, the Company expects related amortization expense for the five succeeding fiscal years to approximate €183,000, €148,000, €130,000, €125,000, and €115,000.

In each reporting period, disclosure must be made for each cash-generating unit of the amount of goodwill, the aggregate amount of impairment losses recognized, and the amount of any goodwill included in the disposal of a cash-generating unit. Disclosure also must be made of any significant changes in the allocation of goodwill between cash-generating units. An example follows.

Changes in the carrying amount of goodwill for the year ended December 31, 2008, by reporting segment were

	Geographical information systems	*IT security*	*Total*
Balance at January 1, 2008	€14,600,000	€3,300,000	€17,900,000
ABC Acquisition	2,200,000		2,200,000
Contingent consideration—ABC Co.	200,000		200,000
Contingent consideration—DEF Co.		170,000	170,000
Adjustment to acquired goodwill—ABC Co.	(80,000)		(80,000)
Goodwill impairment—ABC Co.	(710,000)		(710,000)
Goodwill impairment—DEF Co.		(360,000)	(360,000)
Balance at December 31, 2008	€16,210,000	€3,110,000	€19,320,000

If adjustments are made in the current period to the allocation of the purchase price that was recorded in a prior period, the nature and amount of the adjustment should be disclosed. An example follows.

The Company acquired the Templar Security Agency in December 2008. The purchase price of the acquisition exceeded the preliminary fair value of the net assets acquired by €652,000, which was assigned to goodwill. During 2009, the Company completed its fair value analysis of Templar's intangible assets and expensed €70,000 of the excess purchase price representing licensing agreements that had previously been assigned to goodwill. The Company's management concluded that Templar would not recognize significant cash flow from the licensing agreements. The €70,000 charge is aggregated into the "Other operating expenses" line item in the accompanying consolidated statement of income and comprehensive income for the year ended December 31, 2009.

If an impairment loss is recognized, disclosure must include a description of the circumstances causing the impairment, the amount of the loss, and the method used to derive fair value. An example follows.

> The Company's judicial case management cash-generating unit is tested for impairment in the fourth quarter, after the annual forecasting process has been completed. Due to the consolidation of the number of case management providers and the increasing conversion of district court software solutions into statewide systems, operating profits and cash flows were lower than expected throughout the reporting year. Based on that trend and expectations of similar performance in the future, the earnings forecast of the case management cash-generating unit for the next five years was revised, and the recoverable value of that unit was estimated using the expected present value of future cash flows. This resulted in a goodwill impairment loss of €1,045,000 being recognized by the case management cash-generating unit.

The amount of R&D expense acquired also must be disclosed, as well as the amount written off in the current period and identification of the line item in the income statement within which this expense is aggregated. An example follows.

> In March 2008, the Company assigned a value of €900,000 to the research and development projects it acquired in a business combination with Squelch, Inc. These projects had not yet been completed as of the date of acquisition; technological feasibility for these projects has not yet been established, nor do they have any future use in research and development activities. The Company recorded the value of these projects, €900,000, as an asset—purchased in-process research and development (IPR&D)—since they are separately identifiable, controlled by the Company, a probable source of future economic benefits, and have a reliably measurable fair value.

JOURNAL ENTRIES

Initial purchase transaction. To record the initial acquisition of another entity. The key elements of this entry are the goodwill asset and the form of payment made to the owners of the acquired entity.

Cash	xxx	
Accounts receivable, net of bad debts	xxx	
Inventory	xxx	
PPE, net of depreciation	xxx	
Intangible assets (various)	xxx	
Goodwill	xxx	
Current liabilities		xxx
Long-term debt		xxx
Notes payable (paid to acquired entity shareholders)		xxx
Cash (paid to acquired entity shareholders)		xxx

Negative goodwill offset. To record the recognition of negative goodwill as income.

Negative goodwill	xxx	
Gain on purchase		xxx

Write-off of impaired goodwill. If the recoverable value of a cash-generating unit is less than its carrying value, then some portion of the goodwill asset originally created as part of the acquisition of that cash-generating unit must be charged to expense in the current period. The entry is shown next.

Impaired goodwill expense	xxx	
Goodwill		xxx

Increased investment in subsidiary. If the acquiring entity does not initially purchase all outstanding shares of an acquiree, but later purchases additional shares, then the additional payment is recorded as an increase in the investment in the subsidiary. The entry is shown next.

Investment in subsidiary	xxx	
Cash		xxx

Spin-off of subsidiary. When a parent company spins off a subsidiary to its shareholders in which it held a majority ownership interest, it must remove the carrying value of the subsidiary's assets and liabilities from its books. If the net carrying value of the subsidiary is positive, the parent company records this as a retained earnings reduction, as shown.

Accounts payable	xxx	
Debt	xxx	
Other liabilities	xxx	
Retained earnings	xxx	
Cash		xxx
Accounts receivable		xxx
Inventory		xxx
PPE		xxx
Other assets		xxx

If the net carrying value of the subsidiary is negative, the parent company records this as an addition to the additional paid-in capital account, as shown.

Accounts payable	xxx	
Debt	xxx	
Other liabilities	xxx	
Cash		xxx
Accounts receivable		xxx
Inventory		xxx
PPE		xxx
Other assets		xxx
Additional paid-in capital		xxx

9 CURRENT LIABILITIES, PROVISIONS, CONTINGENCIES, AND EVENTS AFTER THE REPORTING PERIOD

DEFINITIONS OF TERMS

Accrued liability (or accrued expenses). A liability for which there is a clear commitment to pay, but for which an invoice has not yet been received. Typical accrued liabilities are wages payable, payroll taxes payable, and interest payable.

Adjusting events after the reporting period. Those post–reporting period events that provide evidence of conditions that existed at the statement of financial position date and that thus require recognition in the financial statements.

Authorization date. The date when the financial statements would be considered legally authorized for issue.

Constructive obligation. An obligation resulting from an entity's actions such that the entity

- By an established pattern of past practice, published policies, or a sufficiently specific current statement has indicated to third parties that it will accept certain responsibilities; and
- As a result, has created a valid expectation in the minds of third parties that it will discharge those responsibilities.

Contingent asset. A possible asset that arises from past events and whose existence will be confirmed only by the occurrence or nonoccurrence of one or more uncertain future events not wholly within the control of the reporting entity.

Contingent liability. An obligation that is either

- A possible obligation arising from past events, the outcome of which will be confirmed only on the occurrence or nonoccurrence of one or more uncertain future events which are not wholly within the control of the reporting entity; or
- A present obligation arising from past events which is not recognized either because it is not probable that an outflow of resources will be required to settle an obligation, or where the amount of the obligation cannot be measured with sufficient reliability.

Current liabilities. Entity obligations whose liquidation is reasonably expected to require the use of existing resources properly classified as current assets, or which will result in the creation of other current liabilities. Obligations that are due on demand or will be due on demand within one year or one operating cycle, if longer, are current liabilities.

Estimated liability. An obligation that is known to exist, although the obligee may not be known, and the amount and timing of payment is subject to uncertainty; now referred to as "provisions."

Events after the reporting period. Events that occur after an entity's accounting year-end (also referred to as the statement of financial position date) and the date they are authorized for issue that would necessitate either adjusting the financial statements or disclosure. The concept is comprehensive enough to cover both favorable and unfavorable post–statement of financial position date events.

Guarantee. A commitment to honor an obligation of another party in the event certain defined conditions are not met.

Indirect guarantee of indebtedness of others. A guarantee under an agreement that obligates one entity to transfer funds to a second entity upon the occurrence of specified events under conditions whereby (1) the funds are legally available to the creditors of the second entity, and (2) those creditors may enforce the second entity's claims against the first entity.

Legal obligation. An obligation that derives from the explicit or implicit terms of a contract, or from legislation or other operation of law.

Liability. A present obligation of the reporting entity arising from past events, the settlement of which is expected to result in an outflow from the entity of resources embodying economic benefits.

Nonadjusting events after the reporting period. Those post–reporting period events that are indicative of conditions that arose after the statement of financial position date and which thus would not necessitate adjusting financial statements. Instead, if significant, these would require disclosure.

Obligating event. An event that creates a legal or constructive obligation that results in an entity having no realistic alternative but to settle that obligation.

Onerous contract. A contract in which the unavoidable costs of meeting the obligations under the contract exceed the economic benefits expected to be received therefrom.

Operating cycle. The average length of time necessary for an entity to convert inventory to receivables to cash.

Possible loss. A contingent loss based on the occurrence of a future event or events whose likelihood of occurring is more than remote but less than likely.

Probable loss. A contingent loss based on the occurrence of a future event or events that are likely to occur.

Provision. Liabilities having uncertain timing or amount.

Remote loss. A contingent loss based on the occurrence of a future event or events whose likelihood of occurring is slight.

Restructuring. A program that is planned and controlled by management and that materially changes either the scope of business undertaken by the entity or the manner in which it is conducted.

Trade account payable. A payable for which there is a clear commitment to pay, and that generally involves an obligation related to goods or services. Typically, it also involves a payment due within one year and is considered to include anything for which an invoice is received.

Unearned revenue. Obligation created by payments made by customers prior to delivery of services or products to them.

CONCEPTS AND EXAMPLES[1]

Current Liabilities—Presentation

IAS 1 requires that the reporting entity must present current and noncurrent assets, and current and noncurrent liabilities, as separate classifications on the face of its statement of financial position, except when a liquidity presentation provides more relevant and reliable information.

IAS 1 also makes explicit reference to the requirements imposed by IAS 32 concerning financial assets and liabilities. Since such common statement of financial position items as trade and other receivables and payables are within the definition of financial instruments, information about maturity dates is already required under IFRS. While most trade payables and accrued liabilities will be due within 30 to 90 days, and thus are understood by all financial statement readers to be current, this requirement would necessitate additional disclosure, either on the face of the statement of financial position or in the footnotes thereto, when this assumption is not warranted.

If a company has a long-term payable that is approaching its termination date, then any amount due under its payment provisions within the next year must be recorded as a current liability. If only a portion of total payments due under the liability are expected to fall within that time frame, then only that portion of the liability should be reported as a current liability. A common situation in which this issue arises is for a copier leasing arrangement, where the most recent payments due under the agreement are split away from the other copier lease payments that are not due until after one year. This situation commonly arises for many types of long-term equipment and property rentals.

Current Liabilities—Accounts Payable

Accounts payable arise primarily from the acquisition of materials and supplies to be used in the production of goods or in conjunction with providing services. Payables that arise from transactions with suppliers in the normal course of business, which customarily are due in no more than one year, may be stated at their face amount rather than at the present value of the required future cash flows.

Current Liabilities—Notes Payable

Notes payable are more formalized obligations that may arise from the acquisition of materials and supplies used in operations or from the use of short-term credit to purchase capital assets. Although international accounting standards do not explicitly address the matter, it is widely agreed that monetary obligations, other than those due currently, should be presented at the present value of the amount owed, thus giving explicit recognition to the time value of money. Most would agree, however, that this exercise would not be needed to present current obligations fairly. (Of

---

[1] *Much of the information in this section is adapted with permission from Chapter 18 of Steven Bragg,* ***Ultimate Accountants' Reference*** *(Hoboken, NJ:John Wiley & Sons, 2006).*

course, if the obligations are interest-bearing at a reasonable rate determined at inception, this is not an issue.)

Current Liabilities—Dividends Payable

Dividends payable become a liability of the entity when a dividend has been declared; however, jurisdictions vary as to how this is interpreted. Under most continental European company laws, only the shareholders in general meeting can declare a dividend, so the function of the directors is to propose a dividend, which itself does not give rise to a liability. In other jurisdictions, the decision of the board of directors would trigger recognition of a liability. Declared dividends that are paid within a short period of time after the declaration date, with a statement of financial position prepared in between the two events, are classified as current liabilities.

Current Liabilities—Unearned Revenues or Advances

If a customer makes a payment for which the company has not made a corresponding delivery of goods or services, then the accountant must record the cash receipt as a customer advance, which is a liability. This situation commonly arises when a customer order is so large or specialized that the company is justified in demanding cash in advance of the order. Another common situation is when customers are required to make a deposit, such as when a property rental company requires one month's rent as a damage deposit. This may be recorded as a current liability if the corresponding delivery of goods or services is expected to be within the next year. If the offset is expected to be further in the future, however, it should be recorded as a long-term liability.

Current Liabilities—Agency Liabilities

Agency liabilities result from the legal obligation of the entity to act as the collection agent for employee or customer taxes owed to various federal, state, or local government units. Examples of agency liabilities include value-added tax, sales taxes, income taxes withheld from employee paychecks, and employee social security contributions, where mandated by law. In addition to agency liabilities, an employer may have a current obligation for unemployment taxes. Payroll taxes typically are not legal liabilities until the associated payroll actually is paid, but in keeping with the concept of accrual accounting, if the payroll has been accrued, the associated payroll taxes should be as well.

Accrued liabilities (also referred to as *accrued expenses*) have their origin in the end of period adjustment process required by accrual accounting. They represent economic obligations, even when the legal or contractual commitment to pay has not yet been triggered, and as such must be given recognition if the matching concept is to be adhered to. Commonly accrued liabilities include wages and salaries payable, interest payable, rent payable, and taxes payable.

Current Liabilities—Bonuses

Rather than waiting until bonuses are fully earned and payable to recognize them, one should accrue some proportion of the bonuses in each reporting period if there is a reasonable expectation that they will be earned and that the eventual amount of the bonus can be approximately determined.

Current Liabilities—Commissions

The amount of commissions due to the sales staff may not be precisely ascertainable at the end of the reporting period, since they may be subject to later changes based on the precise terms of the commission agreement with the sales staff, such as subsequent reductions if customers do not pay for their delivered goods or services. In this case, commissions should be accrued based on the maximum possible commission payment, minus a reduction for later eventualities; the reduction can be reasonably based on historical experience with actual commission rates paid.

Current Liabilities—Compensated Absences

A company is required to accrue for compensated absences, such as vacation time, when employees have already earned the compensated absence, the right has vested, the payment amount can be estimated, and payment is probable. If a company is required to pay for earned compensation absences, then vesting has occurred. A key issue is any use-it-or-lose-it provision in the company employee manual, which has a dramatic effect on the amount of compensated absences to be accrued. If such a policy exists, then the accrual is limited to the maximum amount of the carry-forward. If not, the accrual can be substantial if the vested amount has built up over many years. The payment amount typically is based on the most recent level of pay for accrual calculation purposes rather than any estimate of future pay levels at the time when the absence is actually compensated.

Example of vacation accrual

Mr. Harold Jardin has earned 450 hours of vacation time, none of which has been used. He currently earns €28.50 per hour. His employer should maintain an accrued vacation expense of €12,825 (= 450 hours × €28.50/hour) to reflect this liability. Conversely, if the company has a "use it or lose it" policy that allows only an 80-hour carry-forward at the end of each year, then the accrual is only €2,280 (= 80 hours × €28.50/hour).

The amount of sick time allowed to employees is usually so small that there is no discernible impact on the financial statements if the time is accrued or not. This is particularly true if unused sick time cannot be carried forward into future years as an ongoing residual employee benefit that may be paid out at some future date. If these restrictions are not the case, then the accounting treatment of sick time is the same as for vacation time.

Current Liabilities—Debt

There are a number of circumstances under which a company's debt must be recorded as current debt on the statement of financial position. They are

- If the debt must be repaid entirely within the current operating cycle
- If the debt is payable over a longer term, but it is also due on demand at the option of the lender

- If the company is in violation of any loan covenants and the lender has not waived the requirement
- If the company is in violation of any loan covenants, the lender has issued a short-term waiver, but it is unlikely that the company can cure the violation problem during the waiver period
- If the debt agreement contains a subjective acceleration clause, and there is a strong likelihood that the clause will be activated

If only a portion of a company's debt falls under the preceding criteria, then only that portion impacted by the rules must be recorded as current debt, with the remainder recorded as long-term debt.

A company that intends to refinance current debt with long-term debt can classify this debt as long-term on the statement of financial position, but only if the refinancing occurs or a refinancing agreement is signed after the statement of financial position date but before the issuance date. The amount of current debt that can be reclassified as long-term debt, if this approach is taken, cannot exceed the amount of debt to be refinanced; not only that, but it is limited by the amount of new debt that can be acquired without violating existing loan covenants.

Current Liabilities—Employee Terminations

If company management has formally approved of a termination plan designed to reduce headcount, the expenses associated with the plan should be recognized at once if the accountant can reasonably estimate the associated costs. The *first requirement* after plan approval is that the plan clearly outlines the benefits to be granted. This information usually specifies a fixed dollar payout based on the amount of time that an employee has been with the company. The second requirement is that the plan must specify the general categories and numbers of employees to be let go, since the accountant needs this information to extend the per-person benefit costs specified in the first requirement. Further significant changes to the plan should be unlikely; this locks in the range of possible costs that are likely to occur as a result of the plan, rendering the benefit cost accrual more accurate.

Example of accrual for termination benefits

The Good Samaritan Company plans to close its Dunkirk branch office and terminate the employment of all people working there. The action is scheduled for three months in the future. The company's employee manual states that all employees are entitled to one week of severance pay for each year worked for the company. The average number of weeks of severance under this policy is 3.5 for the group to be terminated, and the average pay for the 29 employees affected is €39,500. Thus, the company must immediately accrue a termination expense of €77,101 (= 29 employees × €39,500 average pay / 52 weeks × 3.5 weeks).

Current Liabilities—Property Taxes

A company should accrue the monthly portion of its property tax liability based on its assessed property tax liability during the fiscal year of the taxing authority.

Example of a property tax accrual

The Good Samaritan Company owns property in County Clare, Ireland. Good Samaritan operates under a calendar year, while the county's fiscal year ends on June 30. It sends a notice to Good Samaritan that its property tax assessment will be €33,600 in the current fiscal year, payable in March of the following year. Accordingly, Good Samaritan's controller begins to accrue 1/12 of the assessment in each month of County Clare's fiscal year, beginning in July. The entry is

Property tax expense	2,800	
Property tax payable		2,800

When Good Samaritan pays the assessment in March of the following year, it makes this entry:

Property tax payable	33,600	
Cash		33,600

Since property taxes typically are paid prior to the end of the taxing authority's fiscal year, this series of transactions will likely result in a debit balance in the Property Tax Payable account for the last few months of the fiscal year, since the company will not have recorded the entire property tax expense until that time.

Current Liabilities—Royalties

If a company is obligated to pay a periodic royalty to a supplier of goods or services that it uses or resells, then it must accrue an expense if the amount is reasonably determinable. A sample royalty calculation worksheet can be found in the Forms and Reports section.

Current Liabilities—Wages

Even if a company times its payroll period-end dates to correspond with the end of each reporting period, this will only ensure that no accrual is needed for those employees who receive salaries (since they usually are paid through the payroll period ending date). The same is not usually true for those who receive an hourly wage; in their case, the pay period may end as much as a week prior to the actual payment date. Consequently, the accountant must accrue the wage expense for the period between the pay period end date and the end of the reporting period. This wage expense can be estimated on a person-by-person basis, but an easier approach is to accrue based on a historical hourly rate that includes average overtime percentages. One must also include the company's share of all payroll taxes in this accrual. An example of an unpaid wage accrual form is shown later in the Forms and Reports section.

Provisions

Under IAS 37, *Provisions, Contingent Liabilities, and Contingent Assets*, those liabilities for which amount or timing of expenditure is uncertain are deemed to be provisions.

IAS 37 provides a comprehensive definition of the term "provision." It mandates, in a clear-cut manner, that a provision should be recognized *only* if

- The entity has a present obligation (legal or constructive) as a result of a past event;
- It is probable that an outflow of resources embodying economic benefits will be required to settle the obligation; and
- A reliable estimate can be made of the amount of the obligation.

Many reserves found in financial statements in days past are clearly not permitted under IFRS. IAS 37 offers in-depth guidance on the topic of provisions. The Standard explains each of the key words in the definition of the term "provision" in detail. Explanations and clarifications offered by the Standard are summarized next.

- **Present obligation.** The Standard opines that in almost all cases, it will be clear when a present obligation exists. The notion of an obligation in the Standard includes not only a legal obligation (e.g., deriving from a contract or legislation) but also a constructive obligation. It explains that a constructive obligation exists when the entity from an established pattern of past practice or stated policy has created a valid expectation that it will accept certain responsibilities.
- **Past event.** There must be some past event that has triggered the present obligation—an accidental oil spill, for example. An accounting provision cannot be created in anticipation of a future event. The entity must also have no realistic alternative to settling the obligation caused by the event.
- **Probable outflow of resources embodying economic benefits.** For a provision to qualify for recognition, it is essential that it is not only a present obligation of the reporting entity, but also it should be probable that an outflow of resources embodying benefits used to settle the obligation will in fact result. For the purposes of this Standard, "probable" is defined as "more likely than not." A footnote to the Standard states that this interpretation of the term "probable" does not necessarily apply to other IAS.
- **Reliable estimate of the obligation.** The Standard recognizes that using estimates is common in the preparation of financial statements and suggest that by using a range of possible outcomes, an entity usually will be able to make an estimate of the obligation that is sufficiently reliable to use in recognizing a provision. Where no reliable estimate can be made, though, no liability is recognized.

Twelve other salient features of provisions explained by the Standard are discussed next.

1. For all estimated liabilities that are included within the definition of provisions, the amount to be recorded and presented on the statement of financial position should be the *best estimate*, at the statement of financial position date, of the amount of expenditure that will be required to settle the obligation. Often this is referred to as the "expected value" of the obligation, which may be defined operationally as the amount the entity would pay, currently, either to settle the actual obligation or to provide consideration to a third party to assume it (e.g., as a single-occurrence insurance premium). For estimated liabilities comprised of large numbers of relatively small,

similar items, weighting by probability of occurrence can be used to compute the aggregate expected value; this is often used to compute accrued warranty reserves, for example. For those estimated liabilities consisting of only a few (or a single) discrete obligations, the most likely outcome may be used to measure the liability when there is a range of outcomes having roughly similar probabilities; but if possible outcomes include amounts much greater (and lesser) than the most likely, it may be necessary to accrue a larger amount if there is a significant chance that the larger obligation will have to be settled—even if that is not the most likely outcome as such.

The concept of "expected value" can be best explained through a numeric illustration.

Example: Provision for warranty claims

Wizard Company manufactures and sells pinball machines under warranty. Customers are entitled to refunds if they return defective machines with valid proof of purchase. Wizard estimates that if all machines sold and still in warranty had major defects, total replacement costs would equal €1,000,000; if all those machines suffered from minor defects, the total repair costs would be €500,000. Wizard's past experience, however, suggests that only 10% of the machines sold will have major defects and that another 30% will have minor defects. Based on this information, the expected value of the product warranty costs to be accrued at year-end would be computed as

Expected value of the cost of refunds:

Resulting from major defects:	€1,000,000 × 0.10	=	€100,000
Resulting from minor defects:	€ 500,000 × 0.30	=	150,000
No defects:	€ 0 × 0.60	=	--
	Total	=	€250,000

2. The "risks and uncertainties" surrounding events and circumstances should be taken into account in arriving at the best estimate of a provision. However, as pointedly noted by the Standard, uncertainty should not be used to justify the creation of excessive provisions or a deliberate overstatement of liabilities.
3. The Standard also addresses the use of present values or discounting (i.e., recording the estimated liability at present value, after taking into account the time value of money). Discounting is required when the effect would be material, but it can be ignored if immaterial in effect. Thus, provisions estimated to be due farther into the future will have more need to be discounted than those due currently. As a practical matter, all but trivial provisions should be discounted unless the timing is unknown (which makes discounting a computational impossibility).

   IAS 37 clarifies that the discount rate applied should be consistent with the estimation of cash flows (i.e., if cash flows are projected in nominal terms). That is, if the estimated amount expected to be paid out reflects whatever price inflation is anticipated to occur between the statement of financial position date and the date of ultimate settlement of the estimated obligation, then a nominal discount rate should be used.

4. Future events that may affect the amount required to settle an obligation should be reflected in the provision amount where there is sufficient objective evidence that such future events will in fact occur. For example, if an entity believes that the cost of cleaning up a plant site at the end of its useful life will be reduced by future changes in technology, the amount recognized as a provision for cleanup costs should reflect a reasonable estimate of cost reduction resulting from any anticipated technological changes. In many instances, however, making such estimates will not be possible.
5. IFRIC 1 mandates that changes in decommissioning provisions should be recognized prospectively (i.e., by amending future depreciation charges).
6. Gains from expected disposals of assets should not be taken into account in arriving at the amount of the provision (even if the expected disposal is closely linked to the event giving rise to the provision).
7. Reimbursements by other parties should be taken into account when computing the provision only if it is virtually certain that the reimbursement will be received.
8. Changes in provisions should be considered at each statement of financial position date, and provisions should be adjusted to reflect the current best estimate. If upon review it appears that it is no longer probable that an outflow of resources embodying economics will be required to settle the obligation, then the provision should be reversed through current period results of operations.
9. Use of provision is to be restricted to the purpose for which it was recognized originally. A reserve for plant dismantlement, for example, cannot be used to absorb environmental pollution claims or warranty payments. If an expense is set against a provision that was originally recognized for another purpose, it would camouflage the impact of the two different events, distorting income performance and possibly constituting financial reporting fraud.
10. Provisions for future operating losses should not be recognized. This is explicitly proscribed by the Standard, since future operating losses do not meet the definition of a liability at the statement of financial position date (as defined in the Standard) and the general recognition criteria set forth in the Standard.
11. Present obligations under *onerous contracts* should be recognized and measured as a provision. The Standard introduces the concept of onerous contracts, which it defines as contracts under which the unavoidable costs of satisfying the obligations exceed the economic benefits expected. Executory contracts that are not onerous do not fall within the purview of this Standard. In other words, the expected negative implications of such contracts (executory contracts that are not onerous) cannot be recognized as a provision.

    The Standard mandates that unavoidable costs under a contract represent the "least net costs of exiting from the contract." Such unavoidable costs should be measured at the *lower* of

- The cost of fulfilling the contract; *or*
- Any compensation or penalties arising from failure to fulfill the contract.

12. Provisions for restructuring costs are recognized only when the general recognition criteria for provisions are met. A constructive obligation to restructure arises only when an entity has a *detailed formal plan* for the restructuring which identifies at least: the business or the part of the business concerned, principal locations affected, approximate number of employees that would need to be compensated for termination resulting from the restructuring (along with their function and location), expenditure that would be required to carry out the restructuring, and information as to when the plan is to be implemented.

    Furthermore, the recognition criteria also require that the entity should have raised a valid expectation among those affected by the restructuring that it will, in fact, carry out the restructuring by starting to implement that plan or announcing its main features to those affected by it. Thus, until both the conditions just mentioned are satisfied, a restructuring provision cannot be made based upon the concept of constructive obligation. In practice, given the strict criteria of IAS 37, restructuring costs are more likely to become recognizable when actually incurred in a subsequent period.

    Only *direct* expenditures arising from restructuring should be provided for. Such direct expenditures should be both necessarily incurred for the restructuring *and* not associated with the ongoing activities of the entities. Thus, a provision for restructuring would not include such costs as cost of retraining or relocating the entity's current staff members or costs of marketing or investments in new systems and distribution networks (such expenditures are categorically disallowed by the Standard, as they are considered to be expenses relating to the future conduct of the business of the entity and thus are not liabilities relating to the restructuring program). Also, identifiable future operating losses up to the date of an actual restructuring are not to be included in the provision for a restructuring (unless they relate to an onerous contract). Furthermore, in keeping with the general measurement principles relating to provisions outlined in the Standard, the specific guidance in IAS 37 relating to restructuring prohibits taking into account any gains on expected disposal of assets in measuring a restructuring provision, even if the sale of the assets is envisaged as part of the restructuring.

    A management decision or a board resolution to restructure taken before the statement of financial position date does not automatically give rise to a constructive obligation at the statement of financial position date unless the entity has, before the statement of financial position date, either started to implement the restructuring plan or announced the main features of the restructuring plan to those affected by it in a sufficiently specific manner such that a valid expectation is raised in them (i.e., that the entity will in fact carry out the restructuring and that benefits will be paid to them).

Examples of events that may fall within the definition of restructuring are

- A fundamental reorganization of an entity that has a material effect on the nature and focus of the entity's operations;
- Drastic changes in the management structure—for example, making all functional units autonomous;
- Removing the business to a more strategic location or place by relocating the headquarters from one country or region to another; and
- The sale or termination of a line of business (if certain other conditions are satisfied, such that a restructuring could be considered a discontinued operation under IFRS 5).

Example: Restructuring provision

Wizard Company acquired all of TKK Corporation's assets and liabilities by issuing 20,000 shares of its €4 par value common stock on January 1, 2008. At that date, Wizard shares were selling at €11 per share. Fair values assigned to TKK Corporation's identifiable assets and liabilities were €450,000 and €320,000, respectively. Accordingly, the amount of goodwill arising on acquisition is €90,000 (=€220,000 – €130,000). On that date Wizard Company decided to create a restructuring provision of €50,000 for future restructuring activities related to TKK. The company recorded this provision with a debit of €50,000 to increase the amount assigned to goodwill and a credit of €50,000 to the restructuring provision account. As a result, since the restructuring provision is recorded against goodwill, an expense for the restructuring will never be recorded and will never affect company's profit. Consequently, the creation of this provision protected Wizard's future profits.

Contingencies

IAS 37 defines a contingent liability as an obligation that is either

- A *possible* obligation arising from past events, the outcome of which will be confirmed only on the occurrence or nonoccurrence of one or more uncertain future events which are not wholly within the control of the reporting entity; *or*
- A *present* obligation arising from past events, which is not recognized either because it is not probable that an outflow of resources will be required to settle an obligation or the amount of the obligation cannot be measured with sufficient reliability.

Under IAS 37, the reporting entity is not to give formal recognition to a contingent liability. Instead, it should disclose in the notes to the financial statements this information:

1. An estimate of its financial effect;
2. An indication of the uncertainties relating to the amount or timing of any outflow; and
3. The possibility of any reimbursement.

Disclosure of this information may be forgone if the possibility of any outflow in settlement is remote or if the information cannot be obtained without undue cost or effort.

Contingent liabilities may develop in a way not initially anticipated. Thus, it is imperative that they be reassessed continually to determine whether an outflow of resources embodying economic benefits has become probable. If the outflow of future economic benefits becomes probable, then a provision is required to be recognized in the financial statements of the period in which the change in such a probability occurs (except in extremely rare cases, when no reliable estimate can be made of the amount needed to be recognized as a provision).

Contingent liabilities must be distinguished from estimated liabilities, although both involve uncertainties that will be resolved by future events. Nevertheless, an estimate exists because of uncertainty about the amount of an event requiring an acknowledged accounting recognition. The event is known and the effect is known, but the amount itself is uncertain. For example, depreciation is an estimate, but not a contingency, because the actual fact of physical depreciation is acknowledged, although the amount is obtained by an assumed accounting method.

In a contingency, whether there will be an impairment of an asset or the occurrence of a liability is the uncertainty that will be resolved in the future. The amount is also usually uncertain, although that is not an essential characteristic defining the contingency. Collectibility of receivables is a contingency because both the amount of loss and the identification of which customer will not pay as promised in the future is unknown. Similar logic would hold for obligations related to product warranties. Both the amount and the customer are currently unknown.

It is tempting to express quantitatively the likelihood of the occurrence of contingent events (e.g., an 80% probability), but this exaggerates the degree of precision possible in the estimation process. For this reason, accounting standards have not been written to require quantification of the likelihood of contingent outcomes. Rather, qualitative descriptions, ranging along the continuum from remote to probable, historically have been prescribed.

IAS 37 sets the threshold for accrual at "more likely than not," which most experts have defined as being very slightly over a 50% likelihood. Thus, if there is even a hint that the obligation is more likely to exist than to not exist, it will need to be formally recognized if an amount can be reasonably estimated for it. The impact will be both to make it much less ambiguous when a contingency should be recorded and to force recognition of far more of these obligations at earlier dates than they are being given recognition for at present.

When a loss is probable and no estimate is possible, these facts should be disclosed in the current period. The accrual of the loss should be made in the period in which the amount of the loss can be estimated. This accrual of a loss in future periods is a change in estimate. It is not a prior period adjustment.

According to IAS 37, a contingent asset is a possible asset that arises from past events and whose existence will be confirmed only by the occurrence or nonoccurrence of one or more uncertain future events that are not wholly within the control of the reporting entity.

Contingent assets usually arise from unplanned or unexpected events that give rise to the possibility of an inflow of economic benefits to the entity. An example of a contingent asset is a claim against an insurance company that the entity is pursuing legally.

Under IFRS, contingent assets should not be recognized; instead, they should be disclosed if the inflow of the economic benefits is probable. As with contingent liabilities, contingent assets need to be continually assessed to ensure that developments are properly reflected in the financial statements. For instance, if it becomes virtually certain that the inflow of economic benefits will arise, the asset and the related income should be recognized in the financial statements of the period in which the change occurs. If, however, the inflow of economic benefits has become probable (instead of virtually certain), then it should be disclosed as a contingent asset.

Example of illustrative footnotes—gain contingency/contingent asset

1. During the current year, a trial court found that a major multinational company had infringed on certain patents and trademarks owned by the company. The court awarded €100 million in damages for these alleged violations by the defendant. In accordance with the court order, the defendant will also be required to pay interest on the award amount and legal costs as well. Should the defendant appeal to an appellate court, the verdict of the trial court could be reduced or the amount of the damages could be reduced. Therefore, at December 31, 2008, the company has not recognized the award amount in the accompanying financial statements since it is not virtually certain of the verdict of the appellate court.
2. In June 2008, the company settled its longtime copyright infringement and trade secrets lawsuit with a competitor. Under the terms of the settlement, the competitor paid the company €2.5 million, which was received in full and final settlement in October 2008, and the parties have dismissed all remaining litigation. For the year ended December 31, 2008, the company recognized the amount received in settlement as "other income," which is included in the accompanying financial statements.

In the context of Phase II of its Business Combinations project, the IASB has extensively redebated the accounting for contingent items. In June 2005, the IASB issued an Exposure Draft (ED), *Proposed Amendments to IAS 37, "Provisions, Contingent Liabilities and Contingent Assets,"* as a result of two current projects: the second phase of the Business Combinations project and the Short-term Convergence project. The proposed amendments are principally concerned with definitions and recognition criteria in IAS 37 but also have required some amendments to the measurement requirements. The IASB proposed to eliminate the terms "provisions," "contingent liability," and "contingent asset" from the IFRS literature and replace these with a new term, "nonfinancial liabilities."

The proposals provide a consistent approach to dealing with contingencies within and outside a business combination, and also provide a comprehensive approach to the accounting for nonfinancial liabilities, which represents a significant change in principle for accounting for obligations. The IASB believes that "the most significant effect of the proposed amendments is to require entities to recognize, as non-financial liabilities, items that were not previously recognized (and, in some cases, not considered to be liabilities)."

There is a wide range of possible contingent liabilities for which footnote disclosure is appropriate. A number of examples are shown in the Footnotes section.

Contingencies—Litigation

The most difficult area of contingencies accounting involves litigation. In some nations, there is a great deal of commercial and other litigation—some of which exposes reporting entities to risks of incurring very material losses. Accountants generally must rely on attorneys' assessments concerning the likelihood of such events; unless the attorney indicates that the risk of loss is remote or slight, or that the impact of any loss that does occur would be immaterial to the company, the accountant will require that the entity add explanatory material to the financial statements regarding the contingency. In cases where judgments have been entered against the entity, or where the attorney gives a range of expected losses or other amounts, certain accruals of loss contingencies for at least the minimum point of the range must be made. Similarly, if the reporting entity has made an offer in settlement of unresolved litigation, that offer normally would be deemed the lower end of the range of possible loss and, thus, subject for accrual. In most cases, however, an estimate of the contingency is unknown and the contingency is reflected only in footnotes.

Contingencies—Debt Covenant Violation

If a company violates a debt covenant on long-term debt, it must reclassify the debt as short term. If, however, the lender waives its right to call the debt, the company can leave the existing debt classification alone. The only exception occurs when the lender retains the right to require compliance with the covenant in the future, and the company is unlikely to be able to comply with the debt covenants on an ongoing basis. In this last instance, the debt must still be classified as short term.

Contingencies—Financial Guarantee Contracts

IFRS has been revised to provide guidance on the accounting for financial guarantees. Those that are in effect insurance should be accounted for under the provisions of IFRS 4, while those that are not akin to insurance should be accounted for consistent with IAS 39, which has been amended appropriately. For the purpose of applying the new guidance, a financial guarantee contract is defined as a contract that requires the issuer to make specified payments to reimburse the holder for a loss it incurs because a specified debtor fails to make payment when due. These are generally to be accounted for under provisions of amended IAS 39, as follows:

- Financial guarantee contracts are initially recognized at fair value. For those financial guarantee contracts issued in stand-alone arm's-length transactions to unrelated parties, fair value will be equal to the consideration received at inception—unless there is evidence to the contrary.
- In subsequent periods, the guarantee is to be reported at the higher of either the amount determined in accordance with IAS 37 or the amount initially rec-

ognized less, if appropriate, the cumulative amortization (to income) that was recognized in accordance with IAS 18.

When certain criteria are met, the issuer (guarantor) may elect to use the fair value option set forth in IAS 39. In other words, the guarantee may be designated as simply being carried at fair value, with all changes being reported currently in earnings.

Reporting Events Occurring after the Reporting Period

IAS 10 addresses the extent to which anything that happens during the post-year-end period when the financial statements are being prepared should be reflected in those financial statements. The Standard distinguishes between events that provide information about the state of the company at statement of financial position date and those that concern the next financial period. A secondary issue is the point when the financial statements are considered to be finalized.

The determination of the authorization date (i.e., the date when the financial statements could be considered legally authorized for issuance, generally by action of the board of directors of the reporting entity), is critical to the application of proper accounting for events after the statement of financial position date. It serves as the cutoff point after the statement of financial position date, until the post–statement of financial position events are to be examined in order to ascertain whether such events qualify for the treatment prescribed by IAS 10. This Standard explains the concept through the use of illustrations.

The general principles that need to be considered in determining the authorization date of the financial statements are set out next.

- When an entity is required to submit its financial statements to its shareholders for approval after they have already been issued, the authorization date in this case would mean the date of original issuance and not the date when these are approved by the shareholders; and
- When an entity is required to issue its financial statements to a supervisory board made up wholly of nonexecutives, authorization date would mean the date on which management authorizes them for issue to the supervisory board.

Example of determining the authorization date

1. The preparation of the financial statements of Xanadu Corp. for the accounting period ended December 31, 2007, was completed by the management on February 15, 2008. The draft financial statements were considered at the meeting of the board of directors held on February 18, 2008, the date the board approved them and authorized them for issuance. The annual general meeting (AGM) was held on March 28, 2008, after allowing for printing and the requisite notice period mandated by the corporate statute. At the AGM the shareholders approved the financial statements. The approved financial statements were filed by the corporation with the Company Law Board (the statutory body of the country that regulates corporations) on April 6, 2008.

   Given these facts, the date of authorization of the financial statements of Xanadu Corp. for the year ended December 31, 2007, is February 18, 2008, the date when the board approved them and authorized them for issue (and not the date they were approved in the AGM by the shareholders). Thus, all post–statement of financial position events between December 31, 2007, and February 18, 2008, need to be considered by Xanadu Corp. for the purposes of evaluating whether they are to be accounted or reported under IAS 10.

2. Suppose in the last case the management of Xanadu Corp. was required to issue the financial statements to a supervisory board (consisting solely of nonexecutives, including representatives of a trade union). The management of Xanadu Corp. had issued the financial statement drafts to the supervisory board on February 16, 2008. The supervisory board approved them on February 17, 2008, and the shareholders approved them in the AGM held on March 28, 2008. The approved financial statements were filed with the Company Law Board on April 6, 2008.

   In this case, the date of the authorization of the financial statements would be February 16, 2008—the date the draft financial statements were issued to the supervisory board. Thus, all post–statement of financial position events between December 31, 2007, and February 16, 2008, need to be considered by Xanadu Corp. for the purposes of evaluating whether they are to be accounted or reported under IAS 10.

The Standard distinguishes two kinds of events after the statement of financial position date. These are, respectively, "adjusting events after the reporting period" and "nonadjusting events after the reporting period." Adjusting events are those post–reporting period events that provide evidence of conditions that actually existed at the statement of financial position date, albeit they were not known at the time. Financial statements should be adjusted to reflect adjusting events after the statement of financial position date.

The Standard gives these five examples of *adjusting events*:

1. Resolution after the statement of financial position date of a court case that confirms a present obligation requiring either an adjustment to an existing provision or the recognition of a provision instead of mere disclosure of a contingent liability;
2. Receipt of information after the statement of financial position date indicating that an asset was impaired or that a previous impairment loss needs to be adjusted. For instance, the bankruptcy of a customer subsequent to the statement of financial position date usually confirms the existence of loss at the statement of financial position date, and the disposal of inventories after the statement of financial position date provides evidence (not always conclusive, however) about their net realizable value at the statement of financial position date.
3. The determination after the statement of financial position date of the cost of assets purchased, or the proceeds from assets disposed of, before the statement of financial position date.
4. The determination subsequent to the statement of financial position date of the amount of profit sharing or bonus payments, where there was a present legal or constructive obligation at the statement of financial position date to make the payments as a result of events before that date.

5. The discovery of frauds or errors, after the statement of financial position date, that show that the financial statements were incorrect at year-end before the adjustment.

Examples of commonly encountered situations of adjusting events

- During the year 2008, Taj Corp. was sued by a competitor for €10 million for infringement of a trademark. Based on the advice of the company's legal counsel, Taj accrued the sum of €5 million as a provision in its financial statements for the year ended December 31, 2007. Subsequent to the statement of financial position date, on February 15, 2008, the Supreme Court decided in favor of the party alleging infringement of the trademark and ordered the defendant to pay the aggrieved party a sum of €7 million. The financial statements were prepared by the company's management on January 31, 2008, and approved by the board on February 20, 2008. Taj Corp. should adjust the provision by €2 million to reflect the award decreed by the Supreme Court (assumed to be the final appellate authority on the matter in this example) to be paid by Taj Corp. to its competitor. Had the judgment of the Supreme Court been delivered on February 25, 2008, or later, this post–statement of financial position event would have occurred after the cutoff point (i.e., the date the financial statements were authorized for original issuance). If so, adjustment of financial statements would not have been required.
- Penn Corp. carries its inventory at the lower of cost and net realizable value. At December 31, 2007, the cost of inventory determined under the first-in, first-out (FIFO) method, as reported in its financial statements for the year then ended, was €5 million. Due to severe recession and other negative economic trends in the market, the inventory could not be sold during the entire month of January 2008. On February 10, 2008, Penn Corp. entered into an agreement to sell the entire inventory to a competitor for €4 million. Presuming the financial statements were authorized for issuance on February 15, 2008, the company should recognize a write-down of €1 million in the financial statements for the year ended December 31, 2007.

In contrast with the foregoing, *nonadjusting* events are those post–statement of financial position events that are indicative of conditions that arose after the statement of financial position date. Financial statements should not be adjusted to reflect nonadjusting events after the reporting period . An example of a nonadjusting event is a decline in the market value of investments between the statement of financial position date and the date when the financial statements are authorized for issue. Since the fall in the market value of investments after the statement of financial position date is not indicative of their market value at the statement of financial position date (instead it reflects circumstances that arose subsequent to the reporting period), the fall in market value need not, and should not, be recognized in the financial statements at the statement of financial position date.

Not all nonadjusting events are significant enough to require disclosure, however. The revised Standard gives examples of nonadjusting events that would impair the ability of the users of financial statements to make proper evaluations or decisions if not disclosed. Where nonadjusting events after the reporting period are of such significance, disclosure should be made for each such significant category of nonadjusting event,of the nature of the event and an estimate of its financial effect or a statement that such an estimate cannot be made. The Standard gives nine examples of such significant nonadjusting post–statement of financial position events:

1. A major business combination or disposing of a major subsidiary
2. Announcing a plan to discontinue an operation
3. Major purchases and disposals of assets or expropriation of major assets by government
4. The destruction of a major production plant by fire
5. Announcing or commencing the implementation of a major restructuring
6. Abnormally large changes in asset prices or foreign exchange rates
7. Significant changes in tax rates and enacted tax laws
8. Entering into significant commitments or contingent liabilities
9. Major litigation arising from events occurring after the reporting period

Dividends (on equity shares) proposed or declared after the statement of financial position date should not be recognized as a liability at the statement of financial position date. Such declaration is a nonadjusting subsequent event, in other words. While at one time IFRS did permit accrual of post–statement of financial position date dividend declarations, this has not been permissible for some time. Furthermore, the revisions made to IAS 10 as part of the IASB's Improvements Project in late 2003 eliminated the formerly permitted display of post–statement of financial position date dividends as a separate component of equity. Footnote disclosure is, however, required unless immaterial.

Deterioration in a company's financial position after the reporting period could cast substantial doubts about a company's ability to continue as a *going concern.* IAS 10 requires that an entity should not prepare its financial statements on a going-concern basis if management determines after the reporting period either that it intends to liquidate the entity or cease trading, or that it has no realistic alternative but to do so. IAS 10 notes that disclosures prescribed by IAS 1 under such circumstances should also be complied with.

IAS 39 established new requirements for accounting for *financial liabilities* that are held for trading and those that are derivatives; these have to be accounted for at fair value. Meanwhile, other financial liabilities continue to be reported at amortized historical cost. IAS 39 stipulates that all financial liabilities are to be measured initially at cost, which (assuming they are each incurred in an arm's-length transaction) is also fair value. Any related transaction costs are included in this initial measurement. In rare instances when the fair value of the consideration received is not reliably determinable, resort is to be made to a computation of the present value of all future cash flows related to the liability. In such a case, the discount rate to apply would be the prevailing rate on similar instruments issued by a party having a similar credit rating.

IAS 39 provides that, subsequent to initial recognition, an enterprise should measure all financial liabilities, other than liabilities held for trading purposes and derivative contracts that are liabilities, at amortized cost. Where the initial recorded amount is not the contractual maturity value of the liability (e.g., as when transaction costs are added to the issuance price, or when there was a premium or discount upon issuance) periodic amortization should be recorded, using the constant effective yield method.

In its 2003 revisions, the IASB introduced what is known as the fair value option, which allowed entities to designate any liability as being held at fair value, with changes in fair value flowing through the income statement.

POLICIES

Current Liabilities

- **There shall be no carryforward of sick time past the current year.** A common management problem is for employees to build up massive reserves of unused sick time, for which they must be paid when they eventually leave the company. This policy is designed to eliminate all unused sick time at the end of each calendar year, thereby keeping accrued sick time expense to a minimum.
- **The number of hours of vacation time carried forward past the current year is capped at ____ hours.** Some employees have a habit of not taking vacation time, resulting in large vacation accruals that can grow for years. Not only does this represent a significant current liability, but it also presents a control problem, since employees who do not take vacation may be staying on the job in order to hide fraudulent activities. This policy is designed to resolve both problems by allowing only a modest carryforward of earned vacation time.
- **The vacation accrual shall be based on the maximum year-end carryforward amount of vacation hours.** The accrual of vacation time is subject to a great deal of interpretation, since it can be based on the current amount of vacation time existing, the maximum available for the year, the maximum carryforward amount, or an estimate of the carryforward amount. By switching between various estimation methods, one can easily modify the vacation accrual to alter reported financial results. This policy requires one to use just one estimation method, thereby removing the variability from the calculation method. The approach specified in the policy is used as the basis for the vacation accrual form shown in the Forms and Reports section.

PROCEDURES

Current Liabilities—Accounts Payable

This seven-step procedure describes the entire transaction cycle for accounts payable.

1. An employee fills out a requisition form for any product she wishes the company to purchase and forwards it to the purchasing department.
2. A purchasing staff person locates the best price for the requisitioned product and issues a purchase order. One copy goes to the supplier, one stays in the purchasing department, and one copy goes to the receiving department. If

there is a computerized receiving system, the purchasing person also enters the purchase order into the database.

3. When the product arrives at the receiving dock, the receiving staff compares it to the purchase order and accepts it if the delivery matches the specifications in the purchase order. If the company has a computerized receiving system, the receiving staff calls up the purchase order on the computer and enters the receipt directly into the system. If not, the staff manually enters the receipt in a receiving log and also attaches the bill of lading to the purchase order. These documents are sent to the accounting department at the end of the day.
4. The accounting staff files the documents by supplier name once they arrive from the receiving department.
5. Whenever supplier invoices arrive, the accounting staff matches them to the previously filed purchasing and receiving documents and enters them in the accounting system as approved payables if all documents match. If they do not match, the accounting staff must contact the supplier to resolve any outstanding issues.
6. When a check run is scheduled, the computer system flags those supplier invoices due for payment, and the accounting staff prints the checks. They attach backup materials (invoice, purchase order, and receiving documents) to each check as proof and forward the check packets to an authorized signer.
7. Once signed, the accounting staff removes the second copy of the remittance advice from each check and staples it to the backup materials, which they file by supplier name. They then mail the checks to suppliers.

CONTROLS

Current Liabilities

- **Include an accrual review in the closing procedure for bonuses, commissions, property taxes, royalties, sick time, vacation time, unpaid wages, and warranty claims.** There are many possible expenses for which an accrual is needed, given their size and repetitive nature. This control is designed to force a continual review of every possible current liability as part of the standard monthly closing procedure, so that no key accruals are missed.
- **Review accrual accounts for unreversed entries.** Some accruals, such as unpaid wage accruals and commission accruals, are supposed to be reversed in the following period, when the actual expense is incurred. If an accountant forgets to properly set up a journal entry for automatic reversal in the next period, however, a company will find itself having recorded too large an expense. A simple control point is to include in the period-end closing procedure a review of all accounts in which accrual entries are made, to ensure that all reversals have been completed.
- **Create standard entries for reversing journal entries.** As a continuation of the last control point, an easy way to avoid problems with accrual journal entries that are supposed to be reversed is to create boilerplate journal entry for-

mats in the accounting system that are preconfigured to be reversed automatically in the next period. As long as these standard formats are used, there will never be an unreversed journal entry.

- **Include a standard review of customer advances in the closing procedure.** If a company regularly deals with a large number of customer deposits, there is a significant risk that the deposits will not be recognized as revenue in conjunction with the completion of any related services or product sales. This problem can be avoided by requiring a periodic review of the status of each deposit as part of the period-end closing procedure.
- **Include an accrual review in the closing procedure for income taxes payable.** A common practice is to only accrue for income taxes on a quarterly basis, when estimated taxes are due. The trouble is that this is a substantial expense being excluded from all monthly financial statements not falling at the end of each reporting quarter, so it tends to skew the reported results of those months. By including in the closing procedure a line item requiring the accrual of an income tax liability, the accounting staff is forced to address this issue every time financial statements are issued.
- **Maintain historical expense information about warranty claims both for ongoing product sales and new product introductions.** If a company creates a warranty expense accrual for a new product based on its standard claim rate for existing products, the warranty expense probably will be underaccrued for the initial introductory period of the product, since more product problems will arise early in a product launch that are corrected in later models. A good control over this underreporting is to track warranty expenses separately for new model introductions and ongoing sales; therefore, a reasonable basis of information can be used for each type of accrual.
- **Match the final monthly payroll pay date to the last day of the month.** The unpaid wage accrual can be significant when employee pay dates differ substantially from the last day of the reporting period. This problem can be partially resolved by setting the last (or only) pay date of the month on the last day of the month and paying employees through that date, which eliminates the need for any wage accrual. This control is most effective for salaried employees, who typically are paid through the pay date. There is usually a cutoff for hourly employees that is several days prior to the pay date, so some wage accrual still would be necessary for these employees.
- **Automate the period-end cutoff.** A common closing activity is to compare the receiving department's log for the few days near the period-end to the supplier invoices logged in during that period, to see if there are any receipts for which there are no supplier invoices. This is a slow and error-prone activity. A good alternative is to use the computer system to locate missing invoices automatically. The key requirements are a purchase order system covering all significant purchases as well as rapid updating of the inventory database by the warehouse staff when items are received. If these features exist, a batch program can be written that links the purchase order, inventory, and accounting databases, and that compares inventory receipts to received invoices. If no

invoice exists, the program calculates the price of the missing invoice based on the purchase order. It then creates a report for the accounting staff itemizing all receipts for which there are no invoices and calculates the price of the missing invoices. This report can be used as the basis for a journal entry at month-end to record missing invoices.

- **Create a standard checklist of recurring supplier invoices to include in the month-end cutoff.** A number of invoices that arrive after month-end are related to services, and an accrual should be made for them. The easiest way to be assured of making these accruals is to create a list of recurring invoices, with their approximate amounts, and use it as a check-off list during the closing process. If the invoice has not yet arrived, then accrue for the standard amount shown on the list.
- **Automate or sidestep the matching process.** The most common way to establish the need for a payment to a supplier is to compare an incoming supplier invoice to the authorizing purchase order as well as receiving documentation to ensure that the item billed has been accepted. If both these sources of information agree with the invoice, then the accounts payable staff can proceed with payment. The trouble is that this process is terribly inefficient and highly error prone. There are three ways to improve this critical control point.
    1. **Use matching automation software.** Most high-end accounting software packages offer an automated matching system that automatically compares all three documents and highlights mismatches for further review. The trouble is that this software is expensive, requires linked computer databases for accounting, purchasing, and the warehouse, and also still requires manual labor to reconcile any mismatches it locates.
    2. **Authorize payments at the receiving point.** This advanced concept requires the presence of a computer terminal at the receiving dock. Upon receipt of a shipment, the receiving staff authorizes payment by accessing the purchase order in the computer system that relates to the receipt and checking off those items received. The computer system then schedules a payment without any supplier invoice. This approach is theoretically the most efficient way to control the payables process but requires considerable custom programming as well as training of the receiving staff.
    3. **Shift payments to procurement cards.** A large proportion of all purchases are too small to require any matching process, since the labor expended exceeds the value of the control. Instead, create a procurement card system and encourage employees to make purchases with the cards, up to a maximum limit. This program greatly reduces the number of transactions requiring matching, thereby focusing the attention of the accounts payable staff on just those transactions most likely to contain errors of a significant dollar value.

Contingencies

- **Include an assessment of contingent debt guarantees in the closing procedure.** Companies tend not to review debt guarantees on a regular basis, so the sudden failure of the obligor to pay can come as a considerable surprise, resulting in the recognition of a large debt obligation. This control is designed to force a regular review of any debt guarantees as part of the regular monthly closing schedule.
- **Include an assessment of debt covenant violations in the closing procedure.** It is not at all uncommon for a company to be unaware of debt covenant violations until informed of them by the lender, resulting in the immediate acceleration of debt into the short-term debt category. This problem can be avoided by including a covenant review in the regular monthly closing schedule.
- **Include an assessment of debt covenant violations in the budgeting process and interim financial planning.** Debt covenant violations sometimes are caused inadvertently by specific finance-related activities that could have been avoided if management had been aware of the impact of their actions. These problems sometimes can be avoided by including a covenant violation review in the budgeting procedure.
- **Include an assessment of all provisions and contingency reserves in the monthly closing procedure.** These reserves tend to be set up once and promptly forgotten, although the underlying contingencies may change in size over time. A reasonable control is to require a periodic review of the size of all reserves in the monthly closing procedure as a standard line item, thereby repeatedly bringing the issue to management's attention.

FORMS AND REPORTS

Current Liabilities—Commission Calculation Worksheet

There is an infinite array of possible sales commission plans. Many plans require the creation of a customized spreadsheet or database program to deal with them, sometimes varying by individual salesperson. Given the size of the commissions awarded in some cases, it is important to quickly determine the commission expense accrual at the end of each reporting period, so this information can be reflected accurately in the financial statements. A good way to do this is to update the commission calculation on a weekly basis and also to update it the day before the end of the reporting period, so that the minimum number of additional sales must be added to the report as part of the closing process. An example of such a report is shown in Exhibit 9.1. This spreadsheet itemizes each invoice in the first three columns and also subtracts out any supplier costs associated with a sale, on the assumption that some sales are actually resales of products drop-shipped from other companies. The report also itemizes different commission rates for recurring, split, and new sales, and contains a section at the bottom for override sales commissions.

Exhibit 9-1: Commission Calculation Spreadsheet

Salesperson Name **Smith**

June 2005 Commissions

Invoice Date	Invoice Number	Invoice Amount	Less Supplier Cost	Net Sale	Customer	Product	Commission Type	Commission Rate	Commission Euros
6/1/2005	5527	€ 1,117.00	€ 0.00	€ 1,117.00	Oregon Land Title	LandTitle Database update	Repeat	4%	€ 44.68
6/4/2005	5570	€ (883.75)	€ 0.00	€ (883.75)	Arizona Title Search	Credit on customer return	Split	4%	€ (35.35)
6/30/2005	5638	€14,898.40	€ 8,332.00	€ 6,566.40	Iowa Land Equity	LandTitle Database update	Split	4%	€ 262.66
6/30/2005	5643	€ 9,191.00	€ 0.00	€ 9,191.00	Oregon Land Title	GPS Trak2000 software	Split	4%	€ 367.64
6/5/2005	5577	€ 700.60	€ 0.00	€ 700.60	Oregon Land Title	LandParcel Database update	New	7%	€ 49.04
6/5/2005	5578	€ 9,009.00	€ 0.00	€ 9,009.00	Iowa Land Equity	LandParcel Database update	New	8%	€ 720.72
6/5/2005	5579	€ 7,850.00	€ 5,000.00	€ 2,850.00	Missouri Flood Insurance	GPS Trak2000 software	New	8%	€ 228.00
6/6/2005	5582	€ 400.00	€ 0.00	€ 400.00	Missouri Flood Insurance	LandTitle Database update	New	7%	€ 28.00
6/9/2005	5583	€ 4,229.25	€ 0.00	€ 4,229.25	Arizona Title Search	LandParcel Database update	New	8%	€ 338.34
6/30/2005	5641	€ 686.80	€ 0.00	€ 686.80	Arizona Title Search	GPS Trak2000 software	New	7%	€ 48.08
		€47,198.30	€13,332.00	€33,866.30					€2,051.80
Manager Override Commissions					Sales trainee #1	€ 2,500	Override	2%	€ 50.00
					Sales trainee #2	€ 1,750	Override	2%	€ 35.00
							Total Commission		€2,136.80

Current Liabilities—Wage Accrual Spreadsheet

Typically, there is a gap between the last date through which wages are paid and the end of the reporting period, which can be a substantial time period. To ensure that the expense associated with this unpaid balance is properly accrued, one should use a standard spreadsheet that itemizes the people who are not paid through period-end as well as their wage rates. It is best to have the spreadsheet automatically calculate a journal entry, as is the case for the sample form shown in Exhibit 9.2. By employing this approach, the same account numbers are used consistently across multiple reporting periods, resulting in consistent reported results.

Exhibit 9.2 Wage Accrual Spreadsheet

Wage Accrual Spreadsheet		For the month of:		Jul-08
Department	*Hourly personnel*	*Pay rate per hour*	*Unpaid hours in month*	*Pay accrual*
Marketing	Below, Melissa	€40.00	14.00	€560.00
Production	Brandon, Andrew	18.15	72.00	1,306.80
Production	Gutierrez, Pablo	17.25	72.00	1,242.00
Production	Holloway, Tim	16.43	72.00	1,182.96
Production	Innes, Sean	15.00	72.00	1,080.00
Production	Smith, Michael	15.00	72.00	1,080.00
Consulting	Verity, Thomas	50.00	72.00	3,600.00

Journal Entry:

	Account number	*Debit*	*Credit*
Production Wages	62150-02	5,891.76	
Production Payroll Taxes	62250-02	365.29	
Marketing Wages	62150-01	560.00	
Marketing Payroll Taxes	62250-01	34.72	
Consulting Wages	50050-03	3,600.00	
Consulting Payroll Taxes	62250-03	223.20	
Wage Accrual	22800		10,674.97

NOTE: Hourly personnel are paid through the Sunday prior to the payroll date.

Current Liabilities—Royalty Calculation Spreadsheet

If a company must pay out a significant royalty related to its use or resale of another company's products, it should create a periodic accrual of this ongoing expense, which is easily forgotten if the actual royalty payment occurs only infrequently. Though the basic calculation of a royalty could use the format shown in Exhibit 9.2, the form is not a sufficient reminder for a periodic royalty accrual. Consequently, one should also include a periodic accrual in the period-end closing procedure. The exhibit shows a standard royalty form suitable for delivery to the entity receiving a royalty and is based on an ascending scale of royalty percentages, based on increasing revenue volumes. Given the wide array of possible royalty calculations, this format may require significant tailoring to match a specific royalty agreement.

Exhibit 9.3 Royalty Calculation Worksheet

[Supplier Name] Royalty Statement for the Third Fiscal Quarter Ended [Date]	
Product Name	€128,000
Product Name	34,500
Product Name	98,250
Total Product Revenue	€260,750
Royalty Calculation:	
4% × First €50,000	€2,000
7% × Excess over €50,000, up to €200,000	10,500
11% × Excess over €200,000	6,683
Total Royalty for the Fiscal Year	€19,183
Less: Previous Payments Made	€14,750
Total Payment	€4,433
[Company Name],	
By:________________________ Date:________________	
Signature of Authorized Officer	

Current Liabilities—Vacation Accrual Spreadsheet

The amount of vacation liability is based on the current amount of earned but unused vacation. Nevertheless, because vacation time can fluctuate significantly over the course of a year, it is quite common to maintain an accrued vacation expense balance equating to an expected fiscal year-end or quarter-end amount. An example of such an accrual calculation is shown in Exhibit 9.4, where the accrual is calculated for three company subsidiaries. In the example, only 40 hours of vacation can be carried forward by subsidiaries A and C, while 80 hours are allowed for subsidiary B. For each subsidiary, the spreadsheet lists all employees, their annual pay, and the maximum number of vacation hours they can carry forward into the next year. By allowing a maximum vacation carryforward, the accountant can easily calculate the maximum possible vacation accrual that must be on the books at the end of the year. The spreadsheet also compares the maximum accrual to the amount currently booked and then transfers the required adjustment into a journal entry at the bottom of the page. This is an effective reporting format for periodic adjustments to the vacation accrual.

Exhibit 9.4: Vacation Accrual Spreadsheet

Vacation Accrual

Name	Annualized salary	Maximum hours	Maximum accrual	Division	Maximum accrual	Current accrued balance	Required entry
Adams, Latrone	€ 45,000	40.00	€ 865	Subsidiary A			
Benning, Brian	€103,000	40.00	€1,990	Subsidiary A			
Blotten, Charles	€ 75,250	40.00	€1,447	Subsidiary A	€ 7,253	€ 5,250	€ 2,003
Clarion, Alice	€ 97,000	40.00	€1,865	Subsidiary A			
Corey, David	€ 56,400	40.00	€1,085	Subsidiary A			
Brower Franklin	€ 85,000	80.00	€3,269	Subsidiary B			
Hustle, James	€ 48,000	80.00	€1,846	Subsidiary B			
Innes, Mandy	€ 99,000	80.00	€3,808	Subsidiary B	€13,346	€12,000	€ 1,346
Mandrel, Steven	€ 65,000	80.00	€2,500	Subsidiary B			
Van den Plee, Joe	€100,000	40.00	€1,923	Subsidiary B			
Chao, Brian	€ 60,000	40.00	€1,154	Subsidiary C			
Dunwiddy, John	€ 51,039	40.00	€ 982	Subsidiary C			
Ephraim, Joe	€ 48,900	40.00	€ 940	Subsidiary C	€ 5,225	€ 5,000	€ 225
Horvath, Mark	€ 37,752	40.00	€ 726	Subsidiary C			
McKenna, Jason	€ 74,000	40.00	€1,423	Subsidiary C			

Journal entry	Account description	Account no	Debit	Credit
	Salary expense– Subsidiary A	6000-01	€2,003	
	Salary expense– Subsidiary B	6000-02	€1,346	
	Salary expense– Subsidiary C	6000-03	€ 225	
	Vacation Accrual	22300		€3,574

FOOTNOTES

Disclosure of Employment Contract Liabilities

A company may enter into a variety of obligations when it agrees to employment contracts, such as a minimum number of years of salary payments, health insurance coverage subsequent to employment termination, and payments for life insurance coverage. If material, the term, potential expense, and descriptions of these agreements should be disclosed in a footnote. It generally is adequate to summarize all employment contract liabilities into a single footnote. An example follows.

> The company has entered into five-year employment contracts with its CEO, CFO, and CIO, under which they are collectively guaranteed minimum salaries totaling €748,000 in each of the next five years, assuming their continued employment. In addition, the company has guaranteed payment for all of their term life insurance policies payable to their spouses, aggregating €3,000,000 for the five-year period. Since this is a firm liability, the company has recorded the present value of the expense in the current period, totaling €82,500.

Disclosure of Geographic Risk

If a company's geographic situation renders it more likely to suffer from a future catastrophe based on its geographic location, it can describe this risk in a footnote. Possible situations warranting such disclosure are locating in a floodplain or in a forested area highly subject to wildfires, being near an active earthquake fault line, or in a common area for tornados. An example follows.

> The company's primary chemical processing facility is located directly over the San Andreas fault line, which has a history of producing earthquakes ranging up to 6.9 on the Richter scale. The company has attempted to obtain earthquake insurance, but the nature of its business makes the risk of loss so great for insurers that they will not provide coverage. Accordingly, the company is searching for a new facility in central Nevada, and plans to move there within the next three years, shutting down the California facility at that time. In the meantime, the company remains at risk from any earthquake-related incidents, with losses from such an event being potentially large enough to have a material impact on the company's financial results.

Disclosure of Government Investigation

If a company is being investigated by any government division at any level and material penalties or losses could result, one should describe the investigation in a footnote, including the nature and potential cost of any claims made. An example follows.

> The government's audit agency has audited the company's billings to the federal government for the past three years and claims to have found that the billing rates used for several employees were too high, based on their experience levels. The agency has requested that these invoices be retroactively reduced and the difference paid back to the government. The rebate amount claimed by the agency is €2.4 million. The company considers the claim to be without merit and is vigorously defending its position. If a further government review finds the company to be liable for this payment, the company will also be subject to the suspension of its agency schedule and all contracting with the government for a maximum of two years.

Disclosure of Industry Risk

If the industry in which a company operates has unique risks related to such factors as intense competition, low barriers to entry, rapidly changing technology, and so on, a footnote can describe these issues and their potential impact on company operations. An example follows.

> The company's primary business is the design, manufacture, and sale of Christmas ornaments. The company's financial results are influenced by the rapidity with which designs are copied by foreign competitors and reproduced at much lower prices as well as the company's ability to continue to create new designs finding favor in the marketplace, maintain a large network of distributors, manufacture in sufficient quantities for the Christmas selling season, and dispose of excess inventory without excessive losses. Based on these factors, the company can experience large fluctuations in its future financial results.

Disclosure of Litigation

Companies are frequently the subject of lawsuits for a variety of alleged situations, such as harassment, patent infringement, and environmental liabilities. One should describe in the footnotes the general nature of each lawsuit, the amount of restitution sought, and the opinion of the company's legal counsel regarding the probable outcome of the suit. If there are many similar suits, they may be summarized for descriptive purposes. If lawsuits would have an immaterial impact on company results, then this can be stated in general terms. Three examples follow.

1. The company is the target of a class action lawsuit entitled *Smith v. ABC Company*, currently in the Fourth District Court of Colorado (USA). In the case, current and previous hourly staff claim nonpayment of overtime pay, and seek damages of €20,000,000. The company avers that the case is without merit and continues to vigorously defend its position in the case. It is not possible to determine a probable outcome at this time, and since company management feels a material loss from the suit to be remote, the company has not accrued any related expense.
2. The company is the target of a sexual harassment lawsuit entitled *Jones v. ABC Company*, currently in the Fourth District Court of Colorado (USA). In the suit, a former employee alleges disparaging comments and actions by her immediate supervisor, and seeks damages of €1 million. Per the advice of company counsel, the company offered to settle the case for €100,000 and accrued for this expense. If the offer is not accepted, however, and if the case were to go to trial, then the company could be liable for the €1 million sought in the suit.
3. The company is the target of a variety of legal proceedings as the result of its normal business operations, generally in the area of personal damage claims related to slips and falls in its warehouse facilities. In management's opinion, any liabilities arising from these proceedings would not have a material adverse impact on the company's financial results.

Disclosure of Outsourced Production Liability

Many companies have outsourced their production to third parties but are shackled by contingent liabilities under which they are required to purchase minimum quantities from the third parties and sometimes also to pay for any fixed costs incurred by the suppliers if production is halted before a predetermined quantity of units have been produced. That being the case, the terms, duration, and general description of the agreement should be included in a footnote. An example follows.

> The company has outsourced its production to the ABC Foreign Company, under a five-year contract that requires the company to purchase a minimum of 10,000 golf carts per year from ABC. If not, the company must pay €650 to ABC for each unit under the minimum on which it did not take delivery. In addition, if the contract is terminated early, the company must pay ABC €200,000 for each year of early termination in order to pay it back for a variety of up-front fixed charges it incurred to create a production line.

Disclosure of Postemployment Benefits

If employees are entitled to benefits subsequent to their employment that are material, then the nature of the transaction, the amount of expense involved, and its treatment in the financial statements should be revealed in a footnote. An example follows.

> The company's former president, Mr. Smith, was asked to step down by the board on May 5, 2008. As part of the separation agreement, the company agreed to pay Mr. Smith's medical insurance premiums for the next two years, and also paid a lump-sum settlement of €2 million. The present value of the entire medical cost was charged to expense in the current period, as was the lump-sum settlement. The medical expense was offset against an Unpaid Insurance Premiums liability account, which will be gradually reduced as periodic medical insurance payments are made.

Disclosure of Purchasing Commitments

There may be a minimum purchase agreement extending into future reporting periods that obligates a company to make purchases in amounts that are material. Not only that, but a company may have made guarantees to pay for the debts of other entities, such as a subsidiary. If these commitments are material, then their nature must be disclosed in the footnotes. The rules are not specific about identifying the exact cost or probability of occurrence of each commitment, so the accountant has some leeway in presenting this information. An example follows.

> The company has entered into a contract to purchase a minimum of 500,000 tons of coal per year for the next 20 years at a fixed price of €20.50 per ton, with no price escalation allowed for the duration of the contract. The company's minimum annual payment obligation under this contract is €10,250,000. The price paid under this contract is €1.75 less than the market rate for anthracite coal as of the date of these statements, and had not significantly changed as of the statement issuance date.

Disclosure of Reseller Liability

Distributors sometimes enter into sole-sourcing agreements with suppliers, whereby they guarantee a minimum amount of sales in exchange for exclusive rights to a sales region. If such an agreement exists, one must disclose its duration, description, and potential amount of payments. An example follows.

> The company has entered into an agreement to be the sole-source New Zealand distributor of Merino lambing shears. The sole distribution agreement will exist for a minimum of two years, as long as the company sells at least 10,000 shears per year. During that two-year period ending in June 2009, the company must pay the supplier €5 for each shear not sold below the minimum annual quantity. If the company were to fail to sell any shears, this liability would be €50,000 per year for two years. At this time, year-to-date sales indicate that the company will meet the minimum quantity required under the first year of the agreement, so management has elected not to recognize any expenses associated with this contingent liability.

Disclosure of Royalty Payments

A royalty agreement involving potentially material payments should be disclosed. The information in the footnote should include a description and the terms of the agreement as well as the potential amount of the payments. An example follows.

> The company contracts much of its software game development to third-party developers. These developers receive nonrecoverable advances ranging from €25,000 to €80,000 for each game they create, against which a standard 8% royalty is deducted. Once the full amount of each advance has been earned by a developer, royalty payments

are accrued monthly and paid quarterly. All development advances are accounted for as short-term assets in the Development Advances account, which currently contains €2,628,000. The company periodically compares product sales to the remaining amount of advances on each product and writes off those advances for which sales trends indicate that remaining royalties earned will not be sufficient to eliminate the advances. In the past year, the company wrote off €350,000 of development advances for this reason.

Disclosure of Self-Insurance Liability

If a company has elected to cover some portion of its risk portfolio with self-insurance, one should itemize the types of risk covered by self-insurance, the method by which estimated expenses are calculated, and the recent claims history of the self-insurance program. An example follows.

> The company has set up a self-insurance program to cover its workers' compensation risk. All claims are paid up to an annual limit of €2 million, after which an umbrella policy covers all remaining claims. The company charges to expense all actual claims made during each reporting period as well as an estimate of claims incurred but not yet reported, based on a one-year rolling history of this information. The amount of claims incurred but not reported is currently €158,000 and is recorded as a liability.

Disclosure of No Insurance

A company that is unable to obtain insurance for coverage of any key business risk, will have to make a footnote disclosure about the circumstances of the situation and a statement about potential losses. An example follows.

> Given the spate of wildfires in recent years in the Bavarian region, it is now impossible to obtain fire damage insurance for the company's headquarters, which is located in the midst of a forest in central Bavaria. The company has assertively taken steps to reduce fire danger through the use of forest thinning, in-house fire control teams, and sprinkler systems. Given these risk mitigation steps, the company feels that the potential risk of loss has been much reduced and so has taken no steps to create a self-insurance fund for this risk.

Disclosure of Supplier Concentration Risk

If a company is highly dependent on a few suppliers for the bulk [illegible]s purchases of materials, or if key materials have limited sources, the proportion [illegible] types of materials subject to this issue should be noted as well as comme[illegible] the relationship with these suppliers and how their loss would impact th[illegible]pany. An example follows.

> The printer drum used in the company's prima[illegible] printer product is sole-sourced to a foreign company that is the dominant producer of this part. If the supplier were to reduce or stop delivering this p[illegible]pany would switch to an alternate supplier that is already being used for [illegible]duction volumes. The concern is that the alternate source's prices are 30% hi[illegible] would have a material impact on the company's cost of goods sold and [illegible]nancial results. Also, the alternate supplier has unproven experience i[illegible] volume levels required by the company. Nevertheless, management b[illegible]pany's relations with its primary supplier to be excellent and the poss[illegible]pply shortage to be remote.

Disclosure of Taxation Disputes

A company may be in a variety of stages of investigation by any number of government taxing authorities, ranging from sales and use tax audits to income tax reviews. Disclosure of these reviews can range from a simple statement that an audit is underway, through the initial judgment notice, to a description of a finalized payment settlement. The next footnotes give examples of three options.

1. The company is being reviewed by an Andalusian sales tax audit team. Management is of the opinion that this review will not result in any material change in the company's financial results.
2. The company has been audited by a Andalusian sales tax audit team, which asserts that the company has established a nexus in that state and so must remit sales taxes for all sales into Andalusia for the past three years, which would total €14 million. Management is of the opinion that there are no grounds for establishing a nexus and intends to contest the issue vigorously through the Andalusian appeals process, up to and including litigation. Management believes there is no need to establish any loss accrual related to this matter at this time.
3. The company has reached agreement with Andalusia, under which a payment of €2.5 million for unpaid sales taxes shall be made. The company intends to collect these taxes from its customers, which management believes will substantially reduce the amount of its liability. Accordingly, it has recognized an expense of €600,000 in the current period to cover any sales taxes it cannot collect from customers and will modify this amount in the future based on its sales tax collection experience for the amounts due.

Disclosure of Unasserted Claims

Even if a company has not yet received any claims for a specific liability, it should disclose the possibility if such claims are probable, and if losses will result. An example follows.

The company's construction division has recently learned that some particleboard used in its construction of residential homes contains trace amounts of asbestos. Though the company has received no claims arising from this use, other builders in the industry have [illegible] targeted by lawsuits, with judgments ranging from €50,000 to €150,000 per home. [illegible] the company plans to vigorously pursue legal action against its particleboard su[illegible] if any claims are made, the company feels that the risk of loss, net of pass-throu[illegible]es to the supplier, is reduced to less than €1 million.

Disclosure of V[illegible] Liability

If a company [illegible]ated to pay its employees for future time off that has already been earned, it [illegible] reveal its method for calculating the obligation as well as its amount. An exam[illegible]ws.

The company accr[illegible] and sick time for its employees up to a maximum of two weeks per year, sinc[illegible]es cannot accrue more time under a use-it-or-lose-it policy. The accrual calcul[illegible]ultiply the current hourly rate for each employee, plus related payroll taxes, by [illegible] amount of time earned by each employee, with a cap of 80 hours earned. The [illegible] accrued €182,000 in the Accrued Vacations liability account under this polic[illegible]

Disclosure of Warranty Liabilities

If the amount of warranty liabilities is material, the general product warranty, as well as its duration, should be listed in a footnote. An example follows.

The company warrants its camping equipment products against defects in design and materials for the lifetime of the original owner, and provides replacements at any time with no investigation or evidence of sales receipt. This warranty policy goes well beyond that of the sporting goods industry. Management believes the policy is a key reason why customers consider the company's products to be of high quality, and so intends to retain this policy into the foreseeable future. Warranty reserves are based on the past year of actual warranty claims, which most recently were 5.9% of sales. In addition, warranty reserves may be increased in the short term if there is evidence of problems with specific products that may result in material increases in warranty claims. Reserves are booked at the point of initial sale.

Disclosure of Provisions

Example footnote illustrating disclosures required under IAS 37 with respect to provisions:

Provisions

As of December 31, 2007, provisions consist of the following (all amounts in euros):

	Opening balance	*Additions*	*Provision utilized*	*Unutilized provision reversed*	*Closing balance*
Provision for environmental costs	1,000,000	900,000	(800,000)	(100,000)	1,000,000
Provision for staff bonus	2,000,000	1,000,000	(900,000)	--	2,100,000
Provision for restructuring costs	1,000,000	500,000	(100,000)	(200,000)	1,200,000
Provision for decommissioning costs	5,000,000	500,000	(2,000,000)	--	3,500,000
	9,000,000	2,900,000	(3,800,000)	(300,000)	7,800,000

Provision for environmental costs. Statutory decontamination costs relating to old chemical manufacturing sites are determined based on periodic assessments undertaken by environmental specialists employed by the company and verified by independent experts.

Provision for staff bonus. Provisions for staff bonuses represent contractual amounts due to the company's middle management, based on one month's basic salary, as per current employment contracts.

Provision for restructuring costs. Restructuring provisions arise from a fundamental reorganization of the company's operations and management structure.

Provision for decommissioning costs. Provision is made for estimated decommissioning costs relating to oilfields operated by the company based on engineering estimates and independent experts' reports.

Disclosure of Contingent Liabilities

Example of illustrative footnotes—contingent liabilities:

1. A former plant manager of the establishment has filed a claim related to injuries sustained during an accident in the factory. The former employee is claiming approximately €3.5 million as damages for permanent disability, alleging that the establishment had violated a safety regulation. At December 31, 2007, no provision has been made for this claim, as management intends to defend these allegations vigorously and believes the payment of any penalty is not probable.
2. Based on allegations made by a competitor, the company is currently the subject of a government investigation relating to antitrust matters. If the company ultimately is accused of violations of the country's antitrust laws, fines could be assessed. Penalties would include sharing of previously earned profits with a competitor on all contracts entered into from inception. The competitor has indicated to the governmental agency investigating the company that the company has made excessive profits ranging from €50 million to €75 million by resorting to restrictive trade practices that are prohibited by the law of the country. No provision for any penalties or other damages has been made at year-end since the company's legal counsel is confident that these allegations will not be sustained in a court of law.

Disclosure of Events after the Reporting Period

These three disclosures are mandated by IAS 10:

1. The date when the financial statements were authorized for issue and who gave that authorization. If the enterprise's owners have the power to amend the financial statements after issuance, this fact should be disclosed.
2. If information is received after the statement of financial position date about conditions that existed at the statement of financial position date, disclosures that relate to those conditions should be updated in the light of the new information.
3. Where nonadjusting events after the reporting period date are of such significance that nondisclosure would affect the ability of the users of financial statements to make proper evaluations and decisions, disclosure should be made for each such significant category of nonadjusting event, of the nature of the event, and an estimate of its financial effect or a statement that such an estimate cannot be made.

JOURNAL ENTRIES

Current Liabilities

Accrue benefits. To accrue for all employee benefit expenses incurred during the month, for which an associated payable entry has not yet been made.

Medical insurance expense	xxx	
Dental insurance expense	xxx	
Disability expense	xxx	
Life insurance expense	xxx	
Accrued benefits		xxx

This entry *should be reversed* in the following accounting period.

Accrue bonuses. To record an estimated bonus amount. This entry assumes that a separate bonus expense account is charged, though it is also common practice to charge a salaries expense account. The accrual is reversed when the bonus is actually paid.

Bonus expense	xxx	
Accrued salaries		xxx

Accrue commissions. To accrue the estimated commission expense prior to payment. The liability is recorded in an accrued salaries account in order to conserve the number of liability accounts, but can also be recorded in a separate accrued commissions account. This entry typically is reversed in the following accounting period to offset the actual commission payment.

Commission expense	xxx	
Accrued salaries		xxx

Accrue property taxes. To accrue for the property tax liability incurred during the accounting period based on the known base of fixed assets.

Property tax expense	xxx	
Property tax payable		xxx

This entry *should not be reversed* in the following accounting period, since the tax payment normally will not occur in the following period—only once or twice per year. Instead, the actual payment should be charged directly against the accrual account with this entry:

Property tax payable	xxx	
Cash		xxx

Accrue royalties. To accrue royalties due to a supplier that have been earned but are not yet due for payment. This entry is reversed when the royalty payment is made.

Royalty expense	xxx	
Accrued royalty expense		xxx

Accrue salaries and wages. To accrue for salaries and wages earned through the end of the accounting period but have not yet paid to employees as of the end of the accounting period.

Direct labor expense	xxx	
(Salaries—itemize by department)	xxx	
Payroll tax expense	xxx	
Accrued salaries		xxx
Accrued payroll taxes		xxx

This entry *should be reversed* in the following accounting period.

Accrue vacation pay. To accrue vacation pay earned but not yet used by employees, subject to the year-end maximum vacation carryforward limitation. The same entry can be used to record accrued sick time.

Payroll taxes	xxx	
(Salaries—itemize by department)	xxx	
Accrued vacation pay		xxx

This entry *should not be reversed* in the following accounting period, since the vacation time may not be used in the following period. Instead, the actual vacation-related payment should be charged directly against the accrual account.

Accrue warranty claims. To accrue a reserve for warranty claims when a sale is made.

Warranty expense	xxx	
Accrued warranty expense		xxx

Record customer advances. To record the liability associated with a customer advance prior to completion of services or delivery of goods to the customer. The second entry assumes an advance is actually a deposit on the use of a company asset, and will be returned once the usage period is completed.

Cash	xxx	
Customer advances		xxx
Cash	xxx	
Customer deposits		xxx

RECORDKEEPING

A detailed record should be kept of all advances received by a company from customers, since this is a common area in which liabilities are underreported through the improper immediate recognition of advances as revenue. It is particularly important when the advances are actually deposits and must be returned to customers, since disputes over the amounts payable will be more likely if recordkeeping is inadequate.

Bonus payments can be quite large, so an itemization of the plans under which they are authorized and a detailed proof of their having been earned should be stored. This information usually is kept in the human resources file for each person to whom a bonus is paid.

Perhaps the most disputed of all current liabilities is the commission expense, due to both the complexity of many commission plans and the large proportion of pay that this expense represents for the sales staff. Accordingly, the level of documentation in this area should be very high, including a detailed calculation for each commission paid that itemizes every invoice on which payment was made and a clear notation of all special splits, overrides, and so on related to the payment. One should also retain the annual commission plan for each salesperson, which is used as the basis for the commission calculations.

The amount of accrued vacation and sick time is based on the accrual levels noted in the employee manual, which may change from year to year. A copy of every version of the employee manual should be stored, so that changes in the terms of these compensated absences can be traced. If an override deal is offered to a specific employee, a written copy of the deal should be stored in the employee's human resources file and also documented in the accounting department so it can be readily accessed when compensated absence accruals are made.

If a group of employees is to be terminated, the accrual for termination benefits can be a substantial one, and so should be adequately documented. This should include a copy of the termination plan, the written estimates of the number and types of positions to be eliminated, and a summary calculation of termination benefits based on this information.

Royalty payments can cause special problems for a company because many royalty agreements allow the payee to audit the company's books to ensure that royalty payments are being calculated and paid out properly. Consequently, special care should be made to segregate all royalty information in a separate set of binders where it can be easily accessed. The binders should either include a complete audit trail for the calculation and payment of royalties, or at least document where this information can be located elsewhere in the accounting records.

The wage accrual can be one of the largest period-end accruals, especially if a large proportion of the labor force is paid on an hourly basis, in which case there is typically a lag of several days between the completion of hours worked and the pay date. In these cases, a standard unpaid wage accrual worksheet, such as the one shown earlier in the Forms and Reports section, should be attached to the journal entry recording the accrual and stored in the journal entry binder for future reference.

An accrual for anticipated warranty expenses can be quite large for companies selling particular types of products, such as consumer end products. In these cases, it is worthwhile to record the historical warranty information on which the accrual is based, such as the historical claims information for both new product introductions and products that have been on the market for some time. This information is useful for proving the validity of the accrual if it is challenged during an audit.

Debt covenant violations catch companies by surprise far too often, because companies do not regularly track company performance in relation to the covenants or plan in advance to avoid violations. This problem can be controlled to some extent by separately recording the covenants in a place where they are difficult *not* to see, such as in the lead page of the budget, alongside all other assumptions. Even better, covenants can be included in the monthly financial statements, as part of a general comparison of covenants to actual results on a trend line for the past few months. This presentation ensures high visibility and also makes it quite clear which covenants are close to being violated.

The assumptions used to derive the amount of insurance claims incurred but not yet reported under any self-insurance program should be documented and included in the journal entry binder. This information will be used by auditors to determine the most appropriate amount of liability to record in association with unreported insurance claims.

10 LONG-TERM DEBT

DEFINITIONS OF TERMS

Amortization. The process of allocating an amount to expense over the periods benefited.

termination date of the bond. The issuing company may issue periodic interest payments directly to bondholders, though only if they are registered; another alternative is to send the entire amount of interest payable to a trustee, who exchanges bond coupons from bondholders for money from the deposited funds.

The issuing company frequently creates a sinking fund well in advance of the bond payoff date, so that it will have sufficient funds available to make the final balloon payment (or buy back bonds on an ongoing basis). The bond agreement may contain a number of restrictive covenants that the company must observe, or else the bondholders will be allowed a greater degree of control over the company or allowed to accelerate the payment date of their bonds.

A bond will be issued at a stated face value interest rate. The rate may not equate to the market rate on the date of issuance, in which case investors will either bid up the price of the bond (if its stated rate is higher than the market rate) or bid down the price (if its stated rate is lower than the market rate). The aftermarket price of a bond subsequently may vary considerably if the market rate of interest varies substantially from the stated rate of the bond.

Some bonds are issued with no interest rate at all. These zero-coupon bonds are sold at a deep discount and are redeemed at their face value at the termination date of the bond. They are of particular interest to those companies that do not want to be under the obligation of making fixed interest payments during the term of a bond.

The interest earned on a bond is subject to income taxes, except (in certain jurisdictions) for those bonds issued by government entities. These bonds, sometimes known as municipal bonds, pay tax-free interest. For this reason, they can be sold competitively at lower actual interest rates than the bonds offered by commercial companies.

The serial bond does not have a single termination date for the entire issuance of bonds. Instead, the company is committed to retire a certain number of bonds at regular intervals, so that the total number of outstanding bonds declines over time.

An alternative is the use of attached warrants, which allow the bondholder to buy shares of company stock at a prespecified price. The warrants may be publicly traded, and then their value can be separated from that of the bond so that each portion of the package is recognized separately in a company's statement of financial position.

Though some corporations issue their own bonds directly to investors, it is much more common for corporations to engage the services of an investment banker, who not only lines up investors for the company but may also invest a substantial amount of his or her own funds in the company's bonds. In either case, the board of directors must approve any new bonds. Thereafter a trustee is appointed to control the bond issuance, certificates are printed and signed, and delivery is made either to the investment banking firm or directly to investors in exchange for cash.

Debt Classification

It is generally not allowable to reclassify a debt that is coming due in the short term as a long-term liability on the grounds that it is about to be refinanced as a long-term debt. This treatment likely would result in no debt ever appearing in the current liabilities portion of the statement of financial position. It is allowable only if the company has the intention to refinance the debt on a long-term basis rather than simply rolling over the debt into another short-term debt instrument that will, in turn, become due and payable in the next accounting year. Not only that, but there must be firm evidence of this rollover into a long-term debt instrument, such as the presence of a debt agreement or an actual conversion to long-term debt subsequent to the statement of financial position date.

In the case of a debt that has been called by the creditor, it must be classified as a current liability. If the period during which the creditor can next call the debt is at some point subsequent to one year, however, then it still may be classified as a long-term debt. Also, if the call option applies only when the company defaults on some performance measure related to the debt, and if the company cannot cure the performance measure within whatever period is specified under the terms of the debt, then the debt needs to be classified as a current liability.

Some debt issuances have *put* provisions, which grant the holder the right to demand repayment by the issuing entity. If demand for redemption is out of the control of the issuer, all the debt must be categorized as a current liability. However, if the put option is conditioned on the occurrence of specified events, and those events have not occurred as of the statement of financial position date, then the debt remains as a noncurrent obligation.

Bonds Sold at a Discount or Premium to Their Face Value

When bonds are initially sold, the entry is a debit to cash and a credit to bonds payable. This occurs only when the price paid by investors exactly matches the face amount of the bond, however. A more common occurrence is when the market interest rate varies somewhat from the stated interest rate on the bond, so investors pay a different price in order to achieve an effective interest rate matching the market rate. For example, if the market rate were 8% and the stated rate were 7%, investors would pay less than the face amount of the bond so that the 7% interest they later receive will equate to an 8% interest rate on their reduced investment. Alternatively, if the rates were reversed, with a 7% market rate and 8% stated rate, investors would pay more for the bond, thereby driving down the stated interest rate to match the market rate. If the bonds are sold at a discount, the entry will include a debit to a discount on bonds payable account. For example, if €10,000 of bonds are sold at a discount of €1,500, the entry would be

Cash	8,500	
Discount on bonds payable	1,500	
Bonds payable		10,000

If the same transaction were to occur, except that a premium on sale of the bonds occurs, then the entry would be

Cash	11,500	
Premium on bonds payable		1,500
Bonds payable		10,000

Example of discount calculation

The Astana Company issues €1,000,000 of bonds at a stated rate of 8% in a market where similar issuances are being bought at 11%. The bonds pay interest once a year, and are to be paid off in 10 years. Investors purchase these bonds at a discount in order to earn an effective yield on their investment of 11%. The discount calculation requires one to determine the present value of 10 interest payments at 11% interest as well as the present value of €1,000,000, discounted at 11% for 10 years. The result is

Present value of 10 payments of €80,000	= €80,000 × 5.8892	=	€471,136
Present value of €1,000,000	= €1,000,000 × .3522	=	352,200
			€823,336
	Less: stated bond price		1,000,000
	Discount on bond		€176,664

In this example, the entry would be a debit to Cash for €823,336, a credit to Bonds Payable for €1,000,000, and a debit to Discount on Bonds Payable for €176,664. If the calculation had resulted in a premium (which would have occurred only if the market rate of interest was less than the stated interest rate on the bonds), then a credit to Premium on Bonds Payable would be in order.

Effective Interest Method

The amount of a discount or premium should be written off gradually to the interest expense account over the life of the bond. The only acceptable method for writing off these amounts is through the *effective interest method*, which allows one to charge off the difference between the market and stated rate of interest to the existing discount or premium account, gradually reducing the balance in the discount or premium account over the life of the bond. If interest payment dates do not coincide with the end of financial reporting periods, a journal entry must be made to show the amount of interest expense and related discount or premium amortization that would have occurred during the days following the last interest payment date and the end of the reporting period.

Example of the effective interest method

To continue with our example, the interest method holds that, in the first year of interest payments, the Astana Company's accountant would determine that the market interest expense for the first year would be €90,567 (bond stated price of €1 million minus discount of €176,664, multiplied by the market interest rate of 11%). The resulting journal entry would be

Interest expense	90,567	
Discount on bonds payable		10,567
Cash		80,000

The reason why only €80,000 is listed as a reduction in cash is that the company only has an obligation to pay an 8% interest rate on the €1 million face value of the bonds, which is €80,000. The difference is netted against the existing Discount on Bonds Payable account. The next table shows the calculation of the discount to be charged to expense each year for the full 10-year period of the bond, where the annual amortization of the discount is added back to the bond present value, eventually resulting in a bond present value of €1 million by the time principal payment is due, while the discount has dropped to zero.

Year	Beginning bond present value (4)	Unamortized discount	Interest expense (1)	Cash payment (2)	Credit to discount (3)
1	€823,336	€176,664	€90,567	€80,000	€10,567
2	833,903	166,097	91,729	80,000	11,729
3	845,632	154,368	93,020	80,000	13,020
4	858,652	141,348	94,452	80,000	14,452
5	873,104	126,896	96,041	80,000	16,041
6	889,145	110,855	97,806	80,000	17,806
7	906,951	93,049	99,765	80,000	19,765
8	926,716	73,284	101,939	80,000	21,939
9	948,655	51,346	104,352	80,000	24,352
10	973,007	26,994	107,031	80,000	26,994
	€1,000,000	€0			

(1) = Bond present value multiplied by the market rate of 11%.

(2) = Required cash payment of 8% stated rate multiplied by face value of €1,000,000.

(3) = Interest expense reduced by cash payment.

(4) = Beginning present value of the bond plus annual reduction in the discount.

Debt Issued with No Stated Interest Rate

If a company issues debt that has no stated rate of interest, then the accountant must create an interest rate for it that approximates the rate that the company would likely obtain, given its credit rating, on the open market on the date when the debt was issued. The accountant then uses this rate to discount the face amount of the debt down to its present value and records the difference between this present value and the loan's face value as the loan balance. For example, if a company issued debt with a face amount of €1 million, payable in five years and at no stated interest rate, and the market rate for interest at the time of issuance was 9%, then the discount factor to be applied to the debt would be 0.6499. This would give the debt a present value of €649,900. The difference between the face amount of €1 million and the present value of €649,900 should be recorded as a discount on the note, as shown in the next entry:

Cash	649,900	
Discount on note payable	350,100	
Notes payable		1,000,000

Debt Issuance Costs

The costs associated with issuing bonds can be substantial. Examples include the legal costs of creating the bond documents, accounting fees; commissions; engraving and printing the bond certificates; registration; and (especially) the underwriting costs of the investment banker. These costs should be deducted from the initial carrying amount of the bonds and amortized using the effective interest method; generally the amount involved is insignificant enough that use of the simpler straight-line method would not result in a material difference. These costs do not provide any future economic benefit and therefore should not be considered an asset. Because these costs reduce the amount of cash proceeds, they essentially increase the effective interest rate, and they should be accounted for the in the same way as an unamortized discount.

Notes Issued with Attached Rights

An issuing company can grant additional benefits to the other party, such as exclusive distribution rights on its products, discounts on product sales, and so on—the range of possibilities is endless. In these cases, one should consider the difference between the present value and face value of the debt to be the value of the additional consideration. When this occurs, the difference is debited to the Discount on Note Payable account and is amortized using the *effective interest method* that was described earlier. The offsetting credit can be made to a variety of accounts, depending on the nature of the transaction. The credited account typically is written off either ratably (if the attached benefit is equally spread over many accounting periods) or in conjunction with specific events (such as the shipment of discounted products to the holder of the debt). Though less common, it is also possible to issue debt at an above-market rate in order to obtain additional benefits from the debt holder. In this case, the entry is reversed, with a credit to the Premium on Note Payable account and the offsetting debit to a number of possible accounts related to the specific consideration given.

Example of note issued with attached rights

The Astana Company has issued a new note for €2,500,000 at 4% interest to one of its customers, the Alaskan Company. Under the terms of the five-year note, Alaskan obtains a 20% discount on all services it purchases from Astana during the term of the note. The market rate for similar debt was 9% on the date the loan documents were signed.

The present value of the note at the 9% market rate of interest over a five-year term is €1,624,750, while the present value of the note at its stated rate of 4% is €2,054,750. The difference between the two present value figures is €430,000, which is the value of the attached right to discounted security services granted to Alaskan. Astana should make this entry to record the loan:

Cash	2,500,000	
Discount on note payable	430,000	
Note payable		2,500,000
Unearned revenue		430,000

The unearned revenue of €430,000 either can be recognized incrementally as part of each invoice billed to Alaskan, or can be recognized ratably over the term of the debt. Since Astana does not know the exact amount of the services that will be contracted for by Alaskan during the term of the five-year note, the better approach is to recognize the unearned revenue ratably over the note term. The first month's entry would show where the amount recognized is 1/60 of the beginning balance of unearned revenue, as indicated in the example below:

Unearned revenue	7,166.67	
Services revenue		7,166.67

Notes Issued for Property

When a note is issued in exchange for some type of property, the stated interest rate on the note is used to value the debt for reporting purposes unless the rate is not considered to be "fair." If it is not fair, then the transaction should be recorded at the fair market value of either the property or the note, whichever can be more clearly determined.

Example of debt with an unfair interest rate, exchanged for property

The Astana Company exchanges a €50,000 note for a special order car made for the company president of the Osaka Company. The car is custom-built for Astana, so there is no way to assign a fair market value to it. The note has a stated interest rate of 3% and is payable in three years. The 3% rate appears to be quite low, especially since Astana just secured similar financing from a local lender at a 7% interest rate. The 3% rate can thus be considered not fair for the purposes of valuing the debt, so Astana's controller elects to use the 7% rate instead.

The discount rate for debt due in three years at 7% interest is 0.8163. After multiplying the €50,000 face value of the note by 0.8163, the controller arrives at a net present value for the debt of €40,815, which is recorded in the next entry as the value of the transportation equipment, along with a discount that shall be amortized to interest expense over the life of the loan.

Vehicle	40,815	
Discount on note payable	9,185	
Notes payable		50,000

Extinguishment of Debt

A company may find it advisable to repurchase its bonds prior to their maturity date if, for example, the market interest rates have dropped so far below the stated rate on the bonds that the company can profitably refinance at a lower interest rate. Whatever the reason may be, the resulting transaction should recognize any gain or loss on the transaction, the transactional cost of the retirement, and any proportion of the outstanding discount, premium, or bond issuance costs relating to the original bond issuance.

Example of debt extinguishment

To return to our earlier example, if the Astana Company were to buy back €200,000 of its €1 million bond issuance at a premium of 5%, and does so with €125,000 of the original bond discount still on its books, it would record a loss of €10,000 on the bond retirement (=€200,000 × 5%), while also recognizing 1/5 of the remaining discount, which is €25,000 (=€125,000 × 1/5). The entry would be

Bonds payable	200,000	
Loss on bond retirement	10,000	
Discount on bonds payable		25,000
Cash		185,000

It may happen that the issuing company finds itself in the position of being unable to pay either interest or principal to its bondholders; if so, there are two directions the accountant can take in reflecting the problem in the accounting records. In the first case, the company may be only temporarily in default and may be attempting to work out a payment solution with the bondholders. Under this scenario, the amortizations of discounts or premiums, as well as of bond issuance costs and interest expense, should continue as they have in the past. If, however, there is no chance of payment, then the amortizations of discounts or premiums, as well as of bond issuance costs, should be accelerated, being recognized in full in the current period. This action is taken on the grounds that the underlying accounting transaction that specified the period over which the amortizations occurred has now disappeared, requiring the accountant to recognize all remaining expenses.

If the issuing company has not defaulted on a debt, restructuring its terms instead, then the accountant must determine the present value of the new stream of cash flows and compare it to the original carrying value of the debt arrangement. In the likely event that the new present value of the debt is less than the original present value, the difference should be recognized in the current period as a gain.

Alternatively, if the present value of the restructured debt agreement is *more* than the carrying value of the original agreement, then a loss is *not* recognized on the difference; rather, the effective interest rate on the new stream of debt payments is reduced to the point where the resulting present value of the restructured debt matches the carrying value of the original agreement. This will result in a reduced amount of interest expense being accrued for all future periods during which the debt is outstanding.

In some cases where the issuing company is unable to pay bondholders, it gives them other company assets in exchange for the interest or principal payments owed to them. When this occurs, the issuing company first records a gain or a loss on the initial revaluation of the asset being transferred to its fair market value. Next it records a gain or loss on the transaction if there is a difference between the carrying value of the debt being paid off and the fair market value of the asset being transferred to the bondholder.

Example of asset transfer to eliminate debt

The Astana Company is unable to pay off its loan from a local lender. The lender agrees to cancel the debt, with a remaining face value of €35,000, in exchange for a company truck having a book value of €26,000 and a fair market value of €29,000. There is also €2,500 of accrued but unpaid interest expense associated with the debt. Astana's controller first revalues the truck to its fair market value and then records a gain on the debt settlement transaction. The entries are

Vehicles	3,000	
Gain on asset transfer		3,000
Note payable	35,000	
Interest payable	2,500	
Vehicles		29,000
Gain on debt settlement		8,500

Scheduled Bond Retirement

A bond agreement may contain specific requirements either to create a sinking fund that is used at the maturity date to buy back all bonds or else to buy back bonds gradually on a regular schedule, usually through a trustee. In either case, the intention is to ensure that the company does not suddenly face a large repayment requirement at the maturity date. In this situation, the company usually forwards, at regular intervals, funds to a trustee, who uses the funds to buy back bonds. The resulting accounting is identical to that noted under the Extinguishment of Debt section. In addition, if the company forwards interest payments to the trustee for bonds that the trustee now has in its possession, these payments are used to purchase additional bonds (since there is no one to whom the interest can be paid). In this case, the journal entry that would normally record this transaction as an interest expense is converted into an entry that reduces the principal balance of the bonds outstanding.

Convertible Debt

Revised IAS 32 addresses the accounting for compound financial instruments from the perspective of the issuers. Convertible bonds and bonds with detachable stock purchase warrants are the most common type of such instruments. IAS 32 requires the issuer of that type of financial instrument to present the liability component and the equity component separately on the statement of financial position.

Under the revised IAS 32, it is required that—whether or not fair values are available for all components of the compound instrument—full fair value be allocated to the liability components, with only the residual assigned to equity. This position has been taken in order to be fully consistent with the definition of equity instruments. Equity evidences the residual interest in the assets of an entity after deducting all of its liabilities.

Residual allocation method. As noted, the only acceptable method of allocating proceeds from the issuance of convertible debt is to assign to the equity component (e.g., the conversion feature) the residual amount; but first, the full fair value of the debt, minus the conversion feature, must be assigned to the liability component. To illustrate this approach, consider the next fact situation.

Example of the residual allocation method

Astana Company sells convertible bonds that have an aggregate par (face) value of €25 million to the public at a price of €98 on January 2, 2008. The bonds are due December 31, 2015, but they can be called at €102 anytime after January 2, 2011. The bonds carry a coupon of 6% and are convertible into Astana common stock at an exchange ratio of 25 shares per bond (each bond having a face value of €1,000). Taking the discount on the offering price into account, the bonds were priced to yield about 6.3% to maturity.

The company's investment bankers have advised that without the conversion feature, Astana's bonds would have had to carry an interest yield of 8% to be sold in the current market environment. Thus, the market price of a pure bond with a 6% coupon at January 2, 2008, would have been about €883.48 (the present value of a stream of semiannual interest payments of €30 per bond, plus a terminal value of €1,000, discounted at a 4% semiannual rate).

This suggests that of the €980 being paid for each bond, €883.48 is being paid for the pure debt obligation and another €96.52 is being offered for the conversion feature. Given this analysis, the entry to record the original issuance of the €25 million in debt securities on January 2, 2008, would be

Cash	24,500,000	
Discount on bonds payable	2,913,000	
Bonds payable		25,000,000
Paid-in capital—conversion feature		2,413,000

The discount should be amortized to interest expense, ideally by the effective yield method (constant return on increasing base) over the eight years to the maturity date. For purposes of this example, however, straight-line amortization (€2,913,000 ÷ 16 periods = €182,000 per semiannual period) will be used. Thus, the entry to record the June 30, 2008 interest payment would be

Interest expense	932,000	
Discount on bonds payable		182,000
Cash		750,000

The paid-in capital account arising from the foregoing transaction would form a permanent part of the capital of Astana. If the bonds are later converted, this would be transferred to the common stock accounts, effectively forming part of the price paid for the shares ultimately issued. If the bondholders *decline* to convert and the bonds eventually are paid off at maturity, the paid-in capital from the conversion feature will form a type of "donated capital" to the entity, since the bondholders effectively will have forfeited this capital that they had contributed to the company.

If the bonds are not converted, the discount on the bonds payable will continue to be amortized until maturity. If they are converted, however, the remaining unamortized balance in this account, along with the face value of the bonds, will constitute the "price" being paid for the stock to be issued. To account for this transaction under the popular *book value method*, the principal amount of the bond is moved to an equity account, with a portion being allocated to the capital account at par value and the remainder going to the additional paid-in capital account. A portion of the discount or premium associated with the bond issuance is also retired, based on the proportion of bonds converted to equity.

To illustrate, assume

On July 1, 2011, all the bonds are tendered for conversion to common stock of Astana. The remaining book value of the bonds will be converted into common stock, which does not carry any par or stated value. The first step is to compute the book value of the debt.

Bonds payable		€25,000,000
Discount on bonds payable		
Original discount	€2,913,000	
Less amortization to date (4.4 yrs.)	(1,638,000)	1,275,000
Net book value of obligation		€23,725,000

The entry to record the conversion, given the foregoing information, is

Bonds payable	25,000,000	
Paid-in capital—conversion feature	2,413,000	
Discount on bonds payable		1,275,000
Common stock, no par value		26,138,000

Note that in the previous entry, the effective price recorded for the shares being issued is the book value of the remaining debt, adjusted by the price previously recorded to reflect the sale of the conversion feature. In the present instance, given the book value at the conversion date (a function of when the conversion privilege was exercised), and given the conversion ratio of 25 shares per bond, an effective price of €41.82 per share is being paid for the stock to be issued. This is determined without any reference to the market value at the date of the conversion. Presumably the market price is higher, as it is unlikely that the bondholders would surrender an asset earning 6%, with a fixed maturity date, for another asset having a lower value and having an uncertain future worth. (Although if the dividend yield were somewhat higher than the equivalent bond interest, an unlikely event, this might happen.)

Convertible Debt—Subsequent Change in Offering to Induce Conversion

If a company induces its bondholders to convert their holdings to equity by subsequently improving the conversion feature of the bond agreement, the issuance of these modifications, or sweeteners, should be accounted for as a reduction in the proceeds of the stock offering, thereby reducing the paid-in capital from the transaction.

A previously acceptable alternative accounting treatment, recording the sweetener payments as an expense in the period of conversion, is no longer deemed appropriate due to the proceeds allocation scheme mandated by revised IAS 32.

Example of subsequent change in conversion terms

Mr. Abraham Smith owns €25,000 of the North Brittany Railroad's convertible debt. The bonds were originally issued with a conversion price of €50 per share, which the railroad subsequently lowered to €40 to induce conversion. The shares have a market value of €38 and a par value of €1. Mr. Smith elects to convert to stock, resulting in this calculation:

	Before change in terms	*After change in terms*
Face amount of bonds	€25,000	€25,000
Conversion price	50	40
Total shares converted	500	625
Fair value per share	38	38
Value of converted stock	€19,000	€23,750

The difference between the total values of converted stock before and after the change in terms is €4,750. This amount is recorded as a reduction in paid-in capital from the transaction:

Bonds payable	25,000	
Capital account, par value		625
Additional paid-in capital (€29,125 – €4,750)		24,375

Debt Issued with Stock Warrants

Warrants are certificates enabling the holder to purchase a stated number of shares of stock at a certain price within a certain period. They often are issued with bonds to enhance the marketability of the bonds and to lower the bond's interest rate.

Detachable warrants are similar to other features, such as the conversion feature discussed earlier, which under IAS 32 make the debt a compound financial instrument and which necessitate an allocation of the original proceeds among the constituent elements. Although warrants that will be traded often in the market are easier to value than are conversion features, the revised IAS 32 requires the residual allocation method of accounting for the issuance of these instruments. Under this method, only residual value is assigned to the equity element of compound instruments consisting of both liability and equity components.

DECISION TREE

The decision tree shown in Exhibit 10.1 shows the general set of decisions to be made during the life of a bond, beginning with the treatment of discounts or premiums on the initial sale price and proceeding through the presence of attached warrants and early debt extinguishment. The decisions in the top third of the tree will impact nearly all bonds, since it is unusual *not* to have a discount or premium. The middle third impacts only attached warrants, with most of the action items involving in-the-money warrants.

Exhibit 10.1 Decision Points during Lifetime of Bond

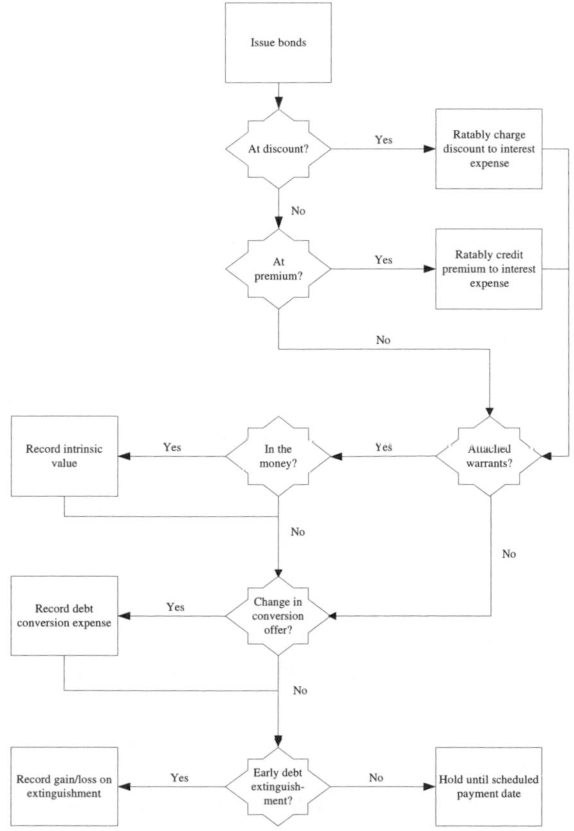

POLICIES

Notes and Bonds

- **All notes and bonds shall only be issued subsequent to approval by the board of directors.** This policy gives the board control over any new debt liabilities. In reality, anyone lending money to the company will require a board motion, so this policy is likely to be imposed by the lender even if it does not exist internally.
- **Debt sinking funds shall be fully funded on scheduled dates.** This policy is designed to force the treasury staff to plan for the timely accumulation of funds needed to pay off scheduled principal payments on debt, thereby avoiding any last-minute funding crises.
- **Recognition of unearned revenue for attached rights shall match offsetting discount amortization as closely as possible.** This policy is designed to avoid the manipulation of revenue recognition for attached rights. For example, if a value is assigned to an attached right, the debit will be to a discount account that will be ratably recognized as interest expense over the term of the debt; however, the credit will be to an unearned revenue account for which the potential exists to recognize revenue much sooner, thereby creating a split in the timing of revenue and expense recognition. Though this split may be valid in some cases, an effort should be made to avoid any significant disparities, thereby avoiding any surges in profits.
- **The fair market interest rate shall be used to value debt transactions where property is being obtained.** This policy is designed to prevent any manipulation of the value assigned to an acquired asset as part of a debt-for-property transaction. By always using the fair market rate, there is no possibility of using an excessively high or low interest rate to artificially alter the cost at which the acquired property is recorded on the company books.
- **Debt shall always be issued at stated rates as close to the market interest rate as possible.** Though there are valid reasons for issuing debt at rates significantly different from the market rate, this causes a problem not only with determining the market rate to be applied to debt present value calculations but also with the amount of interest expense recognized. Instead, this policy avoids the problem by requiring debt issuances to have stated interest rates so close to the market rate that there is no possibility of a significant debt valuation issue.

Extinguishment of Debt

- **Debt shall not be extinguished early if the primary aim is to report a gain or loss on the extinguishment.** If a company buys back its bonds when the stated interest rate on the debt is lower than the current market interest rate, it will recognize a gain on the transaction, but it must refinance the purchase with more expensive debt at current market rates. Thus, this policy is designed to keep company management from creating transactions that appear to increase profits when the underlying results worsen the company's financial situation.

- **When interest rates allow, the company shall repurchase its debt with less expensive debt.** Though it sounds obvious, this policy is designed to force management to make the correct decision always to use less expensive debt, even though this will result in the recognition of a loss when the older, more expensive debt is eliminated from the company records.

Convertible Debt

- **Debt conversions to equity shall always be recorded using the book value method.** This policy keeps the accounting staff from switching between the book value and market value methods, whereby they could use the market value method to recognize gains and the book value method to avoid losses.
- **Debt conversion calculations shall always be verified by the audit staff.** This policy is designed to ensure that any expenses associated with debt conversions to stock shall be calculated correctly. Either internal or external auditors can be used; the main point is to require independent verification of all journal entries related to debt conversions.

Debt Issued with Stock Warrants

- **Debt issuance calculations incorporating attached stock warrants shall always be verified by the audit staff.** This policy ensures that the residual allocation method is applied, under which full fair value is allocated to the liability components, with only the residual value being assigned to equity. This allocation is critical to the amount of bond discount that must be subsequently amortized.

PROCEDURES

Notes and Bonds—Borrowing Short-Term Funds

This nine-step procedure is used by the chief financial officer to borrow funds from the corporate line of credit.

1. Review the short-term cash forecast with the financial analyst and determine the immediate cash need from that report.
2. Alter the expected amount based on any unusual cash flows not noted on the standard report.
3. Verify that there is a sufficient amount left on the line of credit to borrow.
4. Extract a copy of the Loan Borrowing/Paydown Form (see the Forms and Reports section) from the forms cabinet and fill it out, entering the amount determined in the first step.
5. Have an authorized person sign the form.
6. Fax the completed form to the bank.
7. Call the bank to verify receipt of the fax.
8. Send the completed form to the general ledger accountant for proper recording in the general ledger.

9. Follow up with the bank if it does not send a transaction confirmation within a reasonable time period.

Notes and Bonds—Loan Collateralization Report

Use this six-step procedure to update the lender's loan collateralization report (the form is shown in Chapter 2) at the end of each reporting period.

1. Call up the collateralization report in the computer system.
2. Alter the date of the month to reflect the date for which the certificate is being submitted.
3. Alter the month-end balance of accounts receivable and inventory on the report, as well as overdue accounts receivable and obsolete inventory line items.
4. Alter the amount of currently borrowed funds on the report.
5. Review the report and sign it.
6. Mail the loan collateralization report to the lender, along with the detail reports for accounts receivable and inventory that tie to the amounts listed on the report.

Effective Interest Method

Use this five-step procedure to determine the amount of discount or premium to amortize in a given accounting period.

1. Determine the present value of the outstanding bond at the beginning of the calculation period. To do this, determine the present value of all interest payments for the bond instrument as well as the present value of the principal payment at the end of the borrowing period, using the market rate of interest as the basis for the discount factor.
2. Calculate the interest expense in the reporting period by multiplying the market interest rate by the bond's present value for the number of days in the accounting period.
3. Subtract from the calculated interest expense the actual cash payment made for interest expense to the bondholders, which is based on the stated interest rate rather than the market interest rate. Using the difference between the two numbers, create a journal entry offsetting the outstanding discount or premium.
4. Add this interest rate difference to the outstanding present value of the bond if there is a discount, or subtract it from the bond if there is an outstanding premium.
5. Store the new balance of the bond present value as well as the newly reduced discount or premium, which will be used as the basis for the effective interest calculation in the next reporting period.

Extinguishment of Debt

Use this nine-step procedure to process the repurchase of debt by the issuer.

1. Examine the bond documentation to determine the amount of any extra fees required to extinguish debt early, such as termination fees or premium payments. Calculate the full extinguishment cost including these factors, and compare it to the cost of replacement financing to see if the proposed extinguishment will result in increased cash flow for the company.
2. Obtain written approval from the board of directors to retire the debt, and include this document in the corporate minute book.
3. If there is a trustee managing bondholder transactions, notify the trustee of the proposed extinguishment.
4. Contact bondholders to notify them of the date on which conversion shall occur and the price they will receive for each bond held. The bond document may require that this information be published to the general public well in advance of the extinguishment date.
5. If the original record of the bond issuance included a recognition of the equity portion, this recognition must be reversed, with a debit to the Additional Paid-In Capital account.
6. If there is any unamortized discount or premium related to the original bond issuance, recognize that portion of the remaining amount that equates to the proportion of debt being retired.
7. If any premium is being paid to retire the debt, charge this premium to expense at the time of the retirement.
8. On the retirement date, issue settlement funding to the bondholder trustee to retire the bonds.
9. Summarize the transaction and send this information to the general ledger accountant for entry in the general ledger.

Convertible Debt

Use this five-step procedure to process a request by a bondholder to convert that entity's bond holdings to company stock.

1. Verify that a sufficient number of shares are authorized and available to fulfill the request by the bondholder.
2. Send documentation of the request to the general ledger accountant, who records any accrued but unpaid interest expense on the bond, debiting it to expense and crediting the capital account (if the bondholder forfeits the interest). The general ledger accountant should initial the step to signify its completion.
3. Update the bond ledger by recording the retirement of the bond serial number.
4. Create a stock certificate for the bondholder and obtain valid signatures authorizing the certificate. Issue the certificate to the former bondholder by registered mail.
5. Update the stock ledger by recording the stock certificate number and the number of shares issued.

Debt Issued with Stock Warrants

Use this seven-step procedure to determine the proper valuation of each component of a debt offering with a warrant attachment.

1. Obtain written approval from the board of directors to issue debt with attached stock warrants, and include this document in the corporate minute book.
2. Conduct the bond offering.
3. Determine the value of the bond components of the offering. This can be obtained from the investment banker handling the transaction, who can estimate it based on the value of similar offerings for other clients. Another alternative is to wait until the bonds and warrants are publicly traded and assign values to the bond components based on their initial trading prices.
4. To assign a price to the warrants, use the residual allocation method under which full fair value is allocated to the liability components, with only the residual value being assigned to equity.
5. Have an independent party, such as the internal audit staff, review the calculations splitting the value of the offering between bonds and stock warrants.
6. Credit the resulting warrant value to the Additional Paid-In Capital account, and credit the full face value of the bond to the Bonds Payable account. Debit the total cash received from the transaction to the Cash account, and enter any remaining difference to either the Discount on Bonds Payable (if a debit) or to the Premium on Bonds Payable (if a credit).
7. If bond issuance costs were incurred, these costs should be deducted from the initial carrying amount of the bonds and amortized using the effective interest method.

CONTROLS

Notes and Bonds

- **Require evidence of intent and ability to recategorize debt from short term to long term.** A company may shift the classification of its short-term debt to the long-term debt category, but this can mislead investors and creditors regarding the company's short-term obligations. A good control is to require evidence supporting the reporting shift, such as a board motion to take on replacement long-term debt, plus a signed long-term loan to pay off the short-term debt. This documentation should be attached to the journal entry that shifts short-term debt into the long-term debt category.
- **Require approval of the terms of all new borrowing agreements.** A senior corporate manager should be assigned the task of reviewing all prospective debt instruments to verify that their interest rate, collateral, and other requirements are not excessively onerous or conflict with the terms of existing debt agreements. It may also be useful from time to time to see if a lending institu-

tion has inappropriate ties to the company, such as partial or full ownership in its stock by the person responsible for obtaining debt agreements.

- **Require supervisory approval of all borrowings and repayments.** As was the case with the preceding control point, high-level supervisory approval is required for all debt instruments—except this time it is for final approval of each debt commitment. If the debt to be acquired is extremely large, it may be useful to have a policy requiring approval by the board of directors, just to be sure that there is full agreement at all levels of the organization regarding the nature of the debt commitment. To be a more useful control, this signing requirement should be communicated to the lender, so that it does not inadvertently accept a debt agreement that has not been signed by the proper person.
- **Investigate the reasoning for revenue recognition related to attached rights that is not ratably recognized.** When a value is assigned to an attached right, the debit is to a discount account that will be ratably recognized as interest expense over the term of the debt; however, the credit will be to an unearned revenue account for which the potential exists to recognize revenue much sooner, thereby creating a split in the timing of revenue and expense recognition. Whenever revenue recognition related to this credit is not calculated on a ratable basis (which would create an approximate match between revenue and expense recognition), the calculation should first be approved by a manager.
- **Gain management approval of the initial debt entry related to debt issued in exchange for property.** It is quite possible that the stated interest rate on any debt issued in exchange for property will not match the fair market rate at the time of the transaction. Since the stated rate can be used to value the debt transaction unless the rate is not considered to be fair, this can lead to some abuse in asset valuation. For example, if the stated rate is below the market rate and is still used to record the property acquisition transaction, the present value of the debt will be higher, resulting in a larger asset valuation. If the asset is depreciated over a longer period than would the interest expense that would otherwise be recognized if the higher market interest were used, then a company effectively has shifted expense recognition into the future and increased its profits in the short term. Consequently, management approval of the interest rate used to value the acquisition should be obtained, while a justification for the interest rate used should be attached to the journal entry.
- **Require written and approved justification for the interest rate used to value debt.** When the stated interest rate on debt varies significantly from the market rate of interest, GAAP requires that the debt be valued using the market rate. Nevertheless, the exact amount of this market rate is subject to interpretation, which has an impact on the amount of interest expense recognized. Requiring justification for and approval of the rate used introduces some rigor to the process.

Effective Interest Method

- **Include in the month-end closing procedure a task to record interest expense on any bonds for which interest payments do not correspond to the closing date.** The payment of interest to bondholders is a natural trigger for the recording of interest expense, but there is no such trigger when there is no payment. To enforce the proper recording not only of unpaid interest expense but also of any amortization on related bond discounts or premiums, a specific task should be included in the closing procedure as well as a required sign-off on the task.

Extinguishment of Debt

- **Include in the debt procedure a line item to charge unamortized discounts or premiums to expense proportionate to the amount of any extinguished debt.** The general ledger accountant may not remember to write off any unamortized discount or premium when debt is extinguished, so the debt extinguishment procedure should include a line item requiring that this task be addressed. Otherwise, expense recognition potentially could be delayed until the original payment date of the debt, which may be many years in the future.
- **Report to the board of directors the repayment status of all debt.** IFRS requires that all unamortized discounts and premiums be recognized in the current period if there is no reasonable chance that the debt will be repaid. Since this acceleration has a significant impact on reported earnings in the current period, there may be some unwillingness to classify debt as unable to be paid. By requiring a standard report to the board of directors regarding the status of debt repayments at each of its meetings, the board can decide on its own when amortization must be accelerated and can force management to do so.

Convertible Debt

- **Verify the market value of debt on the date of issuance of convertible debt.** As noted, the only acceptable method of allocating proceeds from the issuance of convertible debt is to assign the full fair value of the debt, minus the conversion feature, to the liability component. After first assigning the fair value of the debt, the residual amount is assigned to equity. A good control is to require evidence supporting the residual allocation process. This documentation should be attached to the journal entry that records the issuance of convertible debt.
- **Include a review of accrued interest expense on all recently converted debt.** If the terms of a company's bond agreements state that bondholders must forfeit accrued interest on converted debt, then there will be a temptation also to avoid recording this accrual on the books as an expense, as is required by IFRS. Consequently, the formal procedure used to convert debt to equity should include a line item for the general ledger accountant to record this accrued interest expense and also require a signature on the procedure to ensure its completion.

- **Verify expense calculations associated with any sweetened conversion offers.** IFRS requires that the issuance of these modifications, or sweeteners, should be accounted for as a reduction in the proceeds of the stock offering, thereby reducing paid-in capital from the transaction. Although recording the sweetener payments as an expense in the period of conversion used to be an acceptable alternative accounting treatment, it is no longer allowed. A copy of the relevant portions of the original bond agreement should be attached to any journal entry that records a conversion to equity, which provides documentation of the initial conversion price. When the calculation is verified by an internal auditor or senior accounting person, this provides documentation of the initial baseline conversion price.

FORMS AND REPORTS

Notes and Bonds—Loan Borrowing/Paydown Form

It is not sufficient to contact a lender and ask to borrow funds or pay down a loan balance. The bank wants to see a signed form authorizing these changes, preferably on company letterhead. A general-purpose sample form is shown in Exhibit 10.2, which can be used to both borrow funds and to retire debt. The form is designed based on the assumption that there are multiple company accounts or loans outstanding, into or out of which funds can be shifted. The user checks off a "Borrow" or "Paydown" box and circles the appropriate "from" and "to" fields, based on the action requested of the lender, enters the relevant loan number and account number, has an authorized officer sign at the bottom of the form, and faxes it to the lender. Some portions of the form can contain preset information, such as the loan and account numbers, as well as the officer name and confirmation phone number. By using the high degree of standardization in this type of form, one can avoid costly errors in the transfer of funds in and out of loan instruments.

Exhibit 10.2 Loan Borrowing/Paydown Form

Loan Borrowing/Paydown Form
for [Company Name]

To the attention of:
Lending officer name
Lending entity name
Lending entity address

Borrow	Paydown	Dollar Amount		Loan Number		Company Account Number
☐	☐		From To		From To	
☐	☐		From To		From To	
☐	☐		From To		From To	
☐	☐		From To		From To	
☐	☐		From To		From To	

Authorization:

Signature	Printed Name	Title/Date

Confirmation Phone Number

Notes and Bonds—Loan Collateralization Report

A lender usually requires that a loan collateralization report such as the one shown in the Chapter 2 Forms and Reports section be completed at the end of each month. The agreement usually requires that old receivables be stripped from the reported balance to arrive at a core set of receivables most likely to be collected by the lender in the event of default. In addition, each category of assets used as collateral is multiplied by a reduction percentage (shown in bold in the exhibit), reflecting the amount of cash the lender believes it can collect if it were to sell each type of asset. The reduced amount of all asset types is then summarized and compared to the outstanding loan balance; if the collateral amount has dropped below the loan balance, then the company must pay back the difference. The report typically is signed by a company officer.

Notes and Bonds—Bond Status Report

If a company has made a number of bond issuances, it is useful to maintain a status report, such as the version shown in Exhibit 10.3. The report contains a separate line item for each series of bonds issued, listing the sale price, face value, and stated interest rate. It also notes all key dates, including interest payment dates, principal payment dates, and conversion dates (if any) for convertible stock. This report is useful not only for planning when cash payments must be made but also as the basis for a variety of accounting entries.

FOOTNOTES

Disclosure of Loans

If a company has entered into a loan agreement as the creditor, the accountant should describe each debt instrument as well as all maturity dates associated with principal payments, the interest rate, and any circumstances under which the lender can call the loan (usually involving a description of all related covenants). In addition, the existence of any conversion privileges by the lender should be described, and any assets to be used as collateral. Other special disclosures involve the existence of any debt agreements entered into subsequent to the date of the financial statements, related-party debt agreements, and the unused amount of any outstanding letters of credit. An example follows.

> The company has entered into a line of credit arrangement with the Federal Commercial Bank, which carries a maximum possible balance of €5 million. The loan has a variable interest rate that is 1/2% higher than the bank's prime lending rate. The loan's interest rate as of the date of the financial statements is 8 3/4%. As of the date of the financial statements, the company had drawn down €750,000 of the loan balance. Collateral used to secure the loan is all accounts receivable and fixed assets. The loan must be renegotiated by December 31, 2008; in the meantime, the bank can call the loan if the company's working capital balance falls below €2 million, or if its current ratio drops below 1.5 to 1.

Exhibit 10.3 Bond Status Report

Company Name
Bond Status Report

Beginning serial number	*Ending serial number*	*Sale price*	*Face value*	*Stated rate*	*1st interest payment date*	*2nd interest payment date*	*Principle payment date*	*Total principal*	*Conversion date*	*Conversion price*
00001	01000	€950	1,000	9.375%	15-Mar	15-Sep	15-Sep-2015	€1,000,000	15-Sep-2020	€50
01001	02000	975	1,000	9.375%	15-Mar	15-Sep	10-Oct-2015	1,000,000	10-Oct-2020	50
02001	03000	990	1,000	9.375%	15-Mar	15-Sep	20-Nov-2015	1,000,000	20-Nov-2020	50
10000	12000	850	1,000	9.100%	15-Feb	15-Aug	15-Feb-2018	2,000,000	15-Feb-2023	52
12001	14000	860	1,000	9.100%	15-Feb	15-Aug	31-Mar-2018	2,000,000	31-Mar-2023	52
14001	16000	845	1,000	9.100%	15-Feb	15-Aug	20-Apr-2018	2,000,000	20-Apr-2023	52
20000	25000	910	1,000	9.250%	1-May	1-Nov	5-May-2020	5,000,000	5-May-2025	55
30000	34000	935	1,000	9.850%	1-Apr	1-Aug	10-Apr-2021	4,000,000	10-Apr-2026	56
40000	48000	980	1,000	9.950%	1-Jun	1-Dec	5-Jun-2022	8,000,000	5-Jun-2027	60
50000	56000	942	1,000	9.450%	1-Jun	1-Dec	11-Jun-2023	6,000,000	11-Jul-2028	62
								€32,000,000		

Disclosure of LoanGuarantees

If a company is liable for the debt of another entity, a footnote should describe the nature of the indebtedness, the relationship between the two companies, the potential amount of the liability, and the date on which the liability terminates. An example follows.

> The company is contingently liable for the outstanding loans of Excelsior Holdings Ltd., in which it owns a 40% interest. The maximum possible loan balance under the guarantee agreement is €4.2 million, of which €3.8 million is currently outstanding. The loan is a term loan with required periodic principal payments, resulting in complete termination of the loan and the company's loan guarantee as of May 31, 2011.

Disclosure of Unused Credit Facilities

If a company has entered into a credit facility with a lender and some portion of that potential debt is unused, a footnote should disclose the terms of the agreement, the amount of debt outstanding, and the amount available. If there are covenants associated with the facility, the company's ability to meet the covenants should be noted. An example follows.

> The company has a revolving line of credit with a consortium of banks for a total of €100 million. The debt is secured by the company's accounts receivable and inventory balances and carries an adjustable interest rate matching the prime rate. The company must meet the terms of several covenants in order to use the facility; it currently meets all covenant requirements. There was €28.5 million outstanding under the line of credit at year-end, leaving €71.5 million available for further borrowings.

Disclosure of Related-Party Loans

If a company has issued loans to related parties, it should describe the nature of the transactions as well as the amounts involved, interest rates payable, and the timing of subsequent payments in a footnote. Some examples follow.

1. The company is owed €2,000,000 in various notes receivable from its executive management team. The notes carry interest rates ranging from 5.25% to 7.5%, and will mature within the next two to five years. The board authorized year-end bonus payments to the executives owing the notes receivable, all of whom chose to forgo payment in exchange for cancellation of their notes payable.
2. The company loaned €175,000 to the CEO in 2006 at an interest rate of 6.5%. Neither the principal nor the accrued interest on the note has been paid. The board has elected to forgive €100,000 of the outstanding principal and all associated interest, leaving a balance of €75,000 on which interest has continued to accrue since the loan initiation date in 2006.
3. The company has been loaned €350,000 by the CEO. This debt is unsecured, carries an interest rate of 8.2%, and can be repaid only after all bank debt has been retired. The debt is junior to all outstanding bank debt, so the likelihood of debt repayment in the short term is remote. Accordingly, the debt is classified as long-term debt in the financial statements.

Disclosure of Loan Acceleration

A company may not be able to maintain the financial covenants called for in a loan document, at which point the lender usually is entitled to require immediate payment of the loan. In such cases, the company should disclose the nature of the covenant violation, the status of any covenant renegotiation, the portion of the debt subject to acceleration, and any reclassification of the debt in the financial statements as a result of this occurrence. An example follows.

> The company was unable to meet the current ratio covenant on its debt agreement with the Fourth National Bank of Wittenberg. The bank has elected not to waive its right to accelerate the maturity of the debt and, as a result, the bank can require the company to pay the current loan balance of €3,575,000 at any time. Accordingly, the debt has been reclassified as short-term debt on the statement of financial position.

Disclosure of Callable Obligations

A company may have a long-term liability that can be called if it violates some related covenants. That being the case, then the accountant must disclose the nature of the violation, how much of the related liability can potentially be called because of the violation, and if a waiver has been obtained from the creditor or if the company has acted to cancel the violation through some action. An example follows.

> The company has a long-term loan with a consortium of lenders, for which it violated the minimum current ratio covenant during the reporting period. The potential amount callable is one-half of the remaining loan outstanding, which is €5,500,000. However, the consortium granted a waiver of the violation, and also reduced the amount of the current ratio requirement from 2:1 to 1:1 for future periods.

Disclosure of Debt Restructuring

It may be that a company restructures its debt, so it should disclose any changes in the terms of the debt agreement and changes in income tax liability as well as any resulting gain or loss. Two examples follow.

1. The company restructured the terms of its €10 million debt with the Fourth [illegible]tional Bank of Wittenberg to reduce the interest rate from 10% to 7.5%, wh[illegible]cluded that portion of the accrued interest expense payable for the past tw[illegible]. This resulted in a onetime gain on interest expense reduction, net of inc[illegible] effects, of €350,000. This has been recorded as a Gain on Debt Restructu[illegible]
2. In December 2007, the company redeemed a portion of i[illegible]nds payable in 2014, totaling €14.1 million in principal value. In orde[illegible]h the bonds, the company paid a 12% premium to the bondholders, [illegible] an Extraordinary Loss on Debt Reduction of €1.2 million net of a ta[illegible]€508,000. The company paid for the bond redemption with funds o[illegible]ugh a recent preferred stock offering.

Disclosure of Loan Reclassification

The circumstances under which a lo[illegible] to be either short-term or long-term debt may have changed, at wh[illegible]should disclose the reason for the change and the amount of debt affected by the reclassification. Three examples follow.

1. The company is planning to sell its Russian-based rocket engine business in the near future. At that time, it plans to use the proceeds of the sale to pay off €19 million debt that it acquired in order to purchase the business originally. Accordingly, it has reclassified this debt as short-term debt.
2. The company has entered into a five-year, €10 million loan agreement with a set of lenders that will allow it to retire its €450,000 of short-term debt when it comes due for payment later this year. Since it is the intent of the company to pay for this short-term debt with the new long-term credit facility, the short-term debt has been reclassified as long-term debt.
3. The company is uncertain of its ability to make the next scheduled payment of €500,000 on its long-term debt of €28 million. Accordingly, it has reclassified the entire amount of the long-term debt as short-term debt.

Disclosure of Loan Extinguishment

If a company experiences a gain or loss through a debt extinguishment transaction, the accountant should describe the transaction, the amount of debt extinguished, the amount of the gain or loss, the impact on income taxes and earnings per share, and the source of funds used to retire the debt. Three examples follow.

1. The company retired all of its callable Series D bonds during the period, totaling €7.2 million. The funds used to retire the bonds were obtained from the issuance of Series A preferred stock during the period. The debt retirement transaction resulted in a gain of €595,000, which had after-tax positive impacts on net income of €369,000 and on per-share earnings of €0.29.
2. The company used the proceeds from its recent stock sale to retire €2.9 million in debt payable to the Fourth National Bank of Wittenberg. This debt agreement contained a prepayment penalty clause, so the company recorded a €150,000 expense for this penalty at the time of the prepayment. The company had also been amortizing the loan origination cost of the loan, of which €27,000 had not yet been recognized at the time of the prepayment. The company charged the remaining balance of this cost to expense. These charges, net of income tax benefits, resulted in a loss of €124,000 and reduced earnings per share by €0.05.

Disclosure of Convertible Debt

A company can issue debt that is convertible into equity; if that is the case, it should describe the terms of the transaction, including the amount of debt issued, the interest rate, and the conversion features, in a footnote. An example follows.

The company issued €8 million in convertible debt on November 10, 2007, to help pay for its ne[illegible]n production facility. The debt carries an interest rate of 7.25% and requires interest payments, with a single balloon payment in 10 years. Debt holders can convert their debt to company stock at any time at a conversion price of €15 per share. [illegible]ns had occurred as of the date of the financial statements. If all the debt were converted to equity, this would represent dilution of 4.7% for the current common

Disclosure of Stock Warrants Issued with Debt

If a company issues stock warrants as part of a debt issuance, it should disclose the proportion of warrants issued to debt, the date after which the warrants may be used, the allocation of received funds to the debt portions and warrant, how the allocation was derived, and how the allocation was treated in the financial statements. An example follows.

> The company issued €11 million in bonds during January 2007. Each of the 11,000 bonds sold at a price of €1,000 and included a warrant to purchase 100 shares of the company's common stock at an exercise price of €14.25 beginning on February 1, 2009. The warrants expire on February 1, 2017. Of the €11 million received, the company allocated the full fair value of the debt, €9.8 million, to the bonds and the residual amount, €1.2 million, to the warrants. The allocation of funds to the warrants was recorded as an increase in the Additional Paid-In Capital account and resulted in a discount on the bonds, which will be amortized to Interest Expense over the life of the bonds. The unamortized discount is currently €1,150,000.

JOURNAL ENTRIES

Notes and Bonds

Sale of bonds at a discount. The first entry is made when bonds are sold at a discount from their face value, thereby increasing the effective interest rate. The second entry is made periodically to gradually reduce the discount, charging the offsetting debit to the Interest Expense account.

Cash	xxx	
Discount on bonds payable	xxx	
Bonds payable		xxx
Interest expense	xxx	
Discount on bonds payable		xxx

Sale of bonds at a premium. The first entry is made when bonds are sold at a premium from their face value, thereby reducing the effective interes[t] rate. The second entry is made periodically to gradually reduce the premium, [ch]arging the offsetting credit to the Interest Expense account.

Cash	xxx	xxx
Premium on bonds payable		xxx
Bonds payable		
Premium on bonds payable	xxx	xxx
Interest expense		

Sale of debt issued with no stated [...]**st rate.** When there is no stated interest rate on a debt instrument, one mu[...]rd the present value of the note using the market rate of interest at the tim[e of] issuance. The first entry shows the initial recording of the debt sale wh[...] second entry shows the periodic reduction in interest expense payable.

Cash	xxx	
Discount on note pay[able]	xxx	
Note payable		xxx

Account	Debit	Credit
Interest expense	xxx	
Discount on note payable		xxx

Issuance of debt for cash and other rights. When debt is issued in exchange for cash and some other form of consideration, the difference between the present value and face value of the debt is recorded as unearned consideration, to be recognized as the consideration is earned by the issuer. The first entry shows the initial recording of such a transaction while the second entry shows the gradual reduction in unearned revenue.

Account	Debit	Credit
Cash	xxx	
Discount on note payable	xxx	
Note payable		xxx
Unearned revenue		xxx
Unearned revenue	xxx	
Revenue		xxx

Notes issued for property. When a company issues debt in exchange for property, it discounts the note either at the stated interest rate on the debt or at the market rate (if the stated rate is not considered to be a fair rate). In either case, the value of the property acquired shall be debited, usually along with a discount on the note payable. The first entry shows this initial transaction; the second entry shows the periodic reduction in the discount and corresponding recognition of interest expense.

Account	Debit	Credit
Property (various accounts)	xxx	
Discount on note payable	xxx	
Note payable		xxx
Interest expense	xxx	
Discount on note payable		xxx

Effective Interest Method

Interest, imputed. To recognize the additional interest expense on a bond after it has been issued with a stated rate below the market rate (first entry), or to recognize a *reduced* level of interest expense on a bond after it has been issued with a stated rate higher than the market rate (second entry).

Account	Debit	Credit
Interest expense	xxx	
Discount on bonds payable		xxx
Cash		xxx
Interest expense	xxx	
Premium on bonds payable	xxx	
Cash		xxx

Extinguishment of Debt

Repurchase of debt. This entry is used when a company elects to buy back issued debt ahead of its expiration date. There is usually a loss on the retirement to reflect the premium usually paid to investors to give up their bonds; any remaining discount or premium on the debt also must be recognized at this time.

Bonds payable	xxx	
Loss on bond retirement	xxx	
Premium on bonds payable (if applicable)	xxx	
Discount on bonds payable (if applicable)		xxx
Cash		xxx

Asset transfer to eliminate debt. When a company exchanges an asset with a lender to eliminate a debt, the value of the transferred asset is first written up or down to match its book value to its fair market value, as shown in the first entry. Its fair market value, as well as any accrued and unpaid interest expense, is then netted against the remaining debt, as shown in the second entry. Both entries assume a gain on the transaction, although the entry can be reversed to record a loss.

Asset account	xxx	
Gain on asset transfer		xxx

Note payable	xxx	
Interest payable	xxx	
Asset account		xxx
Gain on debt settlement		xxx

Convertible Debt

Record conversion of convertible debt to equity, book value method. If bondholders wish to convert their bonds into company stock, the next entry is used on the assumption that the remaining balance of the bonds represents the value of the resulting equity.

Bonds payable	xxx	
Premium on bonds payable (if premium existed)	xxx	
Discount on bonds payable (if discount existed)		xxx
Capital stock at par value		xxx
Additional paid-in capital		xxx

Record conversion to equity with accrued but unpaid interest expense. It may be that the terms of a convertible debt agreement require bondholders to forgo any accrued interest expense at the time they convert bonds to company stock, so the related journal entry should include the recognition of that expense as well as an offset to the capital account, as noted in the next journal entry.

Interest expense	xxx	
Long-term debt	xxx	
Capital, par value (various stock accounts)		xxx
Capital (various stock accounts)		xxx

Record conversion to equity following a sweetening of conversion feature. If a company induces its bondholders to convert their holdings to equity by subsequently improving the conversion feature of the bond agreement, it must record the issuance of these modifications as a reduction in the proceeds of the stock offering, thereby reducing paid-in capital from the transaction.

Bonds payable	xxx	
Capital account, par value		xxx
Additional paid-in capital		xxx

Debt Issued with Stock Warrants

Initial entry of bonds sale with attached warrants. The first entry is used to assign a value to the bonds and the residual amount to the warrants, based on the residual allocation method. The entry includes a provision for any discount or premium on bonds sold. The second entry shifts funds into an expired warrants account, on the assumption that the warrants are never exercised by the holder.

Cash	xxx	
Discount on bonds payable (if applicable)	xxx	
Premium on bonds payable (if applicable)		xxx
Bonds payable		xxx
Additional paid-in capital		xxx
Additional paid-in capital	xxx	
Additional paid-in capital—expired warrants		xxx

RECORDKEEPING

When there is a discount or a premium on the issuance of any form of debt, it should be amortized over the life of the debt. Since this amount can be substantial and can have an impact on reported results for many years, the calculation of the premium or discount must be fully documented and retained in the accounting archives for the term of the related debt. A copy of the calculation should be retained in the current journal entry binder for easy access by any auditors wishing to review it.

At a time when short-term debt is reclassified as long-term debt on the grounds that the company has the intention and ability to conduct the refinancing, there should be adequate documentation of the company's intent to do so (such as a board motion), as well as ability to do so (such as a signed loan document). This information should be retained in the accounting archives for as long as the short-term debt transfer is shown in the financial statements. For example, if five comparative financial statements are issued, then the supporting documentation should be kept on file until the year in which the reclassification was made has dropped off the financial statements—a period of five years.

When a right is granted to the lender and attached to a debt (such as a discount on future purchases from the company in exchange for a below-market interest rate), the unearned revenue can be recognized either ratably or in association with a particular event. Since the opportunity exists to manipulate the timing of revenue recognition in this instance, a business case should be documented for all revenue recognition entries that do not evenly spread revenue recognition over the duration of the related debt. The business case should describe the type of event that triggers the revenue recognition and why revenue is most properly recognized at that time.

When a company issues debt in exchange for property and elects to record the value of the debt at an interest rate other than the stated rate of the debt, the reason for doing so as well as the reason for the interest rate selected should be noted as an attachment to the journal entry documentation. This information may be reviewed at any time during the life of either the debt or the acquired property (whichever is longer), so the information should be retained for that time period.

Whenever a convertible bond is issued with the strike price already in the money but contingent on a future event, the value of the equity portion of the bond issuance must be recognized whenever the event comes to pass. This means that a note should be placed in the month-end closing procedure, indicating the contingent event and the action to be taken if it comes to pass. It is also useful to note in the procedure the location of the convertible bond documents that describe the amount assigned as well as the accounting entry to be made. This approach will ensure that the equity portion of the convertible bond is accounted for in an appropriate manner.

Convertible bonds may be issued with attached warrants, in which case the cash received will be assigned to both the debt and equity parts of the transaction based on the residual allocation method. Consequently, a record of the value of the bonds and the warrants as of the date of the transaction should be retained and attached to the journal entry recording the transaction.

11 LEASES

DEFINITIONS OF TERMS

Bargain purchase option (BPO). A provision in the lease agreement allowing the lessee the option of purchasing the leased property for an amount that is sufficiently lower than the fair value of the property at the date the option becomes exercisable. Exercise of the option must appear reasonably assured at the inception of the lease.

Economic life of leased property. IAS 17 (revised) defines economic life of a leased asset as either the period over which the asset is expected to be economically usable by one or more users or the number of production or similar units expected to be obtained from the leased asset by one or more users. (This was the definition of *useful life* under the original IAS 17.)

Executory costs. Those costs such as insurance, maintenance, and taxes incurred for leased property, whether paid by the lessor or lessee. If it is the obligation of the lessee, then these are excluded from the minimum lease payments.

Fair value of leased property (FMV). The amount for which an asset could be exchanged between a knowledgeable, willing buyer and a knowledgeable, willing seller in an arm's-length transaction. When the lessor is a manufacturer or dealer, the fair value of the property at the inception of the lease will ordinarily be its normal selling price net of volume or trade discounts. When the lessor is not a manufacturer or dealer, the fair value of the property at the inception of the lease will ordinarily be its cost to the lessor unless a significant amount of time has lapsed between the acquisition of the property by the lessor and the inception of the lease, in which case fair value should be determined in light of market conditions prevailing at the inception of the lease. Thus, fair value may be greater or less than the cost or carrying amount of the property.

Finance lease. A lease that transfers a substantial amount of all the risks and rewards associated with the ownership of an asset. The risks related to ownership of an asset include the possibilities of losses from idle capacity or technological obsolescence and of variations in return due to changing economic conditions; rewards incidental to ownership of an asset include expectation of profitable operations over the asset's economic life and expectation of gain from appreciation in value or the ultimate realization of the residual value. Title may or may not eventually be transferred to the lessee.

Gross investment in the lease. The sum total of the minimum lease payments under a finance lease (from the standpoint of the lessor), plus any unguaranteed residual value accruing to the lessor.

Guaranteed residual value. A fixed fee the lessee must pay the lessor at the end of a lease term, representing the predetermined value of the underlying asset.

Inception of the lease. The date of the written lease agreement or, if earlier, the date of a commitment by the parties to the principal provisions of the lease.

Initial direct costs. Initial direct costs, such as commissions and legal fees, incurred by lessors in negotiating and arranging a lease. These generally include (1) costs to originate a lease incurred in transactions with independent third parties that (a) result directly from and are essential to acquire that lease and (b) would not have been incurred had that leasing transaction not occurred; and (2) certain costs directly related to specified activities performed by the lessor for that lease, such as evaluating the prospective lessee's financial condition; evaluating and recording guarantees, collateral, and other security arrangements; negotiating lease terms; preparing and processing lease documents; and closing the transaction.

Lease. An agreement whereby a lessor conveys to the lessee the right to use an asset (property, plant, equipment, or land) for an agreed-on period of time, in return for payment or series of payments. Other arrangements essentially similar to leases, such as hire-purchase contracts, bare-boat charters, and so on, are considered leases for purposes of the Standard.

Lease term. The initial noncancelable period for which the lessee has contracted to lease the asset, together with any further periods for which the lessee has the option to extend the lease of the asset, with or without further payment, which option it is reasonably certain (at the inception of the lease) that the lessee will exercise.

Lessee's incremental borrowing rate. The interest rate that the lessee would have to pay on a similar lease, or, if that is not determinable, the rate that at the inception of the lease the lessee would have incurred to borrow over a similar term (i.e., a loan term equal to the lease term), and with a similar security, the funds necessary to purchase the leased asset.

Minimum lease payments (MLPs).

1. *From the standpoint of the lessee.* The payments over the lease term that the lessee is or can be required to make in connection with the leased property. The lessee's obligation to pay executory costs (e.g., insurance, maintenance, or taxes) and contingent rents are excluded from minimum lease payments. If the lease contains a bargain purchase option, the minimum rental payments over the lease term plus the payment called for in the bargain purchase option are included in minimum lease payments.

   If no such provision regarding a bargain purchase option is included in the lease contract, the minimum lease payments include

   a. The minimum rental payments called for by the lease over the lease contract over the term of the lease (excluding any executory costs), plus
   b. Any guarantee of residual value, at the expiration of the lease term, to be paid by the lessee or a party related to the lessee.

2. *From the standpoint of the lessor.* The payments described above plus any guarantee of the residual value of the leased asset by a third party unrelated to either the lessee or lessor (provided that the third party is financially capable of discharging the guaranteed obligation).

Net investment in the lease. The difference between the lessor's gross investment in the lease and the unearned finance income.

Noncancelable lease. A lease that is cancelable only

1. On occurrence of some remote contingency
2. With the concurrence (permission) of the lessor
3. If the lessee enters into a new lease for the same or an equivalent asset with the same lessor
4. On payment by the lessee of an additional amount such that at inception, continuation of the lease appears reasonably assured

Operating lease. A lease that does not meet the criteria prescribed for a finance lease.

Penalty. Any requirement that is imposed or can be imposed on the lessee by the lease agreement or by factors outside the lease agreement to pay cash, incur or assume a liability, perform services, surrender or transfer an asset or rights to an asset, or otherwise forgo an economic benefit or suffer an economic detriment.

Rate implicit in the lease. The discount rate at the inception of the lease that, when applied to the minimum lease payments and the unguaranteed residual value accruing to the benefit of the lessor, causes the aggregate present value to be equal to the fair value of the leased property to the lessor, net of any grants and tax credits receivable by the lessor.

Related parties in leasing transactions. Entities that are in a relationship where one party has the ability to control the other party or exercise significant influence over the operating and financial policies of the related party. Examples include

1. A parent company and its subsidiaries
2. An owner company and its joint ventures and partnerships
3. An investor and its investees

Significant influence may be exercised in several ways, usually by representation on the board of directors but also by participation in the policy-making process, material intercompany transactions, interchange of managerial personnel, or dependence on technical information. The ability to exercise significant influence must be present before the parties can be considered related.

Renewal or extension of a lease. The continuation of a lease agreement beyond the original lease term, including a new lease where the lessee continues to use the same property.

Residual value of leased property. The fair value, estimated at the inception of the lease, that the enterprise expects to obtain from the leased property at the end of the lease term.

Sale and leaseback accounting. A method of accounting for a sale-leaseback transaction in which the seller-lessee records the sale, removes all property and related liabilities from its statement of financial position, recognizes gain or loss from the sale, and classifies the leaseback in accordance with this section.

Unearned finance income. The excess of the lessor's gross investment in the lease over its present value.

Unguaranteed residual value. The portion of the residual value of the leased asset (estimated at the inception of the lease) as to which realization by the lessor is not assured, or which is guaranteed by a party related to the lessor.

Useful life. The estimated remaining period over which the economic benefits embodied by the asset are expected to be consumed, without being limited to the lease term. (The former definition of this term, as employed in the original standard IAS 17, has now been assigned to the term "economic life.")

CONCEPTS AND EXAMPLES

Accounting for Leases—Lessee

A typical lease is recorded by the lessee as an *operating lease*. Under IAS 17, the lessee must record a lease as a *finance lease* if a substantial number of all the benefits and risks of ownership have been transferred to the lessee. IAS 17 stipulates that substantially all of the risks or benefits of ownership are deemed to have been transferred if *any one* of these five criteria has been met:

1. The lease transfers ownership to the lessee by the end of the lease term.
2. The lease contains a bargain purchase option (an option to purchase the leased asset at a price that is expected to be substantially lower than the fair value at the date the option becomes exercisable), and it is reasonably certain that the option will be exercisable.
3. The lease term is for the major part of the economic life of the leased asset; title may or may not eventually pass to the lessee.
4. The present value (PV), at the inception of the lease, of the minimum lease payments is at least equal to substantially all of the fair value of the leased asset, net of grants and tax credits to the lessor at that time; title may or may not eventually pass to the lessee.
5. The leased assets are of a specialized nature such that only the lessee can use them without major modifications being made.

Further indicators which suggest that a lease might be properly considered to be a finance lease are

6. If the lessee can cancel the lease, the lessor's losses associated with the cancellation will be borne by the lessee.
7. Gains or losses resulting from the fluctuations in the fair value of the residual accrue to the lessee.
8. The lessee has the ability to continue the lease for a supplemental term at a rent that is substantially lower than market rent (a bargain renewal option).

The decision tree for this transaction is shown later in the Decision Tree section.

The lessee accounts for an *operating lease* by charging lease payments directly to expense. There is no balance sheet recognition of the leased asset at all. If the schedule of lease payments varies in terms of either timing or amount, the lessee should consistently charge the same rental amount to expense in each period, which may result in some variation between the lease payment made and the recorded expense. Nevertheless, if there is a demonstrable change in the asset being leased that justifies a change in the lease payment being made, there is no need to use straight-line recognition of the expense.

Example of accounting for changing lease payments

The Adelaide Botox Clinics (ABC) Company has leased a group of operating room equipment under a five-year operating lease arrangement. The monthly lease cost is €1,000 for the first 30 months and €1,500 for the second 30 months. There is no change in the equipment being leased at any time during the lease period. The correct accounting is to charge the average monthly lease rate of €1,250 to expense during every month of the lease. For the first 30 months, the monthly entry will be

Equipment rent expense	1,250	
Accounts payable		1,000
Accrued lease liability		250

During the final 30 months, the monthly entry will be

Equipment rent expense	1,250	
Accrued lease liability	250	
Accounts payable		1,500

The lessee accounts for a *finance lease* by recording an asset and an obligation (liability) at an amount equal to the lesser of (1) the fair value of the leased property at the inception of the lease, net of grants and tax credits receivable by the lessors, or (2) the present value of the minimum lease payments.

For purposes of this computation, the minimum lease payments are considered to be the payments that the lessee is obligated to make or can be required to make, excluding contingent rent and executory costs such as insurance, maintenance, and taxes. The minimum lease payments generally include the minimum rental payments and any guarantee of the residual value made by the lessee or a party related to the lessee. If the lease includes a bargain purchase option (BPO), the amount required to be paid under the BPO is included in the minimum lease payments. The present value shall be computed using the implicit rate in the lease, if this is practicable to determine; if not, the lessee's incremental borrowing rate should be used.

The lease term to be used in the present value computation is the fixed, noncancelable term of the lease, plus any further terms for which the lessee has the option to continue to lease the asset, with or without further payment, provided that it is reasonably certain, as of the beginning of the lease, that lessee will exercise such a renewal option.

The depreciation of the leased asset will depend on which criterion resulted in the lease being qualified as a finance lease. If the lease transaction met the criteria as either transferring ownership or containing a bargain purchase option, the asset arising from the transaction is to be depreciated over the estimated useful life of the leased property, which will be used by the lessee (most likely) after the lease term expires. If the transaction qualifies as a finance lease because it met either the criterion of encompassing the major part of the asset's economic life or because the present value of the minimum lease payments represented substantially all of the fair value of the underlying asset, then it must be depreciated over the shorter of the lease term or the useful life of the leased property. The conceptual rationale for this differentiated treatment arises because of the substance of the transaction. Under the first two criteria, the asset actually becomes the property of the lessee at the end of the lease term (or on exercise of the BPO). In the latter situations, title to the property remains with the lessor.

Thus, the leased asset is to be depreciated (amortized) over the shorter of the lease term or its useful life if title does not transfer to the lessee; however, when it is reasonably certain that the lessee will obtain ownership by the end of the lease term, the leased asset is to be depreciated over the asset's useful life. The manner in which depreciation is computed should be consistent with the lessee's normal depreciation policy for other depreciable assets owned by the lessee, recognizing depreciation on the basis set out in IAS 16.

Example of a finance lease transaction

The Andorra Barrel Company (ABC) leases a woodworking machine under a five-year lease that has a one-year extension clause at the option of the lessor as well as a guaranteed residual value of €15,000. ABC's incremental borrowing rate is 7%. The machine is estimated to have a life of seven years, a current fair value of €90,000 and a residual value (*not* the guaranteed residual value) of €5,000. Annual lease payments are €16,000.

The first step in accounting for this lease is to determine if it is a finance lease or an operating lease. If it is a finance lease, calculate its present value, and use the effective interest method to determine the allocation of payments between interest expense and reduction of the lease obligation, and then determine the depreciation schedule for the asset. Later, there will be a closeout journal entry to record the lease termination. The steps are

1. **Determine the lease type.** The woodworking machine is considered to have a life of seven years; since the lease period (including the extra year at the option of the lessor) exists for the major part of the machine's economic life, the lease is designated as a finance lease.
2. **Calculate asset present value.** The machine's present value is a combination of the present value of the €15,000 residual payment due in six years and the present value of the stream of annual payments of €16,000 per year for six years. Using the company incremental borrowing rate of 7%, the present value multiplier for €1 due in six years is 0.6663; when multiplied by the guaranteed residual value of €15,000, this results in a present value of €9,995. Using the same interest rate, the present value multiplier for an ordinary annuity of €1 for six years is 4.7665; when multiplied by the annual lease payments of €16,000, this computes to a present value of €76,264. After combining the two present values, we arrive at a total lease present value of €86,259. The initial journal entry to record the lease is

Leased equipment	86,259	
Lease obligation		86,259

3. **Allocate payments between interest expense and reduction of lease liability.** ABC's controller then uses the effective interest method to allocate the annual lease payments between the lease's interest expense and reductions in the lease obligation. The interest calculation is based on the beginning balance of the lease obligation. The calculation for each year of the lease follows.

Year	Annual payment	Interest expense	Reduction in lease obligation	Remaining lease obligation
0				€86,259
1	€16,000	€6,038	€9,962	76,297
2	16,000	5,341	10,659	65,638
3	16,000	4,595	11,405	54,233
4	16,000	3,796	12,204	42,029
5	16,000	2,942	13,058	28,991
6	16,000	2,009	13,991	15,000

4. **Create depreciation schedule.** Although the asset has an estimated life of seven years, the lease term is for only six years, after which the asset is expected to be returned to the lessor. Accordingly, the asset will be depreciated only over the lease term of six years; however, the amount of depreciation will only cover the asset's present value of €86,259 *minus* the residual value of €5,000. Therefore, the annual depreciation will be €13,543 [= (€86,259 present value – €5,000 residual value) / 6-year lease term].

5. **Record lease termination.** Once the lease is completed, a journal entry must record the removal of the asset and its related depreciation from the property, plant, and equipment register as well as the payment to the lessor of the difference between the €15,000 guaranteed residual value and the actual €5,000 residual value, or €10,000. That entry follows.

Lease obligation	15,000	
Accumulated depreciation	81,259	
Cash		10,000
Leased equipment		86,259

Accounting for Leases—Lessor

From the perspective of the lessor, if none of the criteria previously noted for a finance lease is met, a lease must be treated as an operating lease. If at least one of the five criteria is met and (1) lease payments are reasonably collectible and (2) there are minimal uncertainties about future lessor unreimbursable costs, then the lessor must treat a lease as a finance lease and as one of these three lease types:

1. **Sales-type lease.** When the lessor will earn both a profit and interest income on a lease transaction.
2. **Direct financing lease.** When the lessor will earn only interest income on a lease transaction.
3. **Leveraged lease.** The same as a direct financing lease, but the financing is provided by a third-party creditor.

The decision tree for this transaction is shown in the Decision Tree section.

Accounting for Operating Leases—Lessor

If the lessor treats a lease as an *operating lease*, it records any payments received from the lessee as rent revenue. As was the case for the lessee, if there is an unjustified change in the lease rate over the lease term, the average revenue amount should be recognized on a straight-line basis in each reporting period. Any assets being leased are recorded in a separate Investment in Leased Property account in the property, plant and equipment portion of the statement of financial position, and are depreciated in accordance with standard company policy for similar assets. If the lessor extends incentives (such as a month of no lease payments) or incurs costs associated with the lease (such as legal fees), they should be recognized over the lease term.

Accounting for Sales-Type Leases—Lessor

If the lessor treats a lease as a *sales-type lease*, the initial transaction bears some similarity to a standard sale transaction, except that there is an unearned interest component to the entry. A description of the required entry is contained in the next table, which shows all debits and credits.

Debit	*Credit*	*Explanation*
Lease receivable		Sum of all minimum lease payments, minus executory costs, plus actual residual value
Cost of goods sold		Asset cost, plus initial direct costs, minus present value* of actual residual value
	Revenue	Present value* of all minimum lease payments
	Leased asset	Carrying value of the asset
	Accounts payable	Any initial direct costs associated with the lease
	Unearned finance income	Lease receivable, minus the present value* of both the minimum lease payments and actual residual value

* *The present value multiplier is based on the lease term and implicit interest rate.*

Once payments are received, one entry is needed to record the receipt of cash and corresponding reduction in the lease receivable and a second entry is needed to recognize a portion of the unearned finance income as interest income, based on the effective interest method.

At least annually during the lease term, the lessor should record any permanent reductions in the estimated residual value of the leased asset. It cannot record any increases in the estimated residual value.

When the asset is returned to the lessor at the end of the lease term, a closing entry eliminates the lease receivable associated with the actual residual value, with an offsetting debit to the leased asset account.

Example of a sales-type lease transaction

The Albury Boat Company (ABC) has issued a seven-year lease to the Adventure Yachting Company (AYC) on a boat for its yacht rental business. The boat cost ABC €450,000 to build and should have a residual value of €75,000 at the end of the lease. Annual lease payments are €77,000. ABC's implicit interest rate is 8%. The present value multiplier for an ordinary annuity of €1 for seven years at 8% interest is 5.2064. The present value multiplier for €1 due in seven years at 8% interest is €.5835. We construct the initial journal entry with these calculations:

- **Lease receivable.** This is the sum of all minimum lease payments, which is €539,000 (= €7,000/year × 7 years), plus the actual residual value of **€**75,000, for a total lease receivable of €614,000.
- **Cost of goods sold.** This is the asset cost of €450,000, minus the present value of the residual value, which is €43,763 (= €75,000 residual value × present value multiplier of 0.5835).
- **Revenue.** This is the present value of all minimum lease payments, or €400,893 (= €77,000/year × present value multiplier of 5.2064).
- **Inventory.** ABC's carrying value for the yacht is €450,000, which is used to record a reduction in its inventory account.
- **Unearned finance income.** This is the lease receivable of €614,000, minus the present value of the minimum lease payments of €400,893, minus the present value of the residual value of €43,763, which yields €169,344.

Based on these calculations, the initial journal entry is

Lease receivable	614,000	
Cost of goods sold	406,237	
Revenue		400,893
Boat asset		450,000
Unearned finance income		169,344

The next step in the example is to determine the allocation of lease payments between interest income and reduction of the lease principal, which is accomplished through this effective interest table:

Year	*Annual payment*	*Interest income*	*Reduction in lease obligation*	*Remaining lease obligation*
0				€444,656
1	€77,000	€35,572	€41,428	403,228
2	77,000	32,258	44,742	358,486
3	77,000	28,679	48,321	310,165
4	77,000	24,813	52,187	257,978
5	77,000	20,638	56,362	201,616
6	77,000	16,129	60,871	140,745
7	77,000	11,255	65,745	75,000

The interest expense shown in the effective interest table can then be used to record the allocation of each lease payment between interest income and principal reduction. For example, the entries recorded for Year 4 of the lease are

Cash	77,000	
Lease receivable		77,000
Unearned finance income	24,813	
Interest income		24,813

Once the lease expires and the boat is returned to ABC, the final entry to close out the lease transaction is

Boat asset	75,000	
Lease receivable		75,000

Accounting for Direct Financing Leases—Lessor

If the lessor treats a lease as a *direct financing lease*, it will only recognize interest income from the transaction; there will be no additional profit from the implicit sale of the underlying asset to the lessee. This treatment arises when the lessor purchases an asset specifically to lease it to the lessee. The other difference between a direct financing lease and a sales-type lease is that any direct costs incurred when a lease is originated must be amortized over the life of the lease, reducing the implicit interest rate used to allocate lease payments between finance income and reducing the lease principal.

A description of the required entry is contained in the next table, which shows all debits and credits.

Debit	*Credit*	*Explanation*
Lease receivable		Sum of all minimum lease payments, plus the actual residual value
	Leased asset	Carrying value of the asset
	Unearned finance income	Lease receivable minus the asset carrying value

At least annually during the lease term, the lessor should record any permanent reductions in the estimated residual value of the leased asset. It cannot record any increases in the estimated residual value.

Example of a direct financing lease transaction

The Ancona Leasing Company (ALC) purchases a boat from a third party for €700,000 and intends to lease it to the Adventure Yachting Company for six years at an annual lease rate of €140,093. The boat should have a residual value of €120,000 at the end of the lease term. Also, there is €18,000 of initial direct costs associated with the lease. ALC's implicit interest rate is 9%. The present value multiplier for an ordinary annuity of €1 for six years at 9% interest is 4.4859. The present value multiplier for €1 due in six years at 9% interest is 0.5963. We construct the initial journal entry with the following calculations:

- **Lease receivable.** This is the sum of all minimum lease payments, which is €840,558 (=€140,093/year × 6 years), plus the residual value of €120,000, for a total lease receivable of €960,558.
- **Leased asset.** This is the asset cost of €700,000.
- **Unearned finance income.** This is the lease receivable of €942,558, minus the asset carrying value of €700,000, which yields €260,558.

Based on these calculations, the initial journal entry is

Lease receivable	960,558	
Initial direct costs	18,000	
Leased asset		700,000
Unearned finance income		260,558
Cash		18,000

Next, ALC's controller must determine the implicit interest rate associated with the transaction. Though ALC intended the rate to be 9%, she must add to the lease receivable the initial direct costs of €18,000, resulting in a final gross investment of €978,558 and a net investment (net of unearned finance income of €260,558) of €718,000. The determination of the implicit interest rate with this additional information is most easily derived through an electronic spreadsheet. For example, the IRR function in Microsoft Excel will automatically create the new implicit interest rate, which is 8.2215%.

With the revised implicit interest rate completed, the next step in the example is to determine the allocation of lease payments between interest income, a reduction of initial direct costs, and a reduction of the lease principal, which is accomplished through this effective interest table:

Year	*Annual payment*	*Unearned interest reduction*	*Interest income*	*Reduction of initial direct costs*	*Reduction in lease obligation*	*Remaining lease obligation (1)*	*Remaining lease obligation (2)*
0						€718,000	€700,000
1	€140,093	€ 63,000	€59,031	€3,969	€ 81,062	636,938	622,907
2	140,093	56,062	52,366	3,696	87,727	549,211	538,876
3	140,093	48,499	45,154	3,345	94,939	454,271	447,281
4	140,093	40,255	37,348	2,907	102,745	351,526	347,444
5	140,093	31,270	28,901	2,369	111,192	240,334	238,621
6	140,093	21,476	19,759	1,717	120,334	120,000	120,000*
	Totals	€260,558*		€18,000*			

* *Rounded.*

The calculations used in the table are

- **Annual payment.** The annual cash payment due to the lessor.
- **Unearned interest income reduction.** The original implicit interest rate of 9% multiplied by the beginning balance in the Remaining Lease Obligation (2) column, which

does not include the initial direct lease cost. The total at the bottom of the column equals the unearned interest liability that will be eliminated over the course of the lease.

- **Interest income.** The revised implicit interest rate of 8.2215% multiplied by the beginning balance in the Remaining Lease Obligation (1) column, which includes the initial direct lease costs.
- **Reduction of initial direct costs.** The amount in the Unearned Interest Reduction column minus the amount in the Interest Income column, which is used to reduce the balance of the initial direct costs incurred. The total at the bottom of the column equals the initial direct costs incurred at the beginning of the lease.
- **Reduction in lease obligation.** The Annual Payment minus the Interest Income.
- **Remaining lease obligation (1).** The beginning lease obligation (including initial direct costs) less the principal portion of the annual payment.
- **Remaining lease obligation (2).** The beginning lease obligation, not including initial direct costs, less the principal portion of the annual payment.

Based on the calculations in the effective interest table, the journal entry at the end of the first year would show the receipt of cash and a reduction in the lease receivable. Another entry would reduce the unearned interest balance while offsetting the initial direct costs and recognizing interest income. The first-year entries are

Cash	140,093	
Lease receivable		140,093
Unearned finance income	63,000	
Interest income		59,031
Initial direct costs		3,969

Lease Terminations

On the date that a lessee notifies the lessor that it intends to terminate a lease, the lessee must recognize a liability for the fair value of the termination costs, including any continuing lease payments, less prepaid rent, plus deferred rent, minus the amount of any sublease payments. Changes in these estimates are recorded immediately in the income statement.

The lessor may record a lease as a sales-type or direct financing lease, recording the underlying leased asset at the lower of its current net carrying value, present value, or original cost, with any resulting adjustment being recorded in current earnings. At the time of termination notice, the lessor records a receivable in the amount of any termination payments yet to be made, with an offsetting credit to a deferred rent liability account. The lessor then recognizes any remaining rental payments on a straight-line basis over the revised period during which the payments are to be received.

Lease Extensions

If a *lessee* extends an operating lease and the extension also is classified as an operating lease, then the lessee continues to treat the extension in the same manner it has used for the existing lease. If the lease extension requires payment amounts differing from those required under the initial agreement but the asset received does not change, then the lessee should consistently charge the same rental amount to expense in each period, which may result in some variation between the lease payment made and the recorded expense.

If a lessee extends an existing finance lease but the lease structure now requires the extension be recorded as an operating lease, the lessee writes off the existing asset, as well as all associated accumulated depreciation, and recognizes either a gain or a loss on the transaction. Payments made under the lease extension are handled in accordance with the rules of a standard operating lease.

If a lessee extends an existing finance lease and the structure of the extension agreement requires the lease to continue to be recorded as a finance lease, the lessee changes the asset valuation and related lease obligation by the difference between the present value of the new series of future minimum lease payments and the existing balance. The present value calculation must use the interest rate used for the same calculation at the inception of the original lease.

When a lease extension occurs and the lessor classifies the extension as a direct financing lease, the lease receivable and estimated residual value (downward only) are adjusted to match the new lease terms, with any adjustment going to unearned income. When a lease extension occurs and the lessor classifies an existing direct financing or sales-type lease as an operating lease, the lessor writes off the remaining lease investment and instead records the asset at the lower of its current net carrying value, original cost, or present value. The change in value from the original net investment is recorded against income in the period when the lease extension date occurs.

Leveraged Leases

A leveraged lease is defined in IAS 17 as a finance lease which is structured so that there are at least three parties involved: the lessee, the lessor, and one or more long-term creditors who provide part of the acquisition finance for the leased asset, usually without any general recourse to the lessor. Succinctly, this type of a lease is given this unique accounting treatment:

1. The lessor records his or her investment in the lease net of the nonrecourse debt and the related finance costs to the third-party creditor(s).
2. The recognition of the finance income is based on the lessor's net cash investment outstanding in respect of the lease.

Leases Involving Land and Buildings

IAS 17 addresses leases involving both land and buildings; in general, the accounting treatment of such leases is the same as for simple leases of other assets. As revised, the Standard requires leases for land and buildings to be analyzed into their component parts, with each element separately accounted for, unless title to both elements is expected to pass to the lessee by the end of the lease term. It continues the operating lease treatment requirement for the land portion of the lease, unless the title is expected to pass to the lessee by the end of the lease term, in which case finance lease treatment is warranted. The buildings element is to be classified as a finance or operating lease in accordance with IAS 17's provisions.

Under the revised IAS 17, the minimum lease payments at the inception of a lease of land and buildings (including any up-front payments) are to be allocated between the land and the buildings elements in proportion to their relative fair values at the inception of the lease. In those circumstances where the lease payments cannot be allocated reliably between these two elements, the entire lease is to be classified as a finance lease, unless it is clear that both elements are operating leases.

Furthermore, the amendment to IAS 17 has specified that for a lease of land and buildings in which the value of the land element at the inception of the lease is immaterial, the land and buildings may be treated as a single unit for the purpose of lease classification, in which case the criteria set forth in IAS 17 will govern the classification as a finance or operating lease. If this is done, the economic life of the buildings is regarded as the economic life of the entire leased asset.

In accordance with IAS 40, it is possible for a lessee to classify a property interest held under an operating lease as an investment property. If it does, the property interest is accounted for as if it were a finance lease and, in addition, the fair value model is used for the asset recognized.

Subleases

A sublease occurs when leased property is leased by the original lessee to a third party. When this happens, the original lessee accounts for the sublease as if it were the original lessor. This means that it can account for the lease as an operating lease, a direct sales lease, or a sales-type lease. The original lessee continues to account for its ongoing lease payments to the original lessor as if the sublease did not exist.

Sale-Leaseback Transactions

Sale-leaseback describes a transaction where the owner of property (the seller-lessee) sells the property and then immediately leases all or part of it back from the new owner (the buyer-lessor). These transactions may occur when the seller-lessee is experiencing cash flow or financing problems or because there are tax advantages in such an arrangement in the lessee's tax jurisdiction. The important consideration in this type of transaction is recognition of two separate and distinct economic transactions. It is important to note, however, that there is not a physical transfer of property. First, there is a sale of property, and second, there is a lease agreement for the same property in which the original seller is the lessee and the original buyer is the lessor.

A sale-leaseback transaction usually is structured in such a way that the sales price of the asset is greater than or equal to the current market value. The higher sales price has the concomitant effect of a higher periodic rental payment over the lease term than would otherwise have been negotiated. The transaction usually is attractive because of the tax benefits associated with it and because it provides financing to the lessee. The seller-lessee benefits from the higher price because of the increased gain on the sale of the property and the deductibility of the lease payments, which usually are larger than the depreciation that was being taken previously. The buyer-lessor benefits from both the higher rental payments and the larger depreciable basis.

Under IAS 17, the accounting treatment depends on whether the leaseback results in a finance lease or an operating lease. If it results in a finance lease, any excess of sale proceeds over previous carrying value may not be recognized immediately as income in the financial statements of the seller-lessee. Rather, it is to be deferred and amortized over the lease term.

Accounting for a sale-leaseback that involves the creation of an operating lease depends on whether the sale portion of the compound transaction was on arm's-length terms. If the leaseback results in an operating lease, and it is evident that the transaction is established at fair value, then any profit or loss should be recognized immediately. If the sale price is not established at fair value, however, then

a. If sale price is below fair value, any profit or loss should be recognized immediately, except that when a loss is to be compensated by below-fair-market future rentals, the loss should be deferred and amortized in proportion to the rental payments over the period the asset is expected to be used.
b. If the sale price is above fair value, the excess over fair value should be deferred and amortized over the period for which the asset is expected to be used.

IAS 17 stipulates that, in case of operating leasebacks, if at the date of the sale and leaseback transaction the fair value is less than the carrying amount of the leased asset, the difference between the fair value and the carrying amount should be recognized immediately. In other words, impairment is recognized first, before the actual sale-leaseback transaction is given recognition.

Nevertheless, in case the sale and leaseback result in a finance lease, no such adjustment is considered necessary unless there has been impairment in value, in which case the carrying value should be reduced to the recoverable amount in accordance with the provisions of IAS 36.

DECISION TREE

The decision tree shown in Exhibit 11.1 itemizes the criteria required for the correct classification of a lease by both a lessee and lessor. If at least one of a set of the criteria on the left side of the flowchart is met, the lessee treats a lease as a finance lease; if not, the treatment is as an operating lease. The right side of the flowchart continues with more criteria for a lessor. If none is met, the lease is treated as an operating lease. The flowchart terminates in the lower-right corner, where a lessor can subdivide a finance lease into either a sales-type lease or a direct financing lease.

Exhibit 11.1 Decision Tree for Determination of Lease Type

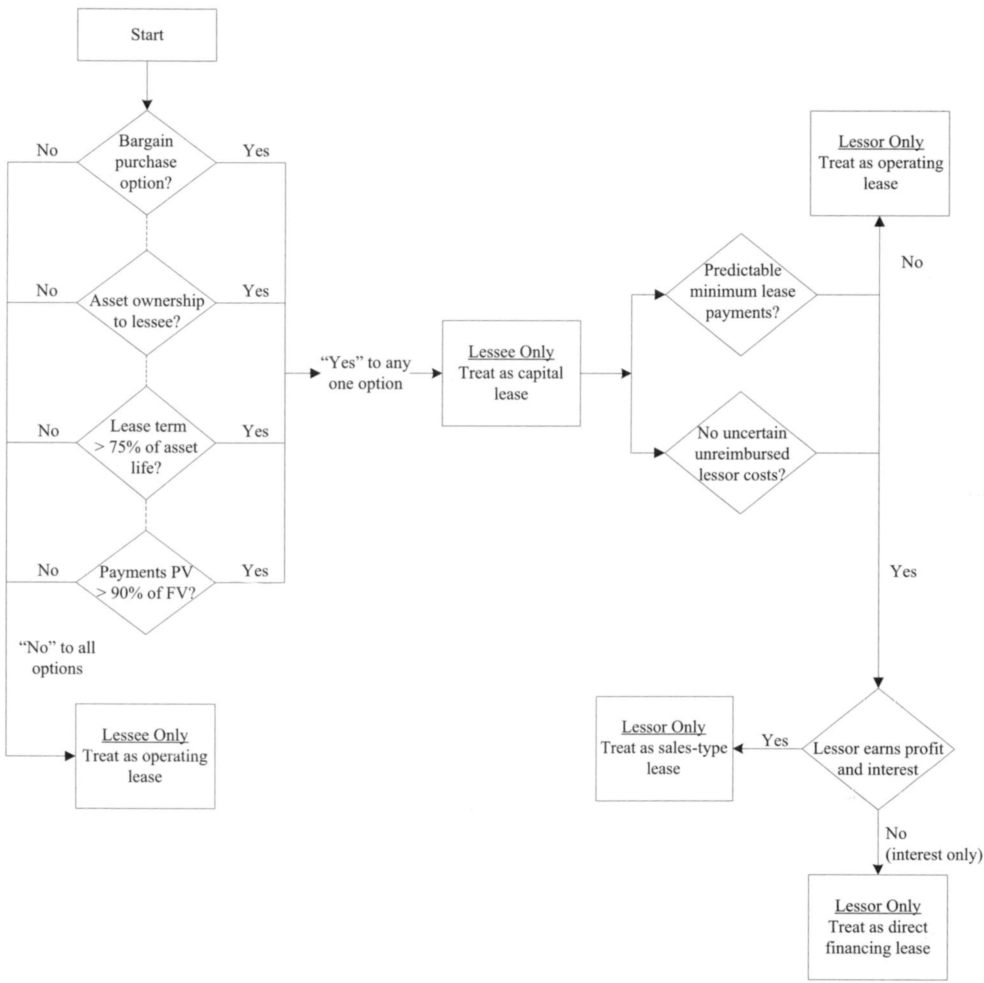

POLICIES

Accounting for Leases—Lessee

- **Lease termination dates shall be regularly reviewed.** It is extremely common for lease agreements to require a written notice of lease cancellation near the end of the lease term. If no written notice is received by the lessor, then the lease payments are contractually required to be continued for some predetermined number of months, which usually is detrimental to the lessee. This policy is designed to ensure a periodic review of lease termination dates, so that lease cancellation notices can be sent in a timely manner.
- **No company leases shall include a guaranteed residual value clause.** A company can negotiate smaller periodic lease payments by guaranteeing the lessor a significant residual value at the end of the lease, typically calling for a

large cash payment back to the lessor. Though such a clause can assist in reducing up-front cash payments, it can also result in an unacceptably high cash liability in the future.

- **The legal department shall send a copy of each signed lease document to the accounting department.** The accounting department must be aware of the amount and timing of all lease payments, so the legal department should be required to provide this information via copies of all signed leases. For larger companies, this policy would require that leases be sent to the finance department instead of accounting, since the finance staff would be more concerned with cash forecasting.

Lease Terminations

- **Only the board can approve lease termination agreements.** IFRS requires that the expenses associated with lease terminations be recognized on the date when the lease termination notice is issued to the lessor. Since the expenses recognized can be substantial, there can be a tendency by management to time the termination notice to alter reported financial results. By requiring the board to issue final approval of such agreements during its regularly scheduled board meetings, management is less likely to alter financial results deliberately through the use of lease termination agreements. The policy is even more effective if the board is informed of the amount of any lease expense to be recognized as part of the termination notification.

PROCEDURES

Accounting for a Finance Lease—Lessee

Use this nine-step procedure to determine the correct accounting for a finance lease during all phases of the lease term.

1. Upon receipt of the finance lease documents, collect this information to be used in the determination of lease-related journal entries:
    a. The lease term
    b. The amount of annual lease payments
    c. Any required lease term extensions (i.e., at the option of the lessor, or if a significant penalty will be incurred if the lease is *not* extended)
    d. The corporate incremental borrowing rate
    e. The interest rate implicit in the lease
    f. The fair value of the asset
    g. The residual value of the asset at the end of the lease term
    h. Any guaranteed residual value to be paid back to the lessor
    i. The dollar amount of any bargain purchase option
    j. Taxes and executory costs
2. Determine the interest rate to be used for a present value calculation. The interest rate used to compute the present value should be the implicit rate in the lease.

3. Calculate the present value of the leased asset. To do so, use a present value table to find the present value multiple for an ordinary annuity of $1 for the lease term, including any required additional lease periods. Multiply this factor by the annual lease payment (not including any legal or executory costs) due to the lessor. Also, if there is a final payment, such as a guaranteed residual value, find the present value multiple for an amount of $1 due at the end of the lease term, including any required additional lease periods. Multiply this multiple by the ending guaranteed residual value due to the lessor. Add together the results of the two present value calculations to arrive at the present value of the leased asset.
4. Assign a value to the asset. Use the lesser of the asset present value, as calculated in the last step, or the fair value of the asset.
5. Record the asset acquisition. Using the value obtained in the last step, record a debit to the appropriate leased asset account and a credit to the Lease Obligation account.
6. Calculate the proportion of each lease payment assigned to interest expense and a reduction in the lease obligation. Create a table with one row assigned to each year of the lease. Number the years in the leftmost column, followed by columns containing the annual payment amount, interest expense, reduction in the lease obligation, and the remaining lease obligation. Fill in all rows in the column for annual payments, using the lease payment schedule contained in the lease agreement. Then multiply the predetermined asset value by the predetermined interest rate, resulting in an entry in the Interest Expense column for the first year. Subtract this expense from the annual payment, with the remainder dropping into the Reduction in Lease Obligation column. Then subtract the amount just placed in the Reduction in Lease Obligation column from the beginning asset value, and put the remainder in the Remaining Lease Obligation column. Continue this process for all years of the lease.
7. Enter the asset in the property, plant, and equipment register, using the predetermined asset value as the acquisition cost. If the asset is to be returned to the lessor at the end of the lease, use the lease term as the asset life for depreciation purposes; otherwise, use the full economic life of the asset. For the purposes of calculating depreciation, reduce the asset value by its expected residual value (not the guaranteed residual value to be paid to the lessor, if any such payment clause exists).
8. Upon termination of the lease, remove the asset from the property, plant, and equipment register and cancel the lease obligation. Record a debit to the Accumulated Depreciation account for the full amount of depreciation expense charged against the asset, with the offsetting credit going against the asset account for the amount of the original asset entry. Also record a credit for the amount of any guaranteed residual value due back to the lessor. Finally, enter a debit to cancel the amount of any remaining lease liability, which should be the difference between the guaranteed residual value and

the residual value used initially to reduce the asset value for depreciation calculation purposes.

9. Send notice of the lease cancellation to the legal department and accounts payable staff, so the legal staff can archive the leasing documents and the accounts payable staff can halt any recurring lease payments set up in the accounting system.

Accounting for a Sales-Type Lease—Lessor

Use this 11-step procedure to determine the correct accounting for a sales-type finance lease by the lessor during all phases of the lease term.

1. Upon receipt of the finance lease documents, collect this information to be used in the determination of lease-related journal entries:
   a. The lease term
   b. The amount of annual lease payments
   c. Any required lease term extensions (i.e., at the option of the lessor, or if a significant penalty will be incurred if the lease is *not* extended)
   d. The implicit interest rate in the lease
   e. The carrying value of the asset
   f. The residual value of the asset at the end of the lease term
   g. Executory costs
2. Create the initial transaction journal entry for the lease by calculating all components of the entry:
   a. Determine the amount of the lease receivable by summing all minimum lease payments, minus executory costs, plus the actual residual value of the asset.
   b. Determine the cost of goods sold by subtracting any initial direct costs from the asset carrying value, minus the present value of the actual residual value. Find the present value by calculating the present value multiplier for $1 due at the end of the lease term, using the lessor's implicit interest rate, and multiplying this by the residual asset value.
   c. Determine the lessor total revenue from the lease transaction by calculating the present value of all minimum lease payments. Find the present value by calculating the present value multiplier for an ordinary annuity of $1 due at the end of the lease term, using the interest rate implicit in the lease, and multiplying this by the annual lease payments from the lessee.
   d. Determine the lessor's inventory reduction by locating the carrying value of the asset being leased to the lessee.
   e. Determine the unearned interest portion of the lessee's prospective lease payments by subtracting from the lease receivable the present value of the minimum lease payments and the actual residual value. Find the present value of the minimum lease payments by calculating the present value multiplier for an ordinary annuity of $1 due at the end of the lease

term, using the lessor's implicit interest rate, and multiplying this by the annual lease payments from the lessee.

3. Once all components of the initial lease entry have been calculated, record the lease receivable and cost of goods sold as debits, and the revenue, inventory, accounts payable, and unearned finance income as a credit.
4. Calculate the proportion of each lessee payment assigned to interest income and a reduction in the lessee's lease obligation. Create an effective interest table with one row assigned to each year of the lease. Number the years in the leftmost column, followed by columns containing the annual payment amount, interest income, reduction in the lease obligation, and the remaining lease obligation. Fill in all rows in the column for annual payments, using the lease payment schedule contained in the lease agreement. Then multiply the predetermined asset value by the predetermined interest rate, resulting in an entry in the Interest income column for the first year. Subtract this revenue from the annual payment, with the remainder dropping into the Reduction in Lease Obligation column. Then subtract the amount just placed in the Reduction in Lease Obligation column from the beginning asset value, and put the remainder in the Remaining Lease Obligation column. Continue this process for all years of the lease.
5. Every time the lessor receives a lease payment from the lessee, record a debit to Cash and a credit to the Lease Receivable account for the full amount of the payment. Also enter a debit to the Unearned Interest account and a credit to the Interest Income account for the amount of the interest income component of the lessee payment, as noted in the effective interest table constructed in the last step.
6. At least annually, record any permanent reductions in the estimated residual value of the leased asset.
7. Near the end of the lease period, issue a written notification to the lessee regarding the approaching termination date and explaining lease renewal and asset return options.
8. Upon receipt of written notice from the lessee to not renew the lease, notify the lessee of the address to which the asset is to be shipped, and issue a receiving approval to the receiving staff.
9. The receiving staff inspects the asset for any unusual damage and notifies the accounting department of the cost of any required repairs to the asset.
10. The accounting department bills the lessee for any indicated asset repair costs.
11. Upon termination of the lease and return of the asset to the lessor, record a debit to the Asset account and a credit to the Lease Receivable account for the residual value of the returned asset.

Accounting for a Direct Financing Lease—Lessor

Use this 12-step procedure to determine the correct accounting for a direct financing finance lease by the lessor during all phases of the lease term.

1. Upon receipt of the finance lease documents, collect this information to be used in the determination of lease-related journal entries:
   a. The lease term
   b. The amount of annual lease payments
   c. The implicit interest rate in the lease
   d. The carrying value of the asset
   e. The residual value of the asset at the end of the lease term
   f. The total of all initial direct costs
2. Create the initial transaction journal entry for the lease by calculating all components of the entry, which are
   a. Determine the amount of the lease receivable by summing all minimum lease payments, plus the actual residual value of the asset.
   b. Summarize all initial direct costs associated with the new lease.
   c. Determine the lessor's asset reduction by locating the carrying value of the asset being leased to the lessee.
   d. Determine the unearned interest portion of the lessee's prospective lease payments by subtracting the asset carrying value from the lease receivable.
3. Once all components of the initial lease entry have been calculated, record the lease receivable and initial direct costs as debits and the asset, unearned finance income, and any cash paid out for the initial direct costs as a credit.
4. Calculate a revised implicit interest rate for the transaction that allows for the amortization of initial direct costs over the lease term. To do so, summarize by year the annual cash inflows and outflows associated with the lease, including the asset purchase price, initial direct costs, annual lease payments from the lessee, and the amount of the residual value. Incorporate this information into the IRR( ) formula in an Excel spreadsheet to determine the lease's internal rate of return.
5. Calculate the proportion of each lessee payment assigned to interest income, a reduction of the initial direct costs, and a reduction in the lessee's lease obligation. To do so, create an effective interest table with one row assigned to each year of the lease. Number the years in the leftmost column, followed by columns containing the annual payment amount, unearned interest reduction, interest income, reduction of the initial direct costs, reduction in the lease obligation, and separate columns for reductions in the remaining lease obligation where the initial lease obligations both include and exclude the initial direct costs. Fill in all rows in the column for annual payments, using the lease payment schedule contained in the lease agreement. Then follow these steps to complete each row of the table:
   a. Multiply the original implicit interest rate by the beginning balance in the second Remaining Lease Obligation column (which does not include the initial direct costs), resulting in an entry in the Unearned Interest Reduction column for the first year.

b. Multiply the revised implicit interest rate by the beginning balance in the first Remaining Lease Obligation column (which includes the initial direct costs), resulting in an entry in the Interest Income column.
c. Subtract the Interest Income from the Unearned Interest Reduction and enter the difference in the Reduction of Initial Direct Costs column.
d. Subtract the Interest Income from the Annual Payment and enter the difference in the Reduction in Lease Obligation column.
e. Subtract the principal portion of the annual lease payment from the Beginning Lease Obligation column that includes initial direct costs and enter the result in that column.
f. Subtract the principal portion of the annual lease payment from the Beginning Lease Obligation column that does not include initial direct costs and enter the result in that column.

6. Every time the lessor receives a lease payment from the lessee, record a debit to Cash and a credit to the Lease Receivable account for the full amount of the payment. Also enter a debit to the Unearned Finance Income account, a credit to the Interest Income account for the amount of the interest income component of the lessee payment, and a credit to the Initial Direct Costs account for the scheduled amortization of that account, as noted in the effective interest table constructed in the last step.
7. At least annually, record any permanent reductions in the estimated residual value of the leased asset.
8. Near the end of the lease period, issue a written notification to the lessee regarding the approaching termination date and explaining lease renewal and asset return options.
9. Upon receipt of written notice from the lessee to not renew the lease, notify the lessee of the address to which the asset is to be shipped, and issue a receiving approval to the receiving staff.
10. The receiving staff inspects the asset for any unusual damage and notifies the accounting department of the cost of any required repairs to the asset.
11. The accounting department bills the lessee for any indicated asset repair costs.
12. Upon termination of the lease and return of the asset to the lessor, record a debit to the Asset account and a credit to the Lease Receivable account for the residual value of the returned asset.

CONTROLS

Accounting for Leases—Lessee

- **Verify existence of leased assets.** A leasing agency could continue to charge a company for lease payments even after the underlying asset has been returned, or a fraudulent employee could sell off or take custody of an asset, leaving the company to continue making the lease payments. In either case, periodically one should trace the assets listed on lease invoices to the actual assets.

- **Verify correct depreciation period for assets acquired under a finance lease.** Under a finance lease, the lessee must depreciate the assets acquired under the terms of the lease. If the asset is to be recorded in the property, plant, and equipment tracking module of the accounting system in the normal manner, it will likely result in a system-designated depreciation period. Such a depreciation period is acceptable if the finance lease involves a transfer of ownership. Nevertheless, if the lessor retains ownership at the end of the lease, the depreciation period must be limited to the lease term. Using a shorter depreciation period will increase the periodic depreciation expense, so this issue has an impact on earnings. Consequently, verification of the depreciation period should be a standard review item in the month-end closing procedure.
- **Ensure that the financial analysis staff is aware of all scheduled lease payments.** If a company uses leases for a large part of its financing needs, lease payments may comprise a significant part of its cash flow planning. If so, the person responsible for the cash forecast should be kept aware of the stream of required lease payments for all leases as well as any changes in those payments and any guaranteed residual values that must be paid to the lessor at the end of a lease. This can be accomplished most easily by requiring the legal department to send a copy of each signed lease document to the accounting department, where the leases can be summarized for cash planning purposes.

Accounting for Leases—Lessor

- **Include in the annual accounting activity calendar a review of residual asset values.** The lessor is required IFRS to conduct at least an annual review of the residual value of all leased assets and to adjust those valuations downward if there appear to be permanent valuation reductions. Any such adjustment will result in the recognition of a loss, so there is a natural tendency to avoid or delay this step. By including it in the standard schedule of activities, the accounting staff is more likely to conduct it.

Lease Terminations

- **Match the date of the lease termination notification to the recognition of any losses associated with the termination.** Management can alter the timing of losses related to lease terminations by recognizing the losses later than the date of the termination notification. This control requires one to ensure that the losses are recognized in the period of notification. The control is best included in a standard review procedure, to ensure that it is consistently followed and enforced.

FORMS AND REPORTS

Lease Payments Report

A company should summarize all outstanding leases in a single document, so it can easily determine scheduled changes in lease payments, lease termination dates, and the amount of guaranteed residual values. An example is shown in Exhibit 11.2.

The report identifies the lessor and the asset being leased as well as the identifying lease number (assuming the leases are stored in some indexed order), payment information, and a "notes" section to cover additional payment information. This report should be reviewed regularly to ensure that all upcoming payments are properly included in the corporate cash forecast; a good way to do so is to schedule a monthly lease review in the accounting department's schedule of activities.

Exhibit 11.2 Lease Payments Report

Lessor	*Asset leased*	*Lease number*	*Monthly payment*	*Final payment date*	*Notes*
Awai Leasing	Router	23790	€358.16	5/15/09	Guaranteed residual value payment of €12,000 on 5/15/12
Enoch Leasing	Band saw	24001	200.50	8/01/08	Bargain purchase option of €1 on 8/01/11
Freitag Leasing	Shredder	25329	628.15	3/31/08	Requires replacement lease at termination

Lease Termination Report

Under some lease agreements, the lessor is obligated to notify the lessee of a lease's upcoming termination date within a certain number of days of the end of a lease. Though this information typically is stored within a lease information database, resulting in automatically batched and printed letters to lessees, it can be useful to have a lease termination report such as the one shown in Exhibit 11.3. This report itemizes the types of assets that will be released from leases shortly, so the lessor can make arrangements for disposition of the assets. Not only that, but the report also notes in the BPO column the existence of a bargain purchase agreement, which makes it less likely that an asset will be returned by the lessee. The Asset Residual column contains the original or revised residual value for each asset and includes a total at the bottom of the report; this information is useful for estimating possible receipts from asset dispositions or at least the gains or losses likely to arise from asset resales.

Exhibit 11.3 Lease Termination Report

Customer number	*Customer name*	*Termination date*	*BPO*	*Asset residual*	*Asset description*
13057	Smith Jones Inc.	8/31/10	No	€42,500	Boston Whaler
14099	Elvis & Sons	8/31/10	No	37,000	Chris Craft
52052	Mobley Assoc.	8/31/10	Yes	128,000	Hudson Boat
				€207,500	

FOOTNOTES

Disclosure of Leases by Lessees

If a company is leasing an asset that is recorded as an operating lease, the accountant must disclose the future minimum lease payments for the next five years as well as the terms of any purchase, escalation, or renewal options. An asset lease may be recorded as a finance lease, in which case the accountant should present the same information as well as the amount of depreciation already recorded for these assets. Finance lease information should also include a summary, by major asset category, of the gross cost of leased assets. An example follows.

> The company is leasing a number of copiers, all of which are recorded as operating leases. There are no escalation or renewal options associated with these leases. All the leases require the company to pay personal property taxes, maintenance, and return shipping at the end of the leases. There are purchase options at the end of all lease terms that are based on the market price of the copiers at that time. The future minimum lease payments for these leases are

2009	€195,000
2010	173,000
2011	151,000
2012	145,000
2013	101,000
	€765,000

Disclosure of Lease Termination Costs

An office or equipment lease agreement typically obligates a company to long-term lease payments with no option to stop those payments even if the company is no longer using the space or equipment. Thus, lease termination costs can be quite high, and generally warrant disclosure. A footnote should include disclosure of the pertinent requirements of the lease agreement, the remaining period over which payments are due, and the potential range of costs involved. An example follows.

> Due to the downturn in the company's principal asparagus distribution market, it no longer requires its San Sebastian transshipment warehouse, for which it has a lease obligation for another six years. The total lease obligation for this facility through the remainder of the lease is €3,025,000. The company is discussing lease termination options with the lessor and is also searching for a sublessee. Given the market conditions, the company does not feel that a sublease can be obtained, and so it assumes that a lease termination fee will be required. Accordingly, it has recorded a lease termination charge in the current period of €2,405,000, which is the present value of the total lease obligation.

Disclosure of Sale and Leaseback Transactions

If a company has entered into a sale and leaseback transaction, it should disclose the total amount of future minimum lease payments as well as the amount of this liability in each of the next five years. It also should note the general provisions of the arrangement and the minimum amount of any payments to be received under the terms of noncancelable subleases. Two examples follow.

1. The company sold its headquarters building under a 20-year sale and leaseback arrangement. Under the agreement, the company is obligated to make aggregate lease payments of €13.5 million over the term of the lease, which is net of €1.25 million in payments from certain noncancelable sublease agreements. The future minimum lease payments for the next five years and thereafter for these leases are

2007	€595,000
2008	613,000
2009	621,000
2010	645,000
2011	701,000
Thereafter	10,325,000
	€13,500,000

2. The company sold its headquarters building under a 20-year sale and leaseback arrangement. Under the agreement, the company is obligated to make aggregate lease payments of €13.5 million over the term of the lease. This is a financing arrangement under which the lessor's up-front payment of €12 million is recorded as a long-term debt, future lease payments net of interest expense will reduce the balance of the debt, and the company continues to carry the property cost on its books and depreciate that cost. The future minimum lease payments are €675,000 per year for each of the next five years, and €10,125,000 in the aggregate thereafter

Disclosure of Leases with Related Parties

A company that has entered into a lease arrangement with a related party should reveal the nature and extent of the transaction. An example follows.

The company's president owns a majority interest in Copier Leases International, from which the company has leased 11 copiers under operating leases. The total amount of payments due under these leases is €93,000, which continues until 2011. Company management is of the opinion that the lease rates obtained are highly competitive to those of other leasing companies.

Disclosure of Treatment of Free Rent Periods

If a company has a rental agreement under which it pays no rent for some portion of the lease period, the proper accounting treatment is to charge to expense the average amount of rent per period, irrespective of the exact timing of payments. This situation should be described in a footnote, as should an explanation of how the liability is recorded. An example follows.

The company has entered into a new five-year rental agreement under which the first five months of rent are free. The company has chosen to charge to expense in each month the average monthly expense over the full lease term rather than no expense at all for the first five months, since this more accurately reflects the periodic lease cost. The excess amount of lease expense recognized early in the lease period, totaling €85,000, has been recorded in the Other Current Liabilities account.

Disclosure of Sublease Rentals

A company that subleased any assets under noncancelable agreements should disclose the minimum amount of payments to be received under these agreements. An example follows.

The company has subleased 25,000 square feet of its office building in County Clare under a three-year noncancelable lease. The total minimum amount of payments to be received under this agreement is €425,000.

Disclosure of Operating Leases by Lessor

A lessor should disclose the cost of leased property, broken down by major asset classifications, and the aggregate amount of accumulated depreciation. It should also note the total amount of minimum lease payments due under noncancelable leases for each of the next five years as well as in total. An example follows.

The company operates a leasing division that issues only leases accounted for as operating leases. The cost of assets leased as of the statement of financial position date were €14,700,000 in the farm equipment category, €29,250,000 in the emergency services category, and €41,000,000 in the municipal government category. The company has recorded €21,750,000 in aggregate accumulated depreciation on the assets recorded in all of these categories. The minimum lease payments due under noncancelable leases in each of the next five years are

2007	€20,000,000
2008	19,250,000
2009	14,750,000
2010	14,500,000
2011	10,000,000
Thereafter	16,500,000
Total	€95,000,000

Disclosure of Direct Financing and Sales-Type Leases by Lessor

A lessor should note the aggregate amounts of unearned finance income and unguaranteed residual values in outstanding lease agreements as well as the total allowance for uncollected lease payments. It should also note the total amount of minimum lease payments due for each of the next five years, with separate deductions for executory costs as well as in total. In the case of direct financing leases, the amount of initial direct costs also must be disclosed. An example follows.

The company leases its tractors to local farmer cooperatives. The total amount of unguaranteed lease residuals the company has estimated in aggregate for its outstanding leases is €3,397,000, which represents 9% of the aggregate minimum lease payments due. The company has also reserved €1,510,000 as an allowance for uncollectible lease payments, which is 4% of the aggregate minimum lease payments due. By comparison, the company reserved 3.8% of its aggregate minimum lease payments in 2008 and 3.2% in 2007. There is currently €6,795,000 of unearned finance income recorded as a liability. The minimum lease payments due under noncancelable leases in each of the next five years are

	Minimum payments due	*Less: executory costs*	*Net minimum payments due*
2007	€7,050,000	€141,000	€6,909,000
2008	5,350,000	107,000	5,243,000
2009	6,800,000	136,000	6,664,000
2010	5,000,000	100,000	4,900,000
2011	4,100,000	82,000	4,018,000
Thereafter	9,450,000	189,000	9,261,000
Total	€37,750,000	€755,000	€36,995,000

JOURNAL ENTRIES

Accounting for Leases—Lessee

Lease, finance (initial record by lessee). To record the initial capitalization of a lease, including imputed interest that is associated with the transaction and both the short-term and long-term portions of the associated account payable. A *second entry* records the interest expense associated with each periodic payment on the finance lease. A *third entry* records the depreciation expense associated with the finance lease in each accounting period.

Finance leases	xxx	
Unamortized discount on notes payable	xxx	
Short-term liabilities		xxx
Long-term liabilities		xxx
Interest expense	xxx	
Unamortized discount on notes payable		xxx
Depreciation expense	xxx	
Accumulated depreciation—finance leases		xxx

Accounting for Leases—Lessor

Initial lease record by lessor (sales-type lease). To record the initial lease transaction by the lessor, including the recognition of a sale, recording of an unearned interest liability, incurrence of a liability for any initial direct costs, and the transfer of the leased asset out of inventory.

Lease receivable	xxx	
Cost of goods sold	xxx	
Sales		xxx
Inventory		xxx
Accounts payable (any initial direct costs)		xxx
Unearned finance income		xxx

Receipt of cash payments by lessor (sales-type lease). To record the receipt of cash and the offsetting reduction in the lease receivable when periodic lease payments are made by the lessee to the lessor.

Cash	xxx	
Lease receivable		xxx

Recording of periodic interest income by lessor (sales-type lease). To periodically record earned interest by shifting interest from the Unearned Finance Income account into the Interest Income account.

Unearned interest	xxx	
Interest income		xxx

Return of asset to lessor at end of lease (sales-type lease). To record the receipt of a leased asset back into inventory upon its return by a lessee who has completed a lease term.

Inventory	xxx	
Lease receivable		xxx

Initial lease record by lessor (direct financing lease). To record the initial lease transaction by the lessor, including the recording of an unearned interest liability, incurrence of a liability for any initial direct costs, and the transfer of the leased asset out of inventory.

Lease receivable	xxx	
Initial direct costs	xxx	
Assets (specify account)		xxx
Unearned finance income		xxx
Cash		xxx

Receipt of cash payments by lessor (direct financing lease). To record the receipt of cash and the offsetting reduction in the lease receivable when periodic lease payments are made by the lessee to the lessor.

Cash	xxx	
Lease receivable		xxx

Recording of periodic interest income by lessor (direct financing lease). To periodically record earned interest by shifting interest from the Unearned Interest account into the Interest income account, with a portion of the Unearned Interest being allocated to an offset of Initial Direct Costs.

Unearned interest	xxx	
Interest income		xxx
Initial direct costs		xxx

Return of asset to lessor at end of lease (direct financing lease). To record the receipt of a leased asset upon its return by a lessee who has completed a lease term.

Asset (specify account)	xxx	
Lease receivable		xxx

Lease Extensions

Conversion of a finance lease to an operating lease. To record a lease extension under which a lease formerly designated a finance lease is now recorded as an operating lease. The existing leased asset is written off, along with all accumulated depreciation. If applicable, either a gain or loss is also recorded on the transaction.

Accumulated depreciation—finance leases	xxx	
Loss on lease conversion	xxx	
Gain on lease conversion		xxx
Finance leases		xxx

Sale-Leaseback Transactions

Sale-leaseback transactions for the lessee (finance lease). The first entry records the initial sale of an asset by the eventual lessee to the lessor, while the second entry records the coincident incurrence of a lease obligation for the same asset. The third entry records any lease payment by the lessee to the lessor, and the fourth entry records depreciation on the leased asset (on the assumption that this is a finance lease). The fifth entry records the periodic recognition of portions of the unearned income on the initial asset sale.

Cash	xxx	
Asset (variety of possible accounts)		xxx
Unearned income on sale-leaseback		xxx
Leased asset (variety of possible accounts)	xxx	
Lease obligation		xxx
Lease obligation	xxx	
Cash		xxx
Amortization expense	xxx	
Accumulated amortization		xxx
Unearned income on sale-leaseback	xxx	
Amortization expense		xxx

RECORDKEEPING

The originals of all signed lease documents should be retained in the legal department, with copies in the accounting department. Auditors will want to review the lease documents in order to prepare footnotes for the audited financial statements, while the accounting staff will want to retain the leases in order to determine the dates on which lease payments change or are paid off. Once a lease has terminated, it can be archived with the accounting records for the year in which the lease expired.

12 PENSIONS AND OTHER POSTRETIREMENT BENEFITS

DEFINITIONS OF TERMS

Accrued benefit obligation. Actuarial present value of benefits (whether vested or nonvested) attributed by the pension benefit formula to employee service rendered before a specified date and based on employee service and compensation (if applicable) prior to that date.

Accrued pension cost. Cumulative net pension cost accrued in excess of the employer's contributions.

Accrued postretirement benefit obligation. The actuarial present value of benefits attributed to employee service rendered as of a particular date. Prior to an employee's full eligibility date, the accrued postretirement benefit obligation as of a particular date for an employee is the portion of the expected postretirement benefit obligation attributed to that employee's service rendered to that date. On and after the full eligibility date, the accrued and expected postretirement benefit obligations for an employee are the same.

Actuarial present value. Value, as of a specified date, of an amount or series of amounts payable or receivable thereafter, with each amount adjusted to reflect (1) the time value of money (through discounts for interest) and (2) the probability of payment (by means of decrements for events such as death, disability, withdrawal, or retirement) between the date specified and the expected date of payment.

Actuarial gains and losses. Include (1) experience adjustments (the effects of differences between the previous actuarial assumptions and what has actually occurred); and (2) the effects of changes in actuarial assumptions.

Actuarial valuation. The process used by actuaries to estimate the present value of benefits to be paid under a retirement plan and the present values of plan assets and sometimes also of future contributions.

Amortization. Usually refers to the process of reducing a recognized liability systematically by recognizing revenues or reducing a recognized asset systematically by recognizing expenses or costs. In pension accounting, the term "amortization" also is used to refer to the systematic recognition in net pension cost over several periods of previously unrecognized amounts, including unrecognized prior service cost and unrecognized actuarial gain or loss.

Asset ceiling. The maximum amount of defined benefit asset that can be recognized is the lower of (1) the surplus or deficit in the benefit plan plus (minus) any unrecognized losses (gains) or (2) the total of (a) any cumulative unrecognized net actuarial losses and past service cost, and (b) the present value of any economic benefits available in the form of refunds from the plan or reductions in future contributions to the plan, determined using the discount rate that reflects market yields at the statement of financial position date on high-quality corporate bonds or, if necessary, on government bonds.

Attribution. The process of assigning pension benefits or cost to periods of employee service.

Contributory plan. A pension plan where employees contribute part of the cost. In some contributory plans, employees wishing to be covered must contribute; in other contributory plans, employee contributions result in increased benefits.

Current service cost. The increase in the present value of the defined benefit obligation resulting from services rendered by employees during the period, exclusive of cost elements identified as past service cost, experience adjustments, and the effects of changes in actuarial assumptions.

Curtailment. An event that significantly reduces the expected years of future service of present employees; or it eliminates, for a significant number of employees, the accrual of defined benefits for some or all of their future services. Curtailments include (1) termination of employee's services earlier than expected, which may or may not involve closing a facility or discontinuing a segment of a business, and (2) termination or suspension of a plan so that employees do not earn additional defined benefits for future services. In the latter situation, future service may be counted toward vesting of benefits accumulated based on past services.

Defined benefit pension plan. Any postemployment benefit plan other than a defined contribution plan. These are generally retirement benefit plans where amounts to be paid as retirement benefits are determinable, usually by reference to employees' earnings and/or years of service. The fund (and/or employer) is obligated, either legally or constructively, to pay the full amount of promised benefits whether sufficient assets are held in the fund or not.

Defined contribution pension plan. Benefit plans under which amounts to be paid as retirement benefits are determined by the contributions to a fund together with accumulated investment earnings thereon; the plan has no obligation to pay further sums if the amounts available cannot pay all benefits relating to employee services in the current and prior periods.

Employee benefits. All forms of consideration to employees in exchange for services rendered.

Expected long-term rate of return on plan assets. The assumption of the rate of return on plan assets reflecting the average rate of earnings expected on the funds invested, or to be invested, to provide for the benefits included in the projected benefit obligation.

Expected postretirement benefit obligation. The actuarial present value as of a particular date of the benefits expected to be paid to or for an employee, the employee's beneficiaries, and any covered dependents pursuant to the terms of the postretirement benefit plan.

Expected return on plan assets. The amount calculated as a basis for determining the extent of delayed recognition of the effects of changes in the fair value of assets. The expected return on plan assets is determined based on the expected long-term rate of return on plan assets and the market related value of plan assets.

Experience adjustments. Adjustments to benefit costs arising from the differences between the previous actuarial assumptions as to future events and what actually occurred.

Fair value. Amount that an asset could be exchanged for between willing, knowledgeable parties in an arm's-length transaction.

Fund. Used as a verb, to pay over to a funding agency (as to fund future pension benefits or to fund pension cost). Used as a noun, assets accumulated in the hands of a funding agency for the purpose of meeting pension benefits when they become due.

Funding. The irrevocable transfer of assets to an entity separate from the employer's entity, to meet future obligations for the payment of retirement benefits.

Gain or loss. Change in the value of either the projected benefit obligation or the plan assets resulting from experience different from that assumed or from a change in an actuarial assumption.

Interest cost component (of net periodic pension cost). Increase in the present value of the accrued benefit obligation due to the passage of time.

Measurement date. Date as of which plan assets and obligations are measured.

Mortality rate. Proportion of the number of deaths in a specified group to the number living at the beginning of the period in which the deaths occur. Actuaries use mortality tables, which show death rates for each age, in estimating the amount of pension benefits that will become payable.

Multiemployer plans. Defined contribution plans or defined benefit plans, other than state plans, that: (1) pool the assets contributed by various entities that are not under common control; and (2) use those assets to provide benefits to employees of more than one entity, on the basis that contribution and benefit levels are determined without regard to the identity of the entity that employs the employees concerned.

Net periodic pension cost. Amount recognized in an employer's financial statements as the cost of a pension plan for a period. Components of net periodic pension cost are service cost, interest cost (which is implicitly presented as part of service cost), actual return on plan assets, gain or loss, amortization of unrecognized prior service cost, and amortization of the unrecognized net obligation or asset existing at the date of initial application of IAS 19.

Other long-term employee benefits. Benefits other than postemployment, termination, and stock equity compensation benefits that do not fall due wholly within one year of the end of the period in which service was rendered.

Past service cost. The actuarially determined increase in the present value of the defined benefit obligation arising on the introduction of a retirement benefit plan, on the making of improvements to such a plan, or on the completion of minimum service requirements for eligibility in such a plan, all of which give employees credit for benefits for service prior to the occurrence of one or more of these events. Past service cost may be either positive (where benefits are introduced or improved) or negative (where existing benefits are reduced).

Plan amendment. Change in terms of an existing plan or the initiation of a new plan. A plan amendment may increase benefits, including those attributed to years of service already rendered.

Plan assets. The assets held by a long-term employee benefit fund and qualifying insurance policies. Regarding assets held by a long-term employee benefit fund, these are assets (other than nontransferable financial instruments issued by the reporting entity) that both:

1. Are held by a fund that is legally separate from the reporting entity and exists solely to pay or fund employee benefits, and
2. Are available to be used only to pay or fund employee benefits, are not available to the reporting entity's own creditors (even in the event of bankruptcy), and cannot be returned to the reporting entity unless either
    a. The remaining assets of the fund are sufficient to meet all related employee benefit obligations of the plan or the entity, or
    b. The assets are returned to the reporting entity to reimburse it for employee benefits already paid by it.

Regarding the qualifying insurance policy, this must be issued by a nonrelated party if the proceeds of the policy both

1. Can be used only to pay or fund employee benefits under a defined benefit plan, and
2. Are not available to the reporting entity's own creditors (even in the event of bankruptcy) and cannot be returned to the reporting entity unless either
    a. The proceeds represent surplus assets that are not needed for the policy to meet all related employee benefit obligations, or
    b. The proceeds are returned to the reporting entity to reimburse it for employee benefits already paid by it.

Postemployment benefits. Employee benefits, other than termination benefits, which are payable after the completion of employment.

Postemployment benefit plans. Formal or informal arrangements under which an entity provides postemployment benefits for one or more employees.

Postretirement benefits. All forms of benefits, other than retirement income, provided by an employer to retirees. Those benefits may be defined in terms of specified benefits, such as health care, tuition assistance, or legal services, that are provided to retirees as the need for those benefits arises, or they may be defined in terms of monetary amounts that become payable on the occurrence of a specified event, such as life insurance benefits.

Prepaid pension cost. Cumulative employer contributions in excess of accrued net pension cost.

Present value of a defined benefit obligation. Present value, without deducting any plan assets, of expected future payments required to settle the obligation resulting from employee service in the current and prior periods.

Prior service cost. Cost of retroactive benefits granted in a plan amendment.

Projected benefit obligation. The actuarial present value as of a date of all benefits attributed by the pension benefit formula to employee service rendered prior to that date. The projected benefit obligation is measured using assumptions as to future compensation levels if the pension benefit formula is based on those future compensation levels (pay-related, final-pay, final-average-pay, or career-average-pay plans).

Retirement benefit plans. Formal or informal arrangements whereby employers provide benefits for employees on or after termination of service, when such benefits can be determined or estimated in advance of retirement from the provisions of a document or from the employers' practices.

Retroactive benefits. Benefits granted in a plan amendment (or initiation) that are attributed by the pension benefit formula to employee services rendered in periods prior to the amendment. The cost of the retroactive benefits is referred to as prior service cost.

Return on plan assets. Interest, dividends, and other revenues derived from plan assets, together with realized and unrealized gains or losses on the assets, less administrative costs including taxes payable by the plan.

Service. Employment taken into consideration under a pension plan. Years of employment before the inception of a plan constitute an employee's past service; years thereafter are classified in relation to the particular actuarial valuation being made or discussed. Years of employment (including past service) prior to the date of a particular valuation constitute prior service.

Settlement. Transaction that (1) is an irrevocable action, (2) relieves the employer (or the plan) of primary responsibility for a pension benefit obligation, and (3) eliminates significant risks related to the obligation and the assets used to effect the settlement. Examples include making lump-sum cash payments to plan participants in exchange for their rights to receive specified pension benefits and purchasing nonparticipating annuity contracts to cover vested benefits.

Short-term employee benefits. Benefits other than termination and equity compensation benefits that are due within one year after the end of the period in which the employees rendered the related service.

Terminal funding. A method of recognizing the projected cost of retirement benefits only at the time an employee retires.

Termination benefits. Employee benefits payable as a result of the entity's termination of employment before normal retirement or the employee's acceptance of early retirement inducements.

Unrecognized prior service cost. Portion of prior service cost that has not been recognized as a part of net periodic pension cost.

Vested benefits. Those benefits that, under the conditions of a retirement benefit plan, are not conditional on continued employment.

CONCEPTS AND EXAMPLES

A pension plan is considered to be an arrangement whereby a company provides benefits under a specific benefit formula to its retired employees. Companies usually fund their pension plans by making periodic contributions to an independent trustee, who then invests the funds and pays benefits to the retired employees.

The accounting for *defined contribution* plans is normally straightforward, with the objective of matching the cost of the program with the periods in which the employees earn their benefits. Since contributions are formula-driven (e.g., as a percentage of wages paid), typically the payments to the plan will be made currently; if they do not occur by the statement of financial position date, an accrual will be recognized for any unpaid current contribution liability. Once made or accrued, the employer has no further obligation for the value of the assets held by the plan or for the sufficiency of fund assets for payment of the benefits, absent any violation of the terms of the agreement by the employer.

For example, contributions might be set at 4% of each employee's wages and salaries, up to €50,000 wages per annum. Generally, the contributions actually must be made by a specific date, such as 90 days after the end of the reporting entity's fiscal year, consistent with local law. The expense must be accrued for accounting purposes in the year the cost is incurred, whether the contribution is made currently or not.

The accounting for *defined benefit* plans is vastly more complex because the employer (sponsor) is responsible not merely for the current contribution to be made to the plan on behalf of participants but also for the sufficiency of the assets in the plan for the ultimate payments of benefits promised to the participants. Therefore, the current contribution is at best a partial satisfaction of its obligation, and the amount of actual cost incurred is not measured by this alone. The measurement of pension cost under a defined benefit plan necessarily involves the expertise of actuaries—persons who are qualified to estimate the numbers of employees who will survive (both as employees, in the case of vesting requirements which some of them may not yet have met; and as living persons who will be present to receive the promised retirement benefits), the salary levels at which they will retire (if these are incorporated into the benefit formula, as is commonly the case), their expected life expectancy (since benefits are typically payable for life), and other factors that will influence the amount of resources needed to satisfy the employer's promises.

Under current IFRS, only the accrued benefit valuation method may be used to measure defined benefit plan pension cost, the key reportable element of the defined benefit pension plan, from the company's perspective. Furthermore, only a single variant of the accrued benefit method—the "projected unit credit" method—is permitted. A number of alternative approaches, which also fell under the general umbrella of the accrued benefit method, are no longer accepted under IFRS. Accordingly, only the projected unit credit method will be discussed in this chapter.

Net periodic pension cost is comprised of the sum of six components:

1. Current (pure) service cost
2. Interest cost for the current period on the accrued benefit obligation
3. The expected return on plan assets
4. Actuarial gains and losses, to the extent recognized
5. Past service costs, to the extent recognized
6. The effects of any curtailments or settlements

Current (pure) service cost. Under IAS 19, service cost is based on the present value of the defined benefit obligation, and is attributed to periods of service without regard to conditional requirements under the plan calling for further service. Thus, vesting is not taken into account in the sense that there is no justification for non-accrual prior to vesting. In the actuarial determination of pension cost, however, the statistical probability of employees leaving employment prior to vesting must be taken into account, lest an overaccrual of costs be made.

Example of service cost attribution

To explain the concept of service cost, assume a single employee is promised a pension of €1,000 per year for each year worked before retirement, for life, upon retirement at age 60 or thereafter. Further assume that this is the worker's first year on the job, and he is 30 years of age. The consulting actuary determines that if the worker, in fact, retires at age 60, he will have a life expectancy of 15 years, and at the present value of the required benefits (€1,000/yr × 15 years = €15,000) discounted at the long-term corporate bond rate, 8%, equals €8,560. In other words, based on the work performed thus far (one year's worth), this employee has earned the right to a lump-sum settlement of €8,560 at age 60. Since this is 30 years into the future, this amount must be reduced to present value, which at 8% is a mere €851, and it is the pension cost to be recognized currently.

In year two, this worker earns the right to yet another annuity stream of €1,000 per year upon retirement, which again has a present value of €8,560 at the projected retirement age of 60. Since age 60 is now only 29 years hence, however, the present value of that promised benefit at the end of the current (second) year is €919, which represents the service cost in year two. This pattern will continue: As the employee ages, the current cost of pension benefits grows apace with, for example, the cost in the final working year being €8,560, before considering interest on the previously accumulated obligation—which would add another €18,388 of expense, for a total cost for this one employee in his final working year of €26,948. It should be noted, however, that in "real-life" situations for employee groups in the aggregate, this may not hold, since new younger employees will be added as older employees die or retire, which will tend to smooth out the annual cost of the plan.

Interest cost for the current period on the accrued benefit obligation. An annual increase in the net periodic pension cost that reflects the time value of money caused by the projected benefits estimated in the previous year now being one year closer to being paid out. As noted, since the actuarial determination of current period cost is the present value of the future pension benefits to be paid to retirees by virtue of their service in the current period, the longer the time until the expected retirement date, the lower will be the service cost recognized. Notwithstanding, over time this accrued cost must be further increased, until the employees' respective retirement dates the full amounts of the promised payments have been accreted. In this regard, the accrued pension liability is much like a sinking fund that grows from contributions plus the earnings thereon.

Consider the example of service cost presented in the preceding section. The €851 obligation recorded in the first year of that example will have grown to €919 by the end of the second year. The increase of €68 in the obligation for future benefits due to the passage of time is reported as a component of pension cost, denoted as interest cost. This cost is determined by multiplying the assumed settlement discount rate by the projected benefit obligation (as defined later in this section) at the beginning of the year.

Expected return on plan assets. Expected return for a given period is determined at the start of that period and is based on long-term rates of return for assets to be held over the term of the related pension obligation. Expected return is to incorporate anticipated dividends, interest, and changes in fair value, and is furthermore to be reduced in respect of expected plan administration costs.

For example, assume that at the start of 2008 the plan administrator expects, over the long term, and based on historical performance of plan assets, that the plan's assets will receive annual interest and dividends of 6%, net of any taxes due by the fund itself, and will enjoy a market value gain of another 2.5%. It is also noted that plan administration costs will average .75% of plan assets, measured by fair value. With this data, an expected rate of return for 2008 would be computed as 6.00% + 2.50% – .75% = 7.75%. This rate would be used to calculate the return on assets, which would be used to offset service cost and other benefit plan cost components for the year 2008.

Actuarial gains and losses, to the extent recognized. Changes in the amount of the actuarially determined pension obligation and differences in the actual versus the expected yield on plan assets as well as demographic changes (e.g., composition of the workforce, changes in life expectancy, etc.) contribute to actuarial gains and losses. IAS 19 does not require immediate recognition of actuarial gains and losses, unless the fluctuations are so great that deferral is not deemed to be wise. If the unrecognized actuarial gain or loss is no more than 10% of the larger of the present value of the defined benefit obligation or the fair value of plan assets, measured at the beginning of the reporting period, no recognition in the current period will be necessary (i.e., there will be continued deferral of the accumulated net actuarial gain or loss). Actuarial gains and losses recognized in other comprehensive income should be presented in the statement of comprehensive income. Those actuarial gains and losses and adjustments that have been recognized should be recognized directly in retained earnings, and should not be reclassified to profit or loss in a subsequent period. If the accumulated net actuarial gain or loss exceeds this 10% corridor, however, the magnitude creates greater doubt that future losses or gains will offset these, and for that reason some recognition will be necessary.

Under IAS 19, this excess should be amortized over the expected remaining working lives of the then-active employee participants, but the Standard actually permits any reasonable method of amortization as long as (1) recognition is at no slower a pace than would result from amortization over the working lives of participants, and (2) that the same method is used for both net gains and net losses. It is also acceptable to fully recognize all actuarial gains or losses immediately, without regard to the 10% corridor.

The corridor and the amount of any excess beyond this corridor must be computed anew each year, based on the present value of defined benefits and the fair value of plan assets, each determined as of the beginning of the year. Thus, there may have been an unrecognized actuarial gain of €450,000 at the end of year one, which exceeds the 10% corridor boundary by €210,000, and is therefore to be amortized over the average 21-year remaining working life of the plan participants, indicating a €10,000 reduction in pension cost in year two. If, at the end of year two, market losses or other actuarial losses reduce the accumulated actuarial gain below the threshold implied by the 10% corridor, accordingly, in year three there will be no further amortization of the net actuarial gain. This determination, therefore, must be made at the beginning of each period. Depending on the amount of unrecognized actuarial gain or loss at the end of year three, there may or may not be amortization in year four, and so on.

Past service costs, to the extent recognized. Past service costs refer to increases in the amount of a defined benefit liability that results from the initial adoption of a plan or from a change or amendment to an existing plan that increases the benefits promised to the participants with respect to previous service rendered. Less commonly, a plan amendment could reduce the benefits for past services, if local laws permit this. IAS 19 requires immediate recognition of past service cost as an expense when the added benefits vest immediately. When these are not vested immediately, however, recognition is to be on a straight-line basis over the period until vesting occurs. For example, if at January 1, 2008, the sponsoring entity grants an added €4,000 per employee in future benefits, and given the number of employees expected to receive these benefits this computes to a present value of €455,000, but vesting will not be until January 1, 2013, then a past service cost of €455,000 ÷ 5 years = €91,000 per year will be recognized. (To this amount interest must be added, as with service cost as described earlier.)

Effects of any curtailments or settlements. Periodic defined benefit plan expense is also affected by any curtailments or settlements that have been incurred. IAS 19 defines a curtailment as arising in connection with isolated events such as plant closings, discontinuations of operations, or termination or suspension of a benefit plan. Many times corporate restructurings will be accompanied by curtailments in benefit plans. The curtailment actually must occur for it to be given recognition.

The effect of a curtailment or settlement is measured with reference to the change in present value of the defined benefits, any change in fair value of related assets (normally there is none), and any related actuarial gains or losses and past service cost that had not yet been recognized. The net amount of these elements will be charged or credited to pension expense in the period the curtailment or settlement actually occurs.

The preceding six components of the net periodic pension cost describe cost types. The net periodic pension cost also can be viewed from the perspective of costs incurred over time. From this perspective, the *accumulated benefit obligation* (ABO) is the actuarial present value of benefit earned based on employee service up until the date of cost measurement. The *projected benefit obligation* (PBO) adds to the ABO the cost of additional benefits associated with expected future compensation increases (assuming that the pension's benefit formula pays more benefits based on increases in compensation, which is not always the case).

POLICIES

- **The expected long-term rate of return must be derived by an independent third party.** A company can significantly alter its reported pension expense each year by changing the expected long-term rate of return that it expects its pension assets to achieve. This policy is designed to keep the expected long-term rate of return from being manipulated internally. Additional layers of control would be requirements to change the third party at regular intervals as well as requirements that the third party hold no investment in the company's securities.

CONTROLS

- **Investigate unusual changes in the expected long-term rate of return.** Since the expected long-term rate of return assumption can have a major impact on the annual pension expense, a recurring audit program should require an investigation of why any changes are made to this rate as well as the independence of the third party that should be providing the estimate.
- **Audit changes in the assumed rate of compensation increases.** The projected benefit obligation is influenced directly by the assumed rate of compensation increases, if benefits are tied to compensation. To ensure that the assumed compensation rate is not being used to artificially inflate or depress the net periodic pension cost, a recurring audit program should require a review of the justifications made for the assumed rate of compensation increases.

FOOTNOTES

Business entities should disclose information that enables users of financial statements to evaluate the nature of its defined benefit plans as well as the financial statements effects of changes in those plans during the period.

If a company has a defined benefit plan or other postretirement plan, in addition to a general description of the type of plan and accounting policy for recognizing actuarial gains and losses, it must disclose a considerable amount of information, as follows.

- The company must reconcile the opening and closing balances of the present value of the defined benefit obligation, itemizing the current service cost, interest cost, participant contributions, actuarial gains and losses, changes in currency exchange rates, benefits paid, past service cost, plan amendments, business combinations, divestitures, curtailments, settlements, and special termination benefits. An example follows.

For the year ended December 31, the changes in the projected benefit obligation of plan assets were

	2008
Net benefit obligation—beginning of year	€257,000
Service costs incurred	4,000
Employee contributions	17,000
Interest costs on projected benefit obligation	15,000
Actuarial loss (gain)	(6,700)
Gross benefits paid	(15,300)
Plan amendment	300
Foreign currency exchange rate change	2,400
Effect of spin-off	(66,000)
Net benefit obligation—end of year	€207,700

- The company must reconcile the beginning and ending balances of the fair value of plan assets, itemizing the expected return on plan assets, actuarial gains and losses, changes in currency exchange rates, employer contributions, employee contributions, the gross benefit payment, business combinations, divestures, curtailments, and settlements. An example follows.

For the year ended December 31, the changes in the projected fair value of plan assets were

	2008
Fair value of plan assets—beginning of year	€295,000
Expected return on plan assets	40,000
Employer contributions (distributions)	1,700
Plan participant contributions	--
Gross benefits paid	(15,300)
Foreign currency exchange rate change	800
Effect of spin-off	(79,500)
Fair value of plan assets—end of year	€242,700

- The company must provide information on the funded status and balance sheet recognition of the unamortized prior service cost, unrecognized net gain or loss, accrued liabilities or prepaid assets, intangible assets, and accumulated other comprehensive income resulting from the recording of an additional minimum liability. An example follows.

The funded status for the year ended December 31 is

	2008
Over/(under) funded status	€50,500
Unrecognized net transition asset	(2,500)
Unrecognized prior service costs	400
Unrecognized net loss	32,800
Prepaid benefit cost recognized in balance sheets	€81,200

As of December 31, the amounts recognized in the statement of financial position consist of

	2008
Prepaid benefit cost (asset)	€81,200
Accumulated other comprehensive loss	--
Net amount recognized at year-end	€81,200

- The company must specify the net benefit cost recognized in the reporting period, showing the service cost, interest cost, expected return on plan assets, amortization of unrecognized transition assets or obligations, any recognized gains or losses, prior service costs, or settlement gain or loss. An example follows.

The next table provides the components of the net periodic pension benefit income for the years ended December 31.

	2006	*2007*	*2008*
Service costs incurred	€ 3,601,000	€ 4,052,000	€ 2,768,000
Interest costs on projected benefit obligation	15,173,000	14,580,000	10,927,000
Expected return on plan assets	(3,603,000)	(2,953,000)	(2,133,000)
Amortization of prior service cost	165,000	192,000	87,000
Amortization of actuarial cost	--	--	15,000
Amortization of transitional obligation	773,000	772,000	586,000
Net periodic pension benefit (income) expense	€16,109,000	€16,643,000	€12,232,000

- The company must list the assumed weighted-average discount rate, weighted-average expected long-term rate on plan assets, and weighted-average compensation rate increase. An example follows.

Assumptions used in the actuarial calculation include the discount rate selected and disclosed at the end of the previous year as well as other assumptions detailed in the next table, for the year ended December 31.

	2008
Discount rate	6.0%
Average salary increase rate	4.5%
Expected long-term rate of return on assets	7.5%

- The company must list the percentage of the fair value of total plan assets invested in each category of plan assets. An example follows.

The next table compares target asset allocation percentages as of the beginning of 2008 with actual asset allocations at the end of 2007.

	Target allocations	*Actual allocations*
Equities	40–80%	62%
Fixed income	20–50%	11%
Real estate	0–10%	4%
Other	0–20%	23%

- The company must provide a description of the investment strategies used. An example follows.

The plan's established investment policy seeks to balance the need to maintain a viable and productive capital base and yet achieve investment results superior to the actuarial rate consistent with our funds' investment objectives. Such an investment policy lends itself to a new asset allocation of approximately 50% investment in equities and property and 50% investment in debt securities. Asset allocations are subject to ongoing analysis and possible modification as basic capital market conditions change over time (interest rates, inflation, etc.).

- The company must describe the logic used to derive the expected long-term return on assets. An example follows.

  Investment return assumptions for the plan have been determined by obtaining independent estimates of expected long-term rates of return by asset class and applying the returns to assets on a weighted-average basis.

- It also must cite the accumulated benefit obligation (if the plan is a defined benefit plan). An example follows.

  The Company's accumulated benefit obligation was €85,886,000 in 2007 and €80,450,000 in 2006.

- The company must list the benefits it expects to pay in each of the next five fiscal years and the aggregate expected payment for the following five years. An example follows.

  The next table provides the expected benefit payments for our pension plan.

2008	€8,553,000
2009	8,447,000
2010	8,377,000
2011	8,466,000
2012	8,527,000
2013–2017	49,231,000

- The company must specify the expected amount of contributions to be paid into the plan during the next fiscal year. An example follows.

  The Company's funding policy, with respect to its qualified pension plan, is to contribute annually not less than the minimum required by applicable law and regulations, or to directly pay benefit payments where appropriate.

- It must cite the measurement dates used to calculate the plan benefits. An example follows.

  The Company uses a December 31 measurement date for its pension plan.

- The company must list the trend rate in health care costs used to measure the expected cost of benefits as well as the time when the company expects that rate to be achieved. An example follows.

	2008	2007
Initial health care cost trend rate	10.0%	10.5%
Ultimate health care cost trend rate	5.0%	5.5%
Number of years to ultimate trend rate	6	6

- The company must specify the effect of a 1% increase and decrease in the assumed health care costs trend rate on the aggregated service and interest costs. An example follows.

  Assumed health care cost trend rates have a significant effect on the amounts reported for the retiree health care plan. A one-percentage-point change in assumed health care cost trend rates would have had these effects:

	One-percentage-point increase	*One-percentage-point decrease*
Effect on total service and interest cost for the year ended December 30, 2007	€ 454,000	€ (357,000)
Effect on postretirement benefit obligation as of December 30, 2007	4,406,000	(3,986,000)

- The company must list he amount and types of related-party securities included in the plan. An example follows.

> Equity securities include the Company's common stock in the amounts of €1.8 million (less than 1% of total pension plan assets) and €2.9 million (less than 1% of total pension plan assets) at December 31, 2008 and 2007, respectively. In addition, due to investment strategies used by the Company's asset managers, the pension plan trust also holds short positions in the Company's common stock, which had a value of €800,000 at December 31, 2007.

If a company has a defined contribution plan, it must disclose its cost as well as a description of the effect of significant changes affecting the plan.

JOURNAL ENTRIES

Record net pension cost. The basic entry needed to record changes in the net pension cost is to itemize changes in the service cost, interest cost, and amortization of unrecognized prior service costs. The entry is shown next.

Net periodic pension cost	xxx	
Accrued/prepaid pension cost		xxx

Contribution to pension plan. Whenever a company pays cash into its pension plan, this reduces the amount of its accrued/prepaid pension cost. The entry is shown next.

Accrued/prepaid pension cost	xxx	
Cash		xxx

Record postretirement benefits. The recording of postretirement benefits besides those contained within a pension plan are very similar to the entry used for a pension plan. Only the name of the expense and related cost change, as noted in the next entry.

Postretirement expense	xxx	
Cash		xxx
Accrued/prepaid postretirement cost		xxx

13 SHAREHOLDERS' EQUITY

DEFINITIONS OF TERMS

Additional paid-in capital. Amounts received at issuance in excess of the par or stated value of capital stock and amounts received from other transactions involving the entity's stock and/or stockholders. It is classified by source.

Allocated shares. ESOP shares assigned to individual participants. These shares usually are based on length of service, compensation, or a combination of both.

Appropriation (of retained earnings). A segregation of retained earnings to communicate the unavailability of a portion for dividend distributions.

Authorized shares. The maximum number of shares permitted to be issued by a corporation's charter and bylaws.

Callable. An optional characteristic of preferred stock allowing the corporation to redeem the stock at specified future dates and at specific prices. The call price is usually at or above the original issuance price.

Compensatory plan. A stock option plan including elements of compensation that are recognized over the service period.

Compensatory stock option plans. Plans that do not meet the criteria for noncompensatory plans. Their main purpose is to provide additional compensation to officers and employees.

Constructive retirement method. Method of accounting for treasury shares that treats the shares as having been retired. The shares revert to authorized but unissued status. The stock and additional paid-in capital accounts are reduced, with a debit to retained earnings or a credit to a paid-in capital account for the excess or deficiency of the purchase cost over or under the original issuance proceeds.

Contributed capital. The amount of equity contributed by the corporation's shareholders. It consists of capital stock plus additional paid-in capital.

Convertible. An optional characteristic of preferred stock allowing the stockholders to exchange their preferred shares for common shares at a specified ratio.

Cost method. Method of accounting for treasury shares that presents aggregate cost of reacquired shares as a deduction from the total of paid-in capital and retained earnings.

Cumulative. An optional characteristic of preferred stock. Any dividends of prior years not paid to the preferred shareholders must be paid before any dividends can be distributed to the common shareholders.

Date of declaration. The date on which the board of directors votes that a dividend be paid. A legal liability (usually current) is created on this date in the case of cash, property, and scrip dividends.

Date of grant. The date on which the board of directors awards the stock to the employees in stock option plans.

Date of payment. The date on which the shareholders are paid the declared dividends.

Date of record. The date on which ownership of the shares is determined. Those owning stock on this date will be paid the declared dividends.

Deficit (formally known as accumulated deficit). A debit balance in the retained earnings account. Dividends generally may not be paid when this condition exists.

Discount on capital stock. Occurs when the stock of a corporation is issued originally at a price below par value. The original purchasers become contingently liable to creditors for this difference.

Employee stock ownership plan (ESOP). A form of defined contribution employee benefit plan, whereby the employer facilitates the purchase of shares of stock in the company for the benefit of the employees, generally by a trust established by the company. The plan may be leveraged by borrowings either from the employer-sponsor or from third-party lenders.

Fixed options. Options that grant the holder the rights to a specified number of shares at fixed prices. It is not dependent on achievement of performance targets.

Graded vesting. A vesting process whereby the employee becomes entitled to a stock-based award fractionally over a period of years.

Grant date. The date at which the entity and another party (including an employee) agree to a share-based payment arrangement, which is when the entity and the counterparty have a shared understanding of the terms and conditions of the arrangement. At grant date the entity confers on the counterparty the right to cash, other assets, or equity instruments of the entity, provided the specified vesting conditions, if any, are met. If that agreement is subject to an approval process (e.g., by shareholders), grant date is the date when that approval is obtained.

Intrinsic value. The difference between the fair value of the shares to which the counterparty has the (conditional or unconditional) right to subscribe or which it has the right to receive and the price (if any) the counterparty is (or will be) required to pay for those shares.

Issued stock. The number of shares issued by the firm and owned by the shareholders and the corporation. It is the sum of outstanding shares plus treasury shares.

Legal capital. The aggregate par or stated value of stock. It represents the amount of owners' equity that cannot be distributed to shareholders. It serves to protect the claims of the creditors.

Liquidating dividend. A dividend distribution that is not based on earnings. It represents a return of contributed capital.

Measurement date. The date on which the price used to compute compensation under stock-based compensation plans is fixed.

No-par stock. Stock that has no par value. Sometimes a stated value is determined by the board of directors. In this case, the stated value is accorded the same treatment as par value stock.

Outstanding stock. Stock issued by a corporation and held by shareholders (i.e., issued shares that are not held in the treasury).

Par value method. A method of accounting for treasury shares that charges the treasury stock account for the aggregate par or stated value of the shares acquired and charges the excess of the purchase cost over the par value to paid-in capital and/or retained earnings. A deficiency of purchase cost is credited to paid-in capital.

Participating. An optional characteristic of preferred stock whereby preferred shareholders may share ratably with the common shareholders in any profit distributions in excess of a predetermined rate. Participation may be limited to a maximum rate, or it may be unlimited (full).

Performance-based options. Options that are granted to employees conditional on the achievement of defined goals.

Retained earnings. The undistributed earnings of a firm.

Service period. The period over which a stock-based compensation award is earned by the recipient. If it is not otherwise defined in the plan, it is the vesting period.

Share-based payment arrangement. An agreement between the entity and another party (including an employee) to enter into a share-based payment transaction, thereby entitling the other party to receive cash or other assets of the entity for amounts that are based on the price of the entity's shares or other equity instruments of the entity, or to receive equity instruments of the entity, provided the specified vesting conditions (if any) are met.

Share-based payment transaction. A transaction in which the entity receives goods or services as consideration for equity instruments of the entity (including shares or share options), or acquires goods or services for amounts that are based on the price of the entity's shares or other equity instruments of the entity.

Share option. A contract that gives the holder the right, but not the obligation, to subscribe to the entity's shares at a fixed or determinable price for a specified period of time.

Share rights. Enables present shareholders to purchase additional shares of stock of the corporation. It is commonly used if a preemptive right is granted to common shareholders by some state corporation laws.

Treasury shares. Shares of a corporation that have been repurchased by the corporation. This stock has no voting rights and receives no cash dividends. Some states do not recognize treasury stock. In such cases, reacquired shares are treated as having been retired.

Vesting. The process whereby the recipient of a stock-based compensation award earns the right to control or exercise the award.

Vesting period. The period during which all the specified vesting conditions of a share-based payment arrangement are to be satisfied.

CONCEPTS AND EXAMPLES[1]

Presentation and Disclosure of Equity

IAS 1 categorizes shareholders' interests in three broad subdivisions: issued capital, reserves, and accumulated profits or losses. This Standard also sets forth requirements for disclosures about the details of share capital for corporations and of the various capital accounts of other types of enterprises.

Disclosure Relating to Share Capital

- *The number or amount of shares authorized, issued, and outstanding.*
- *Capital not yet paid in.* IAS 1 requires that a distinction be made between shares that have been issued and fully paid, on one hand, and those that have been issued but not fully paid, on the other hand.
- *Par value per share.* This is also generally referred to as legal value or face value per share.
- *Movements in share capital accounts during the year.* This information usually is disclosed in the financial statements or the footnotes to the financial statements. Under the provisions of IAS 1, reporting entities must present either a statement showing the changes in all the equity accounts (including issued capital, reserves and accumulated profit or loss) or a statement reporting changes in equity other than those arising from transactions with, or distributions to, owners.
- *Cumulative preference dividends in arrears.* If an entity has preferred shares *outstanding* and does not pay *cumulative* dividends on the preference shares annually when due, it will be required by statute to pay these arrearages in

---

[1] *Much of the information in this section is adapted with permission from Steven Bragg,* ***Ultimate Accountants' Reference*** *(Hoboken, NJ: John Wiley & Sons, 2006), Chapter 20.*

later years, before any distributions can be made on common (ordinary) shares.

- *Reacquired shares.* Shares that are issued but then reacquired by a company are *referred* to as *treasury shares.* The entity's ability to reacquire shares may be limited by its corporate charter or by covenants in its loan and/or preferred share agreements. *Shares outstanding* refers to shares other than those held as treasury shares.
- *Shares reserved for future issuance under options and sales contracts, including the terms and amounts.* Companies may issue share options that grant the holder of these options rights to a specified number of shares at a certain price. A common example of a share option is that granted under an employee share ownership plan (ESOP).

Disclosures Relating to Other Equity

- *Capital paid in excess of par value.* This is the amount received on the issuance of *shares* that is the excess over the par value. It is called additional paid-in capital in the United States; in many other jurisdictions, including the European Union, it is referred to as share premium. Essentially the same accounting would be required if a stated value is used in lieu of par value, where permitted.
- *Revaluation reserve.* When a company carries property, plant, and equipment at *amounts* other than historical costs, as is permitted by IAS 16 (revaluation to fair value), the difference between the historical costs (net of accumulated depreciation) and the fair values is credited to the revaluation reserve. The Standard requires that movements of this reserve during the reporting period (year or interim period) be disclosed, which usually is done in the footnotes. This disclosure also will appear in the statement of changes in equity and the statement of comprehensive income. Also, restrictions concerning distributions of this reserve to shareholders should be disclosed.
- *Reserves.* Reserves include capital reserves as well as revenue reserves. Statutory reserves and voluntary reserves also are included under this category. Finally, special reserves, including contingency reserves, are included as well. The use of general reserves and statutory reserves, once common or even required under company laws in many jurisdictions, is now in decline.
- *Retained earnings.* By definition, retained earnings represents a corporation's accumulated profits (or losses) less any distributions that have been made therefrom. IAS 8 requires that two other adjustments be shown as adjustments to retained earnings:

    1. Correction of accounting errors that relate to prior periods should be reported by adjusting the opening balance of retained earnings. Comparative information should be restated, unless it is impracticable to do so.
    2. The adjustment resulting from a change in accounting policy that is to be applied retrospectively should be reported as an adjustment to the opening balance of retained earnings. Comparative information should be restated unless it is impracticable to do so.

- *Total comprehensive income for the period,* showing separately the total amounts attributable to owners of the parent and to noncontrolling (i.e., minority) interest in the subsidiaries. A comprehensive income includes all components of "profit or loss" and of "other comprehensive income." Changes in other comprehensive items during the period are reported in other comprehensive income while the cumulative amounts are presented in equity.

Other comprehensive income is comprised of five components:

1. Changes in revaluation surplus (see IAS 16, *Property, Plant and Equipment*, and IAS 38, *Intangible Assets*)
2. Gains and losses arising from translating the financial statements of a foreign operation (see IAS 21, *The Effects of Changes in Foreign Exchange Rates*)
3. Gains and losses on remeasuring available-for-sale financial assets (see IAS 39, *Financial Instruments: Recognition and Measurement*)
4. The effective portion of gains and losses on hedging instruments in a cash flow hedge (see IAS 39)
5. Actuarial gains and losses on defined benefit plans recognized in accordance with paragraph 93A of IAS 19, *Employee Benefits*

IFRS provides only minimal guidance regarding the actual accounting for capital transactions, including the issuance of shares of various classes of equity instruments. The next section offers suggestions concerning the accounting for such transactions within the spirit of IFRS, although largely drawn from other authoritative sources. This is done to provide guidance that conforms to the requirements under IAS 8 and to illustrate a wide array of actual transactions that often need to be accounted for.

Legal Capital and Share Capital

The owners of common shares are the true owners of the corporation. Through their shared ownership, they have the right to dividend distributions, to vote on various issues presented to them by the board of directors, to elect members of the board, and to participate in any residual funds left if the corporation is liquidated. If the company is liquidated, they will not receive any distribution from its proceeds until all creditor claims and claims of holders of all other classes of shares have been satisfied. There may be several classes of common shares, which typically have different voting rights attached to them; the presence of multiple types of common shares generally indicates that some shareholders are attempting some degree of preferential control over a company through their type of common shares.

Most types of shares contain a par value, which is a minimum price below which the shares cannot be sold. The original intent for using par value was to ensure a residual amount of funding was contributed to the company that could not be removed from it until the dissolution of the corporate entity. In reality, most common shares now have a par value that is so low its original intent no longer works. Thus, although the accountant still tracks par value separately in the accounting records, it has little meaning.

If an investor purchases shares at a price greater than par value, the difference is credited to an Additional Paid-in Capital account. For example, if an investor buys one common share at a price of €82, and the share's par value is €1, then the entry would be

Cash	82	
Common shares—par value		1
Common shares—additional paid-in capital		81

When a company initially issues shares, there will be a number of costs associated with it, such as the printing of share certificates, legal fees, investment banker fees, and security registration fees. These costs can be charged against the proceeds of the share sale rather than being recognized as expenses within the current period.

If a company accepts property or services in exchange for shares, the amount listed on the books as the value of shares issued should be based on the fair value of the property or services received. This amount may not be easily determined, in which case the current market price of the shares issued should be used. If neither is available, then the value assigned by the board of directors at the time of issuance is assumed to be the fair value.

Preferred shares come in many varieties. Essentially they are shares that have fewer (or none) of the rights conferred on common shares but that offer a variety of incentives, such as guaranteed dividend payments and preferential distributions over common shares, to convince investors to buy them. The dividends also can be preconfigured to increase to a higher level at a later date, which is called *increasing rate preferred shares*. This is an expensive form of funds for a company since, in most countries, the dividends paid to investors are not tax deductible as interest expense.

The dividends provided for in a preferred share agreement can be distributed only after the approval of the board of directors (as is the case for dividends from common shares) and so may be withheld. If the preferred shares have a cumulative provision, then any dividends not paid to the holders of preferred shares in preceding years must be paid prior to dividend payments for any other types of shares. Also, some preferred shares will give their owners voting rights in the event of one or more missed dividend payments.

Because these shares are so expensive, many companies issue them with a call feature stating the price at which the company will buy back the shares. The call price must be high enough to give investors a reasonable return over their purchase price, or else no one will initially invest in the shares.

Convertible Preferred Shares

Preferred shares also may be converted by the shareholder into common shares at a preset ratio, if the preferred share agreement specifies that this option is available. If this conversion occurs, the accountant must reduce the par value and Additional Paid-in Capital accounts for the preferred shares by the amount at which the preferred shares were purchased and then transfer these balances into corresponding Common Share accounts.

Example of a preferred share conversion to common shares

If a shareholder of preferred shares was to convert one share of the Tallinn Logistics Company's preferred share into five common shares, the journal entry would be as shown, on the assumption that the preferred share was bought for €145 and that the par value of the preferred share is €50 and the par value of the common shares is €1.

Preferred share—par value	50	
Preferred share—additional paid-in capital	95	
Common shares—par value		5
Common shares—additional paid-in capital		140

In the journal entry, the par value account for the common shares reflects the purchase of five shares, since the par value of five individual shares (i.e., €5) has been recorded, with the remaining excess funds from the preferred share being recorded in the additional paid-in capital account. If the par value of the common shares were to be greater than the entire purchase price of the preferred share, however, the journal entry would change to bring in extra funds from the retained earnings account in order to make up the difference. If this were to occur with the previous assumptions, except with a common shares par value of €40, the journal entry would be

Preferred share—par value	50	
Preferred share—additional paid-in capital	95	
Retained earnings	55	
Common shares—par value		200

Share Splits

A share split involves the issuance of a multiple of the current number of shares outstanding to current shareholders. For example, a one-for-two split of shares when there are currently 125,000 shares outstanding will result in a new amount outstanding of 250,000 shares. Share splits are effected to reduce the market price on a per-share basis. In addition, dropping the price into a lower range can make the shares more affordable to small investors, who may then bid up the price to a point where the split shares are cumulatively more valuable than the presplit shares.

A share split typically is accompanied by a proportional reduction in the par value of the share. For example, if a share with a par value of €20 were to be split on a two-for-one basis, then the par value of the split share would be €10 per share. This transaction requires no entry on a company's books. Nevertheless, if the split occurs without a change in the par value, then funds must be shifted from the Additional Paid-in Capital account to the Par Value account.

A reverse split also may be accomplished if a company wishes to proportionally increase the market price of its shares. For example, if a company's common share sell for €2.35 per share and management wishes to see the price trade above the €20 price point, then it can conduct a 10-for-1 reverse split, which will raise the market price to €23.50 per share while reducing the number of outstanding shares by 90%. In this case, the par value per share would be increased proportionally, so that no funds were ever removed from the Par Value account.

Example of a share split with no change in par value

If 250,000 shares were to be split on a one-for-three basis, creating a new pool of 750,000 shares, and the existing par value per share of €2 were not changed, then the accountant would have to transfer €1,000,000 (the number of newly created shares times the par value of €2) from the Additional Paid-in Capital account to the Par Value account to ensure that the legally mandated amount of par value per share was stored there.

Share Subscriptions

Share subscriptions allow investors or employees to pay in a consistent amount over time and receive shares in exchange. When such an arrangement occurs, a receivable is set up for the full amount expected, with an offset to a common share subscription account and the Additional Paid-in Capital account (for the par value of the subscribed shares). When the cash is collected and the shares are issued, the funds are deducted from these accounts and shifted to the standard common share account.

Example of a share subscription

If the Koszalin Molasses Company sets up a share subscription system for its employees and they choose to purchase 10,000 shares of common shares with a par value of €1 for a total of €50,000, the entry would be

Share subscriptions receivable	50,000	
Common shares subscribed		40,000
Additional paid-in capital		10,000

When the €50,000 cash payment is received, the Share Subscriptions Receivable account will be offset, while funds stored in the Common Share Subscribed account are shifted to the Common Shares account, as noted in the next entry.

Cash	50,000	
Share subscriptions receivable		50,000
Common shares subscribed	50,000	
Common shares		50,000

Retained Earnings

Retained earnings is that portion of equity not encompassed by the various par value or additional paid-in capital accounts. It is increased by profits and decreased by distributions to shareholders and several types of share transactions.

Retained earnings can be impacted if the accountant makes a prior period adjustment that results from an error in the prior financial statements; the offset to this adjustment will be the Retained Earnings account, and will appear as an adjustment to the opening balance in the Retained Earnings account. A financial statement error would be one that involved a mathematical error or the incorrect application of accounting rules to accounting entries. A change in an accounting *estimate* is not an accounting error and so should not be charged against retained earnings.

Retained earnings can be restricted through the terms of lending agreements. For example, a lender may require the company to restrict some portion of its retained earnings through the term of the loan, thereby giving the lender some assurance that funds will be available to pay off the loan. Such a restriction would keep the company from issuing dividends in amounts that cut into the restricted retained earnings.

Share Warrants

A share warrant is a legal document giving the holder the right to buy a company's shares at a specific price, and usually for a specific time period, after which it becomes invalid. It is used as a form of compensation instead of cash for services performed by other entities to the company and also may be attached to debt instruments in order to make them appear as more attractive investments to buyers.

If the warrant attached to a debt instrument cannot be detached and sold separately from the debt, then it should not be accounted for separately. If it can be sold separately by the debt holder, however, then the fair value of each item (the warrant and the debt instrument) should be determined, and the accountant should apportion the price at which the combined items were sold between the two, based on their fair values.

Example of value allocation to warrants

For example, if the fair value of a warrant is €63.50 and the fair value of a bond to which it was attached is €950, and the price at which the two items were sold was €1,005, then an entry should be made to an additional paid-in capital account for €62.97 to account for the warrants, while the remaining €942.03 is accounted for as debt. The apportionment of the actual sale price of €1,005 to warrants is calculated as

$$\frac{\text{Fair value of warrant}}{\text{Fair value of warrant} + \text{Fair value of bond}} \times \text{Price of combined instruments}$$

or

$$\frac{€63.50}{(€63.50 + €950.00)} \times €1005 = €62.97$$

If a warrant expires, then the funds are shifted from the outstanding warrants account to an additional paid-in capital account. To continue with the last example, this would require the next entry:

Additional paid-in capital—warrants	62.97	
Additional paid-in capital—expired warrants		62.97

If a warrant is subsequently used to purchase one share of the entity's equity, then the value allocated to the warrant in the accounting records should be shifted to the common share accounts. To use the preceding example, if the warrant valued at €62.97 is used to purchase a common share at a price of €10.00, and the common share has a par value of €25, then the par value account is credited with €25 (since it is mandatory that the par value be recorded), and the remainder of the funds are recorded in the additional paid-in capital account. The entry follows.

Cash	10.00	
Additional paid-in capital—warrants	62.97	
Common shares—par value		25.00
Common shares—additional paid-in capital		47.97

Dividends

The board of directors must authorize distribution of dividends. The board is not allowed to make such a distribution if the company is insolvent or would become insolvent as a result of the transaction.

The date on which the board of directors votes to issue dividends is the *declaration date*. At this time, by the board's action, the company has incurred a liability to issue a dividend. Unless the dividend is a share dividend, the accountant must record a dividend payable at this time and debit the retained earnings account to indicate the eventual source of the dividend payment.

The dividend will be paid as of a *record date*. This date is of considerable importance to shareholders, since the entity holding a share on that date will be entitled to receive the dividend. If a share is sold the day before the record date, then the old shareholder forgoes the dividend and the new one receives it. As of the payment date, the company issues dividends, thereby debiting the Dividends Payable account and crediting the Cash account (or the account of whatever asset is distributed as a dividend).

On rare occasions, a company will choose to issue a *property dividend* to its shareholders. Under this scenario, the assets being distributed must be recorded at their fair market value, which usually triggers the recognition of either a gain or loss in the current income statement.

Example of a property dividend

The Ryga Book Binders Company declares a property dividend for its shareholders of a rare set of books, which have a fair market value of €500 each. The 75 shareholders receive one book each, which represents a total fair market value of €37,500. The books were originally obtained by the company at a cost of €200 each, or €15,000 in total. Consequently, a gain of €22,500 (= €37,500 minus €15,000) must be recognized. To do so, the accountant debits the Retained Earnings account for €37,500, credits the Gain on Property Disposal account for €22,500, and credits its Dividends Payable account for €15,000. Once the books are distributed to the shareholders, the accountant debits the Dividends Payable account for €15,000 and credits the Inventory account for €15,000 in order to eliminate the dividend liability and reflect the reduction in book inventory.

A dividend also may take the form of a *share dividend*. This allows a company to shift funds out of the Retained Earnings account and into the Par Value and Additional Paid-in Capital accounts, which reduces the amount of funding that the tax authority would see when reviewing the company for an excessive amount of retained earnings (which can be taxed). In most countries, these distributions are not taxable to the recipient. If the amount of a share dividend represents less than one-quarter of the total number of shares currently outstanding, then this is considered to be a distribution that will not greatly impact the price of existing shares through dilution; accordingly, the accountant records the fair market value of these shares in the Par Value and Additional Paid-in Capital accounts and takes the offsetting funds out of the Retained Earnings Account.

Example of a small share dividend

If the Hellas Fishing Equipment Company wishes to issue a share dividend of 10,000 shares and their fair value is €32 per share, with a par value of €1, the entry would be

Retained earnings	320,000	
Common shares—par value		32,000
Additional paid-in capital		288,000

If more than one-quarter of the total amount of outstanding shares is to be distributed through a share dividend, then we assume that the value of the shares will be watered down through such a large distribution. In this case, funds are shifted from retained earnings only to cover the amount of the par value for the shares to be distributed.

Example of a large share dividend

Using the preceding example (and assuming that 10,000 shares were more than 25% of the total outstanding), the entry would change to

Retained earnings	32,000	
Common shares—par value		32,000

If there are not sufficient funds in the retained earnings account to make these entries, then the number of shares issued through the share dividend must be reduced. Nonetheless, given the small size of the par values that many companies have elected to use for their shares, the amount of retained earnings required actually may be less for a very large share dividend than for a small one, since only the par value of the shares must be covered in the event of a large distribution.

A **liquidating dividend** is used to return capital to investors; thus, it is not strictly a dividend, which is intended to be a distribution of profits. This transaction is impacted by the laws of the state of incorporation for each organization, so it cannot be readily summarized here. Alternatively, in most cases the general entry is to credit cash and debit the Additional Paid-in Capital account.

If a corporation declares a dividend payable in *scrip* that is interest bearing, the interest is accrued over time as a periodic expense. The interest is not a part of the dividend itself.

A summary of the entries required for the various types of dividends is provided in the Decision Tree section.

Treasury Shares (Buy-Back Shares)

If the board of directors elects to have the company buy back shares from shareholders, the shares that are brought in-house are called *treasury shares*. IFRS does not specifically address the accounting for treasury share transactions. As a general principle, however, profit or loss cannot be affected by transactions in an entity's own shares, and thus the proper accounting would be to report these as capital transactions only. US GAAP offers explicit guidance on the accounting for treasury share transactions, and this guidance forms the basis for suggested approaches in this section.

A corporation's purchase of its own shares normally is accounted for under the *cost method*. Under this approach, the cost at which shares are bought back is listed in a treasury share account. When the shares are subsequently sold again, any sale amounts exceeding the repurchase cost are credited to the Additional Paid-in Capital account; any shortfalls, however, are charged first to any remaining additional paid-in capital remaining from previous treasury share transactions and then to retained earnings if there is no additional paid-in capital of this type remaining. For example, if a company chooses to buy back 500 shares at €60 per share, the transaction would be

Treasury shares	30,000	
Cash		30,000

If management later decides to permanently retire treasury shares that were recorded originally under the cost method, it backs out the original par value and additional paid-in capital associated with the initial share sale and charges any remaining difference to the retained earnings account. To continue with the previous example, if the 500 shares had a par value of €1 each originally had been sold for €25,000, and all were to be retired, the entry would be

Common shares—par value	500	
Additional paid-in capital	24,500	
Retained earnings	5,000	
Treasury shares		30,000

If instead the company subsequently chooses to sell the shares back to investors at a price of €80 per share, the transaction is

Cash	40,000	
Treasury shares		30,000
Additional paid-in capital		10,000

If a treasury share subsequently is sold for more than it was originally purchased, the excess amount also may be recorded in an additional paid-in capital account that is specifically used for treasury share transactions. The reason for this segregation is that any subsequent sales of treasury shares for less than the original buy-back price require the accountant to make up the difference from any gains recorded in this account; if the account is emptied and there is still a difference, then the shortage is made up from the additional paid-in capital account for the same class of shares and then from retained earnings.

In the less common case where there is no intention of ever reselling treasury shares, transaction is accounted for at the point of purchase from shareholders under the *constructive retirement method*. Using this approach, the shares are assumed to be retired, and so the original common shares and additional paid-in capital accounts will be reversed, with any loss on the purchase being charged to the retained earnings account and any gain being credited to the additional paid-in capital account. For example, if a company were to buy back 500 shares at €60 per share and the original issuance price was €52 (par value of €1), then the transaction would be

Common shares—par value	500	
Additional paid-in capital	25,500	
Retained earnings	4,000	
Cash		30,000

Note that under the constructive retirement approach, no treasury account is used, since it is assumed that the shares are retired from use immediately rather than being parked in a treasury shares holding account.

A special case arises when a company is forced to buy back shares at above-market prices under the threat of a corporate takeover. When this happens, the difference between the repurchase price and the market price must be charged to expense in the current period.

Options

A share option is an agreement between a company and another entity (frequently an employee), allowing the entity to purchase shares in the company at a specific price within a specified date range. The assumption is that the options will be exercised only if the fixed purchase price is lower than the market price, so that the buyer can turn around and sell the shares on the open market for a profit. For example, a company could issue options that give an employee the right to acquire shares in the company at €5 each, with the options having to be exercised before December 31, 2008. The option holder is taking a risk that the share price may not reach €5 (the option is "out of the money") or the share price may exceed €5 (the option is "in the money").

Under IFRS 2, *Share-Based Payment*, the fundamental approach for equity-settled transactions is to expense the value of share options granted over the period during which the employee is earning the option, that is, the period until the option vests (becomes unconditional). If the options vest (become exercisable) immediately, the employee receiving the grant cannot be compelled to perform future services, and accordingly the fair value of the options is compensation in the period of the grant. More commonly, however, there will be a period (several years, typically) of future services required before the options may be exercised; in those cases, compensation is to be recognized over that vesting period. There are two practical difficulties with this: (1) estimating the value of the share options granted (true even if vesting is immediate); and (2) allowing for the fact that not all options initially granted will ultimately vest or, if they vest, be exercised by the holders.

IFRS 2 directs that where market prices are not available (which is virtually always the case for employee share options, since normally they cannot be sold), the entity must estimate fair value using a valuation technique that is "consistent with generally accepted valuation methodologies for pricing financial instruments, and shall incorporate all factors and assumptions that knowledgeable, willing market participants would consider in setting the price."

Appendix B of the Standard notes that all option pricing models take into account

- The exercise price of the option
- The current market price of the shares

- The expected volatility of the share price
- The dividends expected to be paid on the shares
- The risk-free interest rate
- The life of the option

In essence, the grant date value of the share option is the current market price, less the present value of the exercise price, less the dividends that will not be received during the vesting period, and adjusted for the expected volatility. The time value of money arises because the holder of an option is not required to pay the exercise price until the exercise date. Instead, the holder can invest funds elsewhere while waiting to exercise the option.

Example of options issued

On March 29, 2007, a company issues 200 options valued at €10 each to a key executive as payment for past services. Each option entitles the executive to acquire a share in the company at a price of €40 on a date when the market price is €35. Assume that on May 29, when the share prices reach €45, the executive exercises the option. This journal entry should be recorded on March 29, the date of grant:

Wages expense	2,000	
Additional paid-in capital—Options*		2,000

**This account may be called "Option reserve" or "Other equity."*

The journal entry required on May 29, the date of exercise, is:

Cash	8,000	
Additional paid-in capital—- Options	2,000	
Share capital		10,000

Under IFRS 2, if the share price did not reach €40 within the specified life of the option, the option would lapse, and the company could then transfer the balance of the Additional Paid-in Capital—Options Account to Additional Paid-in Capital (or "Other equity").

If the options were sold to investors, the company would record an increase in equity ("Other equity" or "Options reserve")

Share Appreciation Rights

Sometimes the management team chooses not to issue share options to employees, either because employees do not have the funds to purchase shares or because no shares are available for an option plan. An alternative, however, is the share appreciation right (SAR). Under this approach, the company essentially grants an employee a fake share option and issues compensation to the employee at a future date if the price of company shares has risen from the date of grant to the date at which the compensation is calculated. The amount of compensation paid is the difference between the two share prices.

To account for a SAR, the accountant must determine the amount of any change in company shares during the reporting period and charge the amount to an accrued compensation expense account. If there is a decline in the share price, then the accrued expense account can be reduced. If an employee cancels the SAR agreement (perhaps by leaving the company), then the entire amount of accrued compensation expense related to that individual should be reversed in the current period.

If the company pays the recipients of SAR compensation in shares, then it usually grants shares on the payment date based on the number of shares at their fair value that will eliminate the amount of the accrued compensation expense. The journal entry required is a debit to the Accrued Compensation Liability account and a credit to the Share Rights Outstanding—Other Equity account.

If a service period is required before a SAR can be exercised, the amount of the compensation expense should be recognized ratably over the service period.

Example of a SAR transaction

A company decides to grant 2,500 SAR to its chief designer. The share price at the grant date is €10. After one year, the share price has increased to €12. After the second year, the share price has dropped to €11. After the third year, the price increases to €15, at which point the chief designer chooses to cash in his SAR and receive payment. The related transactions would be

End of year 1

Compensation expense (€2 net gain × 2,500 shares)	5,000	
SAR liability		5,000

End of year 2

SAR liability	2,500	
Compensation expense (€1 net loss × 2,500 shares)		2,500

End of year 3

Compensation expense (€4 net gain × 2,500 shares)	10,000	
SAR liability		10,000
SAR liability (payment of employee)	12,500	
Cash		12,500

Employee Share Ownership Plans

An employee share ownership plan (ESOP) is one where employees receive additional compensation in the form of shares purchased by the ESOP from the corporation. Since the company usually has a legal obligation to provide shares or contributions to the ESOP (which then are used to buy its shares), the ESOP should be considered an extension of the company for accounting purposes. This means that if the ESOP obligates itself to a bank loan in order to buy shares from the company, the company should record this liability on its books even if the company is not a guarantor of the loan. The entry would be a debit to cash and a credit to loans payable. However, a loan from the company to the ESOP does not require an accounting entry, since the company is essentially making a loan to itself.

In addition, if the company has obligated itself to a series of future contributions of shares or cash to the ESOP, it should recognize this obligation by recording a journal entry that debits the full amount of the obligation to an Unearned ESOP Shares account (this is reported as a contra equity account) and credits the Common Shares account.

When the company makes a contribution to the plan, the funds usually are shifted to the lender who issued a loan to pay for the initial purchase of shares. Accordingly, the Note Payable and Related Interest Expense accounts are both debited, while a second entry also debits a Compensation Expense account and credits the

Additional Paid-in Capital and Unearned ESOP Shares accounts to reflect the coincident allocation of shares to ESOP participants. Of particular interest is the treatment of dividends issued by the sponsoring company. When declared, a compensation expense must be recognized for all shares in the ESOP that have *not* been allocated to ESOP participants, rather than the usual charge to Retained Earnings. This requirement tends to be a disincentive for the board of directors to declare a dividend, since the declaration immediately triggers an expense recognition.

Example of ESOP transactions

The Brisbane Security Company establishes an ESOP for its employees. The ESOP arranges for a bank loan of €100,000 and uses it to purchase 10,000 shares of no-par-value shares. The entry is

Cash	100,000	
Notes payable		100,000
Unearned ESOP shares	100,000	
Common shares		100,000

Brisbane then contributes €10,000 to the plan, which is used to pay down both the principal and interest components of the debt. The entry is

Interest expense	2,000	
Notes payable	8,000	
Cash		10,000

The ESOP plan requires an allocation of shares to plan participants at the end of each calendar year. For the current year, 2,000 shares are allocated. On the date of allocation, the fair value of the shares is €13. Since the fair value is €3 higher than the original share purchase price of €10, the difference is credited to the Additional Paid-in Capital (Other equity) account. The entry is

Compensation expense	26,000	
Additional paid-in capital		6,000
Unearned ESOP shares		20,000

Brisbane then declares a dividend of €0.50 per share. The dividend applied to the 8,000 remaining unallocated shares is charged to a compensation expense account while the dividend applied to the 2,000 allocated shares is charged to the Retained Earnings account. The entry is

Retained earnings	8,000	
Compensation expense	2,000	
Dividend payable		10,000

DECISION TREE

Dividends—Recording of Different Types

The decision tree shown in Exhibit 13.1 itemizes the journal entry required for each of the various types of dividends as of the declaration date.

Exhibit 13.1 Dividend Entries on Declaration Date

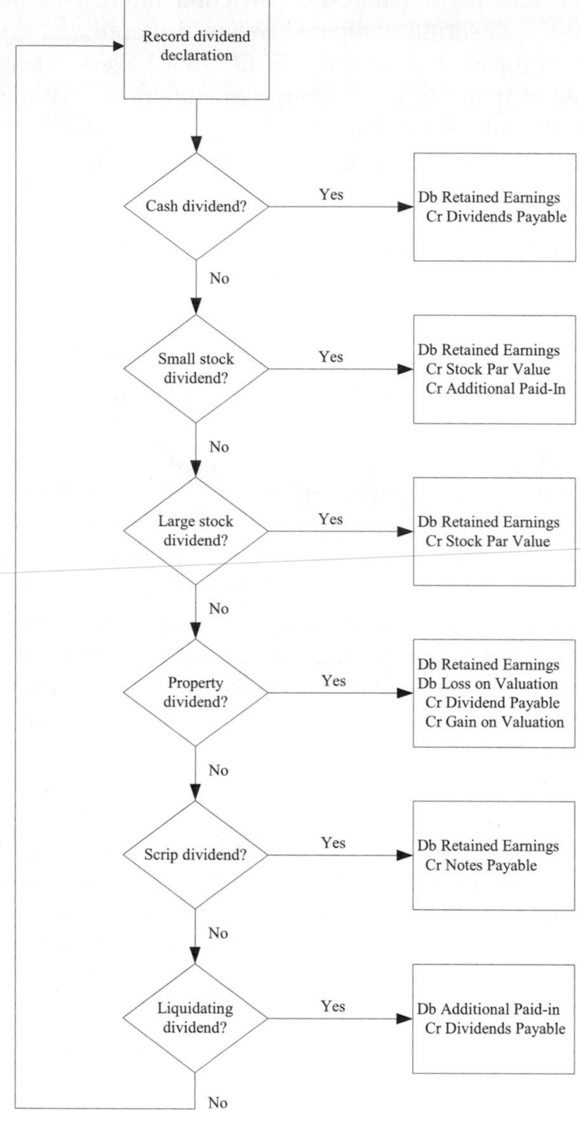

POLICIES

Legal Capital and Share Capital

Share issuance costs shall include only certificate printing, security registration, and legal and underwriting fees. This policy is designed to strictly limit the types of expenses that can be charged against the proceeds from a shares offering. By doing so, there is little room for extraneous expenses to be netted against a shares sale.

Shares Subscriptions

Shares subscription plans for employees must be approved by the board of directors. This policy requires the board to authorize the number of shares that may be sold to employees, as well as any discounts on those purchases. By requiring ongoing approval of additions to the number of shares authorized for distribution, the board can maintain effective control over this program.

Dividends

The board of directors shall not time property dividend declarations in order to influence reported earning levels from gains or losses recognized on property to be distributed. A gain or loss on assets must be recognized on the date of a dividend declaration if there is a difference between the fair market and carrying values of the assets. This can give rise to deliberate timing of dividend declarations in order to recognize gains or losses in specific reporting periods. This policy points out to directors that such behavior is not acceptable.

The board of directors shall not time scrip dividend declarations to influence reported levels of indebtedness. A scrip dividend is a note payable issued to shareholders in place of cash; generally, it is a bad idea unless there is an immediate expectation of cash receipts to pay off the resulting notes. Furthermore, a board could time a scrip dividend declaration to immediately follow the issuance of year-end financial statements, so that readers of the statements will not be aware of the sudden increase in indebtedness until the next financial statements are released. This policy is designed to bring the potential reporting issue to the attention of the board, though it still has the ability to override the policy.

Treasury Shares

The initial sale price of all shares shall be recorded by share certificate number. When shares are repurchased into the treasury, it is possible that the original sale price of each share repurchased must be backed out of the shares account, depending on the accounting method used. This policy requires that sufficient records be kept to allow such future treasury shares transactions to be properly recorded.

The circumstances of any greenmail shares repurchases shall be fully documented. This policy is designed to provide proper documentation of the amount of any shares repurchased under the threat of a corporate takeover. By doing so, one can more easily determine the price under which shares were repurchased as well as the market price of the shares on that date. This is critical information for the recognition of expenses related to excessively high repurchase costs because it can have a major negative impact on reported earnings levels.

Options

The current dividend yield shall be used for all option valuation assumptions. When a company uses different option pricing formulas to determine the compensation expense associated with its options, it can reduce the amount of expense recorded by assuming an increased dividend yield in the future. This policy is designed to freeze the dividend assumption, thereby nullifying the risk of deliberate expense modifications in this area.

The expected term of all options shall be based on the results of the last ___ years. When a company records compensation expense, part of the calculation is an estimate of the time period over which options are expected to be held by recipients. If this assumed period is shortened, the value of the options is reduced, resulting in a lower compensation expense. Consequently, there is a tendency to assume shorter expected terms. This policy is designed to force the accounting staff always to use a historical basis for the calculation of expected terms, so there is no way to modify the assumption.

Option-based compensation expense shall be adjusted at regular intervals for the forfeiture of options. An estimate of option forfeitures should be made at the time when option compensation expenses are first recognized. If actual experience with option forfeitures varies from expectations, the difference must be recognized as a change in accounting estimate in the current period. The trouble is that accountants can ignore the changes for some time and only record them in accounting periods where their impact is most useful to the accountant. This policy is designed to avoid the timing of adjustments by requiring regular adjustments at set intervals. Including this action item in the month-end closing procedure is a good way to ensure compliance with the policy.

Option vesting periods shall be identical for all option and shares grants. When a company reduces the vesting period for its options, it can reasonably justify using a shorter option life if it expenses its share options using, for example, the Black-Scholes-Merton model. This policy discourages the board of directors from shortening vesting periods by making it necessary also to shorten all types of share grants at the same time, thereby also introducing some vesting consistency to the complete range of corporate share grants.

Compensation expenses shall be recognized for both new option grants and those still outstanding from prior years. When a company elects to charge its option grants to expense, a common practice is to ignore outstanding options issued in prior years, and instead only charge new options to expense. This underreports the prospective compensation expense. This policy is designed to force full disclosure of the expense associated with all option grants.

The minimum value model shall be used to calculate compensation expense for option grants as long as the company is privately held. When a company is privately held, it can still use the fair value method promulgated under IFRS 2. The problem is that the fair value method requires the use of a shares volatility measure as part of the calculation—a matter of opinion when shares are not publicly traded. To avoid the potential manipulation associated with volatility calculations under this scenario, the policy recommends the use of the minimum value model; this is the same as the fair value method, minus the shares volatility calculation.

Share Appreciation Rights

Vesting periods for share appreciation rights (SAR) shall not exceed the standard vesting period used for other share grants. Since the gradual increases in the value of a SAR grant must be charged to expense in the period when the increases occur, a company could delay this expense recognition by lengthening the service period required before the SAR is earned by an employee. This policy is designed to require the use of a standard vesting period for all types of share grants, thereby avoiding extremely long SAR vesting periods.

Employee Share Ownership Plan (ESOP)

The board of directors shall not time dividend declarations in order to influence the recognition of a compensation expense for unallocated ESOP shares. When shares held in an ESOP have not yet been allocated to employees, a declared dividend on those shares is charged to compensation expense in the current period. Since this may represent a significant alteration in reported profit levels, there can be a temptation to time the dividend declaration in order to avoid reporting a profit reduction. This policy is designed to bring the potential reporting issue to the attention of the board, though it still has the ability to override the policy.

Periodic accruals of ESOP compensation costs shall be based on the fair market value of company shares at the end of the current reporting period. It is common practice for a company to allocate shares from its ESOP to plan participants only at the end of each year, at which point compensation expense is recognized for the fair value of the allocated shares. The amount of this compensation expense should be estimated and partially accrued in each month of the year leading up to the actual allocation. Estimating what the fair value of the shares will be at the end of the year may be problematic because it can result in significant variances in estimates from month to month, with wildly fluctuating compensation expense accruals based on these estimates. The best approach is to use this policy to create the accrual based on the assumption that the actual fair market value at the end of the current reporting period shall match the year-end fair market value, thereby removing valuation estimates from the calculation.

PROCEDURES

Issue Share Capital

Use this 13-step procedure to initially issue shares to the public. This procedure assumes that shares are to be publicly traded and so lists additional registration steps.

1. Locate an underwriter and negotiate either a best-efforts or firm-commitment share sale.
2. Determine the initial price at which shares are to be offered to the public.
3. Sign a letter of intent with the underwriter.
4. Undergo a due diligence review by the underwriter.

5. Create a registration statement and send it to the Securities Commission (e.g., the Securities and Exchange Commission in the United States) or other national enforcement agency. Respond to any questions the commission may have.
6. Issue a prospectus version of the registration statement to potential investors.
7. Conduct a road show to meet with institutional investors.
8. Apply to the shares exchange on which the company wishes to list its shares.
9. Submit filings in accordance with the securities laws of all states in which the company expects to sell shares.
10. File the final offering prospectus with the Securities Commission.
11. Sign a lockup agreement, which prevents management from selling shares to the public for a predetermined period.
12. Sell shares to the underwriter if the sale is a firm-commitment arrangement or issue shares as sold under a best-efforts arrangement.
    a. Remove share certificates from locked storage. On each one, print the certificate number, the number of shares issued, and the date of issuance. Have the corporate officers sign the certificates as indicated.
    b. Record the number of shares purchased, the purchase price, and the purchaser's name in the share register and store this document as an attachment to the corporate minute book.
    c. Send the share certificates to the share purchasers (possibly just the underwriter) by registered mail.
13. Upon receipt of payments from investors, debit Cash and credit the Par Value and Additional Paid-in Capital accounts.

Manage Share Subscriptions (Employees)

Use this seven-step procedure to deduct fixed amounts automatically from employee paychecks and use them to purchase discounted shares on behalf of employees.

1. Obtain authorization from the board of directors to create a share subscription plan, and record the authorization in the corporate minute book.
2. Notify employees of the plan details, including maximum withholdings allowed and any discounts on share purchases.
3. Obtain signed withholding authorizations from participating employees. Forward them to the payroll department for entry in the payroll database as deductions. Then file the forms in employee payroll files.
4. As cash is received, debit the Cash account and credit the Common Share Subscribed account, noting in the attached journal entry detail the name and Social Security number of each employee from whom the funds were withheld, and the amount withheld.
5. At the end of each month, calculate the fair market price of the shares, less any discount allowed to employees under the share subscription plan. Issue

shares to employees based on the amount of cash withheld. Debit the Common Shares Subscribed account and credit the Additional Paid-in Capital and Par Value accounts for the amount of shares issued.

6. If there is any excess cash remaining that cannot be used to purchase full shares, it is left in the Common Shares Subscribed account until the next month.
7. Periodically calculate the number of shares authorized and not yet issued under the employee share subscription plan and report this information back to the board of directors.

Issue Property Dividends

Use this four-step procedure to ensure that the board is aware of any potential gains or losses on property dividends and that the transaction is properly recorded.

1. If the board discusses distribution of property, look up the carrying value net of any amortization or depreciation and compare it to the fair market value. If there is no ready market for the asset, consult with an appraiser to obtain an approximate valuation range.
2. Determine the difference between the net carrying value of the property and the fair market value and note the amount of this gain or loss to be recognized as part of the property dividend. Report this amount to the board of directors.
3. If the dividend is approved, record the gain or loss on the dividend declaration date. Credit the Dividends Payable account for the carrying value of the distribution, the Retained Earnings account for the fair value of the property, and either credit the Gain on Property Disposal or debit the Loss on Property Disposal accounts to show the gain or loss on the adjustment of the property's carrying value to its fair value.
4. On the distribution date, debit the Dividends Payable account for the net carrying value of the asset and credit the asset account to remove the property from the company's accounting records.

Treasury Shares—Record Gains and Losses on Resale of Treasury Shares

Use this four-step procedure to record any gains or losses on the resale of treasury shares. The procedure assumes the use of the cost method when recording the sale of treasury shares.

1. Upon the purchase of shares, record a debit to the Treasury Shares account and a credit to the Cash account for the full amount of the purchase.
2. Note the share certificate numbers and number of shares purchased in the corporate share register.
3. When the shares are resold, record a credit for the full amount of the Treasury Shares account, such that the inflow and outflow to and from this account net to zero. Debit the Cash account for the amount of the cash received. If the difference requires a credit to balance the entry (a gain on the sale), enter a credit to the Additional Paid-in Capital account. If the differ-

ence requires a debit to balance the entry (a loss on the sale), enter a debit to the Additional Paid-in Capital account for treasury shares and then to retained earnings if this account balance drops to zero.
4. Note the share certificate numbers and number of shares sold in the corporate share register.

Treasury Shares—Shares Repurchased under a Greenmail Agreement

Use this four-step procedure to determine the proper allocation of a forced share repurchase under the threat of a corporate takeover between equity and expense accounts.

1. If there is a documented agreement to repurchase shares from an investor at above-market rates, charge the difference between the market rate and the rate paid on the date of the repurchase to the Excess Shares Repurchase expense account.
2. If the shares are not publicly traded and the value of other consideration granted by the shareholder is more clearly measurable, assign the value of the consideration to the Excess Shares Repurchase expense account and record the difference as the repurchase of shares.
3. If there is no way to determine any value for the other consideration granted and the shares are not publicly traded, record the entire amount of the transaction as the repurchase of shares.
4. After determining the proper method for recording the transaction from among the preceding three choices, document the reason for the method chosen and include it in the financial statements as a footnote.

Options—Measurement Using IFRS 2 Requirements

Use this 10-step procedure to calculate the initial compensation expense when options are first granted, using the guidelines of IFRS 2.

1. Obtain the signed options agreement.
2. Verify that the option grant has been authorized under a board-approved option program.
3. Determine the fair value of options.
4. Input the exercise price of the options, as listed in the signed options agreement.
5. Input the number of options granted.
6. Input the expected term of the options, based on the most recent rolling three-year history of exercised options.
7. Input the expected percentage of forfeited options, based on the most recent rolling three-year history of forfeited options.
8. Input the risk-free interest rate (e.g., the rate on the most recent issuance of government-issued 90-day notes).
9. Input the share volatility percentage, using the measured volatility for the most recent rolling three-year period. Ignore this step if the company is privately held.

10. Record the compensation expense ratably over the vesting period of the options granted.

CONTROLS

Legal Capital and Capital Shares

- **Independent substantiation must be obtained to verify the valuation of shares issued in exchange for goods and services received.** When shares are swapped for goods or services, the shares are valued at the fair value of the goods or services. Since the offsetting debit is to an expense, the amount of this valuation can have a major impact on reported profit levels. This control is designed to force the accounting staff to go through the steps of obtaining outside verification of the fair value at which they have chosen to record the transaction.

Share Subscriptions

- **Periodically compare employee-authorized payroll deductions to actual deductions.** If a company's shares are performing well, it is quite possible that employees will complain if the amounts of payroll deductions being taken from their paychecks to pay for the shares have been too low, were ignored, or were started significantly later than the authorization date of the deduction, since employees will be losing money on the appreciation of their shares if any of these problems have arisen. If employees can prove their case, the company may even compensate them for the lost share appreciation. Consequently, a periodic comparison of authorized to actual deductions ensures that there is no room for complaints by employees over this issue.

Retained Earnings

- **Password-protect the Retained Earnings account.** Though there are a few instances when the Retained Earnings account can be rightfully altered under IFRS, it is best to control access to the account with password protection, thereby forcing accounting adjustments into the current period, where they can be seen more clearly as a component of the income statement. Adjustments to the Retained Earnings account should be authorized only by the controller after being personally reviewed and possibly also approved by the external auditors.

Dividends

- **Require board approval of the fair value justification for all assets used in property dividends.** Since the recognition of the difference between the fair and carrying value of assets being distributed can have a major impact on reported earning levels, the board should be made fully aware of the justification for any asset fair values departing significantly from carrying value and the impact the resulting gain or loss will have on reported earnings.

- **Obtain board approval of a specific date range within which dividends are to be declared each year.** This control is designed to keep the board of directors from deliberately altering reported financial results through the timing of dividend declarations. For example, the board can declare either property or scrip dividends on specific dates that are designed to result in gains or losses (for property dividends) or changes in debt levels (for scrip dividends). The same problem applies when dividends are declared for ESOP shares, since the dividends for unallocated ESOP shares are charged to compensation expense in the current period.

Treasury Shares

- **Require the use of a separate additional paid-in capital account for treasury share transactions.** If a treasury share is resold to investors at a loss, the loss is first charged to any remaining gains from previous treasury share sales, with remaining losses being offset against the Retained Earnings account. Since a reduction in the Retained Earnings balance can be construed as a reduced level of financial performance, there is an incentive to charge these losses elsewhere. A typical ploy is to charge the losses to the General Additional Paid-in Capital account, which usually contains a much larger balance than the Additional Paid-in Capital account for treasury shares. By creating the separate Additional Paid-in Capital account for treasury shares and requiring its use in all treasury share procedures, it is much less likely that treasury share losses will be diverted away from the Retained Earnings account.
- **Require board approval of all share repurchases conducted under greenmail situations.** A normal treasury share transaction has no impact on expenses, but a greenmail situation does, since the difference between the market price and the usually much higher price paid must be charged to expense. It is clearly in the interests of a company to not record this incremental expense because it can result in a massive reduction in profits during the period when the payment is made. Consequently, the board should be made aware of the expense consequences when it approves a greenmail share repurchase.

Share Appreciation Rights

- **Include SAR compensation expense accruals in the standard closing procedure.** A company could delay or ignore any changes in the value of SAR grants to its employees, thereby avoiding the recognition of any associated compensation expense. This problem can be avoided by including the accrual as a standard action item in the monthly closing procedure. The issue also can be highlighted by including it as a footnote attached to the financial statements, thereby requiring periodic updating of the footnote information.
- **Use a standard share valuation form when calculating SAR compensation expense.** A company can use a variety of methods for determining the market value of company shares as part of its recognition of compensation expense, especially when the shares are not publicly traded. This can give rise to different methods being used over time, depending on which one results in the

smallest compensation expense recognition. The best way to avoid this problem is to create a standard calculation form, such as the one shown in the Forms and Reports section, which forces the use of a single calculation format for all SAR-related compensation expense calculations.

Options

- **Review the assumptions used to determine the compensation cost for options.** Even small changes in the assumptions to develop the compensation cost associated with share option grants can result in a significant change in compensation costs, so there is a risk of formula manipulation in order to alter reported financial results. In particular, compensation expenses can be lessened by reducing the assumed share volatility or the assumed life of an option or by increasing the assumed risk-free interest rate or dividend yield. A periodic review of these assumptions, particularly in comparison to the assumptions used for prior calculations, can spot significant or clearly incorrect assumptions.
- **Verify that option grant extensions are measured on the date of authorization.** When the term of an option grant is extended, one may have to recognize compensation expense on the extension date if there is an unrecognized difference between the market and exercise prices of the shares. This rule can give rise to some variation in the date on which the measurement is made, in the hope that the market price of the shares will drop, thereby resulting in a lower compensation expense. By creating a procedure that clearly requires the calculation to be made on the date of authorization, this problem can be eliminated.
- **Use a consistent fair market value estimation method.** If a company is privately held, it may be difficult to determine the fair value of the shares, which can result in reduced fair value estimates in order to avoid recognizing any compensation expense. One should require a consistent valuation estimation methodology so a company does not alter its valuation formula every time options are granted.

FORMS AND REPORTS

Legal Capital and Share Capital

When share certificates are issued, a company must keep track of the number of certificates issued, the number of shares listed on each certificate, to whom the certificates are issued, information about the dates of issuance, and any subsequent cancellation or transfer dates. The example share record shown in Exhibit 13.2 indicates a typical layout for this type of report.

Exhibit 13.2 Share Record

Certificate number	*Issued to*	*Number of shares*	*Issue date*	*Cancel or transfer date*
1	Joel Henderson	1,410,000	3/22/07	
2	Gary Simms	570,000	3/22/07	5/25/07 to Mary Simms
3	Richard Rondo	695,000	3/22/07	5/9/07 cancelled
4	Mark Abercrombie	716,000	7/14/07	
5	Brad Hanley	115,000	7/14/07	

Share Subscriptions

When a company issues shares to its employees as part of an ongoing share subscription program, it can assume that employees will ask periodically for a statement detailing the amount of their payroll deductions for this purpose, the number of shares issued based on those deductions, and the residual amount of deductions not yet used to purchase company shares. An example of such a share subscription statement is shown in Exhibit 13.3. The example assumes payroll deductions twice a month, with a 10% discount from the share market price for employees.

Exhibit 13.3 Share Subscription Statement by Employee

Payroll Deductions		Share Purchases				
Date	*Amount*	*Date*	*Share value*	*10% discount*	*Number of shares*	*Cash remainder*
01/15/2007	€300.00					
01/31/2007	300.00	01/31/2007	€12.15	€10.94	54	€9.24
02/15/2007	300.00					
02/28/2007	300.00	02/28/2007	13.10	11.79	51	7.95
03/15/2007	300.00					
03/31/2007	300.00	03/31/2007	14.05	12.65	48	0.75
04/15/2007	300.00					
04/30/2007	300.00	04/30/2007	13.75	12.38	48	6.51
05/15/2007	300.00					
05/31/2007	300.00	05/31/2007	13.25	11.93	50	10.01

Share Option Detail Report

If there are many option grants to a large number of employees, it is necessary to maintain a report listing the number of options granted, the exercise price for each grant, and the expiration date of each set of options. The report shown in Exhibit 13.4 shows this information for one sample employee as well as the number of options vested and the prospective purchase price (good for equity planning) if each block of options were to be purchased.

Exhibit 13.4 Share Option Detail Report

Date granted	*Options granted*	*Exercise price*	*Options vested*	*Purchase price*	*Expiration date*
Clay, Alfred					
02/01/03	1,317	0.6800	€ 878	€ 597.04	01/31/13
04/03/03	2,633	0.8200	1,755	1,439.10	04/02/13
12/01/03	2,633	0.9000	878	790.20	11/30/13
09/01/04	5,266	0.9800	5,266	5,160.68	08/31/14
12/31/04	1,317	1.0300	1,317	1,356.51	12/30/14
03/08/05	2,633	1.0800	2,633	2,843.64	03/07/15
Totals	15,799		€12,727	€12,187.17	

Share Appreciation Rights

For many privately held companies, there is no ready method for determining the value of their shares, which can cause problems when the value of share appreciation rights is calculated. The form shown in Exhibit 13.5 presents a standard approach for creating this valuation, using the revenue multiple for publicly held companies as the benchmark valuation figure. The form is divided into three sections, each one being labeled in the upper left corner in bold. The first section allows one to split the business into its component parts and multiply the revenue for each part by the public sector valuation multiple to arrive at a total estimated company valuation. It is especially important always to use the same "market basket" of public sector companies to derive the valuation multiple in order to achieve consistency in the valuation derivation. The second section is used to itemize the types and amounts of shares outstanding, along with the liquidation participation of each share type, resulting in a valuation per SAR. In the example, a class of preferred shares is assumed to have a double distribution. The third section itemizes the SAR grants by date, listing the number of shares issued on each date and their issuance price. This information is used in the final column on the right to determine the difference between the SAR issuance price and current estimated valuation, resulting in a compensation expense accrual in the lower right corner that can be used as the basis for a journal entry to recognize compensation expense.

Exhibit 13.5 Standard Calculation Form for Share Appreciation Rights

Share Appreciation Rights
Standard Calculation Form

Company Valuation:

Business Segment	*Segment revenue*	*Public sector valuation multiple*	*Estimated company valuation*
Outdoor advertising	€ 4,500,000	1.2	€ 5,400,000
Publishing	12,250,000	1.7	20,825,000
Rentals	8,050,000	1.0	8,050,000
	€24,800,000		€34,275,000

Share Valuation:

Share type	*Number of shares*	*Participation percentage*	*Estimated value per share*
Common	12,000,000	100%	€2.2624
Preferred series A	1,500,000	200%	4.5248
Share appreciation rights	150,000	100%	2.2624
	13,650,000		

SAR Compensation Expense:

Date of SAR issuance	*Number of shares*	*Issuance price*	*Compensation expense*
05/15/2007	50,000	€1.10	€58,119
08/21/2007	80,000	1.38	70,590
11/03/2007	20,000	1.75	10,248
	150,000		€138,956
	SAR compensation already recognized:		€120,000
	SAR compensation expense accrual:		€18,956

FOOTNOTES

Disclosure of Capital Structure

The financial statements should include a footnote describing the number of shares authorized, issued, and outstanding, their par values, and the rights and privileges associated with each class of shares. A description of these rights and privileges should include dividend preferences and special privileges or unusual voting rights. An example follows.

> As of October 31, 2007, the company capital structure consisted of common shares and Series A preferred shares. There were 10 million common shares authorized and 4.2 million shares outstanding, while there were 1 million preferred shares authorized and 800,000 shares outstanding. Both classes of shares have par values of €0.01 per share. The Series A preferred shareholders are entitled to a full return of their original investments in the event of a liquidation or sale of the company as well as an additional 100% return, before any distributions are made to common shareholders. These shareholders also are entitled to dividend payments matching any declared for shares of common shares. In addition, a two-thirds majority of the Series A shareholders must approve any sale of the company or a significant portion of its assets. Also, Series A shareholders are entitled to elect two members of the company's board of directors. Common shareholders are entitled to elect all other members of the board.

Disclosure of Subsequent Equity Transactions

If a company enters into any equity-related transactions subsequent to the date of the financial statements but before their issuance, these transactions should be described in a footnote. Examples of typical transactions falling into this category include share splits, share issuances, and purchases of shares back into the treasury. An example follows.

> Subsequent to the reporting period, the company issued an additional 100,000 common shares at an average price of €24 per share, resulting in receipts, net of transaction fees, of €2,250,000. Management intends to use the funds to renovate its headquarters building.

Disclosure of Change in the Number of Authorized Shares

If a company elects to either increase or decrease its number of authorized shares through a change in its certificate of incorporation, a footnote should disclose the board's approval of this action, the change in the number of authorized shares, and any impact on the par value of the shares. An example follows.

On April 17, 2007, the board authorized the amendment of the company's certificate of incorporation to increase the number of authorized shares of common shares by 90 million from the prior level of 10 million. There was no change in the stated par value of the shares as a result of this transaction.

Disclosure of Shares Sale

If a company sells shares, a footnote should disclose the type and number of shares sold, the price at which the shares were sold, and the general use of the proceeds. An example follows.

During May 2007, the company sold 4,210,000 shares of its Series B preferred shares at a price of €12 per share, netting €48,500,000 after sale and issuance costs. Management intends to use the proceeds to fund several anticipated acquisitions.

Disclosure of Share Subscriptions

If investors have subscribed to company shares, the company should reveal the number of subscribed shares not yet issued. An example follows.

The company offered its common shares for sale to a limited group of investors during the reporting period. The investors subscribed to €4,250,000 of shares at €20.00 per share. Of the amount subscribed, €3,650,000 has been received, resulting in the issuance of 182,500 shares. The share issuance is reflected in all earnings per share information in these financial statements. The unpaid €600,000 of subscriptions will result in the issuance of an additional 30,000 shares when payment is received, which would have reduced earnings per share in the reporting period by €.03 if the subscription payments had been received during the period.

Disclosure of Converted Bonds

If the holders of convertible bonds have elected to convert their bonds into shares, one should disclose the dollar amount of bonds converted, the conversion ratio, and the resulting number of shares issued. An example follows.

During the past quarter, 45% of the holders of the company's convertible 8% bonds elected to convert their holdings into the company's common shares. The debt converted was €32 million, leaving €39 million still outstanding. The bond conversion transaction resulted in the issuance of 3,764,705 shares, which is an increase in the company's outstanding common shares of 4.2%.

Disclosure of Redeemable Preferred Shares

If there are any outstanding redeemable preferred shares, a footnote should itemize any determinable redemption requirements in each of the next five years, including call prices and the dates on which they are effective. An example follows.

The company has 50,000 redeemable preferred shares outstanding. Under the sale agreement for these shares, the company is obligated to repurchase 10,000 shares per year under the following pricing schedule:

Year	*Shares to repurchase*	*Aggregate price*
2007	10,000	€50,000
2008	10,000	53,000
2009	10,000	56,000
2010	10,000	59,000
2011	10,000	62,000

Disclosure of Cash Dividends

If a company issues a cash dividend, a footnote should reveal the amount of the dividend, the date on which the dividend was declared, the date on which the dividend will be payable, and the date on which shareholders of record will be identified for the distribution. An example follows.

> On September 10, 2007, the board declared a cash dividend of €1.07 per share, payable on November 2, 2007, to shareholders of record on September 25, 2007. This dividend distribution does not violate any covenants associated with the company's existing loans.

Disclosure of Noncash Dividends

If a company chooses to pay shareholders dividends with assets other than cash, a footnote should disclose the nature of the assets being used for payment, the fair market value of the amount distributed, any gain or loss recognized by the company as part of the transaction, and how the transaction was handled in the financial statements. An example follows.

> The company distributed inventory dividends to its shareholders of record on April 30, 2007, issuing 10 pounds of its hard candy for every 100 shares of common shares held. The candy had a fair market value of €2,000,000 at the time of the dividend distribution. The company recorded no gain or loss on the transaction. It reduced the inventory asset by the amount of the distribution.

Disclosure of Dividends Deferred

If the decision is made to defer payment of declared dividends, a footnote should reveal the reason for the decision while also specifying which dividends were deferred and the aggregate amount of the deferral, as well as the amount of cumulative and per share dividends in arrears. Two examples follow.

1. The board deferred the full amount of dividends declared on November 10, 2007, totaling €1,050,000, due to a short-term cash flow problem related to the company's foreign sales receipts. The dividends deferred include €600,000 for common shares and €450,000 for preferred shares.
2. The company has deferred payment of its last two dividend declarations, which total €729,000 in deferred dividends. Based on the number of shares outstanding as of the date of the statement of financial position, there is €1.29 of deferred dividends per share. Due to its declining cash flows, the company is unable to predict when the deferred dividends will be distributed to shareholders.

Disclosure of Employee Share Ownership Plan

If a company has set up an employee share ownership plan (ESOP), it should disclose which employees participate in the plan, how dividends received by the plan are used, the formula used to make contributions to the ESOP, how contributed shares are used as collateral on any ESOP debt, how share valuations are assigned to employees, and how the company treats ESOP transactions in its financial reports. The footnote should also disclose any compensation cost recognized during the period. An example follows.

> The company makes monthly contributions to its employee share ownership plan (ESOP) sufficient to make principal and interest payments on its outstanding debt. Shares held by the plan are used as collateral on the debt, but a portion of the shares are released as collateral at the end of each year in proportion to the amount of debt paid down. At that time, the shares are allocated to qualified employees, who are defined as those working at least 30 hours per week as of year-end. Once allocated, shares are included in earnings-per-share calculations. The company records compensation expense each month based on the market value of the shares expected to be released from collateral at year-end. The compensation expense thus recorded in the past year was €189,000. The fair value of shares still held as collateral as of year-end was €4,050,000. At year-end, the ESOP contained 410,000 shares, of which 270,000 was used as collateral and 140,000 had been released from collateral and recorded as compensation expense.

Disclosure of Employee Share Purchase Plan

If an employee share purchase plan is in place, a footnote should disclose the amount of any discounts granted to employees, how the discount is calculated, and maximum amounts employees are allowed to purchase. The number of shares reserved for this purpose and the actual number purchased should also be disclosed. An example follows.

> The company operates an employee share purchase plan that allows its employees to purchase the company's common shares at below-market rates, subject to certain restrictions. Shares are offered at a discount of 10% of the shares' fair market value at the end of each month, as determined by the posted Euronext share price on that date. Employees may purchase shares up to a maximum of 15% of their gross pay. Under the plan, 2.5 million common shares have been reserved for purchase by employees, of which 312,987 shares have thus far been purchased, leaving 2,187,013 available for purchase. In the past year, 82,067 shares were purchased at an aggregate price of €15.85 each.

Disclosure of New Type of Shares

If a company is creating a new type of shares, a footnote should disclose the rights of the new shares, the date on which it was authorized, the number of shares authorized, and the number of any shares issued. An example follows.

> The board authorized an amendment to the certificate of incorporation that created a new Series B preferred share in the amount of 10 million shares, with a par value of €0.01 per share. The share has preferential liquidation rights of 200% of the initial investment prior to the participation of common shareholders and is also entitled to the same dividend granted to common shareholders. Two million shares of the Series B pre-

ferred share were issued on December 15, 2007, at €8.10 per share, resulting in total proceeds of €16.2 million. The company expects to use these funds to pay down its existing debt.

Disclosure of Par Value Change

Though rare, companies will sometimes alter their certificates of incorporation to change the par value of their shares. This change is typically in a downward direction, resulting in the shifting of funds from the shares account to the additional paid-in capital account. When this happens, a footnote should include the date and amount of the change as well as the aggregate amount of funds shifted into or out of the shares account. An example follows.

A majority of the company's shareholders voted on October 10, 2007, to amend the company's certificate of incorporation to reduce the par value of its common shares to €0.01 from €1.00. Due to this change, €990,000 was shifted from the Common Shares account to the Additional Paid-in Capital account.

Disclosure of Retained Earnings Segregation

The board of directors may set aside some portion of retained earnings for a specific purpose. If so, a footnote should describe the amount segregated as well as the reason for and amount of the segregation. An example follows.

The company has been judged liable for asbestos claims amounting to €14,500,000. The company intends to contest this initial judgment vigorously and has appealed the decision. Nonetheless, the board of directors has segregated the full amount of the initial judgment from retained earnings, so that the company will not find itself with negative retained earnings in the event that the appeal is denied and it must pay the full amount of the claim.

Disclosure of Reserved Shares

A company may set aside unissued shares for specific purposes, such as the expected exercise of options or warrants or the conversion of shares from a debt instrument. In these cases, one should disclose the number of shares set aside and the reason for the reservation. An example follows.

The board authorized the reservation of 4,025,000 shares as of May 14, 2007. Of this amount, 2 million shares were set aside in expectation of the conversion of the company's 5 7/8% bonds to share capital by its bondholders. The remaining 2,025,000 shares were set aside in expectation of the exercise of share options by employees.

Disclosure of Share Capital Repurchase Program

One should describe the date on which a share capital repurchase program was authorized by the board of directors, the maximum number of shares to be repurchased, and the current status of the repurchase program. An example follows.

The company's board of directors authorized a share capital repurchase program for its Series A preferred shares on June 30, 2007, up to a maximum of 2 million shares. As of the statement of financial position date, the company had repurchased 1,255,000 shares for a total of €58,500,000. The repurchased shares are held in the corporate treasury and cannot be released without board approval.

Disclosure of Treasury Shares Held

One should reveal the cost basis used to record any shares held by a company. An example follows.

The company records the value of its common and preferred shares held in the treasury at cost.

Disclosure of Greenmail Share Repurchase

If a company elects to buy back shares at a high price under the threat of a takeover or similar situation, it should note the market price of its shares on the date of the transaction, the price per share actually paid, and the amount of the transaction charged to expense. An example follows.

The company repurchased 450,000 shares from a major shareholder on May 15, 2007. The shareholder had indicated that he was willing to pursue a change of corporate ownership if the company did not agree to pay a premium for his shares. The board elected to do so, and paid €15 per share for shares having a market price of €11.50 on the date of the transaction. The company charged the difference between the purchase and market prices of €1,575,000 to expense in the current period.

Disclosure of Sale of Treasury Shares

If a company elects to sell some portion of its treasury shares, a footnote should reveal the number of shares sold, the aggregate sale price, the aggregate price at which the shares were originally purchased by the company, and the treatment of any gain or loss on the sale. An example follows.

The company sold 450,000 common shares for a total of €8,565,000. The company had previously purchased these shares for €8,750,000 and stored them as treasury shares. Since the sale price exceeded the original purchase price by €185,000, the difference was charged to the Additional Paid-in Capital account.

Disclosure of Share-Based Compensation

If a company has paid employees or outside entities compensation in the form of shares, the number of shares granted, the effective date of the transaction, and its fair market value should be itemized in a footnote. Three examples follow.

1. The board authorized share compensation to the company's executive team as of July 31, 2007, in the amount of 340,000 shares of common shares. The shares had a fair market value of €14,900,000 on the date of the grant.
2. The board authorized the granting of 10,000 shares of common shares with a fair value of €52,000 to the company's legal advisor. The advisor accepted this payment in lieu of a cash payment for ongoing legal services performed.
3. The board authorized the granting of 150,000 shares of common shares to a director in exchange for the elimination of €800,000 in accrued interest on a loan the director had extended to the company in 2006.

Disclosure of Share Contribution

If a company donates shares to a nonprofit organization, a footnote should disclose the date of the contribution, the number of shares involved, their aggregate market value, how the transaction was handled in the financial statements, and the amount of any gain or loss recognized as a result. An example follows.

> The company contributed its entire share holdings in XYZ Corporation to the My Way Foundation, including 500,000 common shares and 125,000 preferred shares. The market value of the contribution on the transaction date was €842,000. Of this amount, €200,000 was recognized as a pretax loss, while the remaining €642,000 was charged to the Donations Expense account.

Disclosure of Share Redemption Agreements

If a company has agreements with its shareholders to buy back their shares upon the occurrence of certain events, a footnote should describe the terms of the arrangement and the potential monetary impact. Three examples follow.

1. The company has required all purchasers of its Series B preferred shares to sign redemption agreements under which the company has the right of first refusal if they wish to sell their shares, at fixed prices of €12.50 in 2007 and increasing in increments of €0.75 per share for each year thereafter. If all Series B shareholders were to request redemption of their shares, the total cash payment required of the company would be €31.25 million. The company maintains a sinking fund to cover these payments. The sinking fund currently contains €10 million; the company plans to add €5 million per year to this fund until the full redemption commitment is met.
2. A major company shareholder died during the past quarter. Under the terms of the standard company redemption agreement, the company is required to buy back her shares at their fair market value, which was derived using the average value compiled by three independent appraisers. The fair market value of her shares as determined by this means was €18,900,000, of which €10,000,000 was paid by a company-maintained life insurance policy. Of the remainder, €5,000,000 was paid in cash, and €4,900,000 is payable to her estate at year-end as well as 7% interest on the unpaid balance.
3. The company redeemed 100,000 shares of its Series A preferred shares, which it issued as part of a financing package arising from its bankruptcy proceedings in 2006. As per the redemption agreement, the company paid a 100% premium over the original €10 sale price of each share, resulting in a total payment of €20 per share or €2,000,000 in aggregate. The incremental increase over the original share price of €1,000,000 was charged to the Additional Paid-in Capital account.

Disclosure of Share Splits

All share splits and reverse share splits should be fully documented in a footnote, itemizing the date on which board of directors approval was granted, the ratio of the share split, and the date on which the split took effect. The footnote also should contain assurances that all share-related information in the financial statements has been adjusted to reflect the share split. Two examples follow.

1. The company's board of directors authorized a three-for-one reverse share split on November 15, 2007, to take effect on November 18, 2007. All share and related op-

tion information presented in these financial statements and accompanying footnotes has been adjusted retroactively to reflect the reduced number of shares resulting from this action.

2. The company's board of directors authorized a three-for-one share split on November 15, 2007, to take effect on December 20, 2007. Each shareholder of record on November 25, 2007, received two additional shares of common shares for each share held on that date. Additional funds were shifted from the Additional Paid-in Capital account to the Common Shares account to equal the amount of additional par value represented by the additional shares issued under the share split. All share and related option information presented in these financial statements and accompanying footnotes has been adjusted retroactively to reflect the increased number of shares resulting from this action.

Disclosure of Share Options

If a company has a share option plan, it must give a general description of the plan, report the number of shares authorized for option grants, and note vesting requirements and maximum option terms. The next footnote provides an example of this "header information."

> The company maintains a share option plan under which all employees are awarded option grants based on a combination of performance and tenure. All options may be exercised for a period of 10 years following the grant date, after which they expire. All options fully vest after recipients have worked for the company subsequent to the grant date in a full-time capacity for a period of four years. The board has authorized the use of 2 million shares for option grants.

Disclosure of Share Appreciation Rights (SAR)

If a company issues share appreciation rights, it should indicate in a footnote the group of people covered by the SAR plan, the terms of the plan, the amount of compensation expense accrued, and the amount of compensation expense to be accrued in future vesting periods. An example follows.

> The company has issued a total of 150,000 share appreciation rights to the executive management team, using a baseline share price of €4.50 per share. Subsequent share appreciation has resulted in an increase in the value of the SAR of €129,400, of which one-half has vested, resulting in the recognition of compensation expense of €64,700. Of the unvested portion of the increase in share value, €32,350 will be recognized in 2007 and an additional €32,350 will be recognized in 2008, assuming no further changes in the share price. No cash payments have yet been made to the SAR holders, which are at the option of the holders until the termination of the plan in 2014.

Disclosure of Warrants Issued

Warrants to purchase shares may be issued, so a footnote should be included to disclose the reason for the transaction, the number of warrants issued, the exercise price at which they can be used to purchase shares, and the vesting period and expiration date. Two examples follow.

1. The company issued 80,000 warrants to a group of venture capital firms. The warrants allow the firms to purchase the company's common shares at an exercise price of €5.10. There is no vesting period, and the warrants expire in 10 years. The war-

rants were issued as part of the compensation package earned by the firms in assisting the company in the placement of a recent issuance of common shares.

2. At the end of 2006, certain holders of warrants to purchase shares of the company's common shares exercised a total of 32,000 warrants to purchase 64,000 shares for a total of €326,400.

JOURNAL ENTRIES

Legal Capital and Share Capital

Initial sale of share capital. When a company sells shares to an investor, it allocates a portion of the sale price to a par value account matching the stated par value of each share sold, with the remainder being credited to an additional paid-in capital account, as noted in the following entry.

Cash	xxx	
Share capital—par value		xxx
Share capital—additional paid-in capital		xxx

Netting of share issuance costs against sale proceeds. To net share capital issuance costs, such as legal, underwriting, certificate printing, and security registration fees, against the proceeds of a share sale.

Additional paid-in capital	xxx	
Share capital issuance expenses		xxx

Share capital issued for services rendered or goods received. To record the fair value of services or goods received in exchange for share capital.

Expense [reflecting specific services or goods received]	xxx	
Share capital—par value		xxx
Additional paid-in capital		xxx

Conversion of preferred shares to common shares. To record the conversion of preferred shares to common shares under a conversion option. The second entry shows this conversion when the par value of the common shares is greater than the entire purchase price of the preferred shares, requiring an additional contribution from the retained earnings account.

Preferred shares—par value	xxx	
Preferred shares—additional paid-in capital	xxx	
Common shares—par value		xxx
Common shares—additional paid-in capital		xxx

Preferred shares—par value	xxx	
Preferred shares—additional paid-in capital	xxx	
Retained earnings	xxx	
Common shares—par value		xxx

Share split with no change in par value. To record a share split where the par value of the shares is not reduced proportionately to match the number of new shares issued. This requires a transfer from the Additional Paid-in Capital account to fund the additional amount of par value required for the new shares.

Shares—additional paid-in capital	xxx	
Shares capital—par value		xxx

Share Subscriptions

Share subscription, initial entry. To record the initial commitment by potential investors to purchase company shares, with no cash yet received.

Share subscriptions receivable	xxx	
Common shares subscribed		xxx
Additional paid-in capital		xxx

Share subscription, payment of. To record the receipt of cash from investors to fulfill their earlier commitments to purchase shares under a share subscription agreement.

Cash	xxx	
Share subscriptions receivable		xxx
Common shares subscribed	xxx	
Common shares		xxx

Warrants

Initial entry of bonds sale with attached warrants. The first entry is used to assign a value to the warrants attached to the sale of bonds, based on the relative values of the warrants and bonds. The entry includes a provision for any discount or premium on bonds sold. The second entry shifts funds into an expired warrants account, on the assumption that the warrants are never exercised by the holder. The third entry shows the proper treatment of a warrant that is converted to shares with an additional cash payment included.

Cash	xxx	
Discount on bonds payable [if applicable]	xxx	
Premium on bonds payable [if applicable]		xxx
Bonds payable		xxx
Additional paid-in capital—warrants		xxx
Additional paid-in capital—warrants	xxx	
Additional paid-in capital—expired warrants		xxx
Cash	xxx	
Additional paid-in capital—warrants	xxx	
Common shares—par value		xxx
Common shares—additional paid-in capital		xxx

Dividends

Dividend declaration, cash payment. To separate the sum total of all declared dividends from retained earnings once the dividends have been approved by the board of directors.

Retained earnings	xxx	
Dividends payable		xxx

Dividend declaration, property dividend. To record the gain or loss on any property to be distributed as a dividend to shareholders, based on the fair value of the asset to be distributed on the date of declaration.

Retained earnings [asset fair value]	xxx	
Loss on property disposal [if applicable]	xxx	
Gain on property disposal [if applicable]		xxx
Dividends payable [asset net carrying value]		xxx

Dividend payment, property dividend. To eliminate the dividend payable obligation and remove the asset being distributed from the company's records, including all related accumulated depreciation or amortization.

Dividend payable	xxx	
Accumulated amortization [if needed]	xxx	
Accumulated depreciation [if needed]	xxx	
Asset		xxx

Dividend declaration, small share dividend. To record a small share dividend, record the fair value of the issued shares on the declaration date by removing the funds from the Retained Earnings account and shifting them to the Shares and Additional Paid-in Capital accounts.

Retained earnings	xxx	
Shares—par value		xxx
Shares—additional paid-in capital		xxx

Dividend declaration, large share dividend. To record a large share dividend, record the par value of the issued shares on the declaration date by removing the funds from the Retained Earnings account and shifting them to the Shares account.

Retained earnings	xxx	
Shares capital—par value		xxx

Dividend declaration, scrip dividend. To record the creation of a note payable to shareholders instead of the usual cash dividend.

Retained earnings	xxx	
Notes payable		xxx

Dividend declaration, liquidating. To record a return of capital to investors, rather than a more traditional dividend that theoretically is based on a distribution of profits.

Additional paid-in capital	xxx	
Dividends payable		xxx

Dividend payment in cash. To issue cash payment to shareholders for dividends declared by the board of directors. The first entry shows the payment of a traditional cash dividend, while the second entry shows the payment of a scrip dividend.

Dividends payable	xxx	
Cash		xxx
Dividends payable	xxx	
Notes payable		xxx

Treasury Shares

Treasury shares, purchase under the cost method. To record the acquisition by a company of its own shares.

Treasury shares	xxx	
Cash		xxx

Treasury shares, retirement under the cost method. This method is used when there is an assumption that repurchased shares will be permanently retired. The original Common Shares and Additional Paid-in Capital accounts are reversed with any loss on the purchase being charged to the Retained Earnings account, and any gain being credited to the Additional Paid-in Capital account.

Common shares—par value	xxx	
Additional paid-in capital	xxx	
Retained earnings [if there is a loss on the repurchase]		xxx
Cash		xxx

Treasury shares, sale at price higher than acquisition price. To record the sale of treasury shares to investors by the company at a price higher than the price at which the company acquired the shares, with payments in excess of treasury shares cost being credited to the Additional Paid-in Capital account. This entry uses the cost method of accounting for treasury shares.

Cash	xxx	
Treasury shares		xxx
Additional paid-in capital—treasury shares		xxx

Treasury shares, sale at price lower than acquisition price. To record the sale of treasury shares to investors by the company at a price lower than the price at which the company acquired the shares, with the loss on the sale being charged to the Additional Paid-in Capital account until that account is emptied and any remaining loss being charged to the Retained Earnings account. This entry uses the cost method of accounting for treasury shares.

Cash	xxx	
Additional paid-in capital—treasury shares	xxx	
Retained earnings	xxx	
Treasury shares		xxx

Treasury shares, purchase under the constructive retirement method. This method is used when there is an assumption that the repurchased shares will be permanently retired or when mandated by state law. The original Common Share and Additional Paid-in Capital accounts are reversed, with any loss on the purchase being charged to the Retained Earnings account and any gain being credited to the Additional Paid-in Capital account.

Common shares—par value	xxx	
Additional paid-in capital	xxx	
Retained earnings [if there is a loss on the repurchase]		xxx
Cash		xxx

Treasury shares, repurchase under a greenmail agreement. When a company is forced to buy back shares at above-market prices under the threat of a corporate takeover, the difference between the repurchase price and the market price must be charged to expense, as noted in the next entry.

Account	Debit	Credit
Treasury shares	xxx	
Excess share repurchase expense	xxx	
Cash		xxx

Options

Options issued with strike price below the market price. If share options are issued, compensation expense is recognized at the fair value of options. The entry is

Account	Debit	Credit
Compensation expense	xxx	
Options—additional paid-in capital		xxx

Options used to purchase shares. When an option holder exercises the option to purchase shares, the journal entry is

Account	Debit	Credit
Cash	xxx	
Options—additional paid-in capital		
Common shares—par value		xxx
Common shares—additional paid-in capital		xxx

Share Appreciation Rights (SAR)

Record increase in value of SAR grant payable in cash. When an initial SAR grant is made, no entry is required. When there is an increase in value of the underlying share value over the share price at which the SAR was granted, the difference is recorded as compensation expense. The entry is

Account	Debit	Credit
Compensation expense	xxx	
SAR liability		xxx

Record increase in SAR grant payable in shares. When there is an increase in value of the underlying share value over the share price at which the SAR was granted, the difference is recorded as compensation expense while the offsetting credit is to a Share Rights Outstanding equity account. The entry is

Account	Debit	Credit
Compensation expense	xxx	
Share rights outstanding		xxx

Record exercise of SAR grant payable in cash. When the holder of a SAR wishes to exercise it and the payment is in cash, the amount of the accumulated SAR liability is reversed, with the difference being credited to Cash, representing the payment to the SAR holder. The entry is

Account	Debit	Credit
SAR liability	xxx	
Cash		xxx

Record exercise of SAR grant payable in shares. When the holder of a SAR wishes to exercise it and the payment is in shares, the amount of the accumulated share rights outstanding is reversed, with the difference being credited to the Par Value account and Additional Paid-in Capital account, representing the payment to the SAR holder. The entry is

Account	Debit	Credit
Share rights outstanding	xxx	
Share—par value		xxx
Share—additional paid-in capital		xxx

Employee Share Ownership Plan (ESOP)

Incurrence of loan to purchase shares. To record a loan on the company books when either it or its ESOP obtains a loan with a third-party lender in order to purchase shares from the company.

Cash	xxx	
Notes payable		xxx

Purchase of shares by ESOP from sponsoring company. To record the transfer of company shares to the ESOP entity when it purchases the shares from the company. The shares have not yet been allocated to employees.

Unearned ESOP shares	xxx	
Common shares		xxx

Payments against note payable by ESOP. To record a reduction in the note payable incurred by the ESOP or the company on its behalf. The second entry records the allocation of shares to plan participants, as triggered by the reduction in the note payable.

Interest expense	xxx	
Notes payable	xxx	
Cash		xxx
Compensation expense	xxx	
Additional paid-in capital		xxx
Unearned ESOP shares		xxx

Dividends declared on shares held by ESOP. To record either a reduction in retained earnings (for shares allocated to employees by the ESOP) or compensation expense (for shares held by the ESOP) at the time of a dividend declaration.

Retained earnings [for allocated shares in ESOP]	xxx	
Compensation expense [for unallocated shares in ESOP]	xxx	
Dividends payable		xxx

RECORDKEEPING

When shares are issued, the transaction should be recorded in a share capital record, an example of which was shown earlier in the Forms and Reports section. This document should be considered a permanent corporate record. It should be set aside in a separate archival area to ensure that it is not batched with other documents for destruction at some point in the future. It is common practice to have the corporate law firm or a share transfer agent maintain this document. If so, one should verify the third party's document safekeeping procedures to ensure that the information is at minimal risk of damage or destruction.

When shares are issued in exchange for goods or services received, the offsetting debit is to an expense account, which can be manipulated by making incorrect assumptions about the value of the goods or services received. Accordingly, one should document thoroughly the reason for the valuation. If the valuation cannot be determined, then the alternative of using the fair value of the shares issued also should be documented, since this valuation can also be subject to opinion when the share capital is not publicly traded.

Earnings can be manipulated to a significant extent if the board of directors authorizes a property dividend for which there is a significant difference between the book and fair value of the property to be distributed. The asset must be marked up or down to its fair value prior to the distribution to shareholders, so it is necessary to fully document the reasoning behind the determination of fair value. This documentation is necessary in case the basis for the fair value determination is called into question later.

The price of each initial share sale should be recorded permanently for each numbered share certificate. This information could be required many years in the future, if those shares are ever bought back into the treasury and the constructive retirement method is used to record the purchase. Under this method, information about the original sale is required in order to determine what part of the share repurchase price is backed out of the share capital account and how much is charged to retained earnings. This information also is required if a share repurchase is recorded initially using the cost method, and then it is determined that the shares will be permanently retired.

When a company agrees to repurchase shares at an excessively high price, usually due to the threat of a corporate takeover by a shareholder, it should document the circumstances of the repurchase, including the amount by which the repurchase exceeded the market value of the shares on the date of the repurchase. If the shares are not publicly traded, then the estimated market value can be quite difficult to ascertain, so the reasoning for the market value used should be documented clearly. The documentation likely will be reviewed and incorporated into the working papers of any external auditors, who will use it as proof of the reasonableness of any excess payments charged to expense.

If a company expenses its share option grants, it should fully document the inputs to its use of the option valuation model, which is used to calculate the compensation expense associated with the option grants. This information is likely to be reviewed carefully by auditors as well as by analysts and investors, since changes in the assumptions can be used to alter reported profit levels. For example, if a company has reduced the vesting period for its share options, this is reasonable evidence for a reduction in the option life assumption in the Black-Scholes-Merton model, so a listing of the reduced option vesting periods and the authorizing board motion should be attached to the journal entry as supporting evidence.

When a company recognizes the compensation expense associated with its option grants, it should document the method under which it ratably spreads the expense over time. There are two techniques available, yielding significantly different expense recognition amounts (as discussed earlier under the Option Vesting Period heading), so this information should be attached to the journal entries used to record the expense.

When a company records a periodic compensation expense as part of its grant of share appreciation rights to employees, the amount of compensation expense granted may be called into question, unless the company can provide a standard means of calculating the expense at the end of each reporting period. Accordingly, the calculation should be noted in a standard format that is attached to the journal entry used to record the expense.

When a company uses an ESOP to allocate shares to its employees, there may be ongoing concerns about who qualifies for the plan, since this determination can completely block an employee from participation or impact the proportion of total shares allocated. Consequently, all plan documents, including revisions to them, should be stored in the permanent file and tagged by date, so it is clear when each revision became effective. Additionally, the calculations for share allocations should be retained in the permanent file. These calculations should clearly state the basis for share allocation, show the calculation for each employee, and attach any supporting documentation required as evidence of the allocation, such as hours worked by employee and pay levels on the allocation date.

14 INTERIM REPORTING

DEFINITIONS OF TERMS

Discrete view. An approach to measuring interim period income by viewing each interim period separately.

Estimated annual effective tax rate. An expected annual tax rate that reflects estimates of annual earnings, tax rates, tax credits, and so on.

Integral view. An approach to measuring interim period income by viewing each interim period as an integral part of the annual period. Expenses are recognized in proportion to revenues earned through the use of special accruals and deferrals.

Interim financial report. Either a complete set of financial statements for an interim period (prepared in accordance with the requirements of IAS 1), or a set of condensed financial statements for an interim period (prepared in accordance with the requirements of IAS 34).

Interim period. A financial reporting period shorter than a full financial year (e.g., a period of three or six months).

Last-12-months reports. Financial reporting for the 12-month period that ends on a given interim date.

Seasonality. The normal, expected occurrence of a major portion of revenues or costs in one or two interim periods.

Year-to-date reports. Financial reporting for the period that begins on the first day of the fiscal year and ends on a given interim date.

CONCEPTS AND EXAMPLES

Interim reporting refers to a requirement by the securities regulator for most publicly held companies to file quarterly or semiannual information. The intent of this requirement is to provide users of the financial statements with more current information, which often is somewhat abbreviated compared to full annual financial reporting.

There are two views of how interim financial statements should be prepared. The first is the *integral view*, under which each interim period is considered to be an integral part of the annual accounting period. As such, annual expenses that may not arise specifically during an interim period nonetheless are accrued within all interim periods, based on management's best estimates. This heightened level of accrual usage likely will result in numerous accrual adjustments in subsequent periods to deal with any earlier estimation errors. It also calls for the use of the estimated annual tax rate for all interim periods, since the annual tax rate may vary considerably from the rate in effect during the interim period if the company is subject to graduated tax rates.

The second approach to interim statement preparation is the *discrete view*. Under this methodology, each interim period is considered to be a discrete reporting period and as such is not associated with expenses that may arise during other interim periods of the reporting year. A result of this thinking is that an expense benefiting more than one interim period will be fully recognized in the period incurred rather than being recognized over multiple periods.

Although IAS 34, *Interim Financial Reporting*, generally favors a discrete view, some of the examples given in Appendix 2 to IAS 34 (e.g., those explaining the accounting treatment of income taxes and employer payroll taxes, or the example that explains the application of the standard to the treatment of contingent lease payments) exemplify an approach that is a combination of the discrete and the integral views.

IAS 34 sets forth these three important aspects of interim financial reporting:

1. Permitting presentation of condensed financial information by the standard is not intended to either prohibit or discourage the reporting entity from presenting a complete set of interim financial statements, as defined by IAS 1.
2. Even when the choice is made to present condensed interim financial statements, if an entity chooses to add line items or additional explanatory notes to the condensed financial statements, over and above the minimum prescribed by this Standard, the Standard does not, in any way, prohibit or discourage the addition of such extra information.
3. The recognition and measurement guidance in IAS 34 applies equally to a complete set of interim financial statements as to condensed interim financial statements. Thus, a complete set of interim financial statements would include not only the disclosures specifically prescribed by this Standard but also disclosures required by other IFRS. For example, disclosures required by IAS 32, such as those pertaining to interest rate risk or credit risk, would need to be incorporated in a complete set of interim financial statements, in addition to the selected footnote disclosures prescribed by IAS 34.

IAS 1 (as revised in 2007) defines a complete set of financial statements to be comprised of the following:

- A statement of financial position as at the end of the period;
- A statement of comprehensive income for the period;
- A statement of changes in equity for the period;
- A statement of cash flows for the period;
- Notes, comprising a summary of significant accounting policies and other explanatory information; and
- A statement of financial position as at the beginning of the earliest comparative period when an entity applies an accounting policy retrospectively or

makes a retrospective restatement of items in its financial statements, or when it reclassifies items in its financial statements.

IAS 34 provides minimum requirements in relation to condensed interim financial reports. The Standard mandates that these financial statements components be presented when an entity opts for the condensed format:

- A condensed statement of financial position
- A condensed statement of comprehensive income, presented as either
    1. A condensed single statement, or
    2. A condensed separate income statement and a condensed statement of comprehensive income
- A condensed statement of changes in equity
- A condensed statement of cash flows
- A set of selected footnote disclosures

IAS 34 sets forth five requirements in relation to form and content of interim financial statements:

1. IAS 34 mandates that if an entity chooses to present the "complete set of (interim) financial statements" instead of opting for the allowed method of presenting only "condensed" interim financial statements, then the form and content of those statements should conform to the requirements set by IAS 1 for a complete set of financial statements.
2. However, if an entity opts for the condensed format approach to interim financial reporting, IAS 34 requires that, at a minimum, those condensed financial statements include each of the headings and the subtotals that were included in the entity's most recent annual financial statements, along with selected explanatory notes, as prescribed by the Standard.
3. IAS 34 requires disclosure of earnings per share (both basic EPS and diluted EPS) on the face of the interim income statement. This disclosure is mandatory whether condensed or complete interim financial statements are presented.
4. IAS 34 mandates that an entity should follow the same format in its interim statement showing changes in equity as it did in its most recent annual financial statements.
5. IAS 34 requires that an interim financial report be prepared on a consolidated basis if the entity's most recent annual financial statements were consolidated statements. Regarding presentation of separate interim financial statements of the parent company in addition to consolidated interim financial statements, if they were included in the most recent annual financial statements, this Standard neither requires nor prohibits such inclusion in the interim financial report of the entity.

IAS 34 includes a list of 10 minimum disclosures required to accompany the condensed interim financial statements, which are outlined next.

1. A statement that the same accounting policies and methods of computation are applied in the interim financial statements compared with the most recent annual financial statements, or if those policies or methods have changed, a description of the nature and effect of the change
2. Explanatory comments about seasonality or cyclicality of interim operations
3. The nature and magnitude of significant items affecting interim results that are unusual because of nature, size, or incidence
4. Dividends paid, either in the aggregate or on a per-share basis, presented separately for ordinary (common) shares and other classes of shares
5. Revenue and operating result for business segments or geographical segments, whichever has been the entity's primary mode of segment reporting
6. Any significant events occurring subsequent to the end of the interim period
7. Issuances, repurchases, and repayments of debt and equity securities
8. The nature and quantum of changes in estimates of amounts reported in prior interim periods of the current financial year, or changes in estimates of amounts reported in prior financial years, if those changes have a material effect in the current interim period
9. The effect of changes in the composition of the entity during the interim period, such as business combinations, acquisitions, or disposal of subsidiaries, and long-term investments, restructuring, and discontinuing operations
10. The changes in contingent liabilities or contingent assets since the most recent annual financial statements

IAS 34 provides examples of the disclosures that are required. For instance, an example of an unusual item is "the write-down of inventories to net realizable value and the reversal of such a write-down."

Finally, in the case of a complete set of interim financial statements, the Standard allows additional disclosures mandated by other IFRS. However, if the condensed format is used, then additional disclosures required by other IFRS are *not* required.

IAS 34 furthermore mandates not only comparative (condensed or complete) interim income statements (e.g., the second quarter of 2005 presented together with the second quarter of 2004) but the inclusion of year-to-date information as well (e.g., the first half of 2005 and also the first half of 2004). Thus, an interim income statement would ideally be comprised of four columns of data. In the case of the remaining components of interim financial statements (i.e., balance sheet, statement of cash flows, and statement of changes in equity), however, the presentation of two columns of data would meet the requirements of IAS 34.

The next example explains these requirements of IAS 34.

The White Nights Security (WNS) Company presents quarterly interim financial statements and its financial year ends on December 31 each year. For the second quarter of 2007, WNS should present these financial statements (condensed or complete) as of June 30, 2007:

1. A statement of comprehensive income with four columns, presenting information for the three-month periods ended June 30, 2007, and June 30, 2006; and for the six-month periods ended June 30, 2007, and June 30, 2006.

2. A statement of financial position with two columns, presenting information as of June 30, 2007, and as of December 31, 2006.
3. A statement of cash flows with two columns presenting information for the six-month periods ended June 30, 2007, and June 30, 2006.
4. A statement of changes in equity with two columns presenting information for the six-month periods ended June 30, 2007, and June 30, 2006.

IAS 34 recommends that, for highly seasonal businesses, the inclusion of additional income statement columns for the 12 months ending on the date of the most recent interim report (also referred to as rolling 12-month statements) would be deemed very useful. Rolling 12-month statements are recommended because seasonality concerns would be thereby eliminated, since by definition each rolling period contains all the seasons of the year. (Rolling statements, however, cannot correct cyclicality that encompasses more than one year, such as that of secular business expansions and recessions.) Accordingly, IAS 34 encourages companies affected by seasonality to consider including these additional statements, which could result in an interim income statement comprising six or more columns of data.

In general, the same inventory costing principles should be utilized for interim reporting as for annual reporting. However, the use of estimates in determining quantities, costs, and net realizable values at interim dates will be more pervasive. For example, normal year-end closing would require the use of a physical inventory count or perpetual recordkeeping system to ensure that the correct cost of goods sold is recorded. However, it is acceptable instead to use the gross profit method for an interim period. Under the gross profit method, one can estimate the cost of goods sold based on the expected gross profit percentage.

Two particular difficulties regarding inventory costing principles are addressed in IAS 34. These are the matters of determining net realizable values (NRV) at interim dates and the allocation of manufacturing variances. Regarding net realizable value determination, the Standard requires that the determination of NRV at interim dates should be based on selling prices and costs to complete at those dates. Projections should therefore not be made regarding conditions that possibly might exist at the time of the fiscal year-end. Furthermore, write-downs to NRV taken at interim reporting dates should be reversed in a subsequent interim reporting period only if it would be appropriate to do so at the end of the financial year. IAS 34 requires that the price, efficiency, spending, and volume variances of a manufacturing entity are recognized in income at interim reporting dates to the extent those variances would be recognized at the end of the financial year.

Example of interim reporting of product costs

The White Nights Security (WNS) Company encounters the next product cost situations as part of its quarterly reporting.

- It conducts inventory counts only at the end of the second quarter and end of the fiscal year. Its typical gross profit is 30%. The actual gross profit at the end of the second quarter is determined to have been 32% for the first six months of the year. The actual gross profit at the end of the year is determined to have been 29% for the entire year.

Coventry University

Lanchester Library

Tel 02476 887575

Returned Items 15/10/2013 14:26

Item Title

38001003654880

Financial management for non-specialists

Thankyou for returning items

Date

013

2013

* Indicates items borro

Thankyou

www.coventry.ac.uk

Coventry University
Lanchester Library

Borrowed Items 15/10/2013 14:27
XXXXXX1437

Item Title Due Date

* 38001003654182 Financial management 28/10/2013
* 38001005778659 Wiley IFRS 05/11/2013

* Indicates items borrowed today
Thankyou
www.coventry.ac.uk

- It determines that, at the end of the second quarter, due to peculiar market conditions, there is a net realizable value (NRV) adjustment to certain inventory required in the amount of €90,000. WNS expects that this market anomaly will be corrected by year-end, which indeed does occur in late December.
- It suffers a decline of €65,000 in the market value of its inventory during the third quarter. This inventory value increases by €75,000 in the fourth quarter.
- It suffers a clearly temporary decline of €10,000 in the market value of a specific part of its inventory in the first quarter, which it recovers in the second quarter.

WNS uses these calculations to record these situations and determine quarterly cost of goods sold:

	Quarter 1	Quarter 2	Quarter 3	Quarter 4	Full Year
Sales	€10,000,000	€8,500,000	€7,200,000	€11,800,000	€37,500,000
(1-Gross profit percentage)	70%		70%		
Cost of goods, gross profit method	7,000,000		5,040,000		
Cost of goods, based on actual physical count		5,580,000[1]		8,255,000[2]	25,875,000
Temporary net realizable value decline in specific inventory[3]		90,000		(90,000)	0
Decline in inventory value with subsequent increase[4]			65,000	(65,000)	0
Temporary decline in inventory value[5]	10,000	(10,000)	0	0	0
Total cost of goods sold	€7,010,000	€5,660,000	€5,105,000	€8,100,000	€25,875,000

[1] *Calculated as [€18,500,000 sales × (1– 32% gross margin)] – €7,000,000 Quarter 1 cost of goods*

[2] *Calculated as [€37,500,000 sales × (1 – 29% gross margin)] – €17,620,000 Quarters 1–3 cost of sales*

[3] *Even though anticipated to recover, the NRV decline must be recognized.*

[4] *Full recognition of market value decline, followed by recognition of market value increase, but only in the amount needed to offset the amount of the initial decline.*

[5] *No deferred recognition to temporary decline in value.*

A number of expenses can be assigned to multiple interim reporting periods, even if they are incurred in only one interim period. The key justification is that the costs must clearly benefit all periods in which the expense is recorded. Examples of such expenses are

- Advertising expense
- Bonuses (if they can be reasonably estimated)
- Contingencies (that are probable and subject to reasonable estimation)
- Contingent rental expense (if the contingent expense appears probable)
- Income taxes (based on the estimated annual effective tax rate)
- Profit sharing (if they can be reasonably estimated)
- Property taxes

Example of interim reporting of various expenses

The White Nights Security (WNS) Company incurs the next costs as part of its quarterly reporting.

- It pays €15,000 of trade show fees in the first quarter for a trade show that will occur in the fourth quarter.

- It pays €32,000 in the first quarter for a block of advertisements that will run throughout the year in *Security Now* magazine
- The board of directors approves a profit-sharing plan in the first quarter that will pay employees 20% of net annual profits. At the time of plan approval, full-year profits are estimated to be €100,000. By the end of the third quarter, this estimate has dropped to €80,000 and to €70,000 by the end of the fourth quarter.

WNS uses these calculations to record these scenarios:

	Quarter 1	*Quarter 2*	*Quarter 3*	*Quarter 4*	*Full year*
Trade show[1]				€15,000	€15,000
Advertising[2]	€8,000	€8,000	€8,000	8,000	32,000
Profit-sharing[3]	5,000	5,000	3,000	1,000	14,000

1 *The trade show payment is recorded initially as a prepaid expense and then charged to trade show expense when the show occurs in the fourth quarter.*

2 *The advertising payment is recorded initially as a prepaid expense and then proportionally recognized in all quarters as it is used.*

3 *A profit-sharing accrual begins in the first quarter, when the plan is approved. At that time, one-fourth of the estimated full-year profit-sharing expense is recognized. In the third quarter, the total estimated profit-sharing expense has declined to €16,000, of which €10,000 has already been recognized. When the profit-sharing expense estimate declines again in the fourth quarter to €14,000, only €1,000 remains to be recognized.*

The fact that income taxes are assessed annually by the taxing authorities is the primary reason for the requirement that taxes are to be accrued based on the estimated average annual effective tax rate for the full fiscal year. Further, if rate changes have been enacted to take effect later in the fiscal year (while some rate changes take effect in midyear, more likely this would be an issue if the entity reports on a fiscal year and the new tax rates become effective at the start of a calendar year), the expected effective rate should take into account the rate changes as well as the anticipated pattern of earnings to be experienced over the course of the year. Thus, the rate to be applied to interim period earnings (or losses) will take into account the expected level of earnings for the entire forthcoming year as well as the effect of enacted (or substantially enacted) changes in the tax rates to become operative later in the fiscal year.

When an interim period loss gives rise to a tax loss carryback, it should be fully reflected in that interim period. Similarly, if a loss in an interim period produces a tax loss carryforward, it should be recognized immediately, but only if the criteria set forth in IAS 12 are met. Specifically, it must be deemed probable that the benefits will be realizable before the loss benefits can be given formal recognition in the financial statements.

IAS 34 prescribes that where volume rebates or other contractual changes in the prices of goods and services are anticipated to occur over the annual reporting period, these should be anticipated in the interim financial statements for periods within that year.

The rule regarding depreciation and amortization in interim periods is more consistent with the discrete view of interim reporting. Charges to be recognized in the interim periods are to be related to only those assets actually employed during the period; planned acquisitions for later periods of the fiscal year are not to be taken into account.

IAS 34 stipulates that an entity should apply the same impairment testing, recognition, and reversal criteria at an interim period as it would at the end of its financial year. However, this does not mean that a detailed impairment calculation as prescribed by IAS 36 would automatically need to be used at interim periods; instead, an entity would need to review for indications of significant impairments since the date of the most recent financial year to determine whether such a calculation is required.

Where IAS 21 provides for translation adjustments to be recognized in the income statement in the period in which they arise, IAS 34 stipulates that the same approach be applied during each interim period. If the adjustments are expected to reverse before the end of the financial year, IAS 34 requires that entities not defer some foreign currency translation adjustments at an interim date.

A change in accounting policy other than one for which the transition is specified by a new standard should be reflected by restating the financial statements of prior interim periods of the current year and the comparable interim periods of the prior financial year. However, a change in accounting *estimate* is to be accounted for only on a go-forward basis, so no retrospective application is allowed.

While year-to-date financial reporting is not required, although the Standard does recommend it in addition to normal interim period reporting, in general, adjustments should *not* be made to results of earlier interim periods. By measuring income and expense on a year-to-date basis and then effectively backing into the most recent interim period's presentation by deducting that which was reported in earlier interim periods, the need for retrospective adjustment of information that was reported earlier is obviated. However, there may be the need for disclosure of the effects of such measurement strategies when this results effectively in including adjustments in the most current interim period's reported results.

Example of interim reporting of contingencies

The White Nights Security (WNS) Company is sued over its alleged violation of a patent in one of its products. WNS settles the litigation in the fourth quarter. Under the settlement terms, WNS must retroactively pay a 3% royalty on all sales of the product to which the patent applies. Sales of the product were €150,000 in the first quarter, €82,000 in the second quarter, €109,000 in the third quarter, and €57,000 in the fourth quarter. In addition, the cumulative total of all sales of the product in prior years is €1,280,000. Under provisions of IAS 34, WNS cannot restate its previously issued quarterly financial results to include the following royalty expense, so instead it will report the royalties expense, including that for earlier years, in the fourth quarter:

	Quarter 1	*Quarter 2*	*Quarter 3*	*Quarter 4*	*Full year*
Sales related to lawsuit	€150,000	€82,000	€109,000	€57,000	€398,000
Royalty expense	0	0	0	11,940	11,940
Royalty expense related to prior year sales	0			38,400	38,400

POLICIES

- **A combination of the discrete and the integral views shall be used for the preparation of all interim financial reports.** This policy is needed to ensure that each interim period is a discrete accounting period, with status equal to a fiscal year, while the accounting treatment of income taxes, employer payroll taxes, or contingent lease payments is consistent with the integral view.

- **The estimated annual effective tax rate shall be used for the income tax accrual in all** interim **periods.** This policy is needed to ensure that excessively low tax rates are not used in earlier interim reporting periods and higher tax rates in later periods as the result of graduated tax rates.
- **The lower of cost or net realizable value (NRV) analysis shall be conducted at interim reporting dates.** Write-downs to NRV taken at interim reporting dates should be reversed in a subsequent interim reporting period only if it would be appropriate to do so at the end of the financial year.
- **Calculation of the cost of goods sold.** A normal year-end closing would require the use of a physical inventory count or perpetual recordkeeping system to ensure that the correct cost of goods sold is recorded. However, it is acceptable instead to use the gross profit method for an interim period. Under the gross profit method, one can estimate the cost of goods sold based on the expected gross profit percentage.

PROCEDURES

Use this two-step procedure to ensure that accruals recorded in interim periods that are based on year-end estimates are updated regularly based on revisions to the estimates:

1. Collect the backup information used to compile all accruals from the immediately preceding interim period.
2. For each accrual, review the estimated full-year expense. If the estimate has changed from the preceding reporting period, subtract from the new estimate the expense already accrued and divide by the number of interim periods left to be reported in the fiscal year. The result is the amount to be accrued in the current period. If the estimate has not changed from the preceding reporting period, then use the last period's accrual amount in the current reporting period.

Use this four-step procedure to ensure that the lower of cost or NRV analysis in an interim period is correctly reported in subsequent interim periods:

1. Record the detail of all write-downs to NRV in each interim reporting period.
2. As part of the next interim reporting period, examine the market value (NRV) of items whose values were written down in a previous interim period. If the market value has increased, then record a gain to the extent of the previous loss.
3. Record all gain recognition in the detailed write-down to NRV report, so that no additional gain will be recorded in a subsequent interim period.
4. Obtain the approval of the controller before recording the gain.

CONTROLS

- **Verify that the discrete view of interim statement preparation is being used.** A recurring internal audit program should specify that the expense recognition within any interim period be examined to ensure that expenses applying to the annual financial statements are being recognized appropriately.
- **Verify that the estimated annual effective tax rate is used in each interim statement.** A recurring internal audit program should specify that the income tax rate used in each interim period is based on the estimated annual effective tax rate.
- **Verify that accruals are being reviewed and adjusted in each interim period.** Part of the closing procedure should require that all accruals involving the recognition of estimated full-year expenses be reviewed and adjusted, based on any changes in the estimated total expense to be incurred.
- **Verify the extent of market value increases for inventory items.** Part of the closing procedure for each interim period should include a review of all inventory items for which a loss was recorded from the write-down of inventories to net realizable value. This reduces the risk that the company will not recognize the reversal of such a write-down in a subsequent period to the extent of the earlier loss.

FOOTNOTES

Disclosure must be made of any changes in accounting principles or the methods of applying them from the preceding interim periods of the current fiscal year or the prior fiscal year. The disclosure must be included not only in the current interim period's financial statements but also in all remaining interim periods of the current year and the annual financial statements. An example follows.

> In the third quarter of 2007, the Company changed its depreciation calculation methodology from the straight-line method used in prior years to the double-declining balance method. The new calculation method has been applied to property, plant, and equipment acquired in previous years and interim periods. Management believes that the new method more accurately reflects the Company's level of equipment usage.

If a company's revenue varies materially with the seasons, it should disclose the seasonality of its sales. This is needed to keep users of the interim financial statements from being misled by large activity changes. Two examples follow.

1. The Company's theme park business is highly seasonal, with 80% of its sales occurring in the second and third quarters.
2. The Company has historically experienced considerable variability on a quarterly basis in its reported level of revenue and net income. A large proportion of this variability is due to seasonal fluctuations in business activity, with activity in its first and fourth quarters being adversely affected by downturns in attendance at its theme parks, particularly in northern climates, where low temperatures can shut down some theme parks entirely. Therefore, the results of operations presented for the three months ended September 30, 2007, are not necessarily indicative of the results of the Company's full-year operations.

RECORDKEEPING

Recordkeeping for interim reporting periods is concerned primarily with tracking variations in inventory levels between interim periods. Recordkeeping is as described next.

- **Inventory affected by lower of cost or NRV rule.** Retain information about any inventory for which a valuation write-down occurred during an interim period. This information should include the part number, part description, quantity affected, and the total value of the write-down. The information will be needed if subsequent NRV increases result in the recognition of a gain to the extent of the previous loss.
- **Net realizable value determination at interim dates.** The determination of NRV at interim dates should be based on selling prices and costs to complete at those dates.

Once the annual report has been completed, the preceding recordkeeping can be archived, while similar information must now be tracked within each successive year.

15 SEGMENT REPORTING

DEFINITIONS OF TERMS

Chief operation decision maker. The person or group responsible for making decisions about resource allocations to business segments as well as the evaluation of those segments.

Operating segment. A component of a business entity that earns revenues and incurs expenses, for which financial information is available, and about which the chief operating decision maker (see preceding definition) makes decisions regarding resource allocations and performance assessments.

Reportable segment. A distinct revenue-producing component of a business entity, for which separate financial information is produced internally, whose results are regularly reviewed, and which meets any of these quantitative thresholds: (1) Its reported revenue, including both sales to external customers and intersegment sales or transfers, is 10% or more of the combined revenue, internal and external, of all operating segments; (2) the absolute amount of its reported profit or loss is 10% or more of the greater, in absolute amount, of (a) the combined reported profit of all operating segments that did not report a loss and (b) the combined reported loss of all operating segments that reported a loss; or (3) its assets are 10% or more of the combined assets of all operating segments. Operating segments that do not meet any of the quantitative thresholds may be considered reportable, and separately disclosed, if management believes that information about the segment would be useful to users of the financial statements.

Segment manager. That person who is accountable to the chief operating decision maker (see earlier definition) for a segment's operating results, financial results, forecasts, and plans.

CONCEPTS AND EXAMPLES

Segment information is required only for public companies but optionally may be provided for privately held companies, which would also be required to comply with the provisions of IFRS 8. It is reported in order to provide the users of financial information with a better knowledge of the different types of business activities in which a company is involved. This information otherwise would be hidden in the consolidated financial information that a company normally releases in its financial statements.

The determination of a segment is based on how a company organizes its financial information internally, so that external users of the segment information will have access to approximately the same information that company managers use to make decisions. This determination, set forth by IFRS 8, is identical to that under US GAAP (FAS 131) and superseded earlier and quite different requirements established under IAS 14. (Note that IFRS 8 becomes mandatorily effective in 2009 but that earlier adoption is encouraged. For a detailed discussion of predecessor standard IAS 14, see *Wiley IFRS 2007*.)

The general requirement for segment reporting is that the revenue, profit or loss, and assets of each segment be reported, as well as a reconciliation of this information to the company's consolidated results. In addition, it must report the revenues for each product and service, and by customer, as well as revenues and assets for domestic and foreign sales and operations. This information is to be accompanied by disclosure of the methods used to determine the composition of the reported segments.

A reportable segment is a distinct revenue-producing component of a business entity, for which separate financial information is produced internally, and whose results are reviewed regularly by the chief operating decision maker. Some business activities, such as corporate overhead and postretirement benefit plans, are not included in segment reporting.

A segment is considered to be reportable if it is significant to the company as a whole. Significance is assumed if it passes any one of these three tests:

1. Segment revenue is at least 10% of consolidated revenue.
2. Segment profit or loss, in absolute terms, is at least 10% of the greater of the combined profits of all operating segments reporting a profit or the combined losses of all operating segments reporting a loss.
3. Segment assets are at least 10% of the combined assets of all operating segments.

When evaluating whether a segment would be reportable based on these tests, a segment should not be separately reported if it becomes reportable due only to a one-time event. Conversely, a segment should be reported, even if it does not currently qualify, if it did qualify in the past and is expected to do so again in the future.

Further, a company may aggregate the results of segments that do not meet any of the 10% tests in order to create a segment that can now be classified as reportable, but only if they have similar economic characteristics and similar products, production processes, customer types, distribution methods, and regulatory environments.

In addition, the combined revenue of the segments designated as reportable must be at least 75% of consolidated revenue. If not, then additional segments must be designated as reportable.

Finally, it is generally best to limit the number of reported segments to no more than 10, after which similar segments should be aggregated for reporting purposes.

As an example of these concepts, the next tables show how the three 10% tests and the 75% test may be conducted. The first table shows the operating results of six segments of a reporting entity.

Segment name	*Revenue*	*Profit*	*Loss*	*Assets*
A	€101,000	€5,000	--	€60,000
B	285,000	10,000	--	120,000
C	130,000	--	€(35,000)	40,000
D	500,000	--	(80,000)	190,000
E	440,000	20,000	--	160,000
F	140,000	--	(5,000)	50,000
Totals	€1,596,000	€35,000	€120,000)	€620,000

Because the total reported loss of €120,000 exceeds the total reported profit of €35,000, the €120,000 is used for the 10% profit test. The tests for these segments are itemized in the next table, where test thresholds are listed in the second row. For example, the total revenue of €1,596,000 shown in the preceding table is multiplied by 10% to arrive at the test threshold of €159,600 that is used in the second column. Segments B, D, and E all have revenue levels exceeding this threshold, so an "X" in the table indicates that their results must be reported separately. After conducting all three of the 10% tests, the table shows that segments B, C, D, and E must be reported, so their revenues are itemized in the last column. The last column shows that the total revenue of all reportable segments exceeds the €1,197,000 revenue level needed to pass the 75% test, so that no additional segments must be reported.

Segment name	*Revenue 10% test*	*Profit 10% test*	*Asset 10% test*	*Revenue 75% test*
Test threshold	€159,600	€12,000	€62,000	€1,197,000
A				
B	X		X	285,000
C		X		130,000
D	X	X	X	500,000
E	X	X	X	440,000
F				
			Total	€1,355,000

DECISION TREE

The decision tree in Exhibit 15.1 shows how to determine which segments must be reported separately as well as which segments should be aggregated and which ones can be summarized into the "all other" segments category.

Exhibit 15.1 Decision Tree for Determination of Reportable Segments

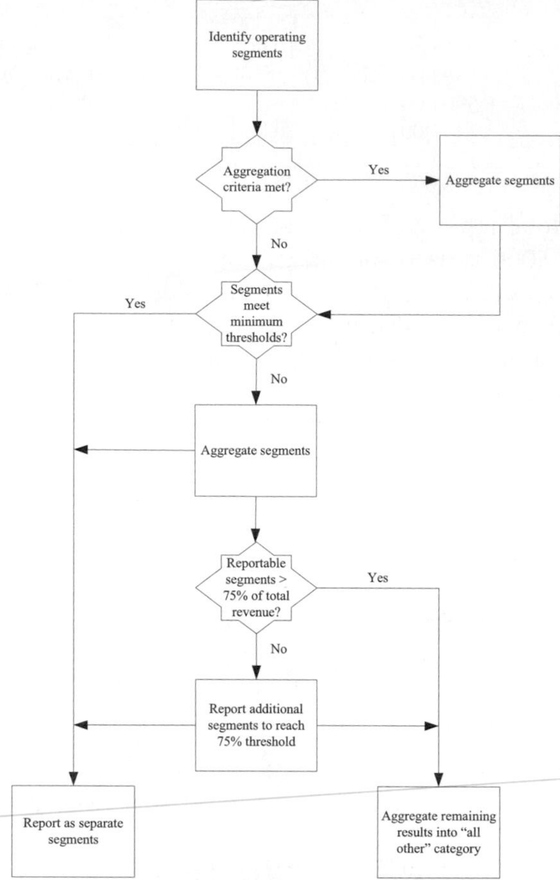

POLICIES

- **Transfer prices used for segment reporting shall match the pricing used for internal reporting purposes.** This policy prevents a company from altering the reported level of segment profitability by shifting profits between segments through the use of transfer pricing.
- **Overhead cost allocations for segment reporting shall match those used for internal reporting.** This policy ensures that financial statement users see the same results shown in internal segment-related financial reports.

PROCEDURES

Segment Determination Procedure

Use this seven-step procedure to determine which business segments must be included in segment reporting.

1. For each business segment, summarize in a table its revenues, profits, losses, and assets. Profits and losses are to be itemized in separate columns.
2. Individually calculate 10% of consolidated company revenues and consolidated segment assets. Also calculate 10% of either total segment losses or profits, whichever is greater.
3. Highlight any segment whose revenues, profits, losses, or assets exceed the 10% threshold figure for each of these categories.
4. Highlight any segments that do not meet these thresholds but have done so in the past and are expected to do so in the future.
5. Remove the highlight from any segment that has exceeded a threshold only as the result of a one-time event, and for which there is minimal expectation that it will exceed a threshold in the future.
6. Summarize the combined revenues of all highlighted segments. If their combined revenue levels do not meet or exceed 75% of consolidated company revenues, then add more segments until this threshold is met or exceeded.
7. If the total number of reportable segments exceeds 10, then aggregate the results of those segments having similar economic characteristics, products, production processes, customer types, distribution methods, and regulatory environments.

Major Customer Reporting Procedure

Use the next five steps to determine which customers comprise 10% or more of consolidated revenues.

1. Print a report showing the trailing 12 months' revenue for all customers, sorted in declining order by total revenue.
2. Aggregate all government sales by top-level entity, so that (for example) all sales to a state government are aggregated into a single sales number. Use the same approach for federal and foreign government sales.
3. Aggregate all customer sales if they are known to be under common control.
4. Calculate the consolidated corporate revenue for the last 12 months, net of intercompany sales. Multiply this amount by 10%.
5. Compare the customer sales (including revenue figures for aggregated governments and customers under common control) to the 10% figure. Report all customers whose sales equal or exceed the 10% figure.

CONTROLS

- **Verify matching of internal and external segment reporting.** The quarterly and annual closing procedures should include a step in which the information issued for segment reporting is compared to the internal segment reports. This information should match. The controller should be notified of any variations between the two reports, which should be reconciled before the segment reports intended for external consumption are released.

FOOTNOTES

The disclosures noted in this section shall be made even if a company has only a single reportable segment. They are

- A description of how management identifies segments, and whether segments have been aggregated
- Total revenues for product or service, or group of products and services, unless it is impractical to provide this information
- Total revenues from domestic and foreign customers (as well as sales to individual foreign countries, if the amounts are material)
- The amount of long-term assets located in foreign countries, which shall include the amounts held in individual countries if those amounts are material
- Total revenues from any customer with whom its transactions total at least 10% of corporate revenues as well as the identity of the segments reporting these revenues

For the purposes of these reporting requirements, a group of customers known to be under common control shall be considered one customer, while a local, state, federal, or foreign government shall be considered a single customer. Several examples of segment disclosure follow.

1. **Determination of segment profitability.** Segment profit is determined based on internal performance measures used by the chief operating decision maker to assess the performance of each business in a given period. In connection with that assessment, the chief operating decision maker may exclude matters such as charges for restructuring, rationalization and other similar expenses, in-process research and development and certain other acquisition-related charges and balances, technology and product development costs, certain gains and losses from dispositions, and litigation settlements or other charges.
2. **Foreign operations (1).** The Company is engaged in business in foreign markets. Our foreign manufacturing and service facilities are located in Australia, Canada, China, Indonesia, and Singapore. Sales to nondomestic customers were €2,500 million or 32% of total sales, €2,200 million or 38% of total sales, and €1,900 million or 33% of total sales for the years ended December 31, 2007, 2006, and 2005, respectively. These countries have experienced volatile exchange rate fluctuations and interest rates, while cash transfers out of Indonesia are restricted at this time. The Company will continue to be affected by economic conditions in these countries and their surrounding regions, though it is not possible to predict the extent or resulting impact on the Company of these issues.
3. **Foreign operations (2).** The Company earns revenues from both domestic and foreign sources. For the purposes of the next table, revenues are attributed to countries based on the store location from which sales are generated or the country to which merchandise is delivered.

	Revenue	*Long-lived assets*
Country of domicile	€23,470,000	€4,950,000
Foreign countries	12,050,000	2,030,000
Total	€35,520,000	€6,980,000

4. **Reporting of segment results—single segment.** The Company operates a single business segment that includes the installation and servicing of oil rigs for independent oil exploration and production (E&P) companies. The next table summarizes the Company's revenues and long-lived assets in different countries.

	2007	2006
Revenues:		
Country of domicile	€67,000,000	€61,000,000
Canada	31,000,000	26,000,000
Other foreign countries	11,000,000	9,000,000
Total	€109,000,000	€96,000,000
Long-lived assets:		
Country of domicile	€29,000,000	€28,000,000
Canada	17,000,000	13,000,000
Other foreign countries	4,000,000	4,000,000
Total	€50,000,000	€45,000,000

5. **Reporting of segment results—multiple segments.** The Company has determined that there are two reportable segments: (1) geographic information systems, and (2) information technology (IT) security audits. Two unreported segments are the Company's customer relationship management software division and its case management software division, whose results do not meet any of the quantitative thresholds under IFRS 8, *Operating Segments*. The next table reveals the operations of the Company's reportable segments.

	Geographic information systems	*IT security audits*	*Other segments*	*Totals*
Revenues	€2,450,000	€5,100,000	€320,000	€7,870,000
Interest revenue	3,400	--	--	3,400
Interest expense	--	63,000	14,000	77,000
Depreciation	93,000	32,000	156,000	281,000
Segment profit	317,000	1,080,000	(43,000)	1,354,000
Segment assets	453,000	190,000	590,000	1,233,000
Expenditures for segment assets	89,000	43,000	25,000	157,000

6. **Major customer reporting (1).** No single customer represents 10% or more of the Company's consolidated revenues.
7. **Major customer reporting (2).** The Company derives a significant portion of its net revenues from a limited number of customers. For the fiscal year ended December 31, 2007, revenues from one client totaled approximately €15.7 million, which represented 12% of total net revenues. For the fiscal year ended December 31, 2006, revenues from two clients totaled approximately €13.6 million and €10.9 million, which represented 16% and 12% of total net revenues. Net revenues derived from sales to government agencies were approximately €126 million and €84 million for the years ended September 30, 2007 and 2006, respectively.

16 FOREIGN CURRENCY

DEFINITIONS OF TERMS

Closing rate. The spot exchange rate (defined below) at the statement of financial position (balance sheet) date.

Comprehensive income. The change in equity of an entity during a period from transactions and other events and circumstances from nonowner sources. It includes all changes in net assets during a period, except those resulting from investments by owners and distributions to owners. It comprises all components of “profit or loss” and “other comprehensive income.”

Conversion. The exchange of one currency for another.

Exchange difference. The difference resulting from reporting the same number of units of a foreign currency in the presentation currency at different exchange rates.

Exchange rate. The ratio for exchange between two currencies.

Fair value. The amount for which an asset could be exchanged, or a liability could be settled, between knowledgeable willing parties in an arm’s-length transaction.

Foreign currency. A currency other than the functional currency of the reporting entity (e.g., the Japanese yen is a foreign currency for a US reporting entity).

Foreign currency financial statements. Financial statements that employ as the unit of measure a foreign currency that is not the presentation currency of the entity.

Foreign currency transactions. Transactions whose terms are denominated in a foreign currency or require settlement in a foreign currency. Foreign currency transactions arise when an entity (1) buys or sells on credit goods or services whose prices are denominated in foreign currency, (2) borrows or lends funds and the amounts payable or receivable are denominated in foreign currency, (3) is a party to an unperformed foreign exchange contract, or (4) for other reasons acquires or disposes of assets or incurs or settles liabilities denominated in foreign currency.

Foreign currency translation. The process of expressing in the presentation currency of the entity amounts that are denominated or measured in a different currency.

Foreign entity. When the activities of a foreign operation are not an integral part of those of the reporting entity, such a foreign operation is referred to as a foreign entity.

Foreign operation. A foreign subsidiary, associate, joint venture, or branch of the reporting entity whose activities are based or conducted in a country other than the country where the reporting entity is domiciled.

Functional currency. The currency of the primary economic environment in which the entity operates, which thus is the currency in which the reporting entity measures the items in its financial statements, and which may differ from the presentation currency in some instances.

Group. A parent company and all of its subsidiaries.

Monetary items. Money held and assets and liabilities to be received or paid in fixed or determinable amounts of money.

Other comprehensive income. Items of income and expense (including reclassification adjustments) that are not recognized in profit or loss as required or permitted by other IFRS. The components of other recognized income include: (1) changes in revaluation surplus (IAS 38); (2) actuarial gains and losses on defined benefit plans (IAS 19); (3) translation gains and losses (IAS 21); (4) gains and losses on remeasuring available-for-sale financial assets (IAS 39); and (5) the effective portion of gains and losses on hedging instruments in a cash flow hedge (IAS 39).

Net investment in a foreign operation. The reporting entity's interest in the net assets of that operation.

Nonmonetary items. All statement of financial position items other than cash, claims to cash, and cash obligations.

Presentation currency. The currency in which the reporting entity's financial statements are presented. There is no limitation on the selection of a presentation currency by a reporting entity.

Reclassification adjustments. Amounts reclassified to profit or loss in the current period that were recognized in other comprehensive income in the current or previous periods.

Reporting entity. An entity or group whose financial statements are being referred to. Under this Standard, those financial statements reflect (1) the financial statements of one or more foreign operations by consolidation, proportionate consolidation, or equity accounting; (2) foreign currency transactions; or (3) both of the foregoing.

Spot exchange rate. The exchange rate for immediate delivery of currencies exchanged.

Transaction date. In the context of recognition of exchange differences from settlement of monetary items arising from foreign currency transactions, this refers to the date at which a foreign currency transaction (e.g., a sale or purchase of merchandise or services the settlement for which will be in a foreign currency) occurs and is recorded in the accounting records.

CONCEPTS AND EXAMPLES

IAS 21 provides the needed guidance on how to include foreign currency transactions and foreign operations in the financial statements of an entity and how to translate financial statements into a presentation currency. The gains and losses resulting from various translation adjustments are treated in different ways, with some initially being stored in the statement of financial position and others being recorded at once in the income statement.

An entity may present its financial statements in any currency (or currencies). If the presentation currency differs from the entity's functional currency, the entity should translate its results and financial position into the presentation currency.

The concept of *functional currency* is key to understanding translation of foreign currency financial statements. Functional currency is defined as the currency of the primary economic environment in which an entity operates. This is normally, but not necessarily, the currency in which that entity principally generates and expends cash.

In determining the relevant functional currency, an entity should give primary consideration to these two factors:

1. The currency that mainly influences sales prices for goods and services as well as the currency of the country whose competitive forces and regulations mainly determine the sales prices of the entity's goods and services
2. The currency that primarily influences labor, material, and other costs of providing those goods or services

Note that the currency which influences selling prices is most often that currency in which sales prices are denominated and settled; the currency that most influences the various input costs is normally that in which input costs are denominated and settled. There are many situations in which input costs and output prices will be denominated in or influenced by differing currencies (e.g., an entity that manufactures all of its goods in Mexico, using locally sourced labor and materials, but sells all or most of its output in Europe in euro-denominated transactions).

The two techniques used to translate the financial results of a foreign entity's operations into the presentation currency of its parent are explained next.

Translation into the Presentation Currency

Most businesses transact and record business activities in the foreign currency (currency of the country in which the foreign entity is located), which is its functional currency. The key consideration when making foreign currency translations is that the underlying economic relationships presented in the foreign entity's financial statements should not be distorted or changed during the translation process into the presentation currency. For example, if the foreign entity's functional currency statements report a current ratio of 2:1 and a gross margin of 40% of net sales, these relationships should pass through the translation process into the presentation currency. When the translation is complete, the performance of the foreign entity's management can be evaluated with the same economic measures used to operate the foreign entity.

To complete the translation into the presentation currency method, the first order of business is to determine the functional currency of the subsidiary. In some locations, a subsidiary may deal with a variety of currencies, which makes this a less-than-obvious decision. The functional currency is the currency in which the bulk of its transactions and financing take place. Next, convert all of the subsidiary's transactions to this functional currency. One should continue to use the same functional currency from year to year in order to provide a reasonable basis of comparison when multiple years of financial results are included in the corporate parent's financial results.

The next step is to convert the results and financial position of an entity whose functional currency is other than the presentation currency (except for the currency of a hyperinflationary economy) using the next procedure:

- Translate all assets and liabilities at the closing rate of that statement of financial position (i.e., including comparatives).
- Translate income and expenses for each income statement (i.e., including comparatives) at the exchange rate at the dates of the transactions (or at the average rate for the period when this is a reasonable approximation).
- Recognize exchange differences in other comprehensive income of the statement of comprehensive income. The cumulative amount of the exchange differences is reported as a separate component of the equity section of the corporate parent's consolidated statement of financial position (Foreign Currency Translation Reserve) until disposal of the foreign operation. This account is cumulative, so one should separately report in the footnotes to the financial statements, as well as in the statement of changes in equity, the change in the translation adjustments account as a result of activities in the reporting period.
- On the disposal of a foreign entity, the cumulative amount of the exchange differences relating to that foreign operation, recognized in other comprehensive income and in a separate component of equity, should be reclassified from equity to profit or loss (as a reclassification adjustment) when a gain or

loss on disposal of this entity is recognized (IAS 1, *Presentation of Financial Statements* as revised in 2007.

This approach to translating foreign currency financial statements usually is selected when a foreign entity's operations are not integrated into those of its parent, if the foreign currency is the currency in which sales prices for its goods and services are denominated and settled, its financing is primarily in that of the foreign currency, or if the subsidiary conducts most of its transactions in the foreign currency.

However, one cannot use this method if the country in which the foreign entity is located suffers from a high rate of inflation, If the functional currency is the currency of a hyperinflationary economy, an entity should restate its financial statements in accordance with IAS 29, *Financial Reporting in Hyperinflationary Economies,* and cannot avoid restatement under IAS 29 by adopting a stable currency (such as the functional currency of its parent) as its functional currency. Hyperinflation is indicated by characteristics of the economic environment of a country, which include: the general population's attitude toward the local currency, prices linked to a price index, and the cumulative inflation rate over three years approaching or exceeding 100%.

If the foreign economy ceases to be hyperinflationary, then the entity no longer restates its financial statements in accordance with IAS 29; it should use as the historical costs for translation into the presentation currency the amounts restated to the price level at the date the entity ceases restating its financial statements.

Example of translation into the presentation currency

A division of the Ulm Clock Company is located in Switzerland. This division maintains its books in francs; generates and expends cash in francs, since it conducts the majority of its operations within Switzerland; and borrows francs from a local bank Accordingly, its functional currency is the franc, which requires the parent's accounting staff to record the division's results in the presentation currency, the euro.

The francs exchange rate at the beginning of the year is assumed to be .08 to the euro, while the rate at the end of the year is assumed to be .10 to the euro. For the purposes of this example, the blended full-year rate of exchange for the franc is assumed to be .09 to the euro. The Swiss division's statement of financial position is shown in Exhibit 16.1 while its income statement is shown in Exhibit 16.2. Note that the net income figure derived from Exhibit 16.2 is incorporated into the retained earnings statement at the bottom of Exhibit 16.2 and is incorporated from there into the retained earnings line item in Exhibit 16.1. For simplicity, the beginning retained earnings figure in Exhibit 16.2 is assumed to be zero, implying that the company is in its first year of existence.

Exhibit 16.1 Statement of Financial Position Translation into the Presentation Currency

	Francs	*Exchange rate*	*Euros*
Assets			
Cash	427	.08	34
Accounts receivable	1,500	.08	120
Inventory	2,078	.08	166
Property, plant, and equipment	3,790	.08	303
Total assets	7,795		623

	Francs	Exchange rate	Euros
Liabilities & Equity			
Accounts payable	1,003	.08	80
Notes payable	4,250	.08	340
Share capital	2,100	.10	210
Reserves	428	.10	43
Retained earnings	14	Note 1	0
Foreign currency translation reserve	--	--	(50)
Total liabilities & equity	7,795		623

Note 1: As noted in the income statement.

Exhibit 16.2 Income Statement Translation into the Presentation Currency

	Francs	Exchange rate	Euros
Revenue	6,750	.09	608
Expenses	6,736	.09	607
Net income	14		1
Beginning retained earnings	0		0
Add: Net income	14	.09	0
Ending retained earnings	14		0

Translation into the Functional Currency

A second method of translating foreign entities' financial statements is used when the functional currency of the foreign entity is not its local currency. Another clear indicator of when this method is used is when: the subsidiary has close operational integration with its parent (direct production or sales arm of the parent); sales prices are influenced by the currency other than the local currency; or most of its financing, sales, and expenses are denominated in the currency other than the local currency, but it uses the local currency to record and report its operations.

Under this method, we translate monetary items, including cash, and also any transactions that will be settled in cash (mostly accounts receivable and payable as well as loans) at the spot exchange rate as of the date of the financial statements. All other assets and liabilities (such as inventory; prepaid items; property, plant, and equipment; trademarks; goodwill; and equity) will be settled at the historical exchange rate on the date when these transactions occurred.

IAS 21 defines monetary items as units of currency held and assets and liabilities to be received or paid in a fixed or determinable number of units of currency. Nonmonetary items that are measured at fair value in a foreign currency (e.g., property, plant, and equipment) should be translated using the exchange rates at the date when the fair value was determined.

Under revised IAS 21, there is no distinction between integral foreign operations and foreign entities. Rather, an entity that was previously classified as an integral foreign operation will have the same functional currency as the reporting entity and will have to remeasure foreign currency items into its functional (and presentation) currency as if these items had been recorded initially in the functional currency. Accordingly, the next procedure should be used for reporting foreign currency items in the functional currency:

- Foreign currency monetary items should be translated using the closing rate.
- Nonmonetary items that are measured at historical cost in a foreign currency should be translated using the exchange rate at the date of transaction.
- Nonmonetary items that are measured at fair value in a foreign currency should be translated using the exchange rates at the date when the fair value was determined.
- Exchange differences arising should be recognized in profit or loss in the period in which they arise.

In a few cases, the income statement is impacted by the items on the statement of financial position that have been translated using historical interest rates. For example, the cost of goods sold will be impacted when inventory that has been translated at a historical exchange rate is liquidated. When this happens, the inventory valuation at the historical exchange rate is charged through the income statement. The same approach is used for the depreciation of plant and equipment and the amortization of intangible items.

Other income statement items primarily involve transactions that arise throughout the reporting year of the subsidiary. For these items, it would be too labor-intensive to determine the exact exchange rate for each item at the time it occurred. Instead, one can determine the weighted-average exchange rate for the entire reporting period and apply this average to the income statement items that have occurred during that period.

Example of translation into the functional currency

A simplified example of the statement of financial position of a foreign subsidiary (located in Switzerland) is shown in Exhibit 16.3 (the same statement of financial position shown in Exhibit 16.1). The Swiss franc exchange rate at the beginning of the year is assumed to be .08 to the euro while the rate at the end of the year is assumed to be .10 to the euro. The primary difference in calculation from the method shown earlier (translation into the presentation currency) in Exhibit 16.1 is that the exchange rate for the inventory and property, plant, and equipment accounts has changed from the year-end rate to the rate at which they are assumed to have been originated at an earlier date. Also, there is no translation adjustment account in other comprehensive income, as was the case under the translation into the presentation currency method.

A highly abbreviated income statement is also shown in Exhibit 16.4. For the purposes of this exhibit, the blended full-year rate of exchange for the franc is assumed to be .09 to the euro. Note that the net income figure derived from Exhibit 16.4 is incorporated into the retained earnings statement at the bottom of Exhibit 16.4 and is incorporated from there into the retained earnings line item in Exhibit 16.3.

Exhibit 16.3 Statement of Financial Position Translation into the Functional Currency

	Swiss Francs	*Exchange rate*	*Euros*
Assets			
Cash	427	.08	34
Accounts receivable	1,500	.08	120
Inventory	2,078	.10	208
Property, plant, and equipment	3,790	.10	379
Total assets	7,795		741
Liabilities & Equity			
Accounts payable	1,003	.08	80
Notes payable	4,250	.08	340
Share capital	2,100	.10	210
Reserves	428	.10	43
Retained earnings	14	Note 1	68
Total liabilities & equity	7,795		741

Note 1: As noted in the income statement.

Exhibit 16.4 Income Statement Translation into the Functional Currency

	Francs	*Exchange rate*	*Euros*
Revenue	6,750	.09	608
Goodwill amortization	500	.08	40
Other expenses	6,236	.09	561
Exchange differences (gain)	--		61
Net income	14		68
Beginning retained earnings	0		0
Add: Net income	14		68
Ending retained earnings	14		68

A major issue is that, under the translation into the presentation currency method, there was a translation (exchange difference) *loss* of €50, while the translation into the functional currency approach resulted in a translation *gain* of €61. This was caused by a difference in the assumptions used in deriving the exchange rate that in turn was used to convert the inventory and property, plant, and equipment accounts from francs into euros. Consequently, the choice of conversion methods used will have a direct impact on the reported level of profitability.

For smaller companies that only rarely deal with foreign exchange transactions, there is no need to formally recall the details of the preceding translation methods. Instead, if they participate in only an occasional sale transaction, they can simply record the initial sale and related account receivable based on the spot exchange rate on the date when the transaction is initially completed. From that point forward, the amount of the recorded sale will not change—only the related receivable will be altered based on the spot exchange rate as of the date of the statement of financial position on which it is reported, adjusting it up or down to reflect the existence of a potential gain or loss at the time of the eventual collection of the receivable. The final gain or loss will be recorded when the receivable is settled, using the spot rate on that date. This procedure will cover the most common transactions that a small business will encounter.

The amendments to IAS 21 published in December 2005 clarify that monetary items (receivable or payable) between any subsidiary of the group and a foreign operation may form part of the group's investment in that foreign operation. Thus, these monetary items can be denominated in a currency other than the functional currency of either the parent or the foreign operation itself, for exchange differences on these monetary items to be classified in other comprehensive income and equity.

Translation of Foreign Currency Transactions

Foreign currency transactions should be recorded, on initial recognition, in the functional currency, by applying to the foreign currency amount the spot exchange rate between the functional currency and the foreign currency at the date of the transaction. Additionally, at the date of each statement of financial position—interim as well as annual—account balances denominated in a currency other than the entity's presentation currency must be adjusted to reflect changes in exchange rates during the period since the date of the last statement of financial position or since the foreign currency transaction date if it occurred during the period. Exchange differences are recognized in profit or loss in the period in which they arise.

Here are the key rules to remember:

- If a company is directly engaged in foreign exchange transactions that are denominated in foreign currencies, then any translation adjustments to the presentation currency that result in gains or losses should be recognized immediately in the income statement. It can continue to make these adjustments for changes between the last reporting date and the date of the current financial statements, and may continue to do so until the underlying transactions have been concluded.

Example of foreign currency transaction reporting

The Louisiana Backhoe Company (LBC) sells backhoes to a variety of countries in the European Union, all of which are paid for in euros. It sold $200,000 of backhoes to Germany on March 15. The receivable was still outstanding on March 31, which was the date of the quarterly financial statements. As of that date, the exchange rate of the euro has dropped by 1%, so LBC has an unrecognized loss of $2,000. It records this as a loss on foreign currency transactions and credits its accounts receivable account to reduce the amount of its receivable asset. When payment on the receivable is made to LBC on April 15, the exchange rate has returned to its level on the sale date of March 15. LBC must now record a gain on its books of $2,000 to offset the loss it had previously recorded.

- Do not report gains or losses on transactions of a long-term nature when accounted for by the equity method. These transactions are defined as those with no settlement date planned in the foreseeable future. Instead, include these transactions in the standard translation procedure used to translate the financial statements of a subsidiary into the currency of its corporate parent.

- If a foreign entity has multiple distinct operations, it is possible that some have different functional currencies. If so, the accountant should review their operations regularly to determine the correct functional currency to use and translate their financial results accordingly. However, if the results of a selected operation on the financial reports of a foreign entity are insignificant, there is no requirement to break out its financial statements using a different functional currency.
- If there has been a material change in an exchange rate in which a company's obligations or subsidiary results are enumerated, and the change has occurred subsequent to the date of financial statements that are being included in a company's audited results, then the change and its impact on the financial statements should be itemized in a footnote that accompanies the audited results. An example is noted in the Footnotes section.

Exchange Rates Used for Calculations

There can be some confusion regarding the precise exchange rate to be used when conducting foreign currency translations. Here are some guidelines.

- If there is no published foreign exchange rate available on the specific date when a transaction occurred that requires translation, one should use the rate for the date that most immediately follows the date of the transaction.
- If the date of a financial statement that is to be converted from a foreign currency is different from the date of the financial statements into which they are to be converted into the presentation currency, then use the date of the foreign currency financial statements as the date for which the proper exchange rate shall be used as the basis for translation.
- If there is more than one published exchange rate available that can be used as the basis for a translation, use the rate that could have been used as the basis for the exchange of funds, which could then be used to remit dividends to shareholders. Alternatively, use the rate at which a settlement of the entire related transaction could have been completed.

Intercompany Transactions

When the results of a parent company and its subsidiaries are combined for financial statement reporting purposes, the gains or losses resulting from intercompany foreign exchange transactions must be reported in the consolidated statements. This happens when the parent has a receivable denominated in the currency of the subsidiary, or vice versa, and a change in the exchange rate results in a gain or loss. Thus, even though the intercompany transaction is purged from the consolidated financial statement, the associated gain or loss must still be reported.

Example of an intercompany transaction

The Seely Furniture Company owns a sawmill in Canada that supplies all of its wood raw materials. The subsidiary holds receivables from the corporate parent that are denominated in US dollars. During the year, there has been a steady increase in the value of the dollar, resulting in a conversion into more Canadian dollars than was the case when each receivable was originally created. By the end of the year, the subsidiary has recorded a gain on currency transactions of C$42,000. Accordingly, the Seely corporate parent records the gain on its books, denominated in US dollars. Because the year-end exchange rate between the two currencies was C$0.73 per US dollar, the subsidiary's gain is recorded as a gain in US dollars of $30,660 (C$42,000 × 0.73 exchange rate) on the books of the parent.

DECISION TREE

The decision tree shown in Exhibit 16.5 can be used to determine which method should be used to translate the financial statements of a foreign subsidiary into the currency of the parent company.

Exhibit 16.5 Type of Translation Method Decision Tree

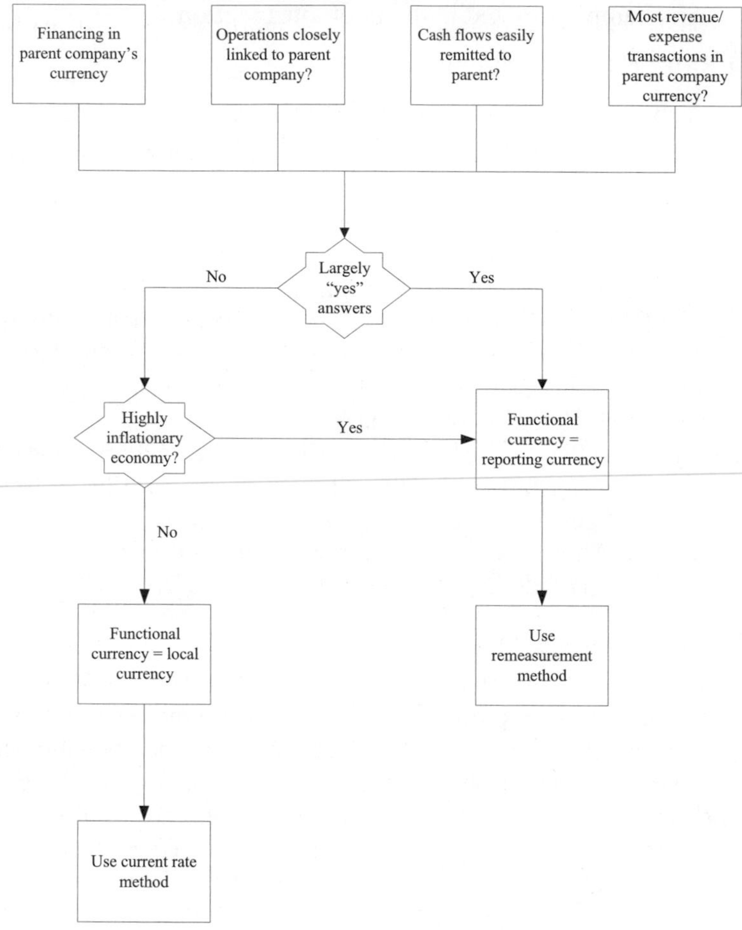

POLICIES

Translation of Foreign Currency Financial Statements

- **Periodically review the status of hyperinflationary economies where subsidiaries are located.** This policy is designed to determine the date when a local economy either becomes highly inflationary or is no longer defined as such under accounting rules. This is of importance in determining what type of translation method to use.

Translation of Foreign Currency Transactions

- **Maintain or have access to a database of daily exchange rates for all currencies in which the company conducts transactions.** This policy allows the accounting staff to have ready access to exchange rates for its translation and currency transaction activities.

PROCEDURES

Financial Statement Translation—Hyperinflationary Economy Determination

Use these six steps to determine status changes for highly inflationary economies.

1. Analyze characteristics of the economic environment of a country, where a foreign entity is located, indicating hyperinflation, which include the general population's attitude toward the local currency (attitude to keep its wealth in nonmonetary assets or in a relatively stable foreign currency) and prices linked to a price index.
2. Establish the three-year date range over which inflation will be measured.
3. Determine the data source containing inflationary information for the selected time periods.
4. Locate the data source and extract the inflation information.
5. Add together the inflation information for the designated three years. The period over which the inflation is measured in the source document may be different from the corporate fiscal year. If so, also obtain the inflation rate for the year in which any portion of the company's fiscal year falls and construct a weighted-average inflation rate based on the number of months in each measured year. For example, if a company's fiscal year ends in October, then multiply the inflation rate for year 1 by 2/12 (to address the two beginning months of the fiscal year falling into year 1) and multiply the inflation rate for year 2 by 10/12 (to address the 10 final months of the fiscal year falling into year 2). Then add these two calculations together to determine the inflation rate for the first year. Perform the same calculation for years 2 and 3.
6. If characteristics of the economic environment of a country indicate hyperinflation and the cumulative inflation rate for the three-year period exceeds 100%, the financial statements of the foreign entity need to be restated in terms of the measuring unit current at the statement of financial position

date, in accordance with IAS 29, before translation. The gain or loss on the net monetary position should be included in profit or loss and disclosed separately. After restating, the financial statements should be translated into the presentation currency, with exchange differences recognized in other comprehensive income and not reclassified from equity to profit or loss until the disposal of the operation.

Application of the Translation into the Presentation Currency

Use the next five steps to translate a subsidiary's financial results into the presentation currency.

1. Identify the subsidiary's functional currency.
2. Measure all parts of the subsidiary's financial statements in its functional currency.
3. Use exchange rates to translate the subsidiary's financial statements from its functional currency to the currency of the corporate parent. The next items note the different exchange rates to be used for different accounts:

   a. **Use the weighted-average exchange rate.** All revenues and expenses as well as changes to retained earnings within the current reporting period.
   b. **Use closing exchange rates.** All assets and liabilities.

4. Record resulting exchange differences in other comprehensive income. The cumulative amount of the exchange differences is presented within the equity section of the statement of financial position (Foreign Currency Translation Reserve) until disposal of the foreign operation.
5. Footnote any changes in the translation adjustment account (and record in the statement of changes in equity) that arose during the reporting period, including the amount of income taxes allocated to the changes.

Application of the Translation into the Functional Currency

Use these four steps to translate a subsidiary's financial results into the functional currency.

1. Verify that the subsidiary's functional currency is not the foreign (local) currency in which transactions were recorded.
2. Use exchange rates to translate the subsidiary's financial statements into the functional currency. The next items note the different exchange rates to be used for different accounts:

   a. **Use historical exchange rates.** All asset and liability accounts that will not be settled in cash (nonmonetary) measured at historical cost in a foreign currency, such as depreciation, intangibles, and inventories carried at cost.
   b. **Use exchange rates at the date when the fair value was determined.** Nonmonetary items that are measured at fair value in a foreign currency.

   c. **Use the weighted-average exchange rate.** All revenues and expenses, except those for which historical exchange rates have already been used.
   d. **Use closing exchange rates.** All cash accounts, as well as any account, such as accounts receivable or payable, that will be settled in cash.
3. Record any exchange differences in profit or loss.
4. Apply translation into the presentation currency if the functional currency is different than the presentation currency.

Translation of Foreign Currency Transactions

Use these six steps to record gains or losses on foreign currency transactions at the end of each reporting period.

1. Obtain a list of all accounts receivable, accounts payable, notes receivable, and notes payable that are outstanding at the end of the reporting period.
2. Obtain the spot exchange rate at the end of the reporting period for the currencies in which all transactions listed in the first step are denominated.
3. Determine the settlement amount of each transaction, assuming that the spot exchange rate will be the exchange rate on the date of settlement.
4. Print out all measurement calculations and attach them to a journal entry form. Note on the form the amount of each spot exchange rate used as well as the source document and date of the source document for each spot exchange rate. If there is a transaction gain, credit the Gain on Foreign Exchange Transactions account and debit the offsetting asset or liability account associated with the transaction. If there is a loss, then debit the loss on Foreign Exchange Transactions account and credit the offsetting asset or liability account associated with the transaction.
5. Have the assistant controller verify the calculations and sign off on the journal entry form.
6. Submit the form to the general ledger accountant for entry into the general ledger.

CONTROLS

Translation of Foreign Currency Financial Statements

The next controls should be used to ensure that translation methods are not arbitrarily switched in order to show or avoid translation gains or losses.

- **Gain external auditor approval of any changes in translation method.** A key difference between the two translation approaches is that exchange differences arising from translation into the presentation currency are placed in the statement of financial position as Foreign Currency Translation Reserve whereas adjustments from translation into the functional currency are recognized on the income statement as gains or losses. The accounting staff could be tempted to shift between the two methods in order to show specific financial results on the corporate income statement. For example, if there were a translation gain, one would be more likely to use translation into the functional currency in order to recognize it on the income statement. This problem is especially likely when the criteria for using one method over the other could be construed either way. The best way to avoid this problem is to have a disinterested third party (i.e., the auditors) approve any change in method over what was used in the preceding year.

- **Require management approval of calculations for the status of inflationary economies.** It is possible to alter the translation method based on the inflationary status of a foreign economy, possibly resulting in the recognition (or not) of translation gains or losses on the income statement. If one were inclined to shift the translation method, a defensible basis for doing so is the inflationary status of the economy in which a foreign entity does business. The inflationary status could be altered by either using incorrect inflation data or shifting the beginning and ending dates of the calculation to correspond to inflation data more in line with one's required result. This issue can be resolved by requiring management or internal audit reviews of these calculations, especially when a change in inflationary status has occurred recently.

Translation of Foreign Currency Transactions

- **Verify that all gains and losses on incomplete currency transactions are updated in the periodic financial statements.** If there have been unusually large fluctuations in the exchange rates of those currencies in which a company has outstanding transactions, there may be a temptation to avoid recording any interim gains or losses prior to settlement of the transactions, on the grounds that the temporary fluctuations will even out prior to settlement. However, this ongoing delay in recognition of gains and losses not only misstates financial statements but also can build over time into much larger gains or losses, which can come as quite a shock to the users of the financial statements when the changes eventually are recognized. Accordingly, the Standard checklist for completing financial statements should itemize the recognition of interim gains and losses on incomplete foreign exchange transactions.

FORMS AND REPORTS

Translation of Foreign Currency Financial Statements

When creating journal entries that include calculations based on a specific exchange rate, it is useful to itemize in the entry not only the exchange rate being used but also the source and date of this information. Accordingly, the journal entry form shown in Exhibit 16.6 has been modified to include the additional information.

Exhibit 16.6 Modified Journal Entry Form

Journal Entry Form

Date: ____________ Approval: ______________________

Account No.	Account Name	Debit	Credit

Reason for journal entry: ____

Exchange rate used: ______________________

Exchange rate source document: ______________________

Date of source document: ______________________

FOOTNOTES

Aggregate transaction gains or losses related to foreign exchange must be disclosed either within the financial statements or in the attached footnotes. If the latter option is chosen, a sample footnote would be

> The company conducts business with companies in several South American countries as part of its ongoing fruit import business. This results in a number of payables denominated in the currencies of those countries, with about €250,000 to €500,000 of such payables being outstanding at any one time. The company does not engage in hedging activities to offset the risk of exchange rate fluctuations on these payables. During the reporting period, the company benefited from foreign exchange gains on these accounts payable totaling approximately €7,500.

The translation of financial statements into the presentation currency results in exchange differences, and the cumulative amount of this adjustment is shown in the equity section of the statement of financial position under the caption Foreign Currency Translation Reserve. In addition, the accompanying footnotes should describe changes in the amount of this balance, the amount of income taxes allocated to it, and any amounts shifted out of this account and recognized as part of the sale or termination of a company's investment in a foreign entity. An example is shown in the next footnote.

> The company summarizes in the equity section of the statement of financial position all exchange differences resulting from the translation of the financial statements of its three foreign subsidiaries into the consolidated corporate statements. During the reporting period, the balance in this account declined by €42,500 to a new balance of €108,250, reflecting the cumulative impact of translation losses incurred during the period. Approximately 20% of this decline was attributable to the sale of the company's travel subsidiary located in Indonesia. In addition, 50% of this decline was attributable

to the partial write-down on the company's investment in its Peruvian trekking subsidiary.

If there has been a significant change in a foreign currency in which a company has significant outstanding transactions, and this change has occurred subsequent to the financial statement date, the impact of this change should be reported as a footnote to the statements. An example follows.

About 40% of the company's revenue is earned from sales to China. On January 14, subsequent to the date of these financial statements, the exchange rate of the China Yuan renminbi dropped 12% from its value on the financial statement date. Since all of the company's sales to China are denominated in renminbis, this represents a potential loss of 12% when those revenues are eventually paid by customers in renminbis. At this time, the drop in value would represent a foreign exchange loss to the company of approximately $412,000. As of the release date of these statements, no accounts receivable related to the sales had been paid by customers. All receivables related to the sales should be collected by the end of February and so are subject to further fluctuations in the exchange rate until that time.

JOURNAL ENTRIES

Translation of Foreign Currency Financial Statements

Financial statement translation adjustment. To record the difference between the exchange rate at the end of the reporting period and the exchange rate applicable to individual transactions. The sample entry shows credit adjustments to several accounts, but these entries could easily be debits instead, depending on changes in applicable exchange rates during the reporting period.

Foreign currency translation reserve	xxx	
Various noncash asset accounts		xxx
Deferred tax liability		xxx

Translation of Foreign Currency Transactions

Translation of foreign currency transactions. To record any changes in the spot rate of exchange at which transactions denominated in a foreign currency would be recorded at the date when financial statements are issued. The **first journal entry** records a loss on a decline in the spot rate on an account receivable (resulting in a reduction in the amount of the receivable in the presentation currency) while the **second entry** records a loss on a decline in the spot rate for an account payable (resulting in an decrease in the payable in the presentation currency), and the **third entry** does so for an outstanding loan payable (resulting in an decrease in the loan payable in the presentation currency).

Loss on foreign exchange transaction	xxx	
Accounts receivable		xxx
Accounts payable	xxx	
Gain on foreign exchange transaction		xxx
Loans payable	xxx	
Gain on foreign exchange transaction		xxx

Recognition of the sale of a foreign subsidiary. To recognize any accumulated translation gains or losses as the result of the sale or write-down of a company's investment in a foreign subsidiary. The entry can be reversed if a gain is to be recognized.

Loss on sale of business entity	xxx	
Foreign currency translation reserve		xxx

RECORDKEEPING

The key recordkeeping issue for foreign currency transactions is to keep a continuing record of the exchange rates used to derive transactions. This record should include the exchange rate, the source of this information, and the date of the source document. For example, the exchange rate for transactions used as of the March 31 financial statements might be the *Financial Times* on March 31. This information will be used by the external auditors to determine whether the correct exchange rates were used to derive accounting transactions.

Coventry University Library

M

R

- Slippers
- Pin (for board)
- hol
- [illegible]
- toilet roll
- kitchen towel
- Stapler pins

[illegible]

- Aubergine
- Onions
- Red pepper
- Apples